Appraisal Procedures for Counselors and Helping Professionals

THIRD EDITION

Robert J. Drummond
University of North Florida

Merrill,
an imprint of Prentice Hall
Englewood Cliffs, New Jersey   *Columbus, Ohio*

Library of Congress Cataloging-in-Publication Data

Drummond, Robert J.
　　　Appraisal procedures for counselors and helping professionals /
　Robert J. Drummond.—3rd ed.
　　　　　p.　cm.
　　　Includes bibliographical references and index.
　　　ISBN 0-02-330681-5
　　　1. Psychological tests. 2. Educational tests and measurements.
　3. Counseling.　I. Title.
　BF176.D78 1996
　150′.28′7—dc20　　　　　　　　　　　　　　　95-4256
　　　　　　　　　　　　　　　　　　　　　　　　　　CIP

Cover art: © Karen Guzak
Editor: Kevin M. Davis
Developmental Editor: Carol S. Sykes
Production Editor: Stephen C. Robb
Text Designer: Mia Saunders
Cover Designer: Proof Positive/Farrowlyne Associates, Inc.
Design Coordinator: Jill E. Bonar
Production Manager: Pamela D. Bennett
Electronic Text Management: Marilyn Wilson Phelps, Matthew Williams, Karen L. Bretz, Tracey B. Ward
Illustrations: Romark Illustrations; J. R. Bidwell

This book was set in Bitstream ITC Garamond and Bitstream Swiss 721 by Prentice Hall and was printed and bound by Quebecor Printing/Book Press. The cover was printed by Phoenix Color Corp.

© 1996 by Prentice-Hall, Inc.
A Simon & Schuster Company
Englewood Cliffs, New Jersey 07632

Earlier editions © 1992 by Macmillan Publishing Company and © 1988 by Merrill Publishing Company.

All photos by the author.

Printed in the United States of America

10 9 8 7 6 5 4 3 2

ISBN: 0-02-330681-5

Prentice-Hall International (UK) Limited, *London*
Prentice-Hall of Australia Pty. Limited, *Sydney*
Prentice-Hall of Canada, Inc., *Toronto*
Prentice-Hall Hispanoamericana, S. A., *Mexico*
Prentice-Hall of India Private Limited, *New Delhi*
Prentice-Hall of Japan, Inc., *Tokyo*
Simon & Schuster Asia Pte. Ltd., *Singapore*
Editora Prentice-Hall do Brasil, Ltda., *Rio de Janeiro*

To those who have inspired and guided me:

> *my mother*
> *my father*
> *my wife, Gloria*
> *my daughters, Robin and Heather*
> *my brother, Paul*
> *my doctoral advisor, Robert L. Thorndike*

Preface

The purpose of this text is to help current and future workers in the helping professions to become better consumers of psychological and educational tests and assessment procedures. First of all, users need to know the philosophical and ethical principles that relate to the field of testing. Second, they need to know when tests should be used and why. Third, they need to know how to locate and select the most valid and reliable instruments to aid in their decision making. Fourth, they need to know how to interpret and report test and assessment results. They need to be alert to the standards developed by various professional organizations and designed as guidelines for test authors and test users.

A systems approach was used to organize the knowledge base and the basic skills and competencies needed by test users. The book focuses on seven components.

1. Models for test use and selection. The first chapter presents a framework for conceptualizing when to use tests and why. It includes some dimensions of the historical, philosophical, and social backgrounds of the testing movement. It also introduces accountability and the competency-based movement, as well as the basic skills and competencies that test administrators and examiners must master.

2. Basic competencies needed. Chapters 2 through 6 identify the basic measurement, statistical, and research skills needed to select, administer, and interpret tests and assessment information.

3. Types of tests and assessment procedures. Chapters 7 through 15 introduce the different types of tests and assessment techniques that are commonly used in the helping professions. This portion of the text covers the assessment of learn-

ing and cognitive styles and the testing of intelligence, aptitude, interest, and personality. Assessment of the environment and development of the test taker are also discussed. The traditional pencil-and-paper tests and inventories are discussed, as are projective tests, situational tests, and the use of behavioral observation.

4. Alternate measurement and appraisal techniques. Chapter 16 focuses on computer-assisted and adaptive testing. Chapter 17 concerns the movement toward alternate and authentic assessment.

5. Testing special populations. Chapters 18 through 21 focus on appraisal procedures and techniques, as well as issues, for working with different special populations, such as clients with disabilities, multicultural groups, test clients with anxiety, and school systems.

6. Communicating test results. Chapter 22 presents strategies for communicating test results to clients, parents, and other professionals, and Chapter 23 looks at guidelines for writing test reports.

7. Current issues and trends. Chapter 24 presents the legal and ethical standards concerned with testing that helping professionals need to know. The final chapter, Chapter 25, recapitulates some of the major trends and issues introduced in the text and predicts some future directions.

CHANGES IN THE THIRD EDITION

Since the second edition was published, there have been major revisions of some tests, such as the Millon, Peabody Picture Vocabulary Test, and WPPSI, and some major new tests have been published. There are many new sources of information available on testing. Many computer versions of tests and interpretative reports are now available to test users. Also, professional organizations have looked more closely at the qualifications and competencies needed by test users. This new edition provides an update on current issues and thinking on testing.

Three chapters have been added to expand the scope of the text: Chapter 24 deals with the legal and ethical issues in testing, Chapter 17 considers alternate and authentic assessment, and Chapter 19 covers working with multicultural groups. Additional issues, such as those raised by the Commission on Fair Testing Practices, are discussed in the relevant chapters. New reference sources have been added to guide further study on the topics, and case studies on the issues are presented in each chapter.

The chapters on disseminating test results and consulting with parents, teachers, and professionals have been combined into one chapter, Chapter 22. The chapter on interviewing and observational techniques has been expanded to include alternate and authentic assessment. Material on employment testing is now included in Chapter 10. Information on mental health testing is now included in Chapter 12. The order of the chapters has been changed so that statistical concepts are presented before measurement concepts, and test administration is discussed before test interpretation.

STRUCTURE OF THE TEXT

Each chapter has a similar format. A chapter overview is followed by learning objectives and a discussion of the topics related to those objectives. A brief summary is included in each chapter, in addition to discussion questions, suggested activities, case studies, and additional readings. Publishers whose tests are cited in the text are listed in Appendix B, and key terms are defined in the Glossary. Separate indexes are provided for topics, tests, and authors.

I have avoided evaluative critiques of most of the tests cited. Most are widely used and accepted in the field. The reader is encouraged to consider the critical reviews of the tests in the *Mental Measurements Yearbooks*, *Test Critiques*, or professional journals. Selection decisions should be situationally specific rather than generalized; tests should have demonstrated validity for the proposed use. A myriad of tests are available in almost all areas. The annotated lists included in the text are not exhaustive, nor do they represent all the exemplary tests in the field. Their purpose is to indicate the range and scope of tests in each area. The text attempts to encourage the reader's curiosity and interest and stimulate further investigation, research, reading, and experimentation to broaden knowledge, skills, and competencies in measurement and evaluation.

ACKNOWLEDGMENTS

I express my appreciation to the following colleagues whose review improved this edition: Rick Bruhn, Sam Houston State University; Judith E. Dobson, Oklahoma State University; Betty N. Dodd, Kean College of New Jersey; Bruce Growick, Ohio State University; Patrick Hardesty, University of Louisville; Roger Herring, University of Arkansas–Little Rock; Mark J. Miller, Louisiana Tech University.

Robert J. Drummond

Table of Contents

CHAPTER 11

Personality Testing   201

CHAPTER 12

Assessment of Adjustment   225

CHAPTER 13

Learning Styles   247

CHAPTER 24

Legal and Ethical Concerns and Issues in Testing   435

CHAPTER 25

Current Trends and Issues   449

CHAPTER 1

Models for Test Use and Selection

Overview

Decision makers want to use their best judgment and appropriate information that is both relevant and accurate. Sometimes certain tests can be identified that will provide this information. Most standardized tests require objective observation and assessment of behavior under controlled conditions. Standards guide the selection, administration, and interpretation of tests.

Objectives

The chapter should enable the reader to

- discuss the steps in a decision-making model
- identify the purposes for giving tests
- list the competencies required of test users
- explain the social, philosophical, and historical foundations of the testing movement as well as some of the current issues

DECISION-MAKING MODEL

In a three-step decision-making model the first step is preparation, which involves

1. specifying the judgments and decisions to be made

2. describing the information needed
3. locating the information already available in files or records
4. deciding what information is needed and when and how this information can be obtained
5. selecting data-gathering instruments and tests to be used and reviewing the instruments for validity, reliability, usability, and interpretability

The second step of the decision-making process is data collection, which involves

1. securing the information needed through testing, observation, and other appropriate methods
2. recording, analyzing, and interpreting the information

The third step of the decision-making process is evaluation, which involves

1. forming hypotheses
2. making decisions or judgments
3. reporting decisions and judgments

Tests are just one source of information; they provide a measure of an individual's behavior at a given moment. Tests only sample the domain being measured. If the limitations of the testing process are recognized, test information can be a valuable tool in decision making.

VALUE OF TESTING

Test information can be valuable to the test taker. It can improve one's self-understanding and reinforce an individual's learning. Test information can also be valuable to society. Many professions now require certification tests to screen incompetent professionals in a given field. Counselors and psychologists, for example, are required to take licensing examinations in many states. Testing programs are also designed to identify or discover talent. This was one of the purposes of the National Defense Education Act several decades ago. A fourth value of testing is that test information can help us learn more about human behavior. If the information is used properly, it can help us to make more efficient use of our social resources. For example, knowing the work values of employees aids in developing an environment that fosters job satisfaction and productivity.

Test information can be especially valuable in educational decision making because it enhances placement decisions. Public Law 94–142 requires exceptional students to be placed in the least restrictive environment, and test information helps educational personnel place these individuals in environments that will best facilitate their learning. Test data are utilized with different criteria in the selection of students for gifted programs, for admission to colleges and universities, and for admission to vocational and technical programs. Advanced Placement Examinations and College Level Examination Programs (CLEP) are examples of widely used placement programs. Teachers are also aided by test data in their selection of instructional strategies and in their evaluation of curriculum programs.

Another way of looking at the value of test data is to consider how the data are used by different groups such as administrators, teachers, counselors, psychologists, curriculum experts, students, researchers, the public, and the legislature. All these groups are consumers of test information.

USES OF TESTS

In a position statement on the use of tests, the task force of the American Association for Counseling and Development (now the American Counseling Association) (1988) identified four major uses of tests. First, test data are used in the placement and selection of individuals—in business and industry as well as in education. Second, tests can help predict success in training programs, educational programs, or actual job experiences. Third, tests can serve descriptive and diagnostic purposes. For example, a test might describe the skills a student has mastered or failed to master in reading or mathematics. Thus, the test might help diagnose why a student is having trouble in reading or math. Fourth, testing that is conducted over a long period can produce data that provide a picture of growth. For example, tests might show growth in achievement from one year to another or growth in self-concept after involvement in group therapy sessions.

The model proposed by the task force of the American Association for Counseling and Development has two other dimensions. It focuses on the type of test to be used and lists four general categories: aptitude and ability tests; achievement tests; interest, attitude, and value tests; and perceptual-motor tests. The third dimension distinguishes between individual and group tests. Often concern focuses primarily on the individual—for counseling, placement, or diagnosis. At other times decisions must involve group testing results.

COMPETENCIES REQUIRED OF TEST USERS

Certain competencies are required to use tests properly. Many negative attitudes toward testing have resulted from certain abuses or misuses of testing. The professional standards of different associations have set explicit guidelines for the selection, use, administration, and interpretation of tests. Those guidelines can be translated into competencies. Test users should be able to do the following tasks:

1. Understand basic measurement concepts such as scales of measurement, types of reliability, types of validity, and types of norms.
2. Understand the basic statistics of measurement and define, compute, and interpret measures of central tendency, variability, and relationship.

*Counselors follow the proce-
dures for administering and
scoring a test exactly as specified.*

3. Compute and apply measurement formulas such as the standard error of measurement and Spearman-Brown prophecy formula.

4. Read, evaluate, and understand test manuals and reports.

5. Follow exactly as specified the procedures for administering, scoring, and interpreting a test.

6. List and discuss major tests in their fields.

7. Identify and locate sources of test information in their fields.

8. Discuss as well as demonstrate the use of different systems of presenting test data in tabular and graphic forms.

9. Compare and contrast different types of test scores and discuss their strengths and weaknesses.

10. Explain the relative nature of norm-referenced interpretation and the use of the standard error of measurement in interpreting individual scores.

11. Help test takers and counselees to use tests as exploratory tools.

12. Aid test takers and counselees in their decision making and in their accomplishment of developmental tasks.

13. Pace an interpretative session to enhance the client's knowledge of the test results.

14. Use strategies to prepare clients for testing to maximize the accuracy of the test results.

15. Explain the test results to test takers thoughtfully and accurately but in a language they understand.

16. Use the communication skills needed in test interpretation and identify strategies for presenting the results to individuals, groups, parents, students, teachers, and professionals.

17. Shape the client's reaction to and encourage appropriate use of the test information.

18. Be alert to the verbal and nonverbal cues expressed by the client, not only in the testing situation but also during feedback situations.

19. Use appropriate strategies with clients who perceive the test results as negative.

20. Be familiar with the test interpretation forms and computerized report forms so that they can guide the client to the information and explanation.

21. Be familiar with the legal, professional, and ethical guidelines related to testing.

22. Be aware of the client's rights and the professional's responsibilities as a test administrator and counselor.

23. List and discuss the current issues and trends in testing.

24. Present results from tests both verbally and in written form and know what types of information should be presented in case studies and conferences.

25. Discuss and utilize strategies to assist an individual in acquiring test-taking skills and in lowering test anxiety.

26. Identify and discuss computer-assisted and computer-adaptive testing and show application to their fields.

The Test User Qualifications Working Group (1988) identified seven factors through a factor analysis of 86 generic subelements of good testing practices. The seven factors are

1. comprehensive assessment—follow-up to get facts from psychosocial history to integrate with test scores as part of interpretation

2. proper test use—acceptance of responsibility for competent use of the test

3. psychometric knowledge—consideration of standard error of measurement

4. maintaining integrity of testing—making clear that cut-off scores imposed for placement in special programs for the gifted are questionable because they disregard measurement error

5. accuracy of scoring—using checks on scoring accuracy

6. appropriate use of norms—not assuming that a norm for a given job or group applies to a different job or group

7. interpretive feedback—willingness and ability to give interpretation and guidance to test takers in counseling (p. 3)

In some states, individuals who wish to become school counselors must pass a certification examination. In Florida, candidates need to demonstrate competencies in eight areas. They must

1. understand basic measurement concepts such as validity, norming, reliability, standard error of measurement, and standardization
2. identify conditions that may affect test results
3. demonstrate knowledge of major functions, strengths, and limitations of standardized and nonstandardized appraisal procedures
4. demonstrate knowledge of appropriate procedures for collecting, storing, and safeguarding assessment instruments and data
5. develop oral and written reports that provide meaningful information based upon assessment data
6. demonstrate an understanding of statistics essential for interpretation to individual students and groups of students
7. interpret assessment data for professional personnel and parents in terms of growth and development of students
8. interpret individual student data from records and professional reports

The National Association of College Admission Counselors (NACAC) believes that counselors need certain competencies to be effective in counseling students from elementary through postsecondary school. One of the competencies that deals with testing is the ability to develop, collect, analyze, and interpret data. Every school counselor should be able to establish effective systems for conveying important data and information about students between educational levels. Specifically, counselors need to understand the proper administration and use of standardized tests and be able to interpret test scores and test-related data to students, parents, educators, institutions, agencies, and the public. The tests included in the NACAC list are

Preliminary American College Test (P-ACT)

American College Test (ACT)

Preliminary Scholastic Aptitude Test (PSAT)

National Merit Scholarship Qualifying Test (NMSQT)

Scholastic Aptitude Test (SAT)

Achievement Tests

Advanced Placement Test

Test of English as a Foreign Language (TOEFL)

College Level Examination Program (CLEP)

Career/vocational aptitude and interest instruments

General aptitude batteries

General achievement tests

Tests of learning disabilities

State/institutional tests

Counselors should also understand how individual and group data and statistics are used in building class and institutional profiles, constructing student transcripts, and preparing reports.

HISTORICAL CONTEXTS

Testing is not a new idea, even though the objective test movement began only at the turn of the century (see Table 1.1). About 2200 B.C. the Chinese used essay examinations to help select civil service employees. The philosophies of Socrates and Plato emphasized the importance of assessing an individual's competencies and aptitudes in vocational selection. Throughout the centuries philosophers and educators have devised certain scales or items to provide teachers and parents with useful information to help their children. Fitzherbert (1470–1538) identified some items to screen retarded from nonretarded individuals—for example, being able to count to 20 pence, being able to tell one's age, and being able to identify one's father and/or mother. Juan Huarte (1530–1589) was probably the first writer to suggest formal mental testing. His book title was translated as *The Trial of Wits: Discovering the Great Differences of Wits Among Men and What Sorts of Learning Suit Best with Each Genius*. Jean Esquirol (1772–1840), a French physician, proposed that there are several levels of mental deficiency and that language is a valid psychological criterion for differentiating among levels. Edouard Seguin (1812–1880) also worked with mentally retarded individuals and believed that these individuals should be trained in sensory discrimination and in the development of motor control. His form board had been adapted and incorporated in some widely used performance and nonverbal IQ tests.

Alfred Binet (1857–1911) became the director of the first physiological/psychological laboratory in France, at the Sorbonne, and did his early work on the relationship of intelligence, palmistry, and phrenology. Binet and Henri were commissioned in 1896 by the Ministry of Public Education in Paris to recommend procedures whereby mentally retarded children might receive the benefits of an education. Binet claimed that his scale provided a crude means of differentiating between those children who could function in the regular classroom from those who could not.

The Victorian era marked the beginning of modern science and witnessed the influence of Darwinian biology on the studies of individuals. In 1879 in Leipzig, Wundt founded the first psychological laboratory. His work was largely concerned with sensitivity to visual, auditory, and other sensory stimuli and simple reaction time. He followed scientific procedures and rigorously controlled observations. He influenced the measurement movement by using methodology that required precision, accuracy, order, and reproducibility of data and findings. The interest in the exceptional individual broadened to include personality and behavior. Freud, Char-

Table 1.1
Major events in testing during the 20th century

1900	Jung Word Association Test	1930	Thurstone's primary mental abilities
to	Binet and Simon Intelligence Scale	to	Buros's *First Mental Measurement Yearbook*
1909	Standardized group tests of achievement	1939	Johnson's test scoring machine
	Stone Arithmetic Test		Graduate Record Examination
	Thorndike Handwriting, Language, Spelling,		Wechsler Bellevue Intelligence Scale
	and Arithmetic Tests		1937 revision of the Stanford-Binet
	Spearman's measurement theory		Murray's Thematic Apperception Test
	Pearson's theory of correlation		Bernreuter Personality Inventory
	Thorndike's textbook on educational		Leiter International Performance Scale
	measurement		Kuder Preference Scale
	Goddard's translation of Binet into English		Lindquist's Iowa Every-Pupil Test
1910	Army Alpha, Army Beta		Bender-Gestalt Test
to	Stenquist Test of Mechanical Abilities		Marino's *Sociometric Techniques*
1919	Porteous Maze Test		Piaget's *Origins of Intelligence*
	Seashore Musical Aptitude Test		Tiegs and Clark's Progressive Achievement Test
	Spearman's *Factors in Intelligence*		Gesell Maturity Scale
	Stanford-Binet Test	1940	Minnesota Multiphasic Personality Inventory
	Otis Absolute Point Scale	to	Wechsler Intelligence Scale for Children
	Stern's concept of mental quotient	1949	United States Employment Service General
	Woodworth Personal Data Sheet		Aptitude Test Battery
1920	Founding of the Psychological Corporation		P. Cattell's Infant Intelligence Scale
to	Goodenough Draw-a-Man Test	1950	Lindquist's electronic test scoring
1929	Strong Vocational Interest Blank	to	*Standards for Educational and Psychological*
	Terman, Kelley, Ruch Stanford Achievement Test	1959	*Testing*
	Clark's *Aptitude Testing*		Guilford's Structure of the Intellect
	Spearman's *The Abilities of Man: Their Nature and*		Stevenson's *The Study of Behavior:*
	Measurement		*Q-Technique and Its Methodology*
	Morrison's School Mastery Tests		Osgood's semantic differential
	Rorschach Ink Blot Test		National Defense Education Act
	Hartshorne and May's *Character Education Inquiry*		Frederikson's in-basket assessment technique
	Kohs's block design		Bloom's *Taxonomy of Educational Objectives*

cot, and Pinel were interested in persons with personal and social adjustment problems.

Many of the innovations and changes in the testing movement resulted from major crises. Both World War I and World War II stimulated major movements in testing. The armed services found that they needed a quick way of screening the level of mental functioning of recruits. They adapted the work of Otis, who developed an objective group test of intelligence and developed the Army Alpha. The original purpose of the army test was to identify those recruits whose lower intelligence would create problems for the military organization. The typical recruit had only a fifth-grade education, and many candidates were illiterate. Another problem was that America had many foreign-born candidates who had little command of the English language and thereby required a nonverbal test or pictorial form with pantomime substituted for written directions. This became the Army Beta.

The first major personality assessment was also developed for use during World War I. The armed services wanted a way to screen psychotics and other emotionally

1960
to
1969
	National Assessment of Educational Progress
	Flannigan's Project Talent
	Wechsler Preschool and Primary Scale of
	    Intelligence
	1960 Revision of the Stanford-Binet
	Jensen's *How Much Can We Boost IQ and*
	    Scholastic Achievement?
	Kuder Occupational Interest Survey
	Cattell's *Theory of Fluid and Crystallized*
	    Intelligence
	Kirk and McCarthy's Illinois Test of
	    Psycholinguistic Ability
	Bayley Scales of Infant Development
			1980
			to
			1989
				Thorndike, Hagen, and Stattler's revision of the
				    Stanford-Binet
				Kaufman Assessment Battery for Children
				Ninth and Tenth Mental Measurements Yearbooks
				Minnesota Multiphasic Personality
				    Inventory II
				Revised *Standards for Educational and*
				    Psychological Testing
				Computer adaptive and assisted testing
				Wechsler Adult Intelligence Scale—Revised
				Nader/Nairn *The Reign of ETS*
				Test in Print III
				Mental Measurements Yearbook reviews in
				    Bibliographic Retrieval Service
				Test Critiques, Vol. 1 to 7

1970
to
1979
	Family Educational Rights and Privacy Act
	New York State Truth in Testing Act
	Public Law 94–142
	SOMPA (System of Multicultural Pluralistic
	    Assessment)
	Wechsler Intelligence Scale for Children—Revised
	Revised Standards for *Educational and*
	    Psychological Testing
	Rokeach Value Survey
	Peabody Picture Vocabulary Test
	Seventh and Eighth Mental Measurements
	    Yearbooks
	Use of computers and microcomputers in testing
	McCarthy Scales of Children's Abilities
			1990
			to
			1999
				Wechsler Intelligence Scale for Children III
				Wechsler Individual Achievement Test
				Revised Scholastic Aptitude Test of CEEB
				Tests III
				Test Critiques 8, 9, & 10
				Authentic Testing (direct or performance
				    assessment)
				The Eleventh Mental Measurements Yearbook
				Standards for Educational and Psychological
				    Measurement, 3rd Ed.
				Computer Adaptive Version of DAT
				Tests in Print IV

disturbed individuals. Such a test was developed from the Woodworth Personal Data Sheet, a forerunner of the modern adjustment inventories.

The successful use of tests by the armed services led to widespread adoption of tests in education and industry. Other factors also contributed to the widespread acceptance of tests. The growth in population, free public education, compulsory school attendance laws, the increase in students going on to institutions of higher education—all were factors that changed the philosophy and practice of testing. In addition, the egalitarian, political, and philosophical movements that championed integration, women's rights, rights of exceptional children and adults, and minority and ethnic group heritage influenced how people viewed testing. Tests were criticized for cultural bias, sexual bias, unfairness to minority groups, and unfairness to handicapped groups. These criticisms led to improved review procedures for the selection of test items and the selection of norming samples.

In recent years, however, the prevailing political philosophy in the United States has changed from a liberal to a more conservative orientation, which has caused a shift from open, humanistic education to back-to-basics and competency-based approaches. We have national assessment, state assessment, minimum- and essential-level skills tests. Many states require students to pass competency examinations prior to graduating. The 1990 Gallup Poll concludes that the public continues to oppose promotion from one grade to the next unless the student can pass examinations—presumably grade- and curriculum-appropriate examinations. Opinions on this topic have not changed significantly over a 20-year period. Sixty-eight percent of the group was in favor of examinations in 1990, whereas 67% favored examinations in 1978. Some states are calling for mandatory examinations for teachers to demonstrate that they can read, write, and communicate effectively, that they know methods of teaching, and that they have mastered the content of what they are to teach.

If we look back at our history, we will find that testing movements have run in recurring cycles. For example, various groups were calling for a moratorium on testing in the early 1960s. Cyclical trends have also characterized the accountability issue, the humanizing of the educational process, human rights, and other issues.

The testing movement has been stimulated by arguments within the profession. Thurstone, Spearman, and E. L. Thorndike debated the nature of intelligence as a single factor or multifactor construct. Cattell, R. L. Thorndike, and Vernon have models including both general and specific factors, or fluid and crystallized intelligence. The debate continues. Sternberg believes that there are different types of intelligence and tests should measure different types of cognitive abilities, and Gardner has proposed a theory of multiple intelligences.

The testing movement has also been affected by technology. The computer and microcomputer have changed the scope and direction of testing administration, scoring, and interpretation. We have computer-assisted and computer-adaptive testing and a myriad of software packages to help us score and interpret everything from biographical data blanks to the Rorschach test.

It is interesting to note the tests that generated the largest number of references in the *Eleventh Mental Measurements Yearbook*. The top test was the Minnesota Multiphasic Personality Inventory-2, which had 637 references. Both the Beck Depression Inventory and the Child Behavior Checklist had more than 200 references. The Wechsler Memory Scale—Revised, the Wechsler Preschool and Primary Scale of Intelligence—Revised, the California Psychological Inventory—Revised Edition, and the Lauria—Nebraska Neuropsychological Battery Forms I and II each had more than 100 references. Of the 703 tests reported in the *Yearbook*, 201 tests were personality tests. In the second major category, vocational tests, 83 were reviewed.

CURRENT ISSUES

Testing has had a history of controversy, both within the field and outside it. Some of the issues involved are recurrent and will be discussed in greater detail in Chapter 25. A test user, though, needs to be aware of the problem areas to follow proper legal and ethical guidelines. It is best to anticipate problem areas and be proactive in communication rather than being surprised by criticism and becoming defensive. The following statements reflect some of the current issues and controversies.

1. Testing is an invasion of privacy.
2. Tests are sex-biased and use inappropriate language, examples, and illustrations.
3. Tests are culturally biased; they are unfair and discriminate against minority groups.
4. Tests may be self-incriminating, and individuals should have the right to rebuttal.
5. Criterion-referenced tests should be used rather than norm-referenced tests.
6. Coaching will help performance of clients on scholastic aptitude tests.
7. Intelligence tests are not measuring the right constructs.
8. There are genetic differences in intelligence.
9. We cannot rely on grades and diplomas; we must have demonstration of competencies on objective tests.
10. Every school scores above the median on achievement tests. The norms are not valid.
11. Athletes should meet the same standards on the SAT as other students. Only a small percentage graduate from college.
12. Multiple-choice tests need to be replaced by authentic and performance assessment.

SUMMARY

This is an information age. Many decisions need to be made, and a decision-making model is a useful guide. Test and assessment data can often help in decision making. It is important to know the types of information that can be gained from testing and the recognized and valid purposes of this procedure.

Test users need to have the skills and competencies necessary to gain reliable and valid information. They also need to be alert to the current issues and controversies in testing and to have an understanding of the historical, social, and political movements that have influenced measurement practices and procedures.

QUESTIONS FOR DISCUSSION

1. What tests have you taken during your lifetime? For what purposes were they given? How can you organize the tests into categories? In what ways was the testing valuable to you? What type of feedback did you get about the results?

2. What types of changes have you noticed in tests and/or testing over time?

3. In the *Ninth Mental Measurements Yearbook*, read the foreword by Anne Anastasi, entitled "Mental Measurements: Some Emerging Trends." She states that "all testing should be considered within a framework of cultural diversity. No test is—or should be—culture free, because human behavior is not culture free. . . ." Why do you agree or disagree with her point of view? What other points in the article should be discussed in class?

4. Should knowledge of the historical foundations of testing be a competency required by workers in the helping professions? Why or why not?

SUGGESTED ACTIVITIES

1. Interview individuals who are working in the helping professions and find out why, when, and how they use testing. Find out what type of decision-making model they use.

2. Look through current newspapers and magazines and cut out or duplicate articles dealing with testing. Discuss those articles in class and identify the types of issues involved.

3. Write a position paper on a current issue in testing.

4. Read further about one of the critical events or one of the key figures in the history of testing and report to the class on what you have learned.

5. Compare the purposes of testing that measurement experts advocate with those that practitioners follow. Is there agreement by both groups as to the roles and functions of testing? Write a position paper on what you believe should be the role of testing and assessment in your field.

6. Report to the class about the certification requirements for your state for a psychological examiner, a school psychologist, a school counselor, or any other professional requiring expertise in testing.

ADDITIONAL READINGS

Buros, O. K. (1977). Fifty years in testing: Some reminiscences, criticisms, and suggestions. *Educational Researcher*, 6(7), 9–15.

This article by one of the important figures in the testing field gives insight into where we are and where we have been.

DuBois, P. H. (1970). *The history of psychological testing*. Boston: Allyn and Bacon.

This is another good book on the history of testing.

Linden, K. W., & Linden, J. D. (1968). *Modern mental measurement: A historical perspective.* Boston: Houghton Mifflin.

This paperback provides readers with a brief history of the modern mental measurement movement.

Zeidner, M., & Most, R. (Eds.). (1992). *Psychological testing. An inside view.*

This book of readings provides an excellent overview of testing. The first chapter by the two editors discusses the context of testing, key concepts, basic assumptions, functions and uses, classification, and major criticisms.

CHAPTER 2

Statistical Concepts

Overview

A worker in the helping professions collects much data on individuals or groups. Statistics provide a means to organize and interpret the data in a way that can be quantified. Statistics play a major role in assessment and measurement. They provide rules and procedures to help summarize and describe data. They provide a frame of reference for interpreting and evaluating test scores. Statistics also help evaluate the psychometric properties of tests or assessment instruments. For example, correlational techniques are used to compute many of the validity and reliability coefficients discussed in Chapter 3.

Objectives

The chapter should enable the reader to understand

- characteristics of the four scales of measurement
- ways to organize and present test data
- measures of central tendency
- measures of the variability of scores
- shapes and types of distributions
- indexes of relative position
- ways of comparing individual performance on two different tests

ROLE OF STATISTICS

A professional needs to know certain statistical concepts to evaluate, use, and interpret standardized and nonstandardized instruments. Workers in the helping professions need to have a good understanding of the four scales of measurement and the different families of statistics.

Descriptive statistics are used to summarize and describe a set of data. Inferential statistics are used to draw inferences about an individual(s) from sample data. For example, do observations of two groups of subjects differ from one another? In Chapter 3 we will look at whether there are differences in the responses of different groups—for example, in the answers of artists and engineers on an interest inventory. Multivariate statistics are used with the simultaneous investigation of two or more variable characteristics measured over a set of individuals. We might explore the relationships among the interests, values, and achievements of different occupational groups.

FOUR SCALES OF MEASUREMENT

Scores on a test, questionnaire, or assessment instrument represent the assignment of numbers to individual items or the total test in order to classify the individual or represent the standing of an individual on some variable. That is measurement—the assigning of numbers to the attributes of individuals, events, or objects according to a set of logical rules. Specific sets of rules define a scale of measurement; four of these scales—nominal, ordinal, interval, and ratio—are used to quantify variables in the behavioral sciences.

Nominal Scale

When numbers stand for names or categories that represent the way individuals differ, that is nominal measurement. Numbers in the nominal scales are arbitrarily assigned to code a specific variable. Here are some examples from interview schedules.

Marital status:

____ 1 never married

____ 2 married

____ 3 widowed

____ 4 divorced

____ 5 separated

Sex:

___ 1 male

___ 2 female

Highest educational level completed:

___ 0 none of the following responses

___ 1 high school diploma or GED

___ 2 vocational, business, or technical school

___ 3 associate of arts or sciences degree

___ 4 bachelor's degree

___ 5 graduate degree

Ordinal Scale

When individuals or objects are ordered or ranked according to some characteristic, that is ordinal measurement. For example, a counselor who is a group facilitator might order his students along an introversion/extroversion continuum. The client who is the most introverted might be assigned the rank of 1 and the most extroverted client the highest rank. Or the percentile of individuals on an achievement test could be ranked from high to low or low to high.

Many items on schedules and questionnaires require a personal ranking on a certain characteristic. Here is just one example. Please rate your degree of competence in the listed behaviors, using the following key: 1 = low, 3 = average, 5 = extremely high.

1.	Oral communication skills	1	2	3	4	5
2.	Written communication skills	1	2	3	4	5
3.	Listening skills	1	2	3	4	5

There are problems with the ordinal scale because the competencies may not be equally spaced. An individual might be extremely strong in certain areas, with minute differences distinguishing those competencies, and extremely weak in some others. Problems also can occur in comparing rankings across groups. The persons with number one rankings in each group might vary tremendously on the variable being ranked. Thus, in rank ordering, the length of the intervals can be unequal. And the numbers used for rankings do not reflect anything quantitative about the variable being ranked. Caution is needed in performing arithmetic operations on measurements derived from ordinal scales and in using and interpreting the information.

Interval Scale

When a scale differentiates among levels of an attribute and has equal distances between those levels, that is interval measurement. It uses numerical values that are equally spaced. Examples of interval scales occur in educational and psychological measurement. We often treat the scores (i.e., the number of correct responses) on aptitude and ability tests as belonging to the interval scale; we assign numbers to levels of an attribute and assume that equal differences in the numbers correspond to equal differences in the attribute. That approach may be meaningful with a variable like temperature, but we can have problems with test results. Can we say a score of 0 indicates an absence of a trait or characteristic or that someone with an IQ of 100 has twice as much intelligence as a person having an IQ of 50?

Ratio Scale

When a true or absolute zero point exists in addition to ranking and equal intervals, that is ratio measurement. Measures such as height and weight are examples of ratio scales. Response time is often an important ratio measurement in interpreting standardized tests: Two minutes are twice as much as one, and there is a true zero point. Both the interval and ratio scale have interval properties and utilize the same statistical procedures.

WHAT SCORES LOOK LIKE

Often a visual picture of what the scores look like is needed. For example, a large number of tests might be organized by setting up the frequency distribution into some type of graphic presentation such as a histogram or frequency polygon.

Let's suppose we have just tested incarcerated youth who have been assigned to our cottage in a correctional facility. The scores of the Nowicki-Strickland Locus of Control Scale, Slosson Intelligence Test, and the Jesness Behavioral Checklist are listed in Table 2.1. We have the scores on 30 youths.

Let's look first at the scores on the Nowicki-Strickland test, given in the column headed LOC. The scale purports to measure locus of control as defined by Rotter (1966). The test measures generalized expectancies for internal versus external control of reinforcement among children. Low scores indicate internality; high scores, externality. As the scores are listed, it is hard to get a picture of the characteristics of this group of offenders. To visualize the data better we could arrange the scores from high to low.

15	9,9,9	6,6	3,3,3
14	8,8,8	5,5,5,5	2,2,2
13	7,7	4,4,4,4,4	1

Arranging the scores in order helps us to see some trends in the data more quickly. We can determine in a glance the highest score and the lowest score, and we can find the approximate middle. However, when a large number of test scores has a greater range (the spread between the high and low scores), it is not as easy to organize and record the scores and see an overall picture.

Table 2.1
Scores on the Nowicki-Strickland Locus of Control Scale (LOC), Slosson Intelligence Test (SIT), and Jesness Behavior Checklist* for Cottage 1

Youth	LOC	SIT	AC	IS	CA	SO	CO	EN	RA	CM	IN	SC	CS	RE	FR	UN
1	1	110	12	27	24	17	23	18	22	20	13	12	28	37	18	26
2	3	120	18	27	28	23	27	16	20	24	15	18	29	33	19	34
3	5	99	15	30	20	21	28	23	19	21	12	16	31	34	18	27
4	3	95	12	22	23	16	22	18	19	21	19	15	26	33	19	33
5	8	93	12	28	18	17	25	18	22	19	12	15	30	36	18	26
6	3	112	15	24	24	20	20	17	22	22	20	12	24	35	19	29
7	9	108	13	26	16	15	23	15	19	17	19	16	18	34	15	31
8	8	82	9	21	19	16	22	16	14	16	18	11	22	30	11	24
9	2	115	11	30	21	17	23	18	19	24	20	18	25	41	21	26
10	14	70	19	20	19	22	21	18	21	14	14	15	30	40	17	30
11	9	99	20	28	22	25	27	13	25	21	13	16	23	37	21	35
12	5	83	8	24	23	15	18	22	18	18	10	9	24	34	15	17
13	5	88	17	29	19	22	26	20	23	18	16	18	24	29	16	31
14	15	75	12	21	15	15	20	15	17	18	17	11	19	34	18	26
15	6	102	15	25	21	21	29	16	19	16	16	14	28	32	16	32
16	7	76	13	28	16	17	19	13	14	19	17	16	22	32	16	27
17	3	85	16	28	15	21	25	17	16	19	17	17	32	41	19	30
18	2	112	14	29	21	19	24	20	18	21	20	18	25	40	20	32
19	13	79	13	17	20	14	27	17	12	18	15	12	25	18	16	25
20	2	117	16	24	22	22	23	17	15	15	15	15	25	32	16	28
21	4	113	15	27	16	20	23	18	22	17	15	15	29	33	22	27
22	9	91	9	27	17	11	18	14	21	16	15	12	26	32	14	18
23	6	107	9	20	18	15	29	16	18	13	18	15	22	28	14	29
24	5	105	18	28	25	23	24	16	20	20	17	15	25	35	19	26
25	4	109	15	27	22	22	22	19	15	20	17	15	26	39	15	23
26	4	107	18	25	25	22	30	17	17	18	18	19	29	38	18	33
27	7	83	17	27	23	22	21	16	23	21	18	15	27	33	17	28
28	4	111	16	16	16	20	25	8	16	13	11	18	21	34	20	32
29	4	109	9	20	13	13	20	18	14	14	16	12	23	28	13	19
30	8	101	17	27	19	21	26	13	21	10	16	16	28	33	20	27

*The Jesness scales are Anger Control, Insight, Calmness, Sociability, Conformity, Enthusiasm, Rapport, Communication, Independence, Social Concern, Consideration, Responsibility, Friendliness, and Unobtrusiveness.

Frequency Distribution

A frequency distribution is a way of summarizing and visually presenting aspects of the test data (see Table 2.2).

These steps must be followed to complete the distribution.

1. Identify three columns to record (a) each score value, (b) a tally of the scores of each score value, and (c) a sum of each tally (frequency).

2. Arrange the scores from high to low in the first column and complete the other two columns as indicated.

A frequency distribution helps to summarize the test data on a particular scale by arranging the scores in order of magnitude and indicating how often each score was obtained.

Sometimes there is a greater range of scores because there are more items on the test and greater variability of performance among the test takers. In such a situation it is easier to group a series of score values; that grouping is called a class interval. We can visualize a frequency distribution if it has between 10 and 20 score intervals. The following formula can be used to determine the range of test score points that should be included in each interval.

$$\text{Class interval size} = \frac{\text{highest score} - \text{lowest score}}{\text{desired number of class intervals}}$$

If we establish 15 as the desired number of class intervals, then the difference between the highest and lowest scores is divided by 15, and the result is an estimate of the number of test score points to be included in each interval.

Table 2.2
Frequency distribution of the Nowicki-Strickland Locus of Control Scale

Score Value	Tally	Frequency
15	1	1
14	1	1
13	1	1
12		0
11		0
10		0
9	111	3
8	111	3
7	11	2
6	11	2
5	1111	4
4	11111	5
3	1111	4
2	111	3
1	1	1

Table 2.3
Group frequency distribution on
the Slosson Intelligence Test

Class Interval	Tally	Frequency
120–124	1	1
115–119	11	2
110–114	11111	5
105–109	111111	6
100–104	11	2
95–99	111	3
90–94	11	2
85–89	11	2
80–84	111	3
75–79	111	3
70–74	1	1

Let's turn back to Table 2.1 and look at the IQ scores, listed under SIT, for the 30 youths. The Slosson Intelligence Test, an individually administered test, yields a total intelligence score, measuring verbal reasoning, vocabulary knowledge, numerical reasoning, and abstract reasoning. To produce a group frequency distribution, we follow these steps.

1. Select the number of class intervals to be used.   10
2. Find the highest score.   120
3. Find the lowest score.   70
4. Subtract the lowest from the highest score.   50
5. Divide the range by the size of the class interval selected to   5
    determine the number of score points to be included in each interval. $10\overline{)50}$
6. Start the frequency distribution with the lowest score.

As we can see from Table 2.3, the grouped frequency distribution provides a good picture of the ability of the group. Because each interval consists of 5 test score points, we lose information about the individual scores. However, the grouping makes the data easier to interpret because there are fewer intervals, only 11 instead of the 51 there would be if individual scores with intervals of 1 were considered.

Graphic Presentations

Two types of graphic presentations of test data will be considered here—the histogram or bar graph, and the frequency polygon, a line graph. Some people prefer a visual mode of learning, and a graph quite often clarifies and simplifies the presentation of the data.

The histogram is a type of bar graph used frequently to portray the distribution of test data. Figure 2.1 presents the histogram of the locus of control scores from Table 2.1. The ordinate, or y axis (vertical line), represents the frequencies of scores

Figure 2.1
Histogram of Slosson Intelligence Test scores

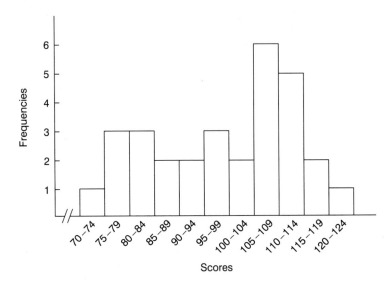

appearing at each score level. The abscissa, or x axis, represents the score points. The intersection of the x and y axes represents the zero point for each.

The frequency polygon is a type of line graph, also used to portray test data. The midpoint of each score interval is used to help plot the graph. In the group frequency distribution of scores on the Slosson Intelligence Test, a score interval of 5 was used. Thus, the midpoint of the interval 70–74 is 72. If the class interval consists of an odd number of score points, the midpoint is a whole number; if it contains an even number of points, the midpoint is a number +.5. Table 2.4 presents information on how the size of the class interval relates to the midpoint. A frequency polygon of the SIT scores is presented in Figure 2.2.

Table 2.4
Size of class interval, score range, and midpoint

Size of Class Interval	Scores	Midpoint
2	70, 71	70.5
3	70, 71, 72	71
4	70, 71, 72, 73	71.5
5	70, 71, 72, 73, 74	72
6	70, 71, 72, 73, 74, 75	72.5
7	70, 71, 72, 73, 74, 75, 76	73
8	70, 71, 72, 73, 74, 75, 76, 77	73.5
9	70, 71, 72, 73, 74, 75, 76, 77, 78	74
10	70, 71, 72, 73, 74, 75, 76, 77, 78, 79	74.5

Figure 2.2
Frequency polygon of scores on
the SIT

Smoothed Curve

If there were many more individuals and a greater number of intervals, the frequency
polygon would be a smoother curve. The shape of the curve provides useful information for the test administrator. When the curve is smoothed out, it gives a better
idea of the shape of the distribution as well as the frequency of the scores. If we
made the intervals progressively smaller and increased the number of individuals
tested on the Nowicki-Strickland Locus of Control Scale, the distribution might look
like Figure 2.3.

Figure 2.3
Frequency polygon of locus-of-control curves, smoothed

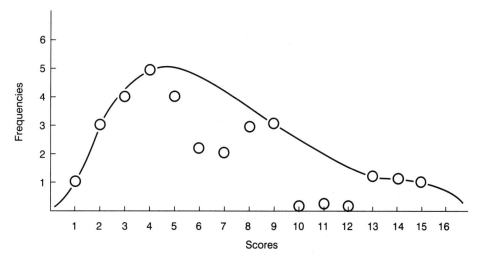

Symmetry and Skewness

When we interpret the curve for a test, we evaluate two major characteristics—skewness and symmetry. There are two major types of curves. The curve for locus-of-control scores is an asymmetrical curve. The curve for the intelligence scores, when smoothed, is more of a symmetrical curve, like that in Figure 2.4. In a symmetrical distribution each side is a mirror image of the other. Later, when we look at interpretation of tests, we will focus on the normal curve, which is a special type of symmetrical curve.

The distribution of locus-of-control scores is a positively skewed distribution. Most of the youths scored near the lower end of the distribution; they were internal in their orientation. A few youths had high scores and were external in their orientation.

If we smoothed the frequency polygon for the scores on the Jesness scales, we would see that most of the scores occur at the higher score levels, with very few scores at the lower levels. This distribution would be negatively skewed. Most of the youths rated their social behavior very positively. The majority of the youths had low scores on the Nowicki-Strickland but high scores on the Jesness.

On criterion-referenced tests, where students tend to get most of the items right, scores pile up at the upper end of the distribution. When tests are easy, most individuals make high scores, and the distribution will be negatively skewed. When test items are difficult, the test takers tend to make low scores on the test, and the

Figure 2.4
Typical curve of scores on intelligence tests

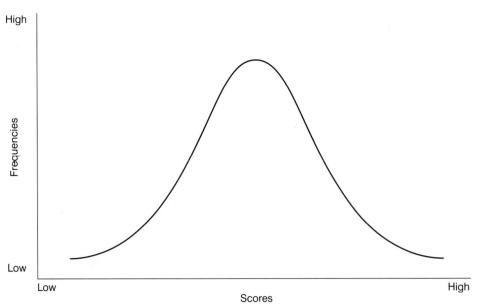

Figure 2.5
Typical curves of scores on Jesness scale

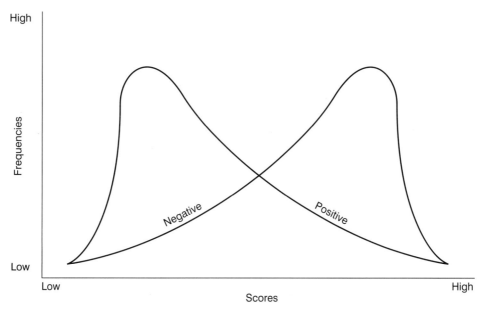

scores pile up at the lower end of the distribution. A few individuals will make high scores. This distribution is positively skewed. The two types of distributions are compared in Figure 2.5.

MEASURES OF CENTRAL TENDENCY

We often want to know about the typical or average performance of a group on a test. There are three measures of central tendency: mean, median, and mode. In part, the measure of central tendency depends on the scale of measurement used. With nominal data the only measure of central tendency is the mode. With ordinal data the median as well as the mode can be used. With the interval and ratio scale all three measures of central tendency can be used. The mode is the score or number that appears most frequently. The mean is the arithmetic average. The median is the middle score, or 50th percentile.

Mode

The mode is the score or numerical value that appears most frequently in a set of scores. In the ordering of the scores on the Nowicki-Strickland test (see Table 2.2), the mode is 4. For the Anger Control Scale on the Jesness, is the mode 9, 12, or 15?

Figure 2.6
Bimodal distribution of boys' and girls' scores on reading achievement tests

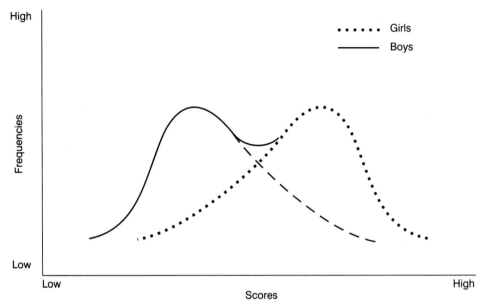

Sometimes there is a bimodal or multimodal distribution; in other words, two or more scores may appear most frequently in the distribution. In the distribution of scores on the Friendliness scale, the same number of people have scores of 16, 18, and 19. Certain achievement subtests produce a distribution such as the one shown in Figure 2.6. Girls tend to score higher than boys on certain scales, and vice versa, thus producing a bimodal distribution.

The mode is often used as a quick measure of central tendency, but it is affected by various factors, such as the number of people taking the test. When the group is small, the mode does not always reflect the typical performance within the group. In a negatively or positively skewed distribution, the mode is quite often not an accurate measure of central tendency.

Mean

The mean is the arithmetic average. It is equal to the sum of the scores on a test divided by the number of individuals who took the test.

$$\overline{X} = \frac{\Sigma X}{N}$$

The mean $(\overline{X})$ is equal to the sum (Σ) of the scores (X) divided by the number of individuals (N). If we added the scores of the 30 individuals taking the Nowicki-Strickland, our total is 178. To compute the mean, we divide 178 by 30. The mean is 5.93.

The mean is the most frequently used measure of central tendency. If we subtract each score from the mean and add up the sum of the differences, the sum is zero. Each score is used to compute the mean, whereas the mode considers just the score with the highest frequency. The mean is affected by extreme scores in the distribution. A few extremely low scores will move the mean down; extremely high scores will move it up.

Median

The median is the middle score, or the score that divides a distribution in half. There will be 50% of the scores falling below the median and 50% above. The median score on the Nowicki-Strickland is 5. When a set of scores consists of an odd number, the median is the middle score. For example, if the scores were 4, 6, 8, the median is 6. With an even number of scores—4, 6, 8, 10—the sum of the two middle scores is divided by 2; the median in this case is 7. Procedures to compute the median from grouped scores in a frequency distribution can be found in most statistical texts.

The median is a better measure of central tendency in a skewed distribution. It is not affected by extreme scores. The relationship of the mean, mode, and median is shown in Figure 2.7 for different types of distributions. The mean, median, and mode have the same score value only in a symmetrical distribution such as the normal curve.

Comparisons of Measures of Central Tendency

There is not one best measure of central tendency. The scale of measurement determines which measure of central tendency can be used, and the purpose of the measure needs to be kept in mind. The mode is the least stable statistic of central tendency. Test makers use the mean and median scores to portray typical or average performance. The mean is a statistic which has algebraic properties; it is used extensively in both descriptive and inferential statistics.

Figure 2.7
Type of distribution and measure of central tendency

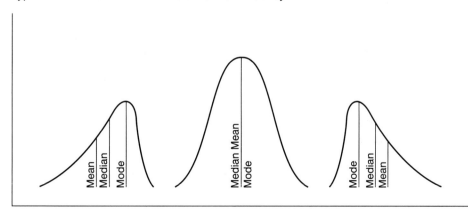

MEASURES OF VARIABILITY

Information about the variability or spread of the scores is necessary for proper interpretation of the data. Two measures of variability are used most often to interpret test scores—range and standard deviation.

Range

A quick measure of the spread of scores can be gotten by computing the range. The range is computed by subtracting the lowest score from the highest score and adding 1 to the difference. If the highest score is 3 and the lowest 1, we add 1 to the difference (2) and calculate a range of 3. The distribution would have three scores— 1, 2, and 3. In the distribution of Nowicki-Strickland scores in Table 2.1, the high score is 15 and the low score 1, making the range 15 ($15 - 1 + 1 = 15$).

The range is easy to compute. However, an extreme score in the distribution can make the range a misleading statistic. For example, a test might produce these scores:

$$1, 2, 2, 3, 3, 3, 4, 4, 5, 5, 6, 6, 40$$

The range here would be 40 even though the other scores are grouped closely together.

The range is a valuable statistic for test interpretation, but it is most often used in conjunction with other statistics such as standard deviation and median, mode, and mean. The range helps tell us how compact or expanded the distribution is but does not always reflect the pattern of variation in the distribution of test scores.

Variance

The variance is a statistic that provides information on how widely spread, or scattered, the scores are from the mean. The variance is computed by subtracting the mean from each score, squaring the difference, and then computing the average squared difference between the scores and the mean. In the formula s^2 represents the variance.

$$s^2 = \frac{\Sigma(X - \overline{X})^2}{N}$$

Standard Deviation

The standard deviation is the square root of the variance and the most widely used statistic of variability. It is a numerical value that describes the spread of scores away from the mean and is expressed in the same units as the original scores. The wider the spread of scores, the larger the standard deviation. Because there is a small range of scores on the Nowicki-Strickland, just 15 points rather than the 51 points of the SIT, the standard deviation on the Nowicki-Strickland Locus of Control Scale will be smaller than the standard deviation on the SIT. Figure 2.8 presents a hypothetical illustration.

To compute a sample standard deviation, let's use just four scores—3, 5, 5, and 7. First, we compute the mean.

$$3 + 5 + 5 + 7 = 20 \div 4 = 5$$

Second, we subtract the mean from each score, square the difference, and then sum the squared differences.

$$
\begin{array}{ll}
3 - 5 = -2 & -2 \times -2 = +4 \\
5 - 5 = 0 & 0 \times 0 = 0 \\
5 - 5 = 0 & 0 \times 0 = 0 \\
7 - 5 = +2 & +2 \times +2 = +4 \\
\hline
 & +8
\end{array}
$$

To find the variance, we divide that sum by the number of scores.

$$8 \div 4 = 2$$

The standard deviation is the square root of the variance; the square root of 2 is 1.414.

It is not always convenient to utilize the definitional formula just illustrated because the mean may be a decimal, making arithmetic operations more complex. A computational formula for raw scores is given here and illustrated, using the scores from the previous example and letting s represent the standard deviation.

$$s = \sqrt{\frac{\Sigma X^2}{N} - \bar{X}^2}$$

X	X^2	
3	9	$s = \sqrt{\dfrac{108}{4} - (5)^2}$
5	25	
5	25	$s = \sqrt{27 - 25}$
7	49	
$\overline{20}$	$\overline{108}$	$s = \sqrt{2} = 1.414$

Figure 2.8
Relationship of size of standard deviation to type of distribution

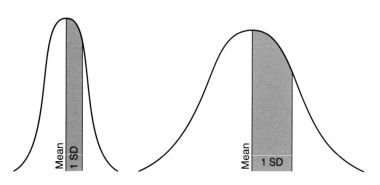

When the scores tend to cluster around the mean, the standard deviation is smaller than when the scores are spread widely around the mean. The standard deviation is an important statistic for interpreting the relative position of an individual within a distribution of test scores. The statistic is stable and is one way of interpreting characteristics of the distribution of the test scores as well as providing a frame of reference for interpreting individual test scores.

MEASURES OF RELATIONSHIP

A statistical measure of relationship can show how two variables are related to one another. We might want to correlate the results of tests given on two different occasions or see how equivalent two forms of an intelligence or achievement test are. For tests with predictive purposes, we might want to know the relationship between intelligence and achievement or scholastic ability and grade point average. Or we might want to correlate two tests that purport to measure the same construct, such as two intelligence tests or two self-concept tests. On other occasions we might want to see whether the scales on a particular test are independent of each other.

To obtain the desired information in these cases, we would use the statistic known as the correlation coefficient. Psychologists and counselors use a number of different types of correlational procedures to measure the relationship of variables. In part, the method utilized will depend on the level of measurement of the variables to be compared, the type of distribution of these variables, and the number of cases to be compared.

Pearson Product Moment Correlation

The Pearson Product Moment Correlation can be computed when we have two continuous variables and data from the interval or ratio scales. If we want to see how consistently a group performed on two different administrations of the same test, we can compute the correlation coefficient. In this case it would be the test-retest reliability coefficient. Let's assume the following scores:

Name	First (X)	Second (Y)
John	1	3
Paul	2	2
Mary	3	4
Jane	4	6
Heather	5	5

The formula is

$$r = \frac{N(\Sigma XY) - (\Sigma X)(\Sigma Y)}{\sqrt{[N(\Sigma X^2) - (\Sigma X)^2][N(\Sigma Y^2) - (\Sigma Y)^2]}}$$

Our first step would be to add each X value to find the sum (15). Our second step would be to add the Y values (20). We then need to square each of the X and Y scores and total those numbers. And we must multiply each individual X and Y score. Because we have five sets of scores, $N = 5$.

X	Y	X^2	Y^2	XY
1	3	1	9	3
2	2	4	4	4
3	4	9	16	12
4	6	16	36	24
5	5	25	25	25
15	20	55	90	68

$$r = \frac{5(68) - (15)(20)}{\sqrt{[5(55) - (15)^2][5(90) - (20)^2]}}$$

$$r = \frac{340 - 300}{\sqrt{[275 - 225][450 - 400]}} = \frac{40}{50} = .80$$

The correlation of 1.80 indicates a degree of association between the two testings. The correlation coefficient ranges from -1.00 to $+1.00$. A correlation of zero indicates no relationship. A coefficient of $+1.00$ indicates a perfect positive relationship.

We could plot the scores using a scatter diagram (see Figure 2.9). The x axis represents the performance on the first test; the y axis represents the performance on the second test. With a correlation of 1.00, we would have a distribution with all the points on a straight line (see Figure 2.10). If there were an inverse relationship, with students performing in reverse order on the two tests, the correlation would be -1.00, and the scores would all fall on a straight line slanted in the opposite direction.

All kinds of combinations of the two sets of scores are possible. The correlation, however, is an index number and we need to square it to find out the percentage of variance in one variable that is predictable from the other variable. The statistic is known as r^2 and is called the coefficient of determination. We can use Venn diagrams to illustrate the statistic (see Figure 2.11). The coefficient of determination represents the intersection of two variables and shows the proportion of variability that those variables share.

Regression

One of the major purposes of testing is prediction, and regression is one of the primary statistical tools for prediction. Regression analysis provides an equation that describes the relationship between two variables. If we know the correlation between an intelligence test and a reading test, for example, we can predict an indi-

Figure 2.9
Bivariate distribution

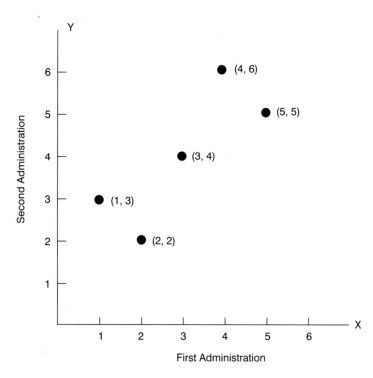

Figure 2.10
Type of distribution and magnitude of correlation coefficient

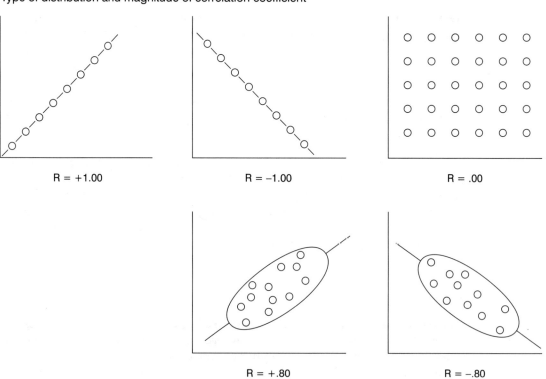

Figure 2.11
Venn diagrams as a way of representing the coefficient of determination

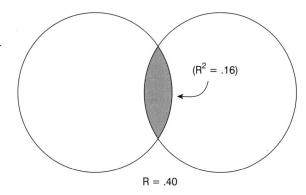

$(R^2 = .16)$

$R = .40$

vidual's reading score from her IQ score. We can compute a regression line if we
know the correlation between two variables and the means and standard deviations
of each. The degree of accuracy of the prediction depends on the strength of the
correlation between the two variables. The weaker the relationship, the larger the
error of estimate; the stronger the relationship, the smaller the error of estimate.

Factor Analysis

Many tests have been derived from factor analysis, which is a statistical technique
used to identify how many factors are needed to explain or account for the intercor-
relation within a set of variables. Items or scales that belong to a factor have usually
moderate to high correlations with the other scales in that factor. Factor analysis is a
method that can systematically summarize a large matrix of correlations. If we had 50
variables, we would have a total of 1,225 correlations. Factor analysis helps remove
the duplicated information from these sets of variables; it results in a smaller set of
derived factors than the original number. Kachigan (1986) identifies five major uses
of this technique:

1. to identify underlying factors that make up a large set of variables
2. to screen variables for inclusion in other required statistical analyses that may
    have to be completed in the future
3. to reduce the number of factors necessary to explain a set of variables
4. to select a small group of representative but uncorrelated variables from among
    a larger set in order to solve a variety of practical problems
5. to cluster people or objects into homogeneous groups based on their intercor-
    relations

Johnson and Holland (1986) studied the structure of the 15 Personal Problems
Inventory and found that four separate and relatively distinct factors accounted for
62% of the variance: performance anxiety problems, interpersonal problems, intrapersonal problems and substance abuse problems.

NORMAL CURVE

The normal curve has many applications in the field of measurement and evaluation. It is a tool that helps us understand the nature of probability. If we obtained a distribution of most educational and psychological characteristics and graphically depicted that distribution, the scores would fall in a bell-shaped curve called the normal curve. The theoretical normal curve serves as an important mathematical model in test interpretation.

The normal curve is a type of symmetrical distribution (see Figure 2.12). It has the following features:

The mean, mode, and median are the same score.

Most distributions accumulate near the mean.

Approximately 68% of the cases fall between −1 and +1 standard deviation.

Approximately 95% of the cases fall between −2 or +2 standard deviations.

Approximately 99.5% of the cases fall between −3 and +3 standard deviations.

We will find that errors of measurement and errors of prediction also have a normal distribution, and the table of the normal curve will help us understand the relative nature of those concepts.

Figure 2.12
Normal curve

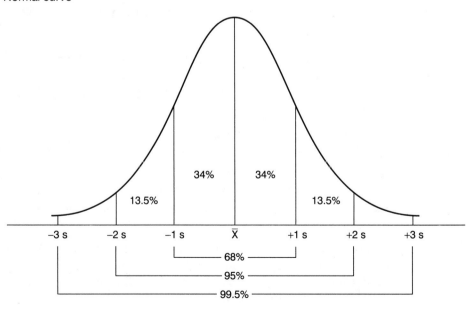

INFERENTIAL STATISTICS

The table of the normal curve is utilized in some types of inferential statistics. We quite often must select samples of individuals because we are unable to test everyone in the population, and we are interested in seeing whether our sample statistics approximate the population statistics, or whether the observed differences between two groups are probably due to something other than chance. One of the major roles of statistics is to provide an inferential measuring tool, to state our degree of confidence in the accuracy of certain measurements. We also like to generalize conclusions beyond the actual sample of observations. Inferential statistics offer the necessary techniques to make statements of certainty that there are real as opposed to chance differences between sets of observations.

An example occurred in the 1978 edition of the Wide Range Achievement Test (WRAT) (Jastak & Jastak, 1978). The males and females in each age group were compared to see whether any of the differences were statistically significant, the hypothesis being that there were no significant mean differences in reading between boys and girls. The test manual presents this information (p. 45):

| | | Male | | Female | | |
Grade	N	Mean	SD	Mean	SD	Significance
5.0	200	14.83	7.43	19.31	7.35	.001
5.5	200	18.32	7.65	20.21	7.56	.05

The conclusion is that there are significant differences between reading scores of boys and girls. Girls have significantly higher means than boys. At the beginning fifth-grade level the observed difference would happen only 1 time in 1,000 by chance. At grade 5.5 the observed difference would happen only 5 times out of 100 by chance.

Test makers utilize inferential statistics to answer questions like these:

1. Are there statistically significant gender differences on the test? Recently one study claimed that the Scholastic Aptitude Test is an unfair instrument to use for assigning scholarship awards because men score significantly higher than women on the test.

2. Are there differences on the scales of the test between normally functioning individuals and those who have psychopathologies?

3. Are there statistically significant racial or cultural differences on the test?

4. Is the correlation coefficient between achievement and aptitude significantly different from chance for the sample selected?

SUMMARY

Statistics provide test developers and users with a way to collect, organize, and interpret test data. Frequency distributions can be used to summarize sets of test scores, and histograms and frequency polygons can help us graphically depict the scores. Measures of central tendency—the mode, mean, and median—help describe what the scores are like on the average. Measures of variability help us understand how the scores are distributed around the averages. Both range and standard deviation are statistics that are used to measure dispersion. Correlation statistics help us quantify the direction and degree of relationship between two variables. Inferential statistics are valuable tools in generalizing results from the sample of behaviors, individuals, events, and items that we have measured.

QUESTIONS FOR DISCUSSION

1. What are the four scales of measurement and what are the advantages and disadvantages of each? Give examples of each type of scale.

2. What are the three measures of central tendency, and what are the strengths and weaknesses of each?

3. Why is variability an important construct in testing? What are the measures of dispersion that are used in testing?

4. Why are measures of relationship important to measurement consumers? What is the coefficient of determination, and how is it used?

5. What are the uses of inferential statistics in measurement contexts? Discuss the uses of multivariate statistical approaches such as factor analysis.

SUGGESTED ACTIVITIES

1. Study a test manual and identify the different types of statistics reported. Make an annotated set of cards with definitions and illustrations of the statistics identified.

2. Compute the mean, mode, and median of the Anger Control and Calmness scores that are included in Table 2.1.

3. Compute the standard deviations and range of the Anger Control and Calmness scores that are included in Table 2.1.

4. Compute a Pearson correlation between Anger Control and Calmness.

5. Construct a frequency distribution of the Sociability or Conformity Scales reported in Table 2.1. Then make a histogram and frequency polygon of the scores.

ADDITIONAL READINGS

Jaeger, R. M. (1990). *Statistics: A spectator sport* (2nd ed.). Newbury Park, CA: Sage.

The author describes basic statistical concepts using nontechnical terms and real world examples. Some chapters include measures of central tendency, variability, correlation, and some fundamentals of measurement.

Kachigan, S. K. (1986). *Statistical analysis: An interdisciplinary introduction to univariate and multivariate methods*. New York: Radius Press.

This text is designed to provide readers with an overview of univariate and multivariate methods of statistical analysis. It provides information verbally, geometrically, graphically, and by example.

CHAPTER 3

Measurement Concepts

Overview

Workers in the helping professions need to be able to understand and apply the fundamental concepts of measurement. Educational and psychological tests are used in a wide variety of contexts, and it is important to select and use the best possible test to obtain the desired information. Decision making should be based on accurate and valid information. However, not all tests are well constructed, and some of the criticisms leveled by practitioners and the general public are justified.

Objectives

In this chapter the measurement concepts necessary for test construction and evaluation are introduced, illustrated, and discussed. After studying this chapter, the reader should understand

- the essential steps in test development and the kinds of evidence with which to judge the adequacy of that development
- the meaning and importance of validity, as well as its different types and uses
- the kind of evidence with which to judge the validity of a test
- the meaning of reliability, errors of measurement, and different types of reliability coefficients

- the kind of factors that influence the reliability of a test and the kinds of evidence with which to judge the reliability of a test
- practical measurement concepts that should be checked before using a test

STEPS IN TEST DEVELOPMENT

Professional standards and ethics of psychologists and counselors focus on test development. Test authors and developers are advised to provide evidence of the reliability and validity of their tests in meeting the purposes for which they were developed. Authors and developers should also provide manuals and norms to help users administer, score, and interpret the tests; they should anticipate how their tests will be used and misused and design correlative materials to foster proper use. Authors and developers have the responsibility to present information in a readily accessible form and to include summaries and interpretations to aid users in reviewing and evaluating the tests.

The test development process may vary somewhat depending upon the type of test being constructed. The following steps are involved in developing an achievement test or aptitude test.

Phase 1: Establishing the Need

1. Consider informal and formal request for such a test.
2. Conduct surveys to see if a need exists.
3. Review and critique other similar tests.

Phase 2: Defining the Objectives and Test Parameters

1. Establish the purpose of the test—who is to be tested and why.
2. Define what objectives will be required of the test takers.
3. Discuss how the test information will be useful to the users as well as test takers.
4. Consider the type of question format and the number of questions to be included.

Phase 3: Involving Advisory Committee Input

1. Select a group of experts in the field (e.g., teachers, administrators, subject area specialists, consumers).
2. Review the objectives, purposes, and parameters of the test.
3. Determine blueprint for the test.

Phase 4: Writing the Questions

1. Use subject area specialists or experts in the test domain to write the test items.
2. Have a measurement specialist review test items prior to field test; have the review panel see whether the test measures the intended domain and whether the items match the specifications in the test blueprint.

Phase 5: Conduct Field Test of the Items

1. Use test sample similar to the targeted group for which the test is being developed.
2. Compute item difficulty and discrimination indices.

Phase 6: Reviewing the Items

1. Check for sexual bias, cultural bias, handicap bias.
2. Eliminate items that might be unfair or offensive to any group.

Phase 7: Assembling the Final Copy

1. Be sure type and number of items meet the coverage specified in the blueprint.
2. Check validity of the scoring key with independent judges.
3. Have the test reviewed by external as well as internal committees.

Phase 8: Securing Necessary Technical Data

1. Determine sampling procedures.
2. Administer and score the test.
3. Compute reliability and validity.
4. Develop appropriate norms.

VALIDITY

Validity is defined in *Standards for Educational and Psychological Testing* (1985) as "the degree to which a certain inference from a test is appropriate or meaningful" (p. 94). The commission producing these standards stated that validity is the most important consideration in test evaluation (p. 9) and includes 25 standards dealing with the concept. Several types of inferences can be made from a score on a single test. One might, for example, be interested in the content that the test items are measuring. Or one might be interested in how the test predicts success in a given program of studies or what type of construct the test is measuring. The evidence for the validity of the test is developed through a number of different procedures. Because tests are used in a variety of ways—for description, for prediction, for measuring growth and development—there are different ways to judge the validity of the test results. Nonetheless, validity is viewed as a unitary concept not a multidimensional one.

Three major categories are used to describe test validity. Most test manuals cite evidence of content, criterion, and construct validity. *Standards for Educational and Psychological Testing* (1985) points out that "these categories are convenient, but the use of these labels does not imply that there are distinct types of validity or that a specific strategy is best for each specific inference or test use. . . . Rigorous distinctions between the categories are not possible. Evidence identified usually with the criterion-related or content-related categories is relevant also to the construct-related category" (p. 9).

Content Validity

Content validity depends on evidence that the items on the test are representative of some defined universe or content domain and that they measure the objectives they are purported to measure. A test user is probably most concerned with the content validity of an achievement test but is also interested in the content validity of other types of tests, such as aptitude tests and interest tests. Test developers may be concerned not only with test items and objectives, but also with the format or response requirements of items. Certain items may demand skills that students are not normally taught at a particular level. For example, they may require abstract reasoning of pupils who are able to use only concrete reasoning.

Content validity is often supported by expert judgment. Test companies enlist, for example, curriculum specialists, subject matter teachers, and college professors to assess the relationship of items to objectives being measured. These reviewers look at whether the items do in fact represent the defined universe or content domain. Another approach utilizes systematic observation of behavior. Experts or trained observers are asked to observe skills and competencies needed to perform a given task; a test or performance checklist is constructed to measure these aspects. Typical statements include the following:

> The main source of words was grade placement lists developed from studies of basal readers.

> The social studies items were selected on the basis of recommendations of 40 authorities in the field.

Face validity, a term quite often referred to by test users, relates to the extent the test appears to be measuring what it claims to be measuring. Usually the term relates to content validity. The test user might quickly skim over the test to see whether it covers the content generally expected in such a test. This method is a quick screening procedure, but a more thorough study of validity should be undertaken.

Criterion-Related Validity

Criterion-related validity is important in demonstrating that test scores are systematically related to one or more outcome criteria. With an aptitude test, for example, one might want evidence that the test can predict success in a training program or job field. The selection of the criterion is related to the context of particular types of clients. They may be students in a school system, clients in a counseling center, or employees in an industrial setting. The test user wants evidence that the test was applied in a context similar to that of the intended clients and that criterion studies were relevant. The goal is to have test scores accurately predicting the criterion performance of interest.

Criterion-related validity is broken down into two categories—concurrent validity and predictive validity. In computing criterion validity, test scores are correlated with criterion measures. In concurrent validity the test scores and criterion information are obtained at the same time. Concurrent validity is usually appropriate for achievement, diagnostic, and certification tests. It may reveal different test profiles for different diagnostic groups with different learning handicaps or different types of psychological adjustment problems. Examples from test manuals include:

> The scores on the Aggressiveness Scale correlated .70 with the rating of teachers of students in their classes.

> The scores on the Mechanical Aptitude Test correlated significantly with supervisory ratings of the worker's performance conducted at the same time.

If test data are used to estimate criterion scores in the future, predictive validity is determined. For example, how well does the SAT test predict a student's grade point average at the end of the freshman year of college? How well does a mechanical aptitude test predict successful performance of a job requiring mechanical aptitude? Some examples:

> The SAT Verbal correlated .30 with grade point average at the end of the first semester at XYZ College.

> The Spatial Relations Scale correlated .70 with success in the metal fabricating training for 136 CETA youth.

Manuals with aptitude or intelligence tests offer considerable evidence on the predictive validity of their tests. However, test users may want to check the utility of the predictor tests. Figure 3.1 presents a useful design for this purpose. A person who is predicted to pass or graduate and subsequently does pass or graduate would be tallied in the positive quadrant; someone who is predicted to pass but fails would be tallied as a false positive. The person who is predicted to fail and does so would

Figure 3.1
Design for predictive validity
check

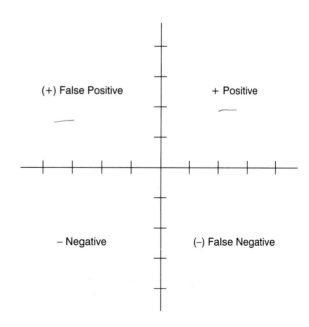

be tallied as a negative; anyone who is predicted to fail but actually passes would be a false negative. Thus, the percentages of correct predictions can be determined and the cut-off score adjusted or a different test selected.

Theorists consider the false positive error the most important to avoid. However, these are value judgments that are partially determined by context perspective. An admissions counselor might argue that enrolling a student who subsequently fails is not all bad; at least this student is given a chance. The parent of that student, who may spend thousands of dollars for a school year with little apparent benefit, might not feel the same.

Both types of criterion-related validity require valid, reliable, and relevant measures of the criterion. The reliability and relevance of the criterion measure selected as well as the type of group tested are factors that affect the validity of the test. A heterogeneous group tends to produce greater variability in scores and therefore higher coefficients than a homogeneous group. Moreover, concurrent validity coefficients are higher than predictive validity coefficients. The criterion used is different, and predictive validity involves a time lag.

Construct Validity

The third type of validity is construct validity. A construct is a grouping of variables or behaviors (e.g., locus of control, state of anxiety, cognitive ability) that is considered to vary across people. The construct is not directly observable but usually has been derived from theory, research, or observation. According to *Standards for Educational and Psychological Testing* (1985), construct validity requires evidence supporting the interpretation of test scores in line with "theoretical implications associated with the construct label" (p. 90). Many authors utilize factor analysis.

For example, the NEO Personality Inventory—Revised (NEO PI-R) authors factored the 240 items and when the five varimax rotated principal components were examined they were found to correspond clearly with the five-factor model of personality.

On the Multidimensional Self-Esteem Inventory 1 (MSEI), a factor analysis was conducted using the total scores from each of the scales. Three factors had eigenvalues greater than 1.0 and accounted for 44.6%, 12.0%, and 9.1% of the variance. Factor I was labeled Overall Self-Evaluation and Effectance; Factor II, Social Self-Esteem; and Factor III, Defensiveness and Private Self-Evaluation.

Most tests attempt to measure one or more constructs. Even achievement tests measure constructs such as reading comprehension. The authors of a test should precisely define each construct and distinguish it from other constructs. Test users also want to know whether a test measures a construct under conditions that have been identified as crucially related to the construct. For example, do clients score differently on a stress scale when under stress and when not?

Authors use many different techniques to demonstrate the construct validity of their tests. A test to measure scholastic aptitude, for example, should demonstrate correlation with achievement in academic subjects and should produce results similar to those of other widely used scholastic aptitude tests. This would be an example of convergent validation, a process in which one test is correlated or compared with other tests, measures, or observations measuring the same construct. A test user would also look for evidence that the construct is unique and is not highly correlated with other scales and tests of other constructs. Anyone interpreting a scale for abstract reasoning would want the scale to have a low correlation with concrete reasoning. This would be an example of discriminant validation, a process in which a test is correlated or compared with other tests, measures, or observations from the one in the test under consideration.

Campbell and Fisk (1959) recommend a multitrait-multimethod approach to provide evidence of the construct validity of a test. They advocate computing correlations between tests measuring the same trait by the same method, tests measuring different traits by the same method, tests measuring the same trait by different methods, and tests measuring different traits by different methods. Some examples of convergent and divergent validity include the following:

> The MSEI was correlated with the Eysenck Neuroticism and Extroversion Scales and the Guilford Zimmerman Temperament Survey. The correlations with the Neuroticism and Extroversion scales were seen as supporting the MSEI in that the most global scales were highly correlated with other measures of global adjustment and modestly correlated with Extroversion, a scale described by Eysenck as being independent of adjustment.

> Convergent validity of the NEO is demonstrated by how the scales are correlated with alternative measures of similar constructs. The Anxiety Scale correlated high with the scores on the State-Trait Anxiety Scale.

A summary of the types of validity is presented in Table 3.1.

RELIABILITY

Reliability is defined as the degree to which test scores are consistent, dependable, and repeatable—in other words, "the degree to which test scores are free from errors of measurement" (*Standards for Educational and Psychological Testing*, p. 19). A client tested on two different occasions would score differently, even on the same test. The difference is caused, in part, by errors of measurement. The test taker may guess better one time than another, know more of the content on one test form than another, or be less fatigued or less anxious at one time. These are all factors that cause errors of measurement, or changes in an individual's scores, from one occasion to another. Changes can also be due to maturation or intervention between testing periods.

Measurement errors reduce the reliability and generalizability of the scores obtained on a given test. However, the intended use of the test results influences the final judgment of the reliability of the test. A test might have sufficient reliability for

Table 3.1
Types of validity

Type	Purpose	Procedure	Types of Tests
Content	To compare whether the test items match the set of goals and objectives	Compare test blueprint with the school, course, program objectives Use panel of experts in content area (e.g., teachers, professors)	Survey achievement tests Criterion-referenced tests Essential skills tests Minimum-level skills tests State assessment tests Professional licensing Examinations Aptitude tests
Criterion: Concurrent	To determine whether there is a relationship between a test and an immediate criterion measure	Correlate test scores with criterion measure at or about the same time Use a rating, observation, or another test as criterion	Aptitude tests Ability tests Personality tests Employment tests
Criterion: Predictive	To determine whether there is a relationship between a test and a criterion measure to be obtained in the future	Correlate test scores with criterion measure obtained after a period of time	Scholastic aptitude tests General aptitude batteries Prognostic tests Readiness tests Personality tests Intelligence tests
Construct	To determine whether a construct exists and to understand the traits or concepts that make up the set of scores or items	Conduct multivariate statistical analysis such as factor analysis, discriminant analysis, multivariate analysis of variance	Intelligence tests Aptitude tests Personality tests

appraising the achievement level of a school district but may not have sufficient reliability to screen individuals for specific placement decisions. The test developer has the major responsibility for providing evidence of a test's reliability and error measurement in each of its intended uses.

A test provides a sample of behavior at a given moment in time; it can sample only the domain being tested. Error of measurement is defined as the difference between a person's observed, or obtained, score and his true score. Thus, the obtained score represents partly a true level of ability, skill, or knowledge and partly an error component that may raise or lower the score. The true score and error score are both theoretical; we can only hypothesize what a true score might be. The standard error of measurement, which is discussed in more detail later in this chapter, is used to estimate a score range in which a true score may fall.

Reliability Coefficients

Test manuals give a number of different reliability coefficients. Reliability coefficients are computed by correlating the results of the same test given on two different occasions, alternate forms of the same test, or part scores or item scores from a single administration of a given test. A number of other coefficients are based on different theoretical assumptions. However, the three methods discussed here follow correlational procedures, which are considered in Chapter 2. The coefficient is a positive index number ranging from .00 to 1.00 with .00 indicating a lack of reliability and 1.00 indicating perfect reliability.

Test-Retest.   When the same test is given twice, the two sets of scores can be correlated and a test-retest coefficient obtained. Usually at least a day and perhaps several years will elapse between the two testings. This type of coefficient is important with aptitude, ability, and personality tests. It is also important when interest tests are used to guide clients in career decisions, which may span many years.

The test-retest method gives a coefficient of stability. Because there are two administrations of the test, a number of variables can influence an individual's performance. One variable might be the way the test was administered. The examiner may have made errors in timing, or an interruption may have occurred. Such errors in test administration reduce reliability. Furthermore, the test taker may vary in performance; motivation, mood, and/or health may fluctuate.

The interval between testings can also be a factor. Normally, this method is not used if the tests are relatively close together; test takers might remember the items and choose the same answers on the second administration, thus inflating the coefficient. The contribution of memory and practice effects must be considered in an interpretation of test-retest coefficients.

Finally, exposure to any intervention such as educational training or psychological therapy affects performance on a second testing. Consequently, the coefficient obtained after such intervention would not be a proper indicator of the stability of the constructs measured. Examples of this phenomenon include:

On the MSEI, the test-retest coefficient on the Global Self-Esteem Scale was .87 over a one-month interval.

The subset of 208 college students in a three-month retest on the five domains of the NEO-PI resulted in coefficients of .79, .79, .80, .75, and .83 for N, E, O, A, and C, respectively.

The test-retest coefficients on the Vocational Preference Scale (VPI) for a group of 100 females on the Realistic Scale were .79 over two weeks, .57 over two months, .86 over one year, and .58 over four years.

Alternative Forms.   Two equivalent forms of a test permit correlation of scores on the two measures to provide an estimate of reliability. This method gives a coefficient of stability because an individual's behavior is being measured at two different times.

The resulting coefficient is considered to be a conservative estimate of reliability. This method also provides a coefficient of equivalence that tells how closely the two tests measure the same constructs. Sources of measurement error occur in both the two forms and the two testings.

Equivalent, or parallel, forms of a test present the same type of format and have almost equal difficulty. They are based on the same blueprint, have the same number of items, and include the same directions for administering, scoring, and interpreting the test. They do not use the same specific items, but a sample of different items form the same domain. This method eliminates the problem of memory and practice, which affects the test-retest reliability. Most survey achievement tests, scholastic aptitude tests, and general aptitude batteries have two or more forms. Alternate forms are especially helpful when pretest and posttest comparisons are needed and high correlation is thus required. For example, on the Primary I Battery, Form F Reading correlated .95 with Form G Reading for 1,326 second grade students.

Split-Half Reliability.   Split-half reliability requires only one administration of a given test. However, the test is divided into two comparable halves—for example, the odd items and even items. The scores on the two subtests are then computed and correlated, and the resulting coefficient provides an estimate of the equivalence of the two forms. Because we are comparing the relationship of two halves rather than full-length tests, we adjust the coefficient, using the Spearman-Brown prophecy formula, to get an estimate of what the coefficient would be if the test halves were full length.

$$\text{total test reliability} = \left(\frac{2r}{1 + r}\right)$$

In the formula r represents the correlation between the two halves. If the correlation is .60, we can substitute the coefficient in the formula and calculate a reliability estimate for the full test.

$$\text{total} = \frac{2(.60)}{1 + (.60)} = \frac{1.20}{1.60} = .75$$

The estimated reliability of the full test is .75. In general this method tends to give a higher estimate of reliability than do the methods previously discussed. As an example, on the reading test portion of the Metropolitan Achievement Test Primary 1 Battery, the split-half coefficient corrected by the Spearman-Brown formula was .96 for a group of second graders.

Other Internal Consistency Methods.   Other methods of computing the reliability of a test consider how certain items on the test relate to other items and to the total test. The Kuder-Richardson formulas (KR 20 and KR 21) are utilized to estimate rational equivalence reliability. The formulas provide an estimate of reliability that is approximately equal to the average of all split-half reliabilities computed for all possible halves.

The KR 20 formula is

$$r = \frac{n}{n-1} \left(1 - \frac{\Sigma pq}{s^2}\right)$$

In the formula r = reliability, n = number of items on the test, Σ = sum of, p = proportion of examinees getting each item correct, q = proportion of examinees getting each item incorrect, and s^2 = variance of the test. The following example illustrates the KR 20 formula.

Item	1	2	3	4	5	
p	.5	.4	.8	.6	.7	
q	.5	.6	.2	.4	.3	
pq	.25	.24	.16	.24	.21	$(\Sigma pq = 1.10)$
						$(s^2 = 2.00)$

$$\frac{5}{4} \left(1 - \frac{1.10}{2.00}\right) = \frac{5}{4} (.45) = .56$$

The KR 21 formula is easier to compute. The procedure is based on the assumption that the difficulty levels are similar for all items on the test. KR 21 tends to underestimate the reliability of a test if the items vary in difficulty.

$$r = \frac{n}{n-1} \left[1 - \frac{\overline{X}(n - \overline{X})}{n s^2}\right]$$

In this formula r = reliability, n = number of items, $\{X\}$ = mean, and s^2 = variance of the test. If n = 80, $\{X\}$ = 50, and s^2 = 100, then the KR 21 reliability is computed like this:

$$r = \frac{80}{79} \left[1 - \frac{50(80 - 50)}{80(100)}\right]$$

$$r = \frac{80}{79} \left[1 - \frac{1500}{8000}\right]$$

$$r = 1.01 \, [1 - .19]$$

$$r = 1.01 \, [.81] = .82$$

Another internal consistency method of computing reliability is Cronbach's Alpha (Cronbach, 1951), which is a method of computing the reliability of a test through using interclass correlation. It can be used when two or more scoring weights are assigned to answers and does not require the right-wrong scoring as does KR 20.

A number of problems are associated with using or interpreting estimates of internal consistency reliability. First, this method works best with a test measuring a single construct, domain, or subject area. The magnitude of the relationship is affected by the degree of homogeneity of the items on a test. If the test items measure heterogeneous dimensions, the coefficients are lower. Second, the method is not appropriate for speeded tests that consist of a series of relatively easy items or tasks, or problems that have to be completed in a strict time (e.g., the clerical speed and accuracy test from the Differential Aptitude Battery). The estimates of these speeded tests are inflated. The Salience Inventory, for instance, reports Cronbach's alpha coefficients on the Participation Scale of .88 for studying, .85 for working, .93 for community service, .87 for home and family, and .88 for leisure activities.

Table 3.2 summarizes the methods for assessing reliability.

Standard Error of Measurement. To apply the reliability information to the interpretation of individual scores, information is needed on the standard error of measurement and is usually contained in the test manual. The standard error of measurement is computed by using this formula.

$$SEM = s \sqrt{1 - r}$$

In the formula SEM = standard error of measurement, s = standard deviation of the test, and r = reliability coefficient of the test. If, for example, the standard deviation on the Erewhon IQ test is 15 and the reliability coefficient is .91, the standard error of measurement is computed thus.

$$SEM = 15 \sqrt{1 - .91}$$
$$SEM = 15 \sqrt{.09}$$
$$SEM = 15 \times .3 = 4.5$$

Table 3.2
Methods of assessing reliability

Method	Procedure	Coefficient	Problems
Test-retest	Same test given twice with time interval between testings	Stability	Memory effect Practice effect Change over time
Alternate forms	Equivalent tests given with time between testings	Equivalence and stability	Hard to develop two equivalent tests May reflect change in behavior over time
Internal consistency	One test given at one time only (test divided into parts in split-half)	Equivalence and internal consistency	Uses shortened forms (split-half) Only good if traits are unitary or homogeneous Gives high estimate on a speeded test Hard to compute by hand

If the reliability of the test is .64 instead, the standard error of measurement is computed like this.

$$SEM = 15 \sqrt{1 - .64}$$
$$SEM = 15 \sqrt{.36}$$
$$SEM = 15 \times .6 = 9.0$$

The standard error of measurement tells the range within which a person's true score may fall. The range variability of an individual's score is a function of the reliability of the test. If the reliability is 1.00, the standard error is zero. The individual's obtained score would be her true score. Standard errors of measurement are distributed normally and form a normal curve. On the Metropolitan Achievement Test the standard errors are present for the raw scores, standard scores, and grade equivalent scores: Reading KR#20 = .93, Split-Half= .95; SEM RS = 2.3; SEM SS = 2.7, and SEM GE = .3.

We can look at the confidence band of the range in which the true score might fall.

$$\pm 1 \text{ SEM} = 68 \text{ times out of } 100$$
$$\pm 2 \text{ SEM} = 95 \text{ times out of } 100$$
$$\pm 3 \text{ SEM} = 995 \text{ times out of } 1000$$

In other words, 68 times out of 100 a person's true score will fall within the range formed by that person's obtained score plus or minus one standard error of measurement. If John scored 100 on the IQ test and the standard error of measurement was 4.5, we can say that 68 chances out of 100 or 68% of the time, John's true score will fall between 95.5 and 104.5. Ninety-five times out of 100, or 95% of the time, his true score will fall between 91 and 109. *Standards for Educational and Psychological Tests* calls for authors and publishers to give users information on the standard error of measurement. Standard 2.9 states that the standard error of measurement should be presented for each major population for which the test is recommended (p. 22).

Factors Influencing Reliability

One of the factors influencing reliability is the length of the test. There is a trend to develop quick methods of assessing individual aptitude as with the Career Ability Placement Survey (CAPS) (see Chapters 8 and 10). However, one of the major ways of increasing the reliability of a test is to increase its length. This works, up to a point, because more items can cover the test domain more completely and can assess a larger sample of behavior. Another version of the Spearman-Brown Prophecy formula indicates the reliability of the test with increased length.

$$r = \frac{(nr)}{1 + (n - 1)r}$$

In the formula r = reliability of the test and n = number of times the test length is increased. If the reliability of a 10-minute spatial aptitude test is .50, the reliability can be increased by increasing the test length.

$$\frac{2(.50)}{1 + (2-1)(.50)} \qquad \frac{3(.50)}{1 + (3-1)(.50)} \qquad \frac{4(.50)}{1 + (4-1)(.50)}$$

Theoretically, if we increase the length of the test two, three, or four times, the reliability increases to .67, .75, or .80. There may be a point at which the test is too long, making it hard to get the test taker to attend to the tasks at hand. Fatigue and frustration may also have an effect on test performance.

A second factor that is crucial to the reliability of the test is the reliability of the scoring. Some types of tests such as multiple choice and true-false are objective, and the accuracy of the scoring can be checked readily. However, this condition is not true of some of the projective personality tests or observation or essay tests. When ratings are used as scores, rater bias can be a major source of unreliability.

A third factor that affects the reliability coefficient is the variability of the group. For instance, the reliability coefficients for individual grades or age groups will be lower than for the coefficients for an age span or grade span.

Grade 4	.82
Grade 5	.83
Grade 6	.85
Grades 4–6	.92

If the group is more homogeneous, the reliability will be lower than it is for a heterogeneous group. There is less variability of scores in a homogeneous group, more in a heterogeneous group.

A fourth factor that affects the reliability of a test is the difficulty of the items. Reliability coefficients are lower when the test is either too easy or too difficult; the distributions of scores become more homogeneous under those circumstances. On difficult tests the test takers increase the unreliability of the test by guessing.

PRACTICAL MEASUREMENT CONCEPTS

A number of practical features need to be considered in the evaluation of a test. Validity and reliability may hold more importance, but other factors merit attention also.

Time of Testing

The time it takes to give a test may be a factor. Can the test be administered during a regular class period, or does the examiner need more time? How many individually administered tests can an examiner reasonably schedule during a day? Is a short, rough approximation of a construct adequate, or is a thorough evaluation necessary?

Time is a factor that is important in decision making. The purpose of the testing may determine how important that factor may be. For example, time constraints may be a critical variable when the concern is with getting information quickly to facilitate decision making. We know that the longer the test, the more reliable the results; but the question might be how much reliability is necessary for a particular purpose.

Cost of Testing

Cost is an important feature because most schools and agencies have limited budgets. Some test companies now lease tests, especially achievement batteries, rather than require the user to purchase them. Also, some test booklets are reusable, requiring the examiner to purchase only answer sheets for another testing. If computer software is available, evaluation of total cost should consider not only the purchase of test materials but also the time needed to administer, score, and interpret the tests. There are many scoring services to which most of the major tests and test batteries can be sent for scoring and interpretation—at an additional cost, of course.

Format of the Test

Just as in the evaluation of other printed material, test users should consider factors such as size of print, attractiveness of format, and clarity of illustrations. Some tests are attractively designed and utilize a variety of colors and print sizes. Some, however, have print that is too small or dark paper that is hard to read. Some tests may utilize double columns to cut down on necessary eye movements; others spread the items across the whole page. The test user should think of the test taker. An attractive format may provide more valid results.

Readability

The readability of the test is an important factor. In general, unless the intent is to test the reading level or verbal facility of the test taker, the reading level should be kept simple so that the construct is measured rather than a reading comprehension factor. Many tests report an index of readability—perhaps Dale Chall or Irving Lorge. Even a test presented on a cassette should use an appropriate reading level and vocabulary. On the Occupational Stress Inventory (Osipow & Spokane, 1987) randomly selected items from each scale and five estimates of reading levels were computed (Dale Chall 8.9; Fog 8.9; Flesch 6.9; Fry 5.0; Smog 6.0). The Millon Adolescent Personality Inventory was developed for youth who read at the sixth grade level or above.

Ease of Administration

Chapter 5 discusses administration of tests in more detail, but it should be noted here that there are different levels of tests. Some require extensive training to administer and score; others do not. Some tests are more difficult to administer because they have a number of individually timed subtests and elaborate instructions for the test taker. The test users should read through the test manual and evaluate the difficulty of test administration.

Ease of Scoring

Some tests have scoring templates and are easy to score by hand or by computer. Other tests require considerable judgment and experience on the part of the examiner. Some utilize differential weighing, for example. Behavioral observations may require specialized training to score. It is possible for scoring to take more time than administering a test. Even when a test is objective and has a predetermined scoring key, the test user should double-check the accuracy of the scoring.

Ease of Interpretation

Results are not useful unless they are interpretable, and both test makers and examiners are expected to provide explanation. Many tests do provide manuals of interpretation for the examiner or detailed sections in the test manual. The better tests have sample or illustrative case studies. Test users should also check to see whether there are special profile sheets or materials to guide the test takers in understanding the results.

Available Aids for Test Administrators

Quite a number of tests now exist on audio cassettes, some on video cassettes. All kinds of software packages are available for users, and many tests and questionnaires are now administered on personal computers. Available aids may make a test easier to administer. For example, a video tape of directions given in sign language might facilitate a test given to a deaf individual.

Usefulness of Test Manual

A test manual should be understandable and thorough. Some of the major components are listed below.

1. The manual should provide evidence to support any use of a single item as a basis of assessment and should caution the user about errors of that approach.
2. The manual should include evidence of the distinctiveness of the constructs being measured. The authors need to discuss how the test was developed and revised.
3. The manual should provide scientific evidence on the test.
4. The manual should provide adequate description of the domains assessed and the types of items included in the domain.
5. The manual should include a description of the course or training program for which the test was designed and the year the materials were prepared.
6. On interest inventories the authors should provide the extent to which average patterns of interests or abilities for an occupation are compatible with the major specialties within that occupation.
7. For adaptive tests the developers need to provide the procedures for selecting items, stopping the test, and scoring the test.

8. The manual should present the implications of the research for test design, interpretation, and use.

9. The manual should summarize evidence derived from research studies to indicate the degree to which improvement can be expected from practice or coaching.

10. The manual should explain in sufficient detail and clarity the procedures for scoring tests locally to maximize the accuracy of scoring. (*Standards for Educational and Psychological Testing*, 1985)

Section 5 of *Standards for Educational and Psychological Testing* (1985) is devoted to standards specifically for test publications: technical manuals and user's guides. Standards are discussed and are summarized in a checklist in Figure 3.2.

Figure 3.2
Checksheet for evaluating a test manual

	Yes	No
1. Technical manual available at time of publication of test	___	___
2. Rationale and uses of test discussed	___	___
3. User cautioned about possible misuses	___	___
4. Studies presented on general uses	___	___
5. Studies presented on specific uses	___	___
6. Special qualifications of users stated	___	___
7. Bibliography of research and studies on test presented	___	___
8. Test manual updated and revised when new edition of test was published	___	___
9. Inquiries invited from potential users	___	___
10. Relationships between test scores and criteria reported	___	___
11. Test administration conditions and modes explained	___	___
12. Interpretive aids provided for test takers	___	___
13. Promotional materials accurately supported by research base	___	___
14. Test interpretation easy to understand	___	___
15. Automated test interpretation service available	___	___
16. Rationale presented and conceptualized if cut-off scores are given	___	___
17. Validity of interpretation discussed	___	___
18. Evidence presented on whether construct being measured corresponds to nature of assessment intended	___	___
19. Rationale for specific combination of subtests and justification of interpretive relationships among scores included	___	___
20. Gender and relevant racial or ethnic group information presented	___	___
21. Method of recommended linguistic modification described in detail	___	___

SUMMARY

This chapter has focused primarily on the measurement concepts of validity, reliability, and practicality. Validity relates to whether the test measures what it purports to measure. Content validity is established by demonstrating a similarity or relationship between what is being measured on the test and what is being taught in the targeted program. A different type of validity is established by comparing test scores with criterion measures. There are two types of criterion validity—concurrent and predictive. Concurrent validity requires that the test scores be compared to a criterion measure taken at or about the same time. In predictive validity the criterion measure is taken at some time in the future. Because most psychological variables cannot be directly measured, a third type of validity—construct validity—has to be established. Construct validity is based on statistical, experimental, and judgmental information that the construct identified is actually measured by the test. Test users need to understand the different types of validity so that they can judge a test's validity for their particular purpose.

Reliability relates to the precision or accuracy of measurement. Different types of procedures are used to establish the reliability of a test—test-retest, alternate forms, split-half and internal consistency methods. Reliability coefficients range from zero to +1.00; the higher the coefficient, the more reliable the test. Errors of measurement interfere with the consistency and accuracy of measurement. Therefore, we use the standard error of measurement as a way of looking at the confidence we can have in interpreting a score.

Another important factor is practicality. Test users are concerned with time; cost; test format; readability; and ease of administering, scoring, and interpreting a test. It is also important to assess the helpfulness of the test manual.

QUESTIONS FOR DISCUSSION

1. What are the different types of validity, and when would each type be important to a test user?

2. What type of validity is represented by each of these questions:
   a. Do the test items match the objectives of our school?
   b. How does the new values test compare with Super's Work Values Inventory?
   c. How well does the Algebra Prognostic Test predict success or failure in Algebra I?
   d. Is there a relationship between the score on the Minnesota Rate of Manipulation Test and workers' rate of assembly of a product?
   e. Is there a relationship between the Mechanical Ability Test and performance of individuals in a six-week training program in mechanics?
   f. Is creativity a distinct factor measured by the test?
   g. Do the abstract thinking items cluster together?

3. What are the different methods of estimating the reliability of a test? What are the advantages and disadvantages of each method?

4. Criterion-reference validity is important in aptitude and ability testing. What are some of the problems in identifying appropriate criterion measures? How would you evaluate criterion measures?

5. Which factor do you believe is more important in selecting a test: validity, reliability, or practicality? Under what conditions would validity be the most important factor? Reliability? Practicality?

SUGGESTED ACTIVITIES

1. Review several standardized tests and identify the types of validity and reliability presented in the test manuals.

2. Interview psychologists and counselors and find out how they use the standard error of measurement in their testing. See whether they have completed any studies of the validity or reliability of the tests they use.

3. Construct an achievement test on the concepts introduced in this chapter and administer it to a number of students in your class. Then compute the reliability of the test using split-half and KR20 or KR21.

4. Write a paper or prepare a class report on one of the following topics: factors that affect test reliability, reliability, reliability of teacher-made tests.

5. Read the critical reviews of some of the tests that you have taken and see what the reviewers say about the validity, reliability, and practicality of the test.

6. Study the following descriptions of two tests and answer the questions that follow the descriptions.

Test A: 40 items

Subscales: General self-esteem, social self-esteem, personal self-esteem, lie
Administration: Self-administering
Item Format: Items in form of questions and test taker checks "yes" or "no" (example: Do you enjoy taking tests? Y N)
Scoring: Hand scoring, one template with the targeted answers and scales identified
Interpretability: Norm tables provided. Illustrative case studies presented
Reliability: Test-retest for adult sample .81
Alpha coefficients: General .78; Social .57; Personal .72, Lie .54
Validity: Content—developed construct definitions for self-esteem and wrote items to cover all areas of the construct; concurrent—correlated scale with Coopersmith's Self-Esteem Inventory $r = .80$, correlation with Beck Depression Inventory and MMPI also presented; construct—factor analysis completed on the scale revealed five subtests for the children's version and four for the adult version; correlations between the scales indicate General correlated .89 with Total, .67 with Social, and .79 with Personal.

Test B: 116 Items

Scales: Global Self-Esteem, Competence, Lovability, Likability, Self-control, Personal Power, Moral Self-Approval, Body Appearance, Body Functioning, Identity Integration, and Defensive Self-enhancement

Administration: Self-administering

Item Format: Client responds to each item on a five point scale ranging from Completely True to Completely False and on section 2, from Almost Never to Very Often (example: People tend to like to include me in their plans)

Scoring: The answer sheet is designed so that it can be scored immediately by ripping the answer booklet to reveal the scoring sheet and counting the numerical weights of the options chosen. There are separate profile sheets for males and females on which the *T* scores and percentile ranks can be identified by circling the computed raw score for each scale.

Interpretability: The manual does not have any case studies illustrating test interpretation. The manual does provide a description of what low scores and high scores mean on each scale.

Reliability: Test-retest coefficients are reported for the test and range form a high of .89 on the Body Functioning Scale to a low of .78 on the Identity Integration Scale. The alpha coefficients range from a low of .78 on Defensive Self-Enhancement to .90 on Global Self-Esteem and Body Functioning.

Validity: The test is a hierarchial model with the first level measuring global self-esteem and the second level corresponding to self-evaluations at an intermediate level of generality.

Convergent and Discriminant Validity: The scale was correlated with the Guilford-Zimmerman Temperament Survey, the Eysenck Personality Inventory, the Body Cathexis Scale among others. The average convergent correlation was .58 and discriminant coefficient was .31. Factor analysis was also conducted on the scaled scores on the test. Three factors were extracted with eigenvalues greater than 1.

a.   Given the following descriptive and technical information, which of the following tests would you select?

b.   What additional information would you want to have to make your decision?

ADDITIONAL READINGS

Feldt, L. S., & Brennan, R. L. (1989). Reliability. In R. L. Linn (Ed.), *Educational measurement* (3rd ed.). New York: Macmillan.

Mesick, S. (1989). Validity. In R. L. Linn (Ed.), *Educational measurement* (3rd ed.). New York: Macmillan.

These two chapters present a thorough review and commentary on two of the important concepts in measurement.

Zeidner, M., & Most, R. (Eds.). (1992). *Psychological testing: An inside view*. Palo Alto, CA: Consulting Psychologists Press.

The book presents an understandable and readable discussion of the major constructs in testing.

CHAPTER 4

Locating and Selecting Tests

Overview

Because workers in the helping professions are often responsible for locating and selecting tests, these professionals need to be familiar with the different sources of test information that are available to them. They need to know the particular strengths and weaknesses of each source. The selection process also calls for familiarity with decision theory. The type of test selected should depend on the kinds of judgments or decisions that must be made. Helping professionals also need to be familiar with the criteria for evaluating educational and psychological tests.

Objectives

After studying this chapter, the reader should be able to

- explain the decision model used to help make judgments and decisions
- list and discuss the sources of test information
- identify and discuss the criteria that should be used to evaluate a test

DECISION THEORY MODEL

A decision theory model provides professionals with a frame of reference to guide them in deciding whether to test and how to locate and select a test. The following questions represent the various steps in a decision theory model.

1. What kinds of judgments or decisions have to be made?

2. What type of information is needed to make the best judgment or decision?

3. What type of information is already available?

4. When and how should the additional information be obtained?

5. What methods and/or instruments are available to help get the information? How should the appropriate test and instruments be located?

6. How should the tests or instruments be evaluated? What criteria should be used in selection?

Decisions and Judgments to Be Made

Workers in the helping professions are often asked to provide information to help child study teams, teachers, or other professionals decide the best type of psychological or educational program to use with a client(s) or the best type of intervention. Helping professionals are often asked to diagnose the strengths and weaknesses of a student with problems in reading or mathematics. Or they may be asked to predict the success of a student in a given educational or vocational program or a client in a treatment program. A school system may want to have a description of the basic skill competencies students have mastered. Or a client may want guidance in what career to consider.

These are only a few examples of the decisions and judgments that must be made. Sometimes the judgments focus on one individual, sometimes on a group. Sometimes their purpose is to predict behavior, sometimes to understand behavior, and sometimes to describe behavior. The key concept is that counselors need to be able to identify clearly the kind of decision or judgment that has to be made. The more specific the problem is, the easier it is to proceed to the next step in the model. The more abstract or vague the issue is, the more difficult it is to ask the right questions.

Type of Information Needed

The second step in the decision-making process is to identify the type of information needed, carefully considering the scope and range of information required. Sometimes, for a particular job a checklist can be developed of the types of information normally needed and the types of questions that should be asked. A career counselor with a client suffering from midcareer crisis might be interested in the individual's employment history as well as current and future job desires. The counselor might also want information about the client's educational background, aptitudes, values, interests, and level of achievement. Cultural and environmental factors, marital status, socioeconomic class, and age are other dimensions that might be relevant. Of course, not all of the information would be gained through testing. It is valuable to discuss a case with colleagues or other professionals to be sure all types of necessary information have been identified. Even though problems may often appear to be unique, a systematic analysis helps develop a systematic approach to identifying needed information.

Information Already Available

The next step is to identify what part of the necessary information is already available. In clinical settings there are intake questionnaires, biographical data banks, and preliminary diagnoses by clinicians and physicians. In school settings there are cumulative folders containing family information, educational history, grades, assessment and test results, anecdotal records, and attendance and health information. Unfortunately, overtesting may sometimes occur—that is, when a client is asked to repeat a recent test or take a similar one. One school district gave all of its students in grades 9 and 10 the Otis-Lennon School Ability Test, the Differential Aptitude Test, the School and College Ability Tests, and the California Test of Mental Maturity. These tests repeatedly assessed the same factors. On an individual basis it is sometimes valuable to have more than one measure of scholastic aptitude or ability. However, when clients are asked to repeat the same test in a short time frame, they may lose motivation or even become hostile. It may be helpful to develop a checklist of information normally available on clients in a particular context. Figure 4.1 presents a sample checklist for a counselor/psychologist in a school setting.

Strategies to Obtain Additional Information

After identifying the type of information needed and the information already available, the professional needs to decide how and when to obtain additional information. If the information needed is to aid in curriculum and instructional decisions for a school system, a schoolwide testing program might be desirable. If the goal is to see whether a student has some type of learning disability, an individual battery of tests would be appropriate.

The time of day, the day of the week, the physical or emotional condition of the client, and the newness of the client to the environment are some of the factors to be considered. In addition, age, grade, level of anxiety and stress, and other issues can be important. And legal aspects need attention in many contexts, especially in testing exceptional students, when parental as well as student approval is sought. Some legal requirements can be quite time-consuming. Because of the total time required to identify and review tests that would be appropriate in a given context and to have the booklets and answer sheets available when needed, many schools and agencies develop an approved list of tests to use for different types of decisions or judgments.

Figure 4.1
Sample checklist of available information

	Needed?	
	Yes	No
Cumulative folder of student		
Birth date	_____	_____
Family information	_____	_____
Record of attendance	_____	_____
Record of marks awarded at each grade level	_____	_____
Previous schools attended	_____	_____
Transcripts of grades from other schools	_____	_____
Minimum level of skills test results	_____	_____
State assessment test results	_____	_____
Survey achievement test results	_____	_____
Scholastic aptitude test results	_____	_____
Health data and records	_____	_____
Hearing tests	_____	_____
Vision tests	_____	_____
Disciplinary actions	_____	_____
Anecdotal records of teachers	_____	_____
Systematic observations of teachers	_____	_____
Child study team action	_____	_____
Class records		
Current attendance	_____	_____
Grades on tests and assignments	_____	_____
Progress in reading	_____	_____
Reading level	_____	_____
Competencies mastered	_____	_____
Samples of work	_____	_____
Anecdotes on or observations of behavior	_____	_____
Notes from parent conferences	_____	_____
Skills mastered	_____	_____
Sociometric data	_____	_____
Guidance counselor's records		
Interest data	_____	_____
Behavior problems	_____	_____
Career and educational goals	_____	_____
Participation in school activities	_____	_____
Cooperative work experience data	_____	_____
Parent or guardian's records		
Nonschool activities and achievements	_____	_____
Health records	_____	_____
Previous achievement records	_____	_____
Transcripts or report cards	_____	_____
Papers or assignments	_____	_____

Testing also has to be coordinated with the school schedule, student schedule, or treatment schedule so that the program is not disruptive or traumatic for the client. The examiner wants cooperative and motivated test takers in order to get valid information from the testing. Students tend to perform better in the morning and quite poorly right before a holiday.

Locating Appropriate Tests

Workers in the helping professions need to know the sources of test information, which will help them get the most appropriate tests for the purposes identified. Many published as well as unpublished instruments are available, some of which are copyrighted and some of which are in the public domain. Counselors and psychologists should be able to identify and evaluate different types of test information. A list of the types of sources and their advantages and disadvantages is given in Table 4.1. The sources range from the specimen copy of the test itself to information provided by colleagues or professionals in the field. It is important to have multiple strategies to locate appropriate tests or instruments. A list of selected sources of test information is included at the end of the chapter. Other reference sources are included in the bibliography at the end of the chapter.

One of the major sources of information is the ERIC Clearinghouse on Assessment and Evaluation housed at the Catholic University of America (209 O'Boyle Hall, Washington, DC, 20064, tel. 202-319-5120). The clearinghouse publishes a brief digest on hot topics in assessment and evaluation as well as the periodic *Measurement Update*. ERIC/AE is a "gopher site." A gopher site or client is a system of software that allows the user to access information both located at the gopher site itself and worldwide via the Internet. Internet is a worldwide network for computers, also known as an information superhighway. The ERIC/AE gopher site includes the ETS Test Collection of more than 9,500 commercial and noncommercial tests. Table 4.2 lists a representative selection of current Test Collection bibliographies from ETS. ERIC/AE also provides Test Review Locator for databases containing the indexes to the *Mental Measurements Yearbooks*, *Tests in Print*, and *Test Critiques*. The clearinghouse also collects essays and bibliographies on current issues in assessment and evaluation. The center also provides the user with direct access to ERIC abstracts, *ERIC Digests*, *Ask ERIC Helpsheets*, Infoguides, and Lesson Plans and can connect the user to CRESST, OERI, SEIS, and other gopher sites. The ERIC/AE gopher site may be directly accessed at gopher.cua,edu, or through telenet or E-Mail (ERIC_AE@CUA.EDU.).

Other Sources of Information on Tests

A number of professional groups publish papers on testing and testing issues. The National Center for Fair and Open Testing (342 Broadway, Cambridge, MA 02139, tel. 616-864-4810) publishes the *Fair Test Examiner*, a quarterly source of up-to-date news and information on testing. The quarterly includes updates on state and federal legislation affecting testing; reports on test misuse and efforts to stop it; and

Table 4.1
Evaluation of sources of information

Type	Advantages	Disadvantages
Specimen sets	Can see test and test format Can read and evaluate technical information about the test Can judge validity, reliability, and interpretability of the test	Does not always include all pertinent information such as technical manual or manual for interpretation or scoring keys
Publisher's catalog	Can get current information on the cost of the test and scoring services available Can get information on new tests and services available	Sometimes presents biased picture of the test Sometimes does not have necessary technical and practical information such as time required, age or grade levels appropriate, sources from which to get complete test package, basic information to screen quickly for appropriateness, such as a description of scales or subtests
Test review volume	Contains critical reviews of the test by experts Contains bibliography of studies done using the test, such as those to assess the validity and reliability of the test	May present dated information because some volumes are published infrequently Can present a spotty or biased review because reviewers do not follow a common format Does not discuss thoroughly the purposes and possible applications of the test
Journal in the measurement field	Contains validity and reliability studies Contains reviews of certain tests Contains research on issues in testing Shows applications of a test or test procedure	Can present theoretical and technical reports Contains spotty reviews without a common format and reviews only a few tests May take two to three years to get information into print because of publication backlog
Newsletter from ERIC center, professional organization, publisher	Keeps abreast of new tests, texts, reference books in field, and issues related to test construction, administration, and interpretation Sometimes offers up-to-date bibliographies of articles and research reports using or evaluating a given test or test procedure	Can be biased Can require a subscription cost Does not index sources, so information may be hard to retrieve

Type	Advantages	Disadvantages
Abstracts (e.g., ERIC, CIJE, *Psychological Abstracts*)	Presents information that is retrievable through computerized searches Includes the major publications and information sources in the field	Identifies sources that are not always readily available May not include information on the instruments used in the study or report May use unfamiliar tests Involves a time lag between article publication and inclusion in the abstract
Test collection, specific annotated bibliography	Identifies from a variety of sources the major tests and instruments developed and used May be updated systematically and published regularly	May include dated and sometimes incomplete sources May not present information on many of the technical and practical issues, such as cost and time
Text, reference books, manual	Provides in-depth information on certain tests, instruments, or procedures Provides information on application	May present dated and biased material Can be highly technical or oversimplified Sometimes presents only one theoretical approach or styled interpretation
Manual or position paper on standards for educational and psychological tests	Provides guidelines for the construction of tests and manuals Presents criteria for interpreting and using tests	Requires background in measurement theory Requires knowledge of the history of trends and issues in testing
Colleague or person working in the field	Is abreast of the field Has first-hand experience in using certain tests Can offer guidance in administration, scoring, and interpretation of tests	May have some biases May not have had sufficient training and experience in utilizing certain tests

profiles of promising new assessment systems at the school, university, and employment testing levels. The center also publishes monographs such as "Sex Bias in College Admissions Tests," "Beyond Standardized Tests," "SAT Coaching Coverup," and annotated bibliographies on assessment of young children, performance assessment, bilingual assessment, and the like.

The Center for the Study of Evaluation, Standards and Student Testing (CRESST) (Center for the Study of Education Annex, 10880 Wilshire Boulevard #700, Los Angeles, CA 90024-4108) publishes a quarterly newsletter on alternative and authentic assessment.

Table 4.2
Representative selection of current Test Collection Bibliographies from ETS

Achievement
Achievement Batteries, Preschool–Gr. 3
Achievement Batteries, Gr. 4–6
Achievement Batteries, Gr. 7 and Above
Achievement Tests, College Level
Algebra Tests
American Government
American History
Art Achievement Tests
Art Education
Basic Skills Competency tests
Biology Achievement
Consumer Competencies
Criterion-Referenced Measures, Preschool–Gr. 3
Criterion-Referenced Measures, Gr. 4–6
Criterion-Referenced Measures, Gr. 7 and Above
Economics, Gr. 1 and Above
Environmental Education
French–Foreign Language
Geography
Geometry
//////////////

Aptitude
Artistic Aptitude
Cognitive Style and Information Processing
Concept Formation and Acquisition
Creativity and Divergent Thinking
Curiosity
General Aptitude, Adults
General Aptitude, Kindergarten–Gr. 6
Intelligence—Group Administered, Preschool–Gr. 3
Intelligence—Group, Gr. 4–6
Intelligence—Group, Gr. 7 and Above

Intelligence—Individually Administered, Preschool–Gr. 3
Intelligence—Individually Administered, Gr. 4–6
Intelligence—Individually Administered, Gr. 7 and Above
Memory
Musical Aptitude
Nonverbal Aptitude
Reasoning, Logical Thinking, Problem Solving
Scholastic Aptitude and Mental Ability
Spatial-Perceptual Relations
////////

Attitudes and Interests
Academic Interests
Children's Attitudes Toward Parents
Curriculum, Attitudes Toward
Educational Techniques, Attitudes Toward
Occupational Attitudes and Job Satisfaction
Racial Attitudes
Religious Attitudes
School and School Adjustment, Attitudes Toward
Sex Roles and Attitudes Toward Women
Social Attitudes
Values
Vocational Interests

Personality
Aggression and Hostility
Alienation
Anxiety
Ascendance-Submission
Depression
Independence-Dependence
Introversion-Extroversion

The National Center on Post Secondary Teaching, Learning, and Assessment (Pennsylvania State University, 403 South Allen Street, Suite 104, University Park, PA 16801-5252). NCPSTLA publishes a quarterly newsletter and occasional publications specifically on assessment.

The following are among the journals that focus on measurement:

Assessment and Evaluation in Higher Education Assessment

Educational and Psychological Measurement

Leadership
Locus of Control
Masculinity-Femininity
Motivation and Need-Achievement
Personality—General
Personality Adjustment
Projective Measures
Psychosexual Development
Responsibility/Perseverance
Self-Concept
Stress
Task Orientation

Sensory Motor
Auditory Skills
Motor Skills
Sensory Motor Abilities
Vision and Visual Perception, Preschool–Gr. 3

Special Populations
Adult Basic Education
American Indians
Brain and Visually Handicapped
Brain-Damaged
Bright Children and Adults
Deaf and Hearing Impaired
Disadvantaged Preschool Children
Educationally Disadvantaged Children
Educationally Disadvantaged Adults
Emotionally Disturbed, Identification
Juvenile Delinquents
Learning Disabilities
Mentally Retarded
Spanish Speakers

Vocational/Occupational
Business Skills
Clerical Aptitude and Achievement
Data Processing
Employment Interviews
Engineering Aptitude and Achievement
Mechanical Aptitude and Achievement
Nurses
Occupational Knowledge, Skilled Trades
Supervisory, Management
Teacher Assessment
Vocational Aptitude
Vocational Rating and Selection Forms
/////

Miscellaneous
Behavior Rating Scales
Biographical Inventories
Child Rearing Practices and Related Attitudes
Counseling Aids
Courtship and Marriage
Culture-Fair and Culture-Relevant Tests
Drugs—Knowledge and Abuse
Educational Record and Report Forms
Environments
Family Interaction and Related Attitudes
Group Behavior and Influences
Human Sexuality
Item Pools
Manual Dexterity
Moral Development
Piagetian Measures
Social Perception and Judgment
Social Skills
Systematic Observation Techniques

College Board Review
Educational Measurement: Issues and Practices
Journal of Educational Measurement
Applied Psychological Measurement
Measurement and Evaluation in Counseling and Development
Applied Measurement
Educational Assessment

There are a number of other journals that publish occasional articles on tests and testing issues such as the *American Psychologist*, the *Journal of Counseling and Development*, and the *Educational Researcher*.

Divisions of professional organizations that focus on testing publish a number of newsletters that emphasize current trends, issues, and news in the field such as *SCORE*, a quarterly published by the division of Evaluation, Measurement and Statistics of the American Psychological Association. The National Council on Measurement in Education also publishes a quarterly newsletter. The Association of Assessment in Counseling of the American Counseling Association publishes *Newsnotes*.

Compendia of Instruments

Many compendia of nonstandardized instruments are now available, including the following:

Goldman, B. A., & Mitchell, D. F. (1990). *Directory of unpublished experimental mental measures*. Dubuque, IA: William C. Brown.

Chun, B. A., Cobb, C. S., & French, J. R., Jr. (1975). *Measures of psychological assessment: A guide to 3,000 original sources and their application*. Ann Arbor, MI: Institute for Social Research.

Fischer, J., & Corcoran, K. (Eds.). (1994). *Measures for clinical practice: Vol. 1. Couples and families* (2nd ed.). New York: Macmillan.

Touliato, J., Perlmutter, B. F., & Straus, M. (Eds.). (1990). *Handbook of family measurement techniques*. Newbury Park, CA: Sage.

Rubin, R. B., Palmgreen, P., & Sypher, H. E. (Eds.). (1994). *Communication research measures: A sourcebook*. New York: Guilford.

After locating a list of tests, the potential user might want more specific information before ordering a specimen set to review. Maintaining a file of publishers' catalogs is helpful in this regard. The type of information found in such catalogs is listed here.

Title	Content	Cost
Author	Range	Complete program
Copyright date	Norms	Manual
Brief description	Scoring/scoring services	Test booklets
Purposes	Working time required	Answer sheets
Features and benefits	Requirements for purchase	

The potential user might also choose to look at what the experts have to say about certain tests and should then consult *Mental Measurements Yearbooks*, *Test Critiques*, or some other specialized collection of reviews. The reviews in the *Mental Measurements Yearbooks* are part of a computer retrieval system. *Test Critiques* uses a standard format: introduction, practical application/uses, technical aspects, critique, and references.

A counselor carefully reviews
and evaluates a test.

If everything appears to be in order, it might be time to send for a specimen copy of the test and consider the test booklet as well as available manuals, answer sheets, and scoring services. The goal is to assess whether the test has validity for the intended purpose(s).

Reviewing and Evaluating Tests

Normally, a checklist should be developed for evaluating tests, and the same procedures should be systematically followed for all tests that are reviewed. Certain universal criteria should be evaluated, of course, such as the validity, reliability, interpretability, and practicability of each test. If possible, a committee should review the criteria that will be used. Perhaps the review schedule could be tried out on one or more tests to see whether it is usable and addresses the desired issues. It is better to have more than one member review each test, to gain more than one perception of the test. However, if small subgroups do the initial screening, the total group should participate in the final screening.

Numerous checklists and schedules can serve as a guide. However, certain unique requirements should be considered, depending on the nature of the decision or judgment to be made. These are some of those issues. The *ERIC/AE Digest* suggests these areas for review:

1. *Test coverage and use*—Is there a clear statement of recommended uses and a description of the population for which the test is intended?

2. *Appropriate samples for test (validation and norming)*— Are there samples of adequate size used for test validation and norming of the test to support conclusions regarding the use of the instrument for the intended purpose?

3. *Test reliability*—Is the instrument sufficiently reliable to permit stable estimates of individual ability?

4. *Predictive validity*—Does the test adequately predict academic performance?

5. *Content validity*—Does the test measure the right psychological constructs?

6. *Test administration*—Does the manual contain detailed and clear instructions for administering the test?

7. *Test reporting*—Are the methods used to report test results (including scaled scores, subtests results, and combined test results) fully described along with the rationale for each method?

8. *Test and item bias*—Is the test biased regarding race, gender, native language, ethnic origin, geographic region, or other factors?

Other criteria to consider are

1. *The nature of the construct*—There are more formalized and standardized approaches to measuring scholastic aptitude but less formalized and standardized approaches to measuring learning style.

2. *The number in the testing group*—Does the examiner get the same result when using a group test as when using an individual test? Is different behavior exhibited when the test is taken in a large group rather than individually? Should a group test be administered orally to just one individual?

3. *The characteristics of the examiner*—Who is qualified to administer the test? Does the examiner have the training necessary to administer some of the individual schedules?

4. *The characteristics of the examinee*—Will any physical handicaps affect test performance? Any emotional or social handicaps?

5. *Practical constraints*—Are there any practical constraints, such as the time allotted to testing? Is cost a concern? What kinds of facilities are necessary for testing?

CRITERIA FOR SELECTING A TEST

A number of schedules and forms have been developed for evaluating a standardized test, but it is always important to have the appropriate components—test booklets, answer sheets, technical manual, administrator's manual, and any manual for interpreting the test. Not all specimen sets include these necessary components. The remainder of this chapter discusses questions that should guide helping professionals in selecting a test.

1. *Was the test designed to measure the behavior under consideration?* Does the test manual describe the purposes of the test? Does the intended purpose correspond to one that the test was designed to accomplish? Does the test manual adequately describe the behaviors that it measures? A good test manual provides a statement of the purpose(s) of the test and a description of the behaviors it measures. Sometimes the descriptions are brief; at other times the authors provide a complex matrix of objectives as well as levels measured.

2. *Do the test items appear to be measuring the traits, objectives, or behaviors that are to be assessed?* The next step is to review the test booklet. A survey achievement battery might have only one item measuring a specific objective in mathematics or only four or five items measuring a specific aptitude. To measure a specific competency in mathematics, a criterion-referenced test with 5 to 10 items on a given objective might be preferable. However, to gain a picture of overall achievement in a school system, the survey achievement test might be sufficient.

   In addition, it is important to look at how test items are phrased. An item could be measuring simple recall of factual information or assessing higher level cognitive skills, such as analysis or evaluation. Items on a personality test may be direct (e.g., "Do you like to take tests?") or less direct (e.g., "In a classroom choose the situation you most prefer . . . taking a test, giving an oral report, doing a workbook page."). A test reviewer must sometimes make subjective judgments about items.

3. *Does the test have validity information?* Validity is the concept that deals with whether a test measures what it was designed to measure. The test reviewer must determine whether the test is valid for the intended purpose. If the test will be used for predictive purposes, the reviewer should check the manual for evidence of criterion-related validity. If test results will be used to describe competencies in a certain subject or in content fields, the reviewer should check the content validity of the test. Because a test includes only a limited sample of items representing the objectives or behavior to be measured, it is important that those items be as representative as possible. In addition, because tests use hypothetical constructs that have been operationally defined by the test authors, the reviewer should check the authors' evidence to support the construct validity of the test.

4. *Is the test reliable?* It is important to know how stable or consistent a test is over time, sample of items, or occasions; how precisely the test results can be interpreted; and how the score is affected by measurement errors. The reviewer should check the reliability information in the test manual, inspecting not only the types of reliability cited but also the magnitude of the coefficients reported. Coefficients will be higher for achievement tests than for personality tests, and higher for high school students than for preschool students. The acceptability of the coefficient depends on the intended use of the test results. If test results will be interpreted for individuals, the reviewer should be sure the manual gives information on the standard error of measurement. A test with a large standard

error of measurement might not be appropriate for individual diagnosis, placement, or prediction.

5. *Does the test provide sufficient information for the psychologist or counselor to interpret the results?* A test should provide the necessary information to make a proper interpretation. In norm-referenced tests like survey achievement tests and scholastic ability tests, an individual's score is compared with the scores of other individuals in a selected reference or norm group. The client being tested should be represented in that norming group. Is there information on how the norming group was formulated? The examiner may want to know about the geographic areas, ages, sexual composition, school locations (e.g., urban, rural, suburban), cultural groups, and educational levels included in the norms. The author should explain the procedures to translate raw scores into derived scores and should provide appropriate tables for different types of scores. The author should also describe techniques for interpreting the test and should adequately explain the meaning of the various scales.

A counselor might be interested in more than just a total score and might want specific item information. Some tests do have computerized reports that give information by objective or by item. The psychologist should study the types of scoring services available and should have sample copies of the printout of results and interpretation.

6. *Does the test provide interpretive feedback for the examinee?* It is important to provide information to clients about their performance on a given test. With achievement tests and school testing programs the information needs to be shared not only with students but also with parents or guardians. In adaptive testing, clients taking tests on a microcomputer can get immediate feedback on the screen as well as a hard copy from the printer. Many tests have self-interpretive leaflets or booklets that examinees can use to interpret and understand their results. However, examiners should never allow self-interpretive booklets to take the place of a counselor's communication and explanation of results. Such tools are an excellent supplement, but the counselor must be sure that all information is understood.

7. *Is the test appropriate for the examinee?* A test may measure appropriate behaviors and have excellent reliability and validity but be inappropriate for the client. One important dimension to be considered is the reading level of the items on the test. If the reading level is too difficult, the client may not be able to understand the vocabulary or sentence structure used. A second important dimension is the physical format of the test. The print size, visual layout of questions, and use of color and white space need to be considered. A third dimension is the manner of responding to questions. Are answers to be recorded on a separate answer sheet or in the test booklet, or are they to be spoken, written, marked, or performed?

Examiners must also consider whether the tasks on the test are age- or grade-appropriate; whether the test is appropriate; whether the test is appropriate for clients of different social backgrounds; whether it is appropriate for individuals with various physical, mental, or academic disabilities; and whether special equipment or facilities are needed to administer the test.

bias free test

8. *Is the test free from bias?* Lately, attention has focused on cultural and sexual bias in test items. Test authors should give evidence in their manuals of the procedures used to eliminate bias. The goal is to have items that are relevant and understandable for the individuals being tested. Some older tests do contain biased language.

level of competency

9. *What level of competency is needed to administer the test?* Some tests can be administered to large or small groups and have easy directions for the examiner. Other tests demand careful monitoring and can be administered only individually. In most testing programs the counselor or psychologist trains examiners and teachers to administer the less complicated group achievement and ability tests. But certain individual intelligence tests and personality tests require specialized training for the examiner. And different levels of psychological tests can be purchased and used only by qualified individuals. Sometimes tapes are available to guide test administration, and there may be separate directions for administering the test to special populations. The proper administration of a test is necessary if results are to be valid. Procedures for administering tests are discussed fully in Chapter 5 of this text.

10. *Is the test a practical one to select?* The cost of the test, answer sheets, and scoring services must be calculated. Consideration must also be given to the time factor. Quite often there is limited time to administer a test—perhaps only one 40- to 50-minute period or a few hours during one morning or afternoon. Another factor is usability. Can the test booklet be reused? Are there hand-scoring as well as machine-scoring systems available? Sending a test to be scored may take 10 days to 2 weeks. Are the results needed immediately? The ease and speed of ordering and securing materials may also be a factor. Practical considerations often are as important as some of the theoretical considerations listed earlier.

SUMMARY

A worker in the helping professions needs to know how and where to locate sources of test information. A number of data bases as well as reference sources are readily available. Other traditional sources of test information include specimen sets, publishers' catalogs, test review collections, professional journals, newsletters, ERIC, CIJE, *Psychological Abstracts*, and *News on Tests*. Peers and colleagues may also be a good source of information.

It is important to secure a specimen set of a test from the publisher and to check the face validity of the test. If the test looks promising, its validity, reliability, usability, and practicality should be checked carefully, as well as various reviews by experts in the field.

QUESTIONS FOR DISCUSSION

1. What are the major steps that an examiner should follow in determining what test to use?
2. What are the different sources of test information that can be used in selecting a test? What are the advantages and disadvantages of each?
3. What practical considerations need to be included in selecting a test?
4. Would you use a test that has received a negative review by the critics? Why or why not?
5. Should a client or representative(s) from the group to be tested be involved in the selection of a test? Defend your position on this issue.

SUGGESTED ACTIVITIES

1. Make an annotated bibliography of the sources of test information.
2. Devise a checklist to use to evaluate tests.
3. Critically review a test in your field. Use the questions in this chapter to guide your evaluation.
4. Interview workers in the helping professions who use tests, and find out the procedures they use to select tests. Report your findings to the class.
5. Compare reviews of the same test found in different editions of *Mental Measurements Yearbooks* and in *Test Critiques* and professional journals. What themes did they agree on, and what were some of the sources of disagreement? What parts of the reviews were helpful to you? Write a composite evaluation of the test from these different reviews.
6. Read the following brief case study and answer the questions that follow it.

   The counselor is implementing a program in (choose level) school to enhance self-concept of the students. The counselor has read in the professional journals that the self-concept of females is lower than males and that enhancing the self-concept of students leads to their increased achievement. The counselor decides to browse through professional journals and see what instruments have been used in previous research. Hearing that the two volumes on self-concept by Wylie are the definitive sources on self-concept, the counselor charges the two volumes from the library.

   a. What is the first step the counselor should have followed to find out what self-concept tests are available?

    b.   What are some of the problems with the approach the counselor has used?

    c.   Should the counselor start out by reviewing the catalogs of the major publishers of psychological tests, given that these catalogs are the most recent source of test information?

    d.   If the counselor was using the ERIC/CIJE or Psych Info systems, what key descriptors and strategies should have been used?

ADDITIONAL READINGS

The reader should become familiar with the structure and organization of these sources of test information.

Conoley, J. C., & Kramer, J. J. (Eds.). (1994). *Supplement to the eleventh mental measurements yearbook*. Lincoln, NB: University of Nebraska Press.

Candidly reviews more than 100 tests.

Crosby-Mulenburg, C. (1988). *Psychological and educational tests: A selected annotated guide*. ERIC Document Reproduction Service, TM 001 545.

Identifies books, reports, and journals about tests and includes extensive listings of references in special education, counseling, and early childhood.

Murphy, L. L., Conoley, J., & Impara, J. C. (1994). *Tests in Print IV*. Lincoln, NB: Buros Institute, University of Nebraska.

Contains a brief description of the instruments. Includes intended purpose; information on the test's population, administration, and scoring; and a reference list of professional literature, citing articles relevant to the instruments.

Science Directorate of the American Psychological Association. (1993). *Finding information about psychological tests: A guide for locating and using both published and unpublished tests*. Washington, DC: Author.

A good guide for helping individuals locate the many test sources and information.

ETS Test Collection Catalogs. (1986). *Vol. 1: Achievement tests and measurement devices.* (1988). *Vol. 2: Vocational tests and measurement.* (1989). *Vol. 3: Tests for special populations.* (1990). *Vol. 4: Cognitive, aptitude and intelligence tests.* (1991). *Vol. 5: Attitude tests.* Phoenix: Oryx Press.

ETS (1987). *Directory of selected national testing programs*. Phoenix: Oryx Press.

Fabriano, E. (1989). *Index to tests used in educational dissertations*. Phoenix: Oryx Press.

Fabriano, E., & O'Brien, N. (1987). *Testing information sources for educators*. Clearinghouse on Tests, Measurement, and Evaluation, American Institutes for Research, Washington, DC. Report TME–94.

Guide to more than 150 books, journals, indexes, and computer-based services and organizations that provide information about student assessment.

CHAPTER 5

How to Administer Tests

Overview

To produce reliable and valid test results, a test has to be administered under standardized or controlled conditions. If the examiner does not administer the test as directed, the results may be different from those obtained under standard procedures, and nonstandard results may affect the correctness of the interpretation. Other chapters will discuss the necessity for accurate scoring and reporting of the results, but administration is the important beginning. This chapter introduces, illustrates, and discusses the guidelines and procedures for test administration. In reviewing the literature on test administration, Saklofske and Kowalchuk (1992) identify five major competencies needed by test administrators: adequate training, knowledge of the content being measured, knowledge of test construction, awareness of measurement concepts, and knowledge of good assessment practices.

Objectives

After studying this chapter, the reader should understand

- what professional standards say about test administration
- what procedures the administrator should follow
- what some of the major issues are in administering tests and how to handle these issues
- what to do when the directions are incomplete or unclear

STANDARDS FOR ADMINISTRATION

Professional standards such as the *Standards for Educational and Psychological Testing* (1995) call for proper procedures in administering tests. The test administrator is cautioned to follow carefully the standardized procedures for administration and scoring specified by the test publishers. Saklofske and Schwean (1992) point out that test administration skills and the interpersonal style of the examiner both influence the test takers' performance. If the test administrator can build a dynamic relationship with the test taker, more valid results will be achieved.

The administrator needs to accept the responsibility for competent use and administration of the test and should be trained and qualified to use appropriate tests and to understand the content that the test measures. The National Board of Certified Counselors' Code of Ethics (1989) reminds counselors that there are many types of assessment techniques. Certified counselors must recognize the limits of their competence and perform only those functions for which they have adequate training.

The various standards call for the administrator to establish a comfortable testing environment with minimal distractions. Test materials need to be carefully selected to meet the developmental level of the client; that is, the test should be readable and understandable. Screens for computer-administered tests should be legible and free from glare.

In addition to being responsible for quality control, the test administrator needs to ensure the validity of the test results by eliminating opportunities for the test takers to attain scores fraudulently. The test giver needs to monitor the testing situation and must refrain from helping any favored person with answers or coaching individuals on the test items.

Any modification of standard administration procedures or scoring should be described in the test report so the reader is alert to the modifications. Users should be cautioned regarding the possible effects of such modifications on the validity of the test results. Test administrators are cautioned not to modify prescribed administration procedures to adapt to particular individuals such as reading test items to an individual, defining specific words in an item, or encouraging an individual to reconsider answers (Test Users Training Work Group, 1993).

PRETESTING PROCEDURES

The AACD (1980, 1988) statement of the responsibilities of users of standardized tests includes under test administration all the procedures to ensure that a test is presented consistently in the manner specified by the test developers and/or used in the standardization and that the individuals being tested have orientation and conditions that maximize their opportunity for optimum performance. The Code of Ethics of the National Board of Certified Counselors (1989) also states that counselors must provide specific orientation of information to an examinee before and after administration of an assessment instrument or technique so that the results may be put in the proper perspective with other relevant factors. The examiner must carry out a number of important duties even before the test date. A decision-making model aids in initially determining whether testing is necessary. Those steps are briefly repeated here.

1. Determine what types of decisions or judgments have to be made.
2. Translate those factors into specific information needed.
3. Check what information is already available.
4. Determine what additional information is needed.
5. Decide how and when to obtain the additional information.
6. Discover which instruments will give the information needed.
7. Determine the most valid and reliable instruments for the intended purpose(s).

When conducting a psychoeducational evaluation or counseling/consultation, the National Association of School Psychologists' Code of Professional Ethics calls for psychologists to consider individual differences such as age, sex, and socioeconomic and ethnic backgrounds and to strive to select and use appropriate procedures, techniques, and strategies relevant to such differences.

In many situations the approval of the examinee is needed before testing can be scheduled. If the client is a minor, it is necessary to get parental approval. Most agencies and school systems have set procedures that must be followed prior to testing. Chapter 24 presents a more complete discussion of the legal and ethical procedures and guidelines that test administrators need to know. In addition to securing the appropriate permission, test administrators need to consider the privacy of the client and any ethical or legal problems that testing might raise. They also need to review the items on the test prior to administering it and to explain why the test will be given and who will get the results.

Examiner Knowledge

The first major responsibility of the examiner prior to testing is to know all about the test. The examiner needs to review the test booklet, test manuals, and answer sheet. The test administrator needs to be familiar with the content of the test, the type of test items, and the directions for administering the test. One of the best ways to become familiar with the test is to follow the procedures and actually take the test. Many tests require the examiner to read directions to the examinees; other tests also require the examiner to read the test items. The AACD (1980, 1988) statement on the responsibilities of users states that effective administration of tests requires that the administrator have knowledge of and training in the actual instruments and processes of presentation. Some individual and group tests require extensive training, and standardized tests should be administered only by qualified, experienced persons. Saklofske and Kowalchuk (1992) feel that the administrators also need to understand test construction, measurement concepts, and good assessment practices.

Management Details

Test companies require purchasers to furnish evidence of their qualifications to use tests. Forms request information on the training level of the purchasers, their professional credentials and educational background, the updating of their professional knowledge and skills, and any other special competencies. They are also questioned about the purposes of the testing. On the Riverside Publishing Company's form, test purchasers are asked to read five principles of effective test use and then sign the form stipulating that they will follow these guidelines. The five principles are these:

1. Maintain the security of testing materials before and after the testing.
2. Avoid labeling students based on a single test score.
3. Adhere strictly to the copyright law and under no circumstances photocopy or otherwise reproduce answer forms, test booklets, or other materials.
4. Administer, score, interpret, and use tests exactly as specified in the manual.
5. Release results only to authorized persons in a form consistent with the accepted principles of test interpretation.

Many management tasks have to be done prior to testing. For example, it is necessary to secure the appropriate number of tests, as well as answer sheets and scoring keys. Any order should be double-checked before it is sent and when it is received. Here are some of the other tasks that need to be accomplished.

1. Scheduling the date for the test
2. Scheduling the room or facilities
3. Counting the number of booklets, answer sheets, pencils, and any other needed materials
4. Securing a stopwatch, if needed, and a do-not-disturb sign
5. Arranging materials for distribution
6. Determining the order in which tests or subtests will be administered
7. Deciding on the procedures for collecting test materials

The client must agree on the date and time of testing, and it is helpful to issue a reminder. It is usually wise to avoid testing the day before a holiday, and it is always important to schedule enough time. Time should be added for giving directions, answering questions, distributing test materials, and collecting test booklets and answer sheets. In school contexts it is important to avoid conflicts with other school activities.

Training Test Administrators

When testing a large number of clients or students, the examiner will need help from other individuals such as teachers, administrators, or counselors. The training of these assistants needs to be specific to the test being administered. They will need a general overview of the test and preferably some practice giving and taking it.

Hands-on experience helps in identifying some of the types of problems that might arise—for example, what to do with clients or students who finish early. All test administrators need to know the guidelines for answering questions about the test and the importance of following standardized procedures in administering the test. Each examiner might benefit from a checklist like the one illustrated in Figure 5.1.

Figure 5.1
Checklist for test administrators

Pretesting Procedures
_____ Send out notice to remind client(s) of testing time.
_____ Send out information on testing program to public and/or parents.
_____ Get informed consent if needed.
_____ Have testing materials on hand.
_____ Check schedule to see whether there is adequate time for testing.
_____ Check date of testing to avoid conflicts.
_____ Arrange for distribution of test materials.
_____ Decide on order of administration of tests.
_____ Decide on procedures for collection of test materials.

Test Knowledge
_____ Review test manuals and test booklets.
_____ Know the makeup of the test.
_____ Read and practice the directions for administering the test.
_____ Check time limits for the test.
_____ Know the directions for recording answers.
_____ Take the test.
_____ Be familiar with scoring procedures.
_____ Prepare answers for specific questions clients might ask.

Management Details
_____ Schedule room and facilities.
_____ Make and check seating arrangements.
_____ Check lighting and ventilation.
_____ Arrange clear and adequate work space.
_____ Organize materials and arrange for distribution.
_____ Highlight directions in the manual.
_____ Develop agenda for the day.

Information for Examinees
_____ Provide sample copies, study guides, and an overview.
_____ Explain purpose of testing.
_____ Communicate the conditions under which the test is to be taken.
_____ Identify any cost of testing.
_____ Identify any special materials or tools needed.
_____ Explain what will happen with the results.
_____ Discuss test scoring procedures.

Awareness and Orientation

A test administrator often must be responsible for awareness and orientation. Codes of test standards remind test administrators that they have responsibility for orientation of the test takers. They recommend that the candidates for testing as well as the relevant institutions or agencies and the community be informed about testing programs. Orientation should describe the purposes of the tests, content areas measured, method of administration, and reporting and utilization of scores. In school contexts students and parents need to be made aware of the testing. If the test is a

Table 5.1
Modes of test administration

Mode	Description	Advantages	Disadvantages
Self-administered	Examinees read the instructions themselves and take the test.	The examiner does not need to be present.	The motivation or attitudes of test takers are not known. They may be confused or unclear about tasks.
Group-administered	Examiner reads the directions to small or large group, answers any questions, and follows the standardized procedures outlined in the manual.	This is the most cost-effective method.	The motivation and attitude of the test takers are unknown.
Individually administered	Examiner administers test to one individual at a time, following the procedures found in the examiner's manual.	The examiner can assess the motivation and attitudes of the test taker as well as thought processes and cognitive level. The examiner can probe to gain more information.	This method is expensive, and only a few individuals can be tested each day. The examiner needs special training and experience in administering individual tests.
Computer-assisted	The directions for taking the test and the test itself are presented on the screen.	The test taker often can get immediate feedback. The examiner does not necessarily have to be present. This method allows for flexibility in scheduling. The computer can score, analyze, and interpret the tests of a large group of individuals.	Some individuals may not perform well because of certain disabilities or because of their attitude toward computers. This method may not be practical if many individuals are to be tested.

part of the system's overall testing program, the examiner should provide news releases not only for the school paper but also for local news media sources. Sometimes agencies or schools publish newsletters that include information on tests and testing programs scheduled in the near future.

Many test publishers provide information sheets and brochures about a test or testing program. These sources usually describe the type of test, the purpose(s) of the test, the types of test items used, type of scoring, and the method of reporting the results. In some cases the cost of the testing is given, along with the time schedule for the testing and the mode of administration (see Table 5.1).

Mode	Description	Advantages	Disadvantages
Videotape-administered	Directions for taking the test and actual test items are presented on the screen.	This method allows for both audio and visual stimuli to be combined. Simulated or real situations can be presented. A wider variety of behaviors can be assessed.	The method may be inappropriate for individuals with certain disabilities.
Audiotape-administered	The test is presented on audiotape.	The examiner can circulate to see whether there are any problems. Testing time can be controlled. The quality of the recording and the type of voice can be uniformly controlled. The method is good to use with individuals with reading problems.	This method is inappropriate for individuals having hearing, listening, or attention deficits.
American Sign Language	The examiner gives directions and presents the test items using sign language.	American Sign Language is the first language of many hearing-impaired individuals.	The examiner needs to be experienced in signing and working with hearing-impaired individuals. Some hearing-impaired individuals might have learned a different system.
Pantomime	The examiner avoids oral or written directions and relies on pantomime to administer the test.	This method is appropriate for certain individuals with disabilities, such as those who are language-impaired.	The examiner must be trained in administering such tests and experienced in working with the various special populations.

The examiner must be sure that orientation makes a test relevant to the test taker(s). Seven general topics should be covered in orientation sessions.

1. Purpose of the test
2. Criteria used for selecting the test
3. Conditions under which the test is to be taken
4. Range of skills or domains to be measured
5. Administrative procedures and concerns (e.g., group or individual administration, time involved, cost)
6. Types of questions on the test and an overview
7. Type of scoring, method, and schedule for reporting results to the test taker

Many standardized tests provide sample items and an overview of the test. The examiner should be sure that all who are going to take a given test have had specific practice with sample problems or have worked on test-taking skills prior to the test. This requirement is especially appropriate for aptitude, achievement, and ability testing.

ADMINISTERING THE TEST

Test administration begins with a final check to see that all is in order—lighting, ventilation, seating arrangements, clear work space for examinees, sharpened pencils, a do-not-disturb sign, and provision for the toilet needs of examinees. The test itself presents further administrative tasks. One of the most important tasks on a standardized test is to deliver verbatim instructions given in the test manual and to follow the stated sequence and timing. Any deviation may change the nature of the tasks on the test and may negate any comparison of test results with those of the norming group.

The examiner also needs to establish rapport with the examinees. For some the test may be a new and frightening experience; they may feel fear, frustration, hostility, or anxiety. In individual testing the examiner can assess these emotional and motivational factors and positively support the test taker. In group testing it is harder to establish rapport, but the examiner can be warm, friendly, and enthusiastic. The goal is for the results to give a valid picture of the attributes measured, so the examiner should encourage the examinees to do their best on each task. Saklofske and Kowalchuk (1992) indicate that the test administrator should demonstrate clear verbal articulation, calmness, and positive anticipation, and also have empathy for and social identification with the examinees. Impartial treatment of all those being tested is essential.

A list of activities for test administrators during testing is included in Figure 5.2. The examiner must be alert to what is going on in the testing situation. In addition, the examiner must be alert to the unique problems of special populations. Young children and individuals with handicaps may need shorter test periods and perhaps

Figure 5.2
Checklist of activities during testing

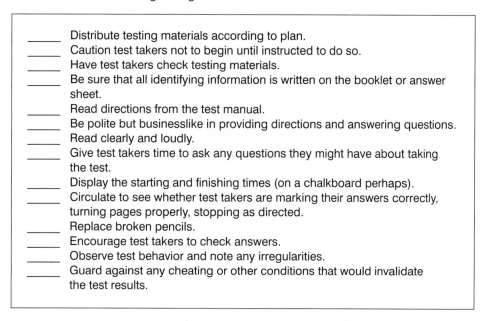

_____ Distribute testing materials according to plan.
_____ Caution test takers not to begin until instructed to do so.
_____ Have test takers check testing materials.
_____ Be sure that all identifying information is written on the booklet or answer sheet.
_____ Read directions from the test manual.
_____ Be polite but businesslike in providing directions and answering questions.
_____ Read clearly and loudly.
_____ Give test takers time to ask any questions they might have about taking the test.
_____ Display the starting and finishing times (on a chalkboard perhaps).
_____ Circulate to see whether test takers are marking their answers correctly, turning pages properly, stopping as directed.
_____ Replace broken pencils.
_____ Encourage test takers to check answers.
_____ Observe test behavior and note any irregularities.
_____ Guard against any cheating or other conditions that would invalidate the test results.

smaller numbers in the testing group. The examiner may have to administer tests individually or make special provisions for visual, auditory, or perceptual-motor handicaps, being sure to record any deviation from standardized administrative procedures. Many tests and assessment inventories are designed to test people with handicaps or give suggested procedures to accommodate various disabilities.

The test administrator must be a keen observer of what is going on in the testing situation. Most individual intelligence tests have observation forms on which an examiner can record test-taking behavior. Independent scales are also available, focusing attention on both normal and abnormal aspects. The examiner should record any critical incidents that may increase or reduce an individual's opportunity to perform to capacity. Chapter 17 discusses observational techniques in greater detail. If a test administrator has no direct responsibility during a test, he should circulate among the examiners and offer assistance if needed.

POSTTESTING PROCEDURES

A routine saves time. The administrator needs to collect materials according to a predetermined order, counting the test booklets and answer sheets and arranging them all face up. In addition, everything should be put back in the testing kit in the proper way so that it is ready for future use. With individual testing the examiner should take time immediately to record any incident that might invalidate scores.

Recording Test Behavior

Test behavior can be recorded on some of the standardized checklists designed to accompany various individual tests or on examiner-made scales (examples are included in Chapter 17). The examiner should determine whether any unusual behaviors might give insight into examinee performance or personality. Different rating forms usually rate examinees on physical reactions, test behavior, social behavior, and observable verbal characteristics. Sometimes it is just as important to know how the individual got an answer as to know whether the answer is right or wrong. Careful observation gives clues to typical behavior as well as to methods of problem solving and reaction to different domains.

The test administrator may want to write a short anecdotal record of an individual or an incident and file it with the test. For example, the examiner might note that John marked all the answers on his answer sheet in about two minutes and put his head down on the desk. When asked what he had done, he said, "I just put marks down on the paper to see how many items I can get right by guessing." Brief accounts can be enlightening.

MAJOR ISSUES AND PROBLEMS IN TEST ADMINISTRATION

Goldman (1971) points out that the problems discovered by the test administrator—such as inadequate motivation, exaggerated tensions, and response sets, with the resulting distortion in client image—are often the result of inadequate preparation for test taking. The awareness/orientation phase is an important element in helping to alleviate response set problems, anxiety, and tension. However, certain problems present themselves only during the testing situation. Some of these, with possible solutions, are detailed in Table 5.2.

Examiner and Bias

A number of factors can bias test results. Rapport (or lack thereof) is one factor. An effective interpersonal relationship must be established between the test administrator and test taker. Partly it involves encouraging test takers to do their best, to be cooperative, and to show responsiveness. Warm interpersonal relationships during testing may improve test results.

The gender, race, or ethnic heritage of the test administrator and test taker may also affect test scores. Administrators need to recognize that race, gender, socioeconomic class, and cultural and educational background can significantly influence test results. The use of reinforcement and encouragement is likewise complex because its effectiveness depends on the aforementioned factors (Saklofske and Schwean,

Table 5.2
Problems encountered in test administration

Problem	Possible Solution
Cheating	Create an environment in which cheating is impossible because of spacing of desks, work areas, and so on.
Client asks question that is not addressed in manual	Respond with good judgment based on experience with similar tests.
Guessing	Encourage examinees to work on known items first, leaving unknown items until the latter part of the testing time. Advise clients to guess if they wish if the test does not penalize guessing.
Lack of effort	Be positive and businesslike in explaining the purpose and importance of the test and exhorting the test taker to do well.
Questions during testing	Explain in the beginning that questions will not be answered during the test session. While circulating around the test room, quietly answer only questions resulting from confusion.
Distractions	Eliminate the distraction if possible. Apologize to test takers and explain as much as possible. Allow extra time.
Refusal to answer	In individual testing repeat the questions and ask whether the test taker understands it. After testing, inquire further if the test taker should have been able to answer.
Examiner indecision in the use of praise and encouragement	Positive reinforcement may help in establishing rapport and reducing anxiety. It should not be artificial and should not be overused.
Examiner effects	Recognize personal biases and be positive but objective. Listen carefully and observe nonverbal cues.

1992). Other factors, such as a lack of sensitivity to the psychological, emotional, and intellectual needs of the test taker, may also bias the test results. One biasing dimension that should not be overlooked is the examiner's beliefs and attitudes. Both verbal and nonverbal cues can demonstrate bias.

In general, examiner bias takes six forms: race, communication skills, attitudes and expectations, gender, competence, and test ethics. Oakland and Parmelee (1985) indicate there is a popular belief that attributes the lower test scores of blacks and other minority individuals to the test administration of a white examiner. Graziano, Varca, and Levy (1982) conclude that the narrow conceptualization of this issue has resulted in oversimplified research questions and a disjointed body of literature. Although there is not strong support in the literature for their premise, Oakland and Parmelee suggest that "white examiners may contribute to anxiety, fears and suspicion, verbal constriction, strained and unnatural reactions, insecurity, latent prejudice, and other such reactions as a result of racial differences" (p. 719). On the other hand, some examiners exhibit paternalism, overidentification, exaggerated concerns or fear of negative client reactions. In general, a test administrator might consider assigning a minority examiner to test minority clients if those clients have a strong preference to work with a minority professional.

In their metanalysis of the effects of examiner familiarity on children's test performance, Fuchs and Fuchs (1986) found that examiner familiarity raised test performance an average of .28 standard deviations. Study results indicated that differential performance favoring the familiar examiner was greater when subjects were of low socioeconomic status, were assessed on comparatively difficult tests, and knew the examiner for a relatively long duration. The authors conclude that the effects of examiner familiarity demonstrate the importance of contextual factors in testing. They see these factors as intervening between the test's sampling of skills or abilities and client performance, bringing into question the view of the test instrument as the most important, if not the exclusive, variable in test performance (p. 257).

A second factor in testing bias is the language and dialect of the examiner and test taker. Communication between the two may be impeded, and verbal and non-verbal cues may be misunderstood. Bilingual and non-English-speaking examinees quite often score higher on performance and nonlanguage tests than on verbal tests. Other factors are the attitudes and expectations of the examiner. The examiner who has warmth, empathy, or genuine concern for the examinee may behave quite differently from the examiner who rejects or is indifferent toward the examinee. Bias and prejudice may prevent an examiner from objectively understanding the characteristics of those being tested.

The fourth factor in testing bias is the sex of the examiner. Sattler (1982) concludes that female examiners tend to elicit slightly better performance than do male examiners. The competence of the examiner is another factor. Some test administrators are poorly prepared to do a clinical, behavioral, and psychoeducational assessment of certain age or cultural groups. Others may conduct the assessment mechanically and superficially. A final factor is the ethical standards of the examiner. The APA (1992) *Ethical Principles of Psychologists* calls for the psychologist to believe in the dignity and worth of the individual and to commit to freedom of inquiry, communication, and concern for the best interests of clients, colleagues, and society in general. The psychologist is responsible for protecting the welfare of all clients.

Feedback on Test and Test Administration

In their chapter of *Educational and Psychological Testing,* Nevo and Jaeger (1993) emphasize the need to get evaluative feedback from the test takers not only on their attitudes toward the test but toward the test administration, testing environment, and test orientation. Here are a few possible questions that could be included in such an evaluation.

1. How would you rate the physical environment for this testing?
2. How would you rate the performance/competencies of the test administrator?
3. Was the time allotted adequate to finish the test?
4. Was the orientation to the test helpful?
5. Do you feel that the test was fair?

SUMMARY

How a test is administered can affect the accuracy and validity of the test results. The test administrator must have important competencies. One key component is knowledge of and training with the test being administered. The attitude of the examiner toward testing and toward clients is crucial. And variables such as environmental conditions can interfere with proper results.

Many tasks—like orientation—must be completed prior to testing. Other tasks—like circulating around the room—are accomplished during testing. The administrator must be a keen observer of what is taking place during testing and should record any factors that might be important in test interpretation. The examiner should try to maintain a positive attitude, maximize achievement and motivation, and equalize advantages.

QUESTIONS FOR DISCUSSION

1. How would you compare the procedures to be followed in administering both group and individual tests?
2. What techniques should the examiner use to establish rapport with the test taker?
3. What types of behavior should an examiner avoid during test administration? Why?
4. An examiner can take certain steps in the first contact with a client prior to the testing to be sure that the test session goes smoothly; for example, the counselor can discuss the purpose of the assessment and can describe the test administrator. What other steps might be taken and why are they important?
5. What dimensions in the testing environment might bias test results?
6. Measurement experts stress that scores are not valid when examiners deviate from standard administrative practices. Should the examiner stick rigidly to the procedures in the manual or maintain the freedom to deviate? Why? Under what circumstances, if any, should the examiner be allowed to depart from the standardized procedures?

SUGGESTED ACTIVITIES

1. Read the manual for test administration for a major controlled testing program such as the Scholastic Aptitude Test or the Graduate Record Examination. Interview the person who is responsible for the administration of the test in your area. What kinds of problems has the person encountered in administering the test? How adequate were the directions in the manual for handling those problem situations?

2. Observe a videotape of a test being administered and use one of the checklists found in the chapter or one you have devised yourself to record and evaluate what the examiner is doing in the session. Rate the individual's ability to administer the test.

3. Review the literature on test bias and write an analysis of what the literature has to say about good and poor test administration practices.

4. Interview a psychologist or counselor who administers a wide variety of individual and group tests to find out that person's attitude on deviating from the standardized procedures. When have they deviated and why?

5. Design a program to train a group of counselors or teachers to administer a specific test.

6. Discuss the following four scenarios.

   Scenario 1

   You are scheduled to do a psychological battery on a 6-year-old child. You usually have no problems establishing rapport but when you get into the testing room the child says to you: "I don't like you. I am not going to take any tests for you!" The child puts her hands over her ears.

   Scenario 2

   You are meeting with Jose prior to setting up a testing appointment. You start to provide an orientation to the testing, the purpose of the tests, the criteria used for selecting the tests—but are interrupted by Jose who says: "I understand of what you are saying, but I think I would do better on the examinations if they were given in Spanish. I am originally from Mexico."

   Scenario 3

   You are administering a national scholastic aptitude examination and you see evidence of a person cheating.

   Scenario 4

   You are administering a test to a group and have read the instructions to the individuals and gotten them started on the test. Five minutes into the test, one of the test takers raises his hand, asks a question loudly, and disrupts others who are taking the test.

7. Read this brief story about XYZ Company and answer the questions that follow:

   A company administered a computer basic skills test for selection purposes. The secretary to the division supervisor administered it. There were a variety of keyboard configurations in the office where the testing took place. Since the secretary administering the test often was interrupted by telephone calls and minor crises, she paid little attention to applicants taking the test. She estimated the time.

   a. What steps could be taken to insure that the computer basic skills test is administered properly and fairly to all applicants?
   b. What other procedures would you implement?

ADDITIONAL READINGS

Clemans, W. V. (1971). Test administration. In R. L. Thorndike (Ed.), *Educational measurement* (2nd ed.). Washington, DC: American Council on Education.

This chapter gives a good overview of the many details involved in administering tests.

Nevo, B., & Jaeger, R. S. (1993). *Educational and psychological testing: The test taker's outlook*. Toronto: Hofrefe & Huber.

The text deals with aspects of psychological tests in general but has specific chapters on systematic study of examinees' reactions to tests. ETS staff members show how collecting feedback from test takers can help test administrators humanize the test environment more.

Sattler, J. M. (1982). *Assessment of children's intelligence and special abilities* (2nd ed.). Boston: Allyn and Bacon.

The text has a general chapter on the examination process and specific information on administering individual intelligence tests.

CHAPTER 6

Scoring and Interpreting Tests

Overview

Scoring errors can affect how a score is interpreted. The test maker has certain responsibilities in making clear to the examiner how the test is to be scored. In addition, the examiner has specific responsibilities to ensure that the test is scored correctly. Most often the examiner calculates how many test answers fit a predetermined key or criterion. That number yields a raw score. Then, depending on the type of test score, some system is used to give meaning to the score. With criterion- or domain-referenced tests, such as a test measuring mastery of basic addition facts, the interpretation of scores relates to a functional performance level. With norm-referenced tests such as the Stanford Achievement Test, the interpretation of the scores is compared to the performance of the standardization or norming group. Counselors must proceed with caution when interpreting performances of minority group members or persons who are not represented in the norm group on which the instrument was standardized (National Board for Certified Counselors, 1989).

Objectives

The chapter should enable the reader to

- list and discuss the important components relative to scoring and interpreting tests that test authors should include in their test manuals

- interpret different types of test scores
- utilize several frameworks to interpret test scores

STANDARDS FOR SCORING

The standards for educational and psychological tests call for test developers to specify in sufficient detail and clarity how a test should be scored (*Standards for Educational and Psychological Testing*, 1985). Accurate scoring and reporting are essential. The standards of the American Association for Counseling and Development (AACD) (1980, 1988) remind us that the measurement of human performance is dependent on accurate and consistent application of defined procedures for crediting the responses made by persons being tested. There are seven specific guidelines for test scoring.

1. Rescore routinely a sample of the test answer sheets to verify the accuracy of the initial scoring.
2. Employ systematic procedures to verify the accuracy and consistency of machine or computer scoring of answer sheets.
3. Obtain a separate and independent verification that appropriate scoring rules and normative conversions are used for each person tested.
4. Verify as accurate the computation and conversion of raw scores and the conversion of raw scores to normative or descriptive scales prior to release of such information to the tested person or to users of the test results.
5. Check routinely for accuracy of computer, machine, or manual reports of test results. The person performing this task must be qualified to recognize inappropriate or impossible scores.
6. Develop and use systematic and objective procedures for observing and recording the conditions and behaviors of persons being tested and make this a part of the scores or test results that are reported.
7. Label clearly the scores that are reported and the date that a particular test was administered.

MODELS OF SCORING

There are three primary models for scoring tests: cumulative, class, and ipsative (Hammer, 1992). Cumulative models assume that the number of items endorsed or responded to that match the key represent the degree of the construct or trait the test measured. The higher the score, the greater the degree of the construct present. Many achievement, aptitude, and personality tests are based on this model.

These test often involve differential weighing of items before summing the items (e.g., individual IQ tests such as the WISC and WAIS).

A second model is the class model that is used to categorize individuals for the purpose of description or prediction. Criterion-referenced and mastery tests are in this category. Responses may be added to compute a score but used only to determine whether the person falls in the appropriate category. Many licensure and certification examinations use this model.

The third is an ipsative model; it indicates how an individual has performed on a set of variables or scales. Certain personality, interest, and value tests utilize this model. The individual ranks the responses internally and the ranks cannot be treated normatively.

SOME EXAMPLES OF TEST SCORING

Some tests demand that the test scorer judge the degree of correctness of the response or compare the responses to standards provided. For example, essay questions on many college placement examinations are scored using a holistic scoring procedure. The raters have model answers that have been given certain weights, and they compare the examinee's essays to those. Such raters are asked to assess answers on a four-point scale and make an overall rating, or holistic judgment, rather than assign a certain number of points to each possible component of the answer.

Many of the individual intelligence tests require the examiner to rate answers on a two-point scale. For example, the criterion might be the degree of abstractness or cognitive level of the answer. One child might say that orange "is a color" and receive one point; another child might say "an orange is a reddish-yellow citrus fruit containing vitamin C" and receive two points. Most test manuals have an elaborate explanation of scoring procedures and examples of typical responses of correct and incorrect answers, or one-point and two-point answers.

Examiners are expected to have supervised training before they use tests where clinical judgment is necessary for scoring. In most situations dealing with individual intelligence testing, examiners are not making blind judgments and need to be alert to factors that may bias their judgment or influence the type of answers the clients give.

On most pencil-and-paper tests there is a predetermined key and a right or wrong answer for each item or a scoring key for a specific scale. These tests don't require individual judgment, just accuracy in calculating the number of right or appropriate answers.

INTERPRETING SCORES

The *Code of Fair Testing Practices in Education* (1988) has five guidelines to help test users interpret scores correctly. The user should first obtain information about the scale used for reporting scores, the characteristics of any norms or comparison groups, and the limitations of the scores. When interpreting scores, the test user should consider any major differences between the norms or comparison groups and the actual test takers and any differences in test administration practices or familiarity with the specific questions on the test. Counselors are cautioned not to use tests for purposes not specifically recommended by the test developer unless evidence is obtained to support an alternate use. The counselor should be able to explain how any passing scores were set, demonstrate what the results of the scores reveal, and provide evidence that the test satisfies its intended purposes.

CRITERION-REFERENCED INTERPRETATION

Criterion- or domain-referenced testing is widely used in educational contexts. Many states and school districts have set standards for students to meet—for example, mastery of essential or basic skills. Popham (1981) states that one meaning of the term *criterion-referenced* relates to referencing an individual's performance to some criterion that is a defined performance level. The individual's score is interpreted in absolute terms, such as the percentage of correct answers. The percentage of correct answers is most widely used in reporting the results of criterion- or domain-referenced tests. Table 6.1 illustrates criterion-referenced interpretation.

Table 6.1
Criterion-referenced interpretation

Writing Tasks	Right Answers	Criterion Needed	Skill Achieved
1. Identify the plural form of nouns.	4	3/4	Yes
2. Use the appropriate forms of common regular verbs.	5	4/5	Yes
3. Make subjects and verbs agree.	4	4/5	Yes
4. Use the appropriate forms of common irregular verbs.	8	7/10	Yes
5. Include necessary information from a phone message.	3	3/4	Yes
6. Include necessary information in a written message.	5	4/5	Yes
7. Identify correct spelling of common words.	5	7/10	No
8. Use commas to separate words in a series	5	4/5	Yes
9. Use commas to separate elements in an address.	2	3/4	No

NORM-REFERENCED INTERPRETATION

Norm-referenced tests call for relative interpretation based on the test taker's position with respect to the normative group. Sometimes it is important for the examiner to be able to differentiate among test takers or to discriminate among individuals on the domain being measured. The procedures utilized to discriminate or differentiate individual performance are based on the use of statistics of variability and central tendency. For example, *T* scores have a fixed mean and standard deviation and can be used to compare how high or low a score is in a distribution.

Norm-referenced test scores can be expressed in a number of different ways. In general, the interest is in the relative position of the individual within the group or in comparison to a norming group. A number of different systems can be used to express the individual's position. Two of the major ways are through the use of percentiles and standard scores.

Percentiles

Percentile ranks are one of the most widely used methods to express the relative position of the test taker on a norm-referenced test. Such rankings range from 1 to 99 and tell the percentage of persons in the norming group who score at or below that particular score. A percentile rank of 50 is the median; a test taker who has a percentile rank of 15 would surpass 15% of the norming group. Percentile rank, percentile score, and percentile are all used interchangeably. Table 6.2 illustrates percentile ranks.

Table 6.2
Simulated percentile norms from a mathematics reasoning test for grade 8

Raw Score	Percentile Rank
45	99
44	99
43	97
42	96
41	94
40	89
39	85
38	81
//	//
31	52
30	50
29	45
//	//
15	5
14	4
13	3
12	2
0–11	1

// = omission of some scores

Table 6.3
Use of percentile bands

Test	Raw Score	Percentile Band
Reading	123	55%–75%
Mathematics	140	91%–99%
Listening	132	71%–89%
Social Studies	111	17%–49%

Many standardized tests report a percentile band as well as a series of other types of scores. Some tests report a percentile band rather than a single score. The upper part of the band corresponds approximately to the percentile rank of a score one standard error of measurement above the obtained raw score. Likewise the lower part of the band corresponds to the percentile rank of the score one standard error below the obtained raw score. The Comprehensive Test of Basic Skills utilizes this format. Table 6.3 illustrates the use of percentile bands.

Standard Scores

Standard scores are a means of presenting the relative position of an individual on a test; such scores describe how many standard deviations an individual's score is from the mean. The standard deviation of the test becomes its yardstick. There are a variety of types of standard scores: z scores, T scores, deviation IQs, stanine, sten scores, and other standard score scales.

z Scores.   The z score is computed by using the formula:

$$z = \frac{x - \overline{X}}{s}$$

In the formula z = standard score, x = a given raw score on a test, $\overline{X}$ = the mean on the test, and s = the standard deviation on the test. If we know that the mean on the test was 100 and the standard deviation 20, and we know that an individual scored 125 on the test, we have the data to compute the z score.

$$z = \frac{125 - 100}{20} = \frac{25}{20} = 1.25$$

Thus, the z score tells us that the person's score is 1.25 standard deviations above the mean. The mean for a distribution of z scores is 0, and the standard deviation 1.0. There are two disadvantages of using z scores. First, they will be expressed in decimals; second, about half of the z scores will have a minus sign if there is a normal distribution of test scores. A test administrator would need to check carefully to see that the scores had been properly computed and recorded, each with the appropriate sign. Table 6.4 illustrates z scores. Because the scores are linear units, they can be transformed in a number of ways without having the properties of the original raw score distribution changed. For example, z scores can be converted into the T scores described in the next section.

T Scores. T scores are standard scores using a fixed mean and standard deviation in units that eliminate the need for decimals and signs. On many tests the arbitrary or fixed mean is 50 and the arbitrary or fixed standard deviation is 10. The formula is

$$T = s(z) + \{X\}$$

If the fixed mean in one example is 50 and the fixed standard deviation is 10, and if z = –.5, then the T score is computed like this:

$$T = 10(-.50) + 50 = -5 + 50 = 45$$

The fixed mean becomes a constant that is added to each score; the fixed standard deviation becomes a constant multiplied by each z score. Negative values and decimals are eliminated through computational procedures, and whole numbers are produced. Another type of T score is known as a normalized standard score. If the distribution is skewed or deviates from a normal distribution, the percentile rank of each raw score is first computed and then the standard score value of the rank is located in the table of the normal curve. This z unit is then used in the computation procedures.

Not all tests use the convention of 50 as the arbitrary mean and 10 as the arbitrary standard deviation. For example, the Analysis of Learning Potential uses 50 as the mean but 20 as the standard deviation. The Army General Classification Test has 100 as the mean but 20 as the standard deviation. On the Wechsler subscales 10 is the mean on the subtests and 3 the standard deviation. On the Scholastic Aptitude Test and the Graduate Record Examinations the formula utilized is

$$100z + 500$$

In this case the fixed mean is 500, and the fixed standard deviation 100.

Table 6.4
Illustration of z scores

Test	Raw Score	Mean	Standard Deviation	z Score
Reading	100	80	10	+2.00
Math	50	50	15	0.00
Science	45	55	5	–2.00
History	98	82	16	+1.00

Deviation IQs.   Most intelligence tests no longer compute intelligence quotients with a formula but use standard scores instead. The mean for a given age group becomes IQ 100, and the test utilizes a fixed standard deviation. In the past the fixed standard deviations have varied depending on the test. For example, on the 1960 revision of the Stanford-Binet the standard deviation was 16 whereas on the Wechsler scales it was 15. On the Army General Classification Test the standard deviation was 20; on Cattell's Culture-Fair Test of Intelligence scaled scores used a standard deviation of 25 as well as 15. Most of the major tests now have selected 15 as the fixed standard deviation.

It is essential for you to know the technical information about the test. What is the arbitrary standard deviation for the test? Scores of 116, 115, 120, and 125 may appear to reflect differences in magnitude but may reflect only that an individual is one standard deviation above the norming group. In looking at scores it is also important to be sure what kind of units are being expressed or reported. Percentile ranks utilize whole numbers containing two digits also.

Stanines.   Stanines are a widely used type of standard score utilizing just nine score units with a mean of 5 and a standard deviation of 2. All the units except 1 and 9 are half standard deviation units. The stanine 5 extends from ¼ *SD* below the mean to ¼ above the mean (e.g., from a *z* score of 2.25 to a *z* score of 1.25). The percentile ranks of stanines are illustrated in Table 6.5.

Sten Scores.   On the personality series—the Early School Personality Questionnaire, the Children's Personality Questionnaire, the High School Personality Questionnaire, and the Sixteen Personality Factor Questionnaire—stens are used instead of stanines. Stens are a normalized standard score scale utilizing 10 units. Characteristics of stens are presented in Table 6.6.

Table 6.5
Characteristics of stanines

Stanine	z Score Range	Percentile Rank (%)	Percent of Scores in Stanine (%)
1	to −1.75	1–4	4
2	−1.75 to −1.25	5–11	7
3	−1.25 to −.75	12–23	12
4	−.75 to −.25	24–40	17
5	−.25 to +.25	41–59	20
6	+.25 to +.75	60–76	17
7	+.75 to +1.25	77–88	12
8	+1.25 to +1.75	89–95	7
9	+1.75 to	96–99	4

Table 6.6
Characteristics of stens

Sten	Percentile Rank	Percentage of Scores in Each Category
1	1–2	2
2	3–7	5
3	8–16	9
4	17–31	15
5	32–50	19
6	51–69	19
7	70–84	15
8	85–93	9
9	94–98	5
10	99–100	2

Other Standard Score Scales. The Iowa Tests of Educational Development and the American College Testing program use standard score scales with a mean of 15 and a standard deviation of 5. Other tests use 50 as the mean and 10 as the standard deviation. Test users need to make sure they know the arbitrary mean and the fixed standard deviation of tests they are using.

Normal Curve Equivalent (NCE) scores have been utilized by many schools, educators, and psychologists in working with research projects for the United States Office of Education, especially Title 1 or Chapter 1 reading projects. NCE scores are normalized standard scores with a mean of 50 and a standard deviation of 21.06. They are computed by calibrating the baseline of a normal curve from 1 to 99 in equal units. Percentile ranks and NCE scores are identical at 1, 50, and 99.

DEVELOPMENTAL INTRAINDIVIDUAL COMPARISON

Other frames of reference can help with interpretation of test performance. Many dimensions of the cognitive, affective, and psychomotor domains develop in a systematic, chronological manner. We are often concerned about the characteristics of individuals at different age or grade levels. Two widely used developmental scales, age norms and grade norms, implicitly compare the test taker's raw score to the average raw score of people at various developmental levels.

Age Norms

Age norms have been developed for many types of behavior and performances that change with age. One of the first authors of intelligence tests, Binet, utilized a system to measure the mental age of children. Age scores can be developed for many different human characteristics but have been used most widely in looking at educational and intellectual variables.

Most age scales are based on what the typical individual can do at a given age. Besides intelligence tests, some of the tests of cognitive and social maturity report age norms. The scores have meaning when the behaviors being measured vary systematically with age; however, for many behaviors the rate of growth varies from year to year (see Figure 6.1). Thus, we do not always have an even progression; there may be rapid growth during some periods and a plateau or no growth during others. The scoring units are not equal units of measurement because of this type of growth pattern.

Age scores are norm-referenced scores. We can compare an individual's performance with what most individuals typically do at that age. We might also be interested in intraindividual comparisons. We could compare an individual's mental age with her chronological age. However, we need to be cautious in our interpretation of age scores because of their psychometric properties and problems of interpretation. High age scores indicate that the individual is ahead of his peers developmentally but not necessarily able to perform the tasks characteristic of the higher age.

Figure 6.1
Age and learning curves

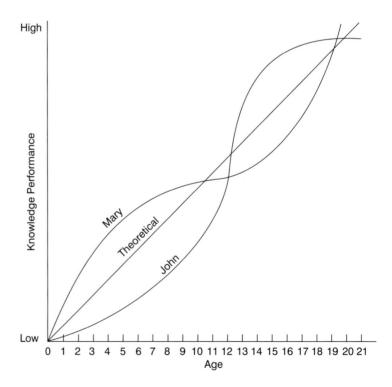

Grade Equivalent and Placement Scores

Grade equivalent scores are widely used by many of the major survey achievement batteries. These scores are based on the same assumptions that age scores are based on, but grade is the frame of reference rather than age. Grade equivalent scores are a means of comparing a student's performance with other students at a given grade level. A score of 5.0 on the Reading Comprehension subtest of the Stanford Achievement Test would mean that the student had a raw score equivalent to that made by a typical fifth-grade student on the test at the beginning of the school year. Test scores are compared to the average or sometimes the median performance at a given grade level.

Teachers, parents, and professionals must be cautious in their interpretation of grade placement scores. Such scores are computed by testing students across grade levels, computing the mean or median for each grade level, plotting the averages with as straight a line as possible and extrapolating this line at the extremes to account for scores above and below the mean. The school year is divided into 10 segments based on a September-to-June school year. Thus, 5.0 would represent a time period at the beginning of the fifth grade, and 5.9 would represent a time period at the end of the fifth grade.

A number of problems are inherent in interpreting grade equivalent scores. A student in Grade 1.9 might get all the items right on the reading comprehension test and receive a score of 4.6. Her raw score is equivalent to the mean or median raw score made by students in the middle of fourth grade. However, this does not mean the first-grade student is actually reading at the fourth grade level. The student has perhaps gotten most of the items right on the lower primary form of the achievement test, but there were no fourth-grade-level items on the test for the first graders.

Other problems and disadvantages of grade equivalent scores are these:

1. The scores are not equal units of measurement but are often ordinal.

2. The scores are often utilized as a standard, and students are expected to be at grade level.

3. Users sometimes fail to recognize that the grade placement scores are based on the average or typical performance in the norming group. Half of the students in the norming group will have higher scores; half, lower.

4. Standard deviations differ for the subtests within a survey achievement test. Some distributions will have small ranges; others, large. The range of grade equivalent scores will then vary for each subtest.

5. Reading comprehension tests of different publishers usually give conflicting grade placement scores.

A summary of the various types of test scores is presented in Table 6.7.

Table 6.7
Comparison of different types of test scores

Type of Score	Advantages	Disadvantages
Raw	Gives precise number of points scored on a test	Cannot be interpreted or compared
Percentile Rank	Easily understood by most test takers Requires no great sophistication in statistics Portrays relative position of scores in percentiles More appropriate for skewed data	Uses ordinal units of measurement Uses unequal units of measurement Does not permit averaging Cannot be compared unless groups are similar Greatly distorts score differences at upper and lower ends of distribution
Stanine	One-digit scores Can be averaged Used for simplicity and utility	May not provide enough scoring units to differentiate among scores Insensitive to sizable differences within a stanine Misleadingly sensitive to small differences on either side of the point separating adjacent stanines
Standard	Derived from properties of the normal curve Reflect absolute difference among scores Can be averaged and correlated Comparable from test to test if reference groups are equivalent	Inappropriate if data are markedly skewed Hard to explain to test takers
Grade and Age	Good if area measured is systematically related with age or grade level Compares an individual's performance with the average for that age or grade	Uses unequal units of measurement Leads to score interpretation that is too literal Can mislead in the case of scores, which do not signify an ability to perform or understand at the higher grade level Has little practical meaning beyond sixth grade or age 12

NORMS

Norms are statistical or tabular data that summarize the test scores of specified groups of test takers. Standards for Educational and Psychological Testing calls for the norms that are presented to refer to clearly described groups. These groups should be those with which users of the test will ordinarily wish to compare the individuals who are tested. In the test manual the test author should (a) describe who was in the norm group and (b) explain the different types of converted scores included in the tables. The test user should ask the following evaluative questions:

1. Does the norming group include the type of person with whom the test taker should be compared?

2. Do the norms include enough cases to be representative of the targeted population?

3. Do the samples include enough cases?

4. Does the manual include differentiated norms or summary information about differences among gender, ethnic, grade, or age groups?

5. Does the manual report include the year in which the normative data were collected, provide descriptive statistics, and describe the sampling design and participation rates in sufficient detail so that the norms can be evaluated?

CONVERSION TABLES

Conversion tables present every possible raw score and the derived score, such as the percentile rank or *T* score for a given norm group (e.g., 12th-grade boys, 10th-grade girls). A conversion table for hypothetical interest scores is presented in Table 6.8. Sometimes tests present multiple group norm tables. At other times a table might present the derived *T* scores for several subtests (see Table 6.9).

Some tests utilize abbreviated or condensed norm tables in which not every raw score value is presented (see Table 6.10). Such tables require interpolation for scores that fall between two of the values presented in the table. Unfortunately, this procedure requires more of the test user's time, and necessary computation introduces greater chance for error.

Table 6.8
Sample conversion table for an interest test

Scale: Technical		
Group: Male	Female	*T*
36	36	80
35	32–35	78
34	30–31	75
33	28–29	72
//	//	//

Table 6.9
Sample norm table reporting different types of scores for several subtests

| Stanine | Standard Score | Percentile Rank (%) | Grade | Raw Scores | | |
				ReadComp	Vocab	Total
5	50	50	11.0	30		60
5	49	48				
5	49	47			30	
5	49	46				59
5	49	45	10.9	29		

Table 6.10
Condensed norm table

Raw Score	IQ
50	140
48	135
45	130
41	125
39	120

PROFILES

Many tests provide profile sheets to aid in interpretation of the results. These forms graphically depict the scores by providing a visual interpretation. Profiles can represent the scores on a single battery or on several tests. Figure 6.2 gives an example of a profile for an individual on the COPSystem Interest Inventory.

Guidelines for interpreting profiles include the following:

1. Small differences should not be overinterpreted.

2. Any score represents a sample of the test taker's behavior in a given domain at a given time.

3. The standard error of measurement should be utilized in interpretation.

4. The normal curve can be used as a frame of reference to interpret the scores on norm-referenced tests.

5. Patterns in the shape of the profile are important (are the scores all high or low?).

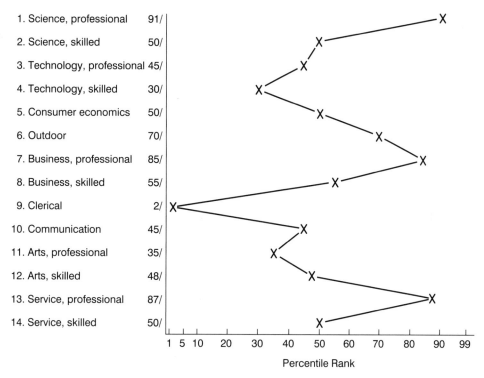

Figure 6.2
Individual profile for COPSystem Interest Inventory

SUMMARY

Studies have shown that examiners make numerous errors in scoring tests. Consequently, a number of standards and guidelines address scoring procedures. Test users need to be sure that they know how to score their tests correctly and follow systematic procedures to achieve accurate scores. Test authors need to be sure that scoring procedures are carefully described, and examiners need to read test manuals carefully.

Raw scores have to be translated into some frame of reference to give meaning to test results. Two major approaches are criterion-referenced and norm-referenced interpretation. Overall, the examiner has to ask two questions about test scores.

1. What is the nature of the score itself: What types of scoring or scaling procedures were used to arrive at the score?

2. What type of system is going to be used to interpret the score?

The examiner must know the advantages and disadvantages of each type of score and be alert to the best way of displaying and explaining the scores on a test.

In norm-referenced testing the reference group is of key importance. Examiners need to study the makeup of the norming group and see whether it is an appropriate comparison group. The validity and usefulness of test results depend on the examiner's knowledge of appropriate test interpretation strategies.

QUESTIONS FOR DISCUSSION

1. How would you handle the situation if certain test results did not appear to be accurate or did not agree with the results of previous tests you had taken? If you were the examiner and found out that you had made some errors in scoring a client's test, what would you do? What steps and procedures should be taken to ensure the accuracy of test scores?

2. What are the differences in scoring and interpreting norm-referenced and criterion-referenced tests?

3. What are the different types of derived scores used in norm-referenced testing? Discuss when you would use each type of score, and analyze the strengths and limitations of each type of score.

4. Should you use a test if there is not an appropriate norm or representative group available for comparison purposes? Take a position and defend it.

5. If you were developing a new achievement test for college-level students, how would you select your norming group? If you were developing a new personality inventory measuring psychological types, how would you select an appropriate norming group?

SUGGESTED ACTIVITIES

1. Interview a director of testing or psychologists and counselors who test extensively. Ask what test scoring procedures they use and how they guard against errors in scoring. Discover what problems arise in scoring individual tests as well as large-group tests.

2. Locate several test manuals and read the sections on test scoring and interpretation. Compare the presentations. How clear and understandable are the procedures? Are possible problems addressed? Are models of correct answers given? Are case studies presented?

3. Write a position paper on one of the following topics: bias in test scoring, use of grade equivalent norms, norm-referenced versus criterion-referenced interpretation, or selecting appropriate norms.

4. Give children of various ages a short, individual vocabulary test. (If vocabulary does not appeal to you, choose some other subject area.) Analyze the answers and develop a scoring system. Try writing a set of procedures for an examiner to follow to score the test.

5. Select several tests measuring the same content or constructs. Compare the types of norming groups presented in the manuals and the ways in which the groups were selected. Evaluate the tests on this dimension.

6. A third-grade teacher has brought you the following results of the spring testing on the Stanford Achievement Test. The teacher doesn't understand the types of scores and the results and wants you to guide her in interpreting the results.

Test	N	Mean Raw	Mean Scale	Percentile Rank	Stanine	Mean Grade Equivalent
Word Study Skills	19	40	613	52	5	4.0
Reading Comp	20	39	599	33	4	3.4
Vocabulary	21	19	587	9	2	2.7
Listening Comp	21	25	614	31	4	3.5
Spelling	21	29	642	94	8	5.1
Language	21	27	617	41	5	3.9
Concept of Numbers	21	19	574	15	3	3.4
Math Computation	21	28	603	43	5	4.4
Math Applications	21	22	580	30	4	3.5
Science	21	26	603	33	4	3.5
Using Information	21	24	613	39	4	3.5
Total Reading	18	78	602	36	4	3.6
Total Listening	21	44	601	15	3	3.1
Total Language	21	56	624	63	6	4.2
Total Mathematics	21	69	586	29	4	3.7

Content Clusters

	Below Average	Average	Above Average
Word Study Skills	5%	79%	16%
Structural analysis	11%	68%	21%
Phonetic analysis consonants	16%	74%	11%
Phonetic analysis vowels	11%	68%	21%
Reading Comprehension	25%	75%	0%
Textual reading	20%	70%	10%
Functional reading	30%	60%	10%
Recreational reading	20%	80%	0%
Literal comprehension	25%	65%	10%
Inferential comprehension	20%	60%	0%
Vocabulary/	48%	48%	5%
Listening Comprehension	14%	81%	5%
Retention	10%	76%	24%
Organization	19%	71%	10%
Spelling	0%	71%	29%
Sight words	0%	43%	57%
Phonetic principles	0%	76%	24%
Structured principles	0%	48%	52%
Language	0%	95%	5%
Conventions	14%	81%	5%
Language sensitivity	24%	62%	14%
Reference skills	19%	62%	19%
Concepts of Number	24%	71%	5%
Whole numbers/place value	38%	57%	5%
Fractions	0%	95%	5%
Operations and properties	29%	71%	0%
Mathematics Computation	19%	71%	10%
Addition of whole numbers	19%	67%	14%
Subtraction of whole numbers	19%	62%	19%
Multiplication of whole numbers	10%	57%	33%
Division of whole numbers	33%	62%	5%
Mathematical Applications	24%	71%	5%
Problem solving	33%	52%	14%
Geometry/measurement	19%	76%	5%
Graphs and charts	10%	67%	24%

Social Science	19%	81%	0%
Geography	19%	81%	0%
History/anthropology	19%	62%	19%
Sociology	48%	24%	29%
Political science	14%	86%	0%
Economics	29%	62%	10%
Inquiry skills	14%	67%	19%
Science	14%	81%	5%
Physical science	14%	57%	29%
Biological science	10%	86%	5%
Inquiry skills	14%	81%	5%

ADDITIONAL READINGS

Davidson, M. L. (1992). Test scores and statistics. In M. Zeidner and R. Most (Eds.), *Psychological testing: An inside view* (pp. 249–295). Palo Alto, CA: Consulting Psychologist Press.

The chapter provides a review of different types of test scores and the statistical procedures used to produce the types of derived scores.

Lyman, H. B. (1991). *Test scores and what they mean* (5th ed.). Boston: Allyn and Bacon.

The text provides guidelines for interpreting tests and examples of good and bad usage of interpretations of test results.

CHAPTER 7

Scholastic Ability and Intelligence Testing

Overview

One of the most controversial areas in testing is the measuring of ability and intelligence. Some of these issues are the nature-nurture controversy, the cultural bias, and the construct validity of intelligence tests. Many types of intelligence tests are widely used in education and clinical settings with all age groups and all types of individuals. Many tests have been developed during this century to measure the dimensions of intelligence—from Binet and Simon's scale to identify students who could not profit from regular classroom instruction in 1905 in France, to the revision of the Stanford-Binet developed by Thorndike, Hagen, and Sattler in 1986. Currently the most influential development in our view of intelligence has come from educational and psychological research on cognitive psychology, especially the conceptualizations by Robert Sternberg, Howard Gardner, and John Horn.

Objectives

This chapter should enable the reader to

- define intelligence
- discuss some of the major theories of intelligence
- list the major types of tests used to measure intelligence
- identify what types of tests should be used and why

- explain how the results of intelligence tests should be reported
- identify the kinds of factors that should be considered in interpreting intelligence test results

DEFINITIONS OF INTELLIGENCE

Many different definitions of intelligence have been given by the authors of intelligence tests. Aiken (1985) indicated that the word was almost unknown in popular speech until the Victorian era. Francis Galton and Herbert Spencer used the Latin word for intelligence to refer to individual differences in mental ability. These individuals as well as other psychologists such as Cattell were influenced by Darwin to look at dimensions of individual differences. They felt that intelligence was a genetic factor, separate from special abilities. Binet (1916) conceptualized intelligence as the capacity of the individual to judge well, to reason well, and to comprehend well, and postulated that intelligence was a general ability. Wechsler (1958), on the other hand, defined intelligence as the "aggregate or global ability of the individual to act purposefully, to think rationally, and to deal effectively with his environment" (p. 7). It is extremely important to check a test manual and study how the test authors define intelligence.

In general, most intelligence tests measure the individual's ability to think abstractly or use verbal, numerical, or abstract symbols. The subjects taking these tests must substitute symbols for actions and manipulate ideas that represent not only current happenings but also events remote in time and space (Stoddard, 1943). Wechsler's definition also includes the dimension of adapting to the environment and adjusting to problems and changing conditions. We must remember that the scores on an intelligence test measure how well an individual performs the set of tasks assessed by the test.

MODELS OF INTELLIGENCE

Many attempts have been made over the past century to develop models that conceptualize the facets of intelligence. One of the first theories was that of Charles Spearman, who postulated a two-factor theory of intelligence. In interpreting his statistical analysis of test performance, Spearman (1927) identified two factors—a G, or general ability, factor that each individual possesses and an S, or specific, factor that varies for each task undertaken. Thurstone (1938), on the other hand, proposed a multifactor theory. He analyzed 57 different tests taken by a high school group and concluded that there was a small group of primary factors rather than a single G factor. Thurstone (1938) termed these factors primary mental abilities and constructed a test called the Primary Mental Abilities Test. The seven primary abilities he identified are these.

1. *Number ability*—to perform basic mathematic processes accurately and rapidly
2. *Verbal ability*—to understand ideas expressed in word form
3. *Word fluency*—to speak and write fluently
4. *Memory*—to recognize and recall information such as numbers, letters, and words
5. *Reasoning*—to derive rules and solve problems inductively
6. *Spatial ability*—to visualize form relationships in three dimensions
7. *Perception*—to perceive things quickly, such as visual details and similarities and differences among pictured objects

One of the major issues during the 1920s concerned controversy over the nature of intelligence. The debate still goes on in psychological circles today. E. L. Thorndike (1927) believed that this type of debate is not productive. He disagreed with the concept of a singular and relatively independent mental process, or *G* factor, and concluded that there were many special or grouped abilities, such as mathematical and mechanical skills. He postulated that there were three major types of intelligence—abstract, practical, and social. Whether one agrees or disagrees depends partly on the individual's theoretical orientation and partly on the type of statistical analysis used with test results. Potential test users should be concerned with the purpose of an intelligence scale and the theories and approaches that will provide the most valid information.

Hierarchical Theory

Vernon (1960) proposed a hierarchical model of intelligence, which identified four levels of factors (see Figure 7.1). The trunk, or first, level includes the *G* factor, which is a general, or cognitive factor. The two main branches of the second level are verbal-educational and practical-mechanical-spatial factors. The third level identifies component factors of these two main branches. The verbal-educational area comprises abilities such as verbal fluency and numerical ability. The practical-mechanical-spatial area includes factors such as mechanical ability, psychomotor ability, and spatial relations. The fourth level of the hierarchy consists of more special and specific factors peculiar to tests in each of the domains above it. Vernon's model presents a conceptual way of including the general intelligence dimension of Spearman's work and the multifactor approach identified by Thorndike, Thurstone, and Guilford.

Guilford's Model of Intelligence

Guilford (1967) developed a multifactor approach to intelligence. He proposed a three-dimensional model that includes five types of operations, four types of content, and six types of products. The model contains 120 cells. Operations include

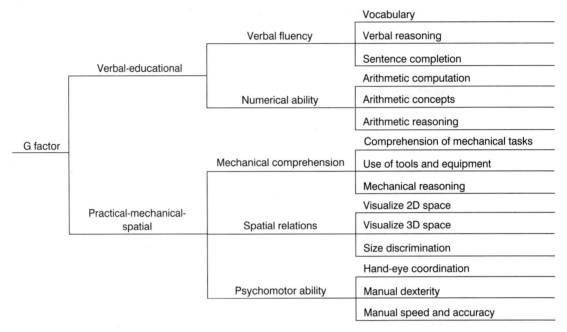

Figure 7.1
Adaptation of Vernon's hierarchical model of intelligence

cognition, memory, divergent thinking, convergent thinking, and evaluation. The four types of content are figural, symbolic, semantic, and behavioral. The six products are units, classes, relations, systems, transformations, and implications. A number of tests have been developed to measure the cells of Guilford's model. His approach is an extension of the multifactor approach advocated by Thurstone.

Cattell's Fluid and Crystallized Intelligence

Cattell (1963) used factor analytic studies to identify a two-factor theory of intelligence based on fluid and crystallized intelligence. Fluid intelligence is general to many different fields and is used in tasks requiring adaptation to new situations. Heredity is an important factor in fluid intelligence. Crystallized intelligence is more specific to a given field such as education. This type of ability depends more on the environment. The Culture-Fair Intelligence Test was designed to measure fluid intelligence.

Horn (1989), a student of Cattell, concluded that the theory can be thought of as a theory of multiple intelligences. These intelligences are "outcroppings of distinct influences operating through development, brain functioning, genetic determination, and the adjustment, adaptations, and achievement of school and work" (p. 76).

Sternberg's Cognitive Approaches to Intelligence

Sternberg (1980, 1985) utilized in his theory the information-processing components of intelligence. He identifies three different types of information-processing components that are important to consider: metacomponents, performance components, and knowledge acquisition components. First, metacomponents are the higher-order control processes used to oversee the planning, monitoring, and evaluating of task performance. He identifies 10 metacomponents as the most important in intelligent functioning.

1. Recognition that a problem of some kind exists

2. Recognition of the nature of the problem

3. Selection of a set of lower-order, nonexecutable components

4. Selection of a strategy for task performance, combining the lower-order components

5. Selection of one or more mental representations for information

6. Decision on how to allocate additional resources

7. Monitoring one's place in the task performance—what has been done and what needs to be done

8. Monitoring one's understanding of internal and external feedback concerning the quality of the task performance

9. Knowing how to act on the feedback that is received

10. Implementing action as a result of the feedback (Sternberg, 1985, p. 62)

Sternberg identifies performance components as lower-order processes used in the execution of strategies needed to perform a task: encoding the nature of the stimulus, inferring the relations between two stimulus terms that are similar in some ways but different in others, and applying a previously inferred relation to a new situation. Knowledge acquisition components are processes involved in learning new information and storing it in memory. Sternberg considers the three most important of these components to be selective encoding, selective combination, and selective comparison. Selective encoding requires sifting out relevant from irrelevant information. Selective combination refers to the combining of information in a way that maximizes its internal coherence or connectedness. Selective comparison relates new information to information already stored in memory to maximize the connectedness of the new knowledge.

Sternberg (1985) postulated six primary sources of individual differences in information processing.

1. *Components*—One individual may use more or fewer components or even different components than those another individual uses.

2. *Combination rule for components*—Different individuals may use different rules to combine.

3. *Mode of component processing*—Different persons prefer to process particular components in different modes.

4. *Order of component processing*—Different persons may use different sequences to order components.

5. *Component time and accuracy*—One person may be able to process a particular component more quickly or accurately than another person.

6. *Mental representations on which components act*—Different individuals may use different representations of information. (pp. 64–65)

Sternberg (1990) argues that memory and analytical reasoning are the operations necessary for success in school and that tacit, informational knowledge, rather than explicit, formal knowledge is required to be successful at work. Most traditional tests are contextualized with respect to the school; the problems are relatively short, have single correct answers, and contain no "real-world" content.

Sternberg (1990) has a research form of test that includes both academic and work contexts called the Sternberg Triarchic Abilities Test. The test has overlapping grade/age levels and can be administered from kindergarten through adulthood. Included on the test are 12 types of items.

Componential: Verbal—measures test taker's ability to learn from context and pick up information from relevant context

Componential: Quantitative—measures inductive reasoning ability in the numerical domain such as extrapolation of a sequence of numbers

Coping with Novelty: Verbal—assesses the ability to think in novel ways and requires hypothetical thinking with counterfactuals or novel verbal analogies which require counterfactual reasoning

Coping with Novelty: Quantitative—assesses coping with novelty skills in the context of the quantitative domain and utilizes a numerical matrix format in which the test taker has to substitute a number in place of a given symbol

Coping with Novelty: Figural—requires test takers to complete the series in a newly mapped domain and includes items similar to the figural completion type

Automatization: Verbal—requires test takers to make rapid decisions as to whether two letters are both the same category (vowel or consonant) or are different (vowel consonant or consonant vowel)

Automatization: Quantitative—requires the test taker to make rapid judgments as to whether two numbers have the same or different properties, such as being odd or even

Automatization: Figural—measures the test taker's ability to judge whether two figures have the same or different properties such as the number of sides

Practical: Verbal—measures the test taker's ability to respond to everyday inferential reasoning problems

Practical: Quantitative—measures the test taker's ability to reason quantitatively with practical everyday problems

Practical: Figural—measures the test taker's ability to perform route planning from information given on a map or diagram (pp. 216–219)

Piaget's Theory of Cognitive Development

Piaget (1970) conceptualized a theory of intellectual development by observing and interviewing children. His task was to discover the basic psychological structures that underlie the formation of concepts fundamental to philosophy and science. He was intrigued by the errors of young children on a test of reasoning and found that older children were not only quantitatively more intelligent, but also qualitatively different from younger children. Piaget focused on the qualitative differences, concluded that learning is fundamentally an internal process of construction, and identified organization and adaptation as two invariant functional properties of all living organisms. Organization is the general tendency to arrange both the physical and psychological processes in a coherent system. Two important dimensions of adaptation are assimilation and accommodation. Assimilation is the process by which a child relates new objects and ideas to familiar objects and ideas. Accommodation is the process by which a child changes behavior and psychological structures in response to environmental events.

Piaget divided intellectual development into four major stages, which are presented in Figure 7.2. These four stages are the sensorimotor period, the preoperational period, the concrete operational period, and the formal operational period. Piaget further identified four factors that affect development and the transition from one stage to another: maturation, experience, transmission, and equilibration. Equilibration can be described as the relative balance that exists between the individual's psychological structures and perceived events in the environment. Developing structures continually move toward greater and greater equilibrium. Piaget's theories have been the basis of the design of curriculum materials and educational programs, and a number of scales have been published to assess an individual's stage of intellectual development.

Figure 7.2
Piaget's stages of cognitive development

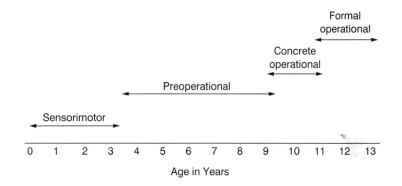

Gardner's Theory of Multiple Intelligence

Gardner (1983) postulated a theory of intelligence that focuses on a symbol system approach and combines both factor analytical and information-processing models. He identified seven forms of intelligence: linguistic, logical mathematical, spatial, musical, body-kinesthetic, interpersonal, and intrapersonal.

Verbal/linguistic intelligence involves word meaning and understanding, reading, grammar, and humor. Logical/mathematical intelligence involves inductive and deductive reasoning, scientific reasoning, mathematical understanding, mathematical operations, and critical and abstract thinking. Visual/spatial intelligence entails understanding relationships of objects in space, mental images, graphic representation, and perception from different angles. Body/kinesthetic intelligence involves complex motor coordination, awareness control of body movements and functions, and mind and body integration. Musical/rhythmic intelligence requires sensitivity to sounds, recognition, creation, and reproduction of both melody and rhythm, and appreciation and enjoyment of the structure of music. Interpersonal intelligence requires effective verbal and nonverbal communication, sensitivity to the feelings of others, and ability to understand and work with others. Intrapersonal intelligence is dependent on metacognition, higher-order thinking, concentration, self-awareness, and other types of self-improvement skills.

Gardner (1993) states that "intelligences work together to solve problems to yield various kinds of endstates—vocations, avocations, and the like" (p. 9). Interpersonal intelligence describes one's ability to detect the moods of other people and to lead those individuals. Intrapersonal intelligence depends on an understanding of one's own feelings and an ability to use self-knowledge productively.

TYPES OF TESTS

A number of methods to classify the various types of intelligence assessments and related tests are used by counselors and psychologists. Individual or group tests, verbal and nonverbal or performance tests, culture-fair tests, and developmental scales are examples. Procedures exist to measure intelligence in every age range from the infant to the senior citizen. Some tests can be classified into more than one category, and not all tests specify an IQ.

Individual Scales

Included in the list of the 38 most cited tests in the *Eleventh Mental Measurements Yearbook* are the Wechsler Preschool and Primary Scale of Intelligence Revised and the Otis Lennon School Ability Test—Sixth Edition.

The Wechsler Scales.   The Wechsler Intelligence Scales are individually administered tests with appropriate forms for different age spans. There are three scales—

A counselor uses a block design test to investigate test takers' visual/motor/spatial and perceptual skills.

the Wechsler Adult Intelligence Scale—Revised (WAIS-R), the Wechsler Intelligence Scale for Children—III (WISC-III), and the Wechsler Preschool and Primary Scale of Intelligence-Revised (WPPSI). The scales have 10 to 12 subtests each, about half belonging to the verbal scale, and the other half to the performance scale. The tests yield a verbal, performance, and total IQ score.

The verbal scale was designed by Wechsler to measure the examinee's ability to work with abstract symbols, the benefit the examinee received from his background, his verbal memory abilities, and his verbal fluency. The six areas included are information, digit span, arithmetic, comprehension, similarities, and vocabulary.

The information test focuses on knowledge and information acquired through educational experiences. Individuals with high scores have a wide variety of experiences, cultural opportunities, and outside interests. Low scores may show a lack of intellectual curiosity or a poor cultural environment.

The digit span test measures short-term or immediate memory. The task is to repeat digits forward as well as backwards. The test demands concentration and attention; examinees with high scores have good short-term memory and can focus their attention well. This ability may relate to low anxiety or stress levels. Low scores may indicate poor attention or an inability to concentrate, resulting from anxiety or stress.

The arithmetic subtest focuses on items that require basic mathematical skills such as addition, subtraction, multiplication, and division, and the ability to apply these skills. High scores are an indication of alertness, ability to concentrate, focus on tasks, and good arithmetic reasoning. Low scores may indicate a poor background in mathematical skills and/or reasoning and an inability to concentrate.

The comprehension subtest focuses on the individual's ability to make social judgments and requires information and knowledge of moral codes, social rules, and regulations. High scores are an indication of reality awareness, capacity for social compliance, and good judgment. Low scores may indicate poor judgment and possibly impulsiveness, antisocial tendencies, or some type of personality disturbance.

The similarities test measures reasoning and conceptual thinking ability. The test taker is presented word pairs and must explain their similarities. The tasks demand inductive reasoning; the individuals must take specific facts and see how they fit a general rule or principle. Individuals with high scores have good verbal fluency and concept formation. Those with low scores have poor ability to think abstractly and see things flexibly.

The vocabulary test contains words from easy to difficult and from concrete to abstract. The test taker is asked to give meanings. The test measures general word knowledge and language development. This subtest is found on almost all general intelligence and scholastic aptitude tests. The performance of the individuals is influenced by cultural experiences and educational backgrounds. Those with high scores on this subtest usually have a wide range of interests, good recall, and high general intelligence. Those with low scores may have had a limited educational background or may be poorly motivated.

The performance scale includes a number of subtests: picture completion, picture arrangement, block design, object assembly, coding, and mazes.

The picture completion test requires the test taker to identify the missing part of a drawing. The subtest measures long-term visual alertness and memory as well as visual acuity. The test taker must be able to differentiate important from minor details. The tasks require perceptual alertness and concentration and an ability to organize visual material. Those with high scores on this subtest have the ability to recognize essential visual information and reveal alertness and good visual acuity. Those with low scores often have poor ability in visual organization and poor ability to concentrate. Impulsive examinees make quick responses without carefully analyzing the whole picture.

The picture arrangement test requires the examinee to put scrambled comic strip pictures in the correct order to tell a story. The test requires temporal visual sequencing, social awareness, planning ability, and nonverbal reasoning. It also requires knowledge of American subcultural values and may be inappropriate for individuals from other cultures. Those with high scores on this test have social intelligence and the ability to anticipate the consequences of initial acts. Those with low scores usually have problems in interpersonal relationships, few ideas, and poor ability to plan ahead.

The block design test requires the examinee to copy a set of designs utilizing colored blocks. The test requires visual-spatial organization, the ability to analyze a whole into parts, and the use of nonverbal problem-solving skills. Those with high scores have good visual-motor-spatial skills and are able to concentrate. Those who score low have poor visual-motor-spatial and perceptual skills and poor visual integration. They may also have problems in concentration.

The object assembly test is a set of jigsaw puzzles that requires visual-motor speed and coordination as well as the ability to configure and organize the parts to the puzzle. Those with high scores on this test have excellent visual organizational abilities and demonstrate perceptual-motor coordination. Those with low scores have problems in visual-perceptual-motor areas and in visual concept formation.

The coding, or digit symbol, test requires quick and accurate coding of symbols that are paired with numbers of geometric shapes. The scale measures visual-motor speed and accuracy as well as short-term visual memory and the ability to follow directions. It demands an ability to learn an unfamiliar task. Those with high scores have effective visual-motor skills and are mentally efficient. They have the ability to memorize by rote new visual material. Those with low scores have poor visual-motor skills and an inadequate capacity for visual associative learning. They may have poor mental alertness.

The maze test requires children to draw an exit route out of each figure. The scale demands visual planning, visual-motor coordination, and perceptual organization. Those with high scores show an ability to plan ahead and a flexible mental orientation. Those with low scores often show impulsivity and poor visual-motor coordination and orientation to reality. A comparison of the dimensions measured in the verbal and performance scales of the Wechsler is given in Table 7.1.

The first step in interpretation of Wechsler results is to analyze the three global estimates of the client's ability—verbal, performance, and full scale. The full scale score is utilized as a summary index of ability, and the examiner is advised to use ± 2 standard errors of measurement to determine where a client's true score falls (LaGreca & Stringer, 1985); that approach translates into FSIQ ± 6. Kaufman (1990) advocates using a 95% confidence band and interprets as a significant strength each scaled score 3 or more points above the mean and as a significant weakness each scaled score 3 or more points below the mean. The examiner can compare the individual's score with the appropriate ability classification listed in Table 7.2.

The second step is to analyze the verbal and performance scores and see whether they are significantly different; a 12-point difference is significant at the .05 level, and a 15-point difference is significant at the .01 level (Kaufman, 1976, 1990). In summarizing the research findings on significant differences between the verbal and performance scales, Groth-Marnat (1990) identified the following possible hypotheses:

1. If the verbal IQ is 15 or more points above the performance IQ, it might show that the individual (a) has a high level of academic achievement, (b) comes from an urban environment, (c) has some type of neurosis (anxiety and tension state, obsessive-compulsion, or depression), (d) has learning problems of a perceptual nature, or (e) has a right-hemisphere cerebral impairment.

2. If the performance IQ is significantly higher than the verbal IQ, it might show that the individual (a) is an underachiever or has not made use of educational opportunities, (b) comes from a lower socioeconomic level or a different cul-

Table 7.1
Comparison of verbal and performance dimensions of the Wechsler Intelligence Scales

Verbal	Performance
General	
Work with abstract symbols	Nonverbal contact with the environment
Utilization of school or educational background	Work with perceptual-motor tasks
	Work with concrete tasks and problems
Verbal memory abilities	
Verbal fluency	
Specific	
Computational skills	Long-term visual memory
Numerical reasoning	Visual alertness
Logical thinking	Ability to differentiate among details
Abstract thinking	Temporal visual sequencing
Ability to form verbal concepts	Social awareness
Word knowledge	Nonverbal reasoning
Language development	Planning ability
Awareness of social rules and mores	Verbal concept formation
	Whole/part analysis
Common sense	Visual-spatial ability
Use of past experience	Sensory-motor feedback
Short-term auditory memory	Visual-motor speed, coordination, and accuracy
Recall of information	Short-term visual memory
	Ability to follow directions
	Visual planning
	Ability to follow a visual pattern

Table 7.2
Classification of range of intelligence scores

IQ Range	Classification	Percentile Range
130 and above	Very Superior	98–99
120–129	Superior	91–97
110–119	High Average	75–90
90–109	Average	25–74
80–89	Low Average	9–24
70–79	Borderline	3–8
69 and below	Below Average	1–2

tural or language background, (c) is a delinquent or a sociopath, (d) has severe reading difficulties, or (e) has left-hemisphere impairment.

The next step is to analyze and interpret the subtests. The examiner might look at the scatter of scores on the subtests and identify the highest and lowest scaled scores on the subtests. Kaufman (1976, 1990) reported that the average scaled score range is 7 points. The examiner might determine the number of subtests that deviate by 3 points or more from the fixed means. The subtests that are 3 points or more above the mean are identified as strengths, and those 3 points or more below the mean are identified as weaknesses. Subtest patterns are then analyzed for commonalities. Bannatyne (1971, 1974), for instance, organizes the subtests into the following categories: (a) verbal conceptual ability—comprehension, similarities, vocabulary; (b) spatial ability—block design, object assembly, picture completion; (c) sequencing ability—arithmetic, coding, digit span; and (d) acquired knowledge—arithmetic, information, vocabulary. The examiner might look at the scatter of the items within a subtest. Is there any pattern of how the individual responds to the items within the test? This is a more qualitative analysis.

The last step is to analyze the content of the responses on the various subtests. The examiner may be able to assess the client's level of thinking and identify any unusual associations as well as certain dimensions of personality and learning style. Spanish versions of the Wechsler scales are also available.

Kaufman Assessment Battery for Children.   The Kaufman Assessment Battery for Children (K-ABC, 1983) is an individually administered measure of intelligence and achievement for children ages 2 years, 6 months to 12 years, 6 months. The K-ABC is based on a theory of intelligence that distinguishes between sequential and simultaneous mental processes. Sequential processing (Kaufman, Kamphaus, & Kaufman, 1985) relates to the ability to solve problems by mentally arranging input in a sequential or serial order. Simultaneous processing refers to the ability to synthesize information from mental wholes to solve the problem. Simultaneous processing is used in such tasks as learning the shapes of letters, deriving meaning from pictorial stimuli, and determining the main idea from a paragraph of a text. Sequential processing is used in learning grammatical relationships and rules, understanding the chronology of events, and making associations between sounds and letters.

The K-ABC contains 16 subtests of mental and processing skills. Three subtests measure sequential processing, seven measure simultaneous processing, and six tests measure achievement. The achievement tests assess school learning in arithmetic, reading-decoding, reading-understanding, general information, early language development, and language concepts. The K-ABC also has a special nonverbal scale designed to assess the intelligence of hearing impaired and limited English proficient children. The 10 subtests to measure mental processing skills are described in Table 7.3.

Table 7.3
K-ABC mental processing subtests

Subtest (ages)	Skill to Be Assessed
Magic Window (2.6 to 4.11)	Identifying and naming an object from a picture rotated behind a narrow slit that permits the picture to be only partially exposed
Face Recognition (2.6 to 4.11)	Attending closely to one or two faces in photographs that are briefly exposed and then selecting the correct face in a group photograph
Hand Movement (2.6 to 12.5)	Copying the precise sequence of taps on the table as performed by the examiner with a fist, palm, or side of the hand
Gestalt Closure (2.6 to 12.5)	Filling in the gaps in a partially completed inkblot drawing and also naming and describing the drawings
Number Recall (2.6 to 12.5)	Repeating in sequence a series of numbers orally presented by the examiner
Triangles (4.0 to 12.5)	Assembling several identical rubber triangles to match a picture of an abstract design.
Word Order (4.0 to 12.5)	Pointing with and without an interference task, to silhouettes of common objects in the same order as the objects were named by the examiner
Matrix Analogies (5.0 to 12.5)	Selecting the picture or design that best completes a 2″ × 2″ visual analogy
Spatial Memory (5.0 to 12.5)	Recalling the locations of pictures arranged randomly on a page
Photo Series (6.0 to 12.5)	Organizing in proper time sequence a randomly arranged array of photographs illustrating an event

CASE OF GEORGE

George Gray
Middletown Elementary School: Grade K
Date of Birth   3/22/80
Chronological Age   7-03
Date of Examination   7/8/87

Tests Used

Kaufman Assessment Battery for Children, Peabody Picture Vocabulary Test—Revised, Developmental Test of Visual-Motor Integration, Goodenough-Harris Drawing Test

Reasons for Referral

George Gray was referred for possible program change. He is currently participating in the language impaired program at Middletown Elementary School.

Background Information

George was previously tested on 7/31/86. He was given the Stanford-Binet Intelligence Scale, Leiter International Performance Scale, Peabody Picture Vocabulary Test, and the Test of Visual-Motor Integration. The Stanford-Binet Intelligence Scale yielded an IQ of 48. The Leiter International Performance Scale was administered because of George's delayed language development, and an IQ score of 77 was obtained. The Peabody Picture Vocabulary Test revealed a standard score below 40, an age-equivalent score of 3 years, 6 months, and a significant deficit in the receptive vocabulary area. A communication evaluation was completed on 11/7/86, indicating that George had an articulation disorder and was severely delayed in language skills. The Vineland Adaptive Behavior Scale was completed on 6/19/87 with these results:

Scale	Age Equivalent
Receptive Language	3–11
Expressive Language	3–3
Written Language	1–6

George's adaptive behavior composite on that evaluation equated to 60.

Another communication evaluation was conducted on 4/24/87. The speech and language pathologist reported that the two communication evaluations were consistent. George was functioning at approximately a 3-year-old level during both evaluations. Vision and hearing were found to be within acceptable limits at the school level.

Examiner Observations

George is a 7-year-old male of average stature for his chronological age. He was somewhat uncooperative by being continually out of his seat and exhibited poor listening skills. His work habits were somewhat slow, but his behavior could be described as extremely active. He was aware of his failures, and he typically gave up on a task at the very beginning if he believed he could not accomplish it. He appeared agitated after his failures. His speech was poor and his language inarticulate. At times his responses were vague, and the examiner had to encourage him to continue responding. He usually spoke only when he was spoken to. On the visual-motor tasks his reaction time was slow; he used a trial-and-error method of problem solving.

Results

Kaufman-Assessment Battery for Children gave these Global Scale standard scores:

Sequential Processing 56 ± 10
Simultaneous Processing 71 ± 9
Mental Processing Composite 63 ± 8
Achievement   Below 40
Nonverbal 67 ± 8

These were the Achievement standard scores:

Spaces and Places 65 ± 13
Arithmetic 62 ± 13
Riddles 59 ± 11
Reading/Decoding 67 ± 7
Reading/Understanding   0

The Mental Processing scaled scores included these scores for Sequential Processing:

Hand Movement   3
Number Recall   1
Word Order   4

These were the scores for Simultaneous Processing:

Gestalt Closure   7
Triangles   10
Matrix Analogies   6
Spatial Memory   2
Photo Series   3

These were the Nonverbal scores:

Hand Movement   3
Triangles   10
Matrix Analogies   6
Spatial Memory   2
Photo Series   3

Significant differences and overall scores were as follows:

Sequential < Simultaneous   .05
Sequential > Achievement   .05
Simultaneous > Achievement   .01
MPC > Achievement   .01

Mean Achievement Standard Score   50.6
Mean Scaled Score   4.5

Scores on the Peabody Picture Vocabulary Test were these:

Raw Score   27
Standard Score < 40
Age Equivalent   3-2

Cognitive Development and Interpretation

George was administered the K-ABC to assess his current mental processing abilities and level of achievement. The K-ABC measures one's style of problem solving. Two types of mental functioning are identified: sequential processing, which involves processing stimuli bit by bit or in serial order, and simultaneous processing, which incorporates a holistic and frequently spatial integration of stimuli.

George's Sequential Processing standard score of 56 ± 10 (95% confidence level) is in the educable mentally handicapped range of functioning. His Simultaneous Processing score of 71 ± 9 is in the borderline range. Thus, there is a significant difference (15 points) between his sequential processing and his simultaneous processing. This difference suggests that George has greater abilities in solving problems holistically or processing many stimuli at one time, rather than stimulus by stimulus.

George's Achievement standard score of below 40 represents a significant discrepancy between his school achievement and mental processing abilities. His Simultaneous Processing standard score of 71 is significantly greater than his Achievement Standard Score. This difference is found in less than 1% of the individuals within George's age group and may be associated with school-related learning tasks on the test, which are usually more sequentially oriented.

George's Mental Processing Composite (MPC) of 63 ± 8 is in the educable mentally handicapped range. His true score has a 95% chance of being between 55 and 71. Thus, his MPC score is significantly higher than the Achievement standard score and indicates that he has greater processing potential than is being exemplified in school-related achievement.

Internal analysis of the K-ABC reveals a mean score of 4.5, which is considered in the handicapped range of functioning. A relative strength is noted on the Triangles subtest, which measures abstract concept formation. A significant weakness is noted in short-term recall via simultaneous processing (Spatial Memory). All his scores on the Mental Processing subtests, except for Triangles, are considered below the average for children within George's age group.

The Nonverbal standard score of 67 was compiled from the subtests Hand Movements, Triangles, Matrix Analogies, Spatial Memory, and Photo Series. George's Nonverbal standard score was not significantly higher than his Mental Processing score, suggesting that his abilities, as measured by the K-ABC, are not significantly different. Language impairment is the major influence, but other factors also appear to be contributing to George's low-functioning intellect.

Receptive Language

On the Peabody Picture Vocabulary Test—Revised, which requires the subject to point to one of four pictures corresponding to a word presented orally by the examiner, George received a standard score below 40. This score is greater than one standard deviation below the mean when considering chronological age and current cognitive functioning, and it represents a process deficit in the receptive language area.

Perceptual-Motor

On the Developmental Test of Visual-Motor Integration, which requires the subject to reproduce geometric designs with pencil and paper, George received a standard score of 4 and an age equivalent of 5.1. This score is within one standard deviation of the mean, when considering chronological age and current cognitive functioning, and represents adequate development in the perceptual motor area. The Goodenough-Harris Drawing Test revealed a mental age of 5.9 and an estimated IQ of 79.

Diagnostic Impressions

George is functioning in the educable mentally handicapped range. He demonstrates significantly greater abilities in simultaneous processing, as compared with sequential processing. He also demonstrates a relative strength in his nonverbal concept formation and his word recognition and letter naming. A significant weakness is noted in his short-term memory recall.

George's Achievement scores are significantly lower than his potential indicates. His nonverbal abilities are not demonstrated as being significantly higher than his Total Mental Processing Composite. A process deficit is noted in receptive language, consistent with his history of poor language development. Perceptual-motor abilities appear to be adequately developed. Just how much George's poor language development has affected his intellectual functioning is not known. Presently his intellectual functioning, as measured by the K-ABC, is somewhere between the educable mentally handicapped and borderline range of functioning. Current remediation strategies should address his language delay as well as his current estimated intellectual functioning.

The K-ABC does have an interpretative manual (Kaufman and Kaufman, 1983), which suggests these five steps.

1. Obtain the derived scores and describe them with bands of error, descriptive categories, national and sociocultural percentile ranks, age equivalents, and grade equivalents.

2. Compare standard scores on the Sequential Processing and Simultaneous Processing scales.

3. Compare standard scores on the Mental Processing and Achievement scales.

4. Determine strengths and weaknesses on the Mental Processing subtests.

5. Determine strengths and weaknesses on the Achievement subtests.

The K-ABC lists these primary goals: to measure intelligence from a strong theoretical and research basis, to separate acquired factual knowledge from the ability to solve unfamiliar problems, to yield scores that translate into educational interventions, to include novel tasks, to be easy to administer and objective to score, and to be sensitive to diverse needs of preschool, minority groups and exceptional children (p. 5).

In a review of the K-ABC, Merz (1984) concludes that the authors have met the goals and that the test will fairly assess minority group members and individuals with language handicaps.

Kaufman Adolescent and Adult Intelligence Test.   The Kaufman Adolescent and Adult Intelligence Test (KAIT) core battery consists of six subtests within two scales. The KAIT measures fluid intelligence, adaptability and flexibility in problem solving through three subtests. The crystallized scale measures ability to solve problems and make decisions based on acquired knowledge, verbal conceptualization, formal and information education, life experiences, and acculturation through subtests on auditory comprehension, double meanings, and definitions. A composite score provides a measure of overall intellectual functioning. The examiner can also add one to four additional subtests to the battery: memory for block designs, famous faces, rebus recall, and auditory recall. A *rebus* is a picture that stands for a word. Individuals are asked to read phrases or sentences composed of rebuses on the fluid scale, then read the phrases or sentences on the on the added recall test that were learned earlier during the rebus learning subtest. The KAIT can measure immediate and delayed recall. The construct validity of the KAIT is shown through studies correlating the KAIT with the WISC-R, WAIS-Rand KABC. Reliability coefficients in the .90s were reported.

Stanford-Binet Intelligence Scale.   The Stanford-Binet Intelligence Scale: Fourth Edition is quite different from the edition published in 1960. The test does retain some content and a variety of tasks but no longer uses the age-scale format. All of the same type of items are grouped together, and the test now has a variety of scales. The purpose of this change is to help examiners obtain a better diagnosis of a test taker's cognitive abilities. The authors claim the test has two major strengths.

1. A continuous scale for appraising the cognitive development of the test taker from age 2 to adulthood

2. An adaptive-testing format that permits testing with a range of tasks best suited to the client's ability level.

The conceptual model for the fourth edition of the Stanford-Binet consists of three levels. The top level is the *G* or generalized reasoning factor. The second level consists of three broad factors: crystallized abilities, fluid-analytical abilities, and short-term memory. The third level measures verbal, quantitative, and abstract/visual reasoning dimensions of intelligence.

The Stanford-Binet contains many of the item types from the previous edition. The criteria for selection required that the items

1. be acceptable measures of the conceptual model utilized

2. be able to be scored reliably

3. be relatively free from ethnic and gender bias

4. function adequately over a wide range of age groups

New items were constructed to increase the pool measuring quantitative reasoning, abstract/visual reasoning, and short-term memory.

The standardization was completed in 1985 and involved 500 examiners, 5,000 subjects, and 160 testing centers from 47 states and the District of Columbia (p. 16). The standardization considered community size, ethnic group membership, age, gender, and socioeconomic status.

The Stanford-Binet consists of four factors. The verbal reasoning factor includes four subtests: vocabulary, comprehension, absurdities, and verbal relations. The abstract/visual reasoning component also includes four subtests: pattern analysis, copying, matrices, and paper folding and cutting. The quantitative reasoning factor has three subtests: quantitative, number series, and equation building. The short-term memory factor includes four scales: bead memory, memory for sentences, memory for digits, and memory of objects. The tests report standard age scores (SAS). Each test has an SAS mean of 50 and a standard deviation of 8. The area scores and overall composite score have a fixed mean of 100 and fixed standard deviation of 15. Tables are available with 16 as the fixed standard deviation.

The items on the test are arranged in levels designated by the letters A through Y. Some tests contain 20 or more levels and cover the entire range from 2 to adulthood; others contain 10 levels and cover a narrower range of chronological age. The purpose of this format is to facilitate adaptive testing. Chronological age and performance on the vocabulary test are used to identify the level at which testing should begin. As in previous editions of the Stanford-Binet, basal and ceiling levels are established.

Other Individual Tests.   The Leiter International Performance Scale (LIPS) is a 54-item, nonverbal test used to assess the intelligence of individuals aged 2 through adulthood. It has been used to test a wide variety of individuals, including those with hearing problems, language disabilities, mental retardation, cultural disadvantages, or non-English-speaking backgrounds. The LIPS measures dimensions of perceptual and conceptual abilities. The perceptual items present tasks involving shapes, colors, block design, and visual closure. The conceptual items require clients to deduce underlying relationships, categories, and classes; demonstrate an understanding of visual-spatial relationships; and understand numerical processes. The categories are labeled symbolic transformation, quantitative discriminations, spatial imagery, genus matching, progression discriminations, and immediate recall. Matey (1984) rates the LIPS valuable for psychologists engaged in the assessment of the mental abilities of hearing impaired children, children with severe expressive or receptive language disabilities, and adults with severe or profound mental retardation. The LIPS is also considered an appropriate instrument for those who have motor and manipulative difficulties in addition to their communication problems.

Arthur Point Scale of Performance Tests—Revised Form II is an individual scale that measures the mental abilities of individuals with reading, hearing and/or speech, emotional, or cultural problems. The Arthur Point Scale contains five tests: Knox Cube Test, Sequin Form Board, Arthur Stencil Design, Healy Picture Completion, and Porteus Maze Test.

The Peabody Picture Vocabulary Test-III measures receptive vocabulary knowledge for standard American English and provides an estimate of the verbal ability and scholastic aptitude of the test taker. The examinee is shown a plate containing four pictures and is asked to point to the picture that corresponds to the stimulus word. A new Spanish version is now available.

The Slosson Intelligence Test-Revised (SIT-R) provides a quick assessment of mental abilities of children and adults, ages 4 to 65. The SIT is a 187-item oral screening instrument with questions arranged on a scale by chronological age. The SIT-R contains 33 vocabulary items, 29 general information items, 30 similarities and difference items, 33 comprehension items, 34 quantitative items, and 28 auditory memory items. The SIT-/R correlates .892 with the WISC-R VIQ and .863 with the WISC-III FSIQ. The KR-20 reliability coefficients are .90 or higher for all age groups. An item analysis identifies the strengths and weaknesses of an individual in eight learning areas.

The Test of Nonverbal Intelligence-2 (TONI-2) provides a language-free measure of cognitive ability. The TONI-2 is used with clients having speech, language, or learning disabilities, who are deaf or hearing impaired, or who have suffered some other form of brain injury. It can also be used with clients who do not speak English or for whom English is not their first language. A 50-item, point-to-the-response test can be given by pantomime to the examinee, who responds by pointing to the selected answer. The test can be given from ages 5 to 85 and 11 months and takes 10 to 15 minutes.

The Raven's Progressive Matrices consist of a series of three nonverbal tests for different ability levels. In measuring the nonverbal component of Spearman's G factor, the items are designed to assess client's ability to make sense of complex situations, derive meaning from events, and perceive and think clearly. It can be group administered and has been utilized with mentally handicapped clients. The Coloured Progressive Matrices (CPM)(1990) is used to spread the scores for the bottom 20% of the general population. Norms are available for children aged 6.5 to 16.5. The Standard Progressive Matrices (SPM)(1993) measures the performance in the average range and consists of five sets of 12 problems each. The Advanced Progressive Matrices (APM) (1993) Test is designed to spread the scores of the top 20% of the population.

Group Intelligence and Scholastic Aptitude Tests

There are quite a number of widely used group intelligence tests. Such tests have been used ever since World War I, when the Army Alpha and Army Beta were used to screen recruits. The Army Alpha was the first widely used group verbal test of intelligence; the Army Beta was the first widely used group nonverbal test. Group tests measure as wide a variety of constructs as do individual tests. All types of theories and approaches are used.

It takes little training for an examiner to be competent in the administration and scoring of group tests. The directions are clearly stated in the manual, and the major task of the examiner is to read the test directions to the examinees and follow rigidly the specified time limits. Scoring keys or stencils are available, as are tables for translating the raw scores into deviation IQs or percentile ranks. Some of the widely used group tests of intelligence are described here.

The Advanced Progressive Matrices Test was constructed by J. C. Ravens and is a 48-item nonverbal group IQ test. The first 12 items are used to give the examinee practice for Part II. The examinee is presented with figure designs or patterns that have parts missing. Examinees are then asked to choose the correct option from among six possible parts. The test can be used with adolescents and adults. The Colored Progressive Matrices Test is similar to the one just described but for ages 5 to 11 and adults. It can be group-administered and has been utilized with mentally handicapped or impaired clients.

Culture-Fair Intelligence Tests are a series of tests developed by R. B. Cattell and A. K. S. Cattell. Scale 1 is used for ages 4 to 8; scale 2 for preadolescents, adolescents, and adults with average abilities; and scale 3 with college students and adults with above-average ability. Scales 2 and 3 are group-administered nonverbal tests measuring perceptual tasks, such as completing a series, classifying, solving incomplete designs, and evaluating conditions. The tests measure the fluid dimension of Cattell's theory mentioned earlier in this chapter.

The Cognitive Abilities Test (CogAT) was originally developed by R. L. Thorndike and E. P. Hagen and is a multilevel battery used to test children from kindergarten to grade 12. Verbal, quantitative, and nonverbal batteries are utilized. The verbal battery measures vocabulary, sentence completion, classification, and analogies. The quantitative battery measures relations, number series, and equation building. The nonverbal battery utilizes figure classification, analogies, and synthesis. The test can be group-administered to classes and hand- or computer-scored. Levels 1 and 2 are designed for kindergarten through grade 3; level A, for grades 3 to 12. Testing time is about 90 minutes. A CogAT *Interpretive Guide for Teachers* and a manual, *Preparing for Testing with the COGAT*, are available to facilitate proper use and interpretation of the test. The current edition of the test is Form 5 (1993).

The Otis-Lennon School Ability Test (OLSAT) was developed by A. S. Otis and later revised by R. T. Lennon. The OLSAT is currently in its sixth edition. The OLSAT has five levels: Primary I for grade 1, Primary II for grades 2 and 3, Elementary for grades 4 and 5, Intermediate for grades 6 to 8, and Advanced for grades 9 to 12. The primary batteries are read to the students by the examiner. Verbal, figural, and numerical items are rotated. The test yields one *G* score. The Otis-Lennon School Ability Test (OLSAT) is used for predicting success in cognitive, school-related areas. The OLSAT also has five forms and yields a school ability index, national PR-S, and national NCE on total verbal and nonverbal Scores. Local norms can also be included in the report. The computer report provides a narrative explaining the student's performance in easy-to-understand language. The student's performance on the test is analyzed by clusters, including verbal comprehension, verbal reasoning, figural reasoning, and quantitative reasoning.

The School and College Ability Tests (SCAT) are a series of group tests measuring verbal and quantitative ability from grade 3.5 to grade 14. The verbal section measures students' understanding of words and analogies, and the quantitative section measures students' understanding of fundamental number concepts. The SCAT reports scores in both verbal and quantitative areas in percentile bands.

The Test of Cognitive Skills (TCS-2) (1992) is a group test used to assess four areas of the cognitive skills of students in grades 2 to 12: analogies, sequences, memory, and verbal reasoning. The analogies test assesses students' ability to see abstract or concrete relationships and to classify objects or concepts according to common attributes. The memory test assesses students' abilities to recall information presented at the beginning of the test. The sequences test assesses students' ability to comprehend a principle or a rule implicit in a pattern or sequence of figures, letters, or numbers. The verbal reasoning test assesses students' ability to discern relationships and reason logically. The TCS yields scores in each of the four areas and provides a verbal, nonverbal, and total IQ.

The Primary Test of Cognitive Skills (PTCS) (1990) was developed by Huttenlocher and Levine to measure the cognitive skills of children in kindergarten and first grade and has four subscales: verbal, spatial, memory, and concepts. These four subscales are combined to yield a cognitive skills index, utilizing a mean of 100 and a standard deviation of 10.

These are not all of the many group tests that are used, but are representative of the types of tests that are available and reflect the variety of approaches used by test authors. For example, the Culture Fair Intelligence Tests yield only one score, whereas the CogAT and TCS yield a series of scores. Scores are reported in different ways. Some tests use percentile bands; others use deviation IQ scores. Certain tests are designed to be culture-free. Some tests—such as the OLSAT, CogAT, SCAT, and TCS—are often given along with major survey achievement batteries because they may provide useful information to the counselor and teacher about students' cognitive abilities that are not assessed as completely on the achievement tests. Some tests utilize primarily verbal and numeric material, while others, such as the Culture-Free Scales, utilize only perceptual stimuli. Some, of course, measure all three areas.

Admissions Tests.   A number of specialized tests are used as one source of information to help admissions counselors in their decision making. Two major national testing programs are used by colleges and universities for admissions decisions: the American College Testing Program (ACT) and the Scholastic Aptitude Test (SAT).

The ACT contains a series of tests: English Usage, Mathematics, Social Studies, and Natural Sciences. The test taker receives scores in each subject area in addition to a composite score. The mathematics test assesses knowledge of algebra and geometry. The science and social studies scales assess the examinee's ability to interpret written paragraphs on science or social studies topics.

The new SAT has two major forms—I and II. SAT I is broken into two sections, verbal and mathematical reasoning. The verbal emphasizes critical reading skills and the understanding of words in context. The mathematics section allows students to use calculators; 29 of the questions require answers generated by the test taker. SAT II includes an English essay and other verbal and quantitative achievement tests in various subject areas. The verbal section measures verbal reasoning and comprehension of textlike material, whereas the quantitative section measures basic principles of algebra and geometry. The PSAT, taken by students in their junior year of high school, helps students become familiar with the types of skills and competencies measured by the test. The SAT is used by high school counselors to help guide students in their educational decisions. Some colleges use the PSAT results to make scholarship decisions. The SAT has been criticized for its inherent bias against minorities and its relative lack of importance in helping make college admissions decisions.

Graduate School Admissions Tests.   On this level also, competitive examinations are used by schools and universities for guidance in admissions decisions. The Graduate Record Examination (GRE) is a scholastic aptitude test required by many graduate and professional schools and scholarship sponsors. The test is given worldwide at testing centers approved by the Educational Testing Service. The test was developed by the Graduate Record Examination Board and is administered by the Educational Testing Service. The GRE general test assesses verbal, quantitative, and analytical abilities. The seven 30-minute sections require 3½ hours of testing time. There are 17 subject tests, each of which requires 2 hours and 50 minutes of testing time. Subject tests are available in biology, chemistry, computer science, economics, education, engineering, French, geology, history, literature in English, mathematics, music, physics, political science, psychology, sociology and Spanish.

The education test contains 200 questions covering five major areas.

1. *Education Goals*—philosophical; historical; psychological, including physical, emotional, intellectual; role of education in a pluralistic society

2. *School Administration and Supervision*—sources of authority; psychological concerns such as grouping practices; sociological considerations such as teacher and student rights

3. *Curriculum*—historical and philosophical considerations; relation to development and learning factors; relation to societal demands

4. *Teaching-Learning*—historical and philosophical concerns; nature of learning and teaching; sociological factors such as social class

5. *Evaluation and Research*—meaning of research conclusions; elementary statistical and measurement concepts; sociological concerns such as uses of pupil records

If requests are made in advance, special arrangements and test materials are available for individuals with verbal, physical, hearing, or learning disabilities. For example, the General Test is available in braille (1972 Nemeth Code), in large type, with large-type answer sheets, and on cassettes. French and Spanish versions of the test are given once a year.

The reliability of the GRE test has been computed using the Kuder-Richardson 20 formula. This coefficient provides an estimate of the internal consistency of the test and alternate form reliability. The test bulletin reports that the reliabilities on the general tests and subject tests range from .88 to .96. The content validity of the subject examinations is extremely critical and is evaluated by a committee of professors working with ETS test development specialists. The main type of validity for the test is its predictive validity—to predict success in graduate school.

The Miller's Analogies Test (MAT) is an objective, group-administered test of mental ability, consisting of 100 multiple-choice analogy items. The content for the analogies comes from literature, social sciences, chemistry, physics, mathematics, and general information. The test is given only at controlled testing centers and requires 50 minutes of testing time. It is used primarily for the selection of students for graduate schools and is published by the Psychological Corporation. The MAT is a short test but seems to have good predictive validity.

Other widely used admission tests in higher education include the Medical College Admissions Test (MCAT), Law School Admissions Test (LSAT), and the Graduate Management Admission Test (GMAT). The most important consideration in the use of these tests is whether the validity of the test for a particular program has been established, especially through studies at a local college or university.

TRENDS AND ISSUES

Intelligence testing is still a center of controversy. Many definitions of the construct of intelligence have led to the development of many different models, theories, and tests. There is no shared agreement as to what intelligence is and how it should be measured. We are not even sure of what words we should use to describe the construct—ability, aptitude, cognitive abilities, intelligence, or potential. The cognitive and information processing movements in psychology have had an impact on the theories and have influenced how we interpret and entitle our tests. Instead of "intelligence" in the title, many tests now refer to "cognitive abilities."

Many models have been developed to help us conceptualize intelligence, such as those by Spearman, Thurstone, E. L. Thorndike, Guilford, Gardner, Horn, Piaget, Sternberg, Wagner, Vernon, and Jensen. The controversy still centers around the issue of whether intelligence is a general attribute or has many specific attributes.

The heredity and environment issue is also still debated. Social scientists have been divided for a long time over the relative importance of heredity and environment in relation to intelligence. Most recently, in their book *The Bell Curve* (1994) Herrnstein and Murray conclude that heredity plays an important role in intelligence. Among other evidence, they note that IQ scores are highly correlated with academic success, job performance, and infant mortality. Children of low-IQ women tend to die more often in infancy that those of higher-IQ parents. Current studies are exploring how the interaction between heredity and environment affects intelligence.

Neither are we in agreement as to the purposes of intelligence testing. Sternberg and Wagner believe the tests should be used to help provide useful information for understanding and improving the learning process of individuals tested.

Much concern is still focused on the biased nature of IQ tests. White middle-class test takers score better than individuals from different racial and cultural groups. Loehlin (1975) concluded that such distinctions reflect biases in the tests themselves, differences in the environments of the groups, and differences in the genetic makeup of the individuals studied. The three factors are viewed as interactive but not necessarily independent. Attempts were made, for example, on the Wechsler Intelligence Scale for Children to minimize bias. Statistics were computed to identify and eliminate items preferential to certain age, ethnic, or gender groups in the current third edition.

Another question often debated deals with the stability of intelligence over time. Research has indicated that IQ scores are very unstable in early childhood. Later, scores may decline with age on some types of items and increase on others. IQ is not viewed as a fixed entity. Some dimensions may be influenced by genetic makeup, but typically one develops greater general knowledge, problem-solving ability, and comprehension with age. On the other hand, the psychomotor performance of an individual might decrease with age.

SUMMARY

The chapter focused on the individual and group-intelligence scales that are most widely used today. The tests cited illustrate that there are many definitions and models of intelligence. They help teachers make instructional decisions about what methods and materials would be best for their students. They help workers in the helping professions to develop realistic expectations for their clients and students. The information from intelligence tests is also valuable in guiding individuals to make educational and vocational decisions. The tests provide a frame of reference for looking at cognitive abilities and making placement and classification decisions on the basis of such scores. Intelligence tests are also used for descriptive and predictive purposes.

QUESTIONS FOR DISCUSSION

1. Compare the different theories of intelligence. What theory do you find most acceptable and why? Why are theories important?

2. What are the advantages and disadvantages of group intelligence tests? Of individual tests? When would you use each?

3. E. L. Thorndike said there were three types of intelligence: abstract, social, and practical. Do you agree with his view? How do they compare with Sternberg's and Gardner's types?

4. Turn back to the "Case of George." He was given the Stanford-Binet, Leiter International Performance Scale, Peabody Picture Vocabulary Test, Goodenough-Harris Drawing Test, and Developmental Test of Visual-Motor Integration. Why was

each test given? Why are there differences in the scores on these tests? Would you have given George any other test? Why or why not?

5. Do you feel that most tests are biased in favor of the white middle-class examinee? Do you believe that we should use only culture-fair tests? Defend your beliefs.

6. What factors influence how an individual performs on an IQ test? Do you believe that items on the intelligence tests should be radically changed so the test can be of more use? Why or why not?

SUGGESTED ACTIVITIES

1. Critique a group or individual intelligence test discussed in this chapter.

2. Interview psychologists and counselors who use intelligence tests. Find out which tests they use and why and when they test. Report your results to the class.

3. Make an annotated bibliography of the intelligence and scholastic aptitude tests you would use in your field.

4. Write a review of the literature or position paper on one of the following topics: bias in intelligence testing, history of intelligence testing, socioeconomic class and intelligence, genetic studies of intelligence, computer-adaptive intelligence testing.

5. Take a group IQ test, score it, and write a report of the results.

6. Read *The Bell Curve* and be prepared to discuss the book in class.

7. Read the following case and answer the questions at the end of it.

Case of Roberta

Roberta is a grade 9 student who was referred to the school psychologists for psychoeducational evaluation to assess possible causes of her unacceptable behavior and poor peer/adult relationships.

School personnel are concerned about Roberta's inability to function in a school setting. She is frequently off task, asks inappropriate questions, comes unprepared, wanders about the classroom, and seeks to make herself the center of attention. Roberta is making just fair grades in average group classes. She appears to be preoccupied and also seems to fear her parents, not wanting them to know what happens in school.

Examiner Observations: Roberta is a thin, pale, young lady with unkempt hair. She has excellent vocabulary and a good sense of humor. However, she does not know how to respond to teasing or correction and seemed to enjoy telling stories about how she got back at people who offended her. Her speech was affected, leaning toward the theatrical, and she appeared to enjoy the attention testing afforded.

She was observed in the class and in the halls. She was unprepared for class, not having paper. This seemed to be a common occurrence. She gave responses to questions in a mumble. When asked to speak louder, she became quite dramatic. In the halls she keeps to herself. She leaves class late and hurries to her next class. She stands out in the crowd. Her mannerisms and dress set her apart.

Results:

Stanford Binet (full scale)   142

Wide Range Achievement Test

Subject	Grade Equivalent	Standard Score	Percentile
1. Reading	12.7	139	99.1
2. Spelling	11.7	127	96
3. Arithmetic	10.0	114	82
4. Arithmetic (Untimed)	12.8	133	99

WISC-III

Verbal Tests	Raw Score	Scaled Score
1. Information	28	16
2. Similarities	29	19
3. Arithmetic	17	14
4. Vocabulary	61	19
5. Comprehension	25	10
6. (Digit Span)	(19)	(13)
7. Verbal Score		78

Performance Tests	Raw Score	Scaled Score
1. Picture Completion	20	9
2. Picture Arrangement	23	7
3. Block Design	52	13
4. Object Assembly	21	7
5. Coding	40	5
6. Performance Score	41	

Composite Scores	Raw Score	Scaled Score	IQ
1. Verbal Score		78	136
2. Performance Score		41	87
3. Full-Scale Score		119	113

a. Describe Roberta's intellectual abilities.

b. Are the results similar for different tests?

c. What additional information would you like to have on Roberta?

ADDITIONAL READINGS

Gardner, H. (1983). *Frames of mind: The theory of multiple intelligence.* New York: Basic Books.

Gardner, H. (1993). *Multiple intelligences: The theory in practice.* New York: Basic Books.

Jensen, A. R. (1969). How much can we boost IQ and scholastic achievement? *Harvard Educational Review, 39,* 1–123.

Jensen, A. R. (1980). *Bias in mental testing*. New York: Free Press.

Jensen, A. R. (1981). *Straight talk about mental tests*. New York: Free Press.

The writings of Jensen have had quite an influence and are enlightening.

Kamphaus, R. W. (1993). *Clinical assessment of children's intelligence: A handbook for professional practice*. Boston: Allyn and Bacon.

The author provides examples and cases to facilitate understanding and interpretation of the WISC-III, Stanford-Binet, Kaufman ABS, Woodcock-Johnson. Information on use of tests for infant and preschool assessment is presented.

Kaufman, A. S. (1990). *Assessing adolescent and adult intelligence*. Boston: Allyn and Bacon.

The author discusses the clinical and neuropsychological assessment of the intelligence of adolescents and adults with special attention given to the Wechsler Adult Intelligence Scale—Revised.

McGrew, K. S. (1994). *Clinical interpretation of the Woodcock-Johnson Tests of Cognitive Abilities-Revised*. Boston: Allyn and Bacon.

The author presents a detailed, step-by-step analysis of the 21 WJTCA tests and includes a special strengths and weaknesses worksheet as well as diagrams and figures to help examiners understand and interpret the test.

Sternberg, R. J. (1985). *Beyond IQ: A triarchic theory of human intelligence*. Cambridge: Cambridge University Press.

Sternberg is one of the leading writers on the topic of the role and function of intelligence.

Sternberg, R. J., & Davidson, J. E. (Eds.). (1990). Intelligence and intelligence testing [Special issue]. *Educational Psychologist, 25*(3–4).

Wagner, R. K., & Sternberg, R. J. (1984). Alternative conceptions of intelligence and their implications for education. *Review of Educational Research, 54*(2), 179–223.

CHAPTER 8

Aptitude Testing

Overview

Aptitude testing has been used in education and psychology since the 1920s to predict what people can learn. Aptitude was considered by some early theorists to be innate but now is viewed as the result of learning experiences. The current operational definition of the construct addresses an individual's ability to learn certain skills or tasks if given the opportunity. Aptitude tests measure an individual's capacity, or potential, for performing a given skill or task and are used to predict behavior—will the individual be successful in a given educational program, vocational program, or occupational situation?

Objectives

After studying this chapter, the reader should be able to identify and discuss the

- uses of major multiaptitude test batteries
- uses of special abilities tests
- uses of work-sample aptitude tests
- problems and issues related to aptitude testing

Chapter 7 discussed the use of scholastic aptitude tests. The content of intelligence, achievement, and aptitude tests overlaps. For example, vocabulary items are a part of all three types as are numerical computation and reasoning items. One of the primary differences among these tests is how the tests are used. Scholastic aptitude, general aptitude, intelligence, and special abilities tests are often used for predictive purposes, whereas achievement tests measure what has been learned and are most often used for descriptive purposes and assessment of growth and change. A variety of specialized achievement tests are used for diagnostic purposes.

MULTIAPTITUDE BATTERIES

Multiaptitude batteries are tests that measure a number of relatively broad ability areas, such as verbal reasoning, numerical reasoning, mechanical reasoning, and abstract reasoning. The most widely used and highly rated multiaptitude batteries are the Armed Services Vocational Aptitude Battery (ASVAB), Differential Aptitude Test Battery (DAT), and the General Aptitude Test Battery (GATB).

Such tests are used primarily for educational and vocational counseling. They permit intraindividual comparisons, showing the highs and lows of an individual's performance on the various subtests. Studies are made of the construct and criterion-reference validity of these tests. The potential test user wants a battery with subtests that are relatively independent of one another (i.e., measuring different abilities and having low intercorrelations) and have a high correlation of success in various educational and vocational programs. Unfortunately, the factors on most aptitude batteries have moderate to high intercorrelations with each other.

Armed Services Vocational Aptitude Battery

The Armed Services Vocational Aptitude Battery (ASVAB) was first developed in 1966 and has gone through a number of revisions since then: Forms 18 and 19 are the current versions. Multiple aptitude batteries are a fundamental component of a comprehensive counseling program. Results from these batteries help students assess their aptitudes, predict performance in academic and occupational areas, select career exploration activities, and make tentative career choices. The ASVAB measures aptitudes for general academic areas and career areas that encompass most civilian and military work. The test is used with clients grade 11 and higher. The authors claim the test is valuable for military and nonmilitary purposes because it can be used for academic and career counseling. The ASVAB consists of 10 subtests, which are described in Table 8.1. The test takes 3 hours to complete—144 minutes of testing and 36 minutes of administrative time. It provides three academic composite scores.

Academic Ability—word knowledge, paragraph comprehension, and arithmetic reasoning

Verbal—word knowledge, paragraph comprehension, and general science

Math—mathematics knowledge and arithmetic reasoning

Table 8.1
Subtests of the Armed Services Vocational Aptitude

Scale	Time (min.)	Items	Description
General Science	11	25	Measures knowledge of the physical and biological sciences
Arithmetic Reasoning	36	30	Measures ability to solve arithmetic word problems
Word Knowledge	11	35	Measures ability to select correct meaning of words in context and best synonym for a given word
Paragraph Comprehension	13	15	Measures ability to obtain information from written passages
Numerical Operations	3	50	Measures ability to perform arithmetic computations in a speeded context
Coding Speed	7	84	Measures ability to use a key in assigning code numbers to words in a speeded context
Auto and Shop	11	25	Measures knowledge of automobiles, tools, and shop terminology and practices
Mathematics Knowledge	24	25	Measures knowledge of high school mathematics principles
Mechanical Comprehension	19	25	Measures knowledge of mechanical and physical principles and ability to visualize how illustrated objects work
Electronics Information	9	20	Measures knowledge of electricity and electronics

From the counselor's manual of the Armed Services Vocational Aptitude Battery (Form 16), 1991. North Chicago, IL: U.S. Military Entrance Processing Command.

The test has four occupational components.

> *Mechanical and Crafts*—arithmetic reasoning, mechanical comprehension, and auto, shop, and electronics information
>
> *Business and Clerical*—word knowledge, paragraph comprehension, mathematics knowledge, and coding speed
>
> *Electronics and Electrical*—arithmetic reasoning, mathematical knowledge, electronics information, and general science
>
> *Health, Social and Technology*—word knowledge and paragraph meaning, arithmetic reasoning, and mechanical comprehension

The number of items included on some of the subtests has been increased to help improve the reliability of the subtests. The test was normed on a national representative sample of 12,000 men and women aged 16 to 23. There are guides for both the counselor and test takers, and a computerized profile is given to the test takers. An example of a profile is given in Figure 8.1.

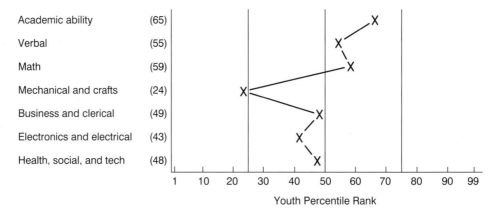

Academic ability	(65)
Verbal	(55)
Math	(59)
Mechanical and crafts	(24)
Business and clerical	(49)
Electronics and electrical	(43)
Health, social, and tech	(48)

Youth Percentile Rank

Figure 8.1
Individual profile of performance on the Armed Services Vocational Aptitude Battery (ASVAB)

Jensen (1988) considers the ASVAB to be a test that measures general ability plus interests rather than differential aptitude. He concludes that the ASVAB is an excellent group test of general ability but states that there are shorter tests available that measure G with satisfactory reliability.

Differential Aptitude Test

The Differential Aptitude Test (DAT) is a battery of eight subtests used for vocational and educational guidance purposes with students in grades 7 through 12 and adults. The test was originally developed in 1947 by Bennett, Seashore, and Wesman and published by the Psychological Corporation. The current revision is the fifth edition (1990). The test takes 235 minutes—181 minutes of actual testing time and 54 minutes of administration. The computer-adapted version takes about 90 minutes. The eight subtests are verbal reasoning, numerical reasoning, abstract reasoning, perceptual speed and accuracy, mechanical reasoning, space relations, spelling, and language usage. The verbal reasoning and numerical ability scores are combined to make a composite index of scholastic aptitude.

The authors claim the results help students plan their futures soundly. The test is also viewed as a tool for the early identification of students with superior intellectual promise.

Available with the DAT is a Career Interest Inventory and a computerized report form that provides a combined assessment of interests and aptitudes which may then be linked to potential occupations.

Reviewers over time, Linn (1982) and Pennock-Roman (1988) consider the DAT useful in exploring a student's academic and vocational possibilities. Test limitations relate to the lack of independence of some of the scales and the separate sex norms. Support materials—a manual and the book *Counseling from Profiles* by Bennett, Seashore, and Wesman (1977), a student workbook, and *Using Test Results for Decision Making: A Guide for Parents and Students*—are valuable to counselors and test takers. Both computerized scoring services and hand scoring stencils are available for the test. A computer-adaptive edition of the DAT is available. The form is parallel to the printed test but results in reduced testing time, and immediate scoring reports are available on the completion of the tests. An example of a profile from the DAT is presented in Figure 8.2.

USES General Aptitude Battery

The United States Employment Service (USES) General Aptitude Test Battery (GATB) is one of the most widely used batteries for assessment in vocational counseling. It is used primarily by the employment service but administered in some secondary schools and in employment projects. The test takes 150 minutes of total time, but only 48 minutes of actual testing time. The GATB is a pencil-and-paper test that measures nine dimensions: verbal, numerical, spatial, form perception, clerical perception, motor coordination, finger dexterity, manual dexterity, and general learning ability. Support systems for the counselor include the *Guide for Occupational Exploration, Dictionary of Occupational Titles*, and the *Bridge of the World of Work*. Keesling and Healy (1988) conclude that the GATB, despite its psychometric limitations, may help clients to make reasonable estimates of their standings on the aptitudes relative to working adults.

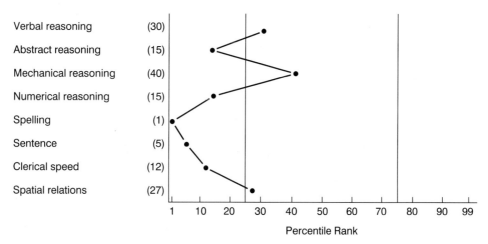

Figure 8.2
Individual profile of performance on the Differential Aptitude Test Battery (DAT)

Career Ability Placement Survey

The Career Ability Placement Survey (CAPS) is a quick, 50-minute battery used to assess abilities for a majority of jobs in 14 occupational clusters. The CAPS contains eight tests.

1. Mechanical reasoning (MR) measures understanding of mechanical principles.
2. Spatial relations (SR) measures the ability to think and visualize in three dimensions.
3. Verbal reasoning (VR) measures the ability to reason with words.
4. Numerical ability (NA) measures the ability to reason with and use numbers.
5. Language usage (LU) measures recognition and use of proper grammar and punctuation.
6. Word knowledge (WK) measures understanding of the meaning and precise use of words.
7. Perceptual speed and accuracy (PSA) measures rapid and accurate perception of small details.
8. Manual speed and dexterity (MSD) measures rapid and accurate hand movement.

There are both self-scoring and machine-scoring forms of the test, and Educational and Industrial Testing Service (EdITS) provides computerized scoring and reporting for CAPS.

The authors purport the test to have five major uses.

1. Classroom career exploration units, matching individual students' ability with occupational requirements
2. School course or training program selection
3. Curriculum evaluation
4. Career development in conjunction with the COPSystem Interest Inventory and COPES, a values profile
5. Employee evaluation

All types of supportive materials are available for the counselor and client. There are a self-interpretation profile sheet and guide, occupational cluster charts, COPSystem Career Briefs Kit, and COPSystem Career Cluster Booklet Kits in addition to an examiner's manual, tapes for administration, and visuals for orientation.

SPECIALIZED BATTERIES

Two of the most widely used specialized aptitude tests historically have been the Minnesota Clerical Test (MCT) (1979) and the Bennett Mechanical Comprehension

Test (1980). The MCT consists of two parts: number checking and name checking. There are 200 pairs of numbers and 200 pairs of names. The test taker is to check each pair in which the items are identical. The test is speeded, and the examinee has eight minutes for the number section and seven minutes for the name section.

The Bennett Mechanical Comprehension Test has both English and Spanish forms to measure an individual's understanding of mechanical relationships and the laws of physics in practical situations. The test is used to screen job applicants for positions requiring complex machine operation and repair and other types of positions requiring practical application of mechanical principles. Norms are available for industrial job applicants, industrial employees, and students. A taped version of the test is available for applicants with limited reading skill. The test requires 30 minutes of testing time.

Clerical Ability

Quite a few clerical tests other than the Minnesota Clerical Test are utilized by counselors.

USES Clerical Skills Test assesses six types of clerical skills—typing from plain copy, taking dictation, spelling, statistical typing, and spelling medical and legal terms.

Clerical Aptitude Test is a three-part pencil-and-paper test that includes number checking; business practice; and date, name, and address checking.

Curtis Verbal-Clerical Skills Test assesses clerical and verbal abilities and measures practical arithmetic, checking and perceptual speed and accuracy, and reading comprehension.

General Clerical Test measures three types of abilities needed for clerical jobs—clerical speed and accuracy, numerical ability, and verbal ability.

Hay Aptitude Test Battery is a general battery that measures number perception, name finding, and number series completion and predicts aptitude for a variety of positions, some of which include accounting, keypunching, typing, filing, stockroom, and mail sorting. Cassette tapes are available for administering and timing the tests.

Office Skills Test assesses clerical abilities of entry-level applicants and contains 12 subtests—checking, coding, filing, forms completion, grammar, numerical skills, oral directions, punctuation, reading comprehension, spelling, typing, and vocabulary.

Personnel Research Institute Clerical Battery consists of a number of tests—alphabetizing, arithmetic reasoning, classification, filing, name comparison, number comparison, spelling, tabulation, shorthand skills, basic checking, audio checking, numeric computation, numerical reasoning, and verbal usage.

PSI Basic Skills Tests for Business, Industry, and Government include a number of subtests—classifying, coding, computation, decision-making, filing names, filing numbers, following oral directions, forms checking, language skills, memory, problem solving, reading comprehension, reasoning, typing practice copy, typing revised copy, typing straight copy, typing tables, visual speed and accuracy, and vocabulary.

SRA Clerical Aptitude Test measures general aptitude necessary for clerical work through three pencil-and-paper tests of office vocabulary, office arithmetic, and office checking.

The descriptions of these tests reveal that some of the subtests are similar to certain subtests on some of the group intelligence and scholastic aptitude tests and to some of the scales on the DAT, ASVAB, and GATB. Verbal and numerical skills are as important as perceptual speed and accuracy skills. Ability to follow directions and short- and long-term memory are also included on some of the tests. In addition, some job-related or job-specific skills such as typing and filing are measured on some of the batteries.

Mechanical Ability

There are a number of other pencil-and-paper tests of mechanical ability besides the Bennett Mechanical Comprehension Test and the mechanical subtests on the multi-aptitude batteries.

Mechanical Aptitude Test is a 45-minute test for high school students and adults that measures comprehension of mechanical tasks, use of tools and materials, and matching tools with operations.

SRA Mechanical Aptitude is a 35-minute test for high school students and adults that measures mechanical knowledge, space relations, and shop arithmetic.

SRA Test of Mechanical Concepts is a 35- to 40-minute test for adults measuring the individual's ability to visualize and understand basic mechanical and spatial interrelationships. It contains three subtests—mechanical interrelationships, mechanical tools and devices, and spatial relations.

Some of these tests of mechanical aptitude contain subtests of spatial relations. The classic tests in the field to measure spatial relations are the Minnesota Spatial Relations Test and the Minnesota Paper Formboard. These two tests require the test taker to visualize objects in three dimensions and manipulate them to produce a particular configuration.

Psychomotor Ability

Quite a few individual tests measure psychomotor abilities, especially fine and gross motor skills and manual dexterity.

Crawford Small Parts Dexterity Test (CSPDT) is designed to measure fine, hand-eye coordination and is used in job selection for occupational areas such as engraving, watch repairing, and telephone installing. Part one requires use of tweezers to assemble pin and collar assemblies; part two requires putting small screws into threaded holes in a plate and screwing them down.

Hand-Tool Dexterity Test involves wrenches and screwdrivers and requires the examinee to take apart 12 assemblies of nuts, bolts, and washers from a wooden frame and then reassemble them.

Minnesota Manual Dexterity Test measures capacity for rapid, simple hand-eye coordination needed for semiskilled shop and clerical operations such as wrapping, sorting, and packing. The test taker is given a long board containing four rows of holes. In the placing test, pegs are to be transferred to the empty board just as they were presented, using only one hand. In the turning test, the pegs are to be removed with one hand one at a time, turned over, transferred to the other hand, and replaced in the same position on the board.

Minnesota Rate of Manipulation Test measures finger-hand-arm dexterity and is used to select employees for jobs that require manual dexterity and in vocational and rehabilitation training programs. There are five subtests in the battery—placing, turning, displacing, one-hand turning and placing, and two-hand turning and placing. The test also uses a test board with round holes arranged in four rows and round blocks painted orange and yellow.

O'Connor Finger Dexterity Test measures finger dexterity and is useful in determining aptitude for assembly jobs requiring rapid handwork. This test uses a smaller board containing a shallow well and many holes arranged in 10 rows. The test taker is given a set of 300 pins and is required to place three in each hole. The test has been useful in predicting success in machine and lathe work, watch and clock repair, and assembly of small parts.

O'Connor Tweezer Dexterity Test measures fine hand-eye coordination and the ability to use small hand tools. The test uses the same smaller board with the same small holes in it. However, the test taker is given 100 pins and is required to put one in each hole, using only a small tweezer. This type of skill is required of laboratory workers, medical personnel, watch repairers, and even stamp collectors.

Purdue Pegboard Test measures hand-finger-arm coordination required for certain types of business or industries. The test taker works with pegs, washers, and collars—putting in the pegs, placing washers over them, and then putting on the collars.

Stromberg Dexterity Test measures manipulative skills in sorting by color and by sequence. The test taker is given an assembly board and disks and is asked to discriminate among, sort, and move and place the biscuit-sized disks as fast as possible.

All of these tests are individually administered and require adequate facilities and space for their administration. The Valpar Component Work Sample System assesses vocational and functional skills and is designed for use with other testing instruments. Valpar System 2000 integrates aptitude, interest, and work history assessment through computer technology. The interest survey is video-based and uses actual job situations. Counselors use both clinical observation and test results from Valpar and other instruments to help clients in selection of training programs and in job placement. The information is also useful in designing educational or rehabilitation plans for a client.

Artistic Aptitude

Three classic tests measure dimensions of art aptitude—Meier Art Test: Art Judgment, Meier Art Test: Aesthetic Perception, and Graves Design Judgment Test. The Meier Art Test: Art Judgment consists of 100 pairs of pictures of famous works of art. One of the pair has been altered, and the test taker is asked to choose the better of the two pictures.

The Meier Art Test: Aesthetic Perception presents four versions of the same work, each differing in terms of proportion, unity, form, or design. The test taker is asked to rank each set in order of merit.

The Graves Design Judgment Test presents 90 sets of two- or three-dimensional designs that vary in unity, balance, symmetry, or other aspects of aesthetic order. The test taker is asked to select the best in each set.

Musical Aptitude

A number of tests have been developed to measure musical aptitude. The classic test in this field is Seashore Measures of Musical Talents. The test takes about 1 hour of testing time and can be administered to students in grade 4 and above and adults. The test presents on tape six subtests measuring dimensions of auditory discrimination: pitch, loudness, time, timbre, rhythm, and tonal memory. Unfortunately, the test lacks sufficient documentation of validity and reliability.

Other tests also purport to measure musical aptitude.

Kwalwasser Music Talent Test is a 50-item orally administered pencil-and-paper test to assess musical aptitude of fourth graders to college students. It presents three-tone patterns that are repeated with variations in pitch, tone, rhythm, or loudness.

Musical Aptitude Profile is an aptitude test that uses violin and cello. Pairs of selections are played, and the test taker is asked whether the two are the same or which of the two represents a better performance. The three subtests are tonal imagery (melody and harmony), rhythm imagery (tempo and meter), and musical sensitivity (phrasing, balance, and style). The test is used for 4th to 12th graders and takes about 2 hours to administer.

Unfortunately, research has been limited on the value of these tests. Music teachers tend to rely more on their own clinical judgment and look for individual performance of music as it is written.

Computer Aptitude

Computer literacy is being taught in kindergarten. Microcomputers have become inexpensive and readily available, and a number of instruments have been developed to assess aptitude in this field.

> Computer Operator Aptitude Battery is a pencil-and-paper test designed to help predict the performance of computer operators. It takes 45 minutes and has three subtests—sequence recognition, format checking, and logical thinking.

> Computer Programmer Aptitude Battery (CPAB) is a 75-minute pencil-and-paper test for adults. It is used to measure potential for success in the computer programming field. The five tests are verbal meaning, reasoning, letter series, number ability, and diagramming, which includes problem analysis and logical solutions.

> Programmer Aptitude Competence Test System (PACTS) assesses the ability to write good computer programs through a simulated experience. The client is given an instruction book to study for 30 to 50 minutes about a general computer programming language for a hypothetical computer. He then is given problems to solve that are scored for correctness, efficiency, compactness, problem difficulty, and completion time.

ISSUES AND PROBLEM AREAS

The trait and factors approach has been a venerable theme in career guidance, rooted in the psychology of individual differences, applied psychology, and differential psychology (McDaniel & Gysbers, 1992). The trait and factor approach views each person as a pattern of traits. These aptitude, achievement, personality, and interest dimensions are identified through objective psychological testing and can be profiled to represent the individual's potential. Occupations are treated in the same way. The degree of fit between the two profiles can be identified. Herr and Cramer (1984) conclude that many variables enter into career decision making—work values, occupational stereotypes and expectations, residence, family socioeconomic status, child-rearing practices, general adjustment, personality factors including needs and propensity for risk taking, educational achievement, level of aspiration, and gender.

Regarding abilities, specific aptitudes tend to correlate more with success in training than with success in performance. Super and Crites (1962) conclude that there might be a level of intelligence necessary to learn a certain occupation, but intelligence tends "to have no special effects on the individual's success in that occupation" (p. 99). The follow-up studies of Thorndike and Hagen (1959) of 10,000 men who had taken the air corps test battery in 1943 found that there were near zero correlations between the scores on that battery and the criteria of success in the occupations. The average variability of the scores within each of the occupational groups was almost as great as the variability of the scales across occupational groups. Project Talent, a large longitudinal study of 440,000 high school students begun in 1960, studied the relation of 22 aptitude and achievement tests, an interest inventory, and a student activities inventory with later educational and career attainments. The results are similar to those found by Thorndike and Hagen.

Emphasis now seems to focus more on decision making and career and educational choice; less emphasis is being placed on aptitude testing. Most of the major batteries are combined with other tests to provide the client more information. In the COP System, interests, values, and aptitude information are combined to provide a starting point to study more about occupations related to these factors.

The various subtests of the special aptitude tests present considerable overlap. The tests are designed to focus on the skills and abilities necessary to be successful in further training or employment in a given field. We must remember, though, that aptitude tests give only one source of information. Brown (1983) points out that there are new trends in this field, such as the integration of testing with cognitive psychology and the use of adaptive testing to individualize testing.

SUMMARY

Multifactor aptitude batteries are used in educational and business contexts. Many aptitude batteries are a part of career guidance systems. The most widely used batteries are the Armed Services Vocational Aptitude Battery (ASVAB), the General Aptitude Test Battery (GATB), and the Differential Aptitude Battery (DAT).

Specialized aptitude tests are designed to measure the ability to acquire proficiency in a specific area of activity, such as art or music. Mechanical and clerical aptitude tests have been used by vocational education and business and industry personnel to counsel, evaluate, classify, and place test takers. Both multifactor and special aptitude tests are designed to help the test takers gain a better understanding of their own special abilities.

QUESTIONS FOR DISCUSSION

1. What are the major multifactor aptitude batteries? When should they be used and why? What are the advantages and disadvantages of this type of test?

2. When would you use special aptitude batteries and why? What are the advantages and disadvantages of such tests?

3. Critics have said that multiaptitude tests provide little differential prediction and are of little value. Do you agree with their evaluation? If you have taken aptitude tests, what value did the results have for you? Did the scores provide a useful framework of looking at your aptitudes and abilities?

4. Some school districts require that all students be given an aptitude battery at some time during their 4 years of high school. Do you agree or disagree with this requirement? Why or why not?

5. Do you feel that there can be a pencil-and-paper aptitude test to measure aptitudes in art, music, and mechanics? Why or why not?

SUGGESTED ACTIVITIES

1. Write a critique of a widely used multiaptitude or special aptitude test.

2. Interview workers in the helping professions who use aptitude tests—employment counselors, career counselors, and school counselors—and find out what tests they use and why. Report your findings to the class.

3. Take a multifactor or specialized aptitude test and write a report detailing the results and your reaction to the test.

4. Make an annotated bibliography of aptitude tests you would use in your field.

5. Write a critical review of the literature on one of the following topics: validity of aptitude tests, new directions in aptitude testing, computer-adaptive aptitude testing, performance aptitude tests.

6. Study the case that follows and answer the questions at the end.

   Case of Albert

   Albert is a 23-year-old caucasian male who dropped out of school in the 10th grade. He is enrolled in a high school equivalency program at a local community college sponsored by the Private Industry Council. He has had numerous jobs in the food service industry but has not been able to hold on to them. He has a wife and three children and realizes now he needs further training and education to support his family.

   The Private Industry Council arranged for some vocational testing. He was administered the DAT with the following results:

   Verbal Reasoning   40%
   Numerical Reasoning   55%
   Abstract Reasoning   20%
   Mechanical Reasoning   55%
   Spatial Relations   30%
   Spelling   3%
   Sentence   5%
   Clerical Speed   45%
   On the Myers-Briggs Type Indicator his code was ISFJ.
   His code on the Self-Directed Search was ARS.

   a. How would you characterize Albert's aptitudes?
   b. What additional information about Albert would you like to have?
   c. If you were a counselor, what educational and vocational directions would you encourage him to explore?

ADDITIONAL READINGS

Hunter, J. E. (1983). *Test validation for 12,000 jobs: An application of job classification and validity generalization analysis to the General Aptitude Battery* (USES Test Research Report No. 45). Washington, DC: Division of Counseling and Test Development, Employment and Training Administration, U. S. Department of Labor.

Kapes, J. T., & Mastie, M. M. (1994). *A counselor's guide to vocational guidance instruments* (3rd ed.). Falls Church, VA: National Vocational Guidance Association.

This text reviews multiaptitude batteries well as other aptitude batteries used with special populations.

CHAPTER 9

Achievement Testing

Overview

Achievement testing is the primary type of testing used in educational programs at all levels. Achievement tests measure acquired knowledge and skills, whereas aptitude tests measure potential, or the ability to learn new tasks. The main distinctions between achievement and aptitude testing relate to the type of learning being measured and the intended use of the test results. Achievement tests come in a variety of types.

1. *Survey achievement batteries*—Partially norm-referenced and partially criterion-referenced tests that measure knowledge and skill in reading, mathematics, language arts, social studies, and science

2. *Subject area tests*—Achievement tests in a single subject area, such as algebra, plane geometry, American history, and chemistry

3. *Criterion-referenced tests*—Tests that measure knowledge and comprehension of a specific skill or competency, such as the ability to draw inferences from pictorial or written matter, or the ability to read a metric scale and give the weight of an object in metric and English units

4. *Minimum level skills tests*—Tests that measure objectives or minimum skills that have to be achieved to pass from one level or grade to another

5. *Individual achievement tests*—Tests that are administered individually across a wide age or grade level to measure achievement

6. *Diagnostic tests*—Tests that are used to assess the strengths and weaknesses of individuals in a subject area by measuring a limited number of skills thoroughly

Objectives

After studying this chapter, the reader should be able to

- list and discuss the different types of achievement tests
- identify situations in which each type of test would be used
- explain the problems and issues in achievement testing
- interpret the results of an achievement test

SURVEY ACHIEVEMENT TESTS

The most widely used achievement test, the survey battery is part of most school testing programs. It usually has a number of subtests—such as reading, mathematics, social studies, and science—and measures the objectives that are typically addressed in grades K–12. A number of different levels or separate tests are in the achievement battery, which is most often given at the beginning or end of the school year. Some districts give the test both times and use the scores as one criterion of whether a student passes to the next grade. The test provides teachers and administrators with a picture of what the student has learned or achieved.

The survey achievement battery subtests are all coordinated with standardized administration and scoring procedures, a common format, and little content overlap. In addition, all of the subtests are normed on the same sampling group. Comparisons between the tests are thus more valid than when each subtest is normed on a different sample. Some widely used achievement batteries are described here.

California Achievement Test (CAT) (Fifth Ed., 1992) is divided into 10 overlapping levels and is administered to students in grades K to 12.9. Level 10 is a readiness instrument for kindergarten students. The test measures achievement in traditional school areas—reading, language, mathematics, reference skills, and spelling.

Comprehensive Tests of Basic Skills (CTBS/4) (1993) is a multilevel achievement battery consisting of 10 levels and measuring three to seven areas, such as reading, language, mathematics, science, social studies, spelling, and reference skills. The CTBS was standardized along with the Short Form Test of Academic Aptitude (California Test of Mental Ability). The test has forms for students in grades K to 12.9.

National Educational Development Series (Educational Services) is used with students in grades 9-10. The test reliably predicts student performance on the PSAT and ACT and provides information useful for career and individual counseling.

Iowa Test of Basic Skills (ITBS) assesses the skills of students in grades K to 9 in reading, language, spelling, capitalization, punctuation, usage, work-study, visual materials, reference materials, mathematics concepts, problem solving, computation, word analysis, and listening.

Metropolitan Achievement Test–7th ed. (MAT-7) is an eight-level achievement test that measures reading comprehension, mathematics, and language skills of kindergartners through 12th-grade students. Social science and science subtests are included in the higher levels of the battery. The MAT-7 has an abridged version containing just the reading, mathematics, and language tests; each test takes about 30 minutes.

Sequential Tests of Educational Progress (STEP) assess English, reading, and mathematics skills. The preschool and primary test diagnoses the instructional needs of students and measures their interests, problem-solving and reading skills, mathematics concepts, and psychomotor skills. The upper grade test measures achievement levels in English expression, reading, mechanics of writing, mathematics computation, mathematics basic concepts, science, and social studies.

SRA Achievement Series (ACH 1-2) measures achievement in reading, mathematics, science, and social studies. Forms are available for grades K to 12.

Stanford Achievement Test (SAT8) measures vocabulary, reading comprehension, mathematics, spelling, and language skills of students in grades K to 12.

CRITERION-REFERENCED TESTS

Criterion-referenced tests, sometimes called domain-referenced tests, measure specific objectives and skills. They differ from norm-referenced tests and survey achievement tests in that they focus on mastery of a given objective or skill. Norm-referenced tests usually include only one or two items to measure a given objective, whereas criterion-referenced tests include many items on a specific objective. The criterion-referenced test is scored to an absolute standard, usually the percentage of correct answers. The teacher may be required to assign grades to the test takers, or students may be required to meet a certain score, say 70%, as evidence of mastery. In systems requiring mastery of objectives, the test taker is not allowed to go on to the next unit until he has passed the one being studied.

Criterion-referenced tests can be used for other purposes also.

1. To evaluate the curriculum

2. To identify topics that should be remediated or enriched

3. To provide information for the counselor to use in educational and vocational planning with students

4. To help students select courses

5. To document student mastery of objectives

6. To provide systematic evidence of student attainment of objectives across levels and fields

A few examples of criterion-referenced tests and testing systems are given here.

Instructional Objectives Exchange (IOX) has a series of tests available for teachers to use to assess specific skills and objectives in reading, mathematics, and writing.

Criterion Test of Basic Skills is a multiple-item criterion-referenced test assessing the reading and mathematics skills of students in grades 1 to 6. The reading subtests measure letter recognition, letter sounding, blending, sequencing, recognition of sight words, and recognition of special sounds. The mathematics subtests assess number and numerical recognition skills, addition, subtraction, multiplication, and division.

Multiscore is a system that provides criterion-referenced assessment of reading, language arts, mathematics, science, social studies, and life skills. It offers a pool of more than 5,500 items and catalogs of instructional objectives. The test service is available from Riverside Publishing Company.

ITEM BANKS

Commercial and public domain test item banks are available for educational purposes. Item banks allow school districts to custom-design achievement tests for specific objectives. Aiken (1985) points out that these item banks have several disadvantages, such as the problem of deciding on an acceptable passing score or mastery level for each test, the limited reliability of the many subtests used to measure given instructional goals or objectives, and the questionable validity of the items as representative of the objective being measured.

Westinghouse Learning Corporation, Science Research Associates, and Houghton Mifflin, among other publishers, provide item banks. Publishers who market survey achievement batteries have a large pool of items from old editions not included in current editions. Many states and consortiums have also developed for school districts item banks that come from tests developed under federal or state grants; these should be screened for local applicability.

MINIMUM-LEVEL SKILLS TESTS

Many districts establish minimum-level skills tests in each subject area that require mastery for a student to pass to the next grade level. Absolute standards are often set, frequently 75%. These essential-skills tests are criterion-referenced and are designed to measure the reading and mathematics skills of students in elementary schools. Often locally constructed, the tests are based upon the instructional management system guiding the progress of students in reading and mathematics. In addition, commercial tests are available that focus on minimum level skills.

Basic Skills Assessment Program (BSAP), used with 10th- to 12th-grade students, is a 210-item pencil-and-paper test measuring skills in reading, mathematics, and writing. The test assesses the ability of students to understand consumer information, read newspapers, and complete job applications.

Everyday Skills Test (EDST) measures routine skills needed in mathematics and reading, such as reading and comprehending labels and telephone directories.

STATE ASSESSMENT TESTS

A number of states require school districts to administer assessment tests in selected grades. Sometimes these tests focus only on essential skills. Other times they survey student knowledge, skills, and understanding in a given subject area such as science, social studies, reading, mathematics, health and nutrition, career education, citizenship, music, and fine arts.

The purpose is to help school districts identify problem areas and evaluate their curriculum. Some states require a minimum level of performance for student advancement. Florida college students are required to pass reading, mathematics, language, and writing tests at a set level to be able to register for upper division courses.

NATIONAL ASSESSMENT OF EDUCATIONAL PROGRESS

The National Assessment of Educational Progress (NAEP) is a national program to assess the knowledge, skills, and attitudes of 9-, 13-, 17-, and 25- to 35-year-olds. Currently, the assessment focuses on 4th-, 8th-, and 12th-grade students. In the past, 10 subject areas were selected for study—art, career and occupational development, citizenship, literature, mathematics, music, reading, science, social studies, and writing. The testing began in 1969 in response to the charge given to the commissioner of education to determine the progress of education in this country. Normally, two subject areas are tested each year, using a stratified random sample. Comparisons are made across age, geographic region, type of community, sex, socioeducational status, and race. Reading is assessed each year, along with two or three other subject areas. In 1990, approximately 87,000 students participated in the national assessment and another 100,000 participated in state assessments of eighth-grade mathematics. The 1992 assessments involved approximately 419,000 students in 12,000 schools. Congress added a new dimension to NAEP in 1990 that makes the tests available for state assessment programs as of 1992.

SUBJECT AREA TESTS

Subject area tests differ from subtests on a survey achievement battery. The survey subtests cover the general curriculum areas of an educational program—reading, mathematics, science, spelling, language, and social studies. These fundamental concepts and skills become competencies upon which more advanced study is based. Survey achievement batteries may provide some measure of students' basic skills but little information on achievement in a given subject. Subject area achievement tests provide more reliable and valid information.

Subject area tests have somewhat the same use as achievement batteries in that student performance can be compared against national norms. A number of subject area tests are available to high schools. Test questions are often derived from instruction across many school districts and states. Some states require students to pass subject area examinations or minimum-level skills tests in all high school subject areas in order to graduate. Subject area tests are also part of major national testing programs used by colleges and universities to determine advanced placement, credit, or one of the criteria for admission. Many states and professional organizations also require licensing examinations, which are really specialized types of subject area achievement tests.

Some of the national achievement testing programs are the College Board Achievement Tests, the American College Testing (ACT) Proficiency Tests, the College Board Advanced Placement Program, and the College Level Examination Program (CLEP). A number of publishers and organizations publish subject area achievement tests. A few examples are given here.

The Riverside Curriculum Assessment System is designed for use with secondary students and tests such areas as algebra, geometry, physics, chemistry, biology, world history, American history, consumer economics, and computer literacy.

Ohio Vocational Education Achievement Testing Program covers most vocational areas—agricultural business, agricultural mechanics, farm management, horticulture, production agriculture, stenography, clerk typing, data processing, general office clerking, word processing, carpentry, construction electricity, air conditioning and refrigeration, cosmetology, auto body mechanics, and so on.

Many professional societies have developed achievement tests. The American Chemical Society, for example, offers achievement tests in general organic-biological chemistry, inorganic chemistry, instrumental determination analysis, general chemistry, and so on.

INDIVIDUAL ACHIEVEMENT TESTS

Workers in the helping professions often utilize individual achievement tests to assess a client's achievement and cognitive processes. The tests provide useful information on the attitudes and motivation of the test takers and may be a single subject or a survey achievement type.

Key Math Diagnostic Arithmetic Test (KMDAT), published by the American Guidance Service, is a single-subject individual test used to diagnose children's strengths and weaknesses in mathematics. It measures the test taker's knowledge of operations—addition, subtraction, multiplication, division, mental computation, and numerical reasoning; mathematical applications—word problems, missing elements, money, measurement, and time; and also content areas such as numeration, fractions, geometry, and symbols. The examiner uses test plates and records the test taker's performance on an individual record form.

Peabody Individual Achievement Test (PIAT), published by the American Guidance Service, can be a survey battery and is given to clients aged 5 to adulthood. The PIAT takes about 30 to 50 minutes to administer and provides information not only on achievement in reading, mathematics, spelling, and general knowledge (science, social studies, fine arts, and sports), but also diagnostic information. The examiner uses easel kits and test plates; the PIAT yields grade equivalents, age percentile ranks, and standard scores by age or grade.

Wide Range Achievement Test—Revised (WRAT-3) is usually administered individually, although the spelling and arithmetic subtests are suitable for group administration. The reading subtest calls for the test taker to recognize and name letters and pronounce printed words; the examiner is encouraged to analyze error patterns. The test is given to both children and adults between the ages of 5 to 75.

Basic Achievement Skills Individual Screener (BASIS), published by the Psychological Corporation, is designed for pupils from grades 1 through grade 8. It includes three subtests—Reading, Spelling, and Mathematics—and an optional writing exercise. Both criterion-referenced and norm-referenced, the test provides beginning-of-the-grade and end-of-the-grade norms as well as age and adult norms. It takes about 1 hour to administer and is designed to help examiners formulate individual educational plans for exceptional and special populations.

Wechsler Individual Achievement Test (WIAT) (1992) was developed for use in conjunction with Wechsler Intelligence Scale for Children, III (WISC-III) and was co-normed. Subtests include Basic Reading, Mathematical Reasoning, Spelling, Reading Comprehension, Listening Comprehension, Mathematics Computation, Oral Expression, and Written Expression. The test can be given to students ages 5 through 19.

Some examiners individually administer other survey and subject area achievement tests, especially if a student has a disability. Individually administered tests do not rely as heavily on reading speed and accuracy. Individual oral administration of a test can be used as a validity check of the scores on a group-administered test.

Woodcock-Johnson Test of Achievement (WJTA) (1990) has two forms that measure achievement in reading, mathematics, written language, and knowledge the way they are typically taught in schools. The WJTA can be given to individuals aged 2 to 90.

ADULT ACHIEVEMENT TESTS

Many tests that can be used to measure the achievement of adults have already been listed and discussed—for example, the Wide Range Achievement Test and the Peabody Individual Achievement Test. Most major testing programs, like the Graduate Record and College Board tests, have achievement tests in subject areas that are used with adults. In 1989 the General Educational Development Test, a high school equivalence examination, was administered to approximately 683,000 people in the United States, Canada, and U.S. territories, over 376,000 of whom earned diplomas.

Certain tests are designed specifically for use with adult populations.

Test of Adult Basic Education (TABE), published by CTB/McGraw-Hill, measures adult proficiency in reading, mathematics, and language. The TABE is used as a diagnostic tool and has three forms—a second- to fourth-grade reading level version, a fourth- to sixth-grade reading level version, and a sixth- through ninth-grade reading level version. The reading test assesses vocabulary and comprehension; the language test measures mechanics, expression, and spelling; and the mathematics test evaluates computation skills, knowledge of concepts, and problem solving. A locator test is used first to determine which is the most appropriate form and then a practice exercise is available to reduce the test taker's anxiety. Depending on the form, the test requires 1½ to 2½ hours of testing time. There is also a Spanish version of the TABE. TABE-PC (1994) is a computer-assisted version of Forms 5 and 6. The locator test is also on the system and places the student at the correct test level. There is also a Spanish PC version.

The Adult Language Assessment Scale (AdultLAS) (1991) is designed to assess how well nonnative English speakers can function. It can be used as a screening test for the ESL population to plan individual instruction, to measure growth in English proficiency, and to help employers design appropriate training.

General Education Performance Index, published by Steck-Vaughn Company, is used by workers in the helping professions to measure an adult's readiness to take the General Educational Development Test. It measures skills in writing, social studies, mathematics, and reading.

DIAGNOSTIC TESTS

One of the major purposes of achievement testing is to diagnose strengths and weaknesses. Diagnostic tests are based on the essential skills and competencies needed for success in a given subject area or educational program, and they use numerous items to measure a skill or objective. The tests can be given individually or in groups, and the information provides a profile of strengths and weaknesses in a particular area of concern. Many of the tests already discussed are utilized for diagnostic purposes—for example, the Peabody Individual Achievement Test, the Wide Range Achievement Test, and the Key Math Test. In addition, some tests are used specifically for diagnostic purposes. One of the most widely used tests, the Wood-cock Johnson Psycho-Educational Battery (WJPEB), is an individually administered test consisting of 27 subtests designed to measure cognitive ability, scholastic apti-tude, academic achievement, interest level, and independent behavior. The test bat-tery is recommended for use in individual assessment, screening, and diagnosis of strengths and weaknesses in cognitive, achievement, and interest areas. It is also used for evaluation of individual growth and program effectiveness, research pur-poses, and teaching purposes (e.g., training in individual test administration).

Some special diagnostic tests concern only reading. The Gates-McKillop-Horowitz Reading Diagnostic Test has 15 individually administered subtests to pro-vide a profile of a student's ability to recognize words and their component sounds. The test enables the teacher to diagnose weaknesses in such areas as coding skills, sight word recognition, auditory blending, auditory discrimination, spelling, and written expression.

USING ACHIEVEMENT TEST RESULTS

Workers in the helping professions can use the results from standardized achieve-ment tests in a variety of ways. One of the primary uses is instructional. Test results can help teachers evaluate individual and group progress as well as materials and methods of instruction. An achievement test is just one source of information, but it is a systematic approach using standardized methods and items that are carefully screened. Achievement test information can be useful in selection and placement decisions; it can be used to help place students and to check on the validity of such placements. Achievement data may show growth in content areas or specific subject areas over time and can serve as one of the criteria to evaluate a school's cur-riculum.

CASE OF JAMES

The case of James illustrates steps in interpret-ing achievement test data from a survey achievement test. James is in fifth grade and is having some academic difficulties in school. He is 10.3 years old, weighs 80 pounds, and is 4 feet 9 inches tall. His profile on the Stanford Achievement Test is given in Figure 9.1. The derived scores plotted in the profile are per-centile ranks and represent how the student performed in relation to students in the national sample.

A profile often has peaks and valleys, rep-resenting the learner's relative strengths and weaknesses. The median is the 50th percentile and represents typical or average perfor-mance. Some tests use different systems to

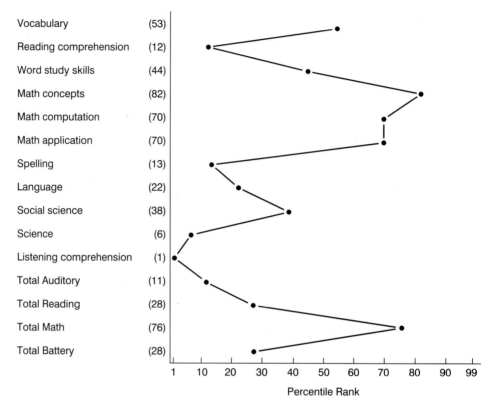

Figure 9.1
Profile of James's scores on the SAT

classify superior or poor performance. Workers in the helping professions need to be familiar not only with what scores mean but also with what is measured by each subtest and which scores are combined to give total scores. In this case the test user needs to be familiar with the *Teacher's Guide for Interpretation* of the intermediate level I battery of the Stanford Achievement Test. A brief description of some of the SAT subtests and types of items is included in Table 9.1.

A total listening score is based on the combination of the Vocabulary and Listening Comprehension scores, which provide data on the learner's ability to understand and remember information presented orally. A total read-

ing score helps test users identify students who might have deficiencies in reading comprehension as well as overall scholastic achievement.

The authors of the test believe that factors other than test scores should be taken into consideration also.

1. *Grade level*—The test measures what has been taught in this and preceding grades.
2. *Number of years at current school*—Students who move often and change schools may be at a disadvantage.
3. *Age*—Students who are in the age range typically served by a grade level tend to

Table 9.1
Sample of dimensions measured by the SAT

Subtest	Type of Items (total number)
Vocabulary (60)	Selecting proper or correct meaning of a word: reading and literature (13), nonfiction and reference (18), mathematics and science (11), social science (14), arts and crafts (4)
Reading Comprehension (72)	Identifying meaning after reading given passage: global meaning (7), explicit meaning (27), implicit meaning (10), meaning determined by context (9), inferential meaning (19)
Word Study Skills (130)	Analyzing words: phonetic analysis (35), consonant sounds (7), long-vowel sounds (10), variant vowels (13), short-vowel sounds (5), structural analysis (30), affixes (8), syllables (7), accent (8), disconnected syllables (7)
Mathematics Concepts (32)	Understanding sets, ordinals, fractions, Roman numerals, powers, value changes, number sentences, associative properties, algorithms, size relationships, length, mean, ordered pairs: numbers (9), notation (7), operations (9), geometry and measurement (7)
Mathematics Computation (40)	Using fundamental facts and solving simple math sentences and algorithms: knowledge of primary facts (18), addition and subtraction algorithms (9), multiplication and division algorithms (13)
Mathematics Application (40)	Selecting proper operation and solving two-step problems: solution of one-step problem (12), analysis and development of solution design (8), rate and scale problems (6), measurement (6), graph reading and interpretation (8)

achieve higher scores than younger students or students who have been retained a year or more.

4. *Out-of-school experience*—Students who travel and read independently and have peers at home who are interested in learning tend to achieve at a higher level.

5. *Health and nutrition*—Healthier individuals who eat a balanced diet tend to score higher than those who do not.

6. *Self-concept*—Students with positive academic and general self-concepts tend to achieve higher scores than those with negative self-concepts.

7. *Socioeconomic level*—Students from lower socioeconomic levels may not have an equal opportunity to learn.

8. *School environment*—The quality of the classroom environment and the attitude of the teacher(s) toward the students can influence performance.

9. *Test content*—The test content may not reflect completely what is taught in a particular district. Also, certain questions may be biased and unfair to certain students, and not all students have the same opportunity to experience and learn certain material.

10. *Test administration*—Proper administrative procedures, time limits, and monitor-

ing of student test-taking behavior are all important.

Additional Information Needed for the Case of James

One of the first questions to consider is how James's test performance compares to his performance in class. His teacher reports that he is an average student in mathematics but has problems in reading comprehension and following directions. He does not seem to listen at times and cannot remember what he is to do. His problems in reading comprehension also create problems in understanding his science and social studies materials.

A second question is how his current test profile compares with other test results. On a local essential skills test (a minimum level or basic skills criterion-referenced test), James failed the following areas (i.e., he had less than 75% of the items correct): vocabulary, listening comprehension, synonyms, antonyms, sequencing, facts and opinions, recalling details, main idea, and sentence completion. The problem of comprehension is very real; James scored at the 12th percentile on the SAT Reading Comprehension, 82 out of a possible 133 right. In mathematics he failed only word problems and association of numbers with words. James scored 111 out of 125 on this test, with a passing score being 94. His reading comprehension problem did not seem to affect his performance on the SAT section on mathematics word problems: he scored at the 70th percentile. Test results are inconsistent in this dimension. Previous standardized achievement scores were low average in reading, average in mathematics, and average in social studies.

A third question is how James performs in relation to his ability. Many school districts no longer include scholastic aptitude testing as part of the school testing program. If the student is referred to a child study team, the counselor may give the student an individual test such as the Peabody Picture Vocabulary Test, or the Slosson Intelligence Test, or even a group IQ test such as the Otis-Lennon School Ability Test. The psychologist may administer the Stanford-Binet or the Wechsler Intelligence Scale for Children. Scholastic aptitude or intelligence testing would help in developing an individually prescribed learning program for James, but no scholastic aptitude or intelligence data were available in his cumulative folder.

A fourth question is whether there are other factors that should be taken into consideration in interpreting the test results. James has progressed normally in school; he was never retained at a grade level and has been at the same school since the beginning of the third grade. He did attend two schools in other states prior to that time. James has had all the normal childhood diseases but is healthy and has not missed many days of school.

James is the oldest child of three siblings; he has an 8-year-old brother and a 3-year-old sister. He lives with his mother and stepfather, who works as a carpenter for a construction company. His mother works part-time as a checkout clerk in a supermarket. His father is in the Navy, and his parents were divorced when James was in kindergarten.

James's mother is concerned about his progress and is open to any suggestions the teacher or counselor may have to improve his academic performance. James relates fairly well with his classmates but gets easily frustrated when he cannot understand his lessons or recite correctly for the teacher. He likes to perform duties around the classroom and has become strongly attached to his teacher.

Two other questions relate to an analysis of the data. How does James perform in relation to the national norms? And how is he mastering the objectives required for the fifth grade? The scores on the SAT profile show that he scored high in relation to other fifth graders in math concepts and just slightly lower in math computation and application. Clearly, his strongest area of achievement is mathematics. In the two listening tests, he scored average in vocabulary and poor in listening comprehension. His total listening performance is below average compared to his peers. He is also below average in spelling, language, science, and reading comprehension. His word study skills are average as are his scores in social science. James is in danger of being retained in the fifth grade because his reading scores are below the criterion for promotion. He has a second chance to pass the essential skills test but needs help to accomplish that task.

Although each item on the survey achievement test relates to a specific behavioral objective, often only one or two items measure a specific objective. An item analysis on such a test may provide good information for the teacher who has a total class profile, but it is of limited value in diagnosing James's educational problem. The Essential Skills Test is based specifically on the behavioral objectives taught in James's class, whereas the SAT is based on a wide sampling of objectives and textbooks from schools across the nation. Teachers and counselors should check the face validity and content validity of a norm-referenced test and determine what percentage of local objectives are assessed by the test battery. Fewer differences are apt to be found in mathematics and reading than in science and social studies.

Postscript

James was referred to the child study team and observed and tested by the school psychologist. On the basis of the information collected by the team, he was assigned to work in a specific learning disabilities resource room.

ANALYSIS OF CLASS PROFILE

A sixth-grade teacher or counselor who had given the Stanford Achievement Test early in the school year (grade level 6.2) might have the test scores reported in Table 9.2 and might want to be able to answer questions like these:

1. How are class members achieving in relation to their ability?

2. How is the class achieving in each subject area?

3. Are there any students who need help or who are having problems in one or more achievement areas?

The achievement test scores in Table 9.2 are reported in grade-equivalent form. The IQ scores are from the Otis-Lennon Mental Ability Test, which yields one score, a deviation IQ with the mean of 100 and standard deviation of 15. The scores are listed to permit comparison of achievement and scholastic ability.

If we assume that the SAT is a valid instrument to measure achievement in this school district, students with average ability should score around grade level, and students with below-average ability should score below grade level. Care should be taken not to overinterpret minor differences in individual scores. Student 19, for example, is technically below grade placement in seven achievement areas, but the

Table 9.2
Achievement test results for a sixth grade class*

Student	Sex	IQ	BM	WM	PM	SP	LG	AC	ACP	AA	SS	SC
1	G	127	8.3	8.7	8.7	10.5	8.0	6.3	6.6	9.6	6.8	9.2
2	G	116	8.3	7.8	8.7	7.0	9.0	5.6	7.3	9.1	8.3	10.0
3	G	130	8.0	7.5	8.0	7.8	10.7	6.5	8.0	9.1	9.0	7.2
4	G	132	7.8	8.0	7.8	8.8	10.5	6.3	7.6	7.4	7.9	7.8
5	G	121	7.3	7.3	9.6	7.0	8.8	6.2	6.3	7.7	8.5	6.0
6	B	122	7.0	6.7	7.0	5.4	8.5	5.8	6.8	7.7	11.4	10.0
7	G	116	6.9	6.9	7.0	8.2	10.0	5.9	6.8	6.8	7.0	5.8
8	B	118	6.8	6.8	7.0	5.6	6.7	5.8	6.3	7.7	7.4	6.9
9	G	110	6.7	7.3	7.2	6.3	6.7	5.8	5.4	7.2	7.2	8.1
10	G	114	6.6	6.6	6.9	8.0	9.3	5.4	6.6	5.7	5.6	6.0
11	B	115	6.5	6.6	6.5	6.0	7.2	5.8	5.9	5.4	8.1	9.2
12	B	104	6.2	5.6	6.2	5.7	6.0	5.8	6.3	7.7	6.3	6.4
13	B	117	6.1	5.4	6.1	4.1	6.2	6.0	7.3	5.9	6.4	9.2
14	G	115	6.0	7.3	6.7	6.6	5.7	5.9	5.9	4.9	6.0	9.0
15	B	115	5.8	5.6	6.1	4.7	7.0	7.0	5.4	6.5	6.6	5.8
16	B	109	5.8	5.5	6.6	4.7	7.1	5.8	4.8	5.6	5.9	6.7
17	B	108	5.6	5.6	5.6	4.3	5.8	5.4	6.3	5.6	5.6	6.7
18	B	103	5.6	3.9	4.9	3.0	5.6	5.2	5.9	5.9	6.8	5.8
19	G	102	5.6	4.7	5.6	3.6	5.3	5.8	6.5	5.6	6.3	4.1
20	G	93	5.5	5.5	5.9	4.7	6.6	4.6	5.4	4.4	6.3	6.6
21	G	112	5.4	4.9	6.4	5.1	5.4	5.6	4.8	5.4	5.3	5.8
22	G	112	5.3	4.7	6.1	6.9	4.6	5.8	5.4	3.8	5.3	4.2
23	B	89	5.1	5.2	4.7	3.4	4.3	5.6	6.1	5.1	5.2	4.3
24	B	96	4.9	5.4	6.1	4.3	5.5	4.4	4.5	3.8	4.9	6.4

*IQ = intelligence quotient, BM = battery median, WM = word meaning, PM = paragraph meaning, SP = spelling, LG = language, AC = mathematics concepts, ACP = mathematics computation, AA = mathematics application, SS = social studies, SC = science

5.8 in Mathematics Concepts is not significantly lower than grade placement when the standard error of measurement is considered.

The teacher might graph the scores of the class or compute some measures of central tendency; the median Battery Median score is 6.15 and the median on the vocabulary, 6.1. The means could be computed: The mean for science is 7.00 and for vocabulary 6.21. Or the teacher might simply count how many students are at or above grade level and how many are below. There are 12 at or above grade placement in vocabulary and 12 below, 11 at or above grade placement in mathematical application and 13 below, and 15 at or above in science and 9 below. This type of analysis is fast, but the ability levels of the group must be kept in mind. The teacher might also be interested in looking at item information, perhaps the specific items that presented problems to the class.

In all cases the purpose of the test should be considered. The scores in this example might be low in some areas because the test was given early in the year, before the students had been exposed to many of the concepts and objectives taught in the sixth grade. Some school districts intentionally give this test at the beginning of the year to obtain an overall estimate of the entry level of the students.

TRENDS AND ISSUES

The major trend and issue in achievement testing is authentic and alternate assessment. Authentic and performance assessment are replacing traditional norm-referenced testing that relies on multiple-choice questions. One such system developed by a major test publisher is the Integrated Assessment System. The series consists of performance tasks in language arts, mathematics, and science for grades 1–8. The ISA Language Arts (1990) consists of a series of reading passages and guided writing activities that assess reading comprehension, writing performance, and higher-level thinking in one integrated activity. The IAS Language Arts portfolio provides a flexible framework for collecting the ongoing work of students. The system encourages collaboration between students and teachers in reviewing the products of the work in the portfolios. Mathematics problems are given requiring students to produce original responses in writing as they select strategies to solve the given problems.

Holistic and analytic scoring procedures are explained in the scoring guide. Scores are based on the quality of work, presence and number of flaws, knowledge of concepts, problem-solving abilities, reasoning skills, computational proficiency, and ability to follow directions.

Criterion-referenced skills analysis is provided by most survey achievement series. For example, the Iowa Test of Basic Skills, Tests of Achievement Proficiency, and the Iowa Tests of Educational Development give users the number of correct answers by objective, number attempted, number correct by each student, class average percentage correct, and national average correct.

More information is presented on authentic assessment in Chapter 21.

SUMMARY

Achievement tests are used at all age and grade levels to measure what individuals have learned. They are used for a wide variety of purposes, such as diagnosis, placement, growth, and description. A variety of achievement tests include individual and group; norm- and criterion-referenced; survey batteries and single-subject; and diagnostic, prognostic, and readiness tests.

Local school districts, states, and the federal government are involved in assessing achievement. Local school districts develop a series of criterion tests to measure how well students are achieving the minimum level skills and essential level skills being taught. The tests are valuable for educational and vocational guidance purposes, evaluation of curriculum and teaching methods, and demonstration of growth from grade to grade.

Achievement tests are used for placement, selection, and classification of students. They should not be used as a primary criterion for evaluating teacher performance. Achievement tests are not free from controversy. Critics are concerned that certain tests and test items may be biased against certain groups.

QUESTIONS FOR DISCUSSION

1. Compare survey achievement and criterion-referenced tests. In what situations would each be the best measure to use?

2. Is it necessary to give both survey achievement tests and minimum-level and essential-level skills tests within one district? Defend your position.

3. How would you go about developing a minimum-level skills test in a content field in junior or senior high school?

4. For what purposes should survey achievement tests be used? For what purposes should we avoid using the tests?

5. Look at the scores found in Table 9.2 and answer these questions: (a) How are class members achieving in relation to their ability? (b) How is the class achieving in each subject area? (c) Are there any students who need help or who are having problems in one or more achievement areas?

6. State your position on one of the following issues: (a) Testing controls what is taught in schools. (b) The best predictor of future success is past achievement, not aptitude. (c) Achievement tests should be banned from use.

SUGGESTED ACTIVITIES

1. Select one of the major achievement tests and write a critique of it.

2. Assemble an annotated bibliography of achievement tests related to your field of interest.

3. Interview workers in the helping professions who utilize achievement tests in their work. Find out what tests they use and why and how they use the results. Report your findings to the class.

4. Administer an individual achievement test or diagnostic test and write a report of the results.

5. Review the research and write a paper on one of the following topics: bias in achievement testing, sex differences in achievement testing, the national assess-

ment program, current trends and issues in achievement testing, criterion-referenced testing.

6. Read the case that follows and answer the questions at the end.

   Case of Danny

   A teacher noticed Danny's constant battle with fellow classmates in class. Danny doesn't seem to have any friends. When his other teachers were asked about him, a mystery seemed to exist.

   Elementary School Record

First Grade		Second Grade		Third Grade		Third Grade (This year)	
Reading	D	Reading	D	Reading	D	Reading	C
Spelling	C	Spelling	D	Spelling	D	Spelling	C
Writing	C	Writing	D	Writing	C	Writing	C
Math	D	Math	D	Math	F	Math	C
				Lang. Arts	F	Lang. Arts	D
				Soc. St.	D	Soc. St.	D
				Science	F	Science	C

   Attendance Record

Absent	23	25	30	21

   Current Test Record:
   Grade 3 (current)
   Minibattery of Achievement

Subject	Score
1. Reading	2.7
2. Math	2.6
3. Writing	2.0
4. Factual	2.2

   WISC-III

Area	Score
1. Verbal	98
2. Performance	105
3. Total	101

Health Record: Danny's physical condition is good. He has had the normal childhood diseases.

Family Background: Danny's father is a heating and air conditioning technician and a high school graduate; his mother is a housewife and has an eighth-grade education. The parents are separated and Danny lives with his grandparents. He has lived with his grandparents since he was 4 years of age when he was taken out of St. John's Orphanage. Home conditions are average considering his grandparents are old. They lack interest in how he is doing at school.

Social Life: Danny belongs to no organizations or clubs and he does not have any close friends. He frequently starts arguments in class and on the playground. He is very outspoken.

Interests and Abilities: Danny has a lot of interest in making things; this is evident in his science projects and art. He has special skills in making things with his hands. He does little reading but watches lots of TV. He fails to do his homework most of the time.

Other Teachers' Assessment of Danny: They comment on his family environment and say that the continual moving of his grandparents has deprived Danny of companions. They say that he acts out to gain attention.

a. Provide a capsule summary of Danny's achievement and aptitude.
b. What additional information about Danny would you like to have?
c. Do his test results correlate with his grades?

ADDITIONAL READINGS

Berk, R. A. (Ed.). (1980). *Criterion-referenced measurement: The state of the art*. Baltimore, MD: Johns Hopkins University Press.

Berk, R. A. (Ed.). (1984). *A guide to criterion-referenced test construction*. Baltimore, MD: Johns Hopkins University Press.

These are two good resource books on criterion-referenced testing.

Farr, R. (1994). *Portfolio and performance assessment*. San Antonio, TX: The Psychological Corporation.

Farr provides specific procedures and techniques for using portfolios and integrating them into the instructional program and school assessment practices.

Millman, J., & Greene, J. (1989). The specification and development of tests of achievement and ability. In R. Linn (Ed.), *Educational Measurement* (3rd ed.). New York: Collier Macmillan.

Mullis, I. V. S. (1990). *The NAEP Guide: A description of the content and methods of the 1990 and 1992 assessments*. Princeton, NJ: Educational Testing Service, National Assessment of Educational Progress.

Nickse, R., & McClure, L. (Eds.). (1981). *Competency-based education: Beyond minimum competency testing*. New York: Teachers College Press.

This book of readings gives a good background in the trends and issues in competency testing.

Wiggins, G. P. (1993). *Assessing student performance: Exploring the purpose and limits of testing*. San Francisco: Jossey-Bass.

Wiggins critically reviews testing practices and the problematic practices operating today in the field. He discusses the usefulness of timely feedback and suggests a new system of assessment that provides teachers and policy makers with more useful and credible feedback.

CHAPTER 10

Career and Employment Testing

Overview

The first part of this chapter discusses tests and assessment procedures to measure interests, values, and career maturity. Many studies of nonintellectual characteristics of individuals and the relationship of those characteristics to achievement and success in different educational and vocational fields have been made. Information about these nonacademic areas is invaluable to counselors working with students or with adults making career and educational decisions. The test results are also important for counselors and psychologists working with clients who have personal problems or teachers and counselors working with children who have educational problems.

The second part of the chapter focuses on employment testing. Tests are widely used in employment contexts both in the public and the private sectors. The usefulness of tests for employment and career development within an organization was demonstrated through the testing programs developed during World War II. Since most employees no longer stay in one career field all their lives, but rather try five to seven careers, these test programs have extended use.

Objectives

After studying this chapter, the reader should be able to

- identify widely used interest, values, and career guidance inventories

* discuss when they are used and explain how they are interpreted
* identify and discuss some of the issues and problems in interpreting tests
* identify specific sources of information concerning vocational and career guidance instruments
* discuss some of the trends in career guidance testing
* identify the roles, purposes, and procedures of employment testing
* discuss the trends, problems, and issues in employment testing

INTEREST INVENTORIES

English and English (1958) define interest as a term of elusive meanings. The first meaning is the attitude or set of attending. The second is the tendency to give selective attention to something. The third is an attitude or feeling that an object or event makes a difference or is of concern to oneself. In psychological theory, some theorists hold to the doctrine that learning cannot take place without a feeling of interest. Sometimes interest is synonymous with motivation. Career developmental theorists have pointed out the importance of interests. Strong (1927) postulated that interest is in the domain of motivation and there are clusters of attitudes, interests, and personality factors related to choice of and satisfaction with an occupation (Shertzer & Linden, 1979, p. 270).

A wide variety of techniques are used to measure interests, such as checklists, structured and unstructured interviews and questionnaires, and informal and standardized inventories. Interest inventories have been used in the helping professions for over half a century. E. K. Strong published his first version of the Strong Interest Blank in 1927. A revised version of the test, the Strong Interest Inventory is a widely used test in the field today. It provides a profile of how an individual's interests compare with those of successful people in certain occupational fields. Another interest inventory, the Kuder Preference Record-Vocational, was first published in 1932. Test takers were asked to choose the item they liked most and the one they liked least in each cluster of three. Kuder's test initially measured interest in 10 general areas, such as outdoor, literary, musical, artistic, and scientific. Interest tests can be one source of information to help with educational and vocational decisions; they are not appropriate for selection purposes, however.

Self-Directed Search

The Self-Directed Search (SDS) is one of the most widely used interest inventories. It was first published in 1971 and has gone through a number of revisions. The SDS guides examinees through an evaluation of their abilities and interests. The test is 16 pages in length and is considered a tool for high school and college students or adults returning to the work force to find occupations that best fit their interests and abilities and by anyone between the ages of 15 and 70 in need of career guidance. The author and publisher claim that the SDS is easy and uncomplicated to administer and score. It can even be self-administered and scored. Special answer sheets, proctors, computer scoring, or scoring stencils are not needed. The SDS is designed to provide immediate feedback, which the author claims aids in examinees' self-understanding and career exploration.

Specifically, the examinees are asked to list their daydreams, activities liked or disliked, competencies, occupations of interest, and self-appraisals in mechanical, scientific, teaching, sales and clerical fields. Examinees use the Occupational Finder (Holland, 1985), which lists 1,156 of the most common occupations in the United States. The occupations are coded by letter to indicate which of Holland's personality types they represent—realistic, investigative, artistic, social, enterprising, or conventional. The manual also gives a single-digit number to indicate the level of general educational development required along with the nine-digit number given by the *Dictionary of Occupational Titles* (DOT) utilized for each occupation listed.

Type	Title	Number
RAS	Cook Apprentice Pastry	313.381-018 ED 4
RAS	Cook Pastry	313.381-026 ED 4

Educational levels of 5 or 6 require college training or more; levels 3 or 4, high school and some college, technical, or business training; and levels 1 and 2 require no special training.

To help the examiner, the *Professional Manual* (1994) provides guidance, and the sourcebook *Making Vocational Choices: A Theory of Vocational Personalities and Work Environments* (Holland, 1985) provides a more complete review of the theory and research behind the test. Additional materials can facilitate the assessment, including the booklet *Occupational Finder, You and Your Career, Leisure Activity Finder*, and *College Majors Finder*. A number of versions are available for counselors to use with clients such as Form CP Career Planning, Form E–Canadian Edition: French, Form E–Canadian Edition: English, Edition En Español, Vietnamese Edition, Form R–Braille Edition, and Form R–Computer Version.

Strong Interest Inventory

The Strong Interest Inventory (SII) is an expansion of the previous editions and includes six general occupational themes (realistic, investigative, artistic, social, enterprising, conventional—i.e., Holland's six personality types, also called RIASEC), 23 basic interest scales, 207 occupational scales (including 34 additional vocational/technical ones), and 12 new professional scales. The inventory also includes an academic comfort scale and 10 administrative indexes. Correlative materials are available to help the counselor and client in interpreting the results, including a *User's Guide*, career exploration worksheet, career finder, college major exploration sheet, introduction for career counselors, guide to understanding results, Strong and Myers-Briggs Type Indicator (MBTI) career development guide, introduction for organizational settings, workshop leader's guide, Strong-Hansen occupational guide, and a video about career options. The authors designed the SII to

1. help individuals make educational choices
2. introduce lifestyle issues for exploration as possible career enhancements
3. stimulate discussions among counselors, students, and parents
4. identify shared interests with people successfully employed in an occupation
5. identify careers to explore for possible midcareer change
6. help identify an interest in management
7. help counselors understand an employee's job satisfaction or dissatisfaction
8. aid in retirement planning

The SII is also proposed as a research tool for individuals, groups, and cultures.

The authors claim that the SII is an interesting exercise and provides a thorough measure of client interests. The profile utilizes John Holland's taxonomy for ease of interpretation. The test takes only about 30 minutes to complete and compares examinee interests with those of persons successfully employed in a wide variety of fields. The authors claim that the occupational scales predict one's eventual occupational choice regardless of sex or racial background. The test can be administered and scored on a microcomputer if the user wants immediate feedback.

In addition to the *User's Guide*, a manual is available that explains the three types of scales—General Occupational Themes, Basic Interest Scales, and the Occupational Scales—and discusses what to do with clients who have either elevated or depressed profiles. The authors also provide suggestions for using the test with adults, cross-cultural groups, and special populations. A number of different types of reports are available such as a profile report, expanded interpretive report, original interpretive report, college major report, and topic reports on areas such as leadership/management style or organizational specialty, leisure, and individual summary.

Career Occupational Preference System

The Career Occupational Preference System (COPS) has three components. The first section is designed to measure interests and presents a profile in 14 areas:

Science Professional	Business Skilled
Science Skilled	Clerical
Technology Professional	Communication
Technology Skilled	Arts Professional
Consumer Economics	Arts Skilled
Outdoor	Service Professional
Business Professional	Service Skilled

The second part of the test battery is an aptitude test (CAPS). It includes eight 5-minute subtests—mechanical reasoning, spatial relations, verbal reasoning, numerical ability, language usage, word knowledge, perceptual speed and accuracy, and manual speed and dexterity.

The third part of the battery measures work values (COPES). It, too, has eight scales—accepting/investigative, carefree/practical, conformity/independence, supportive/leadership, noncompulsive/orderliness, privacy/recognition, realistic/aesthetic, and self-concern/social.

There are several forms of the test. COPS-P measures interest at the professional level. COPS-R is written at a sixth-grade reading level and the unit is presented in a single, easy-to-follow programmed booklet. COPS-II is used to measure the interests of younger students and those at higher grade levels for whom reading or language presents difficulties, or for whom motivation might be a problem.

The test summary provides a profile of the 14 career groups, showing the highs on all three tests, and clients are urged to consider groups in which their interest, abilities, and values are all high. Thereafter, they are instructed to look at the groups for which interests and aptitudes are both high.

The *COPSystem Comprehensive Career Guide* provides support for the client. The COPS interest test can be completed in a 20- to 30-minute period and is self-scoring. COPES takes approximately 40 to 50 minutes, while CAPS requires 50 minutes. Both self-scoring and machine-scoring forms are available. The CAPS also has administration available on tape. A *COPSystem Career Brief Kit* for clients to use with their test results and *Career Cluster Booklets* provide correlative information about the different occupational fields.

Other Interest Inventories

Many other interest tests are available. Critical reviews can be found in *Reports of the AMEG* (now the Association for Assessment in Counseling) *Committee to Screen Career Guidance Instruments* (Association of Measurement and Evaluation in Counseling and Development, 1986), *A Counselor's Guide to Vocational Guidance Instruments* (Kapes & Mastie, 1994), and *Mental Measurement Yearbooks*. A special annotated bibliography on personality and vocational assessment instruments is part of the ETS Test Collection volumes available from Ornx.

Some of the other widely used inventories are identified here.

Campbell Interest and Skills Survey (CISS) focuses on careers that require a postsecondary education and is most appropriate for use with individuals who have completed college or plan to attend. The CISS adds a parallel skill scale that reports the estimate of the individual's confidence in his or her ability to perform various occupational activities.

Career Assessment Inventory (CAI) provides scores on 6 general occupational theme scales, 22 basic interest scales, and 89 occupational scales. The CAI also has administrative indices and four nonoccupational scales.

Harrington-O'Shea Career Decision System–Revised (COM-R) is designed for use with seventh graders to adults and provides scale scores in six interest areas (e.g., crafts, arts, scientific, social). It is designed for use with high school and college students. The COM–R surveys abilities, values, school subject preferences, and interests. A Spanish version is available. Another version is written at the fourth-grade level and is designed for use with individuals with low reading skills, special education students, and adults.

Interest Determination, Exploration, and Assessment System provides scores on such scales as mechanical, electronics, nature/outdoor, science, numbers, writing, arts/crafts, social service, child care, medical service, business, sales, office practice, and food service. The test is designed for use in grades 6 to 12.

Jackson Vocational Interest Survey (JVIS) is used with high school students and adults and has 34 basic interest scales such as creative arts, performing arts, mathematics, skilled trades, dominant leadership, business, sales, law, human relations, management, and professional advising. It also has 10 occupational themes such as assertive, enterprising, helping, and logical. The test reports similarities of examinee interests and 24 areas of major study in college.

Judgment of Occupational Behavior-Orientation (JOB-O) is used with seventh graders to adults and provides scores for 120 job titles, with decision-making information included on the answer sheet.

Kuder General Interest Survey (Form E) is used with 6th- to 12th-grade students. It measures broad vocational interests and is used for counseling and vocational exploration. The 10 scales are outdoor, mechanical, computational, scientific, persuasive, artistic, literary, musical, social service, and clerical.

Kuder Occupational Interest Survey (Form DD) has 126 occupational and 48 college major scales.

Ohio Vocational Interest Survey: Second Edition (OVIS–II) provides scales such as manual work, basic services, machine operations, quality control, clerical health services, crafts and precise operations, skilled personal services, sports and recreation, customer service, regulations enforcement, communications, numerical, visual arts, agricultural and life sciences, engineering and physical sciences, music, performing arts, marketing, legal services, management, education and social work, and medical service.

Vocational Interest, Experience and Skills Assessment (VIESA) is used with 8th- to 12th-grade students and combines two ACT instruments—the ACT Interest Inventory and the Career-Related Experience Inventory. The information is clustered around the themes of data, ideas, people, and things.

OTHER INTEREST ASSESSMENT TECHNIQUES

Other techniques can be used to measure interest. Super and Crites (1962) identified four methods.

1. *Expressed Interests*—what clients say their interests are

2. *Manifest Interests*—what clients are observed doing

3. *Testing*—what clients know about various fields

4. *Interest Inventories*—what clients check about their interests and preferences

The helping professional may want to check the validity of test or inventory results by asking clients about their interests and activities, inquiring about their preferences, and finding out why areas are liked and disliked. Individuals may have had no experience or opportunity in certain areas, and some likes and dislikes may be influenced by parents, spouse, or family attitudes. Interests cannot be determined by how clients spend their time. Time may be spent doing things under pressures from parents, spouse, family, or peers. Or individuals simply may not have time to do the things they most enjoy.

Client performance should be considered on more than just interest tests. In many situations, aptitude and achievement data also help in the decision-making process. Clients may learn and like what they do best, but not necessarily. A number of other factors may be involved, such as opportunity and experience.

VALUES

Values are an important dimension of personality, and value assessment is an important component of career guidance testing. Most large computerized guidance systems include value measurement and definitions as an important part of the system. Some tests measure general values; others only work values.

The Hall Occupational Orientation Inventory (1976) is based on Maslow's personality theory and Roe's theory of occupational choice. The authors argue that occupational decisions reflect inner values, needs and beliefs; abilities; and interests perceived as important. The first 10 scales assess client values and needs—for example, creativity-independence, risk, belongingness, security, aspiration, esteem, location concern, and extremism.

The Work Values Inventory (WVI) measures 15 extrinsic and intrinsic values important to the world of work. The WVI is a short 45-item test yielding scores in areas such as altruism, esthetics, creativity, intellectual stimulation, independence, achievement, prestige, management, economic returns, security, surroundings, supervisory relations, associates, variety and way of life.

The Minnesota Importance Questionnaire measures 20 psychological needs and six underlying values related to work satisfaction. The values assessed are achievement, altruism, autonomy, comfort, safety, and status. The needs scales provide scores in such areas as security, social status, compensation, achievement, authority, creativity, and moral values.

The Salience Inventory (Research Edition) measures the importance of five major life roles—student, worker, homemaker, "leisurite," and citizen. Each role is assessed from three perspectives: participation, commitment, and value expectations. There are 170 behavioral and affective items that are rated on a four-point scale.

The Values Scale is a scale developed to measure intrinsic and extrinsic life/career values. The test has some scales similar to the Work Values Inventory—for example, achievement, aesthetics, altruism, economic returns, prestige, and variety—but it also has scales such as ability utilization, advancement, authority, creativity, lifestyle, personal development, physical activity, risk, social interaction, social relations, working conditions, cultural identity, physical prowess, and economic security.

GUIDELINES FOR INTERPRETING TESTS

These general guidelines might be considered in interpreting interest and values tests.

1. Scale titles should be translated into terms clients can understand. Clients may be confused by actual scale titles such as altruism and aesthetics.

2. Clients may be encouraged to plot their own scores and make profiles, identifying their own high and low scores. This is a type of ipsative interpretation, with clients making their own intraindividual comparisons.

3. Client profiles can be compared with norming groups and available vocational and educational groups.

4. If key items are identified by research, specific responses may be considered and discussed with the client.

5. The meaning of values and interests in work and career fields should be discussed.

CAREER DEVELOPMENT INSTRUMENTS

Career development and maturity instruments were developed to help counselors assess career awareness and knowledge. Used to evaluate the effectiveness of career guidance and education programs, they were widely used when there was more federal and state support of career education programs in the schools. These instruments can provide counselors with valuable information about the career development and educational needs of individual clients and can provide survey information to help in planning career guidance programs.

The Career Awareness Inventory has two forms—an elementary form for grades 3 to 6 and an advanced form for grades 7 to 12. The author says the test can be useful in identifying strengths and weaknesses of individuals or groups and in focusing on specific aspects of career awareness.

The Career Development Inventory has forms for both junior and senior high school and college and university students. The test contains five scales—career planning, career exploration, decision making, world-of-work information, and knowledge of preferred occupational group. The scales are combined to give scores in career development attitudes, career development knowledge and skills, and career orientation.

The Career Maturity Inventory is an instrument for grades 6 to 12 that measures the attitudes and competencies related to variables in the career-choice process. The test has two parts—an attitude test and a competence test. The attitude test measures attitudes toward decisiveness, involvement, independence, orientation, and compromise dimensions of career maturity. The competence test has five subtests—knowing yourself (self-appraisal), knowing about jobs (occupational information), choosing a job (goal selection), looking ahead (planning) and what should they do? (problem solving).

The College Board has also a Career Skills Assessment Program for grades 9 to 14 and adults. The purpose of this assessment is to help individuals gain insight into career planning and decision making. The information helps counselors, teachers, and administrators evaluate the extent to which students have mastered fundamental career development principles. There are six content areas that have books of exercises—self-evaluation and development, career awareness, career decision making, employment seeking, work effectiveness, and personal economics.

The one problem with many instruments is that they do not require students to apply these skills to themselves. It is not enough for clients to gain some understanding of the process; they must also see how this information can be transferred to their own real world.

COMBINED PROGRAMS

The trend in career guidance is for assessment to include interest, values, and other dimensions such as aptitude, career development and maturity. The COPS previously discussed in this chapter includes interest, values, and aptitude assessment.

The Career Planning Program (CPP) of ACT is another example. The system is designed to help students from grade 8 to adult identify and explore personally relevant occupations and educational programs. The assessment stresses career exploration and helps individuals relate information about their interests, experiences, and abilities to the work world.

Another system is Planning Career Goals, developed by the American Institutes for Research and published by CTB/McGraw-Hill. The assessment consists of a number of separate subtests—life and career plans report, interest inventory, information measures, and ability measures. The battery is designed to assist guidance and counseling personnel in working with 8th- to 12th-grade students in career and educational planning. The system takes about 5 hours to administer and looks at the traits and preferences of the client, permitting comparisons with persons actually employed in the preferred career fields.

The World of Work Inventory is another comprehensive system for grade 8 to adulthood that covers interests, temperament, and aptitude and achievement areas. The battery is useful for needs assessment and can clarify for school counselors what types of occupational information are needed. The test information is also useful to personnel working with clients in rehabilitation, correctional, and employment placement contexts.

PROBLEMS OF INTEREST MEASUREMENT

Counselors need to be aware of a number of problem areas when utilizing interest tests.

1. Even though there is much evidence of the stability of interests, especially from the late teens on, some clients change their interests dramatically in their adult years.

2. Tests given before grade 10 or 11 may not be accurate measures of interests. Students may not have had the background of experiences, real or vicarious.

3. Job success is usually correlated more to abilities than interests.

4. Many interest inventories are very susceptible to faking, either intentional or unintentional.

5. Response set may affect the validity of an individual's profile. Clients may choose options they consider more socially desirable or acquiescence may prevail.

6. High scores are not the only valuable scores on an interest inventory. Low scores, showing what people dislike or want to avoid, are often more predictive than high scores.

7. Societal expectations and traditions may prove more important than interest in determining vocational selection. Gender bias was a major concern in interest measurement during the past several decades and needs to be considered when selecting instruments and interpreting profiles.

8. Socioeconomic class may affect the pattern of scores on an interest test. Scores for upper- and middle-class clients are more predictive than scores for lower-class clients.

9. The inventories may be geared to the professions rather than to skilled and semiskilled areas. Many inventories were criticized because they were geared exclusively to college-bound students.

10. A profile may be flat and hard to interpret. In such a situation a counselor should use other tests and techniques to determine interests.

11. Tests use different types of psychometric scoring procedures. Some interest tests use forced-choice items, in which individuals are asked to choose from a set of options. Examinees may like or dislike all of the choices but still must choose. Scoring procedures will have an impact on interpretation of results.

FUTURE TRENDS IN INTEREST MEASUREMENT

Holland (1986) predicts a movement toward more practical inventories. The movement has been stimulated by the inclusion of standard inventories within computer-assisted career systems. Holland believes that inventories will be more helpful to females, people with skilled trade interest, and older citizens (p. 262). The use of more interpretative materials and workbooks will compete with one-to-one counseling strategies. Holland recommends more study of the use of inventories for intervention. He foresees a proliferation of computer-based inventories, scoring, and interpreting systems, along with self-help workbooks. Hansen (1990) reports on the increased use of interest inventories and the expansion of their use to new populations, especially in cross-cultural contexts.

EMPLOYMENT TESTING: ROLES AND PURPOSES

Tests are used in employment contexts for placement decisions, assignment to training programs, promotion, retention, licensing, and certification. Test can be used, for example, to select individuals for entry-level positions, make differential job assignments, select individuals for advanced and specialized positions, decide who will be promoted within an organization, decide who is eligible for training, and provide diagnostic and career development information for individuals. To be effective, tests must be valid for the intended purpose and should be the least discriminating tools for the decisions that need to be made. Tests can help ensure fair treatment of workers in an employment context.

The Psychological Corporation utilizes a two-way grid to identify the human resource applications for the uses of tests. The horizontal dimension lists the job type, while the vertical lists the human resource application. The job types listed include clerical and administrative; accounting and financial; sales and service; supervisory, managerial, and professional; industrial and technical; and a final category, "may fit other jobs." The functions are job analysis, administrative assessment, basic skills (reading, writing, and arithmetic); general aptitude, the ability to think, learn, and succeed; specialized aptitude and ability, managerial, mechanical spatial, manual, visual; personal characteristics and style assessment; assessment for training and development, the ability to benefit and succeed, vocational/career guidance, and vocational rehabilitation (Psychological Corporation, 1994, p. 49).

TEST USE IN THE PRIVATE SECTOR

Employees in the private sector work primarily in manufacturing, retail trades, and service occupations. Clerical workers constitute the largest group, numbering approximately 20 million persons. Tests are used in the private sector to help make decisions in selection, placement, training, and promotion of personnel. Tests are also used to provide credentials or certification.

Types of Tests

Gatewood and Perloff (1990) report employers use general aptitude, cognitive ability, clerical achievement, spatial and mechanical abilities, perceptual accuracy, and motor ability tests for selection and promotion. Clerical workers were tested by two-thirds to four-fifths of the employers. Testing was used more by transportation and communication industries than by manufacturing and more by large corporations (employing 1,000 or more employees) than by smaller companies. Large companies, with many different job categories, tended to rely on in-house experts or consultants to handle test development and administration.

The Bureau of National Affairs Survey (Miner, 1976) provides a good summary of trends. Of companies that used tests it was found that more than 80 percent used them to screen applicants for office-clerical positions. Only 20% used tests to screen applicants for production or maintenance jobs, 14% used tests for data processing jobs, and fewer than 10% used tests to screen applicants for sales or service jobs.

Personality tests are used in some employment contexts. In general, the most widely used personality tests discussed in the text are used in industrial contexts also, such as the Myers-Briggs Type Indicator, the California Psychological Inventory, the Edwards Personal Preference Inventory, and the Guilford-Zimmerman Temperament Scale. Projective tests such as the Rorschach and Thematic Apperception Test and the Sentence Completion Test are reportedly used by some groups. Assessment of attitudes, stress, organizational commitment, and work environment are used to diagnose strengths and weaknesses in the organization and to monitor changes in the work force.

Scales of job satisfaction measure dimensions such as attitude toward supervision, the company, the co-workers, pay, working conditions, promotion, security, subordinates, autonomy, and esteem needs. Some of the standardized tests that are used in business and industry are described here.

Basic Occupational Literacy Test (BOLT) has four subtests of reading and arithmetic. The reading test has four levels of difficulty and assesses vocabulary and reading comprehension. The arithmetic section measures computation and reasoning at the fundamental, intermediate, and advanced levels. The BOLT wide range scale is used as a quick screen to determine whether the employment counselor should give the General Aptitude Test Battery or Non-Reading Aptitude Test Battery.

Comprehensive Ability Battery (CAB) contains 20 pencil-and-paper subtests that measure a single primary-ability factor related to performance in an industrial setting. The subtests are verbal ability, numerical ability, spatial ability, perceptual completion, clerical speed and accuracy, reasoning, hidden shapes, rote memory, mechanical ability, meaningful memory, memory span, spelling, auditory ability, esthetics judgment, organizing ideas, production of ideas, verbal fluency, originality, tracking, and drawing.

Employee Aptitude Survey Series has a number of tests such as verbal comprehension, visual pursuit, visual speed and accuracy, space utilization, numerical reasoning, verbal reasoning, word fluency, mechanical speed and accuracy, and symbolic reasoning.

Employment Barrier Identification Scale assesses the ability of an unemployed client to gain and retain employment. It looks at job skills, education, environmental support, and personal survival skills.

Employers' Test and Service Associates publishes tests such as General Mental Ability Test, Office Arithmetic Test, General Clerical Ability Test, Stenographic Skills Test, Mechanical Familiarity Test, Mechanical Knowledge Test, Sales Aptitude Test, and Personal Adjustment Index.

Industrial Reading Test measures reading comprehension and is used for selecting job applicants and screening trainees for vocational and technical programs.

Aptitude and Intelligence Series includes many subtests—blocks, dexterity, dimensions, factory terms, fluency, judgment, memory, motor, numbers, office terms, parts, secretary, semiskilled worker, senior clerk, skilled worker, unskilled worker, vehicle operator, writer, perceptions, precision, sales terms, tools, contact personality factor, neurotic personality factor, contact clerk, dental office assistant, dental technician, designer, engineer, factory machine operator, factory supervisor, general clerk, inspector, instructor, numbers clerk, office machine operator, office supervisor, office technical, optometric assistant, sales clerk, sales engineer, sales person, sales supervisor, scientist.

Job Effectiveness Prediction System includes tests such as coding and converting, comparing and checking, filing, language usage, mathematical skill, numerical ability, reading comprehension, spelling, and verbal comprehension.

Personnel Tests for Industry (PTI) measures general ability in verbal and numerical areas and is used in the selection of workers needing competencies in these areas.

Wesman Personnel Classification Test assesses general verbal and numerical abilities and is used for selection of employees for clerical, sales, supervisory, and managerial positions.

The Wonderlic Personnel Test measures general verbal, spatial, and numerical reasoning and is used for selection and placement purposes and to predict adjustment to jobs, turnover, and dissatisfaction on routine, simple, labor-intensive jobs.

Employment Reliability Inventory is a 81-item true/false test measuring emotional maturity, conscientiousness, trustworthiness, long-term commitment and safe job performance.

Comprehensive Personality Profile is used in employee selection and professional development situations and measures whether the individual is people- or task-oriented or patient/impatient. The primary traits assessed are emotional intensity, intuition, recognition, motivation, sensitivity, assertiveness, trust, and good impression.

Certification

Friedman and Williams (1982) point out that the trend toward competency testing is strong in industry, too. Job applicants are often required to complete competency testing before they submit their applications. In addition, there are the statutory-based licensing examinations and certification programs. Shorthand reporters, automobile mechanics, respiratory therapists, and mental health counselors all take licensing or certification examinations.

Merely passing the test is not enough; the public is concerned about continued competence and has pressed for continuing education and recertification programs.

Career Planning

Besides screening applicants or certifying applicants for placement purposes, tests are used for career planning. Many industries are interested in helping their workers define the goals they would like to achieve within the company. A testing program is designed to help workers identify interests, values, and competencies and guide them in further professional development and formal educational activities.

TEST USE IN GOVERNMENT

The federal government became involved in employment testing in 1883, when Congress created the United States Civil Service Commission. In 1979 the Office of Personnel Management (OPM) became involved in the testing process and established standards for job classification and competitive examinations for more than 1,000 types of jobs. The OPM has responsibility for two-thirds of the federal civilian work force, and a large percentage of these workers are selected by one of the testing programs.

Other governmental agencies develop and administer their own tests. The Department of State, for example, uses its own tests to select foreign service officers. The United States Employment Service (USES) has developed tests for use in the local and state employment offices. The General Aptitude Test Battery (GATB) is widely used; it compares examinee scores with workers in more than 600 jobs. The USES has also developed interest inventories and tests of proficiency in dictation, typing, and spelling.

Tests are often required for selection purposes by state and local government agencies, also. Tests are frequently required of police officers and fire fighters, as well as clerical workers. Local governmental agencies tend to use tests less than state agencies. It should be mentioned that both state and local agencies use oral and performance examinations more than federal agencies do (Friedman and Williams, 1982). Skilled workers tend to be given tests more than unskilled workers, and tests are not used as a sole criterion. Education, experience, character, and residence requirements are other important factors considered in hiring.

Occupational and Professional Licensing

States often mandate occupational and professional licensing for which some type of examination is required. This is even true in education in many states, with teachers and principals required to pass licensing examinations. States often establish a licensing board for a specific occupation. Occupations requiring licensing examinations include the following: architects, acupuncturists, audiologists, chiropractors, dentists, dental hygienists, engineers, funeral directors, landscape architects, land surveyors, occupational therapists, psychologists, speech pathologists, hearing aid counselors, optometrists, registered nurses, practical nurses, pharmacists, physical therapists, physicians, physician's assistants, podiatrists, and social workers.

TEST USE IN THE MILITARY SECTOR

The military sector makes extensive use of tests for selection and classification purposes. The Armed Services Vocational Aptitude Battery (ASVAB) was developed in 1976 by combining the validated subtests from the various test batteries used by each of the services. One form has been developed to be used in high schools as a guidance tool for counselors and as a recruiting tool. ASVAB helps identify the proper technical training or education needed for various types of occupational areas in the armed forces. In addition, there are specific tests that are used to select candidates for admission to the service academies, reserve officer training programs, officer candidate schools, and specialized programs such as flight training. The Cadet Evaluation Battery, Air Force Officer Qualifying Test, the Flight Aptitude Selection Test, and the Defense Language Aptitude Test are examples.

PERSONNEL SELECTION AND CLASSIFICATION TECHNIQUES

A number of procedures and devices other than psychological tests are used in personnel selection and classification.

Biographical Data

Almost all employers require prospective employees to complete an application blank, a biographical information blank, or a life history. Employers believe that these forms provide information on what the candidate has done in the past and can be used to predict future behavior. Gatewood and Feild (1990) identify three assumptions for the use of biographical data. The best predictor of applicants' future behavior is what they have done in the past. Applicants' life experiences provide an indirect measure of their motivational characteristics. Applicants are less defensive in describing their previous behaviors on the form than discussing their motivations for these behaviors. Research does indicate that biographical information has been a useful predictor of turnover and job success (Perloff, Craft, & Perloff, 1984). Biographical data also have been valuable in assessing individuals and classifying them into subgroups for purposes of better placement and utilization. Personnel directors sometimes divide large groups of current and former employees into categories of successful and unsuccessful workers and determine which items differentiate the two groups. Cook (1988) states that biodata instruments are cheaper than other custom-made tests but are not as valid as cognitive tests.

Interviews

The selection interview is one of the basic tools of the personnel director. The purpose of the interview is to gain information about the candidates' qualifications and experiences relevant to the available job. Perloff, Craft, and Perloff (1984) conclude that limited evidence indicates the procedure is valid and reliable. More systematic, structured, job-related interviews tend to have higher validity. The situational interview, with specific questions based on job-related critical incidents, has also proven to be a valid assessment tool. Studies of the interview show that interviewers tend to make decisions about candidates early in the interview. Negative information tends to be weighed more heavily than positive information, and visual cues tend to be more important than verbal cues. In addition, ratings are affected by how many others are being rated at the same time; clients who share similarities with the interviewer—the same race, sex and so on—tend to be more favorably rated. Often applicants are rated the same in evaluations, either superior (leniency error), average (central tendency error), or poor (stringency error). Sometimes one or two either good or bad characteristics of an applicant tend to influence the ratings of all the other characteristics (halo error). Sometimes the interviewer allows the quality of the applicants who preceded the present applicant to influence the ratings of the present applicant (contrast effect). Interviewers at times are overconfident in their ability to evaluate applicants; as a result, they make hasty decisions.

Interviewers need training and instruction in these skills.

1. Creating an open-communication atmosphere
2. Delivering questions consistently
3. Maintaining control of the interview
4. Developing good speech behavior
5. Learning listening skills
6. Taking appropriate notes
7. Keeping the conversation flowing and avoiding leading or intimidating the interviewee
8. Interpreting, ignoring, or controlling the nonverbal cues of the interview (Gatewood & Feild, 1990, p. 481)

Gatewood and Feild (1990) argue that the selection interview can be valuable if the interviewers are trained in the process, panels are used whenever possible, job-related questions are used, and multiple questions are designed for each KSA (knowledge, skill, and ability) required by the job.

Assessment Center

The most widely used multiple assessment procedure in industry is the assessment center. Primarily, the center has been used to evaluate the potential of candidates for promotion to managerial positions. The center usually analyzes a candidate's performance on several standardized assessment exercises. These are usually selected and/or constructed from a thorough job analysis of the positions for which the assessment is to be made. Perloff, Craft, and Perloff (1984) conclude that the overall evidence suggests that assessment center evaluations are valid and promising predictors for all groups, regardless of sex or minority status. Cook (1988) states that the assessment center is referred to as the "Rolls-Royce" of selection methods because it is expensive and uses a wide range of assessment methods and trained assessors. On the other hand, the range of assessors and assessment methods reduces bias and gives candidates more chance to show their strengths and weaknesses. Byham and Thornton (1986) indicate that the three most widely used techniques are the in-basket exercises, assigned leaderless group discussions, and interview simulations. They emphasize that the assessment center exercises mirror the majority of day-to-day activities of individuals performing in the target jobs.

To evaluate and select the exercises, the observer needs to ask the following questions.

1. Is the exercise appropriate for the targeted job?
2. Does the exercise represent an important component of the job?
3. Have most of the important dimensions of the job been included in the exercises?
4. Are the exercises efficient and cost effective?

5. Are the exercises valid?

6. Do the exercises accomplish their purpose?

Thornton and Byham (1982) identify nine dimensions frequently measured in assessment centers. These are the use of oral communication in individual or group situations, planning and organizing strategies (setting goals, making proper assignments, and allocating resources), delegating responsibilities and utilizing subordinates effectively, control (monitoring and regulating activities and responsibilities), decisiveness (readiness in making decisions, rendering judgments, and taking action), initiative (influencing events to achieve goals), tolerance for stress, adaptability (maintaining effectiveness with various tasks, responsibilities, or people), and tenacity. The administrator of an assessment center should keep in mind the following guidelines:

1. Assessment should be based on clearly defined dimensions of the position or behavior in question.

2. Multiple assessment techniques should be used.

3. A variety of job-sampling techniques should be used.

4. Familiarity with the job and the organization is needed; experience in the job or role is desirable.

5. Thorough training in assessment center procedures is necessary for all observers and raters.

6. All pertinent behavior should be observed, recorded, and communicated to other raters and observers.

7. Group discussion and decision-making procedures are used to integrate observations, rate dimensions, and make predictions.

8. Clients should be assessed against clearly understood external norms, not against each other.

9. Observers should guard against first impressions and other errors commonly made in rating and observation.

Job Analysis

One of the key elements in employee assessment is job analysis. Gatewood and Feild (1990) define job analysis as a purposeful, systematic process for collecting information on the important work-related aspects of a job (p. 251). Familiar terms such as knowledge, skills, ability, effort, responsibilities, and working conditions must all be put together so that they describe the quantity and quality of the work performed. Task analysis of the worker's functions is required, including the instruction and training that are part of the job. Variables will relate to both job content and job context. Effort, responsibility, and working conditions are contextual factors; knowledge, skill, and ability are job content factors. Both how-to aspects of the job and level of performance are important. A job analysis should follow these steps.

1. Read and review existing materials and data on the job to be analyzed.
2. Have supervisors and experienced workers in the field meet and discuss the job requirements, producing a list of tasks and roles that are performed.
3. Write the tasks and job characteristics on a flip chart so those involved in the position can react to what you have written.
4. List outputs, knowledge, skills, and abilities, including use of machines, tools, equipment, and work aids needed to get the job done. Get agreement on the tasks performed.
5. Have the workers determine the percentage of time spent on each task or skill.
6. Group common tasks together.
7. Have the workers tell how they know or recognize excellent, satisfactory, or poor performance of the tasks and the job.
8. Construct an instrument to assess job performance and have supervisors and workers react to the tasks and performance standards identified.

An example of a job analysis interview is given in Figure 10.1.

A number of task inventories are available to counselors. They contain three major sections—background information on the respondents, job tasks, and other miscellaneous information. The Position Analysis Questionnaire (PAQ) is one of the leading commercial measures available. It has six sections.

1. *Information Input*—where and how the worker receives information about how to perform the job
2. *Mental Processes*—the cognitive skills necessary for job performance
3. *Work Output*—tools, equipment, and physical activities needed to perform the job
4. *Relationships with Other Persons*—how other people are related to and interact with the job
5. *Job Context*—the physical and social environment in which the work is performed
6. *Other Characteristics*—characteristics and activities not covered by previous questions

The respondent is asked to rate 194 items on the extent of use, amount of time, importance to the job, possibility of occurrence, and applicability to the job in question. The Psychological Corporation has a similar test called the Common Metric Questionnaire.

Guidelines for Selection

A number of guidelines should be followed by personnel workers developing a selection process.

1. Know the legal and ethical considerations thoroughly.

What is your job title?
Where do you work?
Of what department or division are you a member?

Job Tasks
What do you do? How do you do it? Do you use special equipment?
What are the major tasks you perform on your job? What percentage of time do you spend on each task?

Knowledge Requirements
For each task you perform, what type of knowledge is necessary?
What types of formal and informal knowledge do you need to perform these tasks?
Do you need formal coursework, on-the-job training, etc.?
What level of knowledge is required?

Skill Requirement
What types of manual, mechanical, or intellectual skills are necessary to perform your job?
What types of tasks require these skills?

Ability Requirement
What types of communication skills, oral or written, are required for your job?
Do you have to prepare reports or complete records as part of your job?
What types of thinking, reasoning, or problem-solving skills are required?
What types of quantitative and mathematical abilities are required for your job?
What types of interpersonal abilities are required?
Are you responsible for supervision of other employees?
What types of physical abilities are required?

Physical Activities
What types of physical activities are required to perform your job?
How often are you engaged in physical activities?

Environmental Conditions
What types of environmental conditions do you encounter on your job?

Other
Describe a typical day.
Are there any other facets of your job that need to be described?

Figure 10.1
Schedule for a job analysis interview

2. Know basic measurement concepts.

3. Know the steps in collecting evidence of criterion-referenced validity.

4. Be able to analyze the skills, competencies, and personal qualities that relate to successful performance on the job.

5. Consider practical factors, such as cost, number of employees involved, and time.

6. Locate tests that purport to measure the characteristics identified for the job.

7. Administer the tests to workers on the job as well as to new applicants.

8. Observe the workers tested and have supervisors report on the performance of these workers.

9. Analyze how the test scores and ratings relate to success on the job.

10. If evidence is favorable, formulate an operational plan to utilize the data for selection purposes. If evidence is not favorable, select other instruments and get additional ratings.

11. Systematically monitor and evaluate the system.

Cronbach (1984) advocates more persistent and analytical research, starting with the development of limited and measurable criteria. If the criteria are diverse and dependable, he concludes that it is far more instructive to find out what factors predict each of the criteria rather than combining the criteria into one index.

MBTI IN ORGANIZATIONS

The MBTI can be used in most business or industrial organizations as a tool to help individuals in the organization understand themselves and others and help them to approach problems in different ways (Hirsch & Kummerow, 1990). The test can help organizations in career planning and development; improving teamwork; resolving conflicts; and helping individuals communicate more effectively with supervisors, peers, and employers. For example, if you tested to be an ESTJ, you would learn the following about yourself:

Individuals classified ESTJ (Extroversion, Sensing, Thinking, Judgment) by the MBTI tend to be analytical, decisive, logical, and tough-minded and are adept at planning and organization. Hirsh and Kummerow (1990) see their contribution to the organization as their ability to see flaws in advance; to critique problems logically and to organize people, process, and product.

ESTJs are take-charge leaders who are able to utilize past experiences to solve problems. They tend to make decisions quickly. They like to work in environments that are task-oriented, organized, and structured and where meeting goals are rewarded. They like their associates to be hard-working people who want to get the job done correctly.

These individuals do have potential problem areas. They tend to decide too quickly and may lack diplomacy in working with others to get the job done. Sometimes they may not see the need for change.

Hirsh and Kummerow (1990) suggest that ESTJs need to recognize the need to consider all sides before deciding on strategies and the benefits of change. They need to make sure they show appreciation of others and also take time to reflect on their feelings and values. There are, of course, 15 other profiles possible on the MBTI.

CURRENT TRENDS AND PERSPECTIVES

Employers are showing increased sensitivity in how they use tests for hiring purposes; they do not want to be charged with discrimination and unfair practices. Because employers must go through elaborate validation and documentation procedures when they employ tests for selection purposes, the use of tests for those purposes has declined. However, the use of tests for certification purposes has increased. Industry is moving toward multifactored assessment utilizing references, testing, interview data, health and physical examinations, and an application blank. Interviews are now more heavily evaluated than tests; written tests are used most frequently for selecting clerical or entry-level workers. Some industries have initiated diagnostic and developmental testing. But the traditional pencil-and-paper tests have been replaced by techniques such as leaderless group discussion, in-basket exercises, and other types of simulated procedures.

A concern is growing about the lack of job analysis data and the need for improved validation of the selection procedures used by business and industry. Licensing and certification examinations are being developed and there is a push for periodic reassessment of competencies for licensing.

Tenopyr (1981) concludes that employment testing has been in a storm of controversy because of its association with the civil rights movement. She points out that there are problems with fairness models because employers cannot afford to use different tests for various subgroups or interpret tests differently for each group. "If employment testing were outlawed tomorrow, the effect of employment of women in business and industry would scarcely be noticed" (p. 1120).

Since so many businesses are concerned about the cost of employee theft, they often use integrity testing to assess a person's dependability, reliability, or aversion to rules and has generated much controversy. The polygraph can no longer be used for employee selection purposes. Applicants are often rejected if they have low scores. Critics point out that these tests do not distinguish between taking small items and big items and present no proof that individuals with high scores are likely to steal. They may have high reliability, but the tests have been criticized for the apparent lack of validation evidence. The high percentage of misclassification errors, and the prospect that such instruments can be perceived as an invasion of privacy make their use very controversial (Gatewood & Perloff, 1993).

Research evidence does not support the validity of the interview or the value of variables such as experience and education. Tenopyr (1981) states that a biodata sheet may have promise, but tests tend to be more valid and reliable than the alternative methods (p. 1123). The most commonly used test is the job knowledge test, not the aptitude test. Tenopyr concludes that a complete abandonment of employment testing and the substitution of other alternatives will not work and will be no more useful than a lottery for jobs (p. 1125). She believes that constructive use of tests can benefit everyone.

Schmidt and Hunter (1981) have found that cognitive ability tests of the kind generally used in personnel selection are valid predictors of successful performance for all jobs in all settings. They also conclude that cognitive ability tests are equally valid for minority and majority applicants and do not underestimate the expected job performance of minority groups. They also quote evidence that cognitive ability tests can produce large labor cost savings, since individuals with greater cognitive ability tend to have better skills and require less training.

The revision of the General Aptitude Test Battery (GATB) has concerned civil rights advocates since blacks and Hispanics tend to score on the average one standard deviation lower than whites. Florez (1991) spoke in favor of not using the GATB altogether for employment screening. He claims that the GATB has an adverse impact on the protected groups and that the "liability pool" is increased.

SUMMARY

There are many new approaches to interest and career assessment. The computer has had a tremendous impact on the administration, scoring, and interpretation of these inventories. These tests have proven to be good measures of vocational success, but many factors need to be considered. The maturity, socioeconomic class, and educational level of the client all play important roles in assessing interests. Environment and heredity issues are also involved. A client may not have had the opportunities and experiences necessary to make valid judgments. Family, societal, and peer expectations may influence an individual's pattern of behavior. Temperament may also influence an individual's preferences. The career and vocational counselor needs to have a comprehensive knowledge of the world of work as well as extensive knowledge of assessment techniques and counseling procedures.

For the past three decades employment testing has been a center of controversy. Laws and court decisions have had an impact on employment testing. Testing is more widely used in federal and state agencies than in business and industry. In addition, many skilled and professional workers must take certification or licensing examinations, which then become the prerequisite for hiring. Tests in business and industry are primarily used for selection purposes, most often for clerical personnel. The decline in testing has led to a movement away from objective selection procedures. Analysis of research has indicated that testing does not discriminate against minority groups and women but saves the organization money. Nevertheless, currently there is more reliance on clinical judgment and consideration of the applicant's experience and education. Personnel psychologists need to be guided by the nine specific standards for the use of tests in employment contexts.

QUESTIONS FOR DISCUSSION

1. Do you believe that interest tests are not necessary, that the best way to find out about a person's interests is to ask, "What are you interested in, or what would you like to do or be?" Defend your position.

2. Interest tests have been criticized as sexually and culturally biased. What procedures can ensure that tests are developed and used properly by workers in the field?

3. The format and mode of presentation of career guidance tests are changing. Some tests are presented by video tape and on the computer screen. The test taker can see video pictures of individuals performing a job. Do you believe that these modes of test administration will prove to be more valid than the traditional pencil-and-paper approach? Which type of inventory would you prefer to take and why?

4. What career guidance tests have you taken? What impact have these tests had on your career development? When did you take these tests? How were the results presented to you? Did you agree with the results? If you were displaced from a current job, would you seek testing to help you identify other possible jobs or career fields?

5. More batteries of tests include aptitude, values, and interest tests rather than just interest tests alone. The computerized career guidance systems often include short tests of values and aptitudes rather than just asking individuals to rate their aptitudes and values. What factors do you think an individual needs to consider in making a career choice? Are there other areas you would include in the battery? What specific tests would you use? What types of nontest information would you find important? What type of assessment program would you use with high school students? young adults with handicaps? clients with midcareer crises? older adults?

6. Many employment test experts believe that the guidelines from the courts and government are outdated and make costly demands on employers that are not justified by the latest research. Do you agree or disagree with this position? Why?

7. Do you think that equity for minority group members can be obtained through item selection by test makers following the golden rule procedure? Is the golden rule procedure a threat to the validity of a test? Why or why not?

8. If you were being considered for promotion on your job, what type of assessment procedures would you consider most valid—pencil-and-paper instruments, behavioral assessments, observation, or some other approach? Why?

9. How would you go about the task of setting up a licensing examination for workers in your field? What things would you do to ensure that you met all of the legal guidelines?

10. The use of tests by business and industry has decreased, yet we are hearing more about the need for accountability, worker efficiency, and competence to be competitive in the global marketplace. What do you predict the future of employment testing will be? What trends do you predict for the next 10 years?

SUGGESTED ACTIVITIES

1. Evaluate an instrument listed or discussed in this chapter and write a critical review of it. Be sure to read the evaluations of the test in the *Mental Measurement Yearbooks*, *Test Critiques*, and *A Counselor's Guide to Vocational Guidance Instruments*.

2. Administer several career guidance tests and write an interpretation, tape, or role-play the results for the client.

3. Write a position paper on one of the following topics: the role of assessment in career guidance, gender and cultural bias in interest measurement, computer-assisted career guidance testing, or the history of career guidance testing.

4. Develop a career guidance and testing program for one of the following: an elementary school, a junior high school, a senior high school, an employment agency, a counseling and testing service, a mental health agency.

5. Design some nontest techniques to assess individual interests and values. Try your assessment techniques out on a sample of individuals and write a report of your findings.

6. Study the following hypothetical case and answer the questions that follow it.

   Mary is 35 years old and has gotten tired of the same job. She experienced some "job burnout" and decided to see what other types of careers she might be able to pursue. She agreed with the counselor that an interest inventory might be a good starting point for discussion. The counselor administered the COPSystem Interest Inventory and the Career Ability Placement Survey. She had the following profile on the COPS Interest Inventory.

Cluster	Raw Score	Percentile
1. Science, Professional	26	91
2. Science, Skilled	11	50
3. Technology, Professional	9	45
4. Technology, Skilled	4	30
5. Consumer Economics	11	50
6. Outdoor	18	70
7. Business, Professional	26	85
8. Business, Skilled	14	55
9. Clerical	1	2
10. Communication	15	45
11. Arts, Professional	17	35
12. Arts, Skilled	21	48
13. Service, Professional	30	87
14. Service, Skilled	17	50

   Mary's CAPS scores follow:

1. Mechanical Reasoning	13	83
2. Spatial Relations	15	92
3. Verbal Reasoning	24	98

4. Numerical Ability	18	92
5. Language Usage	22	83
6. Word Knowledge	41	68
7. Perceptual Speed & Accuracy	116	83
8. Manual Speed & Dexterity	230	32

   a.   How would you describe Mary's pattern of interests?
   b.   How would you describe Mary's pattern of aptitudes?
   c.   What further information would you want to have about Mary?
   d.   What further information would you want to have about the tests?
   e.   The CAPS has a self-interpretive profile and guide. How would you use this
        with Mary?

7. Interview an individual who is working in the personnel field in business and
    industry. Find out what types of assessment procedures that person's company
    uses to hire workers and to promote workers. Report your findings to the class.

8. Conduct a task or job analysis of your current job. Get the reactions of others,
    that is, your co-workers and your supervisors. See if they agree. Then design
    assessment instruments to rate individuals in your field. Identify standardized
    instruments and procedures that might already be available.

9. Design an assessment program to hire workers in your field, to identify profes-
    sional development needs, and to identify those who should be promoted to
    managerial levels.

10. Write a critical review of the literature on one of the following topics: assessment
    centers, job analysis, legal aspects of employment testing, leaderless group dis-
    cussion, in-basket and situational testing.

11. Critically analyze one of the widely used tests listed in this chapter.

ADDITIONAL READINGS

Berk, R. A. (Ed.). (1986). *Performance assessment: Methods and applications*. Baltimore, MD:
   Johns Hopkins University Press.

   The book has chapters by a number of experts in each field and covers topics such as job
   analysis, numerical rating scales, behavior-based scales, performance tests, assessment
   centers, appraisal interviews, utility analysis, validity generalization and predictive bias,
   and performance distribution assessment. There are also chapters on the application of
   performance assessment to different applied fields.

Gatewood, R., & Perloff, R. (1990). Testing and industrial application. In G. Goldstein & M.
   Hersen (Eds.), *Handbook of psychological assessment* (2nd ed.). New York: Pergamon
   Press.

   The chapter provides an overview of the many types of assessment procedures currently
   used within business and industry.

Holland, J. L. (1986). New directions for interest testing. In B. S. Plake & J. C. Witt (Eds.), *The
   future of testing*. Hillsdale, NJ: Lawrence Erlbaum.

John Holland presents a discussion of the usefulness, validity, and reliability of interest testing. He identifies some of the current trends as well as the critical issues and opportunities in this area.

Journal of Vocational Behavior, *33*(3) (December 1988).

This is a special issue on fairness in employment testing.

Kapes, J. T., & Mastie, M. M. (1988). *A counselor's guide to vocational guidance instruments* (2nd ed.). Falls Church, VA: National Vocational Guidance Association.

This guide provides critical reviews of the major interest inventories, measures of work values, career development inventories, and instruments for special populations.

Lowman, R. L. (1991). *The clinical practice of career assessment: Interest, abilities, and personality*. Washington, DC: American Psychological Association.

The author explains which tests to use, what to look for, and how to give feedback.

Power, P. W. (1991). *A guide to vocational assessment* (2nd ed.). Austin, TX: Pro-Ed.

The author presents a review of instruments, techniques, and issues related to vocational assessment of disabled clients, including utilization of work samples and computers, independent living with behavioral assessment approaches, and so on.

Tenopyr, M. L. (1986). Needed directions for measurement in work settings. In B. S. Plake & J. C. Witt (Eds.), *The future of testing* (pp. 269–288). Hillsdale, NJ: Lawrence Erlbaum Associates.

Tenopyr presents a review of the major trends and problems in the uses of measurement in business and industry.

CHAPTER 11

Personality Testing

Overview

Personality includes all the special qualities people have that make them different from each other—charm, energy, disposition, attitude, temperament, cleverness— and the feelings and behavior they exhibit. Personality assessment is important in describing and understanding behavior; it is also an area of controversy.

Personality tests are a part of the affective domain and are thus not as valid and reliable as most of the aptitude and achievement tests that make up the cognitive domain. They give us a picture of the individual's typical performance. Personality tests are used in clinical settings to identify personal problems and diagnose psychopathologies as well as in counseling and guidance contexts. Just as values and interests tests are important tools in vocational guidance, so are adjustment and temperament inventories important in personal counseling. Personality tests can help individuals gain insight into their own behavior, and they can be used to evaluate change after therapy, growth groups, and assertiveness training. Personality tests can help describe an individual systematically, diagnose a problem, give an indication of growth or change in behavior, and predict behavior. Such tests are extensively used in research studies.

Workers in the helping professions who plan to use personality tests need more training than is provided in this text. The goal here is to present an overview of the field and a conceptual framework for personality tests. Separate courses are available for individuals who want to develop proficiency in the use of projective and the other clinical-level tests. The potential user needs to have practicum experience under the supervision of an experienced examiner. Specialized in-service training is available for many tests and is valuable even for experienced examiners because of the many innovations in the field.

Objectives

The chapter should help the reader

- understand the role and importance of theory in personality assessment
- be familiar with the techniques of measuring personality
- know the advantages and disadvantages of different formats in assessing personality
- identify tests and instruments to assess specific dimensions of personality
- locate and discuss sources of information related to personality assessment
- be cognizant of the issues and problems in personality assessment

---

ROLE OF PERSONALITY THEORY

Many different theories have been developed to explain human behavior. It is not the purpose of this text to summarize these theories but to state that the examiner does need to know them. Theories give us a frame of reference and a way of conceptualizing and interpreting behavior. Many personality tests do have a base in theory, of which the test is a conceptualization.

Henry A. Murray

One of the personality theorists who has had a tremendous impact on personality assessment in this century is Murray, whose book, *Explorations in Personality* (1938), postulated his concepts of personality. He was aware not only of the biological but also the social and environmental bases of personality. His theory looks at how individuals are affected by external forces and how their attitudes, needs, and values influence their reaction to the world around them. In Murray's theory needs are closely studied. He defined *need* as a constructor—a force that helps individuals organize their perceptions, apperceptions, intellectualizations, connotations, and actions in such a way as to move in a certain direction an existing, unsatisfying situation. He states that needs manifest themselves by leading the organism to search for, or to avoid encountering, or when encountered to attend and respond to certain kinds of press or environment and forces (pp. 123–124). His list of psychogenic, or secondary, needs includes abasement, achievement, acquisition, affiliation, aggression, autonomy, blame avoidance, change, cognizance, construction, counteraction, deference, dominance, exposition, excitement, harm avoidance, nurturance, passivity, play mirth, recognition, rejection, retention, sex, succor, and understanding.

Murray sees environmental forces, or presses, as determinants of behavior. Two aspects of presses are how the individual perceives the press, and how it is in reality. The interaction between needs and presses forms thema, the resulting unit or pattern of behavior. Murray and his associates developed the Thematic Apperception Test (TAT) as an outgrowth of his theories.

The Thematic Apperception Test is a projective personality test that is individually administered and consists of 20 cards with ambiguous pictures on them. The examinee is instructed to make up a story that includes what is occurring in the situation depicted in the picture, what has happened to lead up to that situation, and what will happen in the future. Some of the cards vary according to the age and sex of the examinee, and one blank card is for the examinee to make up her own story. In interpreting the results, the examiner needs to know the common plots for the pictures. If an examinee comes up with a deviation from the normal plots, this information gives some insight into the examinee's characteristic modes of functioning. In the first picture of the TAT a young boy is contemplating a violin that rests on a table in front of him. One person's story might be that the boy was daydreaming about becoming a great violinist. Therefore, he begged his parents to buy him a violin and let him take lessons. They scraped and sacrificed and finally got him the violin, but when they hear him practice, they wish they had spent the money on a haircut instead.

Groth-Marnat (1990) indicates that typical stories given to card 1 revolve around a rebellious boy being forced by his parents or an authority figure to play the violin or around a self-motivated boy who is daydreaming about becoming a violinist. Bellak (1975) points out that this picture deals with the general issue of impulse versus control or the conflict between personal demands and external controlling agents. The stories for this picture can provide information about the client's relationships with parents—whether they are domineering, controlling, indifferent, helpful, understanding, or protective. The stories also give an indication of the need for achievement and how it is accomplished.

Unfortunately, there are no standard scoring procedures that all psychologists accept. Murray used qualitative methods of scoring and focused on five dimensions—the hero; motives, trends, and feelings of the hero (needs); forces of the hero's environment (press); themes and outcomes; and interests and sentiments. Murray believes that the first task is to identify which story character is the focal figure or hero. He believes that examinees identify with this character and project their needs, attitudes, and feelings onto that person.

Murray did try to quantify the degree of each psychogenic need identified in each story by counting the number of times a certain need was mentioned. The same procedure is used for presses. According to Murray's technique, the examiner would thus determine the characteristics of the hero and the patterns of needs and presses. Murray believes that these then combine to make thema, but gives rather vague instructions on how to analyze thema.

Arnold (1962) has identified five categories of thema.

1. Achievement success or failure, happiness/unhappiness, active effort or passivity
2. Right and wrong, ethical considerations, guilt
3. Human relations
4. Reaction to adversity
5. Interests and sentiments

The TAT has been utilized by clinicians, school psychologists, and researchers for over 50 years. It can help access the covert and deeper structures of personality and is less susceptible to faking. With no right or wrong answers, examinees often find the situation interesting and nonthreatening. The test gives a broad measure of personality and has been used to measure cognitive style, creativity, problem-solving skills, verbal fluency, imaginative processes, family dynamics, adjustment, general intelligence, and sexual adjustment (Groth-Marnat, 1984).

Dana (1985) concludes that competent interpretation of the TAT is difficult because there is no consensus on how to score the test. In addition, responses on the TAT are affected by culture, the examiner, and purpose of the assessment. It has been one of the most frequently used assessment procedures, but the validity and reliability of the test are questionable because of unsystematic card stimuli, a lack of standard directions and administration procedures, use of various short forms, an absence of consensual scoring, and a paucity of careful training for interpretation (p. 132).

Listed here are a number of other tests based upon Murray's theories.

Children's Apperception Test is a TAT test with 10 cards depicting animals in human social context. Examinees aged 3 to 10 are asked to tell a story for each picture.

Children's Apperception Test—Human Figure is a TAT projective test utilizing human figures in situations of concern to children. Examinees aged 3 to 10 are asked to tell a story for each picture.

Robert's Apperception Test for Children is a TAT test utilizing 16 line drawings as stimuli for examinee storytelling. The pictures emphasize everyday contemporary events such as parent disagreement, affection, observation of nudity, and school and peer interpersonal events. The test is designed to identify emotionally disturbed children aged 6 to 15.

Adjective Checklist is a pencil-and-paper personality inventory containing 300 adjectives. It measures 37 dimensions of personality, including 15 need scales based on Murray's theory.

Symonds Picture Story Test is a TAT test designed for adolescents.

Edwards Personal Preference Schedule is a pencil-and-paper forced-choice personality inventory designed to measure 15 of Murray's needs. It also yields a consistency score.

Jung. Carl Jung has also influenced personality test authors. Jung (1910, 1918), a contemporary of Freud, utilized the word association techniques of Galton to diagnose mental illness and developed a projective test employing free association with a list of 100 words. Jung's theory has influenced the development of a major inventory, the Myers-Briggs Type Indicator (MBTI). Jung postulated that four dimensions structure an individual's personality—extroversion-introversion, sensing-intuition, thinking-feeling, and judgment-perception. The MBTI is a personality test used in personal counseling, marital counseling, educational programming and research in the business and industrial sector. The test is available in several forms, is self-administering, and is used with high school students and adults.

Other Theory-Based Tests

The Personal Orientation Inventory (POI) is based on Maslow's theory of manifest needs and measures values and behaviors important in the development of actualized individuals. It has scales such as Time Ratio, Support Ratio, Self-Actualization Value, Existentiality, Feeling Reactivity, Spontaneity, Self-Regard, Self-Acceptance, Synergy, Acceptance of Aggression, and Capacity for Intimate Contact. The inventory has been useful in evaluating therapy and assessing an individual's mental health.

The Blacky Picture Story Test (Blum, 1949) is a projective test based upon Freud's theory and consists of 11 cartoons portraying dogs in situations related to the stages of psychosexual development.

The Vocational Preference Inventory (VPI) is based upon Holland's theory of vocational adjustment. A personality-type theory, the first six scales measure the six types—realistic, investigative, social, artistic, enterprising, and conventional. The VPI is a 160-item pencil-and-paper inventory in which examinees are asked to circle occupations they like or might consider.

TECHNIQUES FOR MEASURING PERSONALITY

Koppitz (1982) categorizes personality tests according to techniques—verbal, visual, drawing, manipulative, objective, and others.

Verbal Techniques

Verbal techniques are defined by Koppitz (1982) as those methods that involve both verbal stimuli and verbal responses (p. 276). The stimuli and responses can be transmitted orally or in writing. With this technique the examinee should have adequate to good language skills and should be able to hear or read words and express himself orally or in writing. Such tests provide a sample of the written and oral expression in addition to the content of the responses.

Projective Questions.   Informal techniques such as simple projective questions can be used.

> If you were starting your program of studies over again, would you major in the same field?
>
> If you could be anything you wanted to be, what would you be?
>
> If you had three wishes, what would you wish for?
>
> What do you like most about school?
>
> What do you like least about school?

Sentence Completion.   The sentence completion method is another personality test. Rotter and Rafferty (1950) published Rotter Incomplete Sentence Blank (ISB) in three forms—high school, college, and adult. Each form contains 40 items, which are the stems of sentences to be completed by the examinee. The test can be administered individually, to groups, or it can be self-administered. It can also be given orally. The stems are designed to assess attitudes toward family, peers, school, work, anxiety, guilt, and physical disability.

Koppitz (1982) uses the ISB a number of ways. She analyzes the content of the responses, the quality of language and sentence structure, vocabulary, spelling, and handwriting. Rotter provides a scoring system, which rates the completed sentences on a seven-point scale for the degree of conflict revealed. The responses also can be classified in three categories—unhealthy, neutral, and positive or healthy responses. Koppitz sees the ISB as a useful icebreaker with reluctant and unspontaneous teenagers but believes that it often gives little unconscious or involuntary information about the examinee.

Story Completion.   Thomas (1937), Duss (Koppitz, 1982), and Munsterberg (1955) all have different versions of this technique. Madeline Thomas developed a set of 15 stories about a hypothetical child of the same age and sex as the child being tested. Koppitz (1982) gives an example of a story: "A boy is at the table with his parents. Father suddenly gets angry. Why?" (p. 278). The stories are designed to investigate a child's dreams, fantasies, attitudes, and defense mechanisms, and they can be analyzed for major themes.

Visual Techniques

With this approach visual stimuli are presented to the examinee, who gives a verbal response. The classic example of this technique, the Rorschach consists of 10 bilaterally symmetrical inkblots, part in black and gray and part in color. It is a projective test that asks examinees to tell what the blots remind them of. A Swiss psychiatrist, Herman Rorschach developed this technique and described it in his monograph, *Psychodiagnostik*, in 1921.

The test has two phases. The first is the free association phase in which the examiner presents the first blot and asks, "What might this be?" (Erdberg, 1985). The second phase is the inquiry phase and starts after the client has gone through the 10 blots. The clinician determines the exact location of each precept and ascertains which variable, color or form, was the primary factor in what the examinee saw in the blot. The test is a perceptual-cognitive task. First, perception is involved in scanning and visualizing the blot. Then, cognitive dimensions determine how the individual organizes or structures the response. The examiner considers the location of each response. Was the whole blot used in the interpretation, or an unusual detail? The examiner also looks at the determinants of the perception. Was the response influenced by form, movement, color, texture, or dimensionality? The content of the responses is also coded. A number of scoring procedures are available (see Exner, 1974, 1978; Exner & Weiner, 1982). Hurt, Reznikoff, and Clarkin (1995) claim that cognitive and ideational processes are measured quite extensively by the Rorschach. Cognitive dimensions can be assessed through the examinee's appreciation of consensual reality, capacity to make use of multiple determinants in creative and novel ways, breadth of content categories, ability to integrate disparate symbolism, attention to detail, and integration of affective and ideational aspects of the response (p. 199).

The examiner must be thoroughly trained in the use of the Rorschach. Groth-Marnat (1984) concludes that a clinician can make numerous errors during administration, scoring, and interpretation. He states that the interpretations need to be checked and rechecked against the overall Rorschach configuration and additional test and biographical data (p. 205).

Generally, high consistency exists in the scoring of the Rorschach but less evidence exists of the validity of the test. Anastasi (1982) evaluates four major challenges relating to the validity of the test.

1. Color itself has no effect on response.
2. Scores are influenced by a subject's verbal aptitude.
3. Response productivity is closely tied to age, intellectual level, and amount of education.
4. Earlier validity studies were based on inadequately developed norms.

Overall, the Rorschach continues to be a widely used instrument. Clinicians find it useful because the tasks required bypass the examinee's conscious resistance and help obtain information about unconscious processes.

Other Tests Using Visual Techniques. The previously described Thematic Apperception Test and Children's Apperception Test are other examples of this technique. In addition Solomon, Bernard, and Starr have utilized visual stimuli in the School Apperception Test. The drawings in this test focus on school-oriented fantasies, attitudes, and perceptions. The Hand Test for ages 6 to adult is designed to measure attitudes and action tendencies likely to be expressed in overt behavior, particularly aggression. Ten picture cards present hands in different positions, and the examinee is asked to describe the activities portrayed on each card. The examiner analyzes the responses both qualitatively and quantitatively for potential negative behavior toward people and objects in the environment, pathological inefficiency, and social withdrawal.

Drawing Techniques

A number of widely used drawing tests are used to assess personality. Among them are the House-Tree-Person Test, Draw-a-Person Test, Bender Visual Motor-Gestalt Test, Draw-A-Family Test, and the Kinetic Family Drawing Test. Drawing seems to be a natural medium for expression in children, and artists have given us insights into the process. Drawing is viewed as a projective technique in which the client shares his perceptions and reactions to the world around him. The style of the drawing—how the individual represents his content—varies tremendously from person to person, and drawing to drawing. How the individual approaches drawing reflects how he approaches life situations (Groth-Marnat, 1984, p. 115).

Draw-a-Person Test.   This test was originally developed by Florence Goodenough to assess the intelligence of children but was expanded by Karen Machover (1949) to include a guide for evaluating personality variables. Koppitz (1968) further refined the scoring system and developed a system of identifying different indicators of emotional difficulties. Some of the general guidelines for interpreting drawings are included in Table 11.1.

Koppitz (1968) identified 30 emotional indicators in children's drawings. She advocates grouping these indicators according to the behavior they reflect. For example, poor achievement might be reflected in poor integration, a monster or grotesque figure, omission of body, omission of arms, or omission of mouth (Koppitz, 1982, p. 285). The drawing of a hostile aggressive individual might show a big figure, transparency, crossed eyes, teeth, long arms, big hands, or genitals. Depressed, withdrawn children characteristically include tiny figures and short arms but no eyes. Other attitudes that can be identified through analysis of drawings are impulsivity, insecurity, anxiety, and shyness or timidness.

Family Drawings.   Family drawings can give insight into an individual's perception of her place within the family. In the Kinetic Family Drawing Test (KFD), the individual is asked to "draw the whole family doing something." In analyzing the drawing, the examiner looks for who is present or who is omitted or given a substitute. The size of the figures is important as well as their position, distance, and interaction with one another. Special attention should be given to the individual's self-portrayal.

The KFD test is analyzed for action, symbols, and style. Action refers to the movement of energy between people and/or objects and can indicate the feeling exhibited. Symbols are interpreted according to psychoanalytic theory. Guidelines are provided in the test manual for interpreting the KFD.

The House-Tree-Person (HTP) test requires the individual to draw a house, a tree, and a person. Hammer (1985) states that the house may represent the way the

Table 11.1
General guidelines for interpreting drawings

Dimension	Interpretation
Location/Placement	
Central	Normal, reasonable, secure person
Upper right	Intellectualizing tendencies, possible inhibition of expression of feeling
Upper left	Impulsive behavior, drive toward immediate emotional satisfaction of needs, orientation toward past
High on page	High level of aspiration, extreme optimism
Low on page	Feelings of insecurity, low levels of self-esteem, depressive tendencies, defeatist attitudes
Lower edge as base	Need for support, lack of self-confidence
Size	
Unusually large	Aggressive, expansive, or grandiose tendencies, acting out potential
Unusually small	Feelings of inferiority, timidness, insecurity, ineffectiveness, inhibition, depressive behavior under stress
Pencil Pressure/ Stroke/Line Quality	
Variable	Flexible, adaptive person
Heavy	Sign of tension, high energy level, forcefulness, and possible acting out tendencies
Light, sketchy	Hesitant, indecisive, timid, insecure person; inhibited personality, low energy level
Shaded strokes	Anxiety
Long strokes	Controlled behavior, inhibition
Short strokes	Impulsive behavior
Straight uninterrupted lines	Assertive and decisive behavior
Organization and symmetry	
Bizarre	Schizoid tendencies
Boxed off	Indication of difficulty in controlling life reliance on external structure or organizations
Element encapsulated	Desire to remove an area of conflict from life
Extremely symmetrical	Obsessive-compulsive, overintellectually defensive, cold, distant, hypertensive, and perfectionist tendencies
Lacking symmetry	Insecurity, poor impulse control, unbalanced self-concept
Erasures	
Excessive	Uncertainty, indecisiveness, and restlessness, obsessive-compulsive personality
Occasional/to improve	Flexibility, satisfactory adjustment
Localized	Conflict or concern about what that area represents

Dimension	Interpretation
Detail	
Absent	Psychosomatic, hypertensive conditions or depressive and withdrawing
Excessive	Obsessive-compulsive tendencies, rigidity and/or anxiety, highly emotional
Bizarre	Indicative of psychosis
Internal organs depicted	Likelihood of romantic delusions, schizophrenic or manic conditions, poor judgment, sexual disturbance indicated by sexual organs
Outer clothing	Voyeuristic or exhibitionist tendencies
Distortions and omissions	
Distortions	Confused, psychotic or schizophrenic condition
Omissions	Conflict, denial
Perspective	
From below	Rejection, unhappiness or inferiority, withdrawal tendencies
From above	Sense of superiority, compensation for underlying feelings of inadequacy
Distant	Inaccessibility, desire to withdraw
Close	Interpersonal warmth, psychological accessibility
Shading	
Shaded area	Anxiety
Complete absence	Character disorder
Color	
Black	Depression, suppression, inhibition, inadequacy, self-deprecation
Red	Problem or danger, anger or violent reaction, need for warmth and affection
Orange	Extroversion, emotional responsiveness to outer world, life or death struggle, ambivalence
Yellow	Cheerfulness, intellectualizing tendencies, lack of inhibition, expansiveness, anxiety
Green	Regulation of affective tendencies, healthy ego, peacefulness, security
Blue	Quiet, calm, well-controlled, cold, distant, fading away or withdrawing
Purple	Inner emotional and affective stimulation, internalization of affect, bold exterior, need to control or possess
Brown	Sensuousness, security, fixations, rigidity, in touch with nature
Gray	Noninvolvement, repressions, denial, emotional neutralization
White	Passivity, emptiness, depersonalization, loss of contact with reality

individual sees his home situation and intrafamily relationships. Tree drawings are analyzed in terms of size, shape, and the quality of the trunk, branches, leaves, and the ground on which the tree stands; these aspects represent the individual's deeper, more subconscious personal feelings. The drawing of the person is viewed as a conscious representation of the individual and his environment.

Bender Gestalt Test.   The Bender Visual Motor Gestalt Test consists of nine cards containing abstract designs that the examinee is asked to copy onto a blank sheet of paper. The test was designed to measure visual-motor integration and functions as a developmental test for children aged 5 to 11, the period when perceptual-motor skills develop. With older students the test can indicate problems with visual-motor perception resulting from a developmental lag or malfunctioning in the visual-motor areas.

Koppitz (1975) presents a development scale to accompany the Bender test and identifies 12 emotional indicators found in the copied designs.

1. *Confused order*—sign of mental confusion, poor planning and organization

2. *Wavy line*—poor motor coordination and/or emotional instability

3. *Dashes substituted for circles*—impulsivity or lack of interest

4. *Increase in size*—low frustration tolerance, explosiveness

5. *Large size*—impulsivity, acting out behavior

6. *Small size*—anxiety, withdrawal, constriction, timidity

7. *Fine line*—timidity, shyness, withdrawal

8. *Careless overwork, reinforced lines*—impulsivity, aggressiveness, acting out behavior

9. *Second attempt at drawing figures*—impulsivity, aggressiveness, acting out behavior

10. *Expansiveness, two or more pages*—acting out behavior

11. *Box around one or more figures*—attempt to control impulsivity, weak inner-control, need for outer limits and structure

12. *Spontaneous elaboration and/or additions to designs*—unusual preoccupation with own thoughts, fears, anxieties, serious emotional problems

Manipulative Techniques

Some examinees, especially children, have trouble expressing their feelings or attitudes verbally or through drawing but can express themselves in play through manipulative materials such as puppets, toys, or clay. Koppitz (1982) states that play can become a projective technique when used with selected materials in an environment free from distractions and in the presence of an observer (p. 289). This approach is especially useful with children who have social, language, cultural, or physical disabilities. The advantages to this technique are several. Toys are natural or familiar items to children. The technique has both diagnostic and therapeutic value and children feel comfortable in a play environment.

Many kits and anatomically correct dolls are available, but many psychologists find miniature toys and matchbox cars to be as good. In addition, many different kinds of hand puppets are available in toy stores, and spontaneous play with puppets is quite often the preference of the child. Children often like to involve the observing psychologist in the puppet show.

Objective Techniques

The most popular and widely used technique to assess personality is the personality questionnaire. It can be administered to individuals or to groups and is easily administered and scored. Questionnaires exist to measure all the different dimensions of personality—attitudes, adjustment, temperament, values, motivation, moral behavior, and anxiety.

Minnesota Multiphasic Personality Inventory-2.   The most widely used personality adjustment inventory is the Minnesota Multiphasic Personality Inventory (MMPI-2). Revised in 1989, the new edition (MMPI-2) has been restandardized and is on tape for blind, illiterate, semiliterate, or disabled individuals. Another option is the box form, with each item on a separate card. The client separates the cards into true and false categories. The test can be machine- or hand-scored. The MMPI-2 is designed to be administered to clients 16 and older who have had at least six years of schooling. The reading level of the examinee has to be adequate, and the intelligence level should be 80 or higher. Raw scores are translated into T scores with a mean of 50 and a standard deviation of 10. There are three major validity scales— Lie (L), Infrequency (F), and Correction (K). An additional "?" scale is a compilation of unanswered items throughout the MMPI. MMPI-2 has several new validity scales—Fb (unusual response inconsistency), TRIN (true response inconsistency), and VRI (variable response inconsistency). The test results are considered valid if fewer than 30 items are left unanswered and the other validity scales are within normal limits.

The L or Lie scale consists of 15 items such as "I never get angry." The scale indicates whether the client is consciously or unconsciously presenting herself as a perfectionist. The F scale consists of 64 items but does not measure a trait. Because the items are answered in a deviant direction by fewer than 10% of the normal adult population, a high score indicates that the test taker has endorsed a large number of serious psychological items. There may be a number of reasons for high scores on this scale.

A scoring error may have occurred or the client may be a poor reader with limited comprehension. Also the test taker might be trying to look bad on the test or be confused and have delusions.

The answer pattern might be a plea for help from a patient who is exaggerating symptoms or with an adolescent the score may be an expression of defiance, hostility, or negativism (Graham, 1990).

The K or correction scale measures defensiveness as a test-taking attitude. The scale has 30 items that cover a wide range of content areas. Low scores usually indicate a deliberate attempt to appear bad, but sometimes a self-effacing, self-critical client may actually endorse these pathological tendencies. Ten basic clinical scales of the MMPI are listed in Table 11.2.

Profile analysis is the main interpretive framework of the MMPI. Newmark (1985) indicates that the standard procedure is to interpret profiles according to the two highest clinical scales with T scores above 70, provided both scales are within 10 T-score points of each other. The resulting code reflects the number of the two scales with the highest scores, the most elevated scale listed first. A number of new scales for the MMPI have been derived by researchers and clinicians—Welsh's Anxiety, Welsh's Repression, Ego Strength, MacAndrew Alcoholism Scale, Dependency, Prejudice Scale, Low Back Pain Scale, and so on.

A number of content scales have been modified or added to MMPI-2—anxiety, fears, obsessiveness, depression, health concerns, bizarre behavior, anger, cynicism, antisocial practices, type A behavior, low self-esteem, social discomfort, family problems, work interference, and negative treatment indicators. The use and interpreta-

Table 11.2
Clinical scales on the Minnesota Multiphasic Personality Inventory–2

Scale	Item Total	Item Content
Hypochondriasis (Hs)	(32)	Undue concern with physical health
Depression (D)	(57)	Depression, denial of happiness and personal worth, lack of interest, withdrawal
Hysteria (Hy)	(60)	Specific somatic complaints, denial of psychological or emotional problems, discomfort in social situations
Psychopathic deviate (Pd)	(56)	Identification with culturally conventional masculine and feminine choices, aesthetic interests, activity-passivity
Paranoia (Pa)	(40)	Delusions of persecution and ideas of reference, interpersonal sensitivity, suspiciousness, moral self-righteousness
Psychasthenia (Pt)	(48)	General dissatisfaction with life, difficulty with concentration, indecisiveness, self-doubt, obsessional aspects
Schizophrenia (Sc)	(78)	Feeling of being different, feelings of isolation, bizarre thought processes, poor family relationships, sexual identity concerns, tendency to withdraw
Hypomania (Ma)	(46)	Elevated energy level, flight of ideas, elevated mood, increased motor activity, expansiveness, grandiosity
Social introversion-extroversion	(69)	Introversion-extroversion, social insecurity

tion of the revised scales remain equivalent to the older ones. Users should be cautious of the supplementary and research scales, however, because their validity has not been thoroughly established in clinical settings.

California Psychological Inventory.   In contrast to the MMPI, which is used primarily with abnormal populations, the California Psychological Inventory (CPI) assesses normal personality dimensions concerning an examinee's typical behavior patterns, usual feelings, opinions, and attitudes related to social, ethical, and family matters. The CPI focuses on diagnosing and understanding interpersonal behavior within normal populations. It is a pencil-and-paper personality inventory for individuals aged 12 to 70 who have a fourth-grade or higher reading level. The four clusters of scales are presented in Table 11.3. The CPI is one of the most frequently used personality inventories and has been employed in many contexts and research studies. Anastasi (1982) rates the CPI as one of the best personality inventories currently available (p. 508).

Table 11.3
Cluster and scales in the California Psychological Inventory

Cluster	Scale	Description
Interpersonal effectiveness, style and adequacy	Dominance (Do)	Measures areas of leadership ability
	Capacity for status (Cs)	Assesses relative level of income, education and prestige, and power attained in the individual's social milieu
	Sociability (Sy)	Differentiates between an individual who is outgoing, extroverted, and sociable and one who is introverted, withdrawn, and prone to avoid social visibility
	Social presence (Sp)	Measures an individual's degree of poise, self-confidence, verve, and spontaneity in social interaction
	Self-acceptance (Sa)	Measures individual's sense of personal worth, self-acceptance, and capacity for independent thinking and action
	Well-being (Wb)	Provides a rough estimate of an individual's level of adjustment
Interpersonal controls, values, styles, and beliefs	Responsibility (Re)	Measures whether an individual is conscientious, responsible, dependable and articulate regarding rules and orders and believes life should be governed by reason
	Socialization (So)	Measures the degree to which an individual accepts and adheres to social norms
	Self-control (Sc)	Measures the degree to which a person can self-direct his own behavior

FORMAT OF TESTS

A wide variety of item formats are used to assess personality dimensions. The MMPI and CPI use a true-false format; the Adjective Checklist presents a list of descriptive words to check; the Work Environment Preference Inventory uses a Likert-type attitude format. The Edwards Personal Preference Schedule has a forced choice format: The examinee has a choice between two options on an item. On the Allport-Vernon Lindzey Scale of Values the examinee ranks options in one part of the test.

FACTOR ANALYTIC APPROACHES

Factor analysis is a statistical method used in test development to see how items cluster statistically. It is also used as an explanatory technique. Factor analysis helps us see

Cluster	Scale	Description
	Tolerance (To)	Measures the degree to which individuals are socially intolerant versus the extent to which they hold accepting, permissive, and nonjudgmental social beliefs and attitudes
	Good impression (Gi)	Identifies individuals who are faking goodness
	Communality (Cm)	Measures the degree to which individuals see their surroundings in ways that are similar to the surroundings of others
Intellectual stance, achievement, and academic ability	Achievement via conformance (Ac)	Measures the degree to which individuals prefer to have their criteria of performance clearly specified by some outside source
	Achievement via independence (Ai)	Measures the degree to which independence and learning are rewarded in learning
	Intellectual efficiency (Ie)	Measures the efficiency of an individual's use of personal intelligence
Conceptual interests	Psychological mindedness (Py)	Measures an individual's ability to perceive inner needs and motives
	Flexibility (Fx)	Measures the degree to which an individual is flexible, adaptable, and changeable in thinking, behavior, and temperament
	Femininity (Ff)	Measures the degree to which an individual is psychologically feminine or masculine regardless of sex

how many distinguishable individual differences can be identified in a set of scores and how significant the influence of each dimension is (Cronbach, 1984, p. 283).

Cattell and his associates have developed a series of personality tests based on the factor analytic method. The Early School Personality Questionnaire (ESPQ) is read or presented by tape to children aged 6 to 8. A special answer sheet uses pictures to guide children in marking their answers. The Children's Personality Questionnaire (CPQ) is used with children ages 8 to 12, and the High School Personality Questionnaire (HSPQ) with youth 12 to 18. The Sixteen Personality Factor Questionnaire (16PF) is used with clients 16 or older. These four tests are based upon the factor analytic approach and contain many of the same factors. Consequently, it is possible to look developmentally at the personality dimensions measured on these tests. The publisher offers computer scoring and interpretation of some levels. Special interpretative reports are available on the 16PF—the Personal Career Development Profile, the Karson Clinical Report, and the Marriage Counseling Report.

Eysenck also made use of factor analysis in his test development. The Eysenck Personality Inventory (EPI) for high school students and adults is a 57-item pencil-and-paper inventory that measures two major dimensions—extroversion-introversion and neuroticism-stability. Eysenck found that these two dimensions accounted for most of the variance on personality tests. The Eysenck Personality Questionnaire (EPQ) is a 90-item pencil-and-paper inventory measuring extroversion-introversion, neuroticism-stability, and tough-mindedness or psychoticism. It also has a Lie scale and can be given to individuals 7 and older. The authors claim it can be used for clinical diagnosis, educational guidance, occupational counseling, personnel selection and placement, and market research.

Five-factor tests of personality have recently received much attention in the literature. The NEO-PI-R (1992) is a 240-item test that measures five major domains—neuroticism, extraversion, openness, agreeableness, and conscientiousness. The neuroticism subscales are anxiety, angry hostility, depression, self-consciousness, impulsiveness, and vulnerability. The extraversion subscales are warmth, gregariousness, assertiveness, activity, excitement seeking, and positive emotions. The agreeableness subscales are trust, straightforwardness, altruism, compliance, modesty, and tendermindedness. The openness subscales are fantasy, aesthetics, feelings, actions, ideas, and values. The conscientiousness subscales are competence, order, dutifulness, achievement striving, self-discipline, and deliberation. The test has several forms: R is for men and women, and S is for an observer. There is also a shorter version, the NEO Five Factor Inventory (NEO-FFI) that has only 60 items and yields just the five domain scores.

DIMENSIONS OF PERSONALITY

Many different dimensions of personality exist. Some tests attempt to assess overall personality, while others focus on one dimension. Following is a representative sample of topics and tests.

Self-Concept Scales

Self-concept has been a popular construct in theories of personality and vocational development. Some of the widely used self-concept measures are listed here.

Coopersmith Self-Esteem Inventories assess attitudes toward self in social, academic, and personal contexts. Both short and longer versions present items (25 to 58) to be answered "like me" or "unlike me." Specific scales include general self, school-academic, home-parents, social self-peers, and lie. School and adult forms are available.

Tennessee Self-Concept Scale measures identity, self-satisfaction, behavior, physical self, moral-ethical self, personal self, family self, and social self. All 100 items are to be answered on a 5-point scale, from completely false to completely true. This scale measures self-concept in terms of identity, feeling, and behavior.

Self-Concept and Motivation Inventory (SCAMIN) assesses self-concept in an academic setting, measuring achievement needs, achievement investment, role expectation, and self-adequacy. The four levels are preschool-kindergarten, early elementary (grades 1 to 3), later elementary (grades 3 to 6), and secondary (grades 7 to 12).

Piers-Harris Children's Self-Concept Scale measures self-concept dimensions such as evaluation of behavior, school and intellectual status, physical appearance and attributes, anxiety, popularity, and satisfaction.

Self-Concept Adjective Checklist is a 114-item pencil-and-paper test of self-concept. It checks physical traits, social values, and intellectual abilities. In K to 3 the stem is "I am. . . . " In grades 4 to 8 an additional stem can be used, "I would like to be. . . . "

Inferred Self-Concept Scale is a 30-item scale in which parents, teachers, or counselors rate dimensions of behavior indicative of an individual's self-concept.

Self-Perception Inventory assesses how individuals see themselves and how they think others see them, such as students, adults, teachers, and family.

The Culture-Free Self-Esteem Inventory has three forms, A and B for children and AD for adults (Battle, 1992). The children's scales measure general self-esteem, social self-esteem, academic self-esteem, and parent-related self-esteem. The adult version measures general, social, and personal self-esteem.

The Multidimensional Self-Esteem Inventory (MSEI) is a 116-item scale measuring components and levels of self-esteem. The highest level is assessed on the inventory by a global self-esteem scale. There are eight component scales at the intermediate level: competence, lovability, likeability, personal power, self-control, moral self-approval, body appearance, and body functioning. There is an identity integration scale providing a measure of global self-concept and a defensive self-enhancement scale that serves as a measure of the individual's defensiveness.

Self-concept measurement is reviewed comprehensively by Wylie (1974, 1979, 1990). Shavelson, Hubner, and Stanton (1976) also reviewed some of the major instruments and proposed a model of self-concept.

Many studies have related self-concept to achievement, minority group membership, and locus of control. Self-concept is believed to be a useful personality construct, although its measurement seems to have continued problems because of the lack of validity and reliability of many of the instruments.

Anxiety Tests

A number of scales have been developed to assess the anxiety level in different groups of individuals. One of the most widely used scales has been the Manifest Anxiety Scale for adolescents and adults. It utilizes 50 true-false items to measure an individual's predisposition to react with anxiety in stressful situations. A modified version for children is the Children's Manifest Anxiety Scale, which also includes an 11-item Lie scale.

The State-Trait Anxiety Inventory was developed to identify the anxiety an individual feels at a particular moment versus the way he feels generally. One version is for children in grades 4 to 8; the other, for seventh graders to adults. The test was designed to evaluate the individual's anxiety level to identify those who might need help in coping with anxiety. The inventory can be used with clients in counseling and therapy as well as for research.

PROBLEMS IN PERSONALITY ASSESSMENT

A number of problems can affect the validity of personality assessment. Many responses to assessment procedures are influenced by variables other than the personality characteristics of the test takers. Psychological, sociological, linguistic, and other variables influence how the examinees respond. These systematic biases are called response set or response style. Lanyon and Goodstein (1982) identified two types of response style.

1. The tendency of the test taker to distort responses in a particular direction regardless of the stimulus content

2. The tendency of the test taker to answer deliberately to produce a certain image

The authors conclude that response style can be corrected through careful test construction practices, but deliberate faking is still a major problem.

Acquiescent response style is the tendency of the test taker to respond positively (true or yes) regardless of the item content. Test takers respond the same way to ambiguous items as they do on clearer items.

The social desirability response set is the tendency of the test taker to choose the response that he believes to be socially desirable rather than the response that more accurately reflects the individual's behavior or feelings. Sometimes a test taker deliberately and consciously chooses the socially desirable response; the individual may be faking goodness because he is defensive about his behavior. Sometimes the choice is unconsciously expressed. Extreme degrees of social desirability help to distort results and affect the validity of the interpretation. Some tests such as the Edwards Personal Preference Scale have attempted to control the social desirability of the items by using forced-choice item matching on the basis of social desirability.

Defensiveness also causes the test takers to deliberately slant their responses in a favorable, well-adjusted light. Individuals are able on many tests to come up with fake positive profiles. Some personality tests such as the MMPI have scales that can be used to identify the test taker as a good or bad faker.

Kline (1993) mentions another problem, the influence of ability and attainment on test scores. These variables can be a major source of distortion. He points out that "personality questionnaires are, inevitably, somewhat superficial, are usually transparent and thus easy to fake, and ultimately seem too crude to encapsulate the subtlety and richness of personality" (p. 242).

SUMMARY

Many ways of assessing personality have been described, and different dimensions have been identified. It is important to know what method is best to obtain the desired client information. Personality tests have lower validity and reliability coefficients than achievement and ability tests and produce larger standard errors of measurement. Promising tests and techniques exist, but many procedures and instruments require specialized training and supervision for proper administration, scoring, and interpretation.

QUESTIONS FOR DISCUSSION

1. How important is personality theory in personality assessment? Do tests and assessment techniques have an adequate theoretical foundation?

2. What are the many different ways of measuring personality? Compare the advantages of each approach.

3. Faking is one of the major problems on personality tests. How would you structure a testing situation to minimize faking? Do you believe that everybody fakes on personality inventories? Explain your answer.

4. A wide variety of item content measures dimensions of personality, from food choices to occupations to musical preferences. How important do you think the content of the items is in assessing personality? Another factor is the format of

the items. What are the advantages and disadvantages of the different formats? For what groups would each format work best?

5. Do you believe that pencil-and-paper personality inventories give a valid picture of an individual's personality? Would situational tests or observation in naturalistic, everyday settings provide more valid information?

SUGGESTED ACTIVITIES

1. Operationally define a personality construct and devise several strategies to measure the construct. Develop some preliminary instruments and give them to a sample of individuals. What was the reaction of the test takers to the form of the test? Analyze the forms. Which form or type of test was most valid? most reliable?

2. Identify a personality test of interest to you. Critically analyze the test. Read the reviews of the test in the *Mental Measurement Yearbooks* and *Test Critiques*.

3. Interview workers in the helping professions who use tests and find out which personality tests they use and why. Report your findings to the class.

4. Review the research on one of the current issues in personality testing, and write a critical analysis of your findings.

5. Make an annotated bibliography of personality tests, specific test types, or test areas appropriate for your current or future field.

6. Read the following case and answer the questions at the end of it.

Name: Salinda
Age: 18
Race: African-American
Highest grade completed: Grade 10
Family: Mother is a single parent who works as a practical nurse in a local hospital
Salinda's dependents: 2 children, ages 17 months and 3 months.
Career goal: Telemarketing

Personality Profile

Measures of Psychosocial Development

	T Score		T Score
Trust	24	Mistrust	55
Autonomy	41	Shame & Doubt	38
Initiative	28	Guilt	64
Industry	42	Inferiority	65
Identity	59	Identity Confusion	69
Intimacy	36	Isolation	62
Generativity	24	Stagnation	61
Ego Integrity	55	Despair	65
Total Positive	38	Total Negative	60

Values Scale

Inner Oriented	T Score
1. Ability Utilization	23
2. Achievement	31
3. Aesthetics	42
4. Personal Development	37
5. Altruism	40

Physical Prowess	
1. Physical Prowess	57
2. Risk	56
3. Authority	46

Group Oriented	
1. Social Interaction	36
2. Cultural Identity	45
3. Social Relations	50
4. Working Conditions	43
5. Variety	31

Physical; Activity	
1. Physical Activity	49
2. Variety	31

Material	
1. Advancement	31
2. Economic Rewards	26
3. Economic Security	35
4. Prestige	33
5. Autonomy	49
6. Life Style	31

Checked that she was dissatisfied with her status as a student, occupational, leisure, and community.

On the Adult Career Concerns Inventory she was high on the exploration and implementation stages.

On the Myers-Briggs Type Indicator, she was ESFP.

Self-Directed Search SEC

Self-Concept

Self-Esteem Inventory

		Raw Score	%	Standard Score Percentile
1. (32)	Total	27	63	56
2. (16)	General	15	78	59
3. (8)	Social	7	51	53
4. (8)	Personal	5	50	51

a. How would you describe Salinda's personality?

b. What additional tests would you like to have Salinda take?

     c.   What other types of information would you like to have to enhance your interpretation of the results?

     d.   How would you present the test results to Salinda? What would you tell her?

     e.   Would it make a difference in your interpretation if Salinda was Native American, Asian, Hispanic, or Caucasian?

     f.   Would your interpretation be different if Salinda was seeking career counseling? personal counseling?

ADDITIONAL READINGS

American Psychiatric Association. (1994). *Diagnostic and statistical manual of mental disorders* (4th ed.). Washington, DC: Author.

The manual provides the description of criteria and codes for psychiatric diagnostic classification.

Butcher, J. N. (1990). *MMPI–2 in psychological treatment*. New York: Oxford.

The author discusses the use of the MMPI in psychological treatment selection and planning.

Graham, J. R. (1990). *MMPI–2: Assessing personality in psychopathology*. New York: Oxford.

The book is a guide to the revised MMPI–2 and discusses the new validity and content scales.

Gross, M. (1962). *The brain watchers*. New York: Random House.

The author tells of some of the misuses of personality testing and even discusses how to cheat on personality tests.

Groth-Marnat, G. (1990). *Handbook of psychological assessment* (2nd ed.). New York: Van Nostrand Reinhold.

The book contains chapters on the interpretation of projective drawings, the Thematic Apperception Test, the Rorschach, the MMPI, and the California Psychological Inventory.

The author presents information on the history and development of the tests, their reliability and validity, their assets and limitations, interpretation procedures, and a bibliography of references and resources on each test.

Kline, P. (1993). *The handbook of psychological testing*. New York: Routledge.

The author reviews psychometric theory and methods and discusses the major types of tests. He presents information on the uses of tests and provides a description and evaluation of some of the major instruments.

Newmark, C. S. (Ed.). (1985). *Major psychological assessment instruments*. Boston: Allyn and Bacon.

The book contains chapters on the MMPI, Rorschach, Thematic Apperception Test, House-Person-Tree Test, Draw-A-Person, and Bender Gestalt Test along with chapters on the Kaufmann and Wechsler scales. This is an excellent source on current research, use, and interpretation of these tests.

Rabin, A. I. (Ed.). (1986). *Projective techniques for adolescents and children*. New York: Springer.

The text has chapters on the major projective personality tests used with children such as the Thematic Apperception Test, Michigan Picture Test–Revised, Separation Anxiety Test, Rorschach, Hand Test, Story and Sentence Completion Tests.

Reilley, R. R., & Reilley, B. A. (1991). *MMPI–2 tutorial workbook*. Austin, TX: Pro-Ed.

The workbook contains information on the revised test and is designed for professionals who desire a refresher in the appropriate use of the test. Topics such as computer assessment, report writing, psychometric scaling, and source of information on the MMPI–2 are presented.

Wylie, R. (1990). *Self-concept instruments*. Lincoln, NB: University of Nebraska Press.

CHAPTER 12

Assessment of Adjustment

Overview

Tests are used as a part of the clinical assessment or in individual counseling. In both instances the tests are individualized and given one-to-one. The setting may be in a hospital, mental health clinic, prison, treatment facility, or counselor's office. A wide variety of tests and assessment procedures may be used. A number of problems and issues relate to the use of tests for clinical assessment and counseling.

Objectives

The chapter should help the reader become aware of

- the models of measuring adjustment
- types of tests and techniques that can be utilized effectively
- the ethical standards, legal issues, and standards that need to be followed
- the issues and concerns about the use of tests in clinical assessment and counseling

---

CLINICAL ASSESSMENT

Clinical assessment is the process that counselors and psychologists use to gain information about a client. The examiner is often interested in diagnosing the problems of a client and may also want to describe the client's behavior, predict future behavior, or evaluate therapeutic interventions (Korchin & Schuldberg, 1981). Tests and assessment procedures are selected to provide information useful in decision making while taking into account the special background and characteristics of the client. The client may be a child, adolescent, or adult; a patient in a clinic or hospital; an inmate in a prison; or an outpatient in a clinic.

Types of Tests and Assessment Techniques

A wide variety of tests and assessment techniques is used. The choice is influenced partly by the theoretical orientation of the counselor and partly by the type of decision to be made. In most cases the counselor uses more than one technique, choosing among aptitude batteries, ability tests, personality tests, projective techniques, interview schedules, checklists, rating scales, and behavioral observations in natural or contrived situations. Possible reasons for appraisal are these.

1. To determine which DSM IV classification is appropriate
2. To see whether neurological impairment exists
3. To help decide which type of treatment, counseling, or therapy would be most appropriate
4. To prescribe the proper instructional strategies
5. To identify the client's assets, achievement, aptitude, or personality to guide in rehabilitative, therapeutic, or educational planning
6. To determine whether an inmate should be considered for a release program
7. To evaluate the effectiveness of treatment, counseling interventions, and group sessions

Models of Clinical Assessment

One popular model of clinical assessment is the psychodiagnostic model influenced by the theories of Murray and Rapaport. The model is holistic and is intended to describe the client in a variety of ways. The model calls for the use of a number of procedures, the measurement of various areas of psychological functioning, assessment of conscious as well as unconscious levels, use of projective techniques as well as objective personality instruments, interpretation based on scorable responses and symbolic signs, and a description more personal and individualistic than normative (Holt, 1968).

The counselor or psychologist is the key individual in this processes and has to organize and conceptualize the questions to be asked and decide on techniques. Clinical judgment is crucial.

A second model is psychometric and emphasizes more objective use of tests and assessment instruments. Tests must be reliable and valid for the purposes identified; the test findings rely on the criterion validity of the tests rather than the clinical judgment of the examiner. The two positions have been in contention for several decades and are part of the controversy between clinical and statistical prediction (Meehl, 1954).

Rogers (1942) believed that assessment results were not that valuable. He argued against formal assessment, believing that no discovery about a client makes any difference in psychotherapy until the information becomes evident to the client in the course of the therapeutic encounter. Individuals holding to the humanistic approach do not use tests routinely or as a precondition to therapy. If used, the testing process includes the client as a coassessor, rather than an object being studied by a detached examiner. Behavioral psychologists and counselors look for objective behavioral indicators, not tests, to measure traits, drives, motives, and unconscious wishes.

Standards for the Clinical Use of Tests

Standards for Educational and Psychological Testing lists standards that should be considered when using clinical tests. These standards are important because clinicians deal not only with the diagnostic use of tests but also with the prediction of behavior and response to treatment.

A number of standards relate to the validity of tests and test interpretations. Even though a test is used for clinical purposes, the examiner must still be constrained by the same need for criterion-referenced evidence of validity that exists with other test uses.

The standards also call for the protection of client rights. The counselor or psychologist is expected to share with clients the test results and the interpretations, as well as information about the range of error for interpretations when such information would be beneficial to the client. The sharing of information is to be in words that clients can understand.

TESTS IN COUNSELING

Many counselors use tests as a tool in working with their counselees. Research has shown that standardized tests can be a valuable part of the counseling process.

Counselors tend to use tests to help their clients learn more about their own

1. occupational or work values
2. career goals and vocational interests
3. career development
4. occupational knowledge and preferences
5. educational interests
6. achievement, aptitude, and abilities
7. problem-solving and coping skills

8. study skills
9. relationships with others
10. attitudes and motives
11. developmental needs
12. attitudes toward family, spouse, marriage, and significant others

Techniques

Counselors use all of the different types of tests and techniques listed in Chapters 6 through 11. They use both formal and informal methods—pencil-and-paper inventories, projective techniques, checklists, situational tests, interviews, simulations, inventories, and work samples. For tests to be an effective tool in counseling, counselors need to be skilled in helping their clients understand and interpret the results. Counselors need to be able to facilitate the appropriate use of the data in decision making. Counselors use tests in all types of settings such as agencies, government, industry, private practice, and schools. Test use is influenced by setting as well as the background of the counselor and the test taker.

Standards for Use of Tests in Counseling

Professional standards provide guidelines for the use of tests in counseling. Counselors are responsible for reviewing the following items.

1. Interpretive material provided to the test taker, to check for accuracy, clarity, and usefulness

Counselors use a wide variety of tests in clinical assessment.

2. Technical data, to see if separate norms should be used for males or females (an extremely important step with interest tests and an aid in discussing prior test scores and assessing the accuracy of current scores)

3. Manual, to determine the rationale for the specific combination of tests used and the justification of the interpretive relationships among the scores

4. Distributions of scores by gender, race, and ethnic group (pp. 56–58)

The counselor is also to caution the client not to rely solely on the test results but to consider other test scores, observations, and other relevant information on personal and social skills, values, interests, accomplishments, and experiences. The counselor is further to encourage multiple valid assessments of the client's abilities, interests, and personality. The counselor should look at school or work performance, participation in extracurricular activities, and hobbies. The counselor should also be sure that interpretive materials and illustrations are made relevant to the client.

CURRENT TRENDS

Korchin and Schuldberg (1981) report that there is a decline in the use of clinical testing for a variety of reasons.

Many new roles are available for the clinician such as therapy, administration, teaching, research, and community programs. Several schools of psychology and counseling are opposed to testing, and questions regarding the reliability and practicality of traditional clinical practices have been raised, and research has not supported the value of testing.

Changes also have occurred in graduate programs at universities, and testing courses are not considered as valuable as they once were. Also, problems in testing methods have occurred when the clinician assumes a secondary and passive role.

Many issues, such as invasion of privacy, have been raised concerning the use of psychological tests. The reactions to the process many times have been negative because of the cost in time and money.

BEHAVIORAL ASSESSMENT

Behavioral assessment centers on the circumstances of behavior rather than the reasons for it. The process relies greatly on observation, especially observation that requires few inferences on the part of the observer. Sometimes clients are required to keep a log of their behavior. Counselors use behavioral assessment in naturalistic and contrived settings, role playing, psychodrama, and interviews. Behavioral assessment is also used in a number of different ways, such as screening, identifying a problem, designing the intervention, monitoring progress, following up, and evaluating cases. A number of strategies are utilized. Counselors sometimes use interviewing techniques, behavior checklists, observational schedules, self-monitoring procedures, simulation and analogue methods, physiological assessment, and computer-assisted assessment (Ollendick & Greene, 1990).

Behavioral Observation

One of the major methods of behavioral assessment is observation, normally of a specific, observable set of behaviors. Observations can be carried out in different contexts and environments, but a number of factors should be considered.

1. Observers should be familiar with the behavioral categories to be studied.
2. Observers should have been trained to use video tapes, films and other audio-visual equipment.
3. Observers should have a chance to check their observations with other raters and with the standards established in the training sessions (Ollendick & Greene, 1990; Haynes, 1990).

Several problem areas relate to this technique. First is the problem of reactivity. If the client knows he is being observed, his behavior may be quite different from when he is unaware of it. People want to play roles and put themselves in a good light. Second, when an observer has to assess a number of individuals over time, fatigue and boredom may occur. In addition, observers may have some unconscious or conscious biases that interfere with objective results. Observer expectations can also influence client behavior.

Two major types of observation are participant and nonparticipant. A group leader responsible for conducting a group but also monitoring the behaviors of individuals in the group is an example of participant observation (Haynes, 1990). In nonparticipant observation the observer does not become a part of the situation. For example, a teacher on playground duty might be able to observe a certain student without her knowing she is being observed, thereby eliminating the problem of reactivity.

Observation can be highly structured. When time sampling is a part of the system, every so often the observer might classify the behavior taking place and record the person responsible for it. The procedures for coding can be simple, requiring just a check by a category, or complex, demanding analysis. Unstructured observation might describe or identify the following components:

1. purpose and object of the observation
2. physical environment
3. acts or events that have taken place
4. time dimensions
5. actors or people observed
6. goals of the persons observed
7. feelings of the observer

Students of ethnographic observation follow outlines like this when they are observing. They are interested in naturalistic observation and do not usually have preconceived theories or set observational schedules to follow.

Self-Monitoring

Self-monitoring is a widely used technique in behavioral assessment. It can be used effectively as a therapeutic technique or simply as a data-collecting device to assess low-rate behaviors such as migraine headaches, high-rate or continuous behaviors such as blood pressure, and other behaviors such as eating patterns, smoking, caffeine intake, and the like. It is a reactive type of measurement technique because attention is focused on the targeted behavior, and the individual knows what events are to be observed. It is a valuable strategy to provide accurate information to workers in the helping professions, and it can provide client reinforcement and feedback. The success of the technique depends on the goals of the monitoring, the quality of the instructions given, and the number of behaviors being monitored. The accuracy of this method depends on the motivation and cooperation of the client. A number of recording devices can be used—for example, pocket diaries, golf counters, tape recorders, and phone-answering devices. When using self-monitoring with a client, the counselor should follow these procedures.

1. Give explicit definitions and examples of the targeted events and explain their possible relevance to the problem at hand.
2. Give explicit monitoring instructions on how to record the behavior.
3. Illustrate the use of the form or recording device and provide practice exercises.
4. Ask the client to repeat the target definitions and self-monitoring instructions.
5. Test client understanding of the assignment.
6. Check with the client during the period specified for any questions or problems.

Simulation and Analogue Methods

Often a counselor wants to find out what a person might do in a given situation, testing a hypothesis before the situation develops in reality. This procedure can be used as an evaluation tool to see whether training has had an effect. It also is a means of giving individuals a chance to rehearse or practice a needed skill as well as a non-threatening technique in the therapeutic process. Role playing is often used to evaluate the client's social skills (Haynes, 1990). The procedures are these.

Analyze the task the client is to do.

Develop realistic situations.

Provide role-playing opportunities.

The technique has the advantage of helping clients distinguish between the form and functions of the behaviors being assessed. It also allows the counselor to assess performance in highly personal and intimate situations, and it can provide a more flexible and individualized assessment.

ASSESSMENT APPROACHES

Inventories Used in Assessment

A number of inventories are widely used for assessing individuals in the mental health field. Millon has developed several instruments including the Millon Clinical Multiaxial Inventory (MCMI-II) which is used to assess the DSM-III categories of personality disorders and clinical syndromes. The inventory uses 20 clinical scales, divided into three categories.

Basic Personality Patterns (DSM-IV/Axis II)

1. schizoid (asocial)
2. avoidant
3. dependent (submissive)
4. histrionic (gregarious)
5. narcissistic
6. antisocial (aggressive)
7. compulsive (conforming)
8. passive-aggressive (negativistic)

Pathological Personality Disorders

S = schizotypal (schizoid)
C = borderline (cycloid)
P = paranoid

Clinical Symptom Syndromes (DSM-III/Axis I)

A = anxiety	B = alcohol abuse	PP = psychotic delusions
H = somatoform	T = drug abuse	CC = psychotic depression
N = hypomanic	SS = psychotic thinking	D = dysthymic

The MCMI-II has two validity indicators. The W-Weight factor is a scale that suppresses the distorting effects of either psychological defensiveness and self-enhancement or emotional complaining and self-depreciation. The V-Validity index is a scale that detects those who fail to cooperate, are unable to comprehend the items, or are too disturbed to answer the items relevantly.

Two computerized interpretations are available from the National Computer Systems and MICROTEST assessment software. The first is a clinical interpretative report that includes the profile of the client and a detailed narrative explaining the psychodynamic relationship between the client's personality patterns of behaving and feeling and the clinical symptoms he may be exhibiting (Millon & Davis, 1995).

The second is the correctional interpretive report that distinguishes the enduring personality characteristics from the more acute maladaptive symptoms. The report focuses on difficulties the client may have in adjusting to imprisonment, his or her trustworthiness, problems with authority, and general antisocial behavioral tendencies. The report provides implications for management and rehabilitation strategies.

The Millon Behavioral Health Inventory (MBHI) is intended to help mental health workers design a comprehensive treatment plan for adult medical patients. The MBHI provides information on the client's basic coping styles, problematic psychosocial attitudes and stressors, and information on attitudes toward treatment intervention. The 20 scales on the MBHI are classified in four areas—basic coping skills, psychogenic attitudes, psychosomatic correlates, and prognostic indexes. The scales under basic coping styles relate to the way the individual reacts to health care personnel, services, and medical regimens. The scales are titled introversive, cooperative, confident, respectful, inhibited, sociable, forceful, and sensitive. The six scales under psychogenic attitudes assess problematic psychosocial attitudes and stressors; they are titled chronic tension, premorbid pessimism, social alienation, recent stress, future despair, and somatic anxiety. The three scales under psychosomatic correlates show the similarities of clients to patients with psychosomatic complications; the scales are titled allergic inclination, cardiovascular tendency, and gastrointestinal susceptibility. The three prognostic indexes identify possible treatment problems or difficulties—pain treatment responsivity, life threat reactivity, and emotional vulnerability. The total test consists of 150 true-false items and is written at the eighth-grade reading level.

The Millon Adolescent Personality Inventory (MAPI) is geared to assess the specific concerns and behaviors of adolescents. The MAPI provides information on the social functioning of adolescents, including information on their relationships with family and peers, their self-esteem, impulse control, and social tolerance. The 22 scales are grouped under four categories—personality styles, expressed concern, behavioral correlates, and reliability and validity indexes. Here are some items similar to those asked on this test.

T F   I like to be with people who go to church regularly.

T F   I feel tense when I think of what I will be expected to do in school this year.

T F   I worry about my drug habits getting out of control.

Two types of report forms are used, one for clinical use and the other for educational or guidance use.

The Clinical Analysis Questionnaire (CAQ) (Krug, 1980) is designed to measure both normal and pathological traits and provides a multidimensional profile of the client. The test has 28 scales, 16 of which measure normal personality traits included on the Sixteen Personality Factor Questionnaire, 7 of which measure various primary aspects of depression, and 5 of which measure factors identified in the Minnesota Multiphasic Personality Inventory pool. The clinical scales are hypochondriasis, suicidal depression, agitation, anxious depression, low-energy depression, boredom and withdrawal, paranoia, psychopathic deviation, psychasthenia, and psychological inadequacy. The test can be administered to individuals 16 and older; it has an average reading level of 6.7. A number of second-order factors can be scored by the equations developed through factor analysis—extroversion, anxiety, tough poise, independence, superego, socialization, depression, psychoticism, and neuroticism. The test belongs to the family of factorial-derived tests discussed in the chapter on personality testing.

The Personal Assessment Inventory (PAI) is a 344-item, self-administered, objective inventory used to assess critical clinical aspects of personality. The PAI has 22 nonoverlapping full scales, 4 validity scales, and 11 clinical scales. The clinical scales measure somatic complaints, anxiety, anxiety related-disorders, depression, mania, paranoia, schizophrenia, borderline features, antisocial features, alcohol problems, and drug problems. The treatment scales involve aggression, suicidal ideation, stress, nonsupport, and treatment rejection. The validity scales cover inconsistency, infrequency, negative impression, and positive impression. A short form of the PAI consists of the first 160 items.

The Adolescent Multiphasic Personality Inventory (AMPI) is an MMPI test for adolescents (ages 10 to 19) and has a fourth-grade reading level. The AMPI has 133 items and scales that are parallel to the MMPI.

The Child and Adolescent Diagnostic Scales are self-report tests that can be scored and profiled in five minutes and take about 15 minutes to take. These scales measure DSM-IV dimensions such as attention deficit, hyperactivity disorder, oppositional defiant disorders, overanxious disorders, identity disorders, eating disorders, substance abuse disorders, and so on.

A number of other personality assessment inventories might be useful to mental health counselors such as the Beck Depression Inventory, Beck Anxiety Inventory, Beck Hopelessness Scale, Brief Symptoms Inventory, DSM-IV Multiaxial Evaluation, Global Assessment of Functioning, Reynolds Adolescent Depression Scale, State-Trait Anxiety Inventory, Suicidal Ideation Questionnaire, Rust Inventory of Schizotypical Cognitions, Self-Description Questionnaire, Therapeutic Reaction Scale, Eating Inventory, and Analysis of Coping Style.

Psychodiagnostic Testing

Clinicians quite often have been trained to use and interpret certain classic tests in the field such as the Wechsler tests, the Rorschach, Thematic Apperception Test (TAT), Sentence Completion, Bender Visual Motor Gestalt Test, and Minnesota Multiphasic Personality Inventory (MMPI). Katz (1985) identifies the best tools for assessing different diagnostic categories as follows.

Mentally Retarded—Wechsler Tests, Bender Gestalt, Draw-a-Person (DAP)

Brain Damaged—Wechsler Tests, Bender Gestalt, and specialized tests

Psychotic—Rorschach, MMPI-II, TAT, history

Neurotics—MMPI, Rorschach, TAT, DAP

Sociopathic—TAT, behavior, MMPI

Passive Aggressive—TAT, behavior, sentence completion

Schizoid—Rorschach, TAT, DAP, MMPI-II (p. 118)

Katz looks for patterns when he analyzes the test results. For psychotic individuals he might find withdrawn or disturbed behavior exhibited on a test battery. The Wechsler Adult Intelligence Scale (WAIS-R) might show variation or disturbed and odd thinking. On the MMPI-II, the client might score high on the schizophrenia, paranoia, and psychasthenia scales. On the sentence completion test the sentences will show confused, illogical, and bizarre patterns. The TAT might reveal odd elements, bizarre twists, and possible anguish.

Kellerman and Burry (1991) recommend that the data gained through observation, interviewing, and testing be combined to complete the diagnosis. The crucial elements in determining treatment are the individual's level of intellectual functioning, nature of their anxiety, defensive structures, self-image, self-esteem, sexual identity, and the balance between impulse and control.

Neuropsychological Assessment Batteries

Neuropsychological assessment refers to testing for brain damage or for organicity (Goldstein, 1984). Such tests are sensitive to the condition of the brain. Brain damage most often affects the cognitive functions, such as memory. Some individuals might show loss of speed in performing skilled activities or psychomotor or perceptual-motor activities. Some have deficits in auditory or tactile perception. Others have problems with visual-spatial skills.

One of the most widely used instruments for neuropsychological assessment is the Halstead-Reitan battery. This test utilizes Wechsler intelligence scales, but also includes a number of tests utilized originally by Halstead, some added by Reitan, and several added by others. Some tests within the battery call for tactual performance. For example, the Halstead Tactual Performance Test uses the Seguin-Goddard formboard, but the test taker is blindfolded and has to place all 10 blocks into the formboard using only a sense of touch. The test taker has to do this three times—first, with the preferred hand, then the other, and finally with both hands. On the Klove Roughness Discrimination Test the test taker must order four blocks, each covered with a different grade of sandpaper. The blocks are presented behind a blind, and the test is scored on the time the client takes and the number of errors made with each hand.

Also included in the Halstead-Reitan Battery are visual and psychomotor scales. For example, the Reitan Aphasia Screening Test contains both language and copying tasks. The copying tasks require the test taker to make a copy of a square, Greek cross, a triangle, and a key. The language functions measured are naming, repetition, spelling, reading, writing, calculation, narrative speech, and left-right orientation. The language section is scored by listing the number of aphasic symptoms. The Klove Grooved Pegboard Test requires the test taker to place pegs shaped like keys into a board containing recesses oriented in randomly varying directions. The test taker performs first with one hand and then the other. Some of the other tests on the scale are the Halstead Category Test, the Speech Perception Test, the Seashore Rhythm Test, Finger Tapping, Trail Making Test, Perceptual Disorders, and the Visual Field Examination. The battery takes 6 to 8 hours to administer.

Another widely used battery is the Lauria-Nebraska Neuropsychological Battery. The test has 11 content scales.

1. Motor measures a wide variety of motor skills.
2. Rhythm measures nonverbal auditory perception, such as pitch discrimination and rhythmic patterns.
3. Tactile measures tactual discrimination and recognition.
4. Vision measures visual-perceptual and visual-spatial skills.
5. Receptive speech measures perception of sounds from simple to complex.
6. Expressive speech measures ability to repeat sounds, words, word groups, and to produce narrative speech.
7. Writing measures ability to analyze words into letters and to write under varying conditions.
8. Reading measures ability to make letter-to-sound transformations and to read simple material.
9. Arithmetic measures knowledge of numbers, number concepts, and ability to perform simple calculations.
10. Memory measures short-term memory and paired associate learning.
11. Intellectual processes measures sequencing, problem solving, and abstraction skills.

The test is shorter than the Halstead-Reitan and helps screen a large number of areas that may be affected by brain damage.

INTERVIEWS

The interview, especially the structured interview, has become an important tool in clinical assessment. The DSM-IV provides a structured guidebook. In addition to the verbal content of the interview, a clinician is often interested in a client's nonverbal behavior or cognitive style. Currently, more attention is being placed on the cognitive areas for knowing and understanding a client.

Structured interviews call for the interviewer to ask each interviewee exactly the same questions in the same manner. A specific set of questions is usually read to the client. Unstructured interviews, on the other hand, do not have a specific plan or order in which the topics are presented. Many examiners believe the best rapport is established when they use words familiar to clients and topics the clients are willing to discuss (Wiens, 1990). Consequently, the same set of questions might not be asked, and the interviewer might use more open-ended questions such as "Tell me about yourself." The advantages of the structured interview are that it assures that specific information will be collected from all clients and it does not require as much training because all interviewers have a list of questions in a prescribed order. The advantages of the unstructured interview are that it gives the interviewee a chance to determine what is important to talk about; it allows the examiner to pursue important but unanticipated topics; and it provides an opportunity to judge the interviewee's behavior in an unstructured situation.

Computerized versions of structured interviews are available. The Structured Clinical Interview for the DSM-IV provides several report options, helps clinicians screen clients on axis 1 in approximately 25 minutes, and covers areas such as mood disorders, anxiety disorders, psychoactive substance abuse disorders, somatoform disorders, eating disorders, and psychotic symptoms. A sample structured interview schedule, appropriate for use in an alcoholic treatment facility, is included in Figure 12.1.

Certain general guidelines should be considered before and during an interview.

1. Have a clear idea of why the individual is being interviewed. The kinds of questions asked depend on the types of inferences, decisions, or descriptions to be made after the interview. Better information results from specific goals.

2. Be concerned about the physical setting or environment for the interview. Interviews will go better if the environment is quiet and comfortable. If the room is noisy or has poor lighting, it may detract from the quality of the information gained. Comfortable and private facilities permit the client to relax without the confidentiality and privacy of the interview being threatened.

3. Establish rapport with the interviewee. Good rapport leads the interviewee to be cooperative and motivated.

4. Be alert to the nonverbal as well as verbal behavior of the client. How a person says something may be as important as what is said.

5. Be in charge and keep the goals of the interview in mind. Have the interview schedule readily available but do not suggest answers. Give the client time to answer and do not become impatient during periods of silence.

Psychiatric Interviews

Workers in the helping professions consider the interview one of the most important technical instruments to find out about individuals and their social functioning. The purpose of the psychiatric interview is to help provide information to guide diagno-

```
Name_____  Date _____
Address_____  Home phone _____
_____  Business phone _____
City_____ State _____ Zip _____
Race_____ Sex _____ Height_____ Weight _____ Age _____
Date of birth _____  Place of birth_____
Next of kin_____  Relationship_____
Address _____
Current employment_____ Duration _____ Salary _____
Spouse's employment _____
Other sources of income _____
Referred by _____
Health insurance _____
Current marital status _____ Number of marriages and duration _____
_____
Children (sex and ages) _____
Type of residence_____
Number in household_____ Head of household _____
Church membership_____ Attendance _____
Belief in higher power _____
_____
Current health problems _____
Physical handicaps _____
Serious illness/surgery _____
_____
Current medications _____
Schools attended _____
Years_____ Certificates/diplomas/degrees _____
_____
Vocational and technical training _____
Military service: _____
Army _____ Navy _____ Air Force _____ Marines _____ Coast Guard _____
Length of service _____ Rank_____ Type of discharge _____
VA history_____
Employment history:
Job description              Dates                    Reasons for leaving
_____
_____
Family history:
Brothers _____Sisters _____Birth order _____
Type of family structure _____
Father's occupation _____Mother's occupation _____
Description of mother _____
Description of father _____
Description of home life _____
_____
History of drug abuse in family _____
```

Figure 12.1
Outline of a structured psychosocial interview

Family's attitude toward substance abuse _____
_____
Current relationships with parents _____
Current relationships with siblings _____
Current relationship with spouse_____
Current relationships with children _____
Criminal justice record:
Number of arrests _____
Types _____
Number of convictions _____
Number and duration of times in jail_____
Number and duration of times in prison_____
Number of times on probation or parole _____
Cases/warrants pending_____
Current probation officer_____
Current legal status _____
Alcohol and substance abuse information:
Number of times in detoxification centers _____ Mental hospitals and/or state
hospitals _____ Jail (for substance-abuse-related offenses) _____ Hospital
(for medical attention) _____ Shelters (such as Salvation Army) _____
Dates of DWI convictions _____
History of drug use:
Age of first use _____ Substances tried _____
First contact_____ First drinking experience _____
First intoxication _____ First blackout _____ Convulsions _____
Morning tremors_____ Hallucinations _____ DTs_____ Fights _____
Personality change _____
Substances regularly used_____
_____ Choice _____
Frequency of use _____
Attempts to stop substance abuse _____
_____
Support groups attended _____
Pattern of substance abuse:
Daily _____ Weekends_____ Periodic _____ Alone _____ Bars_____ Friends _____
Use in 24-hour period:
At present _____ Substances_____
At peak _____ Substances_____
Date of last drug/substance abuse and amount_____
Overdoses, withdrawals, or adverse reactions _____
_____
Attempted suicides _____
Problems caused by substance abuse:
Job _____
Family_____
Finances _____
Health_____
Sex _____
Loss of control _____

sis and selection of a treatment plan. The questions are designed to elicit information from the physical, psychological, biochemical, anatomical, social, emotional, family, and educational aspects of a client's life (Beutler, 1995). The following areas are usually included in the interview schedule.

1. *Demographic information*—This information includes the age, sex, educational level, marital status, number of children, and employment of the client.

2. *Chief complaint*—The chief complaint should be recorded in the client's exact words. Sometimes individuals feel that there is nothing wrong with them, but their wives or husbands are sick and need to be receiving treatment.

3. *Present illness and medical history*—It is important to ascertain the background factors related to the client's present illness.

4. *Past psychiatric history*—Any information on the client's past illnesses should be recorded, including the types of disorder, any precipitating factors, and the steps that were taken in treatment.

5. *Mental status*—Any information on the client's appearance, cognitive functioning, affect, moods, and interpersonal style is helpful.

6. *Personal and social history*—The information itself is important, but the way the client presents it also gives the interviewer a look at how the client speaks, thinks, feels, and evaluates situations. The interviewer tries to get a complete family history, including short sketches of the individual's parents, siblings, and other relatives. All dimensions of the client's personal history are important.

Psychological Case Study

The interview is a key component of a psychological case study, which Bromley (1986) defines as an account of a person in a situation, focusing on a relatively short, self-contained part of an individual's life and the unique aspects of that individual's personality. The purpose of the case study technique is to find a solution to the client's problem by looking at how and why a client acted as he did in a given situation. Case studies can refer to many situations and environments—for example, a case study of a business organization. In this text, however, case study refers to a reconstruction and interpretation of a major episode in a client's life.

Case studies are conducted in a context that guides the investigator in what procedures should be used and what end results should be accomplished. For example, the investigator might be concerned about whether a person should be placed on probation or whether a client should seek divorce. Bromley (1986) lists six basic rules in preparation for conducting a case study.

1. Be sure that facts and details are accurate.

2. Have a clear idea of the aims and objectives of the study explicitly and unambiguously stated.

3. Assess the degree to which the stated aims and objectives have been accomplished.

4. Receive training in the case study method and establish rapport and a good working relationship with the client.

5. View the client in an ecological perspective—objects, persons, and events are interpreted in terms of the individual's physical, social, and symbolic environment. Remember, the case study is undertaken because the personal qualities of the client are unusual, or the psychological and situational circumstances are unusual, or both.

6. Be able to write in a good clear manner, direct and objective but not disinterested. (p. 24)

No set formats exist of how to write the psychological case study, but Bromley (1986) identified 14 items to be included.

1. Demographic information about the client and a description of physical appearance

2. Lifestyle and history of the client, including routine activities, material possessions, physical health, and important life events

3. Psychological makeup of the client—attitudes, abilities, motivations, self-concept, and so on

4. Social history of the client—social role and status, social relationships, family, friendships, and loyalties

5. Moral and ethical standards of the client relative to the case

6. The client's problem under investigation in the case study

7. An account of the evidence and arguments related to the analysis of the case study

8. A detailed description of any issue that falls beyond the normal range of events

9. A review of the evidence and arguments in relation to the conclusions and recommendations made

10. A summary of the methods and procedures utilized in conducting the case study and a reminder of the context of the study, the conditions that gave rise to it, and the factors affecting any future course of the study

11. A statement of any reservations, implications, or comments important to the case

12. A title and an abstract

13. Summary and conclusion sections that include a brief statement of the problem; the methods used to study the problem; the main findings; and the conclusions, recommendations, and predictions

14. A list of references and sources used and acknowledgments (p. 28)

The investigator must keep in mind the reasons for conducting the case study and guard against one-sided points of view. Team approaches and case conferences enhance eliciting different points of view. The investigator must also be mindful of the target of the case study. Self-analysis is often doubly valuable. It gives the investigator insight into how the individual perceives himself and may lead the client to better self-understanding. The investigator should avoid merely cataloging behavior and personality characteristics. Human behavior is an interaction between personal characteristics and situational factors, and the case study should provide some general conclusions about the client.

Interviewing Children and Adolescents

A number of specific interview schedules are designed for use with children and adolescents. The Interview Schedule for Children (Kovacs, 1982) is a widely used interview schedule for children aged 8 to 17. The schedule takes about 40 to 60 minutes to administer, after which the interviewer rates the symptoms from the information given in the child's responses.

Another scale is the Child Assessment Schedule (Hodges, Kline, Stern, Cytryn, & Kline, 1982). It includes questions about school, friends, activities, family, fears, worries, self-image, mood, somatic concerns, expressions of anger, and thought disorder and also has questions on delusions, hallucinations, and related symptoms. The schedule has been useful in detecting psychopathology in children.

WELLNESS

The theme for 1991 for AACD (now ACA) was wellness. Wellness looks at the total person, and Hettler's model includes six dimensions—physical, spiritual, emotional, social, intellectual, and occupational. One of the most popular instruments is the Lifestyle Assessment Questionnaire. The LAQ evaluates an individual's habits and knowledge in a wide range of health and wellness dimensions. Eleven questions are in the personal data section. Section 2 concerns lifestyles and has questions on physical exercise, nutrition, and spiritual dimensions of the individual's life. Section 3 is a health risk appraisal, and Section 4 has individuals rate topics for personal growth. A computerized report form is available, and the instrument is also produced on interactive software. The report to the client is entitled Making Wellness Work for You and provides suggestions on how the client can make positive lifestyle changes.

PITFALLS

Fisher (1985) reminds professionals involved in assessment in the mental health field to look carefully at counterproductive behaviors.

1. *Being too sociable or following the "nice-guy" syndrome*—Some examiners are more concerned with being liked than being objective and professional in their tasks.

2. *Being collusive or aloof*—the other end of the scale.

3. *Being a technician*—Some examiners put more emphasis on the procedures and the techniques than on looking at the person as a whole.

4. *Being a rescuer*—Some examiners rush to the rescue of their clients (also called the doctor syndrome).

5. *Being an opponent*—Some examiners act as though they and their clients are on opposite sides.

SUMMARY

A wide variety of assessment models and techniques is used to assess adjustment of clients. Workers in clinical and counseling contexts use tests for a wide variety of purposes. Although the use of clinical testing has declined, many new techniques have been utilized in measuring and evaluating clients. Behavioral assessment techniques such as self-monitoring, behavioral observation, and the use of simulation have been widely used in the field because they center on evaluating actual behavior in naturalistic situations.

Several new instruments and techniques, as well as renewed interest in the classical testing procedures, have resulted from computer scoring and interpretation procedures. Neuropsychological testing has been developed to identify brain damage or organicity. Traditional techniques such as the interview and case study are primary tools of workers in the helping professions.

QUESTIONS FOR DISCUSSION

1. What do you believe the role of testing should be in a mental health setting? What should the goals and objectives be for testing in this context? Some clinicians are opposed to any type of testing in this field. Why do you agree or disagree with their position?

2. What are the advantages and disadvantages of using behavioral assessment techniques? In what types of situations would behavioral assessment procedures be more appropriate than traditional standardized testing?

3. What are the advantages and disadvantages of an interview? What are the different types of interviews and when would you use them? What are the sources of bias operating in the interview and how would you attempt to correct bias in interview situations?

4. What types of interviews are used in the mental health field? What are some of the problems and issues in the use of the interview technique?

5. What are the uses of the case study? What are the advantages and disadvantages of this approach? When would you use case studies in your work?

SUGGESTED ACTIVITIES

1. Interview psychologists and counselors working in the mental health field and find out what tests and assessment procedures they use and why. Report your findings to the class.

2. Critically review a test utilized primarily in mental health settings. Read the reviews of the test in different journals and yearbooks.

3. Design a behavioral assessment instrument and try it out on several individuals. Write an analysis of your experiment.

4. Design an interview schedule and try it out on several individuals. Write an analysis of the results.

5. Critically review a software package used in a mental health setting—for example, a biographic data program or a test interpretive package.

6. Write a review of the literature on a topic such as behavioral assessment, case study approach, use of tests in clinical settings, use of tests in counseling settings, or neuropsychological testing.

7. Make an annotated bibliography of tests utilized in the mental health setting.

8. Study this information about Lawana and answer the questions that follow it.

Lawana is a 16-year-old who has completed her education through grade 10. She says she doesn't have the energy or desire to go anywhere and adds that when she does go out, she feels anxious and scared.

Background information: Lawana's mother is living with a Hispanic and has been married twice—the first time for 11 years, the second for 1½ years. Lawana has two sisters, ages 8 and 12, and an older brother, age 22, who no longer lives with the family. Lawana's mother got pregnant with Lawana during a period of separation from her first husband. Lawana learned about this and maintains regular positive contact with her biological father. She hates her mother's live-in boyfriend, who abuses her when he is drunk. Her mother, who has refused to acknowledge the abuse, believes Lawana's problems are caused by racial prejudice at school. Lawana is earning Bs and Cs in her classes.

Lawana's mother was concerned enough about Lawana's condition to arrange an appointment at the local Mental Health Clinic for Lawana. Lawana was tested with a number of assessment instruments. Her profile follows.

Personal Assessment Inventory

Validity

Inconsistency	52	Infrequency	50
Positive Impression	40	Negative Impression	57

Clinical

Somatic Complaints	55	Anxiety	68
Anxiety-Related Disorders	65	Depression	45
Mania	45	Paranoia	55
Schizophrenia	56	Borderline Features	57
Antisocial Features	48	Alcohol Problems	50
Drug Problems	48		

Treatment

Aggression	55	Suicidal Ideation	62
Stress	62	Nonsupport	58
Treatment Rejection	40		

Interpersonal

| Dominance | 48 | Warmth | 42 |

Beck Anxiety Inventory: 27(severe)

Beck Depression Inventory: 42(moderate)

a. How would you describe her adjustment? (Remember: On the PAI, the mean *T* score is 50 and the SD is 10.)

b. What additional information about Lawana would you like to have?

ADDITIONAL READINGS

Read "The Future of Clinical Assessment" by Jay Ziskin and "Perspectives on the Future of Neuropsychological Assessment" by Raymond Dean in *The Future of Testing*, the second volume in the Buros-Nebraska Symposium on Measurement and Testing, edited by Barbara S. Plake and Joseph C. Witt (1986). The chapters present the current thinking and future projections on testing in these areas.

Several good source books on tests are available for special groups and populations. Pro-Ed has published an interesting assessment series: S. Joseph Weaver edited the volume entitled *Testing Children*; Robert G. Harrington edited a similar volume entitled *Testing Adolescents*; and Dennis P. Swiercinsky's collection is entitled *Testing Adults*. Many chapters are of interest to people working in the mental health field.

Golden, C. J. (1990). *Clinical interpretation of psychological tests* (2nd ed.). Boston: Allyn and Bacon.

The author provides examples of the clinical application of tests such as the Wechsler scales, Wide Range Achievement Test, Peabody Individual Achievement Test, MMPI-II, 16PF, Bender Gestalt, Wechsler Memory Scale, and the Halstead-Reitan Neuropsychological battery.

Katz, L. (1986). *A practical guide to psychodiagnostic testing*. Springfield, IL: Charles C. Thomas.

The author provides practical suggestions on how to conduct psychodiagnostic testing.

CHAPTER 13

Learning Styles

Overview

Learning style is defined as an individual's preferred mode and desired conditions to learn. People differ in how they approach learning. Mann and Sabatino (1985) state that "two individuals with identical IQs, with the same configuration of special abilities, or with exactly the same type and strength of information processing capacities may nevertheless be quite different in the ways that they perceive things, think, solve problems, recall events, come to decisions, play musical instruments, and swing baseball bats" (p. 189).

Assessing learning style has important benefits. It can help us understand how an individual learns and how he perceives, approaches, interacts, and responds to the learning environment (Keefe and Languis, 1983). Dunn, Dunn, and Price (1987) found that when students are taught with approaches and resources that complement their unique learning styles, their achievement is significantly increased and their attitudes are better. Hargrove and Poteet (1984) believe that one of the most neglected aspects of diagnostic activity with exceptional students is the determination of their unique learning styles (p. 10).

Objectives

After studying this chapter, the reader should be able to

- list and explain the purposes and objectives of assessing learning styles

- list the different types of tests to assess learning styles and identify the dimensions they measure
- discuss the issues, trends, and problems in measuring learning styles

PROCESSING STYLE

Processing style, an important component of learning style, can be defined as the individual's method of inputting and outputting information. Input is the reception of sensory information from visual, auditory, or hepatic sources. (Hepatic combines the kinesthetic and tactile stimuli.) Processing involves integrating the information with previously learned information. Individuals store the information in short-term memory and then use a variety of memory strategies to store the information in long-term memory. Output involves using a vocal or motor response to a problem or task.

MODALITY ASSESSMENT

Modalities are the specific sensory or motor abilities that are our pathways to learning. Inghram (1980) states that modality assessment is divided into two types—assessment of acuity and assessment of perception. Assessment of acuity is an attempt to evaluate whether a certain pathway to learning exists. Assessment of perception evaluates the ability to discriminate visually, aurally, tactilely, or kinesthetically to store and recall a stimulus and integrate that stimulus into memory. In summarizing the research on modality preference, Reiff (1992) reports that about 30% will remember what is seen, 30% what is heard, and 30% utilize mixed modalities. The remaining 10% remember kinesthetically. Modality strengths vary with age as the child matures and gains experience; eventually, the modalities blend.

Visual Assessment

Usually perception includes five dimensions, according to Inghram (1980).

1. *Visual discrimination*—the ability to identify differences and similarities in stimuli, such as among letters, numbers, words, or graphic forms
2. *Figure ground*—the ability to locate or identify a figure from a background of irrelevant stimuli, such as finding a certain word on a page
3. *Visual memory*—the ability to recall a sequence of visually presented stimuli, such as letters or numbers
4. *Visual closure*—the ability to make a whole from reduced cues, such as naming an object or scene from an incomplete drawing

5. *Visual motor integration*—the ability to utilize perceived visual stimuli to make body movements more effective and efficient, such as a football player weaving downfield to avoid tackles (pp. 274–275)

Listed here are a number of instruments available to measure both visual acuity and visual perception.

Snellen Eye Chart is used to screen visual acuity.

Keystone Visual Survey Test measures dimensions of visual functioning.

Spache Binocular Reading Test is used to screen a child's visual acuity.

Frostig Developmental Test of Visual Perception measures hand-eye coordination, figure/ground, form constancy, position in space, and spatial relations in children 4 to 8.

Developmental Test of Visual-Motor Integration assesses visual-motor function of children 2 to 15.

Bender Visual Motor Gestalt Test assesses the examinee's ability to reproduce visual stimuli and aids in identifying brain-injured individuals.

Bender Gestalt Test for Young Children is a form of the Bender test for young children.

Memory for Designs Test measures visual perception of individuals 8 and older.

Slosson Drawing Coordination Test is used to diagnose visual-perceptual and visual-motor coordination problems and brain damage.

Metropolitan Readiness Test has a matching and copying subtest.

Detroit Tests of Learning Aptitude measure visual attention to letters and visual discrimination.

Illinois Test of Psycholinguistic Abilities includes subtests on visual closure, visual sequential memory, and visual association.

Visual perceptual difficulties can be informally assessed by observing a client in different contexts. Any of these behaviors might signal trouble.

Holding paper too close to the face

Holding a book too near or too far away

Having poor eye-hand coordination

Stumbling

Being restless, irritable, or nervous when called on to use eyes for close work

Frowning, scowling, and squinting

Blinking eyes frequently

Shutting or covering one eye

Rubbing eyes frequently (Inghram, 1980, p. 281)

Clients with visual perceptual difficulties may complain about different physical problems when they have to use their eyes. They may state they have a hard time reading what is required. Students with visual perception problems may be clumsy in visual motor tasks such as writing, drawing, cutting, and different types of games involving movement and coordination. Such students are easily distracted and are careless about doing assignments sequentially.

Auditory Assessment

The auditory modality has four dimensions.

1. *Auditory discrimination*—the ability of the client to distinguish among sounds, such as the sounds of letters or blends

2. *Sound/ground*—the ability to select an auditory stimulus (e.g., a theme in music) from a background of competing auditory stimuli (e.g., the accompaniment)

3. *Auditory memory*—the ability to recall the sequence of stimuli presented orally, such as following commands and remembering digits

4. *Auditory blending*—the ability to blend distinct sounds into words

Any question about auditory acuity should be referred to an audiologist. A number of standardized measures of auditory acuity can be administered by trained examiners. Examples of some of the auditory assessment instruments are included here.

Wepman Auditory Discrimination Test assesses the ability of children aged 5 to 8 to identify similarities and differences in word pairs.

Goldman-Fristoe-Woodcock Test of Auditory Discrimination assesses skills in auditory discrimination, auditory memory, and sound-symbol associations in individuals aged 3 to 84.

Goldman-Fristoe-Woodcock Auditory Skills Test Battery contains 12 subtests that assess auditory attention, discrimination, memory, and sound-symbol skills in individuals age 3 to 80.

Screening Test for Auditory Perception assesses ability of students in grades 1 to 6 to discriminate types of vowels, consonants, rhyming verses, nonrhyming words, and so on.

Oliphant Auditory Discrimination Memory Test assesses the ability of examinees in grades 1 to 8 to hear and discriminate sounds and words.

Illinois Test of Psycholinguistic Abilities includes subtests on auditory frequency memory and sound blending.

Wechsler Intelligence Scale for Children—Revised and Wechsler Adult Intelligence Scale include a digit span subtest.

Many informal ways of identifying auditory problems are used. If the examinee has problems following directions, asks constantly to have items repeated, is distracted easily by extraneous auditory stimuli, or has pronunciation problems, the individual may have auditory processing problems.

Inghram (1980) identifies seven categories of auditory perception deficits that are included in Table 13.1.

Motor Assessment

An individual can learn through using psychomotor abilities. A number of standardized tests measure different types of sensory motor skills. Sometimes self-concept and academic performance can be improved through development of the individual's motor abilities. Improved coordination may improve participation in sports, games, dancing, and so on. Individuals may become more confident, more accepted, and feel much better about themselves. Some of the tests available in this area are listed here.

Bruininks-Oseretsky Test of Motor Proficiency assesses dimensions such as running speed, agility, balance, bilateral coordination, strength, and upper limb

Table 13.1
Auditory perceptual deficits

Deficit	Characteristic Behavior
Signal/ground	Has difficulty attending to what is said because of the presence of competing noise Has difficulty identifying a sound in its word context
Auditory closure	Cannot supply the missing auditory parts Has trouble in retrieving all that is said
Auditory constancy	Has difficulty in recognizing vowel or word sounds from one day to another Cannot recognize rhyming patterns Does not understand sound families
Sound discrimination	Has difficulty in distinguishing and discriminating between sounds that closely resemble each other
General auditory memory	Has difficulty remembering a sound contained in several different words Has immediate memory and can repeat but may forget the next day
Auditory attention	Is unable to remember something that has just been said by someone else Exhibits poor memory for auditory stimuli and is easily distracted
Sequential auditory memory	Cannot recall appropriate word order to constitute acceptable syntax in a sentence Cannot remember simple instructions Has difficulty in recalling appropriate word order

coordination, and looks at the gross and fine motor coordination of examinees aged 4 to 14.

Devereux Test of Extremity Coordination assesses the level of motor development in children aged 4 to 10.

Lincoln-Oseretsky Motor Development Scale measures 36 motor development tasks in children aged 6 to 14.

Moore Eye-Hand Coordination and Color Matching Test assesses speed of eye-hand movement and ability to match colors in individuals 2 and older.

Primary Visual-Motor Test assesses visual-motor functions in copying geometrical and representative designs in children aged 4 to 8.

Purdue Perceptual-Motor Survey assesses laterality, directionality, and perceptual-motor matching skills in children from preschool to grade 8.

Southern California Sensory Integration Tests measure visual, tactile, and kinesthetic perception as well as motor performance in children aged 4 to 10.

Modality Preference Assessment

Certain tests and assessment instruments can be used to quickly determine the examinee's modality preference. It is important to determine not only effective modalities, but also the modalities that interfere with learning. The Swassing-Barbe Modality Index (Barbe & Swassing, 1979) is used to identify a student's modality strengths. It presents a matching-to-sample task, is individually administered, and takes about 20 minutes. The examiner presents a stimulus sample (circles, triangles, squares, and hearts), and the examinee is asked to reproduce the sample. Testing is conducted with visual, auditory, and tactile stimuli.

The first test in the index is the visual test. The examinee is given several warm-up items and is then shown a set of shapes, beginning with three shapes and ending with nine. The test taker is instructed to assemble the shapes in the sequence just seen. Testing is stopped when the examinee makes errors on two consecutive sets. The second test is an auditory test. The names of shapes are read aloud in sequence at the rate of one per second. The examinee is asked to assemble the sequence of shapes in the sequence just heard. The third test is a kinesthetic test. The examiner holds a shield so that the examinee can feel but cannot see the shapes. Then the examiner removes the shield and asks the examinee to reassemble the shapes in the sequence just felt. Three separate scores are tallied.

COGNITIVE STYLE

Cognitive style is another dimension of learning style. It is the preferred way an individual reacts to environmental stimuli; it is used to describe how individuals differ in organizing and controlling a task. Messick (1989) defines cognitive styles as information processing habits that represent an individual's typical modes of perceiving, thinking, remembering, and problem solving. Witkin (1949) identified two component styles—field dependence and field independence. Field-dependent individuals tend not to restructure situations but to accept them as experiences. They are more attentive to social cues, accept other people readily, and like to be with people. Field-independent people prefer to interpret and restructure their environmental situations. They are less attentive to social cues and prefer to work with ideas and abstract principles. Field-independent individuals are more interested in science and mathematics, like to set their own goals, are more internally oriented, and do not require external reinforcement. Reiff (1992) reports that field-independent individuals are global, benefit from cooperative learning, and need strategies to help organize and comprehend material. Field-independent individuals are analytical, more internally motivated, cognitively flexible, and like independent projects.

Witkin, Moore, Goodenough, and Cox (1977) found that cognitive style is an important factor in academic learning and social behavior. Three of the widely used tests of cognitive style are listed here.

Embedded Figures Test assesses cognitive style in perceptual tasks; it is a 12-item test with cards containing complex and simple figures and requiring the examinee to locate and trace a previously seen simple figure within a larger complex figure.

Group Embedded Figures Test assesses cognitive style through 25 pencil-and-paper items that require individuals to find 1 of 8 simple figures in complex designs.

Children's Embedded Figures Test is a 25-item individually administered test of perceptual process and cognitive style for children aged 5 to 12.

Numerous cognitive styles exist. Kagan (1966) identified the impulsive/reflective style. Examinees with an impulsive style give answers quickly, without thinking through the situation, and often make errors. Reflective examinees are just the opposite. Mann and Sabatino (1985) classify cognitive styles into three general categories.

1. A cognitive style may simply identify particular characteristics or traits that a person possesses in greater or lesser degree, such as authoritarianism.

2. A cognitive style may indicate placement at a particular point on a cognitive personality dimension whose opposite poles indicate opposing cognitive orientations, such as field independence versus field dependence or reflection versus impulsivity.

3. Certain cognitive styles place individuals within a particular cognitive category, such as analytical, categorical, or relational in their thinking. (p. 191)

Some of the cognitive control styles are leveling-sharpening, scanning-focusing, conceptual-differential, constricted-flexible, and field articulation. Leveling-sharpening is defined by Goldstein and Blackman (1978) as representing the characteristic degree to which current precepts and relevant memory traces interact or assimilate in the course or registration of current precepts and memories (p. 8).

Conceptual Tempo

Another popular cognitive construct, conceptual tempo or reflection-impulsivity was studied by Kagan, Rosman, Day, Albert, and Phillips (1964); it relates to the different speeds with which individuals make decisions. Kagan et al. used the Matching Familiar Figures Test to assess reflection-impulsivity. Individuals are presented with 12 pictures and asked to choose the one that most nearly matches a particular picture selected by the examiner. The task requires individuals to scan the alternatives and to make a decision. The time taken to respond is considered a measure of the individual's tendency toward reflection or impulsivity.

Reiff (1992) reports that reflective learners think longer before they answer a question and tend to make fewer errors. They spend time deliberating and analyzing the situation. Impulsive individuals fail to attend to tasks, have difficulty considering quick decisions and alternatives to problems, are less systematic in their information search, produce fewer testable hypotheses, underestimate time intervals, are impatient, and want immediate gratification.

Counselors can help reflective learners by allowing them time to thoroughly examine materials, model risk taking to show error is natural, help them organize proofing of work, provide cooperative learning experiences, and teach them test-taking skills. Impulsive learners can be helped by organizing materials and assignments into smaller components, provide a nondistracting environment, provide explicit guidelines and directions, and structure time into smaller segments (Reiff, 1992).

Brain Preference

Grady (1984) reports that research points toward two hemispheres of the brain. The left hemisphere takes care of linear and sequential operations; the right hemisphere is in charge of simultaneous and visual functions. He concludes that cognitive style is related to hemispheric organization: individuals tend to have a hemispheric preference or dominance (p. 1). Wonder and Donovan (1984) emphasize that the human brain's two halves have different but overlapping skills or ways of thinking. They found individuals with left preferences to be positive, analytical, linear, explicit, sequential, verbal, concrete, rational, active, and goal-oriented. Individuals with right brain preferences were intuitive, spontaneous, emotional, nonverbal, visual, artistic, holistic, playful, diffuse, symbolic, and physical.

According to Gazzaniga (1985) and Sherrod (1985), people tend to prefer one side of the brain over the other, and that preference affects their approach and attitude toward life and work. Sherrod states that an individual's major and minor dominance could serve as a supplemental clue to a career selection. Left-brain-oriented people tend to prefer career fields such as planning, law, editing, technology, writing, and bookkeeping. Right-brain-oriented people tend to prefer roles such as policy-makers, artists, poets, sculptors, politicians, playwrights, and musicians. Two brain preference instruments are identified here.

Your Style of Learning and Thinking (SOLAT) appears in different forms for children, adolescents, and adults and attempts to measure brain preference through

SA	A	D	SD	1.	I prefer to be a listener.
SA	A	D	SD	2.	Daydreaming helps me solve problems.
SA	A	D	SD	3.	I like to do things on the spur of the moment.
SA	A	D	SD	4.	I like to follow my hunches.
SA	A	D	SD	5.	I like to take risks.
SA	A	D	SD	6.	I like to be free to learn without a lot of structure.
SA	A	D	SD	7.	I can express myself well verbally.
SA	A	D	SD	8.	I remember faces easily.
SA	A	D	SD	9.	My mood changes frequently.
SA	A	D	SD	10.	I can remember and sing songs I hear on the radio or TV.
SA	A	D	SD	11.	I like to print when I take notes.
SA	A	D	SD	12.	I like to work in groups.
SA	A	D	SD	13.	I am seldom absentminded.
SA	A	D	SD	14.	I use gestures to express my feelings.
SA	A	D	SD	15.	I prefer hands-on experiences to verbal instructions.
SA	A	D	SD	16.	I like to think before I answer so that I use the right words.
SA	A	D	SD	17.	I can rely on my intuition.
SA	A	D	SD	18.	I can remember and sing lyrics I hear.
SA	A	D	SD	19.	I like to write down the goals and activities I need to accomplish each day.
SA	A	D	SD	20.	I like to learn things by watching how others do them and then imitating.

SA = strongly agree, A = agree, D = disagree, SD = strongly disagree

Figure 13.1
Sample Brain Preference Survey

40 items with three response options per item, one each representing left, right, and integrated ways of functioning.

Brain Preference Indicator uses a 36-item multiple-choice self-report format, with selected options scored for left or right brain preference.

Sample items representative of those often included on such instruments are included in Figure 13.1.

LEARNING PERSONALITIES

Another way to look at differences in learners is through their personality structure. In educational settings one of the most widely used tests to measure personality type is the Myers-Briggs Type Indicator (MBTI). The test is based upon Jung's theory of psychological types and measures personal tendencies or preferences along four bipolar dimensions.

1. extroversion-introversion
2. sensing-intuition
3. thinking-feeling
4. judging-perceptive

Individuals are assigned the initial letter of each bipolar dimension on which they score highest. An individual's type is the combination of the four preferences.

E represents an extrovert, who relates more easily to the outer world of people.

I represents an introvert, who relates more easily to the inner world of ideas.

S stands for sensing, preferring to work with known facts.

N stands for intuition, preferring to look for possibilities and relationships.

T stands for thinking, basing judgments on impersonal analysis and logic.

F stands for feeling, basing judgment more on personal values.

J refers to judging, preferring a planned way of life.

P refers to perceptive, preferring a flexible, spontaneous way of life.

The MBTI profile sheet presents a quick picture of 16 different combinations of the four dimensions. For example, the INFP has the following characteristics.

1. Full of enthusiasm
2. Loyal
3. Not apt to talk of a continuing relationship until a person is known well
4. Concerned about learning
5. Interested in language
6. Fond of independent projects
7. Apt to undertake too much but will somehow get it done
8. Friendly but not always sociable
9. Not concerned with physical environment
10. Not concerned about possessions

Lawrence (1982) states that individuals must follow their inclinations if the best learning is to take place.

The Murphy-Meisgeier Type Indicator for Children (1987) measures the psychological type of children, grades 2 through 8, using the same four preference scales as the MBTI. The authors provide manuals to help teachers and parents use the information from the test. Characteristics of each type of student are identified and suggested activities are given. Teachers are told that an intuitive student needs opportunities to be creative and original, dislikes routine and taking time for precision, has a seemingly sporadic approach rather than an orderly one, and so forth. Some of the suggested activities for intuitive students are to challenge them with problem-solving activities for which there are multiple solutions; to implement role-playing activities, especially improvisation; and to reduce the number of practice examples that are required for assignments.

LEARNING STYLE INVENTORIES

Learning style can be broadly defined as the way an individual learns. Dunn (1983) states that learning style represents the "way individuals concentrate on, absorb, and retain new or difficult information or skills" (p. 496). Keefe and Monk (1988) define learning style as the composite of characteristic cognitive, affective, and physiological factors that serve as relatively stable indicators of how individuals perceive, interact with, and respond to learning environments (p. 3). Many learning style inventories are available. One widely used instrument is the Learning Style Inventory (LSI) (Dunn, Dunn, & Price, 1978), which looks at modality preferences as well as other factors. The test authors look at environmental elements that affect learning—sound, light, temperature, and design. An emotional dimension considers factors such as motivation, persistence, responsibility, and structure. Sociological dimensions relate to whether an individual likes to work alone, with peers, in pairs, in a team, with adults, or in a varied situation. Another level considers the physical factors, including intake of food or drink, time of day, and desire for mobility. The final dimension of the model relates to psychological variables—cerebral dominance, impulsivity, and analytical versus global approaches.

The Learning Style Profile (LSP) (Keefe, Monk, Letteri, Languis, & Dunn, 1988) is a 128-item pencil-and-paper inventory that was developed under the sponsorship of the National Association of Secondary School Principals. The subscales on the test cover cognitive, affective, and physiological dimensions of learning styles. Cognitive dimensions include perceptual preferences, field independence/dependence, simultaneous/successive, inductive/deductive, active/reflective, thinking/feeling, need for structure, sharpening/leveling, focusing/scanning, narrow/broad, reflective/impulsive, and complex/simple. Affective styles include achievement motivation, risk taking/cautiousness, social motivation, anxiety, persistence, inductive/deductive, thinking/feeling, and need for structure. Physiological dimensions are time-of-day preference; need for mobility; anxiety; and environmental elements such as sound, light, temperature, and design.

Other widely used learning style instruments are listed here.

Learning Type Measure assesses four types of learning styles based on doing, watching/watching and feeling/thinking continuums.

Learning Style Inventory presents concrete experience, reflective observation, abstract conceptualization, and active experience for college students and adults.

Learning Styles Inventory measures student attitude toward nine models of instruction—projects, drill and recitation, peer teaching, discussion, teaching games, independent study, programmed instruction, lecture, and simulation.

Canfield Learning Styles Inventory assesses individuals from grade 6 to adult in four areas—conditions (peer, organization, goal setting, competition, instructor, detail, independence, authority), content (numeric, qualitative, inanimate, people), mode (listening, reading, iconic, direct experience), and expectation.

Learning Preference Inventory uses Jung typology, sensing-feeling, sensing-thinking, intuiting-feeling, extroversion-introversion.

Learning Efficiency Test measures visual and auditory memory under both ordered and unordered recall. It measures immediate, short-term, and long-term recall.

Learning styles are also geared to specific subject areas. One such inventory is the Reading Style Inventory (RSI), a diagnostic reading test that identifies a student's natural learning style in reading. The test takes 20 to 30 minutes to administer and has a diskette available to test, score, and produce computerized individual or group profiles. The RSI matches an individual reading style diagnosis with the most appropriate reading methods and materials.

Kolb (1976) has a different type of model. He postulates that learning proceeds in four stages.

1. Concrete experience that directly involves the learner
2. Reflective observation in which the learner reflects on experience from different perspectives
3. Abstract conceptualization in which the learner creates generalizations and theories
4. Active experimentation with application of theories to problem solving and decision making

Kolb's Learning Style Inventory is used to assess an individual's personal preferences along the abstract-concrete and active-reflective dimensions. He identifies four major types of learning styles.

1. Convergers, who like to solve specific problems
2. Divergers, who like to organize many relationships into a gestalt and use their imaginative ability to see commonalities
3. Assimilators, who use inductive reasoning to develop theoretical models
4. Accommodators, who like to carry out plans and conduct experiments and who are action-oriented.

Graska and Riechmann (Eisen, 1984) have a different type of conceptualization of learning style. Their instrument measures six types of learning styles—competitive, collaborative, avoidant, participant, dependent, and independent.

Gregorc (1982) has still another conceptualization of learning styles. His scale is called the Gregorc Style Delineator and consists of 10 sets of four words each, which the examinee is asked to rank. The scale is designed to reveal two types of abilities for managing information—perception and ordering.

Mind Styles

Gregorc looks at perception as the means by which an individual grasps information. It has two dimensions—abstractness and concreteness. Gregorc defines abstractedness as the quality that enables an individual to grasp, conceive, and mentally visualize data through the faculty of reason and to emotionally and intuitively register and deal with inner and subjective thoughts, ideas, concepts, feelings, drives, desires, and spiritual experiences (p. 5). He defines concreteness as the quality that enables an individual to grasp and mentally register data through the direct application of the physical senses. The second type of ability—ordering—also has two qualities: sequence and randomness. Sequence is defined as the quality that helps individuals grasp and organize information in a linear, step-by-step, methodical, predetermined order. Randomness helps individuals grasp and organize information in a nonlinear, galloping, leaping, and multifarious manner. The Style Delineator assesses the perception and ordering abilities individuals use to adapt to their everyday environments at work, school, home, or in social interactions.

Other Instruments

The K-ABC, discussed in Chapter 7, also differentiates between serial and simultaneous information-processing styles. This information is valuable to teachers in planning instruction.

The Florida Analysis of Semantic Traits (Bailey & Siudzinski, 1986) is an individually administered scale that measures six dimensions of learning style. With one dimension the student is asked to respond to a question such as, "What do you want from your school work?" or "What is important about your school work?" Analysis of the response to this question indicates the type of criteria the student thinks is important. The responses are scored on a dimension from aesthetical to practical. Criteria are important motivators; when an individual's criteria are used to describe a task or outcome, the individual becomes invested in that task or outcome.

The other scales measure direction, source, reason, decision factors, and convincers. The Direction Scale measures how students focus or maintain their motivation. The two extremes are toward and away from. Toward describes people who can focus on achieving their goals. These individuals are motivated to have, get, achieve, and attain. Away-from individuals are motivated by a problem or something to get away from, to be avoided, steered clear of, or gotten rid of. These students have trouble maintaining focus on their goals, are distracted, and most respond to negative situations (p. 11).

The Source Scale is analyzed for internality and externality of the responses. The Reason Scale assesses whether the individual prefers options or procedures. Procedures people prefer following the rules. Options people are not satisfied with the way something has always been done. Another scale deals with decision factors and identifies four types. The sameness person does not like change and wants his world to remain the same. The sameness-with-exceptions person wants her world to remain about the same but will adapt as change occurs. The difference and difference-with-exception individual loves change and will force change whenever possible. The both-sameness-with-exceptions-and-difference individual likes normalcy and change and will adapt as change occurs. The last scale measures which modality convinces individuals to do something. A second part of the scale relates to the number of times individuals must experience the modality to be convinced. The information from all six scales is then translated into action strategies to improve instructional strategies and the motivation and attitude of students.

SUMMARY

Learning style and modality assessment may provide useful information for the diagnosis and description of behavior. The information can help provide strategies and methodologies for both the instructor and the learner. It is useful to know both the formal and informal procedures used to assess the different dimensions of learning style. Many of the instruments listed have questionable validity and reliability. Although they might have face validity, they have little concurrent or predictive validity. The research on learning styles is still new, but there are many implications for teaching and learning as well as for understanding interpersonal conflicts and problems.

QUESTIONS FOR DISCUSSION

1. Do you believe all instructors ought to assess the learning styles of their students and use a variety of teaching strategies? Or should the instructor specifically train individuals to cultivate new learning styles and skills?

2. What are the ways you learn best? Review the different types of learning styles discussed in this chapter, and determine the categories or types that pertain to you.

3. Many psychologists have emphasized the importance of cognitive theories and abilities in learning situations. Do you feel that cognitive styles tests provide the instructor and learner with more important information than an aptitude test or interest test does? Defend your position.

4. Do you feel that a better way of investigating differences among students is to look at personality structure rather than learning style or cognitive style? Why or why not? Would you want to give all of your students the Myers-Briggs Type Indicator? Why or why not?

5. The validity and reliability of the instruments discussed in this chapter are usually lower than for traditional types of tests. Would you still use these instruments to make instructional decisions? What would you tell the students about the tests?

SUGGESTED ACTIVITIES

1. Critique a cognitive style or learning style inventory. Take it yourself or administer it to an appropriate test taker. Does the test appear to have face validity? Does the test have construct validity? What are the reliability coefficients reported?

2. Take the Myers-Briggs Type Indicator. How could this test be used in instructional environments? Does the test provide a valid portrait of you? How could this test be used in instructional environments?

3. Make an annotated bibliography of cognitive style and learning style tests.

4. Conduct an experiment. Give one of the learning style tests to a class and instructor. Give the class an attitude test about the class and instructor. Divide the class into two groups: those who have the same type of learning style as the teacher and those who do not. Are there differences in the attitudes of the two groups toward the instructor and the class?

5. Recruit a volunteer and use a learning or cognitive style inventory to identify the individual's style. What would happen if you formed work, growth, or therapy groups that had persons of only one learning or personality type included? Is it better to have mixed types of individuals within a group? Conduct an experiment on this topic or read the research on the topic and write a short position paper.

6. Read the Case of Quille and answer the questions that follow it.

   Quille took the Personal Style Indicator (Controneo, 1983) and had the following profile.

Affiliative	90%
Creative	70%
Enterprising	30%
Ordered	5%
Investigative	35%

   The instrument is an eight-item assessment instrument in which the individual is asked to rank five words based upon their importance to him/her (e.g., "Rank 1 the word that is most important to you and 5 to the word that is least important to you: (a) Thinker (b) Doer (c) Facilitator (d) Coordinator (e) Promoter"). Strengths for affiliatives include learning by interaction, sharing ideas with others, and discussing in peer groups or with an instructor or mentor.

   Quille also took the Learning Type Measure (LTM) (McCarthy & St. Germain, 1993). The LTM is a 27-item instrument. Fifteen items involve ranking preferences (e.g., "I am usually (a) productive (b) creative (c) disorganized or (d) critical"). Twelve of them are items related to the passive/active or watching/doing continuum (e.g, "I prefer a hobby that is (a) active (b) passive. Quille was identified most likely as an "imaginative learner." Imaginative learners are idea people, function through social interaction, need to be involved personally, and learn by listening and sharing. Quille scored lowest as a "common sense learner," one who needs to know how things work, seeks usability, and perceives information abstractly and processes it actively. The two styles in the middle were "analytical learner" and "dynamic learner."

On the Meyers-Briggs Type Indicator, Quille was an ENFP (extraverted intuition with feeling). These individuals usually have as strengths people skills, enthusiasm and energy, adaptability, creativity, and new ideas and possibilities.

a.   How would you characterize Quille's learning style?

b.   What additional information would you like to have on the instruments and Quille before interpreting the assessment data?

c.   The first two instruments were short and could be completed in 5 minutes or less. Would you use these instrument? Why or why not? When might you use these instruments?

d.   If Quille were seeking career possibilities, what do these instruments say about career fields that might fit into her learning style?

ADDITIONAL READINGS

Griggs, S. A. (1991). *Learning styles counseling*. Ann Arbor, MI: ERIC Counseling and Personnel Services Clearinghouse.

The author discusses how counselors can increase their effectiveness by knowing their client's learning style and illustrates how counseling interventions can be prescribed based on learning styles. The research on learning styles in counseling and teaching is presented and strategies for consulting with teachers and parents about learning styles discussed.

Meisgeier, C., Murphy, E., & Meisgeier, C. (1989). *A teacher's guide to type: A new perspective on individual differences in the classroom*. Palo Alto, CA: Consulting Psychologists Press.

This guide provides an introduction to type theory for teachers and suggests activities that can be used with each of the personality types.

Myers, I. B. (1980). *Gifts differing*. Palo Alto, CA: Consulting Psychologists Press.

This book provides a general overview of Jung's theory of personality types and specifically describes the 16 personality types found on the Myers-Briggs Personality Type Indicator.

Reiff, J. C. (1992). *Learning style*. Washington, DC: NEA.

The author presents a conceptual framework of understanding learning styles and shows how the knowledge will help counselors and helping professionals.

CHAPTER 14

Assessment of Development

Overview

One in five American children has a developmental, learning, or emotional problem, according to the 1988 National Health Interview Study of Child Health. Some experts think the statistics should be higher because many parents and helping professionals are unable to recognize certain disorders. Counselors need to know characteristic behaviors at the different developmental stages, be able to assess problems, and recommend special educational assistance. Early competence exerts a subtle influence toward adaptation throughout life. Failure to adapt at one period of development promotes difficulty later.

Objectives

After studying this chapter the reader should be able to

- discuss the general principles of developmental assessment

- describe the major domains assessed in developmental testing

- explain the advantages and disadvantages of the various assessment devices used to measure aspects of development

- identify some of the major instruments used in developmental assessment

GENERAL PRINCIPLES

Developmental and readiness testing has become increasingly important in the early screening and identification of clients who might need remedial help or further assessment. Children are rapidly developing and this must be considered in assessment and treatment (Yule, 1993). The assessment can be a valuable tool in the screening, diagnosis, placement, program planning, and evaluation of programs. Much attention has been placed on identifying preschoolers with disabilities, but many developmental theories now focus on the total life span rather than just childhood and adolescence. Developmental assessment is important in understanding cognitive, ego, interpersonal, moral and psychosocial development as individuals progress through the various stages of their life.

The assessment needs to focus on both the client and the client's environment. The client plays an active role in shaping an environment that fulfills his basic needs. The significant individuals in the client's world need to be identified, and parents, guardians, spouses, friends, and relatives might be needed to provide input to the assessment. Attachments, separations, and losses in a client's life have a dramatic influence. While age is an important factor in assessment, social factors also must be considered (Yule, 1993).

Current functioning is influenced by previous events, and counselors need to evaluate clients with this in mind. Theories point out that conflicts are inevitable and necessary for human development, and some may never be completely resolved.

Developmental assessment focuses on these characteristics.

1. the normality of client functioning in the various domains
2. the historical factors that contributed positively or negatively to the client's functioning
3. the current state of affairs—family, school, or work factors that contribute positively and negatively to the client's functioning
4. the current state of wellness of the client—his physical, psychological, and emotional health
5. the expectations of the client and his significant others
6. the client's current educational, social, and psychological needs

Yule (1993) reminds helping professionals not to treat any assessment finding in isolation but to piece it together with other data on the client's overall adjustment. Isolated symptoms should be viewed cautiously and emphasis placed on patterns of adjustment, their adaptability and flexibility. Behavior is interpreted in light of developmental norms and environmental factors.

DOMAINS

Developmental tests measure typical skills that should be mastered at certain stages. Preschool tests, for example, assess gross motor, fine motor, language, self-help,

Drawings of people provide information on their child's developmental level.

social, emotional, and cognitive skills. A number of domains are common to developmental assessment instruments across the life span.

Communication skills—both verbal and nonverbal, receptive and expressive language skills, listening and comprehension skills

Cognitive skills—reasoning, thinking, memory skills; basic achievement in reading, writing, and mathematics; problem-solving abilities

Physical development—motor and sensory development, general development, balance, locomotion, walking

Emotional development—temperament, adjustment, emotional expression, self-concept, attitudes

Social development—peer and family relationships, friendships, interpersonal relationships

Self-care skills—ability to meet basic self-care needs, drinking, eating, toileting, dressing

Independent living skills—ability to function independently in the home and community, clothing care, cooking, transportation, shopping, money management

Work habits and adjustment—ability to work independently, maintain proper work habits, work with employers and employees, job seeking and keeping skills

Adjustment problems—aggression, hyperactivity, acting out, withdrawal, delinquency, stress, depression

METHODS OF ASSESSMENT

The four major techniques of assessment are direct testing; naturalistic observation; interviewing of parents, teachers, or guardians; and multiple measures. Direct testing is not always possible because of the developmental level of a client, a disability, wariness toward the test administrator, or the presence or nonpresence of parents in the case of young children. The performance of these individuals tends to be inconsistent.

Naturalistic observation provides an opportunity to see how a person behaves and performs in normal everyday functioning. The process is time-consuming and expensive. A number of structured observation schedules exist, and raters need to be trained to use them so that observations are consistent and properly focused.

Helping professionals use a wide variety of interviewing methods. Computerized versions are designed to elicit specific information; life history schedules help guide the collection of appropriate information from parents. Preschoolers or individuals with certain disabilities are not capable of filling out self-report forms, so interviews with parents or guardians are necessary to determine skills and adaptive behaviors not always modeled in school. The validity of personality tests such as the Personality Inventory for Children and self-concept scales such as the Inferred Self-Concept Scale that teachers or parents complete is questionable. Reliability of the data depends on the quality of the scale (content validity) and the accuracy of the people answering the questions.

There are a variety of informal assessment procedures that helping professionals can utilize to achieve a more global perspective of the problem. Sentence completion techniques can be utilized to zero in on important concerns at a particular stage of development (e.g., "In school, when the teacher calls upon me, I _____ _____"). Journaling is also utilized. Individuals are asked to tell how they feel about certain types of experiences, interventions, programs, and the like. A portfolio of these feelings can be kept. Other writing exercises like stories and poems can also be helpful in understanding the client.

Observing individuals while they are playing games, drawing, and in play therapy or other informal situations can provide information on their cognitive and psychosocial development. Clients can be asked to tell a story about a particular picture or situation, or to complete a story.

Self-monitoring requires the individual to keep a record of certain behaviors, feelings, or worries. A client could keep a record of the number of times he blew his cool, felt depressed, spoke out in class when not called upon, felt a craving for certain foods, and the like.

Helping professionals get more complete information when they utilize multiple measures. The process might be more time-consuming and expensive but it allows the counselor to combine information from a number of different sources, individuals, and occasions.

EARLY IDENTIFICATION

Three widely used general batteries to assess preschool children are the Developmental Indicators for the Assessment of Learning—Revised (DIAL-R), the Battelle Developmental Inventory, and the Denver Developmental Screening Test. DIAL-R is used to assess the cognitive, language, motor, social, and emotional development of children ages 2 to 6. In the motor area tests the child is involved in activities like catching a bean bag, jumping, hopping, skipping, building with blocks, touching fingers, and cutting with cutting cards and scissors. The Battelle Developmental Inventory can be given from birth to 8 years and measures personal, social, adaptive, motor, communication, and cognitive skills. The Denver Developmental Screening Test assesses personal-social, fine motor, language, and gross motor skills of children from birth to 6.

Some instruments focus on one domain. The Children's Adaptive Behavior Scale is designed to assess a child's adaptability to different social environments. Five areas covered are language development, independent functioning, family role performance, economic and vocational activity, and socialization. The Matson Evaluation of Social Skills can be used with clients aged 6 through adult and features both a teacher rating and a self-report form.

LANGUAGE DEVELOPMENT

The time between birth and age 6 is viewed as a crucial period for language development. A number of standardized tests are available to help professionals look at qualitative and quantitative differences. A few examples of the tests available are these.

Houston Test for Language Development is designed to measure verbal and nonverbal communication of children from birth to 6. The HTLD is used for differential diagnosis of problems resulting from emotional deprivation, auditory and motor deficits, and other causes. The test provides a profile of strengths and weaknesses that can be valuable when planning specific interventions.

Reynell Developmental Language Scale (RDLS) is used to assess slow development in receptive and expressive language areas of children 1 to 7 years of age.

Test of Language Development (TOLD) assesses receptive and expressive vocabulary and expressive grammatical structure by using picture identification, grammatic completion, word definitions, word discrimination, and word articulation. The primary form can be given to children aged 4 to 8.11, while the intermediate form is used with children aged 8.6 to 12.11.

Test of Adolescent Language–2 (TOAL–2) identifies problems in both the spoken and written language of adolescents. TOAL–2 provides scores in listening, speaking, reading, writing, spoken language, written language, vocabulary, grammar, receptive language, and expressive language.

COGNITIVE STAGES

Piaget's theory of cognitive development involves four major stages. In the sensorimotor stage children from birth to 2 develop schemes and organized patterns of behavior or thought through sensory and motor activities. The preoperational stage occurs between the ages of 2 and 7 when children develop the ability to conserve and decenter, that is, to overcome perceptual centration, irreversibility, and egocentrism in their logical thinking. During the concrete operational stage children between 7 and 11 develop the ability to use mental operations but have difficulty in manipulating conditions without experience. The formal operational stage starts at 11 to 12 when children are able to solve problems, work with abstractions, form hypotheses, and engage in mental operations. Children tend to think, perceive, organize, and understand their personal, physical, and social environment differently at various stages of development.

Two tests assess stages of development.

The Concept Assessment Kit (CAK) measures cognitive development of preschool and primary grade children. The CAK is a multiple item task-assessment and oral-response test measuring conservation. Forms A and B measure conservation of two-dimensional space, number substance, continuous quantity, discontinuous quantity, and weight. Form C measures conservation using area and length.

The Wach Analysis of Cognitive Structures assesses the development of learning ability among young children and suggests activities to stimulate learning and growth. The inventory has 15 clusters of tasks divided into subtests consisting of manipulative, visual-sensory, and body movement actions. The test is culture-free, nonverbal, and has been used with children having language, mental, and hearing deficits.

The tests focus on how we think and reason. They do not present norms and standard scores like traditional cognitive ability tests or have the same level of validity. Some counselors believe this information also provides a frame of reference to look at social and emotional development and is useful in instructional programming.

CASE OF BOBBY

Bobby
Race/Sex: African-American male
Date of Birth: 8/17/88
Grade: Kindergarten
Present School: San Pablo Elementary
Date: 4/11/95

Tests Used

At age 4.5 on 1/27/93
Leiter International Performance Scale
Peabody Picture Vocabulary Test-Revised
Preschool Attainment Record
Developmental Test of Visual-Motor Integration
Stanford-Binet Intelligence Scale, Form L–M

At age 5.8 on 4/23/94
(Speech and Language Evaluation)
Zimmerman Preschool Language Scale
Expressive One-Word Picture Vocabulary Test
Structured Photographic Expressive Language Test-II
Cultural Evaluation of Language Fundamentals—Revised
Goldman Fristoe Test of Articulation
Bracken Basic Concept Scale

At age 6.4 on 12/18/94
Woodcock-Johnson Tests of Achievement—Revised
Vane Kindergarten Test
Vineland Adaptive Behavior Scales

Reason for Referral

Bobby was originally referred to Child Find by the Speech and Hearing Center to obtain a current level of functioning. His parents noted delays in overall developmental skills and significant deficits in the use of speech and language.

Background Information

Bobby's mother reported her pregnancy was normal and without complications. However, at the age of 6 months Bobby contracted bacterial meningitis, after which his speech and language skills were severely delayed.

Review of Records

Bobby's initial evaluation by the psychologist on 1/27/93 (CA 5 4.5) indicated a Stanford-Binet Intelligence Scale IQ of 54, a Leiter IQ of 79, and a Peabody Picture Vocabulary Test score of 52. The examiner noted that the scores obtained appeared to be somewhat depressed due to significant difficulties in speech and language. Placement in a preschool handicapped program was recommended on 3/22/93.

A re-evaluation was completed on 4/23/90. Results of Bobby's performance on the WPPSI were a Verbal IQ of 70, a Performance IQ of 86, and a Full Scale IQ of 75.

Speech and Language assessment was completed in May of 1994. Reported results include these scores.

Clinical Evaluation of Language Fundamentals—Revised	65
Bracken Test of Basic Concepts	50
Expressive One-Word Picture Vocabulary Test	61

The examiner reports that Bobby evidences severe delays in expressive language and a severe phonological disorder. Participation in a program for severely language impaired students was suggested.

Testing was also administered on 12/18/94. The Woodcock-Johnson Test of Achievement—Revised indicated academic skills at a prereadiness level comparable to a preschool youngster below 4 years old.

Vane scoring of the human figure drawing yielded an age equivalent of 5.4, which is in the low average range.

Adaptive skills as measured through teacher ratings of the Vineland Adaptive Behavior Scales showed standard scores in the average range.

Sensory Functioning

In the fall of 1994 Bobby passed the vision screening administered at school. During the evaluation he was observed to shield his right eye during drawing activities. Observations were discussed with his parents and periodic screenings at school were suggested.

Results of the hearing screening indicated auditory acuity in the left ear was adequate. He failed to respond appropriately at all frequency levels presented in the right ear. Significant deficits in speech articulation and language were also reported.

Summary and Conclusions

Bobby is a 6-year, 4-month-old youngster who is placed in a full-time SLD program. He has evidenced significant deficits in acquisition of basic academic skills, and he also sustains substantial delays in speech and language. Results of formal intellectual assessments indicate overall conceptual skills are within the borderline to low average range, but scores should be interpreted with caution due to his significant difficulties in speech and language. Current academic levels are significantly below that expected of his estimated ability.

Adaptive skills show functioning at a level more typical of a much younger child with the most notable deficits in communication skills. Daily living and self-help skills are an area of relative strength although still rated at the preschool level.

Bobby can be expected to continue requiring a comprehensive, well-structured, individualized educational program. Preferential seating and individual presentation of instructions are suggested. Continued placement in the self-contained SLD program seems the most appropriate and least restrictive to meet his overall educational needs. A staffing—a meeting of counselors, psychologists, teachers, and parents—should be scheduled to consider permanent placement and review current assessment results.

PSYCHOSOCIAL DEVELOPMENT

Erikson developed a theory of personality development based upon psychoanalytical, biographical, historical, and anthropological methods of study. He postulates eight stages of psychosocial development. At each stage positive and negative forces produce conflict and a crisis that must be resolved. When the negative forces have a stronger influence than the positive factors, the outcome leads to difficulties in adjustment and development. The developmental crisis that needs to be resolved during the first year is Trust versus Mistrust. For 2- and 3-year-olds it is Autonomy versus Doubt; for 4- to 5-year-olds it is Initiative versus Guilt. Industry versus Inferiority is the crisis from 6 to 11 years, and Identity versus Role Confusion during adolescence, while Intimacy versus Isolation occurs during young adulthood. Generativity versus Stagnation is the crisis during middle age and Integrity versus Despair during old age. The degree and direction of conflict resolution determines the overall health of the individual, but the degree of conflict resolution is relative, since no stage conflict is completely resolved. One of the major instruments to assess Erikson's stages is the Measure of Psychosocial Development. The Case of Anita illustrates the use of this inventory.

CASE OF ANITA

Ms. Moore was a counselor working with a group of unwed African-American teenage mothers. She was eager to find out more about the personality dynamics and conflict resolution of Anita, one of her counselees.

Anita is 16 and will be a senior if she is able to pass her courses. Her pregnancy and birth of a daughter during the school year have hampered her academically, and she is talking about dropping out of school. Anita comes from a single-parent family. Currently, her grandmother is taking care of her baby while she works part-time at Kentucky Fried Chicken. Ms. Moore decided to administer the Measures of Psychosocial Development (MPD), since it is based upon sound personality theory and assesses adolescent and adult personality development. The MPD is a 112-item self-report inventory that has 27 different scales—9 positive scales (trust, autonomy, initiative, industry, identity, intimacy, generativity, ego integrity, and total positive), 9 negative scales (mistrust, shame and doubt, guilt, inferiority, identity confusion, isolation, stagnation, despair, and total negative) and 9 resolution scales, one for each stage, and a total resolution scale. The test taker responds on a 5-point scale ranging from "not at all like you" to "very much like you."

The MPD is easy to score. Ms. Moore just removed the top page of the answer sheet, counted the ratings for each row of items, and recorded the scores on each of the 27 scales on the profile sheet.

Alpha reliabilities ($n = 372$) for the scales ranged from a low of .65 on trust to a high of .84 on identity confusion. The median coefficient was .74. Test-retest coefficients for 108 individuals were also reported and ranged from a high of .91 on total negative to a low of .67 on inferiority.

The MPD reports construct validity through intercorrelations of the scale, correlation of the MPD with the Inventory of Psychosocial Development and the Self-Description Questionnaire. The author claims the data support the discriminant validity of the positive scales, and that there is moderate support for the negative scales and consistent evidence for convergent validity of the scale. Separate norms are presented for males and females ages 13 to 17, 18 to 24, 25 to 49, and 50+. The manual does not provide the means and standard deviations for any of these groups or the standard errors of measurement for the various scales. Despite separate norms, no statistical evidence indicates a gender difference. The norms utilize T scores with a mean of 50 and a standard deviation of 10.

Anita had the following percentile ranks on the MPD.

Positive Scales

Trust	03
Autonomy	42

Initiative	27
Industry	24
Identity	14
Intimacy	01
Generativity	11
Ego Integrity	01
Total Positive	03

Negative Scales

Mistrust	79
Shame and Doubt	50
Guilt	35
Inferiority	69
Identity Confusion	65
Isolation	92
Stagnation	38
Despair	96
Total Negative	79

Resolution Scales

Trust versus Mistrust	08
Autonomy versus Shame & Doubt	50
Initiative versus Guilt	46
Industry versus Inferiority	27
Identity versus Identity Confusion	24
Intimacy versus Isolation	01
Generativity versus Stagnation	27

Ego Integrity versus Despair	02
Total Resolution	05

The MPD manual (p. 9) states that high scorers on mistrust perceive the world as inconsistent, painful, stressful, and threatening, and believe that life is unpredictable. They struggle with the burden of questioning whether others are trustworthy. Their basic mistrust may be characterized as a sense of living precariously, of feeling that good things never last, or doubting that needs will be met. High scorers on isolation tend to remain alone and be self-absorbed from fear of ego loss. Isolation occurs if a person's identity is too weak to sustain the uncertainties of intimacy. The individual may be drawn toward intimate relationships but also be frightened by them (p. 10). Commitments and responsibilities seem unreasonable or too restrictive.

High scorers on despair perceive that their lives have been filled with misdirected energies and lost opportunities. They believe there is no time to undo the mistakes of the past and to begin life anew.

MORAL DEVELOPMENT

Piaget studied the moral development of children and identified two broad stages. Kohlberg expanded the two broad stages into three levels, each with two stages. The first level is preconventional morality and usually extends to the age of 9. The two stages are punishment-obedience orientation and instrumental-relativist orientation. The second level is conventional morality and includes the good boy-nice girl and the law-and-order orientations. This period is typical of youth ages 9 to 20. Level three is postconventional morality and includes social contract and universal ethical principle orientation. A number of instruments have been developed to measure moral reasoning.

The Moral Judgment Interview uses a structured interview technique that involves a minimum of 21 questions about the client's reasoning regarding three moral dilemmas. Raters are used to match the responses against the stage criteria.

Social Moral Reflection Measure is a group-administered version of Kohlberg's Moral Judgment Inventory.

Defining Issues Test is a pencil-and-paper instrument that presents dilemmas about which the client selects preferred responses.

Ethical Reasoning Inventory is a paper-and-pencil inventory that consists of 6 dilemmas from Kohlberg's manual. Questions are followed by two responses and sets of reasons that represent stages of Kohlberg's theory.

The scoring of some of these tests is tedious, time-consuming, and would demand careful study of the manuals and criteria for scoring. Reliability of some instruments is moderate. Gilligan believes that women have a different approach to resolving real-life dilemmas. The question about the criterion-referenced validity of these tests is whether individuals actually behave the way they say they do.

CAREER DEVELOPMENT

Super postulates a five-stage theory of career development. The first is the growth stage in which the preadolescent develops self-awareness and interests. Children role play and fantasize about different jobs and occupations. The exploratory stage extends from early adolescence to early adulthood and has three phases: crystallization, specification, and implementation. Crystallization relates to developing ideas about fields of endeavor and appealing occupations. Specification relates to moving from general preferences to choosing a specific career or job. Implementation requires pursuing chosen fields.

The establishment stage normally takes place in early to middle adulthood and consists of developmental tasks: stabilizing, consolidating, and advancing. Individuals settle down, support their families, and develop appropriate lifestyles in the stabilizing stage. At the consolidating stage individuals are concerned with their place in an occupation or in an organization. Workers have the expectation of moving up the ladder and getting ahead financially in the advancing stage. The maintenance stage extends from middle adulthood to later adulthood and consists of three developmental tasks: holding, updating, and innovating. The disengagement stage extends from the early 60s to retirement and has three phases: disengagement, retirement planning, and retirement living.

Super, Thompson, and Lindeman (1988) point out that it is common for individuals to change career paths after becoming established. This requires individuals to reassess life and career plans and go back to previous developmental stages and tasks.

CASE OF CINDY

Cindy is a 28-year-old caucasian female. She has been married since June 1983 and has a six-year-old daughter. Cindy is interested in re-entering the job market but is unsure about her employment qualifications and interests. She doesn't know whether to return to school, get vocational training, or begin work wherever employment is available. Cindy maintained a high C or low B average throughout high school, but did not particularly like school. After graduation she was employed as a grocery clerk/cashier and a retail sales person but stopped working when her daughter was born. Now Cindy wants to develop her job skills and explore career options. Her husband is employed as a high school teacher and has encouraged her to research her career choices.

Cindy dresses neatly, has good eye contact, and is friendly, verbal, and articulate. She understands the need for career exploration and appears focused and committed to developing an action plan.

The counselor chooses the ACCI as one of the assessment instruments because it is intended for adults rethinking their careers. The ACCI is appropriate for both sexes, is written in American English at the eighth grade reading level, and may be hand- or machine-scored. The test taker is asked to respond to 61 items on a five-point scale, indicating the amount of current concern toward the statement.

The test manual provides a developmental model for assessment and counseling. The authors present content, concurrent, and predictive validity as well as the factor structure of the instrument. Alpha coefficients are reported for two different groups and range primarily in the .80s and .90s. The authors also present the standard error of measurement.

The results on the ACCI indicate considerable concern for Exploration. Specification had an average score of 5.0 while Implementation and Crystallization were 4.5 and 4.0 respectively. The next highest score was 4.6 on Updating. The other scales had scores of 4.0 or less. The Disengagement Stage had the lowest scores.

Other test results are also reported here.

Strong Interest Inventory—General Occupational Theme Scores

Realistic	Average
Investigative	Moderately Low
Artistic	Moderately High
Social	Moderately High
Enterprising	Moderately Low
Conventional	Moderately Low
Academic Comfort	Moderately High
Intro/Extroversion	Average

Salience Inventory:

Participation: High salience—home and family, working

Moderate—studying

Low—leisure, community service

Commitment: High salience—home and family

Moderate—working, studying

Low—leisure

Value
Expectations: High—home and family, community service

Moderate—working, studying

Myers-Briggs Type Indicator:

EIFP Extrovert, Intuitive, Feeling, Perceptive

SUMMARY

Counselors' knowledge of assessing developmental readiness has become increasingly important in the early identification and screening of clients with problems. Developmental tests measure the typical skills expected in normal development. Assessment includes physical, social, cognitive, emotional, communication, self-care, and independent living skills as well as work habits and adjustment. Direct testing, naturalistic observation, interviewing, and a combination of these are used to assess these domains. Much emphasis is placed on the early identification of problems and preschool screening. Developmental theories provide a useful framework for understanding critical periods of development.

QUESTIONS FOR DISCUSSION

1. What are the general principles of developmental assessment?
2. List and discuss the major domains assessed in developmental testing.
3. What are the advantages and disadvantages of the various methods of developmental assessment?
4. What are some of the major instruments used in early identification?
5. What contributions have developmental stage theories made to assessment? Do you agree or disagree that developmental theories have little value in the assessment process?
6. Review the case of Bobby, Anita, or Cindy. Do you feel that the counselor utilized appropriate tests? Why or why not? Did the tests have sufficient reliability and validity for the purposes intended? What is your interpretation of the data and test results given? What additional information would you have found desirable?

SUGGESTED ACTIVITIES

1. Interview counselors and helping professionals about what types of developmental assessment procedures they use and why. Have them identify problems they have had in working in developmental assessment. Report your findings to the class.
2. Visit a Child Find or similar agency and inquire about the assessment procedures they use, the cooperating agencies they work with, the incidence of children with disabilities they have identified, and the type of parent education and training that is available. Report this information to the class.

3. Write a paper or give a report on assessing developmental stages, milestones of development, assessment domains, critical issues or problems in preschool assessment, or a similar topic.

4. Select a developmental screening or stage instrument and administer it to an appropriate subject. Write the results and discuss them in class.

5. Write a critical analysis or review of one of the major developmental assessment instruments.

6. What developmental assessment tools and techniques would you use to help understand the following cases?

Mary is in ninth grade and involved in all types of school activities. She is a cheerleader, a member of the basketball team, and a member of the National Honor Society. She has increased the amount of time she spends in exercising and jogging. She does these activities every day and has placed herself on a stringent diet. She has begun to lose weight. Her mother is concerned and calls you to arrange an appointment with you, the counselor.

John has just started second grade. He has become tearful when school or his teacher is mentioned. He procrastinates when getting ready for school in the morning and misses the bus some mornings. His parents have called you because they are concerned about John's behavior.

Shannon is a junior in high school. She has been concerned because all her friends know what they want to do after high school but she doesn't. She thinks that something is wrong with her and feels she doesn't have the skills and abilities to do much of anything.

ADDITIONAL READINGS

Bagnatto, S. J., & Neisworth, J. (1991). *Assessment for early intervention*. New York: Guilford Publications.

The book focuses on the competencies needed for developmental assessment and presents models of team assessment and intervention.

Blau, T. H. (1991). *The psychological examination of the child*. New York: Wiley.

The book is designed to help the examiner identify anything that might be out of order in the child's development and deals with what is important to learn about all children and their development.

Reynolds, C. R., & Kamphaus, R. W. (1990). *Handbook of psychological and educational assessment of children: Intelligence and achievement: Vol. 2. Personality, behavior, and context*. New York: Guilford Press.

The books cover a broad base of the domains tested and include evaluation and treatment of childhood disorders of development, learning, and behavior.

Vernon, A. (1993). *Developmental assessment and intervention with children and adolescents*. Alexandria, VA: American Counseling Association.

The author provides strategies to assess the normal problems that children and youth face. Case studies are presented along with strategies to help diagnose and remediate the problem.

CHAPTER 15

Environmental Assessment

Overview

Environmental assessment contributes to the understanding of the dynamics of behavior and is used to determine the impact of environment on the development of the individual, the family, and other groups. Knowledge of a client's environment helps the counselor determine possible intervention strategies and resources that could be used effectively. Public Law 94–142 requires determination of the least restrictive environment for children with disabilities. Ecological psychology focuses on specific features of the environment and the interactive effect of individuals within systems. The focus is not only on how situational variables determine the present behavior of individuals and groups, but also on how these variables influence the direction of personal and social growth over time.

Objectives

This chapter should help the reader understand

* the uses of environmental assessment in counseling and in personality appraisal
* the dimensions and models of environmental assessment
* the instruments and techniques available to helping professionals
* the applications of environmental assessment in counseling and educational contexts

THEORETICAL BACKGROUND

Environmental assessment has roots in the phenomenological approaches to counseling because idiographic approaches are often utilized by the counselor. Counselors are interested at times in discovering the laws or factors that guide the behavior of a certain individual rather than laws pertaining to people in general. Barnett and Zucker (1990) state that this approach stresses the personal and social behaviors and constructs that have validity for the client such as overt behaviors of concern to the individual or others; covert or internal events that can be reported; central themes, values, and goals; and the impact of behaviors and situations on the individual (p. 145). The approach is concerned with the perceptions, cognitions, and learning of the individuals involved.

Environmental assessment also has roots in ecological psychology. Bandura (1986) emphasizes that in social transactions people become each other's environments (p. 335). Ecological psychology focuses on groups and their adaptation to their environment, and it is characterized by its naturalistic methodology, site specificity, systems concepts, emphasis on long time periods, transdisciplinary emphasis, and evaluation of natural experiments.

Values

A number of important values in this approach have been identified.

1. Knowledge of the environment can help us understand the behavior and adjustment of children and adults.

2. Ecological assessment helps counselors determine possible intervention strategies and resources.

3. Ecological strategies help counselors evaluate outcomes of the assessment-intervention process.

4. Environmental assessment is important to help determine the extent to which a given environment is likely to facilitate positive development.

5. Environmental assessment helps counselors determine the extent to which certain skills are required for successful placement in those environments.

6. Public Law 94–142 requires assessing environments to determine, across multiple dimensions, the extent to which they are normalized and least restrictive.

Barnett and Zucker (1990) state that child, school, family, and relevant community systems should be assessed for multiple perspectives of adjustment pertaining to the referral question, systems problems, and strengths (p. 146). They believe that it is important to consider not only how situational variables influence the present behavior of clients but also how these variables may later change their personal and social growth and adjustment.

Models and Dimensions

Moos (1973) has developed a model to assess the dimensions related to the psychosocial characteristics and social climates of environments. He claims that environments have unique "personalities" just as people do (p. 1). His model focuses on relationship dimensions, personal development or personal growth dimensions, and system maintenance and system change dimensions. The relationship dimensions identify the nature and intensity of the personal relationships within the environment. Key concepts in the relationship dimensions across environments are involvement, support, spontaneity, expressiveness, affiliation, and peer cohesion. Personal development dimensions are characterized by autonomy, practical orientation, personal problem orientation, independent-task orientation, competition, self-discovery, and anger and aggression. The exact nature of these dimensions, of course, depends on their underlying purposes and goals. System maintenance and system change dimensions assess the extent to which the environment is orderly, is clear in its expectations, maintains control, and is responsive to change. The scales are titled Order and Organization, Clarity, and Control. Moos and his co-workers have developed a number of scales to assess environments in a wide variety of settings, such as the family, school, and correctional setting.

Bailey and Wolery (1989) define the environment to include everything that surrounds us and experiences to which we are exposed. They stress seven important components.

Physical space—amount of space that is available and the way the space is arranged

Organization and supervision of space—space must be organized and well-defined according to use or function

Materials—environment should contain sufficient materials for those who will be using the environment

Peer environment—the number and type of people who are going to share the environment

Organization and scheduling—level of organization of the environment, how activities are scheduled, and the roles of the people involved

Safety—environment that is free of hazards and has adequate supervision

Responsiveness—provides an opportunity to enhance feelings of competency and independence

Moos (1974) points out six ways characteristics of human environments have been identified.

1. Ecological dimensions, which include geographical, meteorological, architectural, and physical design variables

2. Behavior settings, which are characterized by both ecological and behavioral properties

3. Dimensions of organizational structure

4. Dimensions identifying the collective, personal, and/or behavioral characteristics of the people living and functioning in an environment

5. Variables relevant to the functional or reinforcement analyses of environments

6. Dimensions related to psychosocial characteristics and social climates of environments (p. 1)

ASSESSMENT STRATEGIES

The strategy used to assess the environment depends on the referral question or the purpose of the assessment. One of the major techniques, direct observation, is preferred to interviewing because clients may have difficulty assessing their own environment. For example, if there is a concern about safety, the observer might want to draw a schematic of the room and plot the activity and movement within the space. For convenience, observers use checklists and rating scales when assessing the salient features of the environment.

Bailey and Wolery (1989) point out that helping professionals should be aware of the complexities of environmental assessment, appreciate the dynamic and interactive nature of environments, focus on functions rather than forms, and be familiar with a variety of strategies. They believe multiple sources of information and multiple measurement strategies should be used.

FAMILY/HOME ENVIRONMENT

Research has revealed the importance of environmental factors in personal, social, and cognitive growth. The family is one of the most important environments for children and can have a tremendous impact on personal and social growth. Many instruments to assess dimensions of the family environment have been developed. Some of the observational scales used to code different dimensions of family interaction are described here.

Affective Style Measure is used to observe families in situations where the participants discuss problems. The observer codes their interaction in categories, such as criticism, guilt induction, and intrusiveness. The code has been found useful in predicting psychiatric disturbance in adolescents and young adults.

Defensive and Supportive Communication Interaction System is a coding system used to observe the defensive and supportive communication in family interaction, family therapy, and marriage therapy. Some of the defensive categories coded are judgmental-dogmatism, indifference, and superiority. Some of the supportive categories coded are emphatic understanding, equality, and spontaneous problem solving.

Developmental Environments Coding System (DECS) assesses familial variables predicted by structural-developmental theory to affect ego and moral development. Dimensions such as focusing, competitive challenging, noncompetitive sharing of perspective, avoidance, rejection of the task, distortion, support, and affective conflict are coded.

Family Conflict and Dominance Codes measure dominance and conflict in family interaction. Family members are asked to complete a questionnaire separately and are then brought together to fill out one questionnaire that represents the family's opinion or view.

Family Constraining and Enabling Coding System (CECS) is used to analyze transactions in family communication by measuring the frequency of communication events and their sequences. Constraining categories include cognitive constraining and affective constraining; enabling categories include cognitive enabling and affective enabling.

Family Interaction Scales (FIS) is a coding system for observing family interaction and is based on the theories of Jackson and Satir. The purpose of the scale is to promote understanding of individual personal development in the family context. The six major dimensions are agreement/disagreement, clarity, topic, commitment, intensity, and relationship.

Another approach to measure the family environment is through self-report instruments. Some of the widely used instruments are described here.

Children's Version of the Family Environment Scale (CVFES) is a downward pictorial extension of the Family Environment Scale and is used with elementary school children.

Colorado Self-Report Measure of Family Functioning is designed to provide a description of whole family functioning along 15 dimensions under three general headings—relationship, personal growth, and system maintenance dimensions.

Conflict Tactics Scale (CTS) measures the use of reasoning, verbal aggression, and violence as modes of dealing with conflict in relationships within a family.

Family Adaptability and Cohesion Evaluation Scales III (FACES III) measures family cohesion and adaptability and perceived and ideal family functioning.

Family Assessment Measure (FAM) assesses dimensions of family strengths and weaknesses from three perspectives—the family as a system, dyadic relationships, and individual family members.

Family Environment Scale (FES) measures the social environmental characteristics of the family and has three climate dimensions—relationship, personal growth, and system maintenance. The FES has 10 subscales—cohesion, expressiveness, conflict, independence, achievement orientation, intellectual-cultural orientation, active-recreational orientation, moral-religious emphasis, and organization and control.

Family Evaluation Form (FEF) assesses dimensions of family functioning—family centeredness, conflict and tension, open communication, emotional closeness, community involvement, children's relations, children's adjustment, parenting-nurturance, parenting-independence training, parenting–effective discipline, parenting–strict/punitive discipline, parenting–negative style, husband/wife dominance, marital satisfaction, homemaker role, worker role, financial problems, and extrafamilial support.

Family Functioning in Adolescence Questionnaire (FFAQ) measures family functioning in adolescence and has scales such as structure, affect, communication, behavior control, value transmission, and external systems.

Family Process Scales (FPS) assesses the interdependence of family members, the dynamic homeostasis in the family, and the family's ability to provide an environment that fosters healthy psychological development and a sense of well-being in its members.

Family Relationship Questionnaire (FRQ) measures family functioning in the areas of affect, conflict, and dominance and can be used with culturally and economically different types of families.

McMaster Family Assessment Device, Version 3 (FAD) evaluates family functioning on seven dimensions and is used to screen healthy and pathological family functioning. The FAD scales are problem solving, communication, roles, affective responsiveness, affective involvement, behavior control, and general functioning.

Self-Report Family Inventory (SFI) assesses dimensions of the family such as health, communication, cohesion, directive leadership, and expressiveness and can be used along with observational instruments in the Beavers System approach to family assessment.

CASE OF ANN

Ann, a 9-year-old in third grade, was not achieving up to the expectations of her mother. She believed Ann was better than a C or D student and that she was lazy and not trying in school. Ann said she likes school but can't keep up with the work and she has too much homework. Recently Ann's father, a naval officer, was sent to the Middle East on deployment for at least 6 months. Ann is the oldest of three children. Her mother mentioned the problems of being a navy wife and the sometimes stormy relationship with her husband. Ann's mother works part-time as a receptionist for a local business. One of the tests given Ann by the counselor was the Family Environment Scale, Children's Version.

Ann had no problems taking the test, which includes 30 items. She was asked to select from three pictures on each of 10 scales the one that looks most like her family.

The test appears to have face validity and the pictures seem to represent the scales and constructs measured by the test. The authors report the procedures they used to establish the content validity of the items. The test-retest reliability was .80 over a four-week interval. The norms are based on a population of 158 Buffalo, New York area children, grades 1 to 6. According to the authors, the sample represented approximately 26 per grade, an equal number of males and females, and a number of different nationalities. The religious grouping was primarily Roman Catholic. A norm table is available for convert-ing raw scores to standard scores over the combined grades. No information is provided in the manual on the fixed mean and fixed standard deviation of the subscales. Table 15.1 illustrates Ann's scores.

The scales with the highest raw scores were conflict (the amount of openly expressed anger, aggression, and conflict among family members), achievement-orientation (the extent to which school activities are cast into an achievement-oriented or competitive framework), and moral/religious emphasis (emphasis on ethical and religious issues and values).

The lowest raw scores were on intellec-tual/cultural orientation (degree of interest in political, social, intellectual, and cultural activi-ties), active/recreational orientation (extent of participation in social and recreational activi-ties), and independence (the extent to which the family members are assertive, self-suffi-cient, and make their own decisions).

Table 15.1
Case of Ann—results of Family Environment Scale

Scales	Raw Score	Standard Score	Third Grade Means
Relationship			
Cohesion	4.0	28	6.67
Expressiveness	5.0	43	5.78
Conflict	8.0	57	7.14
Achievement-Orientation	7.0	55	7.04
Personal Growth			
Independence	3.5	35	5.53
Intellectual/Cultural	2.0	22	5.89
Active/Recreational	3.0	22	7.00
Moral/Religious	8.0	53	7.32
System Maintenance			
Organization	4.5	30	7.18
Control	7.5	52	5.60

SCHOOL ENVIRONMENT

A number of variables are important not only to the attitudes, personal success, and achievement of students but also to a number of nonachievement behaviors such as attendance, social interaction, number of interruptions, and level of questions (McKee and Wilt, 1990). Assessment needs to focus on seating position, classroom design and furniture arrangement, spatial density and crowding, noise, and lighting. Teacher effectiveness research also has identified teacher behaviors that are related to student achievement such as with-itness, overlapping, signal continuity and momentum, group alerting, and accountability in lessons.

Scales have been developed to measure the psychological attributes of the school environment at all levels from kindergarten to graduate school. Various forms measure the perceptions of groups such as parents, teachers, students, and administrators. Some of the major instruments are described here.

Classroom Environment Scale measures the psychosocial environment of the school on three major dimensions—relationship, personal growth, and system maintenance and change. The scales are involvement, affiliation, teacher support, task orientation, competition, order and organization, rule clarity, teacher control, and innovation.

College Characteristics Index (CCI) measures 30 needs derived in part from Murray's theory discussed in Chapter 11. The first nine scales are abasement, achievement, adaptability, affiliation, aggression, change, conjunctivity, counteraction, and deference.

High School Characteristics Index (HCSI) assesses 30 dimensions of environmental press characteristic of the high school environment.

The College Student Experiences Scale (CSEQ) assesses 14 dimensions of college activities, 8 dimensions of college environment, and 21 estimates of outcomes of colleges. Additional sections call for demographic data and opinions about college.

Institutional Functioning Inventory (IFI) can be used to compare how administrators, faculty, students, trustees, and so on perceive dimensions of the college environment. The 11 scales are intellectual-aesthetic extracurriculum, freedom, human diversity, concern for improvement of society, concern for undergraduate learning, democratic governance, meeting local needs, self-study and planning, concern for advancing knowledge, concern for innovation, and institutional spirit.

The Effective School Battery has a form for students and one for teachers. The teacher inventory has 12 parts—background information, involvement of parents, classroom management and teaching practices, resources, job satisfaction, training and other activities, interaction with students, school rules and discipline, how different groups get along, personal safety, personal opinion, and school climate. The student inventory has four parts—what about you, how you spend your time, your school, and what do you think.

SCHOOL CLIMATE

The National Association of Secondary School Principals developed a model to assess school climate (Howard & Keefe, 1991). Their comprehensive model consisted of four types of variables— school district and community environment, school input, school climate, and student outcomes. The school district and community environment variables were the population in the area in which the school was located and the percentage of school-aged children in the area served by the school. The school input variables were the governance of the school (private, public), percentage of minorities enrolled in the school, number of students receiving free or reduced lunches, percentage of students in remedial programs, number of activities for which budgeted resources are available, number of elective courses in the curriculum, average per-pupil expenditure, principal's attitude toward change, performance of the school's administrative team, average teacher salary, student-teacher ratio, percentage of school employees who are professionals, number of transfers in and out of the school, average daily attendance, number of students whose primary language is English, principal's perception of autonomy of action in the district, principal's perception of participation in school decisions, number of students enrolled in the school, nature of student dress rules in the school, nature of student employment rules in the school, importance of 14 selected school goals, teacher satisfaction, teacher perceptions of autonomy of action in district or school, and teacher perceptions of participation in school decisions.

Two school climate variables were teacher climate and student climate; these were measured by the NASSP Climate Surveys.

There were six student outcomes—total achievement (reading and math scores), percentage of students receiving disciplinary referrals, percentage of students passing all courses, student satisfaction, student self-efficacy (measured by the Brookover Self-Concept of Ability Scale), and percentage of students completing the school year (not dropping out). With the impact of school reform and decentralization of authority, much attention has been placed on the school climate and school environment.

WORK ENVIRONMENT

A number of approaches measure the work environment. Sometimes the instrument measures the social-psychological dimensions of work; other times the scale might focus on measuring leadership, stress, organizational climate, or attitudes toward the bureaucratic structure. A sample of environment scales are described here.

Productivity Environmental Preference Survey (PEPS) assesses how workers prefer to function, learn, and perform their work-related or educational activities.

PEPS is used for employee placement and for counseling as well as to provide information for office design and layout. It has scales such as sound, temperature, light, design, motivation, responsibility, persistence, structure, self-orientation, and peer-orientation. There is a computerized version of the test available for PCs.

Rahim Organizational Conflict Inventories (ROCI) measure the types of conflict and various styles of handling conflict found within an organization.

The Organizational Climate Index (OCI) is based on the need-press paradigm of Murray and measures the psychological climate of the work setting.

Occupational Environment Scale assesses the types of stress people experience in their work environment—role-related stress, responsibility for others, role ambiguity, role insufficiency, role overload, and boundary roles.

Leadership Appraisal Survey evaluates how associates view their leader or supervisor and looks at leadership style and components of leadership.

Work Environment Scale, one of 10 social climate scales developed by Moos and his associates, measures three dimensions of work—relationship, personal growth, and system maintenance and system change. The scales are involvement, peer cohesion, supervisor support, autonomy, task orientation, work pressure, clarity, control, innovation, and physical comfort. There are three forms: the real form measures workers' perceptions of existing work environments; the ideal form measures the workers' perceptions of the ideal work environment; and the expectations form measures workers' expectations about their work settings.

PERSON-ENVIRONMENT-FIT

Person-environment-fit theories stress the need to study the congruence between the client's needs, capabilities, and aspirations and environmental demands, resources, and response opportunities (Holland, 1985). Counselors look for ways that different environmental arrangements and conditions force accommodations in behavior and study the individual-environment interactions. At times counselors focus on whether clients are functioning in the environment as predicted. Person-environment-fit has wide application and is especially important when working with preschool children, students with disabilities who need to be mainstreamed, and workers who are making career-change decisions.

Holland (1985) points out that individuals seek an environment that is reinforcing, satisfying, and congruent with their personality types. Holland developed two instruments that measure personality types—the Self-Directed Search and the Vocational Preference Inventory. These tests are discussed in Chapter 10.

CASE OF SAM

Mr. Brown, a beginning fifth-grade mathematics and science teacher, came to the counselor for help. Sam is causing the teacher "fits" because he acts in an inappropriate manner. The counselor decides to use the Instructional Environment Scale (TIES) (Ysseldyke & Christenson, 1987) as the instrument to help understand the situation.

The authors state that TIES systematically describes how a student's academic behavior problems are a function of factors in the instructional environment. TIES is used to gather data on 12 components of effective instruction—instructional presentation, classroom environment, teacher expectations, cognitive emphasis, motivational practice, relevant practice, informed feedback, adaptive instruction, academic engaged time, progress evaluation, instructional planning, and student understanding.

The counselor followed the procedures outlined in the manual.

1. Conducted a classroom observation and recorded the observations on the green form.
2. Interviewed Sam, the student identified by the teacher as a problem, with the structured interview schedule on page 4 of the green form.
3. Interviewed Mr. Brown and completed page 1 of the green form.
4. Reviewed information from the interviews and observations to see if more information was needed.
5. Observed science and mathematics classes and completed the institutional rating form on the blue sheet and the summary profile sheet.
6. Provided feedback to the teacher and to the student.

The counselor carefully read the directions for scoring TIES and read the interpretive examples. The manual presents inter-rater reliabilities ranging from .83 on Cognitive Emphasis and Motivational Strategies to .96 on Informed Feedback and Student Understanding. The median coefficient was .95.

The authors present evidence on the content validity of the 12 components and support each with evidence from research on effective teaching.

After observing Sam, the counselor asked the teacher whether Sam's performance was typical. Mr. Brown said that Sam put on a big show because he had a bigger audience. The teacher said his instructional goals and expectations were the same for all students. He did not plan for Sam separately and followed the instructional sequence as in the syllabus of the county. Mr. Brown said he taught the class as a whole. He wanted to keep all the students at the same place and did not give Sam any independent assignments or help.

In the interview with Sam the counselor asked about the mathematics and science classes Sam had just attended. Sam said he knew what the teacher wanted him to learn but did not know why he had to learn the "junk." He said, "I will never use this stuff." Sam said he did his homework once in a while if he liked the topic. The boy reported that the teacher asked him questions once in a while, but usually he could not answer them. Mr. Brown yelled at him for being lazy, not completing assignments, and not doing his work neatly. The counselor reviewed the class exercise that had just been assigned and found that Sam had completed 10 of 15 math problems, the first seven of which were correct. When the problems called for more than one operation, Sam appeared to be confused.

The counselor rated the 12 dimensions of teaching after observing the classes. Each item was rated on a four-point scale. A rating of 1 indicated that the description was not at all like the student's instructional environment, whereas a rating of 4 indicated that the description was very much like the student's instructional environment. The purpose is to identify instructional strengths and weaknesses and to identify aspects of the environment that are contributing to the student's difficulties. Domains of 1s and 2s suggest areas of difficulty where change is needed for the student to improve academically.

The counselor rated Mr. Brown 4 on instructional presentation, classroom environment, cognitive emphasis, and teacher expectation. Ratings of 3 were given on relevant practice and academic engage time. Scores of 2 were given on motivational strategies, informed feedback, and instructional planning, and 1s were assigned for student understanding, adaptive instruction, and progress evaluation.

SUMMARY

Environmental assessment contributes to the understanding of the dynamics of behavior of children, adults, and the work, school, or other type of environment. The environment can be viewed in terms of physical space—how the space is organized and supervised, the materials in the environment, the people, how it is scheduled, its safety, responsiveness, and so on. The environment can also be assessed from a psychosocial perspective. Research has pointed to the importance of the family/home environment to personal, social, and cognitive growth. Likewise, the school environment and specifically the classroom environment influences the achievement and self-concept of learners. Research on person-environment-fit supports the importance of the congruence between the environment and the individual's potential.

QUESTIONS FOR DISCUSSION

1. What are the theoretical roots of environmental assessment?
2. Why is environmental assessment valuable to the helping professional?
3. What are some of the major models and dimensions of environmental assessment?
4. What are some of the major strategies used to assess the environment?
5. What approaches are used to measure the family environment?
6. Compare and contrast approaches used to measure the school environments.
7. What approaches are used to measure the work environment?

8. Review the case of Ann. What should the counselor say to Ann's mother when reporting the results of this test? Would you have given Ann this test? From information provided how would you rate this test? What tests would you have given Ann, if any? Why?

9. Review the case of Sam. If you were the counselor, how would you proceed to work with Mr. Brown and Sam to improve the instructional environment as well as Sam's academic performance? Discuss possible strategies with other class members.

SUGGESTED ACTIVITIES

1. Interview family counselors and find out what types of assessment instruments and techniques they use and why. Report your results to the class.

2. Interview school counselors and find out what types of assessment instruments and techniques they use to evaluate the school and classroom environment and why. Report your findings to the class.

3. Administer one of the family, work, or school environment scales, score and interpret the results, and present the report to the class.

4. Write a critical review of one of the major environment instruments.

5. Write a paper on one of the current issues in assessing the environment such as person-environment-fit or a similar topic.

6. Study the following case of Team X and answer the questions at the end of it.

A Fortune 500 company decided that it would change its system and utilize work teams. The company had a general orientation session on total quality management (TQM) but did not provide any team building or group skills training, which are crucial elements in TQM. The organization brought in a consultant to try to "fix" the teams when it appeared the experiment resulted in lower, rather than higher, productivity. The consultant gave the Campbell-Halcum Team Development Survey (TDS) to collect baseline data.

The purpose of the TDS is to stimulate a focused discussion about the team's strengths and weaknesses; to help the team identify, acknowledge, and address its problems; to give team members an opportunity to share their ideas for improving the team; to help the leader see how his/her perceptions compare with those of the rest of the team; to identify training needs; and to provide benchmark data to track the team's progress. Members respond to 93 statements using a six-point scale ranging from "strongly agree" to "strongly disagree." A sample of the statements follows.

1. Team members resent being on this team.
2. The team has an excellent idea of the directions needed to accomplish the goals set for it.

There is also a 23-item observation scale that can be used in conjunction with the team member form. This form also uses a six-point scale and includes statements such as "Group members respect each other."

The results of the Team X group and its leader's scores follow.

Dimension/Scale	Team Average T Score	Chair's T Score
Resources		
Commitment	50	51
Competence	60	59
Material Resources	45	60
Time and Staffing	45	55
Information	58	60
Resource Use		
Mission Clarity	38	36
Leadership	40	38
Planning/Organization	42	40
Team Unity	62	64
Empowerment	45	52
Individual Goals	47	52
Improvement		
Conflict Resolution	58	53
Innovation	60	55
Team Assessment	48	60
Feedback	43	40
Rewards	38	40
Team Success		
Satisfaction	55	58
Performance	47	45
Overall Index	51	52

The mean T score is 50 and the SD is 10. The authors call 45–55 the midrange, 55–60 high, and 60 or more very high, whereas 40–45 is low and 35–40 very low.

a. What would you identify as the strengths and weaknesses of the team?
b. How do the perceptions of the chair and members correlate?
c. What implications do the data have for training and development?

ADDITIONAL READINGS

Grotevant, H. D. (1989). *Family assessment: A guide to methods and measures*. New York: Guilford Press.

The authors discuss observational measures and self-report measures, and present abstracts of major schedules and instruments used in family assessment.

Moos, R. H. (1976). *The human context: Environmental determinants of behavior*. New York: Wiley.

Moos presents his psychosocial model of assessing environments.

Touliastos, J., Perlmutter, B. F., & Straus, M. A. (Eds.). (1990). *Handbook of family measurement techniques*. Newbury Park, CA: Sage Publications.

The authors review tests and assessment devices to measure family interaction, intimacy and values, parenthood, roles and power, and adjustment.

CHAPTER 16

Adaptive Testing

Overview

Computer technology has been applied to all phases of testing. For over 30 years test scoring, computing of norms, derived scores, and reliability and validity coefficients have been computerized. Computers are currently being used in the administration, scoring, and interpretation of many types of tests and assessment instruments. All types of instruments—personality, achievement, intelligence, aptitude, and interest—are being programmed for the computer, which is seen as a tool to facilitate and improve measurement practices. Adaptive testing and interactive testing are current practices. A test can be assembled by the microcomputer with an agreed-upon item response methodology and can be tailored to the test taker. Professional literature has given much attention to the topic, and several special issues of professional journals have dealt with it.

Objectives

This chapter should help the reader understand

- what kinds of uses test developers make of computer-assisted and computer-adaptive assessment
- how pencil-and-paper and adaptive tests can be compared and evaluated
- where information about adaptive tests can be found

- how computer-assisted and computer-adaptive tests can be evaluated
- what the advantages and disadvantages are of these approaches to testing

TEST ADMINISTRATION

One of the most common applications is computer administration of items at a terminal. Green (1984) states that tests thus administered are not very different from conventional pencil-and-paper tests. Normally, the items are multiple choice and are presented one at a time. The examinee indicates an answer by pressing a key on a keyboard. Light pens are used with some programs. Instructions are presented visually, and test takers can proceed only by pressing the key that the program requests. Practice items give the examinee a chance to become familiar with the format. On some tests examinees are required to check whether they have pressed the key they meant to press. Madsen (1986) lists seven advantages for test administration on a terminal.

1. Relatively low equipment costs are required if the testing volume is low.
2. Computer-assisted tests reproduce closely the instructions and presentation formats of pencil-and-paper versions.
3. Testing on a terminal has proven to be as cost-effective as traditional testing after the initial equipment costs are covered.
4. Positive client response to computer-assisted testing is common.
5. Evidence is beginning to show that computer testing does not affect the reliability of the instrument over a wide range of special clients and situations.
6. The collection of ancillary test data is now possible on variables such as response time and patterns for items and scales.
7. Adaptive testing, in which selection of the next question is based on the test taker's responses to previous items, is a near perfect example of computer-assisted testing adjusted to suit the needs of individuals. (p. 9)

Watkins and McDermott (1991) summarize the advantages—ability to do interactive testing, more efficient use of staff time, more efficient scoring, reduced error rate, and potential assistance to persons with visual or auditory disabilities. Kline (1993) also summarizes the advantages of computer testing over traditional methods. He believes the first and greatest advantage is that computer-administered testing allows for almost immediate feedback of results. In addition, he notes, administration procedures are always the same. He also states that where skilled examiners are in short supply, the prewritten interpretation can be valuable. Kline also points out that computer-administered tests can facilitate the testing of individuals with disabilities, who can use special keyboards.

As limitations, Watkins and McDermott (1991) note that computer-administered tests depersonalize the client, interface poorly with clients, reduce efficiency with difficult clients, compromise the confidentiality of clients possibly at risk, cannot discriminate between normal and pathological responses, and may introduce bias into testing.

Madsen (1986) also lists several limitations of computer-assisted test administration, such as increased cost and scheduling problems, problems of some test takers in using the equipment, difficult or impossible adaption of certain types of tests and item formats, and lack of normative data for computer-assisted tests. Kline (1993) states that some subjects, particularly older adults and those with intellectual handicaps, may had difficulty with computer-administered tests. In addition, some counselors believe that a primary tenet of counseling is to establish rapport with the client, and a computer cannot do this.

Jackson (1985) points out the differences between standard and computerized administration.

1. Method of presentation of stimulus material—Only one nonverbal item might be present on the screen rather than several on a page in standard administration.

2. Type of task required of the test taker as a result of computer presentation—The computer may not be programmed to review previous responses.

3. Method of recording responses

4. Method of score interpretation (p. 7)

One other difference is that more information can be gained through computer administration. Green (1984) indicates that the computer can time each response and produce a response rate in addition to the number of correct answers.

EQUIVALENCE OF CONVENTIONAL AND COMPUTER TESTS

Bunderson, Inouye, and Olsen (1989), in reviewing the studies on computer-based testing and conventional testing, conclude that the reliabilities of the computer and conventional tests are very similar and that computer tests tend to yield lower scores than conventional tests. Green (1984) states that when a conventional test is transferred to computer presentation, there is no assurance that the test performance will be equivalent. He concludes that time limit differences and response differences could affect the total test score (p. 5). Research has indicated that when speed tests are translated from pencil-and-paper to a computer mode of presentation, responses come much faster on the computer. In their study of computer and conventional modes, Greaud and Green (1986) found a large mean difference in favor of the computer.

Because the computer normally presents one item at a time in a regular sequence, this type of presentation directs the test takers' attention to each item. The computer also forces a change in how the test takers can take tests. On pencil-and-paper tests the examinee can scan the whole test, skip around, and leave out items. Most computer programs, however, force the examinee to answer questions in order and thus discourage skipping. This procedure may be a potential source of difference on personality and interest tests. Lee, Moreno, and Sympson (1984) reported that individuals taking computer versions of mathematics tests are less likely to turn away from the display and use pencil and scratch paper than are examinees with pencil-and-paper versions. Jackson (1991) concludes that advances in computer technology including touch screens, voice recognition, and rapid access to massive scored data give us a greater capacity to do justice to the complexity of personality. Watkins and McDermott (1991) state that most of the current applications are narrow in scope and application but promise increased efficiency, economy, and reliability.

Allred and Harris (1984) report that on an adjective checklist, people tested by computer are more likely to check more adjectives as applying to themselves than are individuals using conventional formats. Green (1984) concludes that conventional and computer-presented tests may yield scores that are not directly comparable. He calls for different norms for the two versions or some system of scale transformation that will permit the same norms to be used. Jackson (1985) concludes that modifications introduced by computer-aided testing require equivalence studies and, sometimes, restandardization of the test. He believes that it is appropriate to require test makers who publish computer-aided testing to provide evidence of the comparability of pencil-and-paper and computer formats (p. 9).

INDIVIDUALIZATION

One of the major advantages for computer presentations of ability, aptitude, and achievement tests is that the format makes possible individualization of the tasks to be measured. Item banks can be developed, and the computer can be programmed to select items from the set so that each test taker could get a different test. Two types of formats—adaptive and nonadaptive—are used. On adaptive tests the item selection is sequential—that is, the items are selected on the basis of how the test taker performed on the previous items. An estimate of the examinee's skill level is made after each item response and is the basis for selection of the next item. The method gives rough approximations and requires a number of responses before the precision improves. One advantage is the climate created by the process—high-ability individuals are not bored by lots of easy items, and low-ability test takers are not frustrated by questions that are too difficult. Green (1984) concludes that computer tests can be more precise, moving estimates up and down the scale until a sufficiently accurate ability estimate is found—often after half the number of items a conventional test would need (p. 10).

In nonadaptive testing the items are selected at random from the item bank so that each test taker gets a different test form. This method has been used to simplify test security and repetitive testing. It also reduces the advantage of coaching on specific item content. This approach is useful when individuals have to be retested, such as on minimum-level skills or essential-skills tests. However, the item pool must be large so that the items presented on the retake are not likely to have been included on the first test. One problem with this approach is equivalence. If the item bank contains items that are homogeneous in content and of approximately equal difficulty, the tests will be fairly parallel and equal.

COMPUTER-AIDED PERSONALITY TESTING

Computer-aided personality testing is also receiving as much attention as computer applications of testing in the cognitive areas. Jackson (1985) lists the following advantages of computer-aided personality testing.

1. The saving of time of the counselor or psychologist
2. The possibility of using trained assistants to monitor test administration
3. The short time lag between administering the test, scoring it, and interpreting it
4. The elimination of human scoring errors
5. The programming capability of the computer to combine rules and complicated processing
6. The standardization of interpretations, eliminating different points of view
7. The potential for systematically collecting and developing normative databases
8. The ability of the computer to perform complex scoring procedures
9. The ability to use computer-based assessment with special populations for whom standard pencil-and-paper procedures are not feasible (p. 5)

The widespread availability of microcomputers has made possible not only on-line presentation of stimulus material but all types of programs for scoring and interpreting the test data. Studies with computer-assisted testing of psychiatric and physically disabled patients and of individuals at all age levels have been made. Programs have been developed to aid psychiatric diagnosis; diagnosis of alcoholism, type A behavior, personal construct systems; and personal decision making and career guidance.

EVALUATING COMPUTER-BASED ADAPTIVE TESTING

Green (1984) lists five main psychometric criteria for evaluating computer-based adaptive testing—unidimensionality, reliability, validity, quality of the item parameters, and equating. Unidimensionality relates to the domain being measured. In ability and aptitude testing, items should be homogeneous and should correlate highly with the total score. The test or scale usually yields one score. However, evidence should be presented that the domain is unidimensional and measures primarily one dimension.

Reliability for these tests is computed by the use of an internal consistency reliability index. McBride and Martin (1983) found twice as many items are needed on a conventional test to get the same reliability as on a computer-adaptive test. Content, predictive, and construct validity information is also important in evaluating computer-adaptive tests. The criterion-related and construct validity of these tests is computed in the same way as for a pencil-and-paper test. It is important to look at how the content validity of the items was studied.

The quality of parameters relates to the quality of the reliability indexes of the items, and the estimate of the item parameters appears to require a large number of cases and items (Green, 1984, p. 15). Because not all items are used with each test taker, those items selected can affect reliability significantly. Items with low reliability dilute the estimate of time parameters of items with good reliability.

Green (1984) identifies two aspects to equating. Because each individual's test is unique, the tests must be certified as equivalent. This task demands that the test is unidimensional with a small error of measurement and that the item responses fit the item response theory model. The second is being able to equate the computer-adaptive test score with the conventional test score. The Educational Testing Service publication *Computer Based Testing: From Multiple Choice to Multiple Choices* (1994) gives these advantages of computer-adaptive testing.

1. Mastery levels can be demonstrated faster and the test can be terminated (licensure or certification) once a test taker has reached the criterion level of mastery.

2. Testing is more interesting and positive. The test provides questions at a level that is consistently appropriate and challenging to the test taker.

3. Testing time is shortened by focusing on the test taker's ability level.

4. Increased psychometric precision is possible over a broad range of proficiency.

In assessing computer-assisted and computer-adaptive tests, the form included in Figure 16.1 might be useful. Moreland (1992) summarizes four important factors in assessing computer-assisted test interpretations: the credentials of the system author, the documentation of the system, the scholarly review of the system, and the tryouts of the system.

PROFESSIONAL STANDARDS AND GUIDELINES

In *Guidelines for Computer-Based Tests and Interpretations* the American Psychological Association (1985) suggests that automated tests be used as only one of several sources of information about clients. Shertzer (1986) recommends that professional training standards be changed so that all graduate students in the helping professions take a course in computer applications with emphasis on computer-assisted testing and become familiar with the APA guidelines. He calls for five main objectives to be gained.

Test title _____

Description of test _____

Description of scales _____

Potential uses _____

Publisher's address _____

       Phone _____

Author qualifications _____

Hardware requirements _____

      K _____

      Additional equipment _____

System availability	Trial period available	_____ YES
_____ Apple		_____ NO
_____ IBM		
_____ Other_____		

Materials provided

_____ Handbook or guidebook	_____ Video cassettes
_____ Technical manual	_____ Training package
_____ User's manual	_____ Other_____
_____ Discs	

Cost

_____ Number of uses

_____ Software cost per user

_____ Supplemental costs (Other systems, additional hardware) _____

Populations to be served

_____ Primary/preschool	_____ Young adult
_____ Elementary (K–6)	_____ College/junior college
_____ Junior high (7–9)	_____ Adult
_____ High school (10–12)	_____ 65+
_____ Special populations (specify)_____	

Potential users	Sophistication required
_____ Administrators	_____ High
_____ Counselors	_____ Medium
_____ Psychologists	_____ Low
_____ Teachers	
_____ Students/examinees	

Features available on software

_____ Test scoring	_____ Measures of variability
_____ Test score interpretation	_____ Record-keeping features

Figure 16.1
Form to evaluate computer testing programs

Features available on software *(continued)*

_____ Item analysis, difficulty, discrimination   _____ Individual records
_____ Reliability information   _____ Accumulated record keeping
_____ Descriptive statistics   on individuals
_____ Group records   _____ Tabular presentations
_____ Capability of adding other data   _____ Graphic presentations
_____ Measures of central tendency

Administration features

_____ Self-administered   _____ Can add local items
_____ Randomly generated   _____ Computer-adaptive

Technical characteristics (1 = excellent, 2 = good, 3 = poor)

_____ User friendliness   _____ Ease of operation
_____ Display   _____ Ease of input/entry
_____ Documentation   _____ Printing/graphics
_____ Storage capacity   _____ Flexibility
_____ Clarity of score   _____ Profiles
_____ Clarity of reports   _____ Error checking
_____ Ability to change scores   _____ Reading level
_____ Response time between input and feedback   _____ Help options
_____ Reliability data   _____ Internal consistency
_____ Parallel forms   _____ Standard error measurement
_____ Content validity   _____ Construct validity
_____ Predictive validity   _____ Concurrent validity

Item selection/presentation

_____ Access to directions   _____ Skipping features
_____ Type of item selection
    _____ Random   _____ Sequential
    _____ Adaptive   _____ Feedback

Display conventions

_____ Format   _____ Color
_____ Headings   _____ Highlighting
_____ Menus

Answering/scoring

_____ Answer registration methods   _____ Backup and changing answers
_____ Error hopping

Norms

_____ Computer assisted/adaptive format   _____ Pencil-and-paper format
_____ Appropriateness   _____ Adequacy of sample
_____ Types of scores

Figure 16.1, *continued*

1. Basic computer literacy

2. Knowledge of information sources

3. An objective and evaluative attitude toward computer-based tests

4. Understanding of the individual's right to privacy

5. Knowledge of and experience with computer-assisted testing

Because of accelerated advances in computer technology—touch screens, voice recognition, rapid access to data—our knowledge of computer hardware and software needs to keep pace. The field is evolving in its methods and standards. Green (1991) sees the standards as a living document that provides us with an important start but that will require frequent revision.

Standards for Educational and Psychological Testing (1985) also addresses the issue of computer-assisted and computer-adaptive testing. The standards call for adaptive tests to provide estimates of the magnitude of errors of measurement based on the analysis of the results from repeated administrations using different items. Alternate form estimates of reliability are necessary to provide an independent check on the magnitude of errors in measurement in adaptive testing. The guidelines caution against concurrent comparisons between pencil-and-paper and adaptive forms as estimates of the alternate form reliability; however, if the variance in the methods is small, the tests can be considered parallel.

The standards also suggest that the author needs to provide in the manual the rationale and supporting evidence for procedures used in selecting items for administration, deciding when enough items have been presented, and scoring the test.

The scaling, norming, score comparability, and equating procedures used in adaptive testing need to be reported. The authors are responsible for providing specific information about the methods of equating the different forms of the test, as well as studies checking the adequacy of equating procedures.

The environment for the administration of computer-adaptive tests call for the items displayed on the screen to be legible and free from glare, with the terminal properly positioned. The novelty of presentation should be watched since it might have an unknown effect on the test administration.

Green (1991) recommends that a good strategy is to use the system, enter a set of responses, and examine the results and their interpretation. Counselors should review similar systems at the same time so they can compare how the systems react to the same response pattern.

SOURCES OF INFORMATION

Many sources of information on software exist in this field. Journals publish reviews or have articles and research on computer-assisted and computer-adaptive testing. Professional organizations that address computerized testing are concerned with standards and provide useful information to users. Computer networks, reference and resource books, ERIC documents, and annotated bibliographies are plentiful. Several sources are identified at the end of this chapter.

COMPUTER OPTIONS

Several programs are available to help individuals computerize their own tests. These programs address

1. how the items are presented to the test takers—in high-resolution text, color graphics, special characters, and even foreign alphabets

2. how the test is designed—conventional format (everyone gets the same item), sequential (testing continues until the examiner can make a decision), adaptive (maximum information)

3. how the narrative score interpretation is presented—in the test maker's own words and style or geared to the specific needs of the test taker or tester

4. how the data is stored

5. how the data is scored and what type of statistical analysis is completed

ADVANTAGES AND DISADVANTAGES OF COMPUTER APPLICATIONS

Some of the major advantages of the computer applications discussed in this chapter are these.

1. Quick, easy, and economical collection of information

2. Improved scoring accuracy

3. Possible alternate formats

4. Faster feedback to the tester and test taker

5. Reduced time spent on routine tasks, such as intake, interviewing, and initial assessment

6. View of computer-assisted testing and interpretation as legitimate and important

7. Endless computer applications

8. Item response theory allows for persons to get different sets of items

Disadvantages of computer applications include these factors.

1. Computer interpretations are confounded because no allowances are made for the client's emotional state, physical disabilities, or other pertinent characteristics.

2. Some traditional instruments may not be easily adapted to computer formats. Computer-assisted tests have different psychometric properties than the paper-and-pencil tests they replace.

3. Normative data may be inadequate for computer-assisted or computer-adaptive tests.

4. The equipment can be expensive, and multiple scoring problems might arise with inadequate equipment.

5. Adequate client-screening procedures need to be developed to identify clients in crisis, who may be unable to concentrate or respond to a computer-assisted interview or assessment.

6. Costs in equipment, training, and time may not be worthwhile.

7. Computers lack human involvement—some individuals see the computer as cold and inhuman.

8. Clients may see a threat to the confidentiality of test data; computers have the potential to collect, store, and recall much intimate information.

9. The standards for obtaining these tests are not strictly monitored.

10. A big investment of money is needed by publishers to develop this type of testing.

It is important to remember that the examiner does not have access to decisions or rules the authors have developed or selected. The computer can be guided to make decisions, but someone has to program the computer, providing the information or rules for decision making. Individuals in the helping professions certainly need to develop computer literacy, but that literacy may not be sufficient to evaluate computer rules and procedures. Consequently, it is necessary to be cautious in the utilization of computerized reports with clients. Some individuals advocate using the computer for what it can do best—quickly process and store information—and humans for what they can do best—think, interpret, and interact.

Dramatic changes in computer technology make possible a more sophisticated diagnostic analysis of item responses and interpretive reporting of test results. Baker (1989) points out that these two areas depend more on the state of the art in psychology and artificial intelligence than on technology. New systems merge the important components of actuarial and clinical reasoning.

TRENDS AND ISSUES

Wise and Plake (1990) point out that we have gone through several generations of computer applications. Initially paper-and-pencil tests were programmed for the computer. Now new formats and types of items are possible, and computer-based simulations can be used in training and testing of problem solving. Many developments in computer and video technology in the past 25 years have occurred, and we can anticipate even greater impact on the field of testing in the future. Hanson (1986) predicts that society will be moving out of the print medium into ready access to video disk and computer-based information. She states that computers now have the capacity to give tests, compute scale scores, print results, and provide interpretative comments and diagnostic information for objective aptitude, ability, achievement, psychomotor, interest, and personality tests as well as for projective tests such as the Rorschach (p. 50). The systems, she concludes, are all self-contained and require only a client who can read a video display and type or a clerk who can assist with those tasks. Hanson believes that, with videodisks storing visual and auditory information, testing applications will not necessarily be limited to data, graphics, and printed words but can be supplemented with sound and motion picture or still-frame visual materials.

Helping professionals are seeing a tremendous growth in the instruments being adopted, adapted, and created for administration by microcomputer. Meier and Geiger (1986) conclude that confidentiality is the issue most often mentioned in discussions of ethical problems regarding computers. Sampson and Pyle (1983) proposed ethical principles for computer-assisted testing and assessment, addressing the issue of individual rights and confidentiality. They recommend that counselors ensure confidential data are restricted to appropriate professionals, and they propose establishing computer security and proper storage of data.

Bersoff and Hofer (1991) remind us of the many legal issues involved such as copyright of the test, scoring procedures, norms and correlational tables. Authors and publishers are reluctant to release the scoring and interpretation procedures and view these as trade secrets. Questions arise concerning the use of computer reports. Are counselors who are not trained in a certain test interpretation liable when they use computer interpretive reports?

Vale (1990) identifies the 1990s as a period when computer-adaptive testing may thrive or cease to be. He points out the three most important issues affecting this type of testing—technology, economics, and marketability. Is computer-adaptive testing ready to implement? Are there benefits to implementing this approach? Can those benefits be sold to test users? It appears that computer-adaptive testing is increasing. The National Council on Licensure Examinations reported that the Nurses Licensing Testing, for example, has a computer-adaptive form. The Graduate Record Examination, the Professional Assessment of Beginning Teachers, and the examinations of the National Council of Architectural Registration Boards all have computer-adaptive forms available. The Educational Testing Service utilizes the Sylvan Technology Centers to administer its computer-adaptive versions of tests. Convenience is a strong argument for these types of tests: Clients have a choice of time and date and have a more personalized learning experience in a controlled environment. They receive preliminary scores immediately and final results much faster. Computer-adaptive testing in this context provides equal access, sensitivity to the needs of users with disabilities, and test security. The differential item function ensures equality and fairness in testing.

SUMMARY

Computer technology has been utilized in all phases of testing. Many tests now have computer-assisted versions. Computer-assisted testing allows for more efficient use of staff time, more efficient and reliable scoring, and greater flexibility in testing individuals with disabilities. Disadvantages include depersonalization of the client and poor interfaces of the client with the computer. The issue of confidentiality is also of concern. Computer-adaptive testing is becoming more widely available to assess the aptitude and achievement of test takers. Many tests provide computer-generated interpretations of tests. Helping professionals are seeing a tremendous growth in the instruments being adopted, adapted, and created for administration, scoring, and interpretation by the microcomputer. Users need to be certain that these tests meet the professional standards for educational and psychological testing and be alert to the legal and ethical issues involved with computer testing.

QUESTIONS FOR DISCUSSION

1. Do you agree with Meier and Geiger's (1986) recommendation that all graduate students in the helping professions complete a course in computer applications in human services, with special emphasis on computer-assisted testing? Why or why not?

2. In what ways are computer-assisted assessment and traditional assessment techniques alike? In what ways are they different?

3. Should assessing be left to the computer and interpretation to the human service professional? Defend your position on this issue.

4. What do you see as future trends in this field? Hansen (1986) states that traditional computer-based interpretive systems are analogous to the printed medium, whereas videodisc systems move the technology into the visual arena. Do you believe that there will be marked acceptance of the new technologies and innovative approaches in assessment? Why or why not?

5. Adaptive testing is not a new concept but has been adapted for use with the computer. One of the advantages of computer-adaptive testing is that it saves time. Do you believe the results of such approaches will be as valid or reliable as those of traditional testing? Why or why not?

SUGGESTED ACTIVITIES

1. Take a computer-assisted test on a microcomputer. Evaluate your experience and report the findings to the class.

2. Interview test takers who have taken computer-adaptive tests and identify their attitudes toward the experience. What aspects did they like best? What aspects did they like least?

3. Make an annotated bibliography of computer-adaptive and computer-assisted tests that are currently available in your field.

4. Get three or four computerized reports of test results. Analyze them according to criteria such as understandability, attractiveness of format, readability, and psychometric properties.

5. Devise a rating scale to evaluate computer-assisted or computer-adaptive tests and select an instrument to evaluate with your scale. Compare the traditional test form with the computerized form. Are there marked differences in the two versions?

6. Read the following case study and answer the questions at the end.

   Lu is upset to learn that the professional licensing examination is a computer-adaptive test now and given at the XYZ Technology Center. She complains to you, her counselor, and says

   "At my age, I hate computers. I don't use one . . . I don't want one! How can they really say that the results are the same as before? The exam use to be 6 hours and now you say it will only take me 2 hours. How can they cover all the knowledge we are supposed to have in a 2-hour period? Also, I don't type or speak 'computerese' . . . I will be at a disadvantage!"

   a. How would you answer her concerns?
   b. How would you help her to be "up" for the testing and alleviate her anxiety?

ADDITIONAL READINGS

Professional journals:

Behavior Research Methods and Instrumentation

Computer Living

Computers in Human Behavior

Computers in Human Services

Computers in Psychiatry/Psychology

Counseling Psychologist

Educational and Psychological Measurement

International Journal of Man-Machine Studies

Journal of Counseling and Development

Journal of Educational Measurement

Journal of Occupational Psychology

Measurement and Evaluation in Counseling and Development

Psychiatric Annals

Gutkin, T. B., & Wise, S. L. (Eds.). (1991). *The computer and decision-making process.* Hillsdale, NJ: Lawrence Erlbaum.

The book has chapters on computer-assisted personality test interpretation, psychodiagnostic applications, validity of computer-based interpretation, use of computers in behavioral assessment, use in industrial/organizational psychology, legal issues, and guidelines for computer testing.

Moreland, K. L. (1992). Computer-assisted psychological assessment. In M. Zeidner & R. Most (Eds.), *Psychological testing: An inside view* (pp. 343–376). Palo Alto, CA: Consulting Psychologists Press.

The chapter provides the reader with a current overview of what is happening in computer-assisted testing.

Wainer, H. (1990). *Computerized adaptive testing: A primer.* Hillsdale, NJ: Lawrence Erlbaum.

Topics such as history, system design and operation, item pools, item response theory, item calibration and proficiency estimation, scaling and equating, reliability and measurement precision, validity, and future challenges are discussed.

CHAPTER 17

Alternate and Authentic Assessment Techniques

Overview

Observation is one of the primary data-gathering tools of workers in the helping professions. The main purpose of observation is to collect information that will be useful in describing, interpreting, and explaining client behavior. Sometimes an individual is observed in a natural situation such as on the job, in the classroom, or at home. At other times the individual can be observed in a contrived or a simulated situation. Observation is one of the key tools of assessment. Shertzer and Linden (1979) call it humankind's first educational tool and first method of appraisal (p. 366). Observation of test behavior is sometimes as important as the actual answers given by the individual. The interview is also an important assessment tool for workers in the helping professions.

There has been a growing dissatisfaction with traditional testing procedures and a movement toward alternative and authentic assessment techniques. These procedures have been utilized in assessing achievement primarily but are currently being used in other areas.

Objectives

The chapter should help the reader identify

* the different methods of observation and the procedures and techniques utilized

* the methods, procedures, and techniques of alternate and authentic assessment

- the use of rating scales, interview schedules, and checklists
- the use of observation in analyzing test behavior
- the problems that arise in the use of interview schedules and rating scales

OBSERVATIONAL APPROACHES

Observational techniques are used in many types of settings. Workers in the helping professions use observational techniques to assess client behavior in play therapy, sociodrama, psychodrama, simulated experiences, role playing, test performance, discussion groups, conferences, and interviews. The procedures vary considerably. Observations can focus on specific behaviors that are objective and observable or on general, overall behavior or adjustment. Observations can be a one-shot affair or a sampling over a longer span of time. The observer can use rating or record forms,

Attention	1 Low	2	3	4	5 High
Response time	1 Slow	2	3	4	5 Quick
Activity level	1 Passive	2	3	4	5 Active
Security	1 Ill at ease	2	3	4	5 Calm and collected
Anxiety	1 Low	2	3	4	5 High
Relationship to examiner	1 Poor	2	3	4	5 Good
Need for reinforcement	1 Low	2	3	4	5 High
Task orientation	1 Gives up	2	3	4	5 Sticks to task
Reaction to failure	1 Poor	2	3	4	5 Good
Interest in test	1 Low	2	3	4	5 High

Figure 17.1
Sample observational scale for an intelligence test

observation schedules, or devices such as the tape recorder, video equipment, or computers to record the data. Rating scales, anecdotal records, ranking scales, sociometric tests, client-kept records, checklists, and self-appraisal scales are some of the varied recording methods used.

Test Behavior Observational Scales

A variety of scales may be included as part of a testing package. For example, there are observation forms that examiners can use with some of the individual intelligence tests (see Figure 17.1). Some scales can be used with many types of individual tests (see Figure 17.2).

	Low		Moderate				High
Attitudes Toward the Test							
Interest in the test	1	2	3	4	5	6	7
Motivation to perform well	1	2	3	4	5	6	7
Attitudes Toward the Examiner							
Degree of rapport	1	2	3	4	5	6	7
Degree of cooperation	1	2	3	4	5	6	7
Degree of comfort	1	2	3	4	5	6	7
Degree of openness	1	2	3	4	5	6	7
General Behavior							
Degree of anxiety	1	2	3	4	5	6	7
Degree of self-confidence	1	2	3	4	5	6	7
Praise or reinforcement needed	1	2	3	4	5	6	7
Frustration tolerance	1	2	3	4	5	6	7
Work Style							
Attention span	1	2	3	4	5	6	7
Impulsivity	1	2	3	4	5	6	7
Persistence	1	2	3	4	5	6	7
Methodical thinking	1	2	3	4	5	6	7
Interest in being challenged	1	2	3	4	5	6	7
Response time	1	2	3	4	5	6	7
Personality Style							
Introversion	1	2	3	4	5	6	7
Reality orientation	1	2	3	4	5	6	7
Mood swing	1	2	3	4	5	6	7
Seriousness	1	2	3	4	5	6	7
Degree of spontaneity	1	2	3	4	5	6	7
Internality	1	2	3	4	5	6	7

Figure 17.2
Test observation form

Slosson and Callisto (1984) have designed a scale to aid the examiner in the observational process, entitled Observational Analysis. The behavioral profile calls for the examiner to check categories such as outward behavior, relationship with examiner, recall, affective tone, attitude, work habits, and expression. The authors also have a visual scanning form to be used for physical observations of the client, including observations of the head and face; arms, torso, and hands; legs and gait; and miscellaneous other categories. A posttest questionnaire requests verbal answers from the client in response to questions such as "Did you feel comfortable or uneasy about taking the test?" The system involves the observation of the client in the total communication process.

Clinical Observations

The examiner may also want to observe the client in learning, performing, or social situations. Observations may be focused on a specific observable behavior, such as time on task, or may cover a wide variety of behaviors, such as affective, cognitive, psychomotor, and social. The examiner might use a checklist of whether a behavior was present or record anecdotal records of typical behavior. Clinical observation is an extremely valuable tool in working with very young children or with clients who have mental or emotional disabilities.

The examiner might be concerned with dimensions of psychomotor performance. Observation of fine-motor coordination might focus on hand-eye coordination; use of fingers; angle of paper to body; reversals or rotations in copying, drawing or writing; and handedness (Hargrove and Poteet, 1984). Observation of gross-motor behavior might look at balance, activity level, body shifts, body positioning, and coordination.

Observation of social behavior can also be helpful, focusing on the relationships the client has with peers, teachers, authority figures, siblings, and parents. Dimensions of cognitive behavior might also be interesting—not only learning styles but also approaches to reasoning and ways of memorizing. Many affective components are related to learning, such as frustration and fatigue, motivation and effort, attention to task, and distractibility.

Self-Observations

On many occasions self-observations are important. A variety of types of data may be collected. Shapiro and Cole (1993) state that the simplest and most common method for collecting self-monitored data is to have the client record the occurrences of the targeted behavior. The data can be summarized over time and frequency rates complied. Sometimes the client is asked to tally the number of incidences of the targeted behavior in time units. There are mechanical devices to help the client tally such as golf counters and wrist counters.

A counselor is often helped in interpreting a case study by an autobiography, diary, journal, letters, themes, stories, and poems. Aiken (1985) states that most people spend quite a bit of time in observing themselves. He cautions that self-observations are most likely to be more biased than the observations made by others (p. 325). However, individuals can be trained to be more objective and systematic in self-observation. They can be trained to keep records of their thinking, actions, and feelings. Since the data is recorded by the individual, periodic checks for accuracy might be necessary. Often the data is checked against ratings by others.

Autobiographies are used to provide insight into individual behavior, attitudes, and personality dimensions. Counselors can specify a certain format or allow individuals to arrange their thoughts however they want. Autobiographies include the facts the clients think are important about their environments. This form of expression also reveals self-concept; but it does rely on trust, and individuals may be concerned about confidentiality. Autobiographies may give insight into personality dynamics and conflicts, but counselors should interpret the data in light of other available information. One of the problems with this method is that many clients tend to overlook their limitations and weaknesses.

The two major formats are structured and unstructured. The counselor may specify the format or allow the individuals to arrange their thoughts any way they want. The counselor must study the autobiography and then interpret the data along with other types of information collected. Autobiographies may give some insight into the personality dynamics and conflicts of the clients.

Logs, journals, and diaries are other approaches. These sources help counselors discern individual interests and activities, but it is difficult to get people to keep logs and diaries on a day-to-day basis. Themes, poems, letters, and stories authored by the client may also provide valuable information about the individual or at least stimulate discussion in a counseling situation. Content analysis is used in looking at this data; the methodology is described in most textbooks on research methods in the social sciences.

Unstructured Versus Structured Observation

One way of looking at observation is by classifying it into structured and unstructured categories. Unstructured observation is open-ended. The helping professional observes the behavior of the client, recording as much as possible of whatever appears to be useful or important. After the data are collected, the observer attempts to analyze and evaluate the behavior. A different approach is the use of structured observation, in which the helping professional has already determined why the observation is to take place, what is to be observed, and how the data will be recorded. This approach is deliberately systematic. The different purposes of observation lead to different approaches.

Problems in Observation

Sometimes breakdowns happen in the tracking and recoding of observations. Barrios (1993) identified four such problems. The first is lack of a clear definition of the construct to be observed. To prevent this, the definition needs to be more precise, concrete, and observable. A second problem is the demands of the scale. Sometimes the observer has to record too many behaviors. The validity and reliability of the observations can be increased if the number of behaviors, complexity of the coding, or duration of the observation is decreased. The third breakdown is caused by distractions. Occasionally some external or internal event diverts the observer's attention and focus. This could be eliminated or reduced by imposing greater structure on the observation, changing the milieu of the observation, or, in some cases, changing the observer. Mistreatment is the last type of breakdown. Sometimes observers are not treated with dignity and respect. This breakdown can be avoided by ensuring dignity, respect, and greater appreciation for the observers. They should be praised when they do a good job.

Critical Incident Approach

Flanagan (1954) proposed using another form of uncontrolled and naturalistic observation called the critical incident technique. Supervisors are asked to identify specific behaviors that are critical to job performance or that distinguish good or poor work behavior. Analysis of their input provides valuable information on the requirements for effective performance. This technique has been applied to a number of contexts. Shertzer and Linden (1979) point out that having an individual clarify critical events in his life provides insight into the personal and social factors that have affected that person's behavior. Some career planning exercises call for individuals to make a time line and record the 10 most critical events in their lives (see Figure 17.3).

Situation Tests

Situation tests are a form of controlled observation. In one classic example of the technique Hartshorne and May (1928) studied character traits by observing children in a variety of structured situations, some of which permitted them to cheat and win at a game, copy test answers, or steal coins. The researchers found that children's honesty was highly dependent on the situation in which they were observed. For example, no child tended to be totally honest or totally dishonest. A boy who was an excellent student but a poor athlete would not cheat if asked to correct his own paper but would inflate his score in a sports situation. A girl who excelled in physical performance but was a poor speller would record her physical performance correctly but cheat on scoring her spelling.

Another example occurred during World War II when the United States Office of Strategic Services (OSS) had to select special agents to carry out espionage or other special intelligence assignments. The candidates were observed and participated in a wide variety of assessment techniques, including pencil-and-paper tests, stress inter-

		a	b	c	d		e			
0	5	10	15	20	25	30	35	40	45	50

a = Work experience in community agency during high school
b = Graduated from college with degree in psychology, got married,
      did not work
c = Divorced, took job as secretary, went part-time to the university
      to become certified as an elementary teacher
d = Began teaching second grade
e = Felt burnout, decided to change careers and become a guidance
      counselor, went back to the university for master's

Figure 17.3
Critical events exercise

views, problem-solving exercises, and a wide variety of situational tests (OSS Assessment Staff, 1948). The candidates were rated by the assessment staff and by their own peers, but the validity of these procedures was never established because performance on the tasks was never correlated with success on assignments carried out by those selected.

Situational testing has been utilized in a variety of settings, including the selection of clinical psychologists (Kelly and Fiske, 1951). One variation of this technique is a leaderless group discussion in which group process becomes the means of observing individual behavior. Candidates for a position might all be invited to a session in which they are given a problem situation to solve, a controversial topic to discuss, or a plan of operation to devise. Observers focus on certain salient traits that they are looking for, such as leadership or problem-solving ability.

A simulated work experience assessment is the In-Basket Test (Frederiksen, Saunders, & Wand, 1957) in which the examinee is given a variety of materials that provide background information from memoranda to technical reports. The examinee is then presented with a series of problems in the "in" basket and is asked to take action—for example, hiring or firing personnel or handling production problems. A number of versions of this approach have been developed for different groups, such as school administrators and military officers. Candidates demonstrate how they would handle each problem and are evaluated not only on their solutions but also on the processes used. Simulated tests are becoming more popular with the availability of varied software programs for the microcomputer.

Brown (1983) identifies problems that arise in the scoring and interpreting of situational tests. He concludes that the data generated with this technique often have undesirable statistical properties, are based on ratings using ordinal scales, have a limited range of values, and in general are unreliable.

Unobtrusive Versus Participant Observation

Often it is possible to observe an examinee through a two-way mirror. Because the observer in this situation is not seen by the examinee, ethical guidelines call for the examinee to be informed and give approval. Unfortunately, when an examinee realizes he or she is being observed, performance may not be typical. However, when visitors come by regularly, targeted individuals may not be aware of being observed. When there is no interaction between the observer and those being observed, and when the individual's behavior is not affected by the situation, observations are said to be unobtrusive.

Participation observation, a tool of the cultural anthropologist, involves the observer as a part of the observational situation. The observer evaluates the group or individuals while participating in the interaction. Aiken (1985) states that the observer's own behavior affects the reactions of other people in the situation (p. 32), but the technique can aid the observer to understand the dynamics of the situation.

Training Observers

Barrios (1993) points out that a key factor in getting valid and reliable data from observation is the training of observers. The first step is orientation, explaining the purpose and importance of observation. The second step is education, instruction in the definitions and recording schemes. The third step is evaluation, which involves assessing the observer's knowledge of the definitions, coding, and tracking procedures. The fourth step is application, in which observers obtain experience in a number of different situations. The fifth step is recalibration, which involves checking the accuracy and agreement of observers and correcting any deviation. The last step is termination, or seeking the observers' feedback and evaluation of the process. Their contribution to the project needs to be acknowledged. Observers should be reminded of the need to maintain confidentiality.

METHODS OF DATA COLLECTION

The observer may want to focus on a single incident or on all client behavior in a given time period. The records needed depend on the purpose of the observations. The observer might take notes, dictate observations into a tape recorder, or use a checklist, rating scale, or behavior tallying or charting procedure. Decisions beforehand include

1. who will be observed
2. what will be observed
3. where the observation will take place
4. when the observation will take place
5. how the observation will be recorded

Anecdotal Records

One method of recording is the anecdotal record, which is a good way to gather information about a client's social adjustment. Anecdotal records are brief accounts of behavior that are recorded in a log or on index cards. An anecdote is a written description of an observed event. The following information should be included.

1. Name of individual observed
2. Name of observer
3. Date and time of the observation
4. Location of the observation
5. Anecdote
6. Context
7. Interpretation (Ten Brink, 1970, p. 166)

Ten Brink also includes eight procedural suggestions for recording behavioral anecdotes.

1. Focus on a single specific incident.
2. Be brief but complete.
3. Use objective behavioral descriptions.
4. Use phrases rather than sentences as long as the phrases are understandable.
5. List the behaviors in the sequence in which they occurred.
6. Evaluate what you have written. Is it a good snapshot of behavior?
7. Include direct quotations whenever possible and significant.
8. Record both positive and negative statements.

An advantage of the anecdotal record is that it does not depend upon the individual's capacity to communicate with the observer. In addition, this approach uses natural settings to observe behavior, and the systematic collection of such information can help in the understanding of a client's behavior. The major disadvantages are the time and expense of observation, the time it takes to write down the verbal description, and the questionable objectivity and reliability of the records.

Behavior Tallying and Charting.   Many times the easiest way to record certain behaviors is to tally their occurrences. Sometimes concern centers around the number of times a behavior occurs, as is the case in educational environments where precision teaching or behavior modification efforts are taking place. At other times concern focuses not only on the frequency of behavior but also on the duration of a behavior. A teacher might be interested in how much time a student spends in her own seat or what percentage of time a preschooler spends crying. Time sampling might be used for behaviors that occur at high rates; that approach involves the recording of behaviors at certain times rather than continuously. Figure 17.4 illustrates a record used to assess the frequency of behavior, and Figure 17.5 shows a figure used to record the duration of behavior. Before any intervention is tried, it is important to establish the base rate of the behavior to be modified

		Date	2/1 to 2/5

Name _____

Observer _____

Description of Behavior   Physically aggressive - any deliberate body
contact made with any part of the body,
hands, legs, etc.

Days	Tallies	Total
Monday	////////	8
Tuesday	//////////	10
Wednesday	///////	7
Thursday	////////////	12
Friday	///////////////	15
Average = 10.4		

Figure 17.4
Record of the frequency of behavior

Name _____

Observer _____

Description of Behavior   *Out of seat, wandering around classroom.*
                          Cannot state why when away from the desk.

Day	Time	Total minutes
Monday	9:10 – 9:30	20
	10:07 – 10:15	8
	11:00 – 11:07	7
	2:00 – 2:22	22
Tuesday	9:05 – 9:27	22
	9:50 – 10:03	13
	1:15 – 1:38	23
Wednesday		
Thursday		
Friday		

Average _____

Figure 17.5
Record of the duration of behavior

in order to determine later whether the behavior has been strengthened or eliminated.

Checklists.   Checklists are a way to record the presence or absence of specific
behaviors in a given situation. A checklist normally consists of statements about

expected behaviors. The observer checks Yes or No to indicate whether the behavior occurred. A sample checklist is shown in Figure 17.6. Piacentini (1993) suggests that they can be used to assess a broad band or can be global in design to assess specific disorders or problem areas.

Rating Scales.   Rating scales are devices that can be used to record impressions of behaviors that have been selected in advance. Such scales can help focus attention on specific behaviors. Rating scales most often consist of behaviors to be observed and require the rater to indicate the degree or frequency of behavior occurrences. Sometimes the rater is asked to rate the characteristics of the observed behavior or performance. A number of different rating scales are commonly used. Some of the formats are illustrated in Figure 17.7.

Rating scales provide a standardized format for the collection of data, ensuring systematic and comprehensive coverage of the behavior in question (Piacentini, 1993). The structured format reduces subjectivity and increases reliability. Dependence on the rater's experience and day-to-day variability are minimized.

Name_____

Observer_____

Date_____

Time observed_____

Yes	No	
____	____	Interrupted others when they were talking.
____	____	Gave compliments or encouragement when talking to others.
____	____	Argued or quarreled with others.
____	____	Swore and used vulgar language.
____	____	Took kidding without getting upset.
____	____	Looked at people directly when talking to them.
____	____	Had a short temper and got angry quickly.
____	____	Was blunt and direct and got to the point.
____	____	Expressed his/her opinion freely.
____	____	Got loud and noisy in conversation.
____	____	Disagreed and took opposite point of view.
____	____	Was nervous and tense when talking with others.
____	____	Was positive about self and others.
____	____	Spoke slowly and softly.
____	____	Made grammatical errors often.
____	____	Had difficulty pronouncing certain words.

Figure 17.6
Checklist of social behavior

Semantic Differential Type
Behavior with examiner

Reserved ____ ____ ____ ____ ____ ____ ____ Open
       1   2   3   4   5   6   7

Response to testing process

Leery ____ ____ ____ ____ ____ ____ ____ Confident
     1   2   3   4   5   6   7

Graphic Type
Reaction to test environment

Comfortable	Somewhat comfortable	Uncomfortable	Ill at ease
1	2	3	4

Necessity to repeat questions

	Never			Occasionally		Often
	1	2	3	4	5	6	7

Numerical Type
Rapport with examinee

     1   2   3   4   5   6   7
   Low   High

Examples needed by test taker

      1   2   3   4
   Only 1   5 or more

Figure 17.7
Sample formats showing semantic differential, graphic, and numerical types of rating scales

GUIDELINES FOR OBSERVATION

Certain guidelines should be considered for observation.

1. Be objective. Be aware of personal biases and prejudices.

2. Be aware of the halo error—the tendency to be influenced by your first impression of an individual or by an exceptional trait. Such influence can be a source of bias.

3. Recognize personal response tendencies—perhaps rating everyone high (generosity error) or low (severity error), or in the middle (central tendency error). Be alert to only positive or only negative observations.

4. Focus on relevant behaviors. Attend only to the assigned behaviors on the checklist or rating scale.

5. Be as unobtrusive as possible.

6. Observe more than once; the more observations, the better chance of getting a complete and accurate picture.

7. Have more than one person observe to permit comparison of results.

8. Train observers so all focus on and record the same behavior in the same way.

9. Instruct observers and have practice sessions in what behaviors are to be observed and how they are to be recorded.

INTERVIEWING

Another form of a situation test that relies heavily on observation is the interview. Several types of interviews are counseling and employment, structured versus unstructured, clinical, panel, stress, medical history, and diagnostic. Interviewing demands good interpersonal and communication skills on the part of the interviewer; different individuals interviewing the same candidate often do not agree on their findings.

Standardized interviews are designed to collect the same type of information from all the respondents. If it is a structured interview, everyone is asked the same questions in the same order, and the answers are recorded identically. Individual intelligence tests are a form of standardized, structured interviews. For example there are a number of structured interview schedules to classify children, adolescents, and adults on the DSM IV such as the Diagnostic Interview for Children and Adolescents (DICA), the Schedule for Affective Disorders and Schizophrenia for School Aged Children (K-SADS), the Interview Schedule for Children (ISC), and the Children's Assessment Schedule (CAS). In unscheduled interviews the interviewer sometimes varies the sequence of the questions and the order of the topics. The information is recorded on a standardized report form, however, so that the data can be compared and summarized.

Some advantages of interviewing are these.

1. Clients can be guided to answer items completely.

2. Probes can be interpreted or explained.

3. Additional information or understanding can be pursued.

4. Nonverbal behavior and cues as well as different aspects of expressive behavior can be observed.

Interviewing also has disadvantages.

1. Success depends on the skill of the interviewer to ask the right questions and correctly interpret the data.

2. Impressions and interpretations are subjective.

3. The communication of some individuals is inhibited, and clients may be unwilling to answer certain questions.

4. The personality of the interviewer can influence the outcome (Shertzer & Linden, 1979).

Guidelines for Conducting Interviews

Even though the reliability and validity of interviewing may be questionable, it is sometimes the only way to gather some types of information; the interviewer can reword questions, add questions, seek clarification of information not understood, pursue interesting topics as they arise or change the line of questioning altogether (Ten Brink, 1974, p. 170). Here are some general guidelines.

1. Be prepared. Be familiar with the interview purpose, schedule of questions, and method of recording answers. Be set mentally and psychologically for the interview.

2. Practice reading the schedule. Pilot test it on a colleague or someone from the target group.

3. Establish rapport. Show interest in the interviewee.

4. Try to put the interviewee at ease so that he will be friendly, cooperative, relaxed, and patient.

5. Explain the purpose of the interview and assure the client of confidentiality.

6. Start out with questions that are nonthreatening.

7. Remember there are certain questions in employment interviewing that are considered legally unacceptable by the Fair Employment Act—such as those relating to age, race, religion, marital status, arrest record and legal problems, number of children and their ages, membership clubs and organizations, occupation of spouse, and maiden name of a female applicant.

8. Do not react to what is said by agreeing or disagreeing; instead, reinforce the fact that the interviewee is answering the questions. Encourage the interviewee to express thoughts and feelings freely.

9. Guide the session with carefully planned questions so that the interview remains on target. Avoid leading questions.

10. Probe and get more details or explanations when the client does not respond to a question.

11. Change or translate words as necessary for individuals from different educational or cultural backgrounds.

12. Listen carefully, patiently, and intensively but avoid overreacting.

13. Be accepting and courteous.

14. Follow the directions for recording the information from the interview. Be as inconspicuous as possible but discuss with the respondent before the interview begins the type of data recording that will be used. If the session is not electronically recorded, take notes throughout the interview.

15. Observe nonverbal and expressive behavior—not only what is said but how it is said.

16. Check the validity of your information by rephrasing some of the questions and asking the client to expand on the information.

17. Be alert to signals that it is time to terminate the interview.

PROBLEM AREAS

Observational techniques show promise but have psychometric problems. They can be important tools in gaining information, but observers need to be well trained. In many cases observers are asked to rate certain dimensions of individual behavior. Cronbach (1984) states that the most serious rating error is leniency or generosity (p. 509). Some raters prefer to say good about everyone rather than discriminate. The halo error occurs when an observer rates an examinee high on one dimension not clearly observed because the individual performed well on another. Sometimes interviewers are influenced by first impressions, usually by unfavorable information about the interviewee. According to Cooper (1984), five problems can affect observation.

1. Lack of agreement regarding what is to be observed. Different observers have different agendas, goals, and expectations regarding an observation.

2. Failure to achieve a reasonable degree of objectivity. What one person sees as truth may not be perceived as truth by others.

3. Effect of the observer on the behavior of the individual or group being observed. The observer may be too obtrusive.

4. Improper preparation for observation. The observer may not have a good idea of what specific behaviors will be observed or how data will be collected.

5. Generalization from an inadequate sample of behavior. More than one observation may be needed. A given observation may not have been a typical sample of an individual's behavior or performance (pp. 80–81).

AUTHENTIC ASSESSMENT

The major testing movement of the 1990s has been authentic assessment. When the multiple-choice format came under fire in the 1980s, teachers were encouraged to utilize other methods of educational assessment such as essays, projects, portfolios, performance tasks, and open-ended exercises. These assessment procedures are not entirely new, since the National Assessment of Educational Progress initiated similar formats in 1969.

There is much confusion about the terminology (Fisher, 1993): Some refer to *authentic assessment* (Wiggins, 1989) and others to *performance assessment* (Stiggins, 1987). Both approaches involve assessing students by observing things they do. Assessment involves students demonstrating that they have achieved a given outcome.

Authentic assessment focuses on the development of assessment exercises that will be not biased against any group of students and can be reliably scored and validly interpreted. Raters are needed in many cases to score the assessments. Current research on a pilot project in Vermont indicates low reliability of the scoring procedures. Miller and Seraphine (1993) conclude that authentic assessment will probably be useful in low-stake assessment such as in classroom situations. Further, they note that multiple assessments will have value but will take more time from instructors and learning and will increase the anxiety level of students, teachers, and administrators.

GUIDELINES FOR GOOD ASSESSMENT SYSTEMS

The National Council of Teachers of Mathematics listed six standards for alternative or authentic assessment in mathematics; the principles apply to other content areas.

1. Assessment should reflect the mathematics that are most important for students.

2. Assessment should enhance mathematics learning.

3. Assessment should promote equity by giving each student optional opportunities to demonstrate mathematical power and by helping each student meet the profession's high expectations.

4. All aspects of the mathematics assessment process should be open to review and scrutiny.

5. Evidence from assessment activities should yield valid inferences about students' mathematics learning.

6. Every aspects of an assessment process should be consistent with the purpose of the assessment.

NCME (1994) provided criteria for evaluating alternative assessment procedures. First the purpose of the assessment needs to be identified. Multiple measures should be used and the process should have technical rigor. The process must be cost effective, of educational value, and equitable to all students. The information should be useful to decision makers.

Issues and Problems

One of the big challenges for helping professionals in the authentic assessment movement will be to help teachers link assessment to ongoing instruction. Teachers will need a better understanding of their classroom practices and the ethical aspects, reasoning, and consequences of good/poor instruction. Teacher training institutions will have to help preservice interns to improve their assessment skills.

Math teachers, for example, will need to consider that mathematics assessment may demand substantial linguistic ability, and thus be unfair to those who are lacking in those skills. Since performance-based assessment uses only a small number of tasks, these may favor one group over another. Students must be provided with assessment alternatives that are appropriate to their ethnicity, gender, handicap, or language. The use of portfolio assessment requires teachers to adapt to ever-changing curricular and instructional demands (CRESST, 1994).

This brief overview suggests what might happen soon in the professions. Licensing and certification tests might need to become more authentic. Many examinations for skilled and craft trades are performance based.

Portfolio Assessment

Portfolio assessment appears to be one of the most widely used types of alternative or authentic assessment. Many teachers keep portfolios on their students. The purpose of the portfolio is

1. to help document the growth and development of the student
2. to serve as a vehicle for communication between teacher, student, and parents
3. to guide instructional planning for the student
4. to maintain a standard assessment procedure throughout the program

The teacher includes in the folder the assessment record of the child, checklists, teacher communications, writing activities, and reading assignments. Additional information such as the reading log, writing log, goal sheet, journal, teacher's notes, learning log, teacher-student conference log, and screening data might be used.

Portfolios can help show students' growth over time, the process by which work was done as well as the final product, their favorite or personally important work, and the evolution of one or more projects or products. The portfolio can also be used to prepare a sample of the best work for employment or college admissions. It could be used for student placement decisions or to achieve alternative credit for a course. It is a helpful tool in curriculum and program evaluation.

SUMMARY

Observational techniques are widely used in assessing and evaluating clients. Counselors and psychologists use observational techniques in assessing the client's behavior in play therapy, sociodrama, psychodrama, simulated experiences, role playing, test performance, discussion groups, conferences, interviews, and in job, home, or school situations. Sometimes observation is a secondary part of a testing situation. On most individual tests the examiner rates the test taker's behavior as well as her answers. Observational techniques show promise but do have psychometric problems that interfere with their validity and reliability.

QUESTIONS FOR DISCUSSION

1. What are the major types and sources of errors likely to arise in observational situations? How can you eliminate or reduce these sources of error?

2. Some individuals advocate the use of unobtrusive observation, claiming that clients will tend to perform in more natural and typical ways. Think of situations in which unobtrusive observation is not possible. How can you enhance the validity of your observations when it is impossible for you to be unobtrusive? Should contrived situations be used?

3. Interview some counselors and psychologists. Ask them how much time they spend using observational techniques and find out whether they use structured or unstructured observation. What instruments or schedules do they use? How valid and reliable do they feel the observations are?

4. When would you make use of self-observational techniques? What training or instructions would you give a client before assigning self-observation? What psychometric problems do you see with these techniques?

5. Compare structured and unstructured interviews. In what situations or contexts would you use each type? Individual standardized tests are considered a form of structured interview. Is it appropriate to deviate from the sequence established by the test authors? What are some factors to consider when interviewing a client?

SUGGESTED ACTIVITIES

1. Choose a type of behavior that is of interest to you and prepare an operational definition of the behavior. Construct a checklist to record the number of times that the behavior occurs in a given situation.

2. Go to the library and find a copy of *Mirrors of Behavior* (Simon & Boyer, 1974). Choose one of the categorical scales included in the volume and try it out in the appropriate environment. Report on the usability of the scale and comment on the reliability and validity as well as the problems one might encounter in using the scale.

3. Review the different observational checklists that are part of many individual tests. What commonalities exist among these scales? What differences? How observable are the behaviors or constructs to be rated by the examiner?

4. Collect some career autobiographies from a group of individuals. Determine a system to analyze the results. Discuss the rationale for your analysis and the results from your study. How did the instructions you gave in the sample influence the results?

5. Review some of the standardized rating scales that are widely used in your field. What scales have higher reliability—structured or unstructured, self-rating or rating by other scales, categorical or summary-type? Report your findings to the class.

6. Study the case of Alicia that follows and answer the questions at the end.

Alicia is in a college reachout program and is participating in a 2-week session at a community college designed to help students develop skills and see the importance of staying in school and going on to some type of postsecondary education. The program is for rural, underachieving minority students.

The following are entries in Alicia's journal.

Monday: Yesterday when I first got their we went to the dorms got our name log then we went and put our clothes in the dorms. Then I went outside to mess with the boys and we had fun with one of the conselors. We played basket in the gym and I had lots of fun. I also like this boy name Rod but me and him both can't talk to each other because he has a girlfriend and I have a boyfriend. I guess I have to put that in the closet. Well get back to real business I think this program so far have done me some good because sometimes other people can learn things better than others. I ihig over her I catch on easy so you know how that is. Because I really want to learn more because up their in life it's gonabe hard down that long road and because we are black you know they think black people can't be or do anything and tha's why am going to pay atton and make something out of my self. also I think this program is good for us because it keeps you off the streets Keeps you away from drugs it keeps you from lots of things think about. they alway told me my 15 years I been on this earth can't do a thing when you just sit around doing nothing. Also I want to go to college and be in a marching band and major in mathematics. Because me an person that likes to need losts of people and fun things like that you know. Well kind of ran out of words to say But I will always remember to stay in school BECAUSE IF YOU BELIEVE YOU WILL ACHIEVE.

Tuesday: Today's Tuesday, so far so good I got up this moing thank God for waking me up. Well let me get on withit took me a shower put on some clothes and went to breakfast. Well breakfast was pretty good this morning. I got full and started on my way to go back to my room and got my books fo my class we went to reading class we was learning about verbs and good stuff like that then we came to Study Hall and did the homework our english teach gave us it was not much but it was rough. Well sitting her in Study Hall listen to thes boys trip on each other one boy told this other boy that he looked like a snaping turtule that mess was funny to. also Miss Pam told one of my friends that she write to big and told one boy he write to bad She coud not read nothing he say. they she asked one boy how to spell it was that he was not using his studing time all they do is paly stand and tell jokes so I don't pay them no mind. Oh when we was comming to Study Hall we was so sorry we did not want to take the stairs so we took the elavater now tell me is that sorry or what. Well I am running out of words to say gotta go See YA

Wednesday: Today is Wednesday I got up this moing went to the bathroom and brush my teeth. Then I went to my room and putsome clothes on then went to brakfast and got full. Then I went to Reading class and learned a little bit then we went to Study Hall then we started triping you know we started tell jokes and stuff like that we tried to tell Miss Pam that we did not have any work to do but she fooded us She made us work asnway. Then she made us take a test and some of us did not study and probely flunk the test you know. Also I think Shon is very nice because he is always smiling and that's the way I like to see pople smiling all the time. Also when I was going to Study hall I touch rod on his arm I like that you know how that is to touch someone you really want to get to. Well we know some flunk Because he told everybody that he miss eight and he told Miss Pam that he want to take the test over becausse she could not read it with his bad handwriting. Of I flunk the test too. I miss five I think I need to study. Know let me get to yesterday we had so much fund we was in the gym and the boys was playing basketball and Chad and Rod and all of them I was cheering for all of the exspecally Rod I like him as you can see. Oh By the way our team did not win because they say we cheated but we didn't we won fare and squar. After we got finished with the relay we ate snacks then we went to take a shower then went to bed well got to go. See YA when I see YA Peace

a. What are the major themes in Alicia's journal?
b. What kind of system would you develop to analyze these journals?
c. What kind of impact do you think the program had on Alicia? Why?

ADDITIONAL READINGS

Read the current issues of the *Journal of Behavioral Assessment, Behavioral Assessment*, and *Journal of Abnormal Child Psychology*. These journals publish research on observational techniques and instruments.

Goldstein, G., & Hersen, M. (1990). *Handbook of psychological assessment* (2nd ed.). New York: Pergamon.

Three chapters on interviewing and two on behavioral assessment provide good information.

Simon, A., & Boyer, E. G. (Eds.). (1974). *Mirrors for behavior III: An anthology of observational instruments*. Wyncote, PA: Communications Material Center.

CHAPTER 18

Working with Special Populations

Overview

Everyone has different concepts of exceptional and special needs examinees. Haring (1982) described exceptional people as those who differ from the norm so significantly and so repeatedly as to impair their success in very basic social, personal, or educational activities. They are described by professionals as disabled, impaired, disordered, or exceptional.

Haring defined *disabled* as any person whose functioning is reduced as a result of physical deficit, or one who experiences problems in learning or social adjustment. Examples of physical deficits include limb loss, crippling conditions, or damage to the brain. The term *impaired*, according to Haring, is more commonly used to refer to sensory deficits. Blindness or deafness are two examples. *Disordered*, another descriptor, refers to problems in learning or social behavior. Emotional disturbance is an example of a behavior disorder; a language disorder denotes difficulty in comprehension or production of language.

In this chapter we will use the term *disabled* to refer to special needs individuals with physical, intellectual, and/or emotional deficits as compared with the general population. People with special needs also include linguistic minorities and the gifted and talented.

Objectives

After studying this chapter, the reader should be able to

- discuss the standards and ethical considerations in testing special needs populations

- identify the major tests and assessment techniques used with these groups

- list the goals and objectives and explain the issues and problems of testing special needs examinees

STANDARDS FOR TESTING PEOPLE WITH DISABLING CONDITIONS

Standards for Educational and Psychological Testing (1985) identifies standards for testing people with disabling conditions. The majority are primarily intended for test authors who are modifying tests to use with special needs groups.

Test authors are required to have psychometric expertise and experience in working with these groups, and test publishers should caution examiners about the use and interpretation of the test with special needs clients until it has been fully validated. Authors should conduct pilot tests on people who have similar disabilities to check on the appropriateness and feasibility of the modifications and should include a careful statement of steps taken to modify the test so that users will be able to identify any changes that may alter its validity.

Test authors should use empirical procedures to establish time limits for modified forms and explore the effects of fatigue. They also should provide validity and reliability information on the modified forms as well as on the unmodified forms.

Clearly, it is important for the user to study the manual and evaluate the technical information to determine whether the modifications are valid and reliable for the group in question. In addition, counselors and psychologists working with clients who have special needs should know what alternate tests and modes are available and appropriate for these persons. Clients need to be informed of the availability of these other instruments and to be given a chance to take them. Those who are interpreting the test results need to know which set of norms should be used. Regular norms are used when the examiner needs to compare the disabled individual's test performance with the general population. Special norms are appropriate when the examiner is looking at how the individual performs in relation to peers with the same disabling conditions.

The needs of impaired examinees should be considered carefully. Hearing impaired individuals need interpreters who sign the instructions and/or items for them. Some tests have video cassettes with the directions and items presented in sign language. For visually impaired individuals, large print versions, braille forms, and forms on cassette recorders are available. Most national testing programs have provisions for special needs individuals to have more time to complete tests.

Both content and format of tests have to be revised for special needs people. Most publishers have expert panels who review the appropriateness of test items to eliminate bias.

Testing Linguistic Minorities

For many non-English-speaking groups English is a second or third language. Tests written in English may become tests of language proficiency for these individuals, rather than measures of other constructs. Of course, it is sometimes important and necessary to have tests that measure English proficiency—especially for educational diagnosis and placement. Tests not meant to measure proficiency in English are sometimes translated into the appropriate native language. However, there may be problems in translation, and the content and words might not be appropriate or meaningful to the group being tested.

Standards for Educational and Psychological Testing (1985) includes seven standards relating to the testing of linguistic minorities. The selection and use of appropriate tests need to be reviewed carefully. A number of standards are intended primarily for the test authors and publishers, but should be taken into consideration by the test user. If the test is modified, the changes should be spelled out in the manual in addition to specifications for test use. The reliability and validity of the test for the intended linguistic group are also important. If two versions of dual-language tests exist, evidence of the comparability of the forms should be included. The standards also caution users not to require a greater level of proficiency of the test in English than the job or profession requires—a significant concern in developing and selecting employment, certification, and licensing examinations. Another standard is extremely important to users; it cautions users to not judge English language proficiency on the basis of test information alone. Many language skills are not adequately measured by multiple-choice examinations. The counselor needs to use observation techniques and perhaps informal checklists to assess proficiency more completely.

The *Code for Fair Testing Practices in Education* (1988) calls for tests to be developed in ways that make them fair for test takers of different race, gender, ethnic background, or with disabling conditions. Test users are asked to evaluate the procedures used by test developers to avoid potentially insensitive content or language; review the performance of test takers of different races, gender, and ethnic background when samples of sufficient size are available; and evaluate how performance differences may be caused by inappropriate characteristics of tests. When necessary and feasible, test administrators are to use appropriately modified forms of tests or administration procedures for test takers with disabling conditions and then interpret standard norms with care in the light of the modifications that were made.

Public Law 94–142

Public Law 94–142, the Education for All Handicapped Children Act, exemplifies the current philosophical and social attitudes toward people with special needs. Passed by Congress in 1975 and amended in 1990 by substituting the word *disabled* for *handicapped*, the law guarantees disabled children 3 to 21 years old appropriate educational opportunities in the least restrictive environment. The law also sets standards for the types of assessment materials and procedures used. Assessment must not discriminate against a child on the basis of race or culture. Furthermore, test and assessment materials are to

1. be provided and administered in the examinee's language or other mode of communication

2. be validated for the specific purpose for which they are to be used

3. be administered by trained personnel according to specifications in the manual

4. yield useful information in specific areas of educational need

5. give an accurate picture of what is to be assessed, such as aptitude and achievement, rather than reflecting the examinee's impaired skills

6. be utilized and interpreted by a multidisciplinary team of persons, including at least one teacher or specialist in the area of the disability

The targeted student should be assessed in all areas related to the suspected disability; the testing should not be confined to academic performance, but should also include health, vision, general intelligence, communication skills, and emotional status. In other words, a single criterion cannot determine the most appropriate educational program for a test taker.

PRESCHOOL EVALUATIONS

In recent years there has been an effort to identify children with disabilities prior to kindergarten. Bailey and Wolery (1989) pointed out five important assessment domains for this group. These are cognitive skills, motor skills, communication skills, play and social skills, and self-care skills.

An annotated list of preschool assessment instruments and tests is provided here.

Bayley Scales of Infant Development are used to assess the mental and psychomotor development of children from 2 to 30 months of age and to aid in the diagnosis of normal or retarded development.

Cattell Infant Intelligence Scale measures intellectual development of children from 3 to 30 months by assessing verbalizations and motor control.

Denver Developmental Screening Test (DDST) is used to evaluate a child's personal, social, fine-motor, gross-motor, language, and adaptive abilities. The test is appropriate for use with children from birth to age 6 as a screening tool.

Kent Infant Development Scale (KID Scale) uses a 252-item inventory to assess the developmental age of infants and young children chronologically or developmentally under 1 year of age. The test measures cognitive, language, motor, self-help, and social skills.

Developmental Assessment for the Severely Handicapped is an observation scale used to assess the progress of severely disabled children from birth to 9 years of age developmentally. The scale provides information on the sensory-motor, language, preacademic, daily living, and socio-emotional areas used to establish individual education programs.

Dallas Preschool Screening Test is used to assess the learning disabilities of children between the ages of 3 and 6: it measures auditory, language, motor, visual, psychological, and articulation development.

DuBose (1982) reminds us that neither Gesell nor Piaget studied children who were impaired or were developing more slowly than their peers. Thus this paucity of developmental information makes it harder for examiners to assess preschool children with disabilities. Some of the behaviors to be noted and considered are described in Table 18.1.

Public Law 99–457, the Education of the Handicapped Act Amendments of 1986, focuses on identifying and developing programs for infants and toddlers with disabilities. The purpose of the law is to facilitate the development and implementation of statewide interagency programs of early intervention services that are comprehensive, coordinated, and multidisciplinary. The law defines individuals with disabilities

Table 18.1

Performance characteristics of preschool children with disabilities

Disability	Behavior
Deafness	Language skill acquisition affected severely
	Communication skills qualitatively different
	Social skill acquisition delayed
	Cognitive skills not necessarily affected
	Motor skills not necessarily affected
Blindness	Gross- and fine-motor coordination affected severely
	Awareness of spatial relationships, object permanence affected
	Self-care and social skills delayed
	Verbal and cognitive skills development hampered
	Sensory motor skill development hampered
	Language patterns and development restricted
Physical impairment	Motor skills poorly developed
	Some form of visual impairment with some disabilities (e.g., cerebral palsy)
	Possible auditory or perceptual problems
	Possible speech problems
	Delayed skill acquisition in all domains
Social-emotional-behavioral problems	Poor communication skills
	Possible delay in motor behavior
	Possible visual problems and hearing loss in autistic children
Mental disability	All areas of development affected
	Sensory perception problems

as those who are mentally retarded, hard of hearing, deaf, speech, language, or visually impaired, seriously emotionally disturbed, orthopedically impaired, other health impaired individuals, or individuals with specific learning disabilities who require special education and related services. Under the legislation, families with children in these categories should be provided with multidisciplinary assessment of unique needs and identification of services appropriate to meet their unique needs. The targeted group is children from birth to age 2 who are experiencing developmental delays, as measured by appropriate diagnostic instruments and procedures, in one or more of the following areas—cognitive development, physical development, language and speech development, psychosocial development and self-help skills. Also included are those children with a diagnosed physical or mental condition that has a high probability of resulting in developmental delay. The key is early identification. Rossetti (1990) points out the need for the involvement of teams of specialists—speech therapists, occupational therapists, physical therapists, and psychologists—in assessing this group.

COMMUNICATION DISORDERS

A communication disorder is defined as a significant deviation in speech or language from norms based on sex, age, and cultural, ethnic, or social expectations (Haring, 1982, p. 82). Speech pathologists are responsible for the assessment of clients with communication disorders and may use a number of different assessment approaches. Psychologists and counselors testing these individuals may find that examinees are unable to say words correctly or to formulate ideas according to accepted standards. The examiners need to concentrate their attention on what these clients have to say and reward client efforts with warmth and positive reinforcement. Other good practices are these.

1. Demonstrate acceptance and positive regard for the client as an individual.
2. Try to remove any distracting stimuli from the testing environment.
3. Keep instructions and directions simple. Repeat or rephrase questions when appropriate.
4. Be alert to facial expressions, gestures, and tone of voice.
5. Allow the examinee to nod, point, or otherwise indicate the answer in a nonverbal manner.

INTELLECTUAL DISABILITIES

Primarily, tests of intelligence have been utilized to assess whether the examinee has a moderate, severe, or profound intellectual disability. Mildly retarded individuals usually score 2 to 3 standard deviations from the mean and range between 55 and 69 on IQ tests. The moderately retarded score 3 to 4 standard deviations below the mean and range between 40 and 54 on IQ tests. Severely retarded individuals score 4 to 5 standard deviations below the mean and have IQs of less than 25.

The testing of severely disabled individuals presents a challenge to the examiner because of the intensity of their physical, mental, or emotional problems. These individuals do not respond well to even the most pronounced stimuli, and sometimes have temper tantrums. They also lack even the most rudimentary form of verbal control. Assessment of these individuals may have to be done over a period of time in both natural and contrived situations. DuBose (1982) advocated that behaviors be assessed across several settings to ensure generalization and that conditions be modified for specific severe disabilities. Items that are utilized should call for behaviors that are observable and measurable. The American Association on Mental Retardation (AAMR) (1983) definition of being mentally retarded includes three criteria: scoring 2.5 standard deviations below the mean on the Wechsler or Binet scales, showing deficits in adaptive behavior, and exhibiting these symptoms by age 18.

Adaptive Behavior

Adaptive behavior is defined as a person's ability to deal effectively with personal and social demands and expectations. For example, the public school version of the AAMD Adaptive Behavior Scale addresses independent functioning, physical development, economic activity, language development, number and time concepts, vocational activity, self-direction, responsibility, and socialization.

The second part of the scale covers destructive behavior, antisocial behavior, nonconforming behavior, untrustworthiness, withdrawn behaviors, odd mannerisms, interpersonal manners, vocal habits, eccentric habits, psychological disturbances, and use of medication.

Many adaptive behavior schedules have been developed and used to assess the characteristics of special populations, especially individuals with possible mental retardation, emotional disturbance, or other learning disabilities. Evaluation provides diagnostic and prescriptive information for the educational programming and guidance of these individuals. Arrman, Hammer, and Rojan (1993) advocate a multimodal assessment of mental retardation, including the use of direct observation, the adaptive behavior scales such as the AAMD just described or the Vineland Adaptive Behavior Scales, IQ tests, and behavior rating scales such as the Behavior Disturbance Scale of the Psychopathology Instrument for Mentally Retarded Youth.

BEHAVIOR DISORDERS

Behavior disorders are sometimes labeled as emotional disturbance. Disagreement exists with regard to classification and acceptable standards. The *Diagnostic and Statistical Manual of Mental Disorders* (DSM–IV) lists disorders that examiners need to be familiar with in working with diverse groups—attention deficit disorders (with or without hyperactivity), conduct disorders, anxiety disorders, eating disorders, stereotyped movement disorders, pervasive developmental disorders, disorders with physical manifestations, and others. Examiners need to recognize the major symptoms of the different types of behavior, which can vary from extreme withdrawal to extreme acting out and aggressive behavior.

Psychologists or examiners rely on many techniques to screen for intervention and program placement of those identified as having behavior disorders. Observation and rating procedures have been used to assess individual functioning in a natural setting. Reports from family, peers, teachers, and parents are valuable also, and sometimes standardized tests are used.

Some of the general tests and scales to assess individuals in this category are listed here.

Behavior Observation Scale for Autism is used to assess the presence of behaviors characteristic of autism.

Burks' Behavior Rating Scales are used to identify patterns of behavior problems in children and to aid in deferential diagnosis.

Child Diagnostic Screening Battery and Adolescent Diagnostic Screening Battery are used with children in clinical settings to identify all possible DSM–IV diagnoses. The tests have forms for parents or guardians and for the clinician.

Louisville Behavior Checklist measures social emotional behaviors indicative of psychopathological disorders in children and is used by examiners in interviewing parents.

Diagnostic Inventory of Personality and Symptoms uses DSM–IV as the framework for the items and scales used.

Some general guidelines for testing individuals with behavior disorders are these.

1. Have a carefully structured environment for testing.
2. Reinforce appropriate behavior.
3. Be fair and consistent.
4. Be sensitive and try to understand individual frustrations, hopes, and fears.
5. Keep directions and routines simple and establish reasonable rules.

AUTISM AND PERVASIVE DEVELOPMENT DISORDERS

Autism and pervasive development disorders are characterized by qualitative impairment in communication, language, and symbolic development and are marked by a restrictive repertory of activities and interests. Most autistic persons have some degree of mental retardation. They suffer from multiple problems in speech, language, and communication. They sometimes exhibit tantrums, aggressive outbursts, and noncompliance. Marcus and Schopler (1993) recommend multimodal assessment for these individuals, including diagnostic instruments such as the Childhood Autism Rating Scale (CARS) and the Autism Behavior Checklist (ABC), among others. Developmental-educational assessment should also be completed by using such scales as the Psychoeducational Profile-Revised (PEP-R). To meet the challenge of working with this group the authors have allowed altering sequences of items so that stressful language items are balanced by more enjoyable visual and motor tasks. The scale also permits alternative methods of communication to enable appropriate assessment of this type of individual. The test has two sections: the first assesses developmental functions; the second identifies unusual or atypical behavior. The Adult Psychoeducational Profile (APEP) is used with moderately to severely handicapped older autistic persons. Communication and language assessment instruments for this group include the Peabody Picture Vocabulary Test. Social, family, and medical information is also included in the assessment.

ANXIETY DISORDERS

Anxiety disorders take different forms in childhood and adolescence but are characterized by intense subjective distress and maladaptive patterns of cognition and behavior. For children and adolescents these might be separation anxiety, overanxiety, and avoidant disorders. For adults they may take the form of generalized anxiety disorders, panic disorder, phobic disorders, and the like. Strauss (1993) suggests the use of multimodal assessment such as structured interviews, self-report inventories, parent and teacher checklists, client observations, and physiological measurements. Some of the major self-report inventories are the Children's Manifest Anxiety Scale—Revised and the Fear Survey Schedule for Children—Revised. A number of rating scales contain items dealing with anxiety and withdrawal.

CONDUCT DISORDERS

Individuals with conduct disorders show patterns of antisocial behavior, often exhibit impaired functioning at home and school, and are viewed as unmanageable by parents and teachers. The child or adolescent may exhibit the following behaviors: stealing, truancy, destroying property, use of weapons, physical cruelty, deliberately setting fires, and similar actions. Helping professionals assess the disorder by a variety of techniques, including self-report inventories such as the MMPI and Millon or reports by others such as the Sutter-Eyberg Student Behavior Inventory. There are a number of direct evaluative systems such as the Parent Daily Report. Peer evaluations are also sought through sociometric techniques. Kazdin (1993) reports each method has its strengths, methodological weaknesses, and sources of bias, but he advocates the use of multiple measures for accurate assessment.

ATTENTION DEFICIT DISORDER

Although its cause is unknown, attention deficit disorder involves multiple areas of functioning and is a complex and chronic disorder of the brain. Rapport (1993) recommends multimodal assessment, which includes structured and semistructured interviews such as the Diagnostic Interviews for Children and Adolescents (DICA) and the Diagnostic Interview Schedule for Children (DISC), checklists and rating forms such as the Child Behavior Checklist (CBC) and narrow band rating scales and checklists such as the Children's Learning Profile (CLP), observations of classroom behavior, intellectual and achievement testing, and neurocognitive testing such as the Continuous Performance Test (CPT) or the Matching Familiar Figures Test (MFFT).

EATING DISORDERS

Two major eating disorders, anorexia nervosa and bulimia, are characterized by a morbid overconcern with weight and physical appearance. In anorexia nervosa the client starves herself/himself to a point of emaciation, strives for thinness, and has a fear of becoming fat. Bulimia clients also strive for thinness but have strong urges to overeat which leads to binges followed by self-induced vomiting, laxatives, fasting, and other similar behavior. Garner and Parker (1993) advocate multimodal assessment and start out with an initial interview. Sometimes a medical examination is necessary to determine if weight loss is due to some underlying physical disorder. Garner and Parker (1993) provide an outline of a clinical interview checklist that includes items dealing with demographic features and treatment history, weight-controlling behavior, binge eating and eating behavior, attitudes toward weight and shape, physical symptoms, and psychological and interpersonal factors. There are a number of self-report inventories such as the Eating Disorder Inventory-2. The revised scale has three new scales—asceticism, impulse regulation, and social insecurity—along with scales assessing attitudes and behaviors toward eating, weight, and shape.

HEARING IMPAIRMENT

Individuals differ in their degree of impairment, as well as the age of onset of the impairment. Audiologists screen individuals with hearing losses that range from mild to profound and can be caused by a number of factors. Normally, examinees with hearing deficits have had a pattern of retarded speech and language development and problems in social development. Some have poor control of their impulses, and do not have a strongly developed sense of responsibility. They often misinterpret the feelings and behaviors of others and may be significantly behind their peers in educational achievement.

Intelligence tests that do not demand oral language are preferable for this group. Examiners must be careful in reaching conclusions during observations. Individuals who exhibit behavior characteristic of the learning disabled, behavior disordered, or mentally retarded persons may be suffering from a hearing loss that leads to those similar behaviors. Simeonsson (1986) identified three major purposes of assessment of hearing impaired individuals to assess the cognitive competency and achievement discrepancy, to assess the cognitive and linguistic discrepancy, and to assess personal and social functioning.

Many individual differences exist within this group, and it is important to take into consideration the etiology of the impairment as well as the developmental history of the individual. The following guidelines pertain to assessment of hearing impaired persons. Bradley-Johnson and Evans (1991) point out that testing should be supplemented with interviews, review of school records, and use of classroom observation.

Be sure that any individual with problems speaking or understanding spoken language has a hearing evaluation.

Keep the test environment controlled and free from distraction; an individual with a mild hearing loss may be distracted by extraneous noise.

Avoid visual distractions, especially if the examinee is reading lips.

If necessary, have an interpreter to help in communication with the examinee.

Allow the interpreter and deaf person to arrange seating to enhance the lines of communication.

Have more than one test or approach to measure the construct in question.

VISUAL IMPAIRMENT

Visual impairment may be caused by injury or disease that reduces the individual's central vision, accommodation, binocular vision, peripheral vision, or color vision. The impairment affects normal patterns of cognitive, affective, and psychomotor development. Visually impaired preadolescents and adolescents quite often have problems in social development that cause lower self-concepts. Psychologists and educators assess aptitude and achievement of the visually impaired by adapting standard instruments to meet their needs. Chase (1986) points out that test administrators need to become familiar with the nature of the visual disorders and their impact on development. Testers must be aware of the

1. effects of distracting noise in a testing situation

2. need for additional time to complete tasks, if the test is in braille or large type

3. need to structure the testing environment and let the examinee become familiar with the objects by handling them

4. need to describe the setting for the examinee

5. need for several breaks or multiple sessions

Specialized tests are available for assessing children and adults with visual impairments. The Hill Performance Test of Selected Positional Concepts measures the spatial concepts of visually impaired children aged 6 to 10. The Reynell-Zinkin Scales provide a profile of six areas for children up to 5 years old—social adaptation, sensorimotor, exploration of environment, response to sound/verbal comprehension, expressive language, and nonverbal communication. The Hepatic Intelligence Scale is a performance-based scale for the blind and partially sighted 16 years and older and has six tests—digit symbol, object assembly, block design, object completion, pattern board, and bead arithmetic.

GIFTED AND TALENTED PERSONS

Often the gifted individual is thought of by educators as having a high level of intellectual ability. Terman (1954) operationally defined gifted as those individuals who score in the top 1% on the Stanford-Binet or have IQs of 130 or above. The United States Office of Education (1978) definition implies that the gifted individual possesses high performance capabilities in areas such as intellect, creativity, academics, leadership, or the performing or visual arts, and requires services or activities not ordinarily provided by a school.

Examiners of gifted and talented individuals have relied on group and individual intelligence tests; survey achievement batteries; and the ratings of teachers, parents, and even the students themselves. Some of the scales used to assess the gifted and talented are listed here.

Scales for Rating the Behavior Characteristics of Superior Students are completed by teachers, parents, or guidance counselors to measure various dimensions of gifted behavior—learning, motivation, creativity, leadership, art, music, drama, planning, precise communication, and expressive communication.

Torrance Tests of Creative Thinking assess the ability of individuals to visualize and transform words and meanings.

Creativity Checklist is given to counselors, parents, and teachers to rate eight dimensions of creative behavior, such as fluency, flexibility, resourcefulness, constructural skill, ingenuity, and independence. It can be used with individuals from kindergarten to adulthood.

Group Inventory for Finding Creative Talent (GIFT) surveys the creative interests and attitudes of students in grades K to 6.

Group Inventory for Finding Interests: Gifted and Talented Screening Form assesses the creative interests and attitudes of students in grades 6 to 12.

Gifted and Talented Screening Form asks parents and teachers to rate individuals on academic performance, creativity, intelligence, psychomotor ability, and visual-performing arts. The scale is used in grades K to 9.

Thinking Creatively with Sounds and Words measures the ability of individuals to create images for words and sounds. There are two forms, one for grades 3 to 12 and one for adults.

Thinking Creatively in Action and Movement (TCAM) is a nonverbal movement test used to assess the creativity of children aged 3 to 8.

Watson-Glaser Critical Thinking Appraisal measures the individual's ability to think critically and includes dimensions such as inferences, recognition of assumptions, deduction, interpretation, and evaluation of arguments.

Creativity Attitude Survey for grades 4 to 6 assesses confidence in one's own ideas, appreciation of fantasy, theoretical and aesthetical orientation, openness to impulse expression, and desire for novelty.

Examiners testing gifted individuals should not be influenced by stereotypical attitudes. Who is tested and what tests are given depends partly on the operational definition of gifted. It can pertain to exceptional academic achievement, extraordinary creativity, special talents, superior intelligence, and/or some other variable. Examiners should remember that gifted and talented students can have the same testing problems that other students have. They may not want to do well because of peer pressure, they may be bored and frustrated, or they may come from disadvantaged environments and may be overlooked by teachers and administrators.

SUMMARY

Psychometric criteria have an important role in diagnosing mental retardation, learning disabilities, and giftedness and they are used as a secondary tool in diagnosing behavioral and emotional disorders. Clinical judgment is also considered an important factor in the diagnosis of exceptionality, especially in the realm of communication impairment and behavior and emotional disorders. Biomedical information is extremely important when studying visual, auditory, and motor impairment. Examiners need to be aware of the specific standards and guidelines for testing special populations. They need to be experienced and knowledgeable in working with the special group in question.

QUESTIONS FOR DISCUSSION

1. How might the following examiner variables affect the validity of the test results? (a) Personal bias and expectation, (b) Difficulty in understanding what the examinee says, (c) Lack of knowledge of the particular handicap, (d) Lack of experience testing and working with the particular exceptionality, (e) Lack of special communication skills (e.g., American Sign Language)

2. Do you think it is acceptable to adapt and modify a standardized test to accommodate the special needs of the examinee? Why or why not?

3. How important do you feel the testing environment is in the testing of exceptional individuals? How would the following factors affect the validity of the test results? (a) Lighting in the room, (b) Noise level of the testing environment, (c) Physical features of the room, (d) Artificial nature of the setting, (e) Positioning needs of the examinee

4. How do labels and diagnostic criteria affect the types of tests given and the validity of the results? Critics have faulted the designations for not reflecting the presence of a disability or the degree of impairment. How should the examiner address this problem?

5. A large number of individuals are impaired in more than one area. What procedures should the examiner follow to ensure proper diagnosis and/or placement?

SUGGESTED ACTIVITIES

1. Interview psychologists who work with special populations and find out what tests they use and why. Report your findings to the class.

2. Review a videotape of a testing session of an individual with a disability. Were there deviations from standard procedures? In what ways did the examiner test the individual differently from the norm?

3. Interview special needs individuals and find out their experiences and reactions to testing. Report your findings to the class.

4. Locate the public laws and court decisions related to assessing exceptional individuals. Write a summary of the legislation and the court decisions.

5. Locate a test that has been adapted and standardized for use with a special population. Compare the adaptation with the original version. How was the test modified? Why? How do the two sets of norms compare?

6. Study these five brief cases and answer the questions that follow.

Mary, a 12-year-old female, has dropped from 100 to 75 pounds in the last 6 months. She refuses to eat with the family. Fights take place at meal time because of her eating habits.

a.   How would you classify Mary?
b.   What additional information would you like to have about her?
c.   What methods would you use to assess Mary or individuals like Mary?

Jonathan had a full scale IQ of 91 on the WISC-III with a Verbal score of 82 and Performance of 106. He was easily frustrated and impulsive in the tasks he was required to do. He couldn't sit still except on the performance items that interested him. His teacher checked "poor" on the following items on a learning profile checklist.

Quality or neatness of handwriting
Completeness of assignments
Quality of reading skills
Quality of speaking skills
She also noted that he completes his work in a hasty, careless fashion.

a.   How would you classify Jonathan?
b.   What additional information would you like to have on him?
c.   What methods would you use to assess Jonathan or individuals like him?

Robert is an 11-year-old boy from a blended family. He lives with his mother, stepfather, and the stepfather's two children. He had a 121 Full Scale IQ on the WISC-III. His grades were excellent, but lately his disruptive and aggressive behavior has led to frequent suspensions and lower grades. His mother reports that he is unmanageable at home and is increasingly oppositional and angry. When he gets angry, he breaks dishes and starts fires. At school he has been accused of stealing money. When he gets angry, he beats up on any student who happens to be near him.

a.   How would you classify Robert?
b.   What additional information about him would you like to have?
c.   What methods would you use to assess Robert or individuals like Robert?

Mindy is a 9-year-old girl who is normal in intelligence but refuses to go to school. She says she is afraid to leave home because she worries that her mother will leave her or die. She tells her mother she can teach her at home. She often enters her parents' bedroom at night and sleeps on the floor.

a.   How would you classify Mindy?
b.   What additional information about Mindy would you like to have?
c.   What methods would you use to assess Mindy or individuals like her?

Allan's mother is concerned because he shows a lack of affection and little interest in interacting with his peers and parents. His language appears to be delayed. The counselor observing Allan in class noted he had problems communicating and interacting with his classmates.

a.   How would you classify Allan?
b.   What additional information would you like to have about him?
c.   What methods would you use to assess Allan or individuals like him?

ADDITIONAL READINGS

Bradley-Johnson, S., & Evans, L. D. (1991). *Psychoeducational assessment of hearing-impaired students: Infancy through adulthood.* Austin, TX: Pro-Ed.

The authors discuss the issues and procedures related to the assessment of hearing impaired students and review the tests and subtests commonly used with this population. They present a checklist of procedures to use before, during, and after testing.

Hamayan, E. V., & Damico, J. S. (1991). *Limiting bias in the assessment of bilingual students.* Austin, TX: Pro-Ed.

Problems in the education and assessment of students with limited English proficiency are identified.

Haring, N. C. (1982). *Exceptional children and youth* (3rd ed.). Columbus, OH: Merrill.

A good overview of the major areas such as mental retardation, learning disabilities, behavior disorders, hearing impairments, visual impairments, physical and multiple disabilities, gifted and talented, cultural diversity, and exceptionality are surveyed. Each chapter presents definitions, prevalence, causes, characteristics, assessment, intervention, curriculum implications, research, and future directions of working with special needs populations.

Rossetti, L. M. (1990). *Infant-toddler assessment.* Austin, TX: Pro-Ed.

The author discusses the assessment of high-risk infants and toddlers and includes sample questionnaires and evaluation instruments.

Simeonsson, R. J. (1986). *Psychological and developmental assessment of special children.* Boston: Allyn and Bacon.

This text identifies dimensions and issues in assessing special children and provides general strategies and instruments for use with this group. The assessment of hearing impaired, visually impaired, motor impaired, autistic, hospitalized, and chronically ill children is discussed.

CHAPTER 19

Multicultural Assessment

Overview

Numerous cultural and ethnic groups live in this country. The theme of the 1993 American Counseling Association (ACA) meeting was "Diversity, Development, and Dignity." Assessment instruments are often criticized as being biased and unfair for use with minorities. One problem that confuses the issue is the broad range of meanings for ethnicity and diversity. *Ethnicity* often is defined as patterns of behavioral roles, social interaction, social customs, language usage, and values shared by a particular group. Rotheram and Phinney (1986) found that studying four dimensions of social patterns helps in differentiating and understanding various ethnic groups. These dimensions are interdependence versus independence, active achievement versus passive acceptance, authoritarianism versus equalitarianism, and expressive versus restrained styles of communication. The 1990 U.S. census identifies four major ethnic groups: African-Americans, who constitute 12.1% of the population; Hispanics, 9%; Asian-Americans, 2.9%; and Native Americans, .5%.

Chapter Objectives

After completing this chapter, the reader should be able to

- list and discuss the standards for multicultural assessment
- identify factors that help in understanding various ethnic groups

- describe assessment instruments, techniques, and procedures that are appropriate for use with various ethnic groups

- explain the trends and issues in multicultural assessment

STANDARDS FOR MULTICULTURAL ASSESSMENT

The Association for Assessment in Counseling (1993) identified 34 standards relevant to multicultural assessment from five of the major sets of standards. Ten standards concerned the selection of assessment instruments according to content. Nine more related to the use of information about the reliability, validity, and norming of the instruments to be selected. Four involved the administration and scoring of the assessment instruments, and 11 covered the use and interpretation of the assessment results. The major theme of these standards is the selection of appropriate instruments.

Content Considerations

The *Code of Fair Testing Practices in Education* (1988) includes two standards in the area of content. The first standard stresses defining the purpose of testing and the population to be tested and then selecting a test appropriate for that purpose and population. The second standard covers the importance of evaluating the test for any potentially insensitive content or language. The *ACA Responsibilities of Users of Standardized Tests* (1989) contributes four standards. The examiner is to determine the limitations to testing created by the individual's age, racial, sexual, ethnic, and cultural background; give attention to how the test is designed to handle variation of motivation, working speed, language facility, and experiential background among persons taking it; determine whether one common or several different tests are required for accurate measurement of groups with special characteristics; and determine whether persons of groups that use different languages should be tested in either or both languages. Four standards are taken from the *Standards for Educational and Psychological Measurement* (1985). When recommending a test for use with linguistically diverse test takers, the test publisher should provide information necessary for appropriate test use and interpretation. Counselors need to review the interpretive materials from the test to make sure that case studies and examples are not limited to illustrations of people in traditional roles. The type and content of the items need to be studied in relation to the cultural background and prior experiences of the ethnic group to be tested. Research should be conducted to explore whether the item or test performance differences for a particular kind of test are related to age, ethnic, cultural, and gender factors. The test and items should be appropriate and not biased.

Technical Considerations

The *Code of Fair Testing Practices in Education* (1988) calls for examiners to make sure the test content and norming groups are appropriate for test takers from different racial, ethnic, or linguistic backgrounds. The counselor is to select tests that have been developed in ways that attempt to make them as reliable and valid as possible for test takers of different race, gender, or ethnic backgrounds. Counselors should review the data from the manual on the performance of test takers of different race, gender, and ethnic backgrounds. The groups must be of a sufficient size. *Responsibilities of Users of Standardized Tests* (1989) also emphasizes the importance of considering the reliability and interpretability of the test and determining whether the standardization and norming procedures are relevant to the local population and use of the data. *Standards for Educational and Psychological Tests* (1985) emphasizes the importance of reviewing the criterion-related evidence of validity when recommending decisions having an actuarial as well as a clinical impact. Since many tests are translated from one language or dialect to another, the reliability and validity for the uses intended in the linguistic groups must be established. The examiner also needs to review any studies of the magnitude of predictive bias due to differential prediction for groups for which previous research has established a substantial prior probability of differential prediction for the type of test in question.

Administration and Scoring

Responsibilities of Users of Standardized Tests (1989) emphasizes the need for the examiner to demonstrate verbal clarity, calmness, empathy for the examinees, and impartiality toward all being tested but to consider potential effects of examiner-examinee differences in ethnic and cultural background, attitudes, and values. *Standards of Educational and Psychological Testing* (1985) reminds examiners that linguistic modification recommended by the test publishers should be described in detail in the test manual. Testing should be designed to minimize threats to the reliability and validity of the test that can arise from language differences.

Use and Interpretation

The *Code of Fair Testing Practices in Education* reminds examiners that when interpreting scores of these groups, they must take into consideration differences between the norms and the scores of test takers and the familiarity of the test takers with the specific questions on the test. In addition, parents and guardians need to know their rights and what procedures they need to follow if they have problems with the assessment. *Responsibilities of Users of Standardized Tests* (1989) also notes that the socioeconomic status, gender, subculture, and other factors may affect an individual's test performance. The counselor needs to use the norms for the group to which the client belongs. *Standards for Educational and Psychological Testing* explains that in educational, clinical, and counseling situations, test administrators and users should not attempt to evaluate test takers whose special characteristics such as age; disability; linguistic, generational, or cultural backgrounds are outside the range of their academic training or supervised experience.

Multicultural Counseling Competencies and Standards (Sue, Arrendo, & McDavis, 1992) includes three standards related to multicultural assessment.

1. Culturally skilled counselors must be aware of the potential bias of assessment instruments and when interpreting findings keep in mind the client's cultural and linguistic characteristics.

2. They also need an awareness and understanding of how culture and ethnicity may affect personality formation, vocational choices, manifestations of psychological disorders, help-seeking behavior, and the appropriateness of counseling approaches.

3. Counselors not only must understand the technical aspects of the instruments, they must also be aware of the cultural limitations.

The bottom line is that counselors not only need the training and experiences in assessing these clients, but the cultural awareness to protect the welfare of the diverse clients with whom they are working. *Ethical Standards of ACA* (1992) instructs counselors to provide specific orientation or information to the examinees prior to and following test administration so that the results of testing many be placed in proper perspective with other relevant factors such as the effects of socioeconomic, ethnic, and cultural factors on test scores. Counselors then proceed with caution when attempting to evaluate and interpret the performance of minority group members or other persons who are not represented in the norming groups on which the instrument was standardized.

TEST BIAS

Test bias is a complex issue. Valencia and Aburto (1991) argue that the major concern during the 1970s and 1980s was whether IQ tests were biased against racial and ethnic minorities. Jensen (1980) claims bias is strictly statistical and can be defined as the systematic error of individuals' scores that is connected to group membership and bias in context for racial or ethnic groups. An item or subtest is labeled biased when empirical evidence shows that it is more difficult for one group member than another, the general ability level of the two groups is held constant, and no reasonable rationale exists to explain the group differences on the same items. Jensen says that test fairness/unfairness relates more to moral philosophy than to psychometrics.

Reynolds and Brown (1984) list six dimensions of bias—inappropriate content, inappropriate standardization samples, examiner and language bias, inequitable social consequences, measurement of different constructs, and differential predictive validity.

Bilingual children with limited English skills have trouble understanding oral and written directions in addition to the vocabulary and the syntax of the test items. Often they have a hard time giving correct verbal responses, and they may have trouble discriminating among sounds that are not a part of their primary language.

Test Taker Bias Factors

Oakland (1982) advises awareness of points of bias during assessment of culturally different or minority group individuals. Some potential bias centers around the test taker.

Language—The examinee's ability to understand and communicate in English is very important. Conventional measures that require a high level of competence in English are not appropriate.

Test wiseness—The examiner cannot assume that examinees can understand directions, comply with proper test taking procedures, and be involved and attentive during testing.

Motivation and anxiety—The examiner may find an examinee who refuses to cooperate or is too anxious. The examiner needs to consider the attitudinal characteristics of examinees and attempt to get them to do their best.

Cultural differences—Minority examinees may come from restricted environments in expectations, language experiences, formal and informal learning experiences, and upbringing. The examiner needs to understand the background of the examinees and whether the test is appropriate. (pp. 153–154)

Examiner Bias Factors

The examiner may introduce bias in several ways. The examiner needs to recognize personal bias and how it may influence interpretation of results. This requires treating each individual with dignity and respect and pursuing the best interests of the examinee. Baruth and Manning (1991) have identified some of the common barriers to effective multicultural counseling:

1. the counselor makes erroneous assumptions about cultural assimilation
2. there is a difference is class and cultural values
3. there are language differences and both cultural or socioeconomic class misunderstandings
4. the counselor believes in stereotypes about culturally different people
5. the counselor fails to understand the culture
6. there is little understanding of the client's reasoning structures
7. there is a lack of cultural relativity among counselors

DEVELOPING GREATER MULTICULTURAL UNDERSTANDING

In developing an action plan to increase their multicultural understanding, counselors can utilize research on the multicultural counseling process, case studies in the literature, experiences of other counselors they are working with, their own experiences with culturally deferent clients, and other first-hand experiences with the various ethnic groups (Draguns, 1989; Nutall, 1992). For counselors the first step is to develop greater self-awareness and comprehension of their own cultural group. They need to comprehend their own environmental experiences in the mainstream culture and reflect on their sensitivity toward their personal beliefs and values. Specific training in working with certain groups provides greater confidence and knowledge of the group.

Counselors need to develop an awareness and comprehension of the history and experiences of the cultural group with which the client is currently identifying or encountering. In general, the counselor must develop perceptual sensitivity toward the client's personal beliefs and values (Baruth & Manning, 1991).

Ethical Principles

Ethical standards of working with culturally diverse clients require for the counselor to have cultural knowledge based on research and experience. They also must understand their own cultural background and be able to go beyond their own biases and prejudices. The counselor must have respect for the diverse values and beliefs of clients as they affect their view of the world and their psychosocial functioning. The counselor must also be aware of the impact of social, environmental, and political conditions on problems and interventions. Counselors must be advocates and stand against racism and discrimination. In assessment they need to utilize multisource, multilevel, and multimethod approaches to assess the capabilities, potentialities, and limitations of the clients (APA, 1992). During assessment and counseling, counselors need to be careful and active listeners, be genuine, and demonstrate verbally and nonverbally that they understand what they are communicating. They want to show that they care about clients and their situations and are working to help them achieve a realistic solution.

Testing Principles

In testing culturally and ethnically different clients, it is important for the examiner to

1. become familiar with the characteristics and learning styles of different groups
2. avoid stereotypes
3. treat all clients equally and with respect and dignity
4. be sure that the tests used are valid and appropriate for the cultural group

Etic and Emic Perspectives

Etic perspective emphasizes the universal qualities among human beings by examining and comparing many cultures from a position outside those cultures. Emic perspective is culture-specific and examines behavior from within a culture, using criteria relative to the internal characteristics of that culture (Dana, 1993). From the etic perspective, assessment would involve comparing individuals' scores to a norming group and comparing different individuals from different cultures on a construct that is assumed to be universal across all cultures.

Dana (1993) includes as etic measures a broad spectrum of instruments to measure psychopathology, personality measures, and major tests of intelligence and cognitive functioning. Included as etic personality measures are the California Psychological Inventory and Eysenck Personality Questionnaire. Included in the intelligence/cognitive functioning area are the Wechsler Intelligence Scales, System of Multicultural Pluralistic Assessment, Kaufman Assessment Battery for Children, McCarthy Scales of Children's Abilities, and Stanford-Binet Intelligence Scale. Other single construct tests for identification of psychopathology are the State-Trait Anxiety Scale, Beck Depression Inventory, and Michigan Alcoholism Screening Test. The MMPI is also on this list; it has been translated into 150 languages and has reported applications in 50 countries. The other tests listed have been translated into other languages, mainly Spanish.

Emic methods include behavior observations, case studies, studies of life events, picture story techniques, inkblot techniques, word association, sentence completion, and drawings. Most of these methods are classified as projective. These tests can provide a personality description of the individual that reflects the data and mirrors the culture and ethnic group (Dana, 1993). The analysis demands more knowledge of the culture by the examiner but aids the understanding of the individual in a cultural context. There are thematic apperception test versions such as the following.

Thompson Modification of the TAT—10-card version for African Americans.

Themes Concerning Blacks Test—20 charcoal drawings depict aspects of African-American culture and lifestyle.

TEMAS—Tell Me a Story Test, designed for Spanish speaking populations.

Michigan Picture Story Test—designed for use with Hispanic-American and African-American children and adolescents.

Sentence completion methods have been used with many different cultures. The items can be designed to assess the social norms, roles, and values of clients from different cultures. Examples of some of the items are

The thing I like most about America is_____

Anglos_____

If I could be from another culture or ethnic group I_____

There are not always formal scoring systems for the different emic tests.

Acculturation

The degree of acculturation to the dominant society and the extent to which the original culture has been retained provide valuable information in interpreting assessment results. Dana (1993) has developed a checklist to record acculturation information. One item related to the phase of the acculturation process and had five levels: precontact, contact, conflict, crisis, or adaptation. Another item related to the mode and had four categories: assimilation, bicultural, traditional, marginal. Dana also looks at group membership—whether the group consists of native peoples, immigrants, refugees, ethnic groups, or sojourners. The sociocultural pattern is also recorded by looking at settlement patterns, status, status mobility, support network, and group acceptability.

For Americans, two instruments can provide information on the moderating variables that affect assessment interpretation: the Developmental Inventory of Black Consciousness (DIB-C) and the Racial Identity Attitude Scale (RIAS). The DIB-C HAS four stages: preconsciousness, confrontation, internalization, and integration. The RAIS ALSO has four: pre-encounter, encounter, immersion-emersion, and internalization. Another useful scale is the African Self-Consciousness Scale (ASC), which has four dimensions: awareness of black identity; recognition of survival priorities and affirmative practices, customs, and values; active participation in defense of survival, liberation, and the like; and recognition of racial oppression (Baldwin & Bell, 1985).

Dana (1993) advises counselors to use moderator variables whenever there is evidence that a client is not representative of an Anglo-American cultural background. The counselor can get an idea of whether the client is identifying with a culture of origin rather than with the dominant Anglo-American culture.

Strategies

Since each client is unique, the examiner needs to be alert to important behavioral signals. Certain behavior may affect the reliability and validity of the test. Appropriate examiner responses are summarized in Table 19.1.

In working with minority and culturally different groups, the helping professional must have basic knowledge of the trends and issues related to the treatment of these groups, the culture of the individuals being tested, tests and assessment procedures appropriate for the groups, and agency and institutional sources of referral and support for the individuals being assessed.

A variety of modes and tests can be used, ranging from nonverbal culture-free tests in the language of linguistic minorities to tests in standard English. The examiner, as pointed out earlier in this chapter, needs to know the client's level of assimilation into the mainstream culture. Understanding the client's educational level and background, language facility, and receptive and expressive vocabulary can help guide test selection.

Table 19.1
Critical behavior indicators and possible examiner responses

Behavior	Response
Is silent	Establish rapport. Give nonverbal and performance test first, get other indexes of individual behavior
Says "don't know"	Don't assume client cannot respond
Is shy and reserved, lowers eyes	Observe client in other situations, spend time establishing rapport, start with nonverbal and untimed tests, provide reinforcement, try to motivate client
Uses wit or popular language	Be firm and positive, be sure examinee knows why the test/instrument is being given
Interrupts the test or asks questions	Be firm but allow some dialogue, be sure the examinee knows the purpose of the test
Is inattentive and restless	Structure test environment, keep examinee involved
Is uncertain about how to respond	Rephrase question, make meaning clear
Watches the examiner rather than listens to the questions	Be firm, be sure questions are clear, be sure there are no distractions in test situation If the responses are inappropriate, question further
Performs poorly on timed tests	Recognize a culture not oriented to the value of time, avoid drawing conclusions about individual performance until untimed measures have been tried
Shows poor knowledge of vocabulary	Try other ways of measuring the examinee's expressive vocabulary, question individual in primary language
Is unmotivated to take test	Explain purpose and value of test to client and family, try techniques to motivate client performance
Scores poorly on information items	Recognize that some items might be biased and not a part of the examinee's culture, ask examinee to clarify any unusual responses
Is afraid of embarrassing or dishonoring family	Initiate test-wise session, practice session, or some type of warm-up
Is quiet and does not ask questions or interact	Establish rapport, explain examiner's role and purpose of the test, ask client to repeat the question if no answer is given or the answer is inappropriate
Is afraid of a male examiner	Observe examinee, establish rapport before testing

SUMMARY

Many factors can bias the assessment of multicultural groups and individuals and lead to possible sources of misinterpretation. Legal and professional standards call for nonbiased, nondiscriminatory assessment, validation of tests for a specific purpose, and use of multiple sources of information and multiple windows to view and understand diversity. Emic approaches provide this window and increase the credibility of the assessment. Moderating variables such as the degree of assimilation of the majority culture are also important in understanding the individual.

QUESTIONS FOR DISCUSSION

1. How might the following examiner variables affect the validity of the test results? (a) Personal bias and expectations of counselor of a certain ethnic group, (b) Lack of experience of the counselor in working with a certain ethnic group, (c) Lack of knowledge of the client's first language, (d) Lack of knowledge of the specific ethnic group.

2. Do you think it is acceptable to adapt and modify a standardized test to accommodate the ethnic group being represented by the client? Why or why not?

3. What personality characteristics do counselors need to have when testing a member of a minority group?

4. Compare and contrast your culture with that of another ethnic group. What are the similarities? What are the differences?

5. What are the different dimensions of bias that an examiner must be alert to?

SUGGESTED ACTIVITIES

1. Interview a psychologist who assesses a number of multicultural clients and find out what tests he or she uses and why. Report your findings to the class.

2. Make an annotated bibliography of tests designed for administration to one of the following groups: Hispanics, Asian-Americans, African-Americans, or Native Americans.

3. Interview counselors who work with diverse groups and find out how they developed their cultural knowledge and awareness.

4. Locate the public laws and court decisions related to assessing minority group members. Write a summary of the legislation and court decisions.

5. Locate a test that has been adapted for a certain minority or ethnic group. How was the test modified? How do the two sets of norms compare? How does the reliability compare?

6. Study the following brief questions and answer the questions at the end of each.

John was a 15-year-old African-American male. Assessment using Gardner's Typology showed he had high musical and kinesthetic intelligence. His family moved into the city from a suburban area because of the father's job change. He attended an inner-city high school that had a magnet program in engineering and mathematics because his parents didn't want him to be bused to another school 30 minutes away. The school he attended had limited programs in fine arts and music and few resources. One of John's friends was shot by a gang in a shopping center, and another classmate died from a drug overdose. John started to withdraw and showed signs of depression. He became sick on school days. His parents want you to test John and help him.

a. What type of assessment procedures and instruments would you use with John?
b. What factors and issues do you feel need to be addressed?
c. What additional information would you like to have about John?

Claudia was a 14-year-old bilingual Latina who was referred to the child study team because of her truancy, lack of motivation, and negative attitude toward her teachers and school. She was placed in an English as a Second Language class with many students who had negative motivation and poor skills. She told her parents she was going to school, but would skip and go to the local mall. She did well academically when she was in class. One of her teachers said: "She is like all of the other problem students we have in this program: no interest, no discipline, and no motivation."

a. What type of tests would you give and why?
b. What factors might tend to bias her test results?
c. What additional information about Claudia would you want to have?

Tobeka, a 6-year-old African-American, entered first grade but was having considerable academic difficulties and was referred for a multifactor evaluation by the school's multidisciplinary team. The mother refused to let her daughter be tested until she could examine the tests that would be used. The psychologist met with the mother to explain why the tests would be given and discuss what tests would be given.

a. What factors were involved?
b. What test standards were involved in this case?
c. What was the ethical responsibility of the psychologist?

Janie, an 8-year-old Native American of the Penobscot tribe, was referred to a multidisciplinary team by her guidance counselor and teachers for evaluation of her avoidant behavior and assessment of her intellectual potential. She had been refusing to participate in her reading group, cried often, and usually failed to follow directions. Her teacher said Janie isolated herself from others in the class and refused to participate. Her mother indicated that the other students made fun of Janie.

a. What advice would you give to the psychologist before he meets with Janie?

b. What important professional standards for multicultural assessment should
be considered in this case?

c. What assessment techniques and procedures would you use in this case?

ADDITIONAL READING

Canino, I. A., & Spurlock, J. (1994). *Culturally diverse children and adolescents: Assessment, diagnosis, and treatment*. New York: Guilford.

The authors guide clinicians in learning how to determine the impact of cultural differences, poverty, discrimination, and acculturation issues when assessing children and adolescents. The book has numerous clinical vignettes to illustrate the constructs presented.

Dana, R. H. (1993). *Multicultural assessment perspectives for professional psychology*. Boston: Allyn and Bacon.

The author presents a comprehensive model for multicultural assessment and a specific review of instrumentation used to assess African-Americans, Hispanics, Asian-Americans, and Native Americans.

CHAPTER 20

Test-Taking Skills

Overview

Test-taking skills have become an important topic in the field of measurement and research. Much controversy has centered around whether coaching can help individuals raise their test scores, particularly by reducing anxiety. This controversy has focused on programs to help students improve their performance on the Scholastic Aptitude Test (SAT). Goldman (1971) concludes that coaching is of help to at least some individuals and is likely to be of greater assistance to underachievers and persons who are "rusty" in the particular area being tested.

Objectives

This chapter should enable the reader to

* list and discuss the different strategies to help individuals maximize their test performance

* identify and analyze the different factors related to test performance

* evaluate the sources of help available to assist individuals in improving their test performance

TEST ANXIETY

Test anxiety is a general feeling of uneasiness, tension, or foreboding that some individuals experience in testing situations. Excessive anxiety can have a detrimental effect on individual performance (Sarason, 1980; Tobias, 1979; Tryon, 1980). When individuals feel pressure to make high scores on a test, their anxiety level may increase (Deffenbacher, 1978). In reviewing the literature on anxiety and test performance, Goldman (1971) found that individuals with high levels of anxiety tend to do worse on cognitive tests. Wine (1980) concluded that individuals with high test anxiety worry about not doing as well as they would like to do on a test. This mind-set leads to their failure to concentrate on or attend to the test. Individuals with low test anxiety, on the other hand, do not worry and are able to concentrate on their test performance. Zeichner and Most (1992) conclude that maximum performance tests (e.g., problem-solving, situational, and critical-thinking exercises) tend to evoke anxiety in the test takers. High anxiety levels impede performance and lead to cognitive interference and task-irrelevant thinking (Saklofski & Kowalchuk, 1992).

Measures of Test Anxiety

Several published instruments are designed to measure test anxiety. The Test Anxiety Inventory is a 20-item pencil-and-paper test to measure two major components of test anxiety—worry and emotionality. The inventory can be given to students and adults in grade 10 and higher and is similar in structure to the A-Trait Scale of the State-Trait Anxiety Inventory. It can also be self-administered.

The Rocky Mountain Behavioral Science Institute publishes two test anxiety scales—the Suinn Test Anxiety Behavior Scale (STABS) and the Test Anxiety Profile (TAP) by E. R. Oetting and C. W. Cole. The STABS is a 50-item pencil-and-paper test for individuals in grade 7 to adulthood. Clients rate their anxiety concerns on a five-point scale, ranging from "not at all" to "very much." The test items concern clients' experiences related to academic testing situations. The TAP is a 77-item pencil-and-paper test measuring individual feelings about six academic testing situations—multiple-choice exams, mathematics exams, essay exams, unannounced tests, talking in front of a class, and tests with time limits.

The classic test in the field is the Children's Test Anxiety Scale (CTAS), which contains 30 items. Feld and Lewis (1969) identified four components discovered through factor analysis of the CTAS—test anxiety, remote school concerns, poor self-evaluation, and somatic signs of anxiety. Test anxiety is measured by such questions as "Do you worry a lot before you take a test?" and "While you are taking a test, do you usually think you are doing poor work?" To assess remote school concerns, there are such questions as "When you are in bed at night, do you sometimes worry about how you are going to do in class the next day?" and "After you have taken a test, do you worry about how well you did on the test?" Poor self-evaluation is measured by such questions as "When the teacher is teaching you about reading, do you feel that other children in the class understand him or her better than you?" and "Do you sometimes dream at night that other boys and girls in your class can do things you cannot do?" To measure somatic signs of anxiety, there are questions such as "When you are taking a test, does the hand you write with shake a little?" and "When the teacher says that she is going to find out how much you have learned, do you get a funny feeling in your stomach?"

Strategies to Help Test Anxiety

Humbree (1988) reviews the correlates, causes, effects, and treatment of test anxiety. The test examiner must be attentive to the examinee's needs. Examinees should be motivated to do their best on tests but should not be made anxious. Sometimes, however, pressure comes not from the psychologist, counselor, or teacher, but from the parents. Currently in our educational system tests have assumed too much importance in some states. They are used as the sole criterion to judge whether a student should be promoted to the next grade or allowed to move from one level to another.

The examiner should consider these strategies in test administration.

1. To be sure examinees understand test instructions, check with the examinees, asking whether they understand. In a group test, circulate around the room to see if students are following directions and recording their answers properly.

2. To establish rapport and an environment that is relaxed and as stress-free as possible, before the test establish a learning-oriented environment. Examinees may need to be taught more effective study habits and may need more time to prepare for tests. Tests can be an interesting learning experience as well as a motivational one. At test time be friendly and positive but follow standardized procedures. Ensure that examinees have the proper physical facilities, space to work, proper lighting, ventilation, and so on.

3. To remove some of the pressure from major tests and exams, conduct group or class sessions on how to take a test, give the examinees practice tests, and provide a list of guidebooks and study guides that are available for an upcoming test.

Relaxation Techniques

The object of relaxation exercises is to help test takers practice mind calming. The following is an example of what a test administrator might say before a test:

> "Sit down and get very comfortable. Close your eyes and take a deep breath. Exhale and let your body and mind relax completely. Breathe in again and as you breathe out, feel even more relaxed. Forget about everything except what I am saying. Listen carefully. Continue to breathe deeply and slowly. You should begin to feel more and more relaxed.
>
> "You are sitting in a lounge chair on the beach. It is not too warm or too cold. The temperature is just right. Everything is very peaceful and pleasant. You see the waves

coming onto the beach. They are a beautiful blue and the sun is a brilliant yellow. You feel nice and warm and relaxed all over. Take a deep breath in the nice clear air. You loose track of time. The sky gets a deeper blue. . . .

"Now that you are relaxed, think positively of yourself. Say, 'I can remember all I need to know on the test.' Say it several times. Say, 'I will know the right answers.' Say, 'I am alert; my mind is powerful.'"

Stress Reduction

Learning can be increased if stress is reduced. Stress is defined as a force that can cause strain or distortion in the individual. Teaching test-taking skills is one approach to reducing stress on tests; another approach is to improve students' knowledge base. One way to do this is to help teachers improve the quality of their instruction. Effective teachers use analytical and synthetic approaches to the subject matter, organize their material to make it clear, and establish rapport with their students (Whitman, Spendlove, & Clark, 1986, p. 1). Teachers bring more than knowledge to the classroom; they also play the role of motivators, experts, and judges.

Feedback is an important factor in improving future performance and alleviating stress. Five steps are essential to effective feedback.

1. Help students know where they stand.
2. Set specific objectives and state the evaluative criteria for successful performance.
3. Provide written comments on papers, tests, and homework assignments.
4. Test frequently.
5. Talk individually with the learners about the quality of their work.

After reviewing the research, Whitman et al. concluded that the frequency and quality of teachers' contact with students both in and out of the classroom influence how students learn. Positive teacher-learner relationships have been linked with learner satisfaction with school, educational aspirations, and academic achievement.

Teachers need to be alerted to dimensions of stress and know how to help learners develop skills to cope more effectively with its negative aspects. They should identify learners with severe anxiety and refer them to professional mental health counselors. A counselor might provide sessions for students on study skills, time management, self-confidence, and relaxation techniques.

IMPROVING TEST SCORES

As mentioned previously, two of the main approaches to improving test scores are better content preparation and better test-taking skills. Counselors can help individuals become more familiar with types of items and testing procedures. The goal of any consulting sessions is ultimately a valid performance measure of the individual being tested.

Coaching

Coaching is a method used by administrators, teachers, and counselors to help test takers improve their test performance. Prell and Prell (1986) state that although there is no universally accepted definition for coaching, the term is popularly used to mean training test takers to answer specific types of questions and provide the information required by a specific test. Coaching is sometimes referred to as teaching to the test.

The topic of coaching has been the object of much attention lately. Considerable controversy has surrounded coaching to improve performance on the Scholastic Aptitude Test (SAT). Alderman and Powers (1980) reported that almost one-third of the high schools surveyed offered special programs for students taking the SAT. Many commercial seminars are also available. Researchers (Messick, 1980; Messick & Yungeblut, 1981) reported that short high school training programs help examinees gain on the average 10 points on the SAT verbal section and 15 points on the SAT mathematics section. It should be understood, however, that gains of 20 to 30 points result from getting just two to three more items correct. Stockwell, Schaffer, and Lowenstein (1991) wrote about the phenomenon in their book, *The SAT Coaching Coverup: How Coaching Courses Can Raise Scores by 100 Points and Why ETS Denies the Evidence*. Cronbach (1984) concludes that the research stimulated by the SAT controversy indicates the following factors.

1. Many different types of coaching programs are in operation in the schools.
2. A key variable in the success of such programs is client motivation and prior preparation.
3. Because most studies have not utilized true experimental designs, it is difficult to compare an experimental group with a control group. (Anastasi, 1982)

Of significance are concerns about the social, philosophical, and ethical aspects of coaching. Some social scientists believe that individuals from lower socioeconomic groups are at a disadvantage because they cannot afford to participate in such programs. Wigdor and Garner (1982) conclude that there may be a considerable advantage to preparing test takers for an examination if it measures abilities and knowledge which are educationally worthwhile.

Strategies to Increase Test Wiseness

Millman, Bishop, and Ebel (1965) define test wiseness as "a subject's capacity to utilize the characteristics and formats of the test and/or test-taking situation to receive a high score" (p. 710). They note that test wiseness is independent of the examinee's knowledge of the subject matter the items are designed to measure.

Millman et al. (1965) identify two major dimensions of test wiseness—elements dependent on the test construction or purpose and elements independent of that construction or purpose. Four major categories of concern for increasing test wiseness are use of time, avoidance of errors, strategies for guessing, and use of deductive reasoning.

In her publication for the Educational Testing Service entitled *Everything You Wanted to Know About Test-Wiseness*, Ford (1973) expands upon the concepts of Millman et al. and adds instructions specific to different types of item formats. Ford presents a number of general test-taking strategies related to understanding and following directions, knowing how to record responses on tests, using time effectively, and figuring out answers. Here are some general strategies that can be utilized to increase test wiseness.

1. Utilize available practice examinations and brochures describing the test. Practice generally has a positive effect on the test performance, building the confidence of the test takers and improving their ability to perform.

2. Have practice sessions on understanding instructions and developing listening skills. Discuss the problems that arise, and give examinees practice with instructions for different types of test formats and answer sheets.

3. Advise examinees on using time efficiently. They should first scan the test to see the scope of what has to be done. They should answer questions they know, going back to the more difficult and time-consuming questions. And they should allow time to check their answers to see whether they have been recorded properly.

In general, test takers feel more knowledgeable and have less anxiety when they receive instructions in how to take a test. Such sessions reduce errors caused by unfamiliarity with test procedures and lead to scores that better reflect an examinee's knowledge and abilities.

Special strategies apply to each type of item format. For example, test takers on multiple-choice tests are cautioned to examine carefully all of the options or responses before attempting to choose the correct answer. If the examinee stops when he sees a correct answer—say option A—he could miss reading options B, C, D, and E, which might also be correct. Option E might read, "All of the above." At other times options may be similar and vary only slightly; usually these options can be eliminated. The examinee has a better chance of getting a higher score if options known to be incorrect can be eliminated and the choice is made from among the remaining alternatives. Sometimes an option resembles the stem—uses the same names, words, or phrases; usually these options should be selected. Correct answers are often longer and perhaps stated more precisely or specifically than the other alternatives.

Prell and Prell (1986) conclude that the most important aspect of test wiseness is its relationship to test validity. Test wiseness is considered a source of variance on tests that reduces the validity. The goal is to maximize the variance due to the knowledge and abilities measured by the test and not penalize test takers who are not test wise. Urman (1983) found that a lack of test wiseness can penalize test takers and that the bias against test takers who are not test wise extends to standardized tests. Prell and Prell (1986) conclude that student performance on tests will become a more accurate reflection of actual knowledge as test wiseness techniques are taught to students.

Application of Test Wiseness to Teacher-Made Tests

More attention has been focused recently on training in test wiseness to help improve test takers' performance on standardized tests, but that knowledge will also help, even more dramatically, with teacher-made tests. John J. Chiodo (1986) provides rules that instructors should follow to reduce student anxiety and improve test wiseness of students on teacher-made examinations.

1. Review the scope of the exam. The instructor should tell the learners in advance the general area(s) that the test will cover and the relative importance of each.

2. Use practice tests. The instructor should give the learners samples of the types of items they will face and sample answers for essay and short-answer questions. Sample items help learners become familiar with the language the instructor uses.

3. Be clear about time limits. Learners need to know how long the test will take and whether extra time will be allowed.

4. Announce what materials and equipment the learners need to bring to the testing situation—pencils, calculators, notebooks, bluebooks, and the like.

5. Review the grading procedures. Test takers need to know how the test will be scored and interpreted and how much the test will count.

6. Review the policies on make-up exams and retakes. The instructor needs to spell out the rules prior to the testing period. Test takers should know whether they may take a make-up test if they have a legitimate reason for missing class, or whether they may retake the test if they do not do well.

7. Provide study help. Students might benefit from a study guide for the test or some formal review sessions.

8. Make some provisions for last-minute questions. Some test takers come up with questions on the day of the test or even during the testing. The instructor needs to have established a procedure for handling these questions.

9. Allow for breaks during long exams. Test takers should have a chance to stand up or stretch or go to the rest room if needed.

10. Coach students on test-taking skills. The examiner should remind learners to survey the whole exam before they start and plan their time efficiently. Test takers need to understand the directions and be reminded to answer those questions they are sure of first.

WORKSHOP ON TEST-TAKING SKILLS

A workshop or seminar for individuals on test-taking strategies might take several sessions, depending on the test to be taken. These sessions should focus on behavior before the test, behavior during the test, general strategies for taking tests, specific strategies for certain types of items or certain domains, and content review. Here is an outline of a possible series of workshops on test-taking strategies.

A.   SESSION 1—Behavior before the test
   1.   Get psychologically ready for the test.
   2.   Attend any orientation sessions.
   3.   Read informational brochures on test.
   4.   Check domains and objectives to be measured.
   5.   Determine review and study strategies.
   6.   Secure study guides and previous exams if available.
   7.   Check into availability of review or study groups.
   8.   Think positively; pep yourself up.

B.   SESSION 2—Day of the test
   1.   Get good rest, eat properly, dress comfortably.
   2.   Be early; don't rush; allow time.
   3.   Try relaxation techniques.
   4.   Concentrate on task; avoid being distracted; block feelings of anxiety.
   5.   Develop positive mind-set toward test.

C.   SESSION 3—Behavior during the test
   1.   If permitted, skim the test prior to starting to gain a general overview of the tasks to be accomplished.
   2.   Decide how much time to allocate to each part of the test.
   3.   Go through the test and answer all the questions you know.
   4.   Leave the hard or time-consuming questions until the last, but don't skip too many questions.
   5.   Keep an eye on the time.
   6.   Read the test critically.
   7.   Read directions carefully as well as sample questions and answers.
   8.   Double check your answers.
   9.   Check to see whether you recorded your answers correctly.
   10. Identify clues in the item stems of questions.
   11. Identify clues in the options or answer choices.
   12. Know the rules for guessing.
   13. Know how standardized tests arrange items.

D.   SESSION 4—Objective test/multiple-choice
   1.   Work quickly and accurately, but read the whole item.
   2.   Read the directions carefully.
   3.   Watch for more than one correct answer and options such as "all of the above."

4. Read every word in the stem of an item and don't skim.
5. Eliminate implausible options.
6. Look for key words or clues that may be in the item.
7. Don't be afraid to guess.
8. Don't be afraid to change your answer.
9. Be confident and don't get flustered.
10. Know how to answer verbal analogy items.
11. Know how to answer reading comprehension items.
12. Know how to answer mathematical and quantitative reasoning items.

OTHER FACTORS

A number of factors can affect the test-taking behavior and thus test scores.

1. anxiety
2. bluffing
3. changing answers
4. past experience
5. response set and positional preferences
6. reading comprehension
7. speaking ability, enunciation, and voice
8. spelling and grammar
9. penmanship and fluency

Anxiety was discussed earlier in this chapter and can affect all four major types of tests—objective, essay, oral, and performance. Bluffing occurs mainly on essay or oral examinations and can bias an individual's score. Test takers with good verbal facility quite often can express themselves well but must be sure to spend some time organizing their answers, using good topic sentences or opening statements.

Changing answers is another factor. Many people believe that their first choices are best and do not change their answers. In general, however, research has shown that it does pay to check over responses. Reiling and Taylor (1972) found that students who changed their answers tended to improve their scores.

Past experience can also influence results. Many test takers are exposed to a test type and/or item type with which they have had no experience. Goldman (1971) suggested that alternate forms, if available, be given to the examinees in this situation. Sometimes testing in general has not been a part of an individual's cultural or educational experiences. This type of test taker might profit from attending sessions on how to take tests.

Response set and positional preferences affect individual performance especially on personality tests. In general, a good standardized test in the cognitive area randomizes correct answers. If 100 items have four options each, each option should serve as the correct answer approximately 25 percent of the time.

Teacher-made tests often reveal unconscious patterns, such as having more items true rather than false. Examinees should be informed that correct answers will follow a random pattern, and any guessing should take that pattern into consideration.

A major criticism of group tests is that they demand reading comprehension skills. Most test authors, however, try to keep the verbal level of the item simple so that the items measure knowledge or application rather than reading comprehension. Counselors should check an examinee's reading level before arbitrarily administering a test. In some cases a test may have to be administered orally, or a nonverbal test may have to be given.

Voice, enunciation, and oral expression are also factors that can affect an individual's performance on an oral test. Many times, practice or rehearsal sessions and role playing can help individuals learn to present themselves better on oral examinations.

Spelling and grammar, penmanship, and fluency are important factors on essay tests. Errors in spelling and grammar detract from the ideas being presented and influence rate judgment negatively. On the other hand, good penmanship and fluent expression create a positive expectation in raters and encourage high ratings.

INFORMATION ON TEST TAKING

One of the major sources of information on test taking is a test publisher. Many publishers have brochures, study guides, and practice exercises available for their tests. A representative bibliography is included at the end of the chapter. The quality of publisher aids varies, however; some are well done, and some are not. The following outline should guide the helping professional who must develop an awareness brochure for a scholastic aptitude test.

A. General statement and misconceptions about preparing for tests
   1. The test measures innate ability, and there is no way to prepare for the test.
   2. A system can be developed to help improve test scores.

B. General statement of what research says about different factors related to test performance
   1. Previous educational experiences are an important factor in test performance.
   2. Generic skills in verbal reasoning and fluency and mathematical analysis and reasoning—the skills necessary for success in academic programs—are measured by scholastic aptitude tests.

C. General statement of what type of preparation has helped individuals improve their test performance
   1. Test companies and educational publishers often have sample tests and study guides available for test takers.

2. Special short-term or long-term courses in a given area might be considered.

3. Courses in test-taking strategies might be of help to some individuals.

D. General statements about test-taking strategies
1. Test performance is only one indicator of potential; previous achievement and other factors are also valid indicators. Therefore, test takers ought not be overwhelmed by the importance of the test.
2. Test takers should become knowledgeable about the tests they plan to take.
3. Test takers should practice taking sample tests.
4. Test takers should develop the proper mental and psychological set.
5. Test takers should develop time management skills and apply the principles to taking tests.
6. Test takers should learn strategies for problem solving and guessing on tests.
7. Test takers should learn to be careful and check their work.

E. Specific strategies for answering verbal and mathematical types of questions should be discussed.

F. An annotated bibliography of resource information (books, guides, and audiovisuals) should be available.

Most test publishers provide brochures on how to take tests, practice tests, purposes and scope of the test, and so on. For example, ETS for the National Teachers Examination has available a bulletin of information, descriptive booklet on the NTE Core Battery, and descriptive leaflets for the specialty area tests. These guides include a previously administered form of the test, rationale for the answers, test-taking strategies, and an explanation of scoring procedures. They also include a separate answer sheet and answer key. ETS (1988) has developed a test-taking tip sheet to provide general information on test taking. Other tip sheets have been developed on analytical, reading, verbal, and quantitative questions and preparing for achievement tests. The tip sheet provides the following suggestions on test taking.

Be a Good Consumer

1. Get information about tests from the test publisher. Often there are copies of tests that have been previously given available.

2. Know what the test covers and does not cover.

3. Plan to be successful the first time you take the test.

Before the Test

1. Become familiar with the types of questions.

2. Assess your strengths and weaknesses.

3. Develop practice and study strategies.

4. Become familiar with the directions and organization of the test.

5. Learn whether you will be penalized for guessing.

6. Study your guessing pattern.

During the Test

1. Arrive at the test site early.

2. Work carefully.

3. Answer the questions immediately.

4. Decide what questions you might get if you have enough time and the questions you will not get because you have no ideas of the answer.

5. Answer every question if there is no penalty for guessing.

6. Keep focused. Don't let others distract you.

After the Test

1. Cancel your test performance if you had unforeseen health, family, or emotional problems.

2. Review your results on the test along with your goals and aptitude.

3. Plan to take the test again if necessary.

Test Alert

Test Alert (1990) is an instructional program of test-taking strategies published by Riverside Publishing Company. The purpose of the program is to introduce primary school students to effective techniques for taking standardized tests. The goal of Test Alert is to help students achieve test scores that accurately reflect their achievement. The program focuses on strategies for test taking and not on a review of the content being tested. Level A is for grades 1 and 2 and is organized into five lessons, one for each day of the school week. Each lesson takes about 35 to 45 minutes. The five lessons are Good Listening, Good Guessing, A Closer Look at Numbers, A Closer Look at Words, and Using Clues. Level B is for grades 3 and 4 and Level C for grades 5 and 6. The 10 lessons at levels B and C each take approximately 45 minutes. A listing of strategy categories follows.

Mechanics of Test Taking

Lesson 1 Reordering Information and Answers

Lesson 2 Pacing Yourself

Lesson 3 Making Good Guesses

Reading Strategies

Lesson 4 Recognizing Main Ideas

Lesson 5 Drawing Conclusions

Mathematics Strategies

Lesson 6 Improving Computation Skills

Lesson 7 Solving Word Problems

Lesson 8 Understanding Math Units

Language Strategies

Lesson 9 Ordering Ideas

Lesson 10 Developing Paragraphs

The lessons include a focus exercise that is an entertaining activity to demonstrate the major concepts of the lesson. Discussion questions, activity booklets, and a teacher's guide are available. The session ends with a trial test in which questions are presented in both a timed and untimed format.

SUMMARY

Often we neglect to prepare individuals properly to take tests. We fail to teach not only test-taking skills, but also study skills. Many tests now have practice exams and study guides. Practice in test taking is helpful for those with limited recent experience. The goal of tests is to obtain a true measure of individual performance. Factors such as self-concept, self-confidence, and achievement motivation can affect actual test performance as well as participation in test-taking programs.

QUESTIONS FOR DISCUSSION

1. Should counselors, psychologists, and teachers make sure that sessions on test-taking skills are conducted prior to all major examinations? Why or why not?

2. Many different study guides have been published for all of the major national testing programs. How would you go about evaluating these guides? Would you recommend a specific one or series, or would you just tell the client that a number of sources are available in most bookstores? Explain your approach.

3. If an individual came to you for advice about a series of seminars in preparation for the Graduate Record Examination at a cost of $1,400, what would you tell that individual?

4. Do you think that anxiety plays a significant role in test performance? Should we try to assess anxiety before and during testing situations? Why or why not?

5. Have you taken seminars in test-taking strategies or sessions on how to improve your performance on a nationally administered examination? What was your evaluation of the seminar or session? Do you believe your performance improved as a result of the seminar?

SUGGESTED ACTIVITIES

1. Read *How to Take a Test: Doing Your Best* by John E. Dobbin (published by Educational Testing Service, Princeton, NJ) and report your reaction to the class.

2. Critically review the kit designed to help elementary school students improve their skills in taking standardized tests, *It's Good to Know* (published by the Educational Testing Service).

3. Many microcomputer programs are available to help individuals prepare for standardized tests. Review one of these programs. Was it more effective than a book or programmed text designed to accomplish the same purpose?

4. Prepare an annotated bibliography of sources to help an individual prepare to take one of the major standardized tests.

5. Administer one of the tests designed to measure test anxiety, and discuss the results with the class.

6. Try one of the relaxation techniques with a class or group of students prior to a major test. What was their reaction to the experience?

7. Read the following brief cases and answer the questions at the end of each.

   Carolyn needs to take the SAT to complete her file so she will be considered for admission to the college for which she is applying. She says, "I don't have time to go to the test prep sessions at school. It is just an aptitude test and either I have it or don't."

   a. Do you agree with Carolyn?
   b. What approach would you use to help her?

   Helen is a 20-year college senior enrolled in elementary education. She has a 3.0 grade point average on a 4-point system. She has to take 2 years of a modern language and is currently taking Spanish 200. Whenever she has a test in class, she becomes nauseous and faints. She does not report the same feeling when she takes tests in other courses.

   a. What do you think is Helen's problem?
   b. What approach would you use to help her?

   Jorge is from Mexico and had the equivalent of a high school education. He has worked as a short-order cook in a fast food business for the past 5 years and wants to better himself. He wants to enter the local state university and major in business but has been told that he has to take the SAT or ACT test. He has been out of school for 7 years and is quite concerned that he won't be admitted.

a. What is Jorge's problem?

b. How would you help him?

Mary is a 43-year-old displaced homemaker. She has raised her family and was a full-time mother and housewife until her recent divorce. She now wants to become economically independent. She graduated from college with a degree in history when she was 20 years old. To get a current teaching certificate, she is required to take a teacher examination. She failed her first attempt, must take the test over again, and is seeking help.

a. What do you hypothesize is her problem?

b. What strategies would you use to help her?

ADDITIONAL READINGS

Dobbin, J. E. (1986). *How to take a test: Doing your best*. New York: Warner Books.

> Written in nontechnical language and covering topics such as study techniques, practical test-taking strategies, rules of thumb about guessing, and interpretation of scores, the book also provides practice in taking reading comprehension, sentence completion, synonyms and antonyms, analogies, and mathematics questions.

Educational Testing Service. *On your own: Preparing to take a standardized test*.

> This interactive video program intersperses test-taking tips with interactive classroom exercises. (Order from Info-Disc Corp., 4 Professional Drive, Suite 134, Gaithersburg, MD 20879)

Hembree, R. (1988). Correlates, causes, effects and treatment of test anxiety. *Review of Educational Research, 58*(1), 47–77.

Hodges, D. L. (1984). *How to lower your anxiety about tests* (edited transcript of an audio tape for college students—with an outline and introductory comments). Eugene, OR: Lane Community College. (ERIC Document Reproduction Service No. ED 245 758)

Reitz, R. (1989). *Test anxiety*. Bloomington, ID: Phi Delta Kappa.

> The book is a collection of articles on components of test anxiety, attributes of test-anxious students, assessment of treatment strategies, and test anxiety treatment programs.

Tyron, G. S. (1980). The measurement and treatment of test anxiety. *Review of Educational Research, 50*, 343–372.

> Representative test-taking guides are listed here.

CHAPTER 21

School Testing Programs

Overview

Schools are among the biggest consumers of tests; each year hundreds of millions of standardized tests are administered by school personnel. The annual cost has been estimated at between $700 and $900 million (Rothman, 1990) for 20 million school days. Teachers utilize testing extensively for instructional, diagnostic, motivational, and grading purposes and construct many of their tests in addition to utilizing many standardized tests. The text will not focus on teacher-made tests but will look at goals and purposes of school testing programs, the procedures and personnel involved, and the type of tests normally utilized.

Objectives

After studying the chapter, the reader should be able to

- discuss the goals of a school testing program
- list and explain the procedures for selecting tests
- identify who should be involved in a testing program
- discuss the roles and responsibilities of school personnel involved in testing programs
- list and describe what types of tests should be utilized and why
- identify the issues and problems involved with school testing programs

GOALS AND PURPOSES OF A TESTING PROGRAM

Teachers, counselors, and administrators need all types of information about students. They need to know about their cognitive and scholastic abilities, their interests, their achievement, and their problems. In school contexts many goals, purposes, and people are involved in a testing program. Here are some of the possible goals of a school testing program.

1. Identify the readiness of kindergarten and first grade students.
2. Determine whether students have mastered the basic and essential skills required by the school system.
3. Place individuals in educational programs.
4. Identify individuals with special needs.
5. Evaluate the curriculum and specific programs of study.
6. Help individuals make their educational and vocational decisions.
7. Assess the scholastic aptitude and cognitive skills of individual students.
8. Measure achievement in specific courses and subject areas.

STEPS IN PLANNING A TESTING PROGRAM

A number of steps should be followed in designing a school testing program. The first step is to identify the types of information needed to make decisions; data should be valuable and necessary. The test user should look at what is needed, when and where it is needed, and who will use it. For example, is the test to be used for selection, placement or grouping, or diagnosis? For one of these purposes, a test is usually administered near the beginning of the school year. A test used to measure achievement gains or program evaluation might be scheduled both at the beginning and end of the school year.

The second step is to identify the types of tests to be given and establish procedures for selecting them. The third step is to identify the responsibilities of the staff in the testing program and to make sure the program is coordinated so those who need the test data are provided the results. The fourth step is to disseminate the test results to the appropriate individuals so that proper decision making and evaluation can take place. The fifth step is to develop an evaluation strategy to continuously monitor the testing program.

Personnel Involved

Mehrens and Lehman (1986) state that the school testing program should be a cooperative venture from the planning stage through the recording, interpretation, and dissemination of results stages (p. 428). The program should not be planned only by the superintendent's staff, the building principal, the school psychologist, the guidance counselor, nor by a combination of these individuals. It is preferable to get more groups involved in decision making such as parents, students, teachers, and representatives from local postsecondary institutions as well as the administrative leaders in the school district. Widespread involvement promotes acceptance of the program and helps each group understand its stake in the process. Teachers might be concerned about getting valid information for instructional decisions, whereas principals might want information with which to evaluate the curriculum. Students might want tests that will help them in their educational and vocational decision making.

Selecting the Test

After a committee has established the different types of tests to be administered, the instruments must be selected. Especially in nonachievement areas, this is usually the responsibility of counselors and psychologists who are trained in testing. Teachers and curriculum supervisors might be involved in the selection or the development of essential-skills or basic-skills tests, under the guidance of a staff member who is an expert on measurement. It is important that the chairperson or coordinator of the selection subcommittee be familiar with ethical and legal standards, technical standards for educational and psychological tests, and sources of test information.

Scope of Responsibilities

The scope of responsibilities in this process is large because the test information is used for so many different purposes. The committee must decide what type of tests should be given, when, how often, and to whom. In addition, the committee must determine who is responsible for administering the program and the tests, scoring the tests, and reporting and disseminating the results. The committee has to consider a number of dimensions before a testing program can be fully implemented. It might be helpful to develop a list of topics that need to be resolved or clarified and then create a responsibility chart like the one illustrated in Figure 21.1.

Administration

Normally, a person who is trained as a psychologist or counselor is given the responsibility for administering a testing program. The individual should be competent in testing and assessment, communication skills, public relations, administering people and programs, and training and in-service education.

Many administrative duties are required of this individual who will oversee the ordering, distribution, administration, scoring, interpreting, and reporting of the testing program. In addition, the individual has to provide the in-service training for teachers and personnel involved with the tests.

Issue	Decision Maker	Date	Product/ Outcome
1. What are the purposes of the testing program?	Full committee	9/1–10/15	Position paper
2. What types of tests should be used?	Subcommittees	10/15–11/1	Report or plan
3. What specific tests should be selected?	Subcommittees	11/1–12/1	Plan or list
4. Who will administer and score the tests?	Full committee	12/1–12/15	Procedure
5. Where and when will tests be administered?	Full committee and subcommittees	12/16–1/15	Schedule
6. How will the results be used, reported, and recorded?	Subcommittees on dissemination and records	1/16–1/30	Plan and forms
7. What training is necessary to implement the program?	Subcommittee on in-service training	1/31–2/15	In-service training program
8. How can the results be used to stimulate research and evaluation activities?	Research and evaluation subcommittees	2/16–3/1	Research/ evaluation plan
9. What will be the strategies to get the testing plan adopted, accepted, and implemented?	Full committee	3/1–4/1	Marketing plan and board approval

Figure 21.1
School testing program responsibility chart

CATEGORIES OF TESTS

The type of test used in school testing programs is sometimes a function of state requirements as well as school system requirements. Some states mandate certain testing and ban other types, such as intelligence testing. A typical program is delineated in Figure 21.2.

The primary type of test utilized in school testing programs is the achievement test. Some school districts administer survey achievement batteries at the beginning and end of each school year in the elementary grades and use the results as one criterion for promotion.

Many schools give criterion-referenced achievement tests that they develop within the district and call minimum-level and essential-skills tests. Students are expected to obtain a certain level of performance to be promoted from one grade to

Test/Inventory	Grade Level												
	K	1	2	3	4	5	6	7	8	9	10	11	12
Readiness/screening	x												
Essential skills	x	x	x	x	x	x	x						
Survey achievement		x	x	x	x	x	x	x	x				
Scholastic aptitude				x		x							
State assessment				x		x			x			x	
Minimum level skills								x	x	x	x	x	x
General interest								x					
General aptitude battery								x					
Subject area achievement										x	x	x	x
Multifactor aptitude battery										x			
Career maturity										x			
Career interest/career values											x		
Armed Services Vocational Aptitude Battery (VSVAB)											x		
Advanced placement												x	
Preliminary Scholastic Aptitude Test (PSAT)												x	
Scholastic Aptitude Test (SAT)													x
American College Testing Program (ACT)													x
National Merit													x
Interest													x

Figure 21.2
Typical school testing program

the next; that is, students are expected to demonstrate mastery of certain performance objectives at each grade level. The school might require a score of 75% on the items on one objective for the student to be given credit for mastering that objective. On the elementary level, these tests usually assess reading, mathematics, and writing skills. On the secondary level, students generally take subject area achievement tests or minimum-level skills tests in a specific content field—for example, American history, algebra 1, or chemistry.

Many states require examinations in the basic skills in the 3rd, 5th, 8th, and 11th grades. Normally, the tests measure skills in reading, writing, and mathematics. Some states utilize the National Assessment model, which measures 10 subject areas, two areas per year. The following tests also measure student skills:

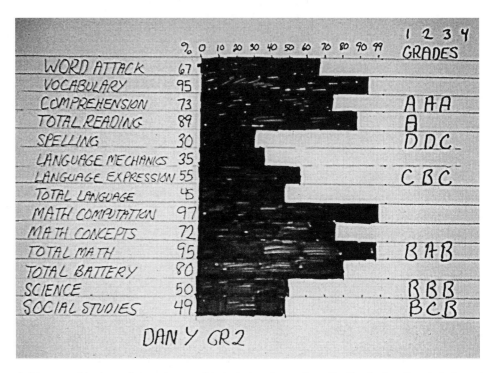

%	0	10	20	30	40	50	60	70	80	90	99	1 2 3 4 GRADES
WORD ATTACK	67											
VOCABULARY	95											
COMPREHENSION	73											A A A
TOTAL READING	89											B
SPELLING	30											D D C
LANGUAGE MECHANICS	35											
LANGUAGE EXPRESSION	55											C B C
TOTAL LANGUAGE	45											
MATH COMPUTATION	97											
MATH CONCEPTS	72											
TOTAL MATH	95											B A B
TOTAL BATTERY	80											
SCIENCE	50											B B B
SOCIAL STUDIES	49											B C B

DAN Y GR 2

Achievement test results can be used to help teachers plan effective instructional strategies to increase achievement.

The American College Testing Service offers a program called the Comprehensive Assessment Program (CAP). The program provides the school district materials to assess achievement, ability, and attitude.

The Developing Cognitive Abilities Test indicates whether students are working at, above, or below anticipated levels of performance.

The School Attitude Measure assesses dimensions of academic self-concept, instructional mastery, control over performance, and student motivation.

End of course examinations are provided by the High School Subjects Tests and the Assessment of Writing.

The National Achievement Test measures achievement K-12 and assesses dimensions of reading, language, mathematics, reference skills, social studies, and science. The Career Survey is also part of the program in grades 7-12.

Scholastic Aptitude Tests

Many school districts still administer scholastic aptitude tests. Some districts utilize these tests only as a rough screening for the gifted program; others give scholastic aptitude tests with the survey achievement tests. Many teachers, counselors, and parents find the test information useful because it describes students' cognitive abilities. The tests are also useful in identifying underachievers and in locating students who are talented and gifted but who have not been previously identified. Nonetheless, in some districts and states scholastic aptitude tests are banned because of their misuse and cultural bias.

Multifactor Aptitude Tests

The state or district often requires administration of a multifactor aptitude test at least once for each student in grades 9 to 12. The Armed Services Vocational Aptitude Battery is the most widely used aptitude test in the high schools. The General Aptitude Test Battery is often administered to high school students by a state employment counselor. Some schools administer aptitude tests that are a part of vocational or career guidance systems, such as the Career Aptitude Placement Series. The information thus gained is helpful to students in thinking about their educational and vocational plans.

Career Guidance Tests

A wide variety of career guidance tests are utilized in the schools, especially at the secondary level. General interest batteries are often given both in junior and senior high schools. In addition to interest tests, schools often administer work values, career maturity, and decision inventories. The results from these tests are helpful not only to the individual student, but also to the counseling staff in planning career guidance activities. Along with achievement and aptitude information, the results from career guidance tests also aid districts in evaluating the educational and vocational needs of students.

The American Business Conference and ETS have developed a system to assess the abilities of noncollege students so that businesses can better evaluate these individuals. The assessment includes performance tests, records of education, training, and work experience.

DEVELOPMENTAL MODEL

Schools need to design systems that are appropriate to their needs. The sample model included in Figure 21.2 looks only at standardized and external testing, but does not represent the full picture. A complete testing program must include other dimensions, such as a method to identify and plan for students who have special needs and a way to assess areas of development not measured by standardized tests. For examples of the types of testing some school districts utilize to assess exceptional students see Table 21.1.

Table 21.1
Identification of exceptional students

Exceptionality	Tests and Procedures
Mental disability	Slosson Intelligence Test (score of 75 or below) Public school version of the American Association of Mental Deficiency Adaptive Behavior Scale Devereux Behavior Rating Scale Wechsler Intelligence Scale for Children (WISC), Wechsler Preschool and Primary Scale of Intelligence (WPPSI), or Stanford-Binet Leiter International Scale Peabody Picture Vocabulary Test Vision, hearing, speech, and language screening Medical, social, and psychological data
Emotional disability	California Test of Personality Wide Range Achievement Test Slosson Intelligence Test Draw-a-Person Test, Kinetic Family Drawing Test Children's Apperception Test Burks' Behavior Rating Scales Behavioral observations Complete social history Documented and dated evidence of two conferences Documented and dated evidence of two interventions or adjustments that have been tried but have not been successful Vision, hearing, speech, and language screening
Specific learning disabilities	Slosson Intelligence Test WISC, WPPSI, Stanford-Binet Peabody Picture Vocabulary Test Wide Range Achievement Test Bender Visual Motor Gestalt Test Survey achievement test results Peabody Individual Achievement Test Behavioral observations Documented and dated alternatives attempted Summaries of two conferences held Vision, hearing, speech, and language screening Woodcock-Johnson Psychoeducational Battery Work samples Attendance record Social, psychological, and medical history
Gifted	Slosson Intelligence Test Renzulli Rating Scale WISC, WPPSI, Stanford-Binet Survey achievement test results

A school system might also be concerned about physical development of its students from K to 12 and want a systematic check on their vision, hearing, speech, and physical fitness. The information from needs assessments can help school personnel determine individual and group needs.

Needs Assessments

A number of different instruments have been designed to assess the needs of students. Some measure primarily the social, psychological, and emotional needs. Others measure the guidance and instructional needs. A variety of such instruments is available from major publishers, but many schools prefer to develop their own based on specific programs and community characteristics. An example of a career guidance needs assessment instrument is given in Figure 21.3.

Read each phrase and then decide the importance of that activity to you. Circle the appropriate number to the left of each phrase, using the scale that follows. Also circle the item number of any area in which you would like to have assistance from the counselor.

0 if you feel the item is not important
1 if you feel the item is of some importance to you
2 if you feel the item is of moderate importance to you
3 if you feel the item is of great importance to you

0	1	2	3	1.	Knowing what jobs are available locally that I can enter immediately after graduating from high school
0	1	2	3	2.	Knowing how to apply for a job
0	1	2	3	3.	Knowing how to write a résumé
0	1	2	3	4.	Knowing how to dress for and what to say in an interview
0	1	2	3	5.	Learning more about my career interests
0	1	2	3	6.	Learning more about the training and education required in my career interest areas
0	1	2	3	7.	Talking with people employed in my career interest areas
0	1	2	3	8.	Arranging for work experience in my career interest fields
0	1	2	3	9.	Learning more about my values and the way they relate to my career choice
0	1	2	3	10.	Learning about what courses I should take if I want to enter certain career fields

---

Figure 21.3
Example of a career guidance needs assessment instrument

EVALUATION OF SCHOOL PROGRAMS

Most schools, elementary and secondary, apply for accreditation from the regional accreditation agency. In the process schools are required to complete self-studies and may opt to survey students, teachers, and parents. The National Study of School Evaluation has not only developed evaluative criteria for the elementary and secondary schools but has also made available four different instruments that can be used to evaluate the school programs—the Teacher Opinion Inventory, Parent Opinion Inventory, and Student Opinion Inventory.

The Teacher Opinion Inventory is a two-part instrument designed to accomplish three goals.

1. Assess teacher opinion about many facets of the school
2. Provide teacher recommendations for improvement
3. Provide valuable data for the school administrator to use in decision making relative to program development, policy formulation, administrative organization, faculty development, and community relations

The first part of the instrument consists of 64 multiple-choice items covering five major categories: organization and administration; curriculum and instruction; student discipline, counseling, and advisement; school and community relations; and job satisfaction.

One example of a multiple-choice question from the Teacher Opinion Inventory follows.

Are you satisfied or dissatisfied with the way students are treated by teachers?

a.   Very satisfied
b.   Satisfied
c.   Neither satisfied nor dissatisfied
d.   Dissatisfied
e.   Very dissatisfied

The second part consists of eight open-ended questions. An example follows.

What curricular changes would you like to see implemented in your school? (p. 12)

The Student Opinion Inventory was developed to accomplish two goals.

1. Assess student attitude toward many facets of school
2. Provide student recommendations for improvement (p. 3)

The inventory utilizes six scales: student-teacher, student-counselor, student-administrator, student-curriculum and instruction, student-participation, and student-school image. There are 35 multiple-choice questions like this one.

How much help do your teachers give you in the selection of courses?

a.   All the help I need
b.   Most of the help I need

    c.   About half the help I need
    d.   Little of the help I need
    e.   None of the help I need

There are 12 open-ended questions like this one.

If you think you need more help at school, what kind of help do you need that you are not getting? (p. 11)

On the Parent Opinion Inventory, there are 53 multiple-choice questions and 11 subscales.

1. Intra-student body relationships

2. School information services

3. Parent involvement

4. Educational objectives

5. Intraschool problems

6. School program factors

7. Innovative programs

8. Student activities

9. Support services

10. Auxiliary services

11. General psychological climate

The following example is similar to the multiple-choice question on the parent inventory.

The school system needs to make numerous curriculum and educational changes to keep up with other schools in the state.

    a.   Strongly agree
    b.   Agree
    c.   Disagree
    d.   Strongly disagree
    e.   No opinion

The open-ended questions are like this one.

What do you think our schools should be trying to do? (p. 11)

One feature of the battery is that there are common items across all three instruments so that the opinions of the school administration and staff, students, and parents can be compared. Comparisons are possible on both the multiple-choice and open-ended items.

A number of other instruments that have value in helping school personnel evaluate different components of the school are available. The Effective School Battery measures dimensions of the school's psychosocial climate as viewed by the teachers and by the students. Psychosocial climate involves constructs such as staff morale, the fairness and clarity of the rules, and the relations with parents and the community. The test also measures population characteristics such as the family educational background of the students, the attachment of the students to the schools and the extent to which students believe in rules.

The teacher form measures job satisfaction, participation in continuing professional development, and attitudes toward education. The teacher form includes scales such as these.

1. *Safety*—how safe teachers report the school environment to be
2. *Morale*—how enthusiastic the teachers are and how confident in the school
3. *Planning and action*—how innovative and experimental the school programs are
4. *Administration*—how teachers view the administration
5. *Resources*—how teachers view the adequacy of supplies and resources
6. *Parent/community involvement*—how the school uses community resources in its programs
7. *Student influence*—how the students participate in school decisions
8. *Use of grades as sanctions*—how teachers use grades as sanctions in response to student misconduct

On the student form there are six scales—safety, respect for students, planning and action, fairness of rules, clarity of rules, and student influence.

On the profile of teacher characteristics, dimensions such as job satisfaction, interaction with students, personal security, classroom orderliness, professional development, nonauthoritarian attitude, and prointegration attitudes are plotted. On the profile of student characteristics, information about the educational background of the parents is also summarized.

ISSUES AND CONCERNS

A number of legal as well as philosophical issues and concerns relate to test programs. Many states have imposed external testing programs, and have, in effect, controlled what is being taught and when. Some citizens argue that the curriculum decisions should be made at the local level and with citizen input. Testing in primary grades has become a controversial issue. Some states have eliminated standardized testing and state assessment testing in grades K to 3.

When both external and internal testing programs are used, much duplication of effort can result. Kubiszyn and Borich (1987) point out that many districts tend to administer more than one test to measure the same thing or to achieve the same purpose. This problem is compounded when tests are required by local, state, and federal agencies. A systematic evaluation of the types of tests given can help determine whether information is redundant. The evaluator might develop a worksheet and make an analysis of the tests being given, listing each measurement objective in a separate column for each grade level and then identifying the tests that meet each objective. The beginning of a sample worksheet is shown here.

Grade 3: Objective 1
Measure vocabulary development

Stanford Achievement Test
Minimum Level Skills Test
State Assessment Test
Reading Skill Packet Test

Grade 3: Objective 2
Measure reading comprehension

Stanford Achievement Test
Minimum Level Skills Test
State Assessment Test
Mathematics Skill Packet Test

This example shows four tests being used to measure each of the first two objectives. Testing takes up a significant portion of instructional time, and needless duplication is certainly to be avoided.

Vermont has developed a plan that combines mixed methods of assessment. The state will assess students in the 4th and 8th grades in writing and mathematics in three ways.

1. A uniform test, primarily performance-based rather than multiple-choice

2. A portfolio, which includes materials collected by the teacher from students during the course of the year

3. A "best piece," which represents what a student considers his or her best efforts of the year.

Portfolios are viewed as providing more complete information about the students' abilities than conventional testing. There are some practical problems, however, that need to be evaluated to see if the process is achieving its goals. The use of portfolio assessment requires teachers to adapt to ever-changing curriculum and instructional demands. The validity and reliability of the process is a problem. Performance-based assessments quite often only use a small number of tasks that may favor one group or another. As a result, scoring reliability is low. The process is time consuming and policy makers need to weigh the costs against the benefits of the proposed assessment changes as well as their educational value before they are implemented. Performance assessment needs to make sure that the purpose of the assessment is clearly identified and multiple measures are used (NCME, 1994). The performance assessment should have technical rigor, be cost effective, protect the student's rights, be equitable, and provide information for decision making.

AMERICA 2000 EDUCATION STRATEGIES

The America 2000 educational goals were developed by an advisory committee during the Bush administration. The major goals included:

1. All children in the United States will start school ready to learn.

2. The high school graduation rate will increase to at least 90%.

3. American students will leave grades 4, 8, and 12 having demonstrated competency in challenging subject matter including English, mathematics, science, history, and geography. Every school in the United States will ensure that all students learn to use their minds, so that they may be prepared for responsible citizenship, further learning, and productive employment in our modern economy.

4. U.S. students will be first in the world in science and mathematics achievement.

5. Every adult American will be literate and possess the skills and knowledge necessary to compete in a global economy and exercise the rights and responsibilities of citizenship.

6. Every school in America will be free of drugs and violence and will offer a disciplined environment conducive to learning.

Blueprint 2000 in Florida, for example, calls for school districts to devise evaluation plans and procedures on a local level. Other groups of citizens and educators are advocating national examinations.

SCHOOL IMPROVEMENT

The school improvement movement has led to the development of several instruments to evaluate the effectiveness of reform. One such assessment is Sizing up Your School System: The District Effectiveness Audit. The audit (Buttram, Corcoran, & Hansen, 1989) focuses on dimensions such as goal setting, curriculum, quality assurance, resource allocation, work environment, school improvement, and community relations. Another set of scales, also published by Research for Better Schools, is Dimensions of Excellence Scales: Survey for School Improvement (Dusewicy & Beyer, 1991). The eight scales cover school climate, leadership, teacher behavior, curriculum, monitoring and assessment, student discipline, staff development, and parent involvement. There are three versions—a school staff survey, student survey, and parent survey.

The educational reform movement and Blueprint 2000 goals have led to focusing on a new design for assessment and evaluation. One such approach is alternate or authentic assessment. The authentic assessment procedures have raised a number of questions such as do racial, cultural, and socioeconomic class gaps narrow or widen with the use of performance assessment. Should choices of alternatives be provided that address differences in ethnicity, gender, or abilities, or should the same sample of behavior be collected for all students?

An example of the general procedures to design an authentic student assessment in mathematics follows.

1. Identify the big ideas.

2. Identify the expected knowledge of the concepts and skills, know-how, effort, and context related to the big idea. The statement should enhance the learning of math.

3. Collect or create several examples of problem situations and questions about those problem situations that could be used to assess students' capabilities on the standard. The assessment should promote equity by giving each student the opportunity to demonstrate math power and by helping each student meet professional expectations.

4. Develop scoring procedures to judge student performance, and review these procedures.

5. Report the results of the student performance.

6. Conduct an equity review of the whole process and its consequences and evaluate the process to see if it is consistent (National Council of Teachers of Mathematics, 1993).

SUMMARY

Schools spend millions of dollars on tests each year. School testing programs are given to screen, group, and place students; to make selections; to measure growth; and to facilitate the accomplishment of educational goals. Test selection should involve a careful study of the goals and should include in the planning all the public involved in using the information gained from the tests. Achievement, scholastic aptitude, general aptitude, and career guidance tests are part of most school testing programs. At times counselors also need information from the affective domain and find attitude and opinion batteries useful, in addition to different types of needs assessments.

QUESTIONS FOR DISCUSSION

1. Study Figure 21.2, a sample school testing program. What tests would you add or drop? Why?

2. Study Table 21.1, which list tests and procedures for identifying exceptional students. Do you see any tests that would be inappropriate for the use suggested in the table? For example, would you use the Slosson Intelligence Test as an initial screen to identify mentally disabled individuals?

3. Teachers may feel that they are under tremendous pressure because of achievement testing. They may dislike the standardized achievement battery selected for their district because it does not measure what they are teaching. In such a situation what steps should the district administrators take to ensure the best test selection and gain the support of district teachers?

4. What types of nonintellectual or noncognitive tests should be included in the school testing program?

5. Should intelligence tests or scholastic aptitude tests be given to students every 2 to 3 years, along with achievement tests? Why or why not? Should all students be required to take some type of personality test, such as the California Test of Personality? Why or why not?

SUGGESTED ACTIVITIES

1. Visit a nearby school and find out what tests are part of that school's testing program.

2. Go to the library and find *School Attitude Measures*, published by the Instructional Objectives Exchange. A number of school attitude inventories are included in the book. Administer one to a friend. Record the results and report them to the class.

3. Assume that you are a school's director of testing and have just received the printout that follows. It summarizes the performance of the school's first-grade students on a recently administered test. In addition to these numbers, you know that the district requires a passing score of 80%. Draft the communication pieces that you would send to teachers, parents, and students.

Report card for High School X: Distribution of students by racial/ethnic group

Objective	Students Tested	Number Failed	Number Passed	Percent Passed
Recognize basic vocabulary	156	24	132	84.6
Recognize Dolch words	156	0	156	100.0
Identify word meanings in context	156	6	150	96.1
Identify rhyming words	156	8	148	94.8
Identify long/short vowels	156	30	126	80.8
Write uppercase and lowercase alphabet	156	5	151	96.7
Discriminate beginning sounds	156	18	138	88.4
Associate ending sounds	156	46	110	70.5

4. Write a position paper on one of the issues related to school testing programs.
5. Interview the counselor responsible for administering the school testing program and report your findings to the class.

	School Percent	District Percent	State Percent
White	78	53	60
Black	14	41	23
Hispanic	3	2	14
Asian	5	3	2
Indian	0	1	1

By Gender	Male Percent	Female Percent
	49	51

School Attendance Rate	School Percent	District Percent	State Percent
	85	92	91

School Mobility	33	45	34

(beginning of year compared with enrollment at end of year)

	School	District	State
Students with mild disabilities (SLD, EMR, Visual, Physical)	5.0	7.0	6.0
Students with moderate disabilities	1.0	2.0	1.0
Limited English Proficiency	1.0	2.0	5.0

Dropouts	Male No.	Female No.	School Percent	District Percent	State Percent
White	40	25	4.0	5.0	4.0
Black	14	7	8.0	4.0	5.0
Hispanic	0	2	4.0	5.0	6.0
Asian	0	2	2.0	2.0	2.0
Indian	0	0	0.0	6.0	6.0
Suspended out of school					
White	162	136	16.0	16.0	11.0
Black	69	56	37.0	21.0	20.0
Hispanic	7	9	25.0	20.0	11.0
Asian	11	8	16.0	10.0	6.0
Indian	0	0	0.0	14.0	13.0

Staff	No.
Teachers	98
Administrators	8
Support Staff	40

Degree	School Percent	District Percent	State Percent
Bachelor's	59	58	55
Master's	40	40	41
Specialist	0	1	3
Doctorate	1	1	1

Teaching Experience	Percent	Racial/Ethnic Group	Percent
First Year	0	White	88
1–3	16	Black	8
4–9	19	Hispanic	2
10–19	19	Asian	2
20+	40	Indian	0

High School Competency Test Grade 11
Communications (Passing Percentage)

	School	District	State
White	95	94	95
Black	80	82	78
Hispanic	82	83	79
Asian	96	83	86
Indian	70	86	89
Unknown	67	76	78

Mathematics

	School	District	State
White	89	86	87
Black	61	53	54
Hispanic	56	73	67
Asian	71	84	86
Indian	70	71	79
Unknown	67	56	62

SAT Average	900	996	880

Expenditure Per Student			
Regular	$3400	$3581	$3826
Exceptional	9020	7417	8429
At Risk	3600	3497	4294
Vocational	4400	5111	4590
Whites			

ADDITIONAL READINGS

Volume two of the *Buros-Nebraska Symposium on Measurement and Testing*, edited by Barbara S. Plake and Joseph C. Witt, has two chapters in Part II: Educational and Academic/Professional Directions that you should read. The first, by Nancy Cole, is entitled "Future Directions for Educational Achievement and Ability Testing." The second, by Ronald Berk, is entitled "Minimum Competency Testing: Status and Potential."

Buros Institute of Mental Measurements. (1994). *Psychological Assessment in Schools*. Lincoln, NB: Author.

The publication discusses tests most frequently used in the assessment of youth.

Jaegar, R. M. (1994, April). What parents want to know about schools: A report on school report cards. *Evaluation Perspectives*, 4(2), 2–3.

CHAPTER 22

Communicating Test Results to Clients, Parents, and Professionals

Overview

Test results are valuable only if they are used. The responsible test administrator reports test data to the client with concern for the client's need for information and with awareness of the client's cognitive level. Results must be communicated in a way that test takers and other targeted individuals can understand.

The first part of the chapter deals with communication of test results. The communication sometimes is between the examiner and parents, teachers, lawyers, police, employers, social workers, and other professionals.

The second part of the chapter deals with the role of the tester as consultant. Consultation may be necessary to help the examiner gain more information about the client. It may also be intended to help the parent, teacher, or other professional better understand the assessment results.

Objectives

The purpose of this chapter is to

- understand the guidelines and standards for communicating test results
- be familiar with different methods and techniques of reporting and disseminating test results
- identify some problem areas in disseminating results and some possible approaches

*   list and discuss the models and techniques used in consulting with parents, teachers, and professionals
*   recognize the importance of communication skills

GUIDELINES FOR COMMUNICATING TEST RESULTS

The AACD (1980) position paper on the Responsibilities of Users of Standardized Tests lists four key elements. The counselor must know the test manual, know the limits of the test, know informed consent procedures, and protect the client's right to privacy.

As was mentioned previously, examiners need to know the information that is contained in the test manual and be prepared to explain difficult concepts. It is important to get clients to understand the limits of a test. When appropriate, the standard error of measurement can help to emphasize that the test results are not absolute; they provide approximations of where true scores might fall. Test results can be influenced by various sources of bias, which may affect the interpretation of the scores. The test taker needs to understand that test data represent just one source of information.

Shertzer and Linden (1979) provide a good summary of the principles needed to guide test interpretation.

1. Select the most valid test available for the purpose.
2. Be skilled and competent in interpreting the test results.
3. Interpret test data in light of the other available information.
4. Present results in terms of probabilities rather than certainties.
5. Be certain that test data help meet a need, and present the results objectively and impersonally. Encourage the client to make his own interpretation and express his own reactions.
6. Interpret with special care results from tests in which clients can vary their responses at will.
7. Realize that the client may react emotionally and even irrationally to the test results, and temper the approach with knowledge of the individual.
8. Use both group and individual approaches to help clients engage in self-appraisal and planning. (p. 501)

Goldman (1971) believes that the counselor needs to look at the process, and he agrees that the first key step is selecting the correct test. In addition, counselors constantly need to sharpen their interviewing skills. The posttest interview gives an opportunity to deal with interpretation and use it in planning and decision making. Counselors need to keep up with the literature on reporting test results.

Lein (1971) adds several other dimensions that should be considered.

1. Be sure that both the examiner and examinee have a clear and immediate goal in mind that serves as the basis of the test report.

2. Avoid specific reporting of derived scores such as standard scores and percentile ranks, if possible.

3. Concentrate on increasing understanding rather than posing as an expert.

4. Recognize that the client may be helped to understand the data but not necessarily accept the results.

5. Never compare one client with another.

6. Be sure that your client or others needing the test information understand the interpretation.

Garfield and Prediger (1982) suggest certain steps and procedures that a counselor should consider in interpreting test results; these are included in the checklist in Figure 22.1.

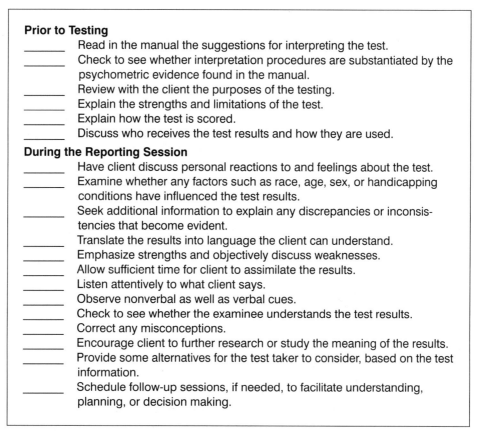

Prior to Testing
_____   Read in the manual the suggestions for interpreting the test.
_____   Check to see whether interpretation procedures are substantiated by the psychometric evidence found in the manual.
_____   Review with the client the purposes of the testing.
_____   Explain the strengths and limitations of the test.
_____   Explain how the test is scored.
_____   Discuss who receives the test results and how they are used.

During the Reporting Session
_____   Have client discuss personal reactions to and feelings about the test.
_____   Examine whether any factors such as race, age, sex, or handicapping conditions have influenced the test results.
_____   Seek additional information to explain any discrepancies or inconsistencies that become evident.
_____   Translate the results into language the client can understand.
_____   Emphasize strengths and objectively discuss weaknesses.
_____   Allow sufficient time for client to assimilate the results.
_____   Listen attentively to what client says.
_____   Observe nonverbal as well as verbal cues.
_____   Check to see whether the examinee understands the test results.
_____   Correct any misconceptions.
_____   Encourage client to further research or study the meaning of the results.
_____   Provide some alternatives for the test taker to consider, based on the test information.
_____   Schedule follow-up sessions, if needed, to facilitate understanding, planning, or decision making.

Figure 22.1
Checklist of steps and procedures for test interpretation

Informed Consent

Certain responsibilities relate to informed consent. The test taker should be informed what will be done with the test results and who will use them. The examiner should also discuss with the test taker any circumstances that could have affected the validity or reliability of the results. The consent of the examinee must be obtained before test results are used for any purpose other than that advanced prior to the testing. The examiner also needs to protect the examinee's right of privacy and all information needs to be accurate.

STANDARDS FOR REPORTING TEST RESULTS

Professional standards and codes of ethics emphasize the importance of how test results are reported. Some of these standards focus on requirements of test authors and publishers. The test manual, for example, should contain information that will facilitate test interpretation. As a matter of fact, all test materials including computerized reports should be designed to facilitate test interpretation. Other standards focus on special types of tests, such as certification and licensing examinations. Reports are to be given promptly to applicants. Test takers who fail should be told their scores and the cut-off score required to pass the test. Applicants should be informed of their performance on all parts of the test for which scores are produced. In addition, rules and procedures used to combine scores or other assessments to determine the overall outcome should be reported to the test taker.

Furthermore, the rights of the test taker must be taken into consideration and there are procedures to handle test irregularities. Some testing organizations offer the test taker the option of prompt and free retesting or the arbitration of the dispute.

Standards call for the clinician to share with clients the test results and interpretations. The clinician is directed to provide information about the range of error for such interpretations when such information will be beneficial to the client. The test information is to be expressed in language that the client or client's legal representative can understand.

METHODS OF REPORTING TEST RESULTS

There are five major methods of reporting test results: individual sessions, group sessions, written reports, programmed and interactive approaches, and video approaches. The role and function of the test taker and counselor vary with each approach.

Individual Sessions

Counselors often use individual interpretation sessions to present test results to clients. How the scores are reported is a function of the counselor's theoretical orientation. Counselors who are more client-centered are apt to present clients with raw and derived scores and encourage the clients to join in the process of interpreting the scores. Counselors might direct more attention to how the clients feel about their scores and interpretations. Counselors who are more direct may review the purpose of the testing, present the results, clarify what the scores mean, and discuss the implications of the results.

When a client interprets and reacts to his own scores, the counselor may gain new insight into the client. By participating in the discussion of the test results, the client may become more accepting of the results and may utilize the information in decision making. Some counselors argue that the more the client participates, the more understanding and learning takes place. Other counselors believe that individual sessions are time-consuming and unproductive.

Group Sessions

Group sessions are used frequently to provide interpretation of test results of clients. Clients with particular learning or personality styles prefer group and social interaction; such clients often learn from each other as well as from the counselor. Most tests now provide interpretive material that the counselor can highlight effectively and efficiently in group sessions. This approach is usually more economical. The counselor can work with a small or large group and can use overhead transparencies, filmstrips and tapes, or videotapes to present material. Such aids are less likely in a one-to-one situation. The use of group sessions does not preclude offering individual sessions, if a client needs further help processing the information.

Written Reports

More and more test publishers are providing some sort of written report of the test results. With many tests clients score themselves, plot the scores on a profile, and have immediate interpretation of the results. School districts often provide parents with interpretive reports of their children's performance on survey achievement testing. Both the language and interpretation are simplified.

Written reports are not valuable to all individuals. Many students and parents have problems reading and understanding test reports even when the language is simple. Many written reports present profiles of scores that are helpful for test takers who have difficulty visualizing test results. Some individuals find written reports impersonal and have aversions to them. Many computerized forms of test interpretation are available now. Computerized reports may be effective in presenting basic facts but probably are ineffective in changing a person's established belief system.

Interactive Approaches

Interactive approaches are another method of presenting test results. With the advent of computer-assisted testing, clients can be provided with immediate results. Many of the computerized guidance information systems, such as CHOICES, are of this interactive type. Holland's Self-Directed Search is a guided exercise that provides the user with useful career information.

Computer-assisted administration of instruments allows for more branching in the programming and immediate feedback. The individual can start over again and see what happens with different choices. This approach relies on written text and visual stimuli. Clients often are freer in responding to a computer than to a counselor and usually rate computer assessment very positively. A few test takers are overwhelmed by the computer and fear they cannot operate a program. Other clients are philosophically opposed to the impersonal nature of the computer.

Video Approaches

A current trend is to combine the technology of the computer with that of video equipment. Scores on certain scales can key individualized reports back to clients, providing audio as well as visual presentation. The presentation can appear more professional and be checked for accuracy before it is used with clients. In addition, the analysis can be more complete and thorough since the rules would be built into the program.

Oral Reports

Quite often the examiner customarily makes an oral report to parents and guardians. The complexity of the report depends upon the familiarity of the parents or client with the concepts and terms used and it is the responsibility of the counselor to translate the information into language the parents can understand. To maximize the effectiveness of the report, parents and guardians need to

1. ask for definitions of unfamiliar terms
2. request examples to support any generalizations that the examiner makes
3. offer examples of the examinee's behavior that contradict test results
4. have the examiner repeat the parts they didn't understand when presented
5. ask for a summary before leaving the session (Shore, Brice, & Love, 1992, p. 110)

Parents should make a list of questions they should ask the examiner, such as the following.

1. What tests did my son/daughter take?
2. What were my child's strengths on each test? Weaknesses?
3. Are there any recommendations or suggestions on how I might help my daughter/son?

PROBLEM AREAS

Counselors may face a number of problems in disseminating test information. Some of the more common problems are discussed here.

Acceptance

The goal of the feedback session with clients quite often is getting them to accept the test results and incorporate that information into their decision making. Negative results frequently prompt resistance of the test takers to change their self-concepts to align with test data. They often resist accepting valid and genuine information about themselves.

Counselors can enhance acceptance of the test information by

1. involving the clients in decision making and general selection of tests prior to the testing
2. establishing rapport with the clients so that they trust the counselor and are relaxed in the sessions
3. spending sufficient time with the clients in interpreting the results—not over-whelming them with too much data
4. translating the results into language that the clients can understand
5. showing the validity of the information for the decision(s) to be made.

Readiness of the Client

The critical factor in the acceptance of the data is client readiness. Test takers who believe that they have a specific need for counseling about the test results and want to learn what meaning data have for them will more readily accept the information presented. If the information is damaging to a client's self-concept or ego, the counselor might have to work on getting that client to extend his acceptance. The counselor can use these techniques to help the client become ready.

1. Have several sessions prior to the report session to build understanding and acceptance.
2. Allow the client to bring up the topic; don't immediately begin the session with test interpretation.
3. Focus on the test rather than on the client.
4. Try to engage the client actively in the learning and planning process both before and after the testing.

Negative Results

Often the results are not what the client wanted, desired, or expected. The client may have failed to pass a certification or licensing examination or to achieve the minimum score for admission to college. Certain results are a threat to the client's self-concept. On a personality test a client may turn up with high scores on the lie scale and become defensive. Or the client may tend to be overly truthful and may have a high score on a neuroticism scale. The test administrator should consider

1. explaining the rationale for cut-off scores and the validity of the established procedures

2. gaining an understanding of the test taker's perceptions and feelings, seeing the whole person complete with irrationalities and blind spots

3. accepting the test taker's right to argue with test implications, without necessarily agreeing with the test taker

4. being genuine and expressing personal feeling, perhaps disagreeing with the clients' views and goals, and pointing out the consequences of a particular course of action

5. identifying other information about the client that supports or does not support the test data

6. discussing the implications of the data and the importance of that information for decision making

Flat Profiles

Many times an individual's pattern of scores has no highs or lows but is just a flat profile. On aptitude and achievement tests this would indicate a similar level of performance in all areas. It might be above average, average, or below average. On interest or career guidance inventories, especially if the client is undecided about future goals, the data are not extremely helpful. Response set might be a factor on a test, with the individual ranking everything high, average, or low. Holland (1979) believes there are major problems in counseling individuals with flat profiles. In the case of flat profiles on interest and career guidance tests, counselors can ask clients to read the descriptions of the six Holland types and rank the three types most characteristic of themselves (Miller, 1985) and discuss the clients' expectations, relevant past experiences, previous work activities, and misconceptions and stereotypes.

In the case of flat profiles on aptitude and achievement tests, counselors can look at the interests, values, and career goals, and assure the clients that their profiles are not abnormal.

The counselor should discuss what an individual considers his or her to be and what he or she can do acceptably. A good procedure is to investigate the individual's performance on previous tests to determine whether this pattern is typical.

Motivation and Attitude

Test results are more significant to clients who are motivated to take a test, come in and discuss the results, and have a positive attitude toward the value of the data. Some clients have a negative attitude toward testing prior to the test and maintain that attitude afterwards. Some clients become negative after they see that the test results are not what they expected.

Workers in the helping professions should recognize that tests can aid clients in developing more realistic expectations about themselves and can be valuable in decision making. However, some clients put too much weight on the results and become overdependent on test data to solve their problems. Other clients use test results as a way of escaping from their feelings and problems. Counselors interpreting test results need to be aware not only of a client's motivation to take or not take a test but also his/her attitude toward the test. Other important information is the immediate goal for the interpretation of the test results, and the client's desire to be involved in decision making about the type of test to be taken and the dissemination of test results.

COMMUNICATION OF TEST RESULTS TO THE PUBLIC

When test results are released to the news media, those responsible for releasing the results should provide information to help minimize the probabilities of misinterpretation. A current movement toward accountability has influenced the use and reporting of test data by the schools. Administrators like to use standardized and criterion-referenced test data to show that the schools are accomplishing the educational goals of society. However, many people have trouble understanding the concepts used in measurement and the many different types of derived scores test makers report. Test data, when properly presented, can be a useful tool in interpreting the school system for the community. Shertzer and Linden (1979) advocate that emphasis be placed on interpretive reporting of group results to show what the scores signify in terms of progress toward the realization of school objectives and vocational plans (p. 504).

General Guidelines

Communication with the public should follow these general procedures.

1. Communication should take place not only after but before testing. News releases can announce a test, and letters and cards can be sent to the parents or guardians. An example of such a letter is included in Figure 22.2. Reports of test results can be made through the local media or can be presented at PTA or community meetings.

2. Because most citizens are not familiar with test jargon and statistical terms, the results should be presented as simply as possible while still remaining accurate and honest.

3. Percentile bands or stanines can be reported graphically or visually using handouts, transparencies, or slides.

4. Data should be presented in summary form—for example, by grade rather than by teacher.

5. Statistical and measurement terms can be defined in nontechnical language with examples provided.

6. The public is not stupid and should not be treated with condescension.

Dear Ocean School Parents and Guardians:

Can you believe it? We have only 9 weeks left in the school year! The time has passed quickly, but there is still much to accomplish. We are confident that with your cooperation we will attain the goals set for this year. We want this to be the best year ever for our children.

As you may know, our school board has adopted promotional criteria for students in Grades K through 8. The criteria are based in part on the Stanford Achievement Test and the Essential Skills Tests. We will begin administering the Stanford Achievement Test next week. The first day of testing will be Monday, April 5. The test will be given over a 2-week period. This time includes makeup testing for children who might be absent, although we hope that every child will be present on testing days and will arrive at school on time. Nonetheless, we do not want any children who are ill to take the tests, so those students will have an opportunity to be tested later.

The Essential Skills Tests will be administered in early May. These tests measure a child's progress in mathematics and reading. We will send home a reminder before the tests.

You can help your child(ren) do well on these tests by following some simple suggestions.

    1. Each child should have a good night's rest prior to a testing day. We suggest 10 hours of sleep.

    2. Each child should have a good, well-balanced breakfast before coming to school on a testing day.

    3. Conflicts and arguments should be avoided. A child's emotional state has great influence on performance.

    4. No child should feel anxious about the test. Pressure has a negative effect.

If you have any questions or suggestions, please do not hesitate to contact the school office, in person or by telephone. We have appreciated your assistance and support throughout the year.

                      Sincerely yours,
                      Ocean School Guidance Counselor

Figure 22.2
Sample letter of information to parents

Any oral or written report should include the following components.

1. A general description of the tests or testing program
2. Uses of the test results
3. Types of skills and competencies measured
4. Types of scores reported and the meaning of those scores
5. Type of norms used
6. Definitions and examples of the summary statistics and measurement concepts needed to understand the presentation
7. The results with appropriate comparisons (national, state, district, and school, year-to-year changes, or grade-by-grade)
8. Factors that might have influenced the results

An oral presentation requires time for questions. The examiner should be prepared to answer the following types of questions about major issues.

Are these tests biased against minority and disadvantaged students?

Why do we test so much?

Why are some schools in the system achieving higher results than others in the system?

Are teachers influenced by the test results?

THE TESTER AS CONSULTANT: LEGAL CONSIDERATIONS

When testers act as counselors they need to be aware of legal requirements, which can be very specific in many situations. The Buckley Amendments became the Family Education Rights and Privacy Act (PL 93–380) and gave parents the opportunity to see all the information affecting the evaluation, placement, or programming of their children. The law covers all personally identifiable educational records collected, maintained, or used. Parents have the right to demand changes in a record if they find the information to be inaccurate, and their consent must be obtained before test scores and records can be released. These rights transfer to the individual at age 18 or to students attending postsecondary schools. Schools are responsible for informing parents of their right to access records and are required to hold a hearing if errors are thought to be included in records. (See also Chapter 24.)

When a client is being assessed for placement, the examiner should remember that the parents probably have useful information. In the screening and placement of students under PL 94–142, the counselor must document contact with the parents and the information received from them. The counselor is required to provide the parents written notice of any proposed change in client identification, evaluation, or placement. Each evaluation procedure and test to be used must be described in writing. Communication must be in a form that is understandable to the parents and in their native language. If the parents are deaf, the information must be transmitted in sign language.

ETHICAL STANDARDS FOR CONSULTATION

Principle 8 of the American Psychological Association's *Ethical Principles of Psychologists* (1992) calls for psychologists to make every effort to promote the welfare and best interests of their clients and to guard against the misuse of assessment results. Principle 5 states that psychologists have a primary obligation to respect the confidentiality of information obtained in the course of their work and should reveal information to others only with the consent of the individual involved or that person's legal representative. The exception to this principle occurs when its exercise would result in clear danger to the individual or to others.

CONSULTING WITH PARENTS

Parents are an important resource in improving children's capacity to cope with the demands of their environment. When parents want to be involved, helping professionals should identify the skills, values, and possibilities of the parents relative to helping their children. *Principles for Professional Ethics* (National Association of School Psychologists, 1980) calls for psychologists to recognize the importance of parental support and obtain it prior to working with a child. Psychologists should secure continued parental involvement through frank and prompt reporting of evaluation findings. They are responsible for telling parents what records consist of, what kind of information goes into the report, who receives the report, and what steps are used to protect the information.

Dustin and Ehly (1984) propose a simple five-step model which involves establishing rapport or phase-in, obtaining information and identifying the problem, providing information for implementation, conducting follow-up and evaluation, and terminating the relationship. The counselor discusses the implications for the child, helps establish goals for the parents, and selects strategies that will be most beneficial to the client and family.

The *Code of Fair Testing Practices in Education* (1988) states that the counselor should tell test takers or their parents or guardians how the test scores will be kept on file and indicate to whom and under what circumstances test scores will be released. Parents should also be informed how to register complaints and have problems resolved about testing. Counselors need to provide parents and guardians with information about the rights of the test taker and discuss whether they can obtain copies of tests and completed answer sheets, retake tests, have tests rescored, or cancel scores.

Brown, Wyne, Blackburn, and Powell (1979) propose a more elaborate model, consisting of seven steps that can be modified to convey test results to parents.

1. Establish a good working relationship.
2. Assess the family and parent dynamics and environment.
3. Check on the validity of assumptions about the family and parents.
4. Explain the test results.
5. Discuss the implications for the child.
6. Establish goals for the parents and select strategies.
7. Involve the child in the conference with the parents.

The consultation can be done with a single parent, a couple, or a group of parents.

Explaining Test Results to Parents

Most parents have little knowledge about testing. Even if various facets of the testing program are explained initially, the examiner should review for parents the purposes of the testing, using nontechnical language. Actual test results might be visually presented through graphs and profiles to help parents understand. Reports need to be comprehensible as well as informational. In reporting specific types of scores, the examiner should be sure that parents understand the type of score being discussed. They should be told the limitations of the test, and the standard error of measurement should be explained. The AACD standards suggest that the examiner discuss the qualifications necessary to interpret and use standardized tests and identify sources of bias that might operate in the situation.

The examiner should walk the parent through the interpretation, being patient and understanding but honest. Working with parents may identify a need for parent education in some group sessions on measurement topics and issues. Goldman (1971) points out that those who work with children and adolescents find that parents rather than the children are most in need of the information provided by tests (p. 438). However, he believes that counselors cannot assume parents will be reasonable and objective about the test report; they may have unreasonable aspirations, blind spots, and defense mechanisms themselves or about their children. It is important to spend enough time with parents, perhaps more than one session, to deal with their feelings and attitudes.

Sattler (1992) proposes a four-stage model for working with parents.

Initial phase of the interview—It is important to have both parents or guardians present at the report session to permit the counselor a more objective assessment of the facts and a chance to get the parents or guardians to share in the responsibilities of the test results. The examiner needs to establish rapport and recognize that parents may have experienced many frustrations and hardships in their family life. They should be encouraged to talk; what they have to say is important. The examiner should assess parents' interest in the test results, their attitudes toward their child's condition, their handling of problems with the child, and their goals and expectations for the child.

Communicating diagnostic findings—The examiner should set the ground rules for the information sharing and should refuse to side with either parent or child. Parents should be encouraged to participate in the session and should be warned that some of the information shared might at times arouse conflict, hostility, or anxiety. They should be free to express their feelings, just as the examiner is honest in portraying the results. The hope is that the parents will develop realistic perceptions and expectations for their child.

Discussion of specific recommendations—The examiner should check to see that the parents have fully understood the test results and their implications. The parents may want specific recommendations or program suggestions, and the examiner should be prepared to provide these.

Termination of the interview—Parents may be unable or unwilling to accept the results of the evaluation. The examiner should accept that difficulty and perhaps provide the names of other professionals or agencies in case the parents want to get a second opinion. The examiner should also be available to see the parents again if necessary and desirable.

Parent-Examiner Conferences

In preparing for a parent conference, it is important for the examiner to gather all pertinent information, including a report of the standardized tests taken by the child and an interpretation of the results. The examiner should also be prepared to record additional information from the parents that might facilitate work with the child. Parents might be asked to describe how the student feels about school, teachers, counselors, testing, grading, or peers. They might also elaborate on the student's special interests. The examiner might have on display the work of other students so that the parents can see not only what books and materials are being used, but also what level of work is expected. The examiner should end the conference on a positive note, thanking the parents for their interest and scheduling another appointment if necessary.

Types of Questions Parents Ask about Tests

Parents tend to ask a number of questions about test scores and reports. Here are some typical questions and some points to include in a response.

What is a standardized test?

This term refers to conditions under which the test was developed, resulting in a number of standards of performance that are representative of a wide sample of test takers. It also refers to conditions under which the test is administered, usually in a uniform manner so that all test takers receive the same directions, same time to take the test, and so on.

How was the test administered?

It was administered by individuals trained and experienced in giving tests such as teachers, counselors, and psychologists.

How are the tests scored, reported, and recorded?

Tests are usually sent back to the publisher to be computer scored. Individual and group reports are sent back to the school district or examiner. Many testing services provide labels on which results are recorded and which can be fastened to the cumulative record or file of the individual. Individual profiles and test summaries are sent to parents; class, grade, and district profiles are sent to the schools.

Often parents ask questions about specific scores used on different tests. The examiner should be prepared to explain scores such as national percentile ranks, grade equivalent scores, stanines, local norms, and standard scores. Specific questions may relate to many areas.

What do these scores really mean?

What is wrong with grade equivalent scores?

Why are our school's scores below the national norms?

Why do you test so much?

How do you use the scores?

How accurately do the tests predict success?

Is there really a relation between the scores and a child's achievement in class?

How much do scores vary and why?

What is scholastic aptitude?

What is intelligence?

What kinds of questions were asked on this test?

Who will see the test results?

Can test scores be improved with coaching?

Is the test fair to members of my race, gender, or ethnic group?

Other Areas of Concern to Parents

Parents also may want to know what to do if they disagree with the results of the testing. For example, the examiner says the child is not ready for kindergarten and the parents think the child is, or the parents think the child should be placed in the gifted program and the examiner doesn't agree. They could be advised of avenues they might take, such as pursuing an independent evaluation on their own, recognizing that the school district may not reimburse them for the evaluation and that it may be difficult to have the client tested with the same tests. Shore, Brice, and Love (1992) remind parents that the people involved in the process are trying to do what is in the best interest of the test taker. Parents should use the information gained from the assessment and discussion with the examiner to make an informed decision about what is best for their child.

Parents may want to know whether test results really matter. The examiner should elaborate on the testing objectives and point out that our society is concerned with accountability. In addition, test results are often a major criterion for promotion or admission to a specific program. Parents should take test results seriously and be supportive of testing programs. They should encourage their children to do their best and praise them for doing as well as they can. Parents' attitudes toward a testing program influence how children view that program.

Parents are sometimes concerned about the anxiety caused by tests and want to know about techniques to help reduce that anxiety. Many bookstores offer audio tapes detailing relaxation techniques. The examiner needs to emphasize that some anxiety is useful, but too much is a problem. Parents should be warned to respond to test anxiety in a realistic manner and not to overreact to test scores.

Parents might ask whether the tests are culturally biased. Many attempts have been made to eliminate as much bias as possible in most test instruments. The essential-skills and minimum-level skills tests are based upon what the students are supposed to learn in schools. Scores would be biased only if individuals did not have an equal opportunity to learn the material included on these tests. Standardized tests use panels of experts to review the items for sexual bias, cultural bias, and bias for individuals with disabilities. On scholastic aptitude tests the item responses for various groups are compared to see if there are differences in how minority and majority groups respond to the test items. However, even with these attempts, some bias might still be operating in the testing situation and may distort a person's true score.

Parents may be concerned about whether scores are fixed or changeable. They need to be reminded that a test measures a sample of behavior at a particular time, using items from a given domain. Tests scores do change; they can go up and down. There may be some ups and downs in the child's test profile from year to year or subtest to subtest. Sometimes a poor performance happens because a student may not be skilled in the areas measured by the test. Most children perform better in some areas than in others. Parents need to understand the dynamics at work and refrain from hasty value judgments.

Parents may also be concerned about whether students ought to be given their own test results. In most cases students should be provided feedback on their performance in words and terms they can understand. The information can help them understand their own strengths and weaknesses and make more realistic educational and vocational choices.

Parents may wonder whether their children are overachievers or underachievers. Overachievers are students who achieve better in the classroom than scholastic aptitude tests predict. These students usually have a positive attitude toward school, internal orientation, and high motivation. The label has been greatly criticized by educators and psychologists from a theoretical and practical standpoint. Under-achievers perform below the prediction of a scholastic aptitude test. Many learning disabled students have normal aptitude but achieve a standard deviation or more below the average for their grade or age.

The Informing Interview

In the informing interview the counselor attempts to communicate assessment results with the parents or guardians. The goal of this session may be partly educational and motivational for the parents and partly therapeutic (Gabel, Oster, & Botnik, 1986). When problems identified are mild or less deviant, parent are more accepting of the results and are less anxious. When the problems are severe, the parents or guardians may become angry, defensive, or blame themselves and others. When parents are defensive, communication is usually ineffective.

Gabel, Oster, and Botnik (1986) suggest that the initial statement and explanation of the problem should be in nontechnical terms. Later the counselor may use medical and psychological terms as support for the assessment. Certain terms, such as mental retardation and brain damage, might stand as an emotional block to communication if not adequately clarified and explained.

The counselor needs to be alert to what questions the parents asked as well as what questions they did not ask. What questions were they really asking? What questions should they be asking? The counselor may want to address practical questions that concern the client such as schooling, therapy, and counseling needs and the like.

Parents as Test Interpreters

Testing companies usually provide self-interpretative report forms for parents, but most parents still have questions about what the test scores mean. A workshop for parents might help them understand and interpret test results properly. Boehm and White (1982) provide four guidelines for parents who present test results to their children.

1. Inform the child about areas of strength or areas needing development.
2. Find out whether the child understands what the test scores mean (e.g., children often confuse the meaning of percentile with percentage).
3. Avoid judgment of an individual's worth. The student whose score is high is no better as a person than the student whose score is low.
4. For a student who is having difficulty, offer to find out the reasons and try to help (pp. 138–139).

Overall, parents need to maintain open communication with their children. Test results should be shared constructively, and steps should be outlined to help with any problem area. Parents also need to listen to their children's view of a test or test result.

CONSULTING WITH TEACHERS

Teachers may need consultation about test use and interpretation, also. They have to administer and score both local and standardized tests, and they need to know the practical implications of the scores for their students.

Again, the first step for the examiner is to establish a working relationship. Brown, Pryzwansky, and Schulte (1995) call for a relationship of mutual trust, open communication, genuineness, and positive regard. The teacher is seeking ways to help a student and wants to have the test results interpreted into language that is easy to understand. The consultation is quite often for the purpose of establishing a plan of action for a particular student.

Caplan (1993) identified four types of problems that arise in teacher consultation.

1. The teacher lacks skills and competencies needed to work with students.
2. The teacher is not objective and unbiased.
3. The teacher lacks confidence and perceives personal deficiencies.
4. The teacher lacks the ability to conceptualize the student's problem.

The NEA and NCME have asserted that student assessment is an essential part of teaching and that good teachers cannot exist without good student assessment. Teachers need to acquire skills and abilities to select, develop, apply, use, communicate, and evaluate student assessment information.

Problems that might interfere with the success of the consultation process might be identified by observing the teacher in class, or by listening carefully to what the teacher has to say.

"Mary has a low IQ. It is impossible to motivate her."

"John comes from a bad family. He will be just like his brothers and not amount to anything."

"Dick scored at the 34th percentile. He did not do well at all."

Part of the problem may be that the teacher does not know enough about basic measurement concepts. This topic could be addressed in a group situation, perhaps through in-service education. If the teacher is biased, the examiner may have to use confrontation and report the objective data collected through observation and feedback. Teacher expectations have a tremendous influence on what happens in the classroom; they should be realistic and communicated regularly and effectively.

Goals should be set for the teacher consultation; they help focus attention on strategies. The collaborative model of consultation calls for strategies to be developed jointly by the consultant and teacher. The theoretical orientation of the consultant partly determines the strategies to be used. Neo-client theory might stress human relation skills, such as problem solving and effective communication, whereas behavior theory might focus on selective use of reinforcement strategies.

The National Association of School Psychologists (1978) calls for establishing professional relationships with school personnel. Standard IV relates to the need of the school psychologist to have a working understanding of the goals, processes, and legal requirements of the educational system and to be familiar with the organization, instructional materials, and teaching strategies of the school. Effective communication skills are essential, and the school psychologist is reminded that the findings and recommendations need to be put into language that is readily understood by the school staff.

Indirect Delivery Model

Gutkin and Curtis (1982) propose an indirect service model that includes these steps that will help teachers and parents and other professionals understand, interpret, and use assessment results more effectively.

1. Develop an open, trusting relationship. Rapport must be established.
2. Establish a collaborative, coordinate relationship. Both parties should have equal authority in the decision-making process.
3. Involve the consultee in the consultation process. The consultant is responsible for helping the consultees become active in the process.
4. Encourage the consultee to accept or reject suggestions. The consultee cannot be forced to accept strategies.
5. Maintain a voluntary relationship. Principals should not force teachers into consultation.
6. Maintain confidentiality. The information shared should be kept confidential.

In this model the consultant may plan to collect data from observations, interviews, and standardized tests if both the consultant and consultee believe the information would be useful. Any tests selected and administered should address specific problems identified in the case.

Problem-Solving Consulting Model

A problem-solving approach helps the parties involved clarify and define the problem of the client and facilitate the analysis of forces that will lead to more effective problem solving. Helping professionals can utilize brainstorming of alternate strategies, evaluate and choose among the alternatives, and then specify the responsibilities of the consultee and consultant. The strategy then must be implemented and evaluated for effectiveness. The process can be recycled if necessary and the steps repeated (Gutkin & Curtis, 1982, p. 805).

When the purpose of the consultation focuses on mental health issues, Caplan (1963, 1970, 1993) proposed a model that includes the focus as well as the goal of consultation. The two major goals are remediation and prevention. The focus may be on individual cases or on administrative programs. Caplan (1970) advocates a consultee-centered case consultation because the primary goal is to improve the consultee's capacity to function effectively in this category of case, in order to benefit many similar clients in the future. Because of the educational emphasis, the consultant uses the discussion of the current case situation, not basically in order to understand the client, but in order to understand and remedy the consultee's work difficulties as manifested in this example (p. 125).

CONSULTING WITH OTHER PROFESSIONALS

Many times an examiner is required to communicate test results to other professionals, such as principals, psychologists, social workers, correctional officers, and judicial staff members. Not all of these professionals understand test information. Again, it is important to work cooperatively to establish good rapport and a working relationship based on mutual respect and recognition of joint proficiencies. Communication skills remain an important variable.

Explanations should be clear and unambiguous. The APA (1981) *Ethical Principles of Psychologists* (Principle 8) calls for the examiner to indicate any reservations regarding test validity or reliability because of assessment circumstances or inappropriate norms. Psychologists and counselors are cautioned to ensure that assessment results and interpretations are not misused by others.

In reporting to other professionals, examiners are faced with a variety of decisions. Goldman (1971) provides some basic guidelines for presenting test information to other professions.

1. Find out exactly what information the recipient needs, what he plans to do with it, and what qualifications he has.

2. Make sure ethical and legal procedures are followed, such as securing a client's written permission to release information.

3. Check to see whether procedures have been established for test information. Normally a policy is already in force.

4. Aim the report as directly as possible to the particular question asked. This practice saves time and provides clear communication of needed information.

EVALUATION OF THE CONSULTANT

Parents, teachers, and other professionals might be asked to evaluate the work of the consultant. Questions such as these are helpful.

1. Did the consultant help you better understand the problem that prompted the testing?

2. Did the consultant help you understand the test results better?

3. Did the consultant provide you with practical suggestions for utilizing the test results?

4. Were you satisfied with the consultant's style in relating to you?

5. Were you happy with the services provided by the consultant?

6. What could be done to improve the services?

A checklist or rating form for consultees might pose questions like these:

1. How many times have you met with the consultant this year?

   1 2 3 4 5 6 7 8 9 10 or more

2. How helpful was the consultant to you?

   Not helpful 1 2 3 4 5 6 7 Extremely helpful

3. How knowledgeable was the consultant about testing?

   Slightly 1 2 3 4 5 6 7 Extremely

SUMMARY

Dissemination of test results is a function of communication. Knowledge of what to communicate requires a thorough background in test interpretation and an understanding of the test manual and the purposes of the test. Group and individual counseling sessions need to be planned prior to testing as well as after testing has been completed. In many types of testing programs, parents and the community need to be informed. It is advantageous to develop a systematic program to inform test users, parents, teachers, and the public about testing. The examiner needs a thorough knowledge of ethical and legal aspects and must be able to translate the test results into language clients can understand.

Consultation demands not only a knowledge of the problem situation but different models of interaction. The consultant needs to know the ethical and legal standards as well as strategies to work with teachers, parents, and other professionals. Communication skills are an important part of the consultation process. In addition, the consultant should include in the process a mechanism for evaluation of his or her services.

QUESTIONS FOR DISCUSSION

1. Which type of test interpretation do you feel is more accurate—group versus individual, computer-based narratives, or standard test profiles?

2. Do you agree that individuals interpreting tests should be extremely careful about interpretation of test results for women, older individuals, minority group

members, and individuals with disabilities? Why or why not? Does the type of test influence the need for caution?

3. What role do you believe counseling theory should have in the interpretation of test results? Should the interpretation be based on a given theory? Defend your position.

4. What are the major problem areas in disseminating results to parents? The community? The test taker? How would you go about evaluating the effectiveness of dissemination efforts?

5. If you could choose the way you were to receive your test results, what system would you choose? Why?

6. Clients value tests more if they see the need for the test information. Are the attitudes of the test taker more important than the system chosen for interpreting results?

7. What do you think are the main issues and problems that consultants face in working with parents, teachers, and other professionals regarding testing results?

8. How important is the role of the consultant for people in the helping professions? What skills does a consultant need?

9. How would you handle a teacher or parent who became excessively dependent on your services and solutions? What should the role of the consultant be in such a case?

10. What model of consultation would you choose if you were asked to work with individuals on testing problems or results? What factors would influence your choice? Would underlying psychological theories be a factor in your decision?

11. Goldman (1971) states that parents are most in need of the information provided by tests. Do you agree with this statement? What kind of program should be established to help parents better understand the test results of their children?

SUGGESTED ACTIVITIES

1. Review the literature on methods and techniques of test interpretation.

2. Talk with the persons responsible for test interpretation and dissemination in several school districts. Assemble a notebook or folder of the sample news releases and examples of the districts' letters to parents, students, and teachers.

3. Interview psychologists and counselors who utilize tests frequently. Find out the systems they use to report test results to their clients and their approaches to problems such as flat profiles, individuals who are disappointed with test results, and so on. Report your findings to the class.

4. Devise a rating scale to evaluate different types of media presentations for disseminating test results.

5. Videotape how you would handle test interpretation sessions with a client who (a) is not ready to accept the results, (b) had a flat profile with all low scores, or (c) who has a really negative attitude toward testing.

6. Devise a workshop for a group of individuals in your field who work with tests and need help in communicating test results.

7. Interview workers in the helping professions who use tests and find out how much time they spend in consultation. Have them discuss the model of consultation they use. Ask them what steps they follow in the consultation process. Also, ask them what types of problems they have had in their roles as consultants. Report your results to the class.

8. Compare the major models of consultation on test results. Identify studies and articles in the literature that deal with test results and test problems.

9. Set up a model consultation program for a consultant who is working with teachers, parents, or other professionals on testing problems and results.

10. Role play a situation in which you have to consult a helping professional on testing problems or results. Examples: A teacher might want to know how she can help her students improve their test scores. She is afraid that she will lose her job if the class does not do well on achievement tests. Or a doctor might want to know whether a child shows any signs of learning disabilities and how that information could be relayed to the child's parents.

11. Write a paper on the skills a consultant needs to be effective with testing problems and results.

12. Design an instrument to evaluate the work of a consultant on testing problems.

13. Review the brief case studies and answer the questions that follow.

    M.W.'s mother was very concerned when she received her second-grader's scores on the CTBS. M.W. scored at the 99th percentile on Math but only at the 81st on Reading. M.W. was at the 94th percentile on the Word Attack Scale and the 95th on Vocabulary, but at the 45th on Language and 54th on Science. M.W. had been tested for the gifted program and was accepted by virtue of a 133 score on the Stanford-Binet. M.W.'s mother can't make any sense out of the test scores and wants the teachers and counselors to help her daughter improve her test scores.

    a. What approach would you use with M.W.'s mother?
    b. What would you tell her about the test results?

    You have been asked to be a consultant on a training and development project. The project involves work with unemployed workers; you are to help explain how to use and interpret different career instruments. The previous consultant who left recently had convinced the project managers to use the Self-Directed Search and the MBTI.

    a. How would you go about developing your role as a consultant?
    b. What steps would you follow?

    c.   The project participants want you to consult with them on how to interpret the two tests. One individual wants you to guide him through the process of analyzing, interpreting, and reporting back to the client the results on the SDS and MBTI. His case is of Albert Smith, a 23-year-old Caucasian male who dropped out of school in the 10th grade. He is enrolled in a high school equivalency program in conjunction with the project. Albert has had numerous jobs in the food service industry but has not been able to hold on to them. He has a wife and three children and realizes that he needs further training and education to support his family. On the MBTI he is a ISFJ. On the Self-Directed Search, he is an ARS. How would you proceed?

ADDITIONAL READINGS

Alpert, J., & Silverstein, J. (1985). Mental health consultation: Historical, present, and future perspectives. In J. Bergan (Ed.), *School psychology in contemporary society*. Columbus, OH: Merrill.

This chapter presents a good overview of the field and gives us information on where it has been and where it is going.

Brown, D., Pryzwansky, W. B., & Schulte, A. C. (1995). *Psychological consultation: Introduction to theory and practice* (3rd ed.). Boston: Allyn and Bacon.

The text presents a good overview of different theories and approaches to consultation. Several chapters deal with evaluation, ethical and legal considerations, and training consultants. The last chapter contains a good discussion of issues in consultation.

Caplan, G., & Caplan, R. B. (1993). *Mental health consultation and collaboration*. New York: Basic Books.

The authors stress the theory and practice of mental health consultation and nature and purpose of mental health collaboration.

Gutkin, T. B., & Curtis, M. J. (1982). School-based consultation: Theory and techniques. In C. R. Reynolds and T. B. Gutkin (Eds.), *The handbook of school psychology* (pp. 519–561). New York: John Wiley and Sons.

This chapter is especially valuable and useful for individuals who work in the school environment.

Harmon, L. W. (1989). Counseling. In R. Linn (Ed.), *Educational measurement* (3rd ed.). New York: Macmillan.

The chapter discusses and illustrates some measurement applications to counseling and issues related to such applications.

Lyman, H. B. (1989). *Test scores and what they mean* (5th ed.). Englewood Cliffs, NJ: Prentice-Hall.

The text has a good presentation on the topic of interpretation of test scores.

Miller, M. J. (1985). Counseling region 99 clients. *Journal of Employment Counseling, 22*, 70–76.

Miller offers a strategy for clients who possess a flat profile and are positioned in Region 99 in the "World of Work Map."

Shore, M. F., Brice, P. J., & Love, B. G. (1992). *When your child needs testing: What parents, teachers, and other helpers need to know about psychological testing.* New York: Crossroad.

The authors cover topics such as why psychological testing, how do I begin, what should the child be told, what about the results, what if I disagree, and what about confidentiality.

Standardized tests and our children: A guide to testing reform in New York. New York Public Interest Research Group, 9 Murray St., New York, NY 10007.

CHAPTER 23

Written Test Reports

Overview

Many times a counselor is required to complete a written report of test results. The type of report depends in part on the purpose of the testing and in part on who will receive the test report. The information age has been affected by widespread use of the computer. Many tests now have computer-generated test reports and software packages available to assist professionals in writing test reports.

Objectives

After studying this chapter, the reader should be able to

- list and discuss ways to format and write test reports for various groups
- identify the proper language and writing style to be used in reports
- discuss the use of computer-generated reports
- locate and evaluate computer-generated reports

PURPOSES OF WRITTEN REPORTS

Counselors are not always in agreement as to what written reports should do. According to Ownby (1990), most authors agree that the report should serve at least four purposes—describe the client who is being assessed and the client's problem, provide a record of the evaluation results for future use, serve as a means of communication to persons wanting or needing the results, and recommend an appropriate course of action. Ownby also recommends that counselors consider the context of the report while writing it and also the referring agent, the client's environment, and the broader context in which interventions are to be made.

CONTENT OF A REPORT

The content of a report depends on the recipients and the purposes of the report (Goldman, 1971; Shore, Brice, & Love, 1992). The information should be communicated in a way that is understandable, usable, adequate, and economical. Normally a test report includes eight components.

1. *Demographic information*—name and address of examinee, date of birth/chronological age, date of examination, race, sex, grade/school, parents or guardians, examiner

2. *Reason for referral and relevant background information*—problem indicated by client; person(s) referring client; relevant educational, social, medical information; family information and history; previous testing results; other personal information

3. *Behavioral observations of the client*—during testing, in nontesting situations, in classroom or work settings

4. *Test results*—tests given; total, scale, and subscale scores; range and spread of scores; basal and ceiling age levels; test items passed or failed

5. *Diagnostic impressions*—strengths and weaknesses affecting performance, diagnostic interpretations

6. *Recommendations*—specific answers to referral questions, predictions, cautions, recommendations

7. *Summary*—brief integrated statement of test findings

8. *Signature*—of the test administrator/report writer

The Case of John and Case of Allen that follow illustrate written reports.

CASE OF JOHN

Student: John
Race/Sex: White/male
Chronological Age: 7–8
School: Middletown
Dates of Evaluation: 10/8/95, 10/15/95, & 12/3/95

Date of Report: 12/3/95

Reason for Referral

John was referred for psychoeducational evaluation because of poor progress in class.

Background Information

John has a history of poor academic achievement. Last year he was frequently absent from school but now attends regularly. The Department of Health and Rehabilitative Services has been involved with the family.

John is having great difficulty doing the work required of him. He does not appear to understand what he is asked to do. Often his response has nothing to do with the question. He wants to please and will fill his paper with attempts to respond. His writing gives evidence of a tendency to reverse and transpose letters and numbers. He does succeed better in math than reading. He does have a concept of numbers and can do simple addition and subtraction.

Behavioral Observations

John is a friendly boy. He was shy at first, but quickly warmed up. His effort and cooperation were good. John seemed to have great difficulty understanding what was said to him. He tends to agree with any suggestion without weighing its merits. John had problems naming common objects. He had difficulty expressing himself. Often, John covered his mouth with his hands or looked down while he spoke as if to give people a reason not to understand him.

During the evaluation, John's affect was somewhat flat. He showed hardly any emotion. Both weeks that John was seen, he had bruises around his face and could not adequately explain their presence.

In class, John was quiet and kept to himself. He tried to work diligently. The teacher overlooked occasions when John copied from other children. He seems to enjoy praise and peer recognition.

Tests Administered

Wechsler Intelligence Scale for Children-III
Woodcock-Johnson Tests of Achievement
Goodenough Draw a Person Test
Peabody Picture Vocabulary Test
Test of Nonverbal Intelligence

Analysis of Test Results

John's scores on the Wechsler Intelligence Scale for Children-III placed him in the borderline range of intellectual ability. A significant discrepancy exists between his verbal and performance scores in favor of the latter. Thus, it can be hypothesized that he performs better with concrete stimuli rather than totally verbal tasks.

This possibility was evaluated by administering the Test of Nonverbal Intelligence and the Peabody Picture Vocabulary Test. These tests also suggest that John has a verbal language deficit and can function better nonverbally. Moreover, the pattern of John's subtests suggests that lack of experience and emotional factors may be depressing his performance. Present test scores should be considered as indicators of current functioning and not as long-range predictors of future progress.

Academically, John is functioning as well as can be expected. He has a very significant deficit in reading achievement and his fund of general knowledge is weak. John cannot yet recognize all the letters of the alphabet or consistently spell his name correctly.

Summary

John is functioning in the borderline range of intelligence. Indications are that his performance may be depressed. He seems to be demonstrating a severe language processing deficit. He has great difficulty with reading and oral information. He is capable of doing some simple math, however.

Recommendations

Based on all available data, an appropriate exceptional student education placement should be discussed.

CASE OF ALLEN

Student: Allen
Race/Sex: White/male
Date of Birth: 8/3/88
Chronological age: 5–7
School: #33
Grade: Kindergarten
Date: 3/27/94

Tests Used

Wechsler Preschool and Primary Scale of
    Intelligence-R
Developmental Test of Visual Motor Inte-
    gration
Sentence Completion Form for Children
California Test of Personality
Peabody Picture Vocabulary Test—Revised
Behavioral Observation

Reason for Referral

Allen was evaluated at the request of the child
study team in consideration of severe behavioral difficulties experienced within the classroom. An estimate of his current intellectual
functioning was also needed.

Background Information

Allen currently resides with his biological
mother. No other children live in the home.
According to information in the child study
team packet, Allen has a short attention span,
often seeks attention at inappropriate times, is
often disruptive and physically aggressive
toward peers, and generally experiences
behavioral difficulties within the classroom.
He refuses to come into the school, runs off,
and talks back. He shows little self-control,
and is argumentative and aggressive. He
recently transferred from another school
within the district.

Burks' Behavior Rating Scale was completed prior to this evaluation. Of the 19 sub-

scales, 6 were found in the very significant
range—poor impulse control, excessive suffering, poor anger control, excessive sense of
persecution, excessive resistance, and poor
social conformity. There were 6 other areas in
the significant range—poor ego strength, poor
coordination, poor intellectuality, poor attention, poor sense of identity, and excessive
aggressiveness. A number of incident reports
and behavioral observations are included in
the child study team's packet. Allen often has
temper tantrums, shows a great deal of disre-
spect (even to the principal of the school),
and has not responded well to any interventions that have occurred thus far. He is quite
oppositional and defiant, and refuses to comply with school rules.

Hearing and vision screening were passed
prior to this evaluation.

Behavioral Observations

Allen was observed prior to the evaluation. He
entered the cafeteria and was instructed to sit
down in his regular seat. He immediately
refused to sit there and wanted to sit somewhere else. He said that other students could
sit at other tables, and was quite verbally
oppositional to his teacher. He also stuck his
tongue out at the teacher and growled. A
number of verbal interventions occurred, in
which the supervising teacher attempted to
modify Allen's inappropriate behavior. In each
case Allen responded either verbally or nonverbally in an oppositional manner. He did
comply to a number of minor requests. As a
rule his behavior was attention seeking, oppositional, and defiant. At the end of the observation Allen began to jab a straw at another student. When instructed to stop, he refused to
give the straw to a teacher, crawled under the
table, and refused to comply with the
teacher's request. At that time he apparently

became quite upset, but calmed down after some teacher interaction.

During the evaluation, Allen repeated many of these behaviors. When brought to the testing room, he immediately became quite upset and lay on the floor crying. He cried for approximately five minutes, refused to be tested, crawled to the door, and began kicking the door. He began to call names and yell. This behavior was not reinforced and he calmed down about 5 minutes later. He appeared to respond well to lack of reinforcement for negative behavior. Stickers and gum were used as reinforcers for test performance.

Even with reinforcers, Allen had a very short attention span and tended to give up easily. He was quite distractible and often wanted to perform tasks other than the ones at hand. He required a good deal of verbal reinforcement and praise to maintain a productive work level. He was quite easily frustrated, particularly with nonverbal reasoning tasks.

Test Results

Intelligence testing on the Wechsler Preschool and Primary Scale of Intelligence-Revised revealed a full scale IQ of 102, which estimates cognitive functioning in the average range. He earned a significantly higher performance IQ (111) than verbal IQ (94). This significant difference may be due to a variety of factors. Within the current evaluation, Allen tended to give up easily on verbal items, and seemed to enjoy the nonacademic, play characteristics of the nonverbal, manipulative items. Considering the short attention span and ease of distractibility noted earlier, Allen does demonstrate that he can work effectively when the stimulus materials are interesting and the tasks are of short duration.

A wide degree of scatter was noted within Allen's profile; his individual subtest scores vary from the low average to superior ranges.

He demonstrated his best abilities on tasks reflecting perceptual organization and planning, and visual-motor control. However, Allen does have difficulty with tasks requiring attention and concentration, which are related to academics. In addition, the overall pattern of scores reflected a significant degree of emotionality, as did the oppositional, defiant, and impulsive behavior exhibited during testing. Individual differences should be interpreted with caution because of these behavioral manifestations.

The Peabody Picture Vocabulary Test— Revised was administered in order to assess receptive vocabulary. Allen obtained a standard score of 108, which represents an average performance for his chronological age. His skills in this language area represent an approximate age equivalent of 6.2 years.

The Developmental Test of Visual-Motor Integration presents tasks of copying geometric forms. On this test of visual-motor skills, Allen demonstrated skills at the 71st percentile, representing above average skills for his chronological age. Consequently, abilities in this area represent a relative strength.

The Woodcock-Johnson Memory Scale assessed short-term memory through auditory processing of verbally presented sentences and digits (repeated backwards). Allen attained a standard score of 92, representing an average performance.

Personality dynamics were assessed through the California Test of Personality, Incomplete Sentences Form, and behavioral observations. Allen reflected significant emotionality throughout the evaluation. Allen is a young man with a quite unsatisfactory adjustment to the school environment. He recognized that he has significant difficulty with peer interactions, primarily because of a lack of social skills and a good deal of egocentrism. He does not believe that he experiences warmth and nurturance from his environment. At one level Allen desires to reach out to the environment in an affectionate manner. However, this desire is blocked by lack of skills and a tendency to act out his feelings. These dynamics were quite apparent throughout the testing situation. Allen was initially quite hostile and aggressive. When he was not rejected because of his behavior, he appeared to be sincerely interested in pleasing the examiner. Allen also related that he likes his classroom teacher a great deal, although he has continual difficulty within and outside the classroom. The difficulty in forming functional relationships may be due to fears or guilt, although these aspects need exploration within the therapeutic milieu. In any event, emotional indicators were reflected, representing a significant degree of severity.

Diagnostic Impressions

Allen appears to be functioning in the average range of cognitive skills. He does demonstrate a better nonverbal ability (in the high average range) than verbal ability (in the average range). He does have a wide degree of scatter, which may be reflective of attentional difficulties as well as oppositional behavior toward the tasks presented. Consequently, the results of this intellectual evaluation should be interpreted with caution. An analysis of Allen's learning abilities reveals adequately developed receptive vocabulary, short-term memory, and visual-motor skills. No difficulties were noted in any of these areas.

Emotionality is the primary concern with Allen. Throughout observations and actual testing, he demonstrated aggressive, oppositional, and defiant behavior. He seems to have a great desire for acceptance and nurturance, but he lacks skills and impulse controls necessary to sustain relationships other than punitive ones. These dynamics may be due to a variety of factors in the clinical history, and may be best explored within a therapeutic setting. In terms of behavioral management,

Allen responded quite well to the nonreinforcement of defiant and angry behavior, as well as positive reinforcement of appropriate on-task behavior.

Allen would benefit from spending time in a very highly structured classroom environment, directing attention to his emotional difficulties. Attention should also be given to the acquisition of basic skills including those in the social/interactional as well as the academic areas. Allen and his parents are currently involved in family therapy at a local clinic. This should certainly continue, and Allen would probably benefit from a long-term relationship in a therapeutic milieu. Temper tantrums, as well as oppositional and defiant behavior, should not be reinforced, within practical limitations. Appropriate behavior as well as on-task and successful academic attempts should be reinforced. Through interventions, Allen may begin to achieve at a rate that is more commensurate with his overall cognitive abilities.

Relative Strengths
1. planning ability, perceptual organization, visual-motor control (WPPSI-R)
2. perceptual ability, visual-motor organization (WPPSI-R)
3. memory, attention, and finger and manual dexterity (WPPSI-R)
4. general range in knowledge and information (WPPSI-R)
5. visual-motor skills (VMI)

Process Deficits
None

Relative Weaknesses
1. numerical reasoning ability (WPPSI-R)
2. verbal social knowledge and practical judgment (WPPSI)

Emotional Indicators
1. distractibility, poor attention, oppositional and defiant behavior (observations during testing)

2. oppositional and defiant behavior, rebelliousness (behavioral observations outside the testing situation)
3. poor personal, social, and overall adjustment (CTP)
4. poor peer relationships, denial (sentence completion)

5. subtest scatter, verbal/performance discrepancy (WPPSI-R)
6. poor impulse control, excessive suffering, poor anger control, excessive sense of persecution, excessive resistance and poor social conformity (Burks' Behavior Rating Scale)

FACTORS AFFECTING THE TEST REPORT

Certain factors should be kept in mind when writing a test report. The first consideration might be the focus of the report. Will it be a test-oriented focus, concentrating on the objective test results, the items, the scales, and the technical aspects of the examinee's performance? Or, will the report focus on the examinee and his characteristics? The decision depends partially on the purpose of the testing and on addressing the referral questions.

The examiner must then decide what material should be included and excluded. Quite often a tremendous amount of information is available. The examiner should have a good understanding of the self-concept, attitudes, interests, motivations, and family background of the examinee and should cite the supporting evidence of diag-

The examiner must carefully review the tests and the purpose of the testing when writing the report.

nostic impressions, attempting to depict the client's individuality and uniqueness. Some judgments are difficult because they are necessarily more subjective. With consistent evidence from a number of sources, the examiner can be more sure of interpretations and conclusions.

Sattler (1992) emphasizes that everything observed from the initial encounter to the end of the contact with the client constitutes data for analysis. The examination is to be viewed not merely as a question-and-answer session, but as an opportunity for interaction between the client and examiner and is as much a part of the examination as are the test questions and the examinee's responses.

Common Problems

Katz (1985) identifies six common problems in psychological report writing.

1. *Overuse of jargon*—Jargon may relate to a certain theory or to psychological testing. Many individuals who are not versed in the particular theory or the technical language will have trouble understanding what is being said. Furthermore, unless operational definitions are included, certain words and terms cause problems because individuals have different concepts of the same term.

2. *Focus on test results rather than the individual*—In this situation test findings are extensively reported but are not related to the behavior of the individual and very few practical suggestions or inferences are reported.

3. *Downplay of test results*—Sometimes a report departs too far from the test findings. It may include more social history of the individual but little evidence from the test results, and the inferences may be based on observations and background information rather than on test information.

4. *Poor organization of the report*—Sometimes each test or subtest is reported, but the test results are not integrated as a whole. At other times historical information is interspersed with the test results, making it hard to separate the components.

5. *Failure of the examiner to take a position*—Examiners often are reluctant to make specific diagnoses or specific treatment recommendations even when the data are there to support them.

6. *Poor written communication skills*—Sometimes a report is poorly written and shows deficiencies in spelling, grammar, syntax, and vocabulary usage.

Tallent (1993) identifies five major categories of problems that are somewhat similar to those just listed: content, interpretation, examiner attitude and orientation, problems of communication, and science and the profession.

WRITING THE REPORT

The goal is to communicate clearly the results of the testing. The examiner should include the purposes of the testing, specific problems or decisions that gave rise to the testing, behavioral descriptions, and sources of information. The examiner should not include hearsay, unverified opinions, generalized statements, nor potentially harmful or damaging information.

Tallent (1958) points out that the style of the report can interfere with effective communication, and he identifies three styles. In the Barnum style the report writer includes many universalities and ambiguities and presents a great deal of hoopla with little substance. In the Aunt Fanny style the writer includes information that is true about all test takers including their Aunt Fanny. The Madison Avenue style contains information to sell an idea or conclusion and is meant to placate someone or to express possible hostility.

Katz (1985) lists eight general guidelines for good report writing.

1. Get to it. It is better to write your report the day of testing or at least within 24 hours of seeing the client. Otherwise, observations and impressions can be forgotten.

2. Remember the basics. Certain basic information must be included, such as date, identifying biographical data, tests administered, behavioral observations, categories of test results, diagnostic prescriptions, recommendations, and a summary.

3. Have in mind the proper organization for the desired report.

4. Keep in mind how long the report should be; aim for clarity and accuracy but keep brevity in mind. Many people might ignore or slight a 10-page report but will read a 2-page report completely and carefully.

5. Say what needs to be said. Examiners should report their findings clearly and directly, using straightforward statements and including specific recommendations. If findings are tentative and nonconclusive, the report should so state.

6. Try to make the report readable and interesting. Carefully choose words and sentences.

7. Ask for feedback. Ask those who read and use the report to give their reaction to it. Feedback helps to improve areas of weakness and reveals areas of strength.

8. Know who is going to read or receive the report. Ethical principles call for the report to be in a language that can be understood by the parties using the report. Consumers of test reports possess a wide variety of skills, interests, and knowledge of educational and psychological tests (pp. 143–149).

Organizing the Report

One of the crucial issues in psychological test report writing is organization. Klopfer (1960) identifies different types of patterns of organization.

1. *Theory-oriented report*—The examiner utilizes a certain personality or psychometric theory as the frame of reference.

2. *Test-oriented report*—The examiner focuses primarily on test information, explaining it in detail and telling how interpretations were derived.

3. *Problem-oriented report*—The examiner focuses on the particular question asked in referral.

4. *Person-centered report*—The examiner focuses on the examinee rather than the sources of information.

5. *Ego-psychological report*—The examiner focuses on the assets and strengths of the individual coping with life demands.

Technical Aspects

The writer needs to be familiar with the *Publication Manual of the American Psychological Association-Fourth Edition* (1994). It describes the mechanical aspects of writing style in sections on punctuation, spelling, capitalization, italics, abbreviations, footnotes, and references. For example, the APA guide permits the use of abbreviations that appear as word entries in *Webster's New Collegiate Dictionary*, such as IQ. Other abbreviations, even if used frequently by journal authors, should always be explained fully when first used. Care should be used even then. For example, SAT is used to designate both the Stanford Achievement Test and the Scholastic Aptitude Test of the College Entrance Examination Board. Even psychologists and counselors may get somewhat confused by isolated or listed abbreviations.

Language

The writer should be specific and concrete rather than abstract and ambiguous. Abstract ideas quite often present problems to readers, who may not be quite sure of meaning. Ambiguous sentences are often misinterpreted because they imply different meanings to different individuals. The sentence "Mary lacks mechanical aptitude" leaves the reader to interpret "lacks" and "mechanical aptitude." It would be better to say "Mary is unable to use the screwdriver or put washers on the bolts." Similarly, in the sentence "John is an extrovert," who is to define an extrovert? It would be better to say, "John likes to be with people and be the center of attention. He talks and laughs loudly and makes sure he introduces himself to everyone in the room."

The examiner should present factual test data directly and accurately, basing interpretations and recommendations on reliable and valid data. It is quite easy to overgeneralize from limited test information. For example, relative to the statement "The examinee is tall for his age and may feel a deficit in his affiliation need," the subject may have a low score on the affiliation scale of the Edwards Personal Preference Schedule, but it is not necessarily a result of his being tall for his age.

Informational statements should also be precise. The sentence "Her IQ was approximately 125 on the WISC-III" leaves the reader unsure. The score is a specific number and can be kept precise by citing the standard error of measurement—for example, an IQ of 125 ($\pm$5).

Revising and Editing the Report

The first draft of the report should be checked for errors and clarity. The following questions address potential problem areas.

1. Do the sentences convey the intended information?
2. Is information presented in an objective manner?
3. Are statements clear, simple, and precise?
4. Are recommendations based upon reliable and sufficient data?
5. Are data factual?
6. Were client records and files reviewed?
7. Are the test results a valid and reliable indicator of client behavior and performance?
8. Are inferences and generalizations based on factual supporting data?
9. Have factors such as previous test results; anecdotal records; behavioral observations; parent, spouse, teacher, or peer reports and observations; medical history; grades; work history; and educational attainment been considered in the synthesis, analysis, and evaluation of current test information?
10. Is the case overstated? Are irrelevant statements eliminated?
11. Is the report organized into logical parts with smooth transitions from part to part, paragraph to paragraph?
12. Are technical details, technical vocabulary, and fancy words minimized? Are terms defined and translated into a common-sense vocabulary?
13. Are sources of information documented?

COMPUTER-GENERATED REPORTS

More and more tests are offering computer-generated test reports and interpretations. This service saves the examiner time and permits complex analyses. The ability of the computer to summarize results from schools, classes, or other types of groups has been widely accepted and utilized. However, social scientists are becoming concerned about the ethical issues in the clinical use of interpretation of computerized test results (Zachary & Pope, 1983). Computerized instruments are used in many fields and may not always be consistent with professional guidelines.

Matarazzo (1983) identifies four of the major concerns.

1. Are there real advantages to computerized interpretation of tests?
2. Will these interpretive reports reach the hands of inexperienced or unqualified individuals who will respond to the halo effect of objectivity projected by a computerized report?

3. Will publishers and developers of computerized interpretive programs reveal their decision rules (their classification or assessment standards) for professional review?

4. Will these computer reviews be sufficiently validated?

Advantages of Computerized Interpretation Programs

A number of advantages can be claimed for computerized interpretive programs. Roid (1986) lists five.

1. Accuracy of scoring and retrieval of norms from complex norm tables

2. Time saved by clinicians

3. Ability of the computer to follow complex decision rules in a fraction of a second

4. Ability to show moderating effects on test interpretation (i.e., that certain age or ethnic groups have different ranges or patterns of scores)

5. Ability to complete elaborate profile and statistical analyses

Types of Computer Interpretive Programs

Moreland (1992) identified two types of commercially available programs besides the scoring only and descriptive types: the clinician-modeled and clinical actuarial. Computerized scoring packages are available for many tests, presenting results on labels or short profile sheets for individuals.

Descriptive scoring gives individuals not only test results but also descriptive phrases, such as "average," "above average," "indicates mastery of." Such programs present certain descriptive words and phrases based upon quantitative criteria. A report, for example, might summarize the results on a given test. The first section might list in descending order the interest clusters measured on the test, with higher scores indicating stronger preferences. The report might use symbols such as 1, 2, or 0 to indicate a positive, negative, or neutral preference.

In the clinician-modeled approach the computer is used to generate an interpretation based upon the interpretive decisions of a renowned clinician or groups of expert clinicians. The information is programmed into the computer. A number of programs are available for the Minnesota Multiphasic Personality Inventory, and Miller (1981) has used this approach with the Louisville Behavior Checklist. Tape recordings of his actual case interpretations were studied, and objective decision rules were extracted from this information.

Computerized actuarial systems have been developed by a number of researchers. McDermot (1980) devised a computer program to identify intelligence, achievement, and adaptive behavior scores that related to quantitative judgments about learning disability status. Barclay (1983) utilized 25 years of multivariate statistical research on self, peers, and teacher ratings of elementary students to design a computerized interpretive program that provides a narrative, diagnostic, and prescriptive report useful to teachers, school psychologists, and other school personnel. Roid (1986) reports that the most widely used actuarial programs are those developed for use with the Minnesota Multiphasic Personality Inventory. The Sixteen Personality Factor Test has reports tailored to be used in vocational counseling as well as marriage counseling. The Strong Campbell Interest Inventory is just one more example of a test using this approach.

Computer interpretation can become very sophisticated because of the logic and memory used to study test patterns and verifiable behaviors or characteristics of examinees. Multivariate statistical analysis can be used to discriminate or distinguish among examinees in various criterion groups and assess the probabilities of group membership quickly and accurately. The computer can aid also in integrating information from a number of sources and tests. It has the ability to analyze patterns of data across situations, individuals, periods of time, and events.

Evaluation

Evaluation of the programs is essential and necessary. Professional standards address computerized interpretations of test results. Many problems arise in the interpretation of these programs because of the lack of information from the test publishers and authors. Here are some of the questions that should be asked of qualified professionals.

1. Does the author present documentation on the validity and reliability of the method?
2. Does the author present information for the examiner about the procedures utilized in the development of the interpretive program?
3. Is the format attractive?
4. Is the presentation clear and precise?
5. Does research compare traditional, clinical, and actuarial interpretation?
6. Is the procedure cost-effective?
7. Are the limitations and problems of this approach discussed by the author?
8. Is the role of the counselor or psychologist spelled out in the manual? What is the role of clinical judgment in using computerized interpretations?
9. Are possible misinterpretations discussed?
10. What are the equipment demands? What size and type of computer can be used?
11. Are backup disks and a hot line available?

SUMMARY

Written test reports are widely used in presenting and interpreting results of testing. The purpose of such a report is to provide a record of the client's performance and to communicate the results, observations, interpretations, and recommendations to a targeted individual or group. The goal of evaluation may vary, but some general guidelines need to be followed in all report writing.

1. Write the results objectively and in a straightforward manner.
2. Edit the report carefully, correcting spelling, grammar, and punctuation errors, and clarifying expressions.
3. Watch how things are said, avoiding jargon, technical language, stereotypical phrases, and ambiguous or abstract terms.
4. Write the report to be interesting and readable.
5. Draw appropriate inferences and provide realistic recommendations.

Computer interpretations are becoming more popular, and much software is available. Many promising types of reports are being generated, but problems arise when these computerized interpretative reports are utilized by inexperienced or unqualified individuals without the proper background knowledge of the tests used.

QUESTIONS FOR DISCUSSION

1. What steps and procedures should an examiner follow to get feedback from consumers of the test reports? How valuable is this type of feedback?
2. Written reports have been criticized for being too mechanical, rigid, and impersonal. Do you believe this criticism is more justified with computerized test reports than with examiner reports? Compare the advantages and disadvantages of both type of reports.
3. Should students in the helping professions have a required course in technical writing that includes a unit on writing test reports? Why or why not? What steps can test examiners take to improve the quality of their test reports?
4. What, if anything, is wrong with the following statements found in test reports? How would you edit each statement? (a) Amy appeared to be emotionally disturbed. (b) The CAT, CPQ, and CTP were administered to Amy. (c) Amy did not know her colors. (d) Amy did not have good psychomotor coordination. (e) Amy was a pretty good student in her class. (f) Amy gave concrete and fabricated explanations to the questions asked. (g) Amy gave distant, highly personalized, slang, and neologistic responses on the Word Association Test. (h) Qualitative analysis suggests that anxiety, obsessiveness, and excessive compulsivity may have had the effect of lowering Amy's score on the Wechsler.
5. Should there be a common format for test reports or should it be dependent on the purpose of the report and the recipient?

SUGGESTED ACTIVITIES

1. Administer one of the tests discussed in the text and write a report of the results for the test taker.

2. Devise a checklist to evaluate a written test report, and use it to critique one of the reports included in the text.

3. Edit the following statements and explain any changes. (a) John's IQ was indicated to be 79. (b) Items that reflect Mary's attitude toward school were not high. (c) Dick's lack of attention and interest may have contributed to his flat profile on the aptitude test. (d) In contrast, Jane's preference for social reinforcement was below average.

4. Write a critical review of the literature on one of the following topics—computerized test reports, reliability and effectiveness of test reports, common errors in written test reports, professional ethics and test reports.

5. Make an annotated bibliography of sources on test report writing.

6. Devise a workshop for teaching people in the helping professions to improve their test report writing skills.

7. Critique several computerized test reports.

8. Read over the following case and answer the questions at the end.

Yvonne was evaluated with the following instruments: Differential Aptitude Test, Myers-Briggs Type Indicator, FIRO-B, Strong Interest Inventory, Self-Directed Search, 16 PF, COP-System Interest Inventory.

Yvonne scored at the 80th percentile on the verbal section of the DAT, which suggested that her capability to understand ideas expressed in words and her ability to think and reason with words is above average. She scored at the 40th percentile on the numerical section of the instrument. This suggests that her numerical capability is average.

She was a ISFJ (Introverted, Sensing, Feeling, Judging) on the Myers-Briggs and can be characterized as being systematic, painstaking, and thorough. This type of individual is very hard-working and adapts well to facts.

On the FIRO-B her scores suggest that she operates within a select or exclusive group of friends. She may be somewhat uncomfortable in social situations, especially if she is not familiar with the people.

Her interest inventory scores indicate that she appears to have general interests in medical service, social service, writing, communication, sales, politics, and business management.

Her 16PF results indicate that she would like to excel in activities of a journalistic nature including writer, editor, and reporter.

Yvonne is a middle-aged woman with a college degree in Christian Education and minors in Speech and English. Her interest in academic areas is very high. Her aptitude scores suggest that she can be successful in advanced college work, especially if she remediates math areas. She seems to be a woman who is selective of the company she keeps.

Specific occupations that may be suitable to Yvonne include broadcast work, print media, writing editor, reporter, media specialist, guidance counselor, social worker, special education teacher, speech pathologist, English teacher, recreation leader, nurse, physician's assistant, emergency medical technician, nursing home administrator, travel agent, salesperson, human resource worker, or school administrator.

a. What problems do you find in this report?
b. What needs to be done to improve this report?
c. What additional information about Yvonne would you like to have?
d. For whom do you think the report was written?

ADDITIONAL READINGS

Fisher, C. T. (1985). *Individualized psychological assessment*. Monterey, CA: Brooks/Cole.

Fisher describes the individualized approach in testing and provides sample reports and information on report writing.

Flesch, R. (1972). *Say what you mean*. New York: Harper and Row.

Flesch, R. (1974). *The art of readable writing* (25th ed.). New York: Harper and Row.

These two books review effective writing skills and techniques to aid in more organized, direct, and interesting report writing.

Katz, L. (1991). *A practical guide to psychodiagnostic testing* (2nd ed.). Springfield, IL: Charles C. Thomas.

The guide has an excellent chapter on writing test reports.

Ownby, R. L. (1990). *Psychological reports: A guide to report writing in professional psychology* (2nd ed.). Brandon, VT: CPPC.

Ownby provides guidelines for writing psychological reports and provides several illustrative examples.

Tallent, N. (1993). *Psychological report writing* (4th ed.). Englewood Cliffs, NJ: Prentice Hall.

The book provides an excellent discussion on the purposes and context of the psychological report and covers topics such as pitfalls in reporting, responsibility, effectiveness, the content of psychological reports, and conceptualizing the psychological report.

Zuckerman, E. L. (1991). *The clinician's thesaurus: A guidebook for writing psychological reports and their evaluations* (2nd ed.). Brandon, VT: CPPC.

The book helps test administrators identify appropriate questions to elicit information about specific symptomatic behavior in the mental, cognitive, and emotional domains.

CHAPTER 24

Legal and Ethical Concerns and Issues in Testing

Overview

Codes of ethics provide a framework for responsible test use. There are probably as many codes of ethics as there are professional societies but to become dynamic helping professionals, individuals must be committed to the ethical standards of their profession and follow them in their practice. A code of ethics expresses the values on which helping professionals build their practice. The American Psychological Association code (1992) includes six general principles: to maintain high competence in one's work; promote integrity in the science, teaching, and practice of psychology; uphold professional standards of conduct and accept responsibility for one's behavior; afford appropriate respect to the fundamental rights, dignity, and worth of all people; contribute to the welfare of those with whom one interacts professionally; and be aware of one's professional and scientific responsibilities to the community and the society in which one works and lives. These principles are translated into specific ethical standards and principles, which will be the focus of this chapter.

There are also a number of laws both on the state and national level that affect testing and testing practices. Professionals need to be familiar with the laws as well as with the court decisions that interpret them.

Objectives

After reading this chapter, the reader should be able to

* list and discuss the major codes of professional ethics as to how they apply to tests and testing practices
* compare and contrast the commonalties and differences among the different codes
* identify the important federal and state legislation that affects tests and testing practices
* discuss the court decisions and their impact on tests and testing practices
* demonstrate knowledge of legal and ethical issues in evaluation and assessment

NBCC CODE OF ETHICS

The National Board of Certified Counselors (NBCC) (1989) identifies in Section C of their code 15 standards dealing with measurement and evaluation. The first deals logically with orientation. The counselor must provide orientation to the examinee prior to and following administration of assessment instruments. In the orientation the counselors must inform the client of the explicit use of the test results.

The counselor is responsible for the appropriate selection of the assessment instruments to be used. The counselor must ensure the validity and reliability of the instrument. Instruments that are biased or otherwise inappropriate will provide invalid information for decision making.

The counselor must be guarded when making statements to the public about specific instruments and techniques. False claims and unwarranted connotations often result from misunderstanding or poor communication.

Counselors must recognize their limitations and only perform techniques or administer assessment instruments for which they have received appropriate training.

Counselors must record when tests are not administered under standard conditions or when irregularities or unusual behavior arise during testing. The behavior might invalidate the results. The code deems unsupervised or inadequately supervised tests as not meeting ethical standards. The exception to this are tests such as interest inventories, which are often designed to be self-administered and self-scored.

Counselors must maintain test security. Coaching and dissemination of test items and materials can invalidate the test results. Counselors, however, must discuss the conditions that might provide more favorable results such as telling test takers that they can guess without any penalty.

Counselors must understand the technical limitations of an instrument when interpreting the results. Counselors need to schedule periodic review and/or retesting of the client to help prevent stereotyping.

The counselor must be concerned about the welfare of the test takers. Who receives the results and how they will be used are important considerations. Interpretations must be made in the light of any limitations in the instruments or norming group.

Computer-generated test administration and scoring programs may be utilized if the counselor is sure that this type of testing will provide the client with accurate results. Computer-based interpretations must be checked for validity by developers before being marketed.

Counselors utilizing tests or making decisions based on test results need appropriate training and skills in educational and psychological measurement, validation criteria, test research, and guidelines for test development and use.

If the tests report insufficient technical data, counselors must explicitly state to examinees the specific purposes for the use of such instruments and why they are being used.

Counselors need to be cautious when evaluating or interpreting the performances of minority group members or other individuals not represented in the standardized sample. Counselors need to recognize that test results only give a picture of the test taker at one moment in time and may become obsolete.

AMERICAN PSYCHOLOGICAL ASSOCIATION STANDARDS

The American Psychological Association (APA) (1992) lists 10 standards for evaluation, diagnosis, and intervention. The first is that psychologists should only perform evaluations, diagnostic services, or interventions within the context of a defined professional relationship and that their assessments, recommendations, and reports are based on information and techniques—such as interviewing test takers—sufficient to substantiate their findings.

The second standard relates to the psychologist having competence in tests and assessment techniques that are used and selecting appropriate instruments and techniques for assessment. The psychologist is to refrain from misusing techniques, results, and interventions and is to prevent others from misusing the information these test results provide.

If psychologists are involved in test development, they are responsible for conducting research with tests and other assessment techniques using scientific procedures and current professional knowledge for test design, standardization, validation, reduction of bias, and recommendations for use.

The fourth standard deals with the use of assessment in general and special populations. Besides proper interpretation, psychologists should recognize the limitations to the certainty with which they diagnose or make judgments or predictions about individuals. They need to consider that in some situations they might be required to adjust administration or interpretation because of factors such as the age, gender, national origin, religion, sexual orientation, disability, language, or socioeconomic status of the individual.

Psychologists must consider the various characteristics of the individual being assessed that might affect their judgments or reduce the accuracy of their interpretation.

They also have a responsibility of not promoting the use of psychological assessment techniques by unqualified examiners.

The freshness of results is a factor. Psychologists do not base their assessment, intervention decisions, or recommendations on outdated test results and measures that are not useful for the current purpose.

Individuals offering assessment or scoring services to other professionals have the obligation to make sure their procedures are appropriate, valid, and reliable.

Results need to be explained in a language that can be understood by the individual being assessed. Appropriate explanations of results must be given by the psychologists.

The last standard holds the psychologist responsible for making reasonable efforts to maintain the integrity and security of tests and other assessment techniques consistent with the law, contractual obligations, and the code of ethics.

ACA CODE OF ETHICS

The American Counseling Association (ACA) (1993) likewise has a code of ethics and with a specific section on measurement and evaluation. The preamble reminds counselors that the primary purpose of educational and psychological testing is to provide descriptive measures that are objective and interpretable in either comparative or absolute terms. Counselors must recognize that there are a wide variety of assessment procedures and that test results provide only one of many sources of information for counseling decisions. The standards are similar to those of the APA and NBCC. Standards deal with orientation; test selection; dissemination of results to the public; competence in administration, scoring, and interpretation; following standardized procedures in test administration; problems of prior coaching; the purpose of testing and the explicit prior understanding of the client; cautious evaluation and interpretation of the performance of minority group members or others not represented in the norming group; and unauthorized reproduction or modifications of tests without the permission of the author and publisher. Counselors are also reminded that they need to be cautious when interpreting the results of a research instrument without sufficient data on its validity, reliability, and interpretability.

CODES OF PROFESSIONAL RESPONSIBILITY

A number of professional responsibility codes have been developed by organizations or consortia concerned with measurement and assessment issues. NCME (1993) published Draft 3 of a Code of Professional Responsibility (CPR) in Educational Assessment. An ad hoc committee of the National Council of Measurement in Education developed the code to promote professionally responsible practices in educational assessment.

The CPR provides a framework of eight major areas of assessment standards that need to be addressed, including responsibilities of those who

1. select assessment products and services
2. market and sell assessment products and services
3. educate others about assessment
4. develop assessment products and services
5. administer assessments
6. score assessments
7. interpret, use, and communicate assessment results
8. evaluate programs and conduct research on assessments

Each section includes more specific standards. In section 7, for example, those who interpret, use, and communicate assessment results are to provide all needed information about the assessment, its purposes, and its uses for the proper interpretation of the results; provide an understandable discussion of all reported scores, including proper interpretations; promote the use of multiple sources of information about persons or programs in making educational decisions; communicate the adequacy and appropriateness of any norms or standards being used in the interpretation of assessment results; discourage unsubstantiated claims, inappropriate interpretations, or otherwise false and misleading statements about assessment results and any likely misinterpretations; and lastly protect the rights of privacy for individuals and institutions.

NCME and the American Association of School Administrators, the National Association of Elementary School Principals, and the National Association of Secondary School Principals (1994) have developed a set of standards for administrator training programs that utilize ethical standards as one criterion for determining competency. Administrators are to demonstrate a working knowledge of the Competency Standards in Student Assessment. One key element in this first standard is the ability to recognize unethical, illegal, and otherwise inappropriate assessment methods and uses of assessment information. As with other standards, the administrator is to understand and be able to apply the basic concepts of assessment and measurement theory; understand the purposes of different kinds of assessment (i.e., achievement, ability, and diagnostic); understand measurement terminology and be able to express that terminology in nontechnical terms; recognize appropriate and inappropriate uses of assessment techniques or results and understand and follow ethical guidelines for assessment; know the mechanics of constructing various types of assessment that are both appropriate and useful; interpret and use assessment information appropriately; know how interpretations of assessments may be moderated by students' socioeconomic, cultural, linguistic, and other background factors; be able to evaluate an assessment strategy or program; and finally be able to utilize computer-based assessment tools that collect input, mediating, and outcome variables that are related to student learning, instruction, and performance.

Throughout this text, references have been made to some of the other major sources of professional codes for test users such as the Standards for Educational and Psychological Testing, the Code of Fair Testing Practices in Education, and the Responsibilities of Users of Standardized Tests. A list of some of the major codes follow.

American Association for Counseling and Development (now American Counseling Association) and the Association for Measurement and Evaluation in Counseling and Development (now the Association for Assessment in Counseling) (1989). *Responsibilities of Users of Standardized Tests*. Alexandria, VA: Author.

American Educational Research Association (1992). *Ethical standards of the American Educational Research Association*. Educational Researcher, *21*(7), October 1992.

American Educational Research Association, American Psychological Association, National Council on Measurement in Education (1995). *Standards for Educational and Psychological Tests*. Washington, DC: Author.

Joint Committee on Testing Practices (1988). *Code of Fair Testing Practices in Education*. Washington, DC: Author.

National Association of College Admission Counselors (1988). *Statement of Principles of Good Practice*. Alexandria, VA: Author.

RESPONSIBLE TEST USE

In each of the following situations, read the scenario and decide what ethical standards are in question.

1. The Browns decide to start a computerized dating service and mail to the clients the NEO Personality Inventory. They score the tests and match clients on the basis of their personality types, using the premise that opposites attract when they match the profiles. The clients are sent a profile sheet of their test results.

2. Jean came to the United States last year from Poland and had been staying with his relatives in New York. He was hit by a taxi crossing a street and had a concussion and other possible head injuries. His lawyer wanted a psychological evaluation. Although Jean was not fluent in English, the examiner administered the Luria-Nebraska Neuropsychological Battery.

3. Robin learned that the CDC Company used the 16PF for screening customer representatives and decided to get a copy of the test and manual to study before applying for the position. Robin called and found out that she had to complete a form to be registered with the company and get the material. She knew that she did not have the qualifications so she asked one of her professors to order the materials for her. Robin studied the test and scoring keys and decided how she would answer the test questions to look like the right type of person for the job.

4. A psychology professor has convinced the student services committee to give all
    new freshmen the MMPI-2. During orientation week, all were administered the
    test but not told its purpose, only that they would be required to take a wide
    variety of types of tests including achievement, aptitude, interest, and personal-
    ity. The professor had some student assistants score the tests. He found that he
    had no time to review the results, so he simply had the test information filed in
    students' cumulative folders.

LEGAL ASPECTS

Counselors not only need to keep up-to-date on current legislation that affects their
practice; they also must keep current with the decisions made in the courts. A number of major pieces of legislation have had implications for testing practices and procedures. Legal rights come from not only the Constitution of the United States, state
constitutions, federal and state laws, but also from interpretations by the courts. This
section briefly discusses some of the major pieces of federal legislation, followed by
some important court decisions brought by individuals or groups who believed they
had been harmed by testing practices.

Family Educational Rights and Privacy Act of 1974 (Buckley Amendment)

The Family Educational Rights and Privacy Act of 1974 protects parents' right to
examine their children's academic records and stipulated the terms under which
others may have access to them. If there is test information in the records, parents
have a right to see these scores as well.

Public Law 94-142

Public Law 94-142 was passed by congress and signed into law on November 25,
1975. The legislation was an effort to reduce the disparities in education opportunities between exceptional children and nonexceptional children. The law directs educators to develop extensive identification procedures, provide special education in
the least restrictive environment, ensure nondiscriminatory testing and evaluation,
and form individualized programs for each handicapped child. The law was passed
to ensure all handicapped children have access to an appropriate education and
related services to meet their unique needs, to ensure protection of their rights, and
to assist schools in providing that education.

The law required that parents give their consent before a child is tested. Parents
must be fully informed of all information relevant to the activity for which consent is
sought in their native language or other mode of communication. Parents must be
fully informed about a particular test to be given and agree in writing to the proce-

dure. Parents have the right to inspect the test protocols. Parents are entitled to inspect and review the educational records of their child related to identification, evaluation, and placement.

Tests and other evaluation materials must be in the child's native language or other mode of communication, unless it is clearly not feasible to do so. The tests must have been validated for the specific purpose for which they are used. Tests have to be administered by trained personnel in conformance with instructions provided by test authors and publishers. Tests must be chosen and administered to ensure that they will accurately reflect a handicapped child's aptitude and achievement level. The philosophy and practice call for multiple criteria in determining appropriate placement. Evaluation must be done by a multidisciplinary team including at least one teacher or other specialist with knowledge of the area of disability. The child is assessed in all areas related to the suspected disability.

Public Law 98-524

Public Law 98-524, the Carl D. Perkins Vocational and Technical Act, was passed by congress and signed into law on October 19, 1984. It was designed to ensure that individuals who are inadequately served under vocational education programs—especially individuals who are disadvantaged or handicapped, men and women entering nontraditional occupations, adults in need of training and retraining, single parents or homemakers, individuals with limited English proficiency, and individuals incarcerated in correctional institutions. The law extended the provisions of the Vocational Educational Act of 1963 by mandating vocational assessment, counseling, support, and transitional services for students identified as handicapped and disadvantaged. "Disadvantaged" was limited to economic and academic, rather than cultural.

Public Law 101-476

Public Law 101-476, The Education of the Handicapped Act Amendments of 1990, was signed into law on October 30, 1990, and was later renamed the Individuals with Disabilities Education Act (IDEA). The act focuses on helping youth with disabilities in the transition from school to vocational rehabilitation, employment, postsecondary education, work, or adult services. Parents have access to all relevant records concerning the identification, evaluation, and educational placement of the child. Parents also have the opportunity to obtain their own independent educational evaluation of the child.

Public Law 101-336

Public Law 101-336, or the Americans with Disabilities Act (ADA), was passed by congress and signed into law on July 26, 1990. The law broadly expands the civil rights laws that apply to women and minorities to more than 43 million Americans who have some form of disability. The law has certain provisions related to testing. Under the reasonable accommodation section, it states

> A private entity offering an examination is responsible for selecting and administering the examination in a place and manner than ensures that the examination accurately reflects an individual's aptitude and achievement level, or other factors the examination purports to measure, rather than reflecting an individual's impaired sensory, manual, or speaking skills, except where those skills are factors that the examination purports to measure.

The test must assess an essential requirement of the job. The test would be invalid if the particular disability would adversely affect test performance on an employment test. Accommodating individuals with disabilities on tests is not necessarily a simple process. Fischer (1994) points out that to comply with ADA, individually modified forms of the standard instrument must be prepared to accommodate a disabled examinee and although the ADA requires reasonable accommodation, the code of ethics and standards for testing requires a much higher standard if the resulting tests scores are to be meaningful (p. 23).

EMPLOYMENT LAWS

Title VII of the Civil Rights Act of 1964 as amended in 1972, 1978, and 1991 outlaws discrimination in employment based on race, color, religion, gender, pregnancy, or national origin. The Age Discrimination in Employment Act of 1967 outlaws discrimination against those who are 40 and above. The Equal Pay Act of 1967 outlaws discrimination in pay based on the gender of the worker and the Vietnam Era Veterans Readjustment Act of 1974 outlaws discrimination against Vietnam era veterans.

The Tower amendment to the Equal Employment Act (1966) provides that an employer may give and act upon the results of

> any professionally developed ability test provided that such test is not designed, intended or used to discriminate because of race. Professionally developed ability test is defined to mean a test which fairly measures the knowledge or skills required by the particular job or class of jobs which the applicant seeks or which fairly affords the employer a chance to measure the applicant's ability to perform a particular job or class of jobs. (Equal Opportunity Commission, 1966)

In 1970 the EEOC redefined discrimination in terms of the effects of selection procedures resulting in adverse impact. Any paper-and-pencil or performance measure including all formal, scored, quantified, or standardized techniques used as a basis for any employment decision that adversely affects hiring, promotion, transfer, or any other employment or membership opportunity of classes protected by Title VII constitutes discrimination unless the test has been validated and evidences a high degree of utility and the person giving or acting on the results can demonstrate that alternative suitable hiring, transfer, or promotion procedures are unavailable.

The Civil Rights Act of 1991 prohibits score adjustment or differential test cutoffs by race. Congress saw score adjustment as violating the principle of fairness.

COURT DECISIONS ON EDUCATIONAL TESTING

Following are a few of the major court decisions on the use of testing in education.

Larry P. v. Riles (1974, 1979, 1984) involved as plaintiffs black elementary school students from the San Francisco United School district who claimed that they had been improperly placed in classes for the educable mentally retarded. The placement had been made on the basis of their scores on an intelligence test that they claimed was inappropriate for use with black students. The district EMR students were 28.5% white and 66% black. The court concluded that the schools had been using an inappropriate test for the placement of blacks in EMR programs and that the test could not be used. The school in the future would have to submit a written statement declaring that tests were not discriminatory and had been validated for EMR placement decisions and provide the statistics on the scores of the students and African-American students.

Diana v. California State Board of Education (1973, 1979) concerned the appropriate use of intelligence tests with Mexican-American students. These students tended to score poorly and were placed in EMR classes. The out-of-court agreement required the schools to test students both in their first language and in English and restricted the administration of many of the verbal sections of the tests.

Debra P. v. Turlington (1979, 1981, 1983, 1984) questioned the fairness of the Florida State Student Assessment Test. The plaintiffs, 10 African-American students, argued that they had been denied due process because they had not been given adequate time to prepare for the test and that the test was used to segregate students by race. The court found the test was not discriminatory. The court concluded that it was the responsibility of the school systems when using a test for granting high school diplomas to show that the test covers only material that was actually taught to the students.

Sharif v. New York State Educational Department (1989) concerned the use of Scholastic Aptitude Test (SAT) scores as the sole basis for awarding state merit scholarships. The plaintiffs claimed that the state was discriminating against girls who were competing for the award. The court ruled that New York could not use the SAT scores alone as a basis for awarding scholarships and needed to have other criteria such as grades or some statewide achievement test data.

COURT DECISIONS ON EMPLOYMENT TESTING

Some of the major court decisions related to tests and testing practices include:

United States v. Georgia Power (1973) first acknowledged the possibility of the unreliability of differential validity.

Griggs v. Duke Power Company (1971) required a two-step process for the case to be considered by the courts. First, the plaintiff has to establish a prima facie case of discrimination. Second, the employer must establish that the test is a "reasonable measure of job performance." A paper-and-pencil test given to prospective coal handlers was struck down.

Washington v. Davis (1976) accepted a selection rule with an adverse impact because the test predicted final marks in police training and was a logical criterion measure.

Bakke v. California (1978) struck down the quota system for minority groups in professional schools.

Golden Rule Insurance Company v. Richard L. Mathias (1980) focused on the out-of-court agreement between the Educational Testing Service and the Golden Rule Insurance Company. The plaintiffs claimed that the test developed by ETS used to license insurance agents was not job-related and unfairly discriminated against blacks.

Contreras v. City of Los Angeles (1981) held that the employer's burden is satisfied by showing it used professionally acceptable methods and that the test was predictive or significantly correlated with important elements of work behavior that comprised or were relevant to the job.

Berkman v. City of New York (1987) struck down an arbitrary conversion process to enhance scores for female firefighter applicants even though the underlying tests did not predict job performance.

Watson v. Fort Worth Bank and Trust (1988) ruled that adverse impact does not apply to subjective criteria. The plaintiff had to identify a specific criterion that produces an adverse impact and show reliable and probative statistical evidence to support an inference of discrimination. The employer needs only to offer a legitimate business reason for the criterion. Employers are not required even when defending standardized tests to introduce formal validation studies showing that particular criteria predict actual on-the-job performance.

Questions and Procedures

Cronbach (1984) identified three crucial questions that need to be considered in using tests in employment contexts.

1. Can an adverse impact be shown such as a greater rejection rate for eligible blacks than for eligible whites?

2. Is the selection rule valid? Was it used as the basis of selection for the job? Are the criterion, content, and construct validity available?

3. Can an alternative selection procedure be used that has less impact?

The Golden Rule Procedure, named for the court case described earlier, calls for simple but specifically prescribed procedures for item analysis, item selection, and monitoring the results of the testing program for minority groups. Ethnic and racial data are collected on the candidates who take the test, and analysis of the test items is completed separately by race or ethnic group and educational level. The percentage of each group passing the items is used to classify the test items. Items for which the correct answer rates of ethnic or minority groups and white examinees are most similar have priority for inclusion on the test. The procedure calls for ongoing analysis of the test items and emphasizes keeping the reading level no higher than grade 12 ability.

CURRENT TRENDS AND PERSPECTIVES

Employers are showing increased sensitivity in how they use tests for hiring purposes; they do not want to be charged with discrimination and unfair practices. Because employers must go through elaborate validation and documentation procedures when they use tests for selection purposes, the use of tests for those purposes has declined. However, the use of tests for certification and licensing purposes has increased.

Tenopyr (1981) concludes that employment testing has been a storm of controversy because of its association with the civil rights movement. She points out that there are problems with fairness models because employers cannot afford to use different tests for various subgroups or interpret tests differently for each group.

SUMMARY

For the past three decades, employment and school testing have been the focus of controversy. Laws and court decisions have had an impact on testing practice. The overall effect has probably been fairer tests and testing practices for minority groups. The role of tests is constantly being redefined by the courts. Helping professionals need to be guided by the code of ethics of their organization, be familiar with the laws and court interpretations, and be careful, critical consumers of assessment practices and procedures.

QUESTIONS FOR DISCUSSION

1. Many employment test experts believe that the guidelines from the courts and legislatures are outdated and make costly demands on employers that are not justified by the latest research. Do you agree or disagree with this position? Why?

2. Do you think that equity for minority group members can be obtained through item selection by test makers following the golden rule procedures? Are the golden rule procedures a threat to the validity of the test? Why or why not?

3. Are codes of ethics something every group advocates but very few members follow?

4. What position would you take if your code of professional ethics conflicted with a recent ruling of the court?

5. Do you feel ethical behavior is more situation-specific than a general trait?

SUGGESTED ACTIVITIES

1. Interview the affirmative action officer at your place of work or at the school you are attending. What are his views on testing? Report your findings to the class.

2. Make a content analysis of two or three of the codes of ethics as they relate to testing. How are they alike? How are they different?

3. Stage a mock trial on one of the major issues in testing such as due process, appropriateness of certain tests for a particular function, misuse of tests, appropriateness of a certain test for a minority group member, and the like.

4. Discuss some of the cases presented in the Responsible Test Use section.

5. Do legal research and see if any cases in your local court system involved testing issues.

6. Study the following cases and answer the questions at the end of each.

A private liberal arts college was working toward getting regional accreditation. The school had usually admitted a large percentage of their students from the bottom half of their high school class, including any student who had a 2.00 on a 4.00 scale. The college did not require the SAT or ACT. The admissions committee was under pressure to increase the academic respectability of the college by changing the standards to require the scores of 400 on both the verbal and quantitative sections of the Scholastic Aptitude Test. The committee was told that enrollment would increase if the school used an established assessment test and that fewer students would drop out.

a. What are the testing issues in this situation?
b. What factors or testing practices are involved?
c. If you were a consultant invited by the college to help the admissions committee in the selection and retention of students, what would you advise?

To remain competitive, Memorial Hospital has decided they need to cut its budget by downsizing, especially semiskilled workers such as orderlies, custodians, cafeteria personnel, stock room clerks, file room clerks, and similar positions. The hospital would like to help these workers qualify for higher level jobs and to remain with the organization. From the attrition rate, the hospital administrators know they will need workers with advanced technical skills and will have to recruit from the outside to fill these positions if they have no one qualified internally. The personnel department has decided to give all the targeted workers who will lose their position the Wide Range Achievement Test and the Wonderlick and select those with the highest scores to be retrained. Eighty percent of the workers are women and minority group members.

a. What are the ethical and legal issues related to this case?
b. What testing factors are involved?
c. If you were a consultant hired by the hospital to help identify workers to be retrained and do outplacement counseling for those who are to be let go, what would you advise Memorial to do?

ADDITIONAL READINGS

American Psychological Association. (1993). *Responsible test use. Case studies for assessing human behavior*. Washington, DC: Test User Training Work Group of the Joint Committee on Testing Practices.

The workbook contains 78 cases to train professionals to use tests wisely. Cases are from seven different settings ranging from counseling to speech-language-hearing contexts and cover 86 elements of proper test use.

Tucker, B. P., & Goldstein, B. A. (1991). *The educational rights of children with disabilities. A guide to federal law*. Horsham, PA: LRP Publications.

The authors provide an overview of the Education for All Handicapped Children Act. Chapter 15 lists the procedures for testing and evaluation.

CHAPTER 25

Current Trends and Issues

Overview

The public perspective toward testing has changed many times during this century. People are concerned about the use of testing and its consequences. Glaser and Bond (1981) argue that changes have been stimulated by legal, social, political, and scientific advances. Plake and Witt (1986) conclude that the field of testing and measurement is a conservative science that has experienced many advances in technology. There are seeds for change as evidenced by the fairness in testing and authentic assessment movements. Glaser and Bond (1981) point out that creative advances in knowledge result from unrestricted free inquiry. Indeed, the critics of testing have demanded changes that were positive and needed.

Objectives

This chapter should enable the reader to identify

- some of the current trends and issues in testing
- some of the future trends and issues in testing

MINIMUM COMPETENCY TESTING

Minimum level competency testing is a movement that has focused not only on public education but on all areas of education and life. More than 800 occupations and professions require licensing or minimum level competency examinations (Shimberg, 1982). On the state, federal, and professional levels licensing boards administer these programs, operating on the premise that

1. a test can be a satisfactory measure of competence
2. a particular test measures critical and important abilities, knowledge, and skills necessary to perform a particular job at the minimum level of competency
3. the test is capable of screening out those who lack the necessary level of competence

Lerner (1981) concluded that the minimum level competency program in education was a genuine grass-roots movement. Florida and Georgia were the first two states to establish minimum competency programs. In the 1980s, 49 states had such programs. Currently 46 states have state-wide testing programs. Thirty-four use standardized norm-reference tests. Some use both, because 34 states also use criterion-referenced tests. Passing such state tests is a requirement for high school graduation in 18 states (Burger & Burger, 1994).

It is easy to see why minimum competency testing came to be thought of as a solution. The 1983 report by the National Commission on Excellency in Education presents relevant information.

1. About 75 million adults are considered functionally illiterate as measured by tests of everyday reading, writing, and comprehension.
2. About 13% of all 17-year-olds are functionally illiterate—as many as 40% in minority groups.
3. Scores on the College Board Scholastic Aptitude Test have declined from 1963 to 1980. The average verbal score fell more than 50 points, and the average mathematics score nearly 40 points.
4. The number and proportion of students who demonstrate superior achievement have declined.
5. Many 17-year-olds lack higher cognitive skills. About 40% cannot draw inferences from written material, only 20% were able to write a persuasive essay, and only 33% could solve a mathematics problem requiring several steps.
6. Between 1975 and 1980, 25% of all mathematics courses were remedial, an increase of 72%.
7. Business, industry, and military leaders state they are to spend millions of dollars on remedial education and training programs. (pp. 8–9)

Minimum competency testing programs have some common characteristics that have been summarized by Pipho (1978). The tests emphasize the acquisition of minimum skills or competencies, most often academic skills such as reading, mathematics, and writing and/or survival skills such as following directions, filling out an employment application, or balancing a checkbook. An absolute performance for pass-fail decisions is set so that the examiner can separate the competent from incompetent candidates. The tests are used for educational and instructional decisions about an individual—graduation, promotion, retention, or appropriate instructional strategies.

An excellent summary of the pros and cons of minimum competency testing is found in Perkins's (1982) article published by the National Council on Measurement in Education. She lists 26 benefits and 24 costs. Because we have already identified benefits, we will list here some of the disadvantages.

1. Leads to an erosion of liberal education

2. Leads to teaching for the test

3. Promotes further stigmatization of the underachiever

4. Encourages labeling of students

5. Causes more dropouts

6. Places the burden of failure on students

7. Ignores the needs of gifted students and average students by emphasizing minimum standards

The National Commission on Testing and Public Policy (1990) found that too many tests emphasized lower-order thinking skills and are devouring valuable instructional time. Pressure to show improved reading and mathematics scores tends to turn teaching these critical subjects into test preparation. Students read isolated paragraphs and practice answering questions. Tests should measure what students are ready to learn next, not what they are unable to learn. Testing practices are changing from multiple choice to alternate assessment procedures so that higher-order thinking skills can be assessed. Goals for Blueprint 2000 emphasize the importance of students being able to use higher-order cognitive skills.

Other issues related to minimum competency testing include possible bias against various groups and a question of whether students with disabilities should be expected to meet the same standards as other students. Hambleton and Eignor (1980) have identified five trouble spots in minimum competency testing. These are: identifying the set of competencies, establishing the performance standard, collecting appropriate validity evidence, computing the reliability of scores and decisions, and equating the scores on alternate test forms.

About 68% of the states in 1990 required minimum competency testing for teachers, responding to the public belief that colleges and universities in some cases have granted diplomas to graduates who were not competent. Teacher competency tests can include basic skills, instructional content, and teaching methodology. In Florida, principals have been required to pass a competency test since 1987.

Georgia, one of the first states to initiate this testing, has dropped performance-based tests for teachers. Viadero (1990) reports that of the 30,000 teachers who took the test, 99% of the teachers passed. Two hundred failed it six times—the maximum number of tries. Another 13% quit before taking it six times. The test is not considered redundant, since principals conduct yearly on-the-job assessments of teachers.

The testing programs have been a target for legal cases. *Debra P. v. Turlington* called for the state to demonstrate that the competencies measured were actually part of classroom instruction in Florida. As of 1990, 47 of the 50 states have statewide student testing and about half of the states have expanded their programs to include more grades, subject areas, and higher-order skills.

The public currently supports minimum competency testing; opposition to it is equated with support for incompetency. Berk (1986) concludes:

> These trends in minimum competency testing and competency-based education during the past decade strongly indicate that public pressure will continue and probably intensify in the 1990s. The state mandates for educational change demand immediate action and long-term planning, at least until the discontent over incompetence has abated and the meaning of the high school diploma has been restored.

LICENSURE AND CERTIFICATION EXAMINATIONS

As was pointed out previously, licensing and certification examinations have been related to the minimum competency movement; they now constitute a major use of testing in our country. The purpose of this testing is to ensure that applicants have the knowledge and skill for practice in their fields. Most programs require successful completion of an approved educational program. The examination then provides an additional check on the preparation of the candidates for licensing. The examination also provides an external check on the quality of educational programs and forces some schools to improve their curriculum. In addition, candidates are often required to provide evidence of good character and knowledge of ethics in their fields.

The validity of these examinations is a crucial issue. Kane (1986) points out "the interpretation of licensure examination scores as predictors of future performance in practice is appealing because it implies a high degree of utility for the licensure process" (p. 155). Kane sees two important components of validity—the need for evidence that the abilities measured are crucial for practice in the field, and the need for test scores to reflect competence in the critical abilities identified as crucial for the job.

Establishing valid criteria that can be generalized to cover the wide variety of licensure situations fairly is a technical problem that requires more research. Conversely, the fact that many applicants may test well does not necessarily mean they will perform a job well if they do not use their knowledge and skills effectively.

Kane (1986) considers licensure a matter of public policy, shaped by public expectations. He identifies five questions relevant to policy decisions about licensing examinations.

1. What types of situations occur most frequently in practice or have the most serious potential consequences?

2. What abilities, including knowledge and skills, are needed to deal with these situations effectively?

3. How well are these abilities taught and assessed in educational programs preparing practitioners?

4. How well does the examination assess competencies in critical abilities, and what sources of variance other than differences in competence (e.g., reading level, response bias) influence examination scores?

5. What are the implications of setting standards at different levels? (p. 179)

The public will probably demand even more examinations and will want more input into the activities of the licensing and certifying agencies.

TRUTH IN TESTING

The truth in testing movement was a product of the 1970s, partly motivated by the accountability movement. Proponents believe that the test makers should be more accountable for the intellectual quality and social consequences of the tests they produce. New York passed a law on truth in testing (effective in 1980) that required disclosure of the questions and answers determining examinees' scores on postsecondary and professional admissions tests within 30 days of the release of the test scores. Nader's report on the Educational Testing Service (ETS) (Nairn, 1980) stimulated interest in this legislation. The authors concluded that ETS has not protected and represented the public interest. They also found that admissions tests such as the SAT have little predictive validity for how well students will do in school and noted such tests are biased against minority groups and students from lower socioeconomic levels. Their findings also indicated that coaching can help boost test scores on aptitude and admissions tests.

Most professional testing organizations were opposed to the legislation. The APA Committee on Psychological Tests and Assessment raised two areas of concern—disclosure of items from low-volume tests or tests with finite items and test interpretation that depends on a long history of research. The truth-in-testing law has possibly been expensive for test publishers, but it has led to more positive public attitudes toward testing.

INVASION OF PRIVACY

Invasion of privacy has been one of the major issues in testing. Some people are concerned about the confidentiality of the results. Others are offended by some of the questions, and still others are concerned about how the questions will be used. Some individuals feel that they are coerced into responding to items if their school or company gives the test. Computer-assisted and adaptive testing and computer data banks and retrieval systems have renewed interest in this issue.

Legal statutes and current standards of professional organizations remind us of the rights of the test taker. Tests are not to include questions that require the client to reveal these kinds of information:

1. Political affiliation
2. Mental and psychological problems potentially embarrassing to the client and his family
3. Sexual behavior and attitudes
4. Illegal, antisocial, self-incriminating, and demeaning behavior
5. Critical appraisals of individuals with whom respondents have close family relationships
6. Legally recognized privileges and analogous relationships, such as those of lawyers, physicians, and ministers
7. Income (Public Law 95–561)

The public is concerned about the type of information gathered, its use, and its storage. Ethical procedures require informed consent before tests are given, an explanation of why the tests are administered, the type of information they yield, who will get a copy of the results, and how the information will be stored or filed.

FAIRNESS TO MINORITY GROUPS

One of the major concerns with admissions, achievement, and intelligence testing has been the question of fairness to minority groups. A disproportionate number of minority students do achieve low or failing scores on minimum competency examinations, and earn lower scores on the SAT. Mehrens and Lehman (1986) state, "If a test does tend to discriminate (differentiate) between races, sexes, or other subcultures, and if the differential scores are not related to what is being predicted (such as on-the-job success), then the test is unfair" (p. 471). This issue has been raised not only in the area of selection for higher education and in minimum competency testing, but also in employment testing. Some of the key issues were discussed in Chapter 24.

Testing requirements for athletes have been the subject of some controversy. The NCAA requirements in 1994 were a combined SAT of 700 or an ACT of 17 with a grade point average of 2.00 to be eligible to participate in college sports.

A 1969 article by Arthur Jensen stimulated much debate; he stated that "genetic factors are strongly implicated in the average Negro-White intelligence difference" (p. 82). Herrnstein (1971) and currently in his book *The Bell Curve* (1994) also concluded that data on IQ and social class differences indicated a pattern of inherited stratification. Nonetheless, the items on IQ tests are criticized for being unfair to minority groups. And some states, such as California, have banned the use of IQ tests in making assignments to special education classes. The relative importance of heredity and environment will continue to be debated as steps are taken through test development and student intervention to eliminate bias and improve minority group performance on tests.

Girls are also seen as being discriminated against on the Scholastic Aptitude Tests. A disproportionately small number of females are semifinalists on the National Merit Examination also.

HOSTILE GATEKEEPER

The National Commission on Testing and Public Policy calls for a broad overhaul of educational and employment tests. The commission argues that tests developed to screen out students and job applicants are inconsistent with today's best policies. Our current testing system has been labeled by a Ford Foundation-funded study as a "hostile gatekeeper." The report concludes that schools and businesses are increasingly relying on multiple-choice tests to make critical judgments about individuals and institutions, causing limited opportunity particularly for women and minority groups. The report calls for schools and businesses to shift to alternate forms of assessment to measure performance. They also advocate a national board to oversee and monitor the use of standardized tests.

THE PAST

Educational and psychological tests have become a widely accepted social enterprise in this century, because of their utility in dealing with large numbers of people and because of their association with technology. After the success of the Army Alpha in World War I, many tests were developed between 1920 and 1940. Buros's first bibliography in 1937 contained 44 pages (as compared with 1,183 in the *Eleventh Mental Measurements Yearbooks*) and included many tests of questionable validity and reliability. This period was not entirely devoid of criticism, but tests were well accepted and results rarely questioned.

Political and philosophical movements influenced the 1950s, 1960s, and 1970s. Schools were desegregated, and concern grew over ethnic, cultural, and gender bias in testing. The misuses of testing were exposed, and some states banned the use of IQ tests. Legislation was enacted to protect the rights of individuals with disabilities and to foster equal opportunity. Also, programs supported ethnic heritage, women's rights, and sexual equity.

THE PRESENT

Current test use reflects the philosophy of the beginnings of the testing movement: "If it exists, it can be measured." ETS (1993) states in its report, *Testing in American's Schools,* that the volume of testing in U.S. schools has increased markedly over the past 20 years and probably will continue unless the alternative assessments under development begin to take the place of traditional standardized tests. Philosophical and political ideology has shifted toward a conservative point of view from humanistic approaches in education to emphasis on basic skills. Accordingly, more emphasis has been placed on accountability, which has led to increased use of licensing and minimum level competency testing. Society is relying even more heavily on testing than it did in the past. The testing companies have accommodated the changes dictated by laws, such as the truth-in-testing law, and by legislation to eliminate cultural, ethnic, and sexual bias. The technology of testing has been stimulated by these political and social events as well as the impact of the computer. More sophisticated procedures are now possible to select items and generate criterion validity. Nonclassical psychometric models are currently being accepted. The information age has led to a greater concern for who has access to information, how it is stored, and how the rights of the individual will be protected.

THE FUTURE

Influenced by technology and society, the future will bring more changes in the practices and procedures used in testing. Preliminary studies and research indicate that computer-adaptive and computer-assisted testing will be used more extensively. Cost effective and labor-saving, the computer is able to collect psychological data along with traditional test information, providing immediate feedback and remediation. More tests that use multiple input and output devices for displaying results continue to be developed. In the past, tests have been transferred from pencil-and-paper format to computer format. Different types of items now are being devised that are unique to the potential of the computer. Video disk technology, CD-ROM, and virtual reality technology can simulate real situations. The items don't have to depend upon words; an item on an interest test can give a visual display of an occupation.

The future will see continued reliance on tests as the primary means of establishing mastery of competencies. Selection tests and large-scale admissions programs will be under increased scrutiny. Various groups in undergraduate education have advocated dropping the Scholastic Aptitude Test as an admissions requirement. Selection tests have had questionable predictive validity; the best single predictor of future achievement is past achievement. SAT results may increase the efficiency of prediction slightly, but studies have shown that 50% or more of the variance related to success in college is unaccounted for by the predictors used.

Schools, states, and institutions will share more in the future. Consortia of states now are working together to construct criterion-referenced and minimum-level skills tests. More reliance on using and refining tests and item banks already available will be generated. Alternate assessment and performance testing will be refined and will have freer formats. Glaser (1994) states that students will be able to observe and reflect on their own performance so they can judge their own level of achievement and develop self-direction. Assessment programs will be judged in terms of the contributions they make to encourage students and teachers to devote their energies to certain content, concepts, and student performance.

The future will see more movement toward assessing cognitive aspects of intelligence. Cognitive interpretation is more practical in helping psychologists and teachers derive individually prescribed programs. Also more emphasis will be placed on the development of multiple intelligences in school and counseling. Gardner and Sternberg and others working in this field will have an increased influence on test development and test interpretation.

In personality measurement, behavioral assessment techniques will become more widely used, and traditional pencil-and-paper inventories will diminish in importance. Certain clinicians will probably be reluctant to change, even though many studies have already indicated that the old standby tests lack validity and reliability. Professional licensing and certification examinations will also include performance assessment. Test items must reflect qualities and skills needed for job performance, not just knowledge demonstrated on pencil-and-paper tests.

Test authors and test publishers will need to withdraw some tests from public access since they do not meet the standards set by professional organizations. Test companies will need to revise problem tests so that they conform to ethical and professional standards or discontinue them. If the test industry does not voluntarily address this issue, the public and the professions will demand compliance.

Movements come in cycles. Criticism of testing will increase again, especially when studies look at the long-term effects of accountability. States have mandated testing but have not put funds into research to establish the validity of the tests. More court cases and judicial opinions will be forthcoming, and the values and priorities of the legislature will change. The future will probably question whether established policies have led to better practice, quality education, or more competent professionals in the work force.

The history of testing has included misuses and abuses and controversies. Many states require teachers as well as counselors and psychologists to take a number of semester hours in testing and demonstrate their testing competencies. However, this requirement does not yet pertain to all professionals who make heavy use of testing. Future movements will ensure the competency of all workers using tests.

Helping professionals need to look at their role in the future. They need to develop the knowledge, skills, and competencies to be good consumers of tests.

Measurement writers have stressed the need for a decision-making model for using tests and have emphasized that tests are only one source of information, the results of which are not absolute. Many leaders in the field have also advocated using a multimodal approach to get information needed for decision making.

Unfortunately, leaders in the field sometimes forget what they espouse. They base their judgments on attitudes, past training and practices, and feelings rather than on disinterested, objective analysis. Helping professionals need to remember the steps of the scientific method and encourage freedom of thought, divergent opinions, and the ability to step back and take another look. Too often test experts take refuge in their factor and discriminant analysis and fail to consider the practical significance of the results. Helping professionals must be competent, knowledgeable, scientific, analytical, and evaluative. In most businesses the consumer is right, and consumer wishes and desires are honored. In testing, the consumer must be protected.

SUMMARY

Current trends and issues in testing are influenced by political, social, economic, and technological developments in our world. Current issues receiving much attention are minimum competency testing, licensure and certification, truth in testing, invasion of privacy, and fairness of tests for minority groups. The history of testing has included criticism from within and without. Some of the controversies periodically resurface. In this information age, the roles and functions of testing are changing. Computer-assisted and computer-adaptive testing are becoming widely used and accepted. All changes have implications for the competencies needed by those who test. Helping professionals must always keep in mind the ethical and professional standards in the field in their selection, use, and interpretation of tests.

QUESTIONS FOR DISCUSSION

1. What are the major issues and controversies in testing today? Which ones are the most critical? Why?

2. What do you predict will be the issues and controversies in testing 10 years from now? 20 years from now? Why?

3. Discuss the major issues in testing and analyze the factors impinging on those issues. Are the forces legal, educational, political, psychological, social, or psychometric? What force do you think is the most influential?

4. What do you predict will be the future trends in testing?

5. Some critics think that there is too much use and reliance on testing today. Do you agree or disagree with this position? Why?

SUGGESTED ACTIVITIES

1. Write a position paper on one of the issues in the field of testing.

2. Write a critical review of the literature on one of the trends or innovations in testing.

3. Interview workers in the helping professions and have them identify what they think are the current issues, trends, and controversies. Report your findings to the class.

4. Conduct a survey of workers in the helping professions to learn their attitudes toward testing and the current issues and trends. Construct your instrument, administer it, and analyze the results. Report the results to the class.

5. Write a paper on where we have been in testing, where we are, and where we will be in the future.

ADDITIONAL READINGS

Conferences such as those sponsored by the Educational Testing Service and the Buros Institute are held annually, and their proceedings are usually published. Additionally, many yearbooks deal in testing, and journals in the field have special publications. Newsletters of professional organizations and the ERIC center on assessment and evaluation are excellent sources. To keep current and well-informed about appraisal procedures and issues, helping professionals need to be aware of these sources as well as others provided by newspapers, magazines, and television.

Appendix A: Tests

AAMD Adaptive Behavior Scale
Nihira, K., Foster, R., Shellhaas, M., Leland, H. Lambert, N. M., & Windmiller, M. (1975). Monterey, CA: CTB/ McGraw-Hill.

ACT Assessment Program
American College Testing Program. (1988). Iowa City: Author.

Adaptive Behavior Inventory of Children
Mercer, J. R., & Lewis, J. F. (1978). San Antonio, TX: The Psychological Corporation.

Adjective Checklist
Gough, H. G., & Heilbrun, A. Jr. (1980). Palo Alto, CA: Consulting Psychologists Press, Inc.

Adolescent Diagnostic Screening Battery
Smith, J. J., & Eisenberg, J. M. (1985). Towson, MD: Reason House.

Adult Career Concerns Inventory
Super, D. E., Thompson, A. S., & Lindeman, R. H. (1988). Palo Alto, CA: Consulting Psychologists Press.

Adult Language Assessment Scale
Duncan, S. E., & DeAvila, E. A. (1991). Monterey, CA: Publishers Test Service.

Advanced Progressive Matrices
Raven, J. C. (1962). London: H. K. Lewis & Co. Ltd.

Affective Perception Inventory
Soares, A. T., & Soares, L. M. (1985). Trumbull, CT: Soares Associates.

Affective Style Measure
Doane, J. A. (1981). Los Angeles, CA: UCLA Family Project.

African Self-Consciousness Scale
Baldwin, J. A., & Bell, Y. R. (1985). *Western Journal of Black Studies, 9*(2), 65–68.

Allport-Vernon-Lindzey Study of Values
Allport, G. W., Vernon, P. E., & Lindzey, G. (1970). Chicago: Riverside Publishing Co.

Analysis of Coping Style
Boyd, H. F., & Johnson, G. O. (1981). San Antonio, TX: Psychological Corporation.

Analysis of Learning Potential
Durost, W. N., Gardner, E. F., Madden, R., & Prescott, G. A. (1970). Orlando, FL: Harcourt Brace Jovanovich Analysis.

Aptitude-Intelligence Series
Industrial Psychology, Inc. (1960). New York: Author.

Armed Services Vocational Aptitude Battery #14, 16, 17, 18
U.S. Military Enlistment Command. (1984). Washington, DC: U.S. Department of Defense.

Arthur Point Scale
Arthur, G. (1947). Arthur Point Scale of Performance Tests: Revised Form II. San Antonio, TX: The Psychological Corp.

Auditory Discrimination Test
Wepman, J. M. (1973). Los Angeles: Western Psychological Services.

Basic Achievement Skills Individual Screener
The Psychological Corporation. (1982). San Antonio: Author.

Basic Occupational Literacy Test
U.S. Employment Service. (1974). Washington, DC: U.S. Department of Labor.

Basic Skills Assessment Program
Educational Testing Service. (1979). Monterey, CA: CTB/ McGraw-Hill.

Battelle Development Inventory
Newburg, J., Stock, J., Wnek, L., Guidobaldi, J., & Suinick, J. (1984). Allen, TX: DLM Teaching Resources.

Bayley Scales of Infant Development
Bayley, N. (1969). San Antonio: The Psychological Corporation.

Beck Anxiety Inventory
Beck, A. T. (1990). San Antonio: Psychological Corp.

Beck Depression Inventory
Beck, A. T. (1987). San Antonio: Psychological Corp.

Beck Hopelessness Scale
Beck, A. T. (1987). San Antonio: Psychological Corp.

Behavior Observation Scale for Autism
Freeman, B. J. (1978). Los Angeles: Betty Jo Freeman.

Bem Sex-Role Inventory
Bem, S. L. (1981). Palo Alto, CA: Consulting Psychologists Press, Inc.

Bender Gestalt Test for Young Children
Koppitz, E. M. (1975). Orlando: Grune & Stratton.

Bender Visual Motor Gestalt Test
Bender, L. (1964). New York: American Orthopsychiatric Association, Inc.

Bennett Mechanical Comprehension Test
Bennett, G., & Owens, W. A. (1980). San Antonio: The Psychological Corporation.

Bernreuter Personality Inventory
Bernreuter, R. G. (1938). Palo Alto, CA: Consulting Psychologists Press.

Brain Preference Indicator
Wonder, J., & Donovan, P. (1984). New York: Morrow.

Brain Preference Survey
Drummond, R. J. (1987). Jacksonville, FL: Educational Services and Research, University of North Florida.

Bruininks-Oseretsky Test of Motor Proficiency
Bruininks, R. H. (1978). Circle Pines, MN: American Guidance Service.

Burks' Behavior Rating Scales
Burks, H. F. (1969). Los Angeles: Western Psychological Services.

California Achievement Test
California Test Bureau. (1978). Monterey,CA: CTB/ McGraw-Hill.

California Psychological Inventory
Gough, Harrison G. (1987). Palo Alto, CA: Consulting Psychologists Press, Inc.

California Short Form Test of Academic Aptitude
Sullivan, E. T., Clark, W. W., & Tiegs, E. W. (1974). Monterey, CA: CTB/ McGraw-Hill.

Campbell-Hallam Team Development Survey
Hallam, G., & Campbell, D. (1992). Minneapolis: NCS Assessments.

Canfield Learning Styles Inventory
Canfield, A. A. (1980). LaCrescenta, CA: Humanics Media.

Career Ability Placement Survey
Knapp, L. F., & Knapp, R. R. (1984). San Diego: Educational and Industrial Testing Service.

Career Assessment Inventory
Johansson, C. B. (1982). Minneapolis: National Computer Systems, PAS Division.

Career Awareness Inventory
Fadale, L. M. (1975). Bensenville, IL: Scholastic Testing Service, Inc.

Career Development Inventory
Super, D. E., Thompson, A. S., Lindeman, R. H., Jordaan, J. P., & Myers, R. A. (1981). Palo Alto, CA: Consulting Psychologists Press.

Career Maturity Inventory
Crites, J. O. (1973). Monterey, CA: CTB/McGraw-Hill.

Career Planning Program
American College Testing Program. (1974). Iowa City: Author.

Career Skills Assessment Program
College Board. (1978). Princeton, NJ: College Board Publications.

Cattell Infant Intelligence Scale
Cattell, P. (1960). San Antonio: The Psychological Corporation.

Child Anxiety Scale
Gillis, J. S. (1980). Champaign, IL: Institute for Personality and Ability Testing.

Child Assessment Schedule
Hodges, K. (1985). Durham, NC: Department of Psychiatry.

Child Behavior Checklist
Achenbach, T. H., & Edenbrock, C. Burlington, VT: Department of Psychiatry, University of Vermont.

Child Diagnostic Screening Battery
Smith, J. J., & Eisenberg, J. M. (1984). Towson, MD: Reason House.

Children's Apperception Test
Bellak, L., & Bellak, S. S. (1974). Larchmount, NY: C. P. S., Inc.

Children's Apperception Test, Human Figures
Bellak, L., & Bellak, S. S. (1965). Larchmount, NY: C. P. S., Inc.

Children's Embedded Figures Test
Karp, S. A., & Konstadt, N. (1971). Palo Alto, CA: Consulting Psychologists Press, Inc.

Children's Learning Profile
DePaul, G. J., Rapport, M. D., & Perriello, L. M. (1990). Boston: Department of Psychiatry, University of Mass. Medical Center.

Children's Manifest Anxiety Scale
Castaneda, A., McCandless, B. R., & Palermo, D. C. (1956). *Child Development, 27,* 317–326.

Children's Personality Questionnaire
Porter, R. B., & Cattell, R. B. (1982). Champaign, IL: Institute of Personality and Ability Testing.

Children's State-Trait Anxiety Inventory
Spielberger, C. D., Edwards, C. D., Montuori, J., & Lushene, R. (1983). Alto, CA: Consulting Psychologists Press, Inc.

Children's Test Anxiety Scale/Children's Anxiety Scale
Sarason, S. B., Davidson, K. S., Lighthall, F. F., Waite, R. R., & Rugbush, B. K. (1960). *Anxiety in elementary school children.* New York: John Wiley & Sons.

Children's Version of the Family Environment Scale
Pineo, C., Simons, N., & Slawinowski, M. (1984). East Aurora, NY: Slosson.

Classroom Environment Scale
Moos, R. H., & Trickett, E. J. (1974). Palo Alto, CA: Consulting Psychologists Press.

Clerical Aptitude Test
Kobal, A., Wrightstone, J. W., & MacElroy, A. J. (1950). Murfreesboro, TN: Psychometric Affiliates.

Cognitive Abilities Test
Thorndike, R. L., & Hagen, E. P. (1982). Chicago: The Riverside Publishing Company.

College Board Scholastic Aptitude Test
College Board. (1996). New York: Author.

College Characteristics Index
Stern, G., et al. (1962). Syracuse, NY: Evaluation Research Associates.

College Level Examination Program
College Board. (1981). New York: Author.

Colorado Self-Report Measure of Family Functioning
Bloom, B. L. (1985). Boulder, CO: Department of Psychology.

Coloured Progressive Matrices
    Raven, J. C. (1983). London: H. K. Lewis & Co., Ltd.

Columbia Mental Maturity Scale
    Burgemeister, B. B., Blum, L. H., & Lorge, I. (1972). San Antonio: The Psychological Corporation.

Comprehensive Ability Battery
    Hakstian, A. R., & Cattell, R. B. (1982). Champaign, IL: Institute for Personality and Ability Testing.

Comprehensive Personality Profile (1992)
    Libertyville, IL: Wonderlic Personnel Test, Inc.

Comprehensive Tests of Basic Skills
    California Test Bureau. (1981). Monterey, CA: CTB/McGraw-Hill.

Computer Operator Aptitude Battery
    Holloway, A. J. (1974). Chicago: Science Research Associates.

Computer Programmer Aptitude Battery
    Palormo, J. M. (1974). Chicago: Science Research Associates.

Concept Assessment Kit
    Goldschmid, M. L., & Bently, P. M. (1968). San Diego, CA: Educational and Industrial Testing.

Conflict Tactics Scale
    Straus, M. A. (1979). Durham, NH: Family Research Laboratory.

Continuous Performance Test (computer program)
    Conners, C. K. (1994). Odessa, FL: Psychological Assessment Resources.

Cooperative Mathematics Tests
    ETS. (1965). Palo Alto, CA: CTB/McGraw-Hill.

Coopersmith Self-Esteem Inventories
    Coopersmith, S. (1981). Palo Alto, CA: Consulting Psychologists Press, Inc.

COPSystem Career Occupational Preference System
    Knapp, R. R., & Knapp, L. F. (1983). San Diego: Educational and Industrial Testing Service.

COPSystem Interest Inventory
    Knapp, R. R., & Knapp, L. (1982). San Diego: Educational and Industrial Testing Service.

Correctional Institutions Environment Scale
    Moos, R. H. (1974). Palo Alto, CA: Consulting Psychologists Press, Inc.

Crawford Small Parts Dexterity Test
    Crawford, J. (1956). San Antonio: The Psychological Corporation.

Creativity Attitude Survey
    Schaefer, C. E. (1971). Creve Cove, MO: Psychologists and Educators, Inc.

Creativity Checklist
    Johnson, D. L. (1979). Chicago: Stoelting Company.

Criterion Test of Basic Skills
    Lundell, K., Brown, W., & Evans, J. (1976). Novato, CA: Academic Therapy Publications.

Culture Fair Series
    Cattell, R. B., & Cattell, A. K. S. (1977). Champaign, IL: Institute for Personality and Ability Testing.

Culture-Free Self-Esteem Inventories (2nd ed.)
    Battle, J. (1992). Austin, TX: Pro-Ed.

Curtis Verbal-Clerical Skills Tests
    Curtis, J. W. (1965). Murfreesboro, TN: Psychometric Affiliates.

Defensive and Supportive Communication Interaction Scale
    Alexander, J. F. (no date). Salt Lake City, UT: Author.

Denver Developmental Screening Test
    Frankenburg, W. F. (1970). Denver: Ladoca Publishing Foundation.

Detroit Tests of Learning Aptitude
    Hammill, D. D. (1985). Austin, TX: Pro-Ed.

Developmental Assessment for Severely Handicapped
    Dykes, M. K. (1980). Austin, TX: Exceptional Resources, Inc.

Developmental Environments Coding System
    Powers, S. J. (1982). Amherst, MA: Author.

Developmental Inventory of Black Consciousness
    Milliones, J. (1980). *Psychotherapy: Theory, Research and Practice, 17*, 175–182.

Developmental Test of Visual-Motor Integration
    Beery, K. E., & Buktenica, N. A. (1967). Cleveland: Modern Curriculum Press.

Devereux Rating Scales
    Devereux Test of Extremity Coordination. (1973). Devon, PA: The Devereux Foundation.

Spivack, G., & Spotts, J. (1966). The Devereux Child Behavior Rating Scale. Devon, PA: The Devereux Foundation.

Diagnostic Interview for Children and Adolescents
Herjanic, B., & Reich, W. (1982). *Journal of Abnormal Child Psychology*, *10*, 307–324.

Diagnostic Inventory of Personality and Symptoms
Vincent, K. R. (1977). Richland, WA: Pacific Psychological.

Differential Aptitude Test
Bennett, G. K., Seashore, H. G., & Wesman, A. G. (1982). San Antonio: The Psychological Corporation.

Dimensions of Excellence Scales
Dusewicy, R. A., & Beyer, F. S. (1991). Philadelphia: Research for Better Schools.

Draw-A-Man Test
Goodenough, F. L., & Harris, D. B. (1963). Goodenough-Harris Drawing Test. San Antonio: The Psychological Corporation.

Early School Personality Questionnaire
Cattell, R. B., & Coan, R. W. (1982). Champaign, IL: Institute for Personality and Ability Testing.

Eating Disorder Inventory
Garner, D. M., Olmsted, M. P., & Polivy, J. Odessa, FL: Psychological Assessment Resources.

Eating Inventory
Stunkard, A. J., & Messick, S. (1983). San Antonio: Psychological Corporation.

Educational Development Series
Anderhalter, O. F., Bauernfeind, R. H., Gried, M. E., Mallison, G., Mallison, J., Papenfuss, J. E., & Vail, N. (1984). Bensenville, IL: Scholastic Testing Service.

Edwards Personal Preference Inventory
Edwards, A. L. (1959). San Antonio: The Psychological Corporation.

Effective School Battery
Gottfredson, G. D. (1984). Odessa, FL: Psychological Assessment Resources, Inc.

Embedded Figures Test
Witkin, H. A. (1971). Palo Alto, CA: Consulting Psychologists Press, Inc.

Employee Aptitude Survey Series
Grimsley, G., Ruch, F. L., Warren, N. D., & Ford, J. S. (1963). Bay Village, OH: Psychological Services, Inc.

Employee Reliability Inventory
Wonderlic Personnel Test, Inc. (1993). Libertyville, IL: Author.

Employment Barrier Identification Scale
McKee, J. M. (1981). Tuscaloosa, AL: Behavior Science Press.

End of Course Tests
CTB/McGraw-Hill. (1986). Palo Alto, CA: Author.

Escala de Inteligencia Wechsler para Adultos
Wechsler, D. (adapted and translated by R. F. Green & J. H. Martinez). (1968). San Antonio: The Psychological Corporation.

Escala de Inteligencia Wechsler para Ninos
Wechsler, D (translated by P. Roca). (1982). San Antonio: The Psychological Corporation.

Everyday Skills Test
California Test Bureau. (1975). CTB/McGraw-Hill.

Eysenck Personality Inventory
Eysenck, H. J., & Eysenck, S. B. G. (1969). San Diego: Educational and Industrial Testing Service.

Eysenck Personality Questionnaire
Eysenck, H. J., & Eysenck, S. B. G. (1976). San Diego: Educational and Industrial Testing Service.

Family Adaptability and Cohesion Evaluation Scales III
Olson, D. H., Portner, J., & Lavee, Y. (1985). St. Paul: Family Social Science, University of Minnesota.

Family, Assessment Measure
Skinner, H. A., Steinhauer, P. D., & Santa-Barbara, J. (1984). Toronto: Addictions Research Foundation.

Family Conflict and Dominance Codes
Henggeler, S. W., & Tavormina, J. B. (1980). *Journal of Genetic Psychology*, 211–222.

Family Constraining and Enabling Coding System
Hauser, S., et al. (1987). Cambridge, MA: Family Development Project, Harvard Medical School.

Family Environment Scale
> Moos, R. H., & Moos, B. S. (1981). Palo Alto, CA: Consulting Psychologists Press, Inc.

Family Evaluation Form
> Emery, R. S., Weintraub, S., & Neale, J. M. (1984). Stoney Brook, NY: Department of Psychology, SUNY.

Family Functioning in Adolescence Questionnaire
> Roelofse, R., & Middleton, M. (1985). *Journal of Adolescence, 8*, 33–45.

Family Process Scales
> Barbarin, O. A., & Gilbert, R. (1985). Ann Arbor, MI: Family Development Project, University of Michigan.

Family Relationship Questionnaire
> Henggeler, S. W., & Tavormina, J. B. (1980). Memphis: Dept. of Psychology, Memphis State University.

Florida Analysis of Semantic Traits Profile
> Bailey, R. C., & Suidzinski, R. M. (1986). Dallas: Bali Screening Co.

Frostig Developmental Test of Visual Perception
> Frostig, M. (1966). Palo Alto, CA: Consulting Psychologists Press, Inc.

Gates-McKillop-Horowitz Reading Diagnostic Test
> Gates, A. I., McKillop, A. S., & Horowitz, E. C. (1981). New York: Teachers College Press.

General Clerical Test
> The Psychological Corporation. (1972). San Antonio: Author.

General Educational Development Test
> General Educational Development Testing Service. (1987). Washington, DC: American Council on Education.

General Education Performance Index
> Seaman, D. F., & Seaman, A. (1980). Austin, TX: Steck-Vaughn Company.

Gifted and Talented Screening Form
> Johnson, D. L. (1980). Chicago: Stoelting Company.

Goldman-Fristoe Test of Articulation
> Goldman, R., & Fristoe, M. (1972). Circle Pines, MN: American Guidance Service.

Goldman-Fristoe-Woodcock Auditory Skills Test Battery
> Goldman, R., Fristoe, M., & Woodcock, R. W. (1976). Circle Pines, MN: American Guidance Service.

Graduate Management Admissions Test
> Educational Testing Service. (1977). Princeton, NJ: Author.

Gregorc Style Delineator
> Gregorc, A. F. (1982). Maynard, MA: Gabriel Systems.

Group Embedded Figures Test
> Oltman, P. K., Raskin, E., Witkin, H. A. (1971). Palo Alto, CA: Consulting Psychologists Press, Inc.

Group Environment Scale
> Moos, R. H. (1981). Palo Alto, CA: Consulting Psychologists Press, Inc.

Group Inventory for Finding Creative Talent
> Rimm, S. B. (1980). Watertown, WI: Educational Assessment Services, Inc.

Group Inventory for Finding Interests
> Rimm, S. B., & Davis, G. A. (1980). Watertown, WI: Educational Assessment Services, Inc.

Hall Occupational Orientation Inventory
> Hall, L. C., & Tarrier, R. B. (1976). Bensenville, IL: Scholastic Testing Service, Inc.

Halstead-Reitan Neuropsychological Test Battery
> Reitan, R. M. (1979). Tucson: Reitan Neuropsychology Laboratory.

Hand Test
> Wagner, E. E. (1983). Los Angeles: Western Psychological Services.

Hand-Tool Dexterity Test
> Bennett, G. K. (1965). San Antonio: The Psychological Corporation.

Harrington-O'Shay Career Decision-Making System
> Harrington, T. F., & O'Shay, A. J. (1982). Circle Pines, MN: American Guidance Service.

Hay Aptitude Test Battery
> Hay, E. N. (1982). Northfield, IL: E. F. Wonderlic Personnel Test, Inc.

High School Characteristics Index
> Stern, G., et al. (1962). Syracuse, NY: Evaluation Research Associates.

High School Personality Questionnaire
Cattell, R. B., & Cattell, M. D., & Johns, E. (1984). Champaign, IL: Institute for Personality and Ability Testing.

House-Tree-Person
Buck, J. N. (1970). Los Angeles: Western Psychological Services.

Illinois Test of Psycholinguistic Abilities
Kirk, S. A., McCarthy, J. J., & Kirk, W. D. (1968). Champaign, IL: University of Illinois Press.

In-Basket Test
Frederiksen, N., Saunders, D. R., Wand, B. (1957). *Psychological Monographs, 71*(9).

Industrial Reading Test
The Psychological Corporation. (1978). San Antonio: Author.

Inferred Self-Concept Scale
McDaniel, E. L. (1973). Los Angeles: Western Psychological Services.

Institutional Functioning Inventory
McGrath, E. J., et al. (1983). Princeton, NJ: ETS.

Interest Determination and Assessment System
Johansson, C. B. (1980). Minneapolis: National Computer Systems/PAS Division.

Interview Schedule for Children
Kovacs, M. (1985). *Psychopharmacology Bulletin, 21*, 991–994.

Iowa Test of Basic Skills
Hieronymus, A. N., Lindquist, E. F., & Hoover, H. D. (1978). Chicago: Riverside Publishing Company.

Iowa Test of Educational Development
Lindquist, E. F., & Feldt, L. S. (1982). Chicago: Science Research Associates.

IPAT Humor Test of Personality
Cattell, R. B., & Tollefson, D. L. (1966). Champaign, IL: Institute of Personality and Ability Testing.

IPAT Music Preference Test of Personality
Cattell, R. B., & Eber, H. W. (1963). Champaign, IL: Institute of Personality and Ability Testing.

Jackson Vocational Interest Survey
Jackson, D. N. (1977). Port Huron, MI: Research Psychologists Press, Inc.

Jesness Behavior Check List
Jesness, C. F. (1984). Palo Alto, CA: Consulting Psychologists Press, Inc.

Job Effectiveness Prediction System
Personnel Decisions Research Institute for Life Office Management Association. (1978). Atlanta: Life Office Management Association.

Judgment of Occupational Behavior Orientation
Cutler, A., Ferry, F., Kauk, R., & Robinett, R. (1972). Belmont, CA: CFKR Career Materials, Inc.

Kaufman Assessment Battery for Children
Kaufman, A. S., & Kaufman, N. L. (1983). Circle Pines, MN: American Guidance Service.

Kent Infant Development Scale
Reuter, J. M., & Katoff, L. (1981). Kent, OH: Kent Developmental Metrics.

Keymath Diagnostic Test
Connolly, A., Nachtman, W., & Pritchett, E. M. (1976). Circle Pines, MN: American Guidance Service.

Keystone Visual Survey Test
Keystone View. (1974). Davenport, IA: Keystone View.

Kinetic Family Drawing Test
Burns, R. C., & Kaufman, S. H. (1972). Actions, styles, and symbols in Kinetic Family Drawings. New York: Bruner/Mazel.

Kohs Block Design Test
Kohs, S. C. (1919). Chicago: Stoelting Company.

Kuder Interest Tests
Kuder, G. F. (1976). Kuder General Interest Survey. Chicago: Science Research Associates.

Kuder, G. F. (1976). Kuder Preference Record, Vocational. Chicago: Science Research Associates.

Kuder, G. F. (1979). Kuder Occupational Interest Survey, Form DD, Revised. Chicago: Science Research Associates.

Kwalwasser Music Talent Test
Kwalwasser, J. (1953). Miami: Belwin-Mills Publishing Corporation.

Lauria-Nebraska Neuropsychological Battery
Golden, C. J., Purisch, A. D., & Hammeke, T. A. (1985). Los Angeles: Western Psychological Services.

Law School Admissions Test
Law School Admissions Council. (1988). Washington, DC: Law School Admissions Service.

Leadership Appraisal Survey
Hall, J. (1986). Woodlands, TX: Telemetrics International.

Learning Efficiency Test
Webster, R. E. (1981). Novato, CA: Academic Therapy Publications.

Learning Preference Inventory
Silver, H. F., & Hanson, J. R. (1978). Moorestown, NJ: Hanson, Silver, Strong and Associates, Inc.

Learning Style Inventory
Kolb, D. A. (1976). Boston: McBer.

Learning Style Profile
Keefe, J. W., & Monk, J. S. (1988). Reston, VA: National Association of Secondary School Principals.

Learning Styles Inventory
Dunn, R., Dunn, K., & Price, G. E. (1987). Lawrence, KS: Price Systems, Inc.

Learning Styles Inventory
Renzulli, J. S., & Smith, L. H. (1978). Mansfield Center, CN: Creative Learning Press, Inc.

Learning Type Measure
McCarthy, B., & St. Germain, C. (1993). Barrington, IL: Excel.

Leiter International Performance Scale
Leiter, R. G. (1952). Chicago: Stoelting Co.

Lincoln-Oseretsky Motor Development Scale
Sloan, W. (1956). Chicago: Stoelting Company.

Louisville Behavior Checklist
Miller, L. C. (1984). Los Angeles: Western Psychological Services.

Manifest Anxiety Scale
Taylor, J. A. (1953). A personality scale of manifest anxiety. *Journal of Abnormal Psychology*, *48*, 265–270.

Matching Familiar Figures Test
Kagan, J., Rosman, B. L., Day, D., Albert, J., & Phillips, W. (1964). Information processing in the child: Significance of analytic and reflective attitudes. *Psychological Monographs*, *78*, (1, Whole No. 578).

McMaster Family Assessment Device, Version 3
Epstein, N. B., Baldwin, L. M., & Bishop, D. S. (1982). Providence, RI: Brown University/Butler Hospital Family Research Project.

Measures of Psychosocial Development
Hawley, G. A. (1985). Odessa, FL: Psychological Assessment Resources.

Mechanical Aptitude Test
Kobal, A., Wrightstone, J. W., Kunze, K. R., & MacElroy, A. J. (1952). Murfreesboro, TN: Psychometric Affiliates.

Meier Art Judgment Test, Meier Art Tests, Meier Aesthetic Perception Test
Meier, N. C. (1963). Iowa City: Bureau of Educational Research and Service, University of Iowa.

Memory for Designs Test
Graham, F. K., & Kendall, B. S. (1960). Missoula, MT: Psychological Test Specialists.

Metropolitan Achievement Tests: Sixth Edition
Balow, I. H., Farr, R., Hogan, T. P., & Prescott, G. A. (1984). San Antonio: The Psychological Corporation.

Metropolitan Readiness Tests: 1986 Edition
Nurss, J. R., & McGauvran, M. E. (1986). San Antonio: The Psychological Corporation.

Michigan Alcoholism Screening Test
Selzer, M. L. (1971). *American Journal of Psychiatry*, *127*, 1653–1658.

Michigan Picture Test
Hutt, M. L. (1980). Orlando: Grune and Stratton.

Miller's Analogies Test
Miller, W. S. (1975). San Antonio: The Psychological Corporation.

Millon Adolescent Personality Inventory
Millon, T., Green, C. J., & Meagher, R. B., Jr. (1982). Minneapolis: National Computer System/PAS Division.

Millon Behavioral Health Inventory
Millon, T., Green, C. J., & Meagher, R. B., Jr. (1982). Minneapolis: National Computer System/ PAS Division.

Millon Clinical Multiaxial Inventory-II
Millon, T. (1987). Minneapolis: National Computer System/ PAS Division.

Minnesota Clerical Test
Andrew, D. M., Peterson, D. G., & Longstaff, H. P. (1959). San Antonio: The Psychological Corporation.

Minnesota Importance Questionnaire
Vocational Psychology Research. (1981). Minneapolis: University of Minnesota.

Minnesota Manual Dexterity Test
Lafayette Instrument Company, Inc. (1969). Lafayette, IN: Author.

Minnesota Multiphasic Personality Inventory-2
Hathaway, S. R., & McKinley, C. (1992). Minneapolis: University of Minnesota Press.

Minnesota Paper Formboard
Likert, R., & Quasha, W. H. (1970). San Antonio: The Psychological Corporation.

Minnesota Rate of Manipulation Test
Employment Stabilization Research Institute, University of Minnesota. (1969). Circle Pines, MN: American Guidance Service.

Minnesota Spatial Relations Test
American Guidance Service Test Division. (1930). Circle Pines, MN: American Guidance Service.

Moore Eye Hand Coordination and Color Test
Moore, J. E. (1968). Atlanta: Joseph E. Moore & Associates.

Multidimensional Self-Esteem Inventory
O'Brien, E. J., & Epstein, S. (1988). Odessa, FL: Psychological Assessment Resources.

Multiscore
Riverside Publishing Co. (1984). Chicago: Author.

Murphy-Meisgeier Type Indicator for Children
Meisgeier, C., & Murphy, E. (1987). Palo Alto, CA: Consulting Psychologists Press.

Musical Aptitude Profile
Gordon, E. (1965). Chicago: Riverside Publishing Company.

Myers-Briggs Type Indicator
Myers, I. B., & Briggs, K. S. (1985). Palo Alto, CA: Consulting Psychologists Press.

National Educational Development Test
Thurstone, T. G. (1994). Park Ridge, IL: SRA/London House.

NEO PI-R
Costa, P. T., Jr., & McCrae, R. R. (1992). Odessa, FL: Psychological Assessment Resources.

Nowicki-Strickland Locus of Control Scale
Nowicki, S., & Strickland, B. R. (1973). *Journal of Consulting Psychology, 40,* 148–154.

O'Connor Tests
O'Connor, J. (1926). O'Connor Finger Dexterity Test. Chicago: Stoelting Company.

O'Connor, J. (1928). O'Connor Tweezer Dexterity Test. Chicago: Stoelting Company.

Ohio Vocational Education Achievement Test Program
The Ohio Vocational Achievement Tests Series. (1987). Columbus: Vocational Instructional Materials Laboratory, The Ohio State University.

Ohio Vocational Interest Survey
D'Costa, A. G., Winefordner, D. W., Odgers, J. G., & Koons, P. B., Jr. (1981). San Antonio: The Psychological Corporation.

Oliphant Auditory Discrimination Memory Test
Oliphant, G. (1971). Cambridge, MA: Educators Publishing Service, Inc.

Organizational Climate Index
Stern, G., et al. (1962). Syracuse, NY: Evaluation Research Associates.

Otis-Lennon Mental Ability Test
Otis, A. S., & Lennon, R. T. (1974). San Antonio: The Psychological Corporation.

Otis-Lennon School Ability Test
Otis, A. S., & Lennon, R. T. (1982). Otis-Lennon School Ability Test. San Antonio: The Psychological Corporation.

Parent Daily Report
Patterson, G. R., & Reid, J. B. (1987). *Behavioral Assessment, 9,* 97–109.

Parent Opinion Inventory
National Study of School Evaluation. (1981). Falls Church, VA: National Study of School Evaluation.

Peabody Individual Achievement Test
Dunn, L. M., & Markwardt, F. C., Jr. (1970). Circle Pines, MN: American Guidance Service.

Peabody Picture Vocabulary Test
Dunn, L. M. & Dunn, L. M. (1981). Circle Pines, MN: American Guidance Service.

Personal Orientation Inventory
Shostrom, E. L. (1968). San Diego: Educational and Industrial Testing Service.

Personal Style Indicator
Controneo, K. (1983). Athens, GA: Academic Excellence Leadership Project.

Personality Assessment Inventory
Morey, L. C. (1991). Odessa, FL: Psychological Assessment Resources.

Personnel Tests for Industry
Wesman, A. G., & Doppelt, J. E. (1969). San Antonio: The Psychological Corporation.

Piers-Harris Children's Self-Concept Scale
Piers, E. V., & Harris, D. B. (1984). Los Angeles: Western Psychological Services.

Planning Career Goals
American Institutes for Research. (1976). Monterey, CA: CTB/McGraw-Hill.

Porteus Mazes
Porteus, S. D. (1965). San Antonio: The Psychological Corporation.

Position Analysis Questionnaire
McCormick, P. R., Jeanneret, P. R., & Meacham, R. C. (1969). West Lafayette, IN: Purdue Research Foundation.

Preschool Language Assessment Instrument
Blank, M., Rose, S. A., & Berlin, L. J. (1978). Orlando: Grune and Stratton, Inc.

Preschool Language Scale
Zimmerman, I. L., Steiner, V. G., & Pond, R. E. (1979). San Antonio: The Psychological Corporation.

Primary Mental Abilities Test
Thurstone, L. L., & Thurstone, T. G. (1974). Chicago: Science Research Associates.

Primary Test of Cognitive Skills
Huttenlocher, J., & Levine, S. C. (1990). Monterey, CA: CTB/McGraw-Hill.

Primary Visual Motor Test
Haworth, M. R. (1970). Orlando: Grune and Stratton, Inc.

Productivity Environmental Preference Survey
Dunn, R., Dunn, K., & Price, G. E. (1981). Lawrence, KA: Price Systems.

Programmer Aptitude Competence Test System
Haverly, C. A., & Seiner, P. (1970). Denville, NJ: Haverly Systems, Inc.

PSI Basic Skills Tests for Business, Industry, & Government
Ruch, W. W., Shub, A. N., Moinat, S. M., & Dye, D. A. (1983). Bay Village, OH: Psychological Services, Inc.

Purdue Pegboard Test
Tiffin, J. (1968). Chicago: Science Research Associates.

Purdue Perceptual-Motor Survey
Roach, E. G., & Kephart, N. C. (1966). San Antonio: The Psychological Corporation.

Racial Identity Attitude Scale
Helms, J. E. (1990). New York: Greenwood Press.

Rahim Organizational Conflict Inventories
Rahim, A. (1983). Palo Alto, CA: Consulting Psychologists Press.

Reading Style Inventory
Learning Research Associates. (1986). Roslyn Heights, NY: Author.

Revised Children's Manifest Anxiety Scale
Reynolds, C. R., & Richmond, B. O. (1985). Los Angeles: Western Psychological Services.

Reynell Developmental Language Scale-Revised
Reynell, J. K. (1977). Windsor, GB: NFER-Nelson Publisher.

Reynolds Adolescent Depression Scale
Reynolds, W. M. (1987). San Antonio: The Psychological Corp. (distributor).

Riverside Curriculum Assessment System
Riverside Publishing Staff. (1991). Chicago: Riverside Publishing Co.

Roberts Apperception Test for Children
Roberts, G. E., & McArthur, D. S. (1982). Los Angeles: Western Psychological Services.

Rokeach Value Survey
Rokeach, M. (1973). Sunnyvale, CA: Halgren Tests.

Rorschach Psychodiagnostic Test, Rorschach Inkblot Test
Rorschach, H. (1945). Bern, Switzerland: Hans Huber.

Rotter Incomplete Sentences Blank
Rotter, J. B., & Rafferty, J. E. (1950). San Antonio: The Psychological Corp.

Rust Inventory of Schizotypal Conditions
Rust, J. (1987). San Antonio: Psychological Corp.

Salience Inventory
Super, D. E., & Nevill, D. D. (1985). Palo Alto, CA: Consulting Psychologists Press, Inc.

Scales for Rating the Behavioral Characteristics of Superior Students
Renzulli, J. S., Smith, L. H., White, A. J., Callahan, C. M., & Hartman, R. K. (1976). Mansfield Center, CN: Creative Learning Press, Inc.

SCAMIN: Self-Concept and Motivation Inventory
Milchus, N. J., Farrah, G. A., & Reitz, W. (1977). Dearborn Heights, MI: Person-O-Metrics.

School and College Ability Test
Educational Testing Service. (1980). Princeton, NJ: Educational Testing Service.

School Apperception Test
Solomon, I. L., Starr, B. D. (1968). New York: Springer Publishing Company.

Screening Test for Auditory Perception
Kimmel, G. M., & Wild, J. (1981). Novato, CA: Academic Therapy Publications.

Seashore Measures of Musical Talents
Seashore, C. E. (1960). San Antonio: The Psychological Corporation.

Self-Concept Adjective Checklist
Politte, A. J. (1971). Creve Coeur, MO: Psychologists and Educators, Inc.

Self-Description Questionnaire 1 and 2
Marsh, H. W. (1988). San Antonio: The Psychological Corporation.

Self-Directed Search
Holland, J. L. (1985). Odessa, FL: Psychological Assessment Resources, Inc.

Self-Report Family Inventory
Beavers, W. R., Hampon, R., & Hulgus, Y. (1985). Dallas: Southwest Family Institute.

Sentence Completion Test
Irvin, F. S. (1979). Creve Coeur, MO: Psychologists and Educators, Inc.

Sentence Comprehension Test
Institute of Psychological Research. (1979). Montreal: Author.

Sequential Tests of Educational Progress
Educational Testing Service. (1979). Monterey, CA: CTB/McGraw-Hill.

Sixteen Personality Factor Questionnaire
Cattell, R. B., & IPAT Staff. (1994). Champaign, IL: Institute for Personality and Ability Testing.

Sizing Up Your School System: The District Effectiveness Audit
Buttram, J. L., Corcoran, T. B., & Hansen, B. J. (1989). Philadelphia: Research for Better Schools.

Slosson Drawing Coordination Test
Slosson, R. L. (1967). East Aurora, NY: Slosson Educational Publications, Inc.

Slosson Intelligence Test
Slosson, R. L. (1981). East Aurora, NY: Slosson Educational Publications, Inc.

Southern California Sensory Integration Tests
Ayers, A. J. (1972). Los Angeles: Western Psychological Services.

Spache Binocular Reading Test
Spache, G. D. (1961). Davenport, IA: Keystone View.

SRA Achievement Series
Naslund, R. A., Thorpe, L. P., & Lefever, D. W. (1981). Chicago: Science Research Associates.

SRA Clerical Aptitudes
Richardson, Bellows, Henry & Co. (1973). Chicago: Science Research Associates.

SRA Mechanical Aptitudes
Richardson, Bellows, Henry & Co. (1970). Chicago: Science Research Associates.

SRA Office Skills Tests
Science Research Associates. (1977). Chicago: Author.

SRA Test of Mechanical Concepts
Stanard, S. J., & Bode, K. A. (1976). Chicago: Science Research Associates.

Stanford Achievement Tests
Gardner, E. F., Rudman, H. C., Karlsen, B., & Merwin, J. C. (1986). San Antonio: The Psychological Corporation.

Stanford-Binet Intelligence Scale
Thorndike, R. L., Hagen, E. P., & Sattler, J. M. (1986). Chicago: Riverside Publishing Company.

State-Trait Anxiety Inventory
Spielberger, C. D. (1983). Palo Alto, CA: Consulting Psychologists Press, Inc.

Sternberg Triarchic Abilities Test
Sternberg, R. J. (in press).

Stromberg Dexterity Test
Stromberg, E. L. (1951). San Antonio: The Psychological Corporation.

Strong Interest Inventory
Strong, E. K., Jr., Hansen, J. C., & Campbell, D. P. (1994). Palo Alto, CA: Consulting Psychologists Press.

Student Behavior Inventory
Funderburk, B. W., & Eyberg, S. M. (1989). *Behavioral Assessment, 11,* 297–313.

Student Opinion Inventory
National Study of School Evaluation Staff. (1981). Falls Church, VA: National Study of School Evaluation.

Suicidal Ideation Questionnaire
Reynolds, W. M. (1987). San Antonio, TX: Psychological Corp. (distributor).

Suinn Test Anxiety Behavior Scale
Rocky Mountain Behavioral Science Institute. (1971). Fort Collins, CO: Rocky Mountain Behavioral Science Institute, Inc.

Swassing-Barbe Modality Index
Swassing, R., & Barbe, R. (1979). Columbus, OH: Zaner-Bloser, Inc.

Symonds Picture Story Test
Symonds, P. M. (1948). New York: Teachers College Press.

System of Multicultural Pluralistic Assessment
Mercer, J. R., & Lewis, J. E. (1979). San Antonio: The Psychological Corporation.

Teacher Opinion Inventory
National Study of School Evaluation Staff. (1981). Falls Church, VA: National Study of School Evaluation.

Tell-Me-A-Story
Costantino, G., Malgady, R. G., & Rogler, L. H. (1988). Los Angeles: Western Psychological Services.

Tennessee Self-Concept Scale
Fitts, W. H. (1965). Los Angeles: Western Psychological Services.

Test Anxiety Inventory
Spielberger, C. D. (1980). Palo Alto, CA: Consulting Psychologists Press, Inc.

Test Anxiety Profile
Oetting, E. R., & Cole, C. W. (1980). Fort Collins, CO: Rocky Mountain Behavioral Science Institute.

Test of Adult Basic Education
CTB/McGraw-Hill. (1987). Test of Adult Basic Education: Form 5 & 6. Palo Alto, CA: Author.

Tests of Cognitive Ability
California Test Bureau. (1976). Monterey, CA: CTB/ McGraw-Hill.

Test of Nonverbal Intelligence
Brown, L., Sherbenu, R. J., & Dollar, S. J. (1982). Austin, TX: Pro-Ed.

Thematic Apperception Test
Murray, H. A. (1943). Cambridge, MA: Harvard University Press.

Thinking Creatively in Action and Movement
Torrance, E. P. (1981). Bensenville, IL: Scholastic Testing Service, Inc.

Thinking Creatively With Sounds and Words
Torrance, E. P., Khantena, J., & Cunnington, B. F. (1973). Bensenville, IL: Scholastic Testing Service, Inc.

Torrance Tests of Creative Thinking
Torrance, E. P. (1974). Bensenville, IL: Scholastic Testing Service, Inc.

USES Clerical Skills Test
  U.S. Employment Service. (1968). Washington, DC: U.S. Department of Labor.

USES General Aptitude Test Battery
  U.S. Employment Service. (1977). General Aptitude Test Battery. Washington, DC: U.S. Department of Labor.

USES Interest Inventory
  U.S. Employment Service. (1981). Washington, DC: U.S. Department of Labor.

Values Scale
  Super, D. L., Nevill, D. D. (1985). Palo Alto, CA: Consulting Psychologists Press, Inc.

Vane Kindergarten Test
  Vane, J. P. (1968). Brandon, VT: CPPC.

Vineland Adaptive Behavior Scale
  Sparrow, S. S., Balla, D. A., & Cicchetti, D. V. (1985). Circle Pines, MN: American Guidance Service.

Vocational Interest, Experience and Skill Assessment
  American College Testing Program. (1983). Iowa City: Author.

Vocational Preference Inventory
  Holland, J. L. (1985). Odessa, FL: Psychological Assessment Resources, Inc.

Watson-Glaser Critical Thinking Appraisal
  Watson, G., & Glaser, E. M. (1980). San Antonio: The Psychological Corporation.

Wechsler Tests
  Wechsler, D. (1981). Wechsler Adult Intelligence Scale, Revised. San Antonio: The Psychological Corporation.

  Wechsler, D. (1991). Wechsler Intelligence Scale for Children, III. San Antonio: The Psychological Corporation.

  Wechsler, D. (1967). Wechsler Preschool and Primary Scale of Intelligence. San Antonio: The Psychological Corporation.

Wepman Auditory Discrimination Test
  Wepman, J. M. (1973). Los Angeles: Western Psychological Services.

Wesman Personnel Classification Test
  Wesman, A. G. (1965). San Antonio: The Psychological Corporation.

Wide Range Achievement Test
  Jastak, S., & Wilkinson, G. S. (1984). Wilmington, DE: Jastak Assessment Systems.

Wonderlic Personnel Test
  Wonderlic, E. F. (1981). Northfield, IL: E. F. Wonderlic Personnel Test, Inc.

Woodcock-Johnson Psycho-Educational Battery
  Woodcock, R. W., & Johnson, M. B. (1977). Allen, TX: DLM Teaching Resources.

Woodcock-Johnson Test of Achievement Revised
  Woodcock, R. W., & Johnson, M. B. (1990). Chicago: Riverside.

Work Environment Preference Schedule
  Gordon, L. (1973). San Antonio: The Psychological Corporation.

Work Environment Scale
  Insel, P., & Moos, R. H. (1974). Palo Alto, CA: Consulting Psychologists Press, Inc.

Work Values Inventory
  Super, D. E. (1970). Chicago: Riverside Publishing Company.

World of Work Inventory
  Ripley, R. E., & Hudson, K. (1977). Scottsdale, AZ: World of Work, Inc.

Your Style of Learning and Thinking
  Torrance, E. P., & Reynolds, R. L. (1980). Athens, GA: Georgia Studies of Creative Thinking.

Appendix B: Test Publishers and Distributors

Academic Therapy Publications
20 Commercial Boulevard
Novato, CA 94949

The American College Testing Program
2201 North Dodge Street
P. O. Box 168
Iowa City, IA 52243

American Guidance Service
4201 Woodland Road
P. O. Box 99
Circle Pines, MN 55014-1796

Behavior Science Press
P. O. Box 020938
Tuscaloosa, AL 35402

Belwin-Mills Publishing Company
15800 N. W. 48th Avenue
Miami, FL 33014

The College Board Publications
45 Columbus Avenue
New York, NY 10023

Consulting Psychologists Press, Inc.
577 College Avenue
P. O. Box 60070
Palo Alto, CA 94306

Creative Learning Press, Inc.
P. O. Box 320
Mansfield Center, CT 06250

CTB/Macmillan/McGraw-Hill
Publishers Test Service
20 Ryan Ranch Road
Monterey, CA 93940

Dallas Educational Services
P. O. Box 831254
Richardson, TX 75083

The Devereux Foundation
19 South Waterloo Road
P. O. Box 400
Devon, PA 19333

Educational and Industrial Test Services
P. O. Box 7234
San Diego, CA 92167

Educational Testing Services
Rosedale Road
Princeton, NJ 08541

Educators Publishing Service, Inc.
75 Moulton Street
Cambridge, MA 02238

Employers Tests & Services Associates
341 Garfield Street
Chambersburg, PA 17201

ERIC Document Reproduction Service
P. O. Box 190
Arlington, VA 22210

Gesell Developmental Test Materials, Inc.
P. O. Box 272391
Houston, TX 77277

Grune & Stratton, Inc.
Orlando, FL 32887

Harrison G. Gough Institute of Personality and
Research
University of California
Berkeley, CA 94720

Haverly Systems, Inc.
78 Broadway
P. O. Box 919
Denville, NJ 07834

Humanics Limited
1389 Peachtree Street, N. E.
Atlanta, GA 30309

Humanics Media
5457 Pine Cone Road
La Cresenta, CA 91214

Industrial Psychology, Inc.
515 Madison Avenue
New York, NY 10022

Institute for Personality and Ability Testing, Inc.
P. O. Box 1188
1602 Coronado Drive
Champaign, IL 61824-1188

IOX Assessment Associates
11411 West Jefferson Boulevard
Culver City, CA 90230

Jastak Assessment Systems
P. O. Box 4460
Wilmington, DE 19807

Kent Developmental Metrics
1325 S. Water Street
P. O. Box 845
Kent, OH 44240-3178

Ladoca Publishing Foundation
Laradon Hall Training and Residential Center
East 51st Ave. and Lincoln St.
Denver, CO 80216

Lafayette Instrument Company
P. O. Box 5729
Lafayette, IN 47903

Life Office Management Association, Inc.
5770 Powers Ferry Road
Atlanta, GA 30327

Meeting Street School
The Easter Seal Society of Rhode Island, Inc.
667 Waterman Avenue
East Providence, RI 02914

National Computer Systems
10901 Bren Road East
Minnetonka, MN 55343

Pacific Psychological
710 George Washington Way
Suite G
Richland, WA 99352

Person-O-Metrics, Inc.
Evaluation and Development Services
20504 Williamsburg Road
Dearborn Heights, MI 48127

Pro-Ed
8700 Shoal Creek Boulevard
Austin, TX 78758

Psychological Assessment Resources, Inc.
P. O. Box 998
Odessa, FL 33556

The Psychological Corporation
555 Academic Court
San Antonio, TX 78204-2498

Psychological Services Bureau
P. O. Box 4
St. Thomas, PA 17252

Psychological Services, Inc.
370 Lake Forest Road
Bay Village, Ohio 44140

Psychological Test Specialists
P. O. Box 9229
Missoula, MT 59807

Psychometric Affiliates
P. O. Box 807
Murfreesboro, TN 37133

Reason House
204 East Joppa Road
Penthouse Suite 10
Towson, MD 21204

Research Psychologists Press, Inc.
1110 Military Street
P. O. Box 984
Port Huron, MI 48060

The Riverside Publishing Company
8420 Bryn Mawr Avenue
Chicago, IL 60631

Rocky Mountain Behavioral Science Institute,
Inc.
2190 W. Drake Road
Suite 144
Fort Collins, CO 80526

Scholastic Testing Service, Inc.
480 Meyer Road
P. O. Box 1056
Bensenville, IL 60106

Sheridan Psychological Services, Inc.
P. O. Box 6106
Orange, CA 92667

Slosson Educational Publications, Inc.
P. O. Box 280
East Aurora, NY 14052

SRA/London House
1550 Northwest Highway
Park Ridge, IL 60068

Stoelting Company
620 Wheat Lane
Wood Dale, IL 60191

U. S. Department of Labor
Division of Testing
200 Constitution Ave.
Employment and Training Administration
Washington, DC 20213

U. S. Military Entrance Processing Command
2500 Green Bay Road
North Chicago, IL 60064

Valpar International Corporation
P. O. Box 5767
Tucson, AZ 85703

Western Psychological Services
12031 Wilshire Boulevard
Los Angeles, CA 90025

E. F. Wonderlic Personnel Test, Inc.
820 Frontage Road
Northfield, IL 60093

Glossary

Ability test An ability test measures the present level of functioning and can provide an estimate of the future performance of an individual on specific tasks or domains in cognitive or psychomotor areas. See also *achievement test* and *aptitude test*.

Accountability Both students and teachers are being required to show that students have mastered course or grade objectives. Minimum level skills, essential skills, survival skills, and other types of achievement tests are used to provide evidence of mastery.

Achievement test An achievement test measures the degree or extent of the knowledge, information, skills, and competencies that a person has acquired through training, instruction, or experience. There are survey achievement tests as well as subject-related tests.

Acquiescence response set Some test takers have a tendency to select positive responses (e.g., "true" or "yes") on attitude and personality tests.

Adaptive testing This procedure adjusts the test questions presented according to an individual's responses to previous items on the test. Test items can thus be geared to the individual's ability or achievement levels, and test takers may start and finish at different levels.

Adjustment test An adjustment test is one of the major types of personality tests. Such tests measure the ability of an individual to function normally in society and achieve personal needs.

Affective domain The affective domain covers dimensions of personality such as attitudes, motives, emotional behavior, temperament, and personality traits.

Age norms Age norms for a particular test provide the median score made by test takers of a given chronological age. In addition to intellectual and social age, many tests provide information on typical characteristic behavior of individuals at given age levels.

Alternate forms For many achievement and aptitude tests it is necessary to have more than one form of the tests available. Alternate forms are constructed according to the same blueprint, that is, with the same set of objectives, the same type of items, and similar difficulty and discrimination values for the test items. The two forms also have similar statistical characteristics; the means, standard deviations, and correlations with other measures should all be approximately equal.

Alternate-forms reliability This type of reliability requires correlating the scores of individuals on one form with the scores they made on the second form. This coefficient provides evidence of the equivalence of the two forms as well as the stability of the individual's performance.

Alternative assessment Alternative assessment emphasizes assessing performance of the test taker through portfolios, interviews, observations, work samples, and the like instead of through multiple choice norm-referenced or criterion-referenced examinations.

Anecdotal records Anecdotal records require a series of observations on an individual(s). The observer should provide an objective description of the behavior observed and an interpretation of the situation. School psychologists are often required to record two observations of the child along with test information.

Aptitude test An aptitude test is used to provide an estimate of future performance on tasks that may or may not be similar to the tasks measured on the test. Aptitude tests are used to assess the educational readiness of individuals to learn or become proficient in a given area if education or training is provided. Aptitude tests may contain the same type of items as achievement tests.

Arithmetic mean See *mean*.

Assessment procedures Assessment procedures are the methods that enable one to appraise or estimate the attributes of a person, group, or programs. The tools of assessment can include checklists, inventories, observational schedules, needs assessments, rating scales, and all types of tests.

Attenuation Attenuation is a phenomenon that takes place in the statistical determination of correlation and regression. The correlation or regression is reduced because of the imperfect reliability of one or both of the measures being correlated or compared.

Attitude Attitude is a dimension of the affective domain and one aspect of an individual's personality. Attitude is reflected in reactions to events, other individuals, objects, or institutions.

Authentic assessment This type of assessment focuses on assessing realistic tasks or activities that relate to the performance on a domain or set of constructs being measured.

Basal age Basal age is the age at which the test taker passes all of the items on a given test.

Basic skills Many achievement tests are designed to measure the basic skills required to be successful in school; these are usually reading, writing, and arithmetic competencies. Such skills are necessary for the student to learn other subjects, such as science and social studies.

Battery A battery is a set of tests usually standardized on the same population. Survey achievement tests are one example of a battery. A battery facilitates comparison of a test taker's performance in different areas.

Behavioral assessment Behavioral assessment focuses on the more objective and observable components of behavior and utilizes a wide variety of techniques, such as observation, checklists, and self-monitoring.

Behavioral objectives Behavioral objectives require counselors and teachers to specify desired behavioral outcomes in objective, observable forms and to identify the conditions of measurement.

Bias Bias in testing results in scores that are higher or lower than they would be if the measurement were more reliable and valid. The error caused by bias is systematic rather than random.

Bimodal distribution A bimodal distribution is a frequency distribution with two modes or high points.

Biographic inventory A biographical inventory is a questionnaire or survey instrument used to obtain information about the individual's educational, social, medical, and work experiences. It is one of the tools used by counselors and employment psychologists.

Buckley Amendment   The Buckley Amendment is federal legislation that gives individuals and their parents or guardians access to information, including the results of standardized tests.

Ceiling   Ceiling is the level or point at which a test taker fails a test or subtest.

Central tendency   Central tendency relates to the typical or average score in a distribution. The three measures of central tendency are the mean, median, and mode. Any one of these statistics summarizes the typical or average performance of a group.

Central tendency error   An error of central tendency occurs when the rater avoids all the extreme judgments, both high and low, and rates all items in the middle.

Checklist   A checklist is a list of words, phrases, or statements describing the behavior of an individual or situation. The rater checks the presence or absence of the item.

Coaching   Coaching occurs prior to the administration of a test and involves short-term instructional activities designed to help test takers increase their test scores. Sessions often include instruction on test-taking strategies and control of test anxiety.

Coefficient alpha   Coefficient alpha is a reliability coefficient that measures the internal consistency of a test. The coefficient is the expected correlation of one test form with an alternate form that contains the same number of items.

Coefficient of determination   The coefficient of determination is computed by squaring the correlation coefficient. It provides an estimate of the proportion of variance in one variable that is predictable from the other variable.

Coefficient of equivalence   The coefficient of equivalence is used to compute the reliability of alternate forms of a test, based either upon two administrations or on a single administration with odd and even items constituting separate forms.

Coefficient of internal consistency   The coefficient of internal consistency is based upon one testing and provides an estimate of the homogeneity of test items. The split-half and Kuder-Richardson methods provide coefficients of internal consistency.

Coefficient of stability   A coefficient of stability provides a picture of how consistent an individual's scores are over a period of time. The test-retest method and alternate forms provide some information on the stability of scores over time.

Cognitive domain   The cognitive domain encompasses the different levels individuals use in perceiving, thinking, and remembering. These levels are knowledge, comprehension, application, synthesis, analysis, and evaluation.

Cognitive style   Cognitive style refers to the strategies or approaches an individual prefers to use in cognitive activities. Some of the styles discussed in the text are internal and external locus of control, field independence-field dependence, and reflectivity-impulsivity.

Competency test   A competency test is an achievement test that assesses a test taker's level of knowledge or skill in some defined domain.

Computer-assisted testing   Computer-assisted testing refers to testing that is presented on the computer rather than in a test booklet.

Computer-based interpretation   Computer-based interpretation is a method of providing the interpretation of test scores according to algorithms built into the computer program. The test user is provided with score reports and narrative statements about the results.

Concurrent validity   Concurrent validity is one type of criterion-referenced validity. Test scores are compared with a criterion measure obtained at about the same time, and the coefficient describes their relationship.

Confidence interval   The confidence interval, or confidence band, is marked by two points that define with specified probability the range that includes an individual's true score.

Construct   A construct is a theory or concept used to explain data in an orderly way. In a psychometric sense it is a psychological attribute or trait.

Construct validity   Construct validity is the extent to which a test measures the intended psychological trait or attribute.

Content validity   Content validity is the degree to which a test measures a defined body of knowledge. This type of validity is extremely important for achievement tests.

Correlation   Correlation is a statistic used to measure the strength and direction of the association between two sets of scores. Coefficients range from +1.00 to -1.00. A correlation of +1.00 indicates a perfect positive relationship between the scores; a correlation of .00 indicates no relationship between the scores; and a correlation of -1.00 indicates an inverse relationship.

Covariation   Covariation refers to the variance that two or more tests or variables have in common.

Criterion-referenced tests   Criterion-referenced tests are designed to assess a rather limited range of objectives or goals. They are usually used as mastery tests to assess whether an individual can demonstrate a specific skill or objective.

Criterion-referenced validity   Criterion-referenced validity is validity based on the correlation of test scores with some type of criterion measure.

Cronbach's alpha   Cronbach's alpha is a procedure for estimating the internal consistency of a test, based on parts of the test. It is one of the procedures used to compute reliability.

Crystallized intelligence   Crystallized intelligence is one of the types of intelligence in Cattell's model. The term refers to the part of intelligence acquired through experience and education.

Culture-fair tests   Culture-fair tests are designed to be fair to all types of cultural and socioeconomic groups. These tests attempt to include only content to which all groups have been exposed during maturation.

Decision theory   Test users are interested in making decisions and predictions on the basis of test results. Such predictions can be classified as positive, false positive, negative, and false negative. Decision theory is also used in selecting a test—to identify the types of information needed and the types of information already available.

Derived scores   A derived score is a score into which a raw score is converted by some type of mathematical operation. Percentile ranks, standard scores, stanines, and grade-equivalent scores are all derived scores.

Descriptive statistics   Descriptive statistics are used to summarize characteristics of a group of scores—for example, central tendency and dispersion or variability of scores. The mean, median, mode, variance, and standard deviation are descriptive statistics.

Deviation IQ   The deviation IQ is the score that compares an individual with his age or grade group. The fixed mean is usually 100, and the standard deviation is 15.

Diagnostic tests   A diagnostic test is an achievement test, most often in mathematics and reading, used to identify the strengths and weaknesses of the individual. Such tests include a wide range of items on a given skill or objective.

Differential prediction   Differential prediction is used in situations of criterion-referenced validity. It indicates the degree to which a test that is used to predict individual attainment yields different predictions for the same criteria for groups with different demographic characteristics, prior experience, or treatment.

Domain-sampling   Domain refers to a given area from which sample items are taken. Often criterion-referenced tests are called domain-referenced tests. The three major domains are cognitive, affective, and psychomotor.

Equivalence reliability   Equivalence reliability gives an estimate of the extent two or more forms of a test are consistent. In split-half reliability, the test is subdivided into two parts; for example, odd items versus even items. In parallel forms the scores from form X of a test are correlated with the scores from form Y to provide an estimate of the equivalence of the forms.

Equivalent forms   Test makers may construct more than one form of a test to measure the same objectives with items of similar difficulty.

Error of measurement   Error of measurement refers to the discrepancy between an individual's observed score and her true score.

Evaluation   Evaluation is the process an individual uses to judge information from one or more sources. That process may focus on test data as well as observations and other sources.

Factor   The term *factor* can describe a psychological construct, such as verbal, spatial, or numerical aptitude. It can also represent the covariance of various subtests that tend to cluster together; that is, it represents their intercorrelations or intersections.

Factor analysis   Factor analysis is a statistical multivariate procedure used to analyze the intercorrelations or covariance of variables. The method results in the identification of a reduced number of factors needed to explain the intercorrelations of variables.

False negative   A false negative is a type of error in which an individual is predicted to fail but actually succeeds if given a chance.

Field dependence   Field dependence is one of the dimensions of cognitive style that relates to an individual's dependence on body cues in space perception.

Field independence   Field independence is a dimension of cognitive style that relates to an individual's dependence on body cues in space perception but independence from the surrounding visual field.

Fluid intelligence   Fluid intelligence is one of the two types of intelligence identified by Cattell. It is the inherited dimension of intelligence and includes problem-solving and thinking ability.

Forced choice   Some interest and personality tests utilize the forced choice method,

whereby the test taker is required to select one or more items from two or more similar or related options. This method helps to control for response set.

Frequency distribution   A frequency distribution is a way of organizing and arranging data in a table. Scores are usually grouped in fewer intervals to summarize overall performance.

g factor.   The *g* factor is a generalized intelligence factor that is measured in most intelligence tests; tests that yield one score are following the *g*-factor approach. Spearman was the leading theorist of this conceptual model.

Grade-equivalent scores   Grade-equivalent scores are a type of derived test score utilized primarily by survey achievement tests. A raw score is translated into the grade level for which the achieved score is the real or estimated mean or median.

Group test   A group test can be given to more than one test taker in a single setting by one test administrator.

Halo effect   Halo effect is the tendency of a rater to let the ratings in other areas of a scale influence the ratings in areas that cannot be observed or are difficult to rate.

Histogram   A histogram is a bar graph that provides a picture or description of scores.

In-basket technique   The in-basket technique requires the examinee to take action on a series of problem situations presented through correspondence, memos, and other documents found in a sample in-basket.

Informed consent   Informed consent requires test takers to give their consent before being tested; it is legally and ethically required. Test takers are to be told what the purposes of the test are, who will have access to the scores, and how the results will be used.

Intelligence test   An intelligence test measures dimensions of aptitude and ability that are needed for success in educational and vocational fields. There are both individual and group tests.

Interest inventory   An interest inventory assesses an individual's likes and dislikes, preferences, and interests. This information is then related to occupational fields and clusters and can sometimes be compared to individuals working in given occupational fields.

Internal consistency   Internal consistency is a method of estimating reliability that is computed from a single administration of a test. The coefficients reflect the degree to which the items are measuring the same construct and are homogeneous. Cronbach's alpha and the Kuder-Richardson formulas are measures of the internal consistency of a test.

Interpretative report   Most interest, aptitude, and achievement tests provide not only a summary of the test scores but also information that helps test takers interpret and understand those scores.

Interval scale   The interval scale is one of the four measurement scales and can be used to classify and order measurements. It plots equal distances between score points but does not have a true zero point. Examples of interval scales include IQ, Celsius, and Fahrenheit scales.

Ipsative measurement   Ipsative measurement is a type of item format, such as forced choice or ranking, in which the variables (options or items) are compared with each other. Ipsative comparisons are only intraindividual and are not appropriate for normative interpretation.

Item bias   An item is said to be biased when the average expected score on the item for the group in question is substantially higher or lower than it is for the overall population and when this difference results from factors that the item is not intended to measure.

Job analysis   The general process of identifying the abilities, competencies, knowledge, and skills needed to perform jobs is called job analysis.

Kuder-Richardson 20/21   The KR 20 and 21 formulas are used to compute reliability in one administration of a test. They are internal consistency measures. KR 20 provides an estimate equal to the mean of all possible split-half coefficients. KR 21 can be substituted for KR 20 if the item difficulty levels are similar.

Least restrictive environment   Public Law 94-142 calls for the placement of each handicapped individual in the most normal situation in which that individual can be successful.

Leniency error   When a person is rated higher on an item than he should be rated, an error of leniency is operating.

Likert scale   A Likert scale is an attitude scale that asks people to rate the intensity of their agreement with certain statements.

Locus of control   Rotter identifies a cognitive and perceptual style that relates to how individuals perceive themselves as being controlled. The two ends of the continuum are external and internal, with external indicating reliance on external reinforcement and a belief in chance and fate.

Mean   The mean is the arithmetic average of a set of scores. It is equal to the sum of the scores divided by the number of scores. The mean is one of three statistics used to indicate central tendency.

Measurement   Measurement is the process used to assign numerals to objects or constructs according to rules so that the numbers have quantitative meaning.

Median   The median is the 50th percentile or the midpoint of a distribution.

Minimum level competency test   A minimum level competency test measures the essential or minimum skills that school systems and states have defined as a standard to be met.

Mode   The mode is the most frequently occurring score or number in a set of scores.

National norms   National norms give the average or median performance of a probability sample representative of the whole country. Most survey achievement batteries and scholastic aptitude tests report national norms.

Nominal scale   The nominal scale is a scale that can be used to classify data into mutually exclusive and exhaustive categories.

Nonverbal test   In a nonverbal test the test taker is not required to respond to the tasks verbally and items are not presented in a written format. The examinee may be shown pictures and asked to point to a specific one. Or the test taker may be asked to manipulate materials, copy block or bead designs, assemble puzzles, and so on.

Norm groups Norm groups are composed of the individuals on whom a test is standardized. These groups provide the basis for interpreting scores.

Norm-reference test A norm-referenced test presents score interpretation based on a comparison of individual performance with that of other individuals in specified groups.

Normal curve The normal curve is a smooth bell-shaped curve that is symmetrical around the mean; the curve can be computed with the use of an equation. Most educational and psychological variables, such as achievement and intelligence, have a normal bell-shaped distribution.

Objective test An objective test has a predetermined scoring key. Multiple choice tests are an example of such a test.

Observational techniques Observational techniques are used to look at the behavior of the test taker, sometimes during the examination and sometimes in naturalistic situations. In behavior assessment self-observation is sometimes used; the client is asked to keep a log or diary of her behavior. Situational tests require raters to observe individual behavior during the test.

Ordinal scale An ordinal scale requires an individual to rank order measurements.

Parallel forms See *alternate* or *equivalent forms.*

Percentile rank Percentile rank places a score in a distribution by identifying the percentage of scores that fall at or below the given score. A percentile rank is a type of derived score utilized on most norm-referenced type of tests.

Performance test A performance test requires the test taker to engage in some type of process, such as manipulating physical objects, rather than marking an answer on an answer sheet.

Personality inventory A personality inventory measures one or more dimensions of personality, such as attitude, adjustment, temperament, and values. The test taker is usually presented with a wide variety of behaviors and asked if they are characteristic of her.

Portfolio Portfolio is a collection of products produced by the person such as the papers, themes, tests, book reports of a student in language arts, or a collection of products produced by a person in a fine arts class.

Predictive validity Predictive validity is a form of criterion-referenced validity in which test scores are compared with performance that is measured sometime in the future. The predictor variable is the test and the criterion variable is the future performance, often on the job or in school.

Predictor A predictor is a measurable characteristic—such as a test score, previous performance, a rating or observation—that is correlated with a criterion variable to indicate future success or failure.

Primary standards Primary standards are the essential and fundamental characteristics that should be met by all tests before they are used.

Profile A profile is a graphic representation of individual or group scores. It provides a picture of the relative magnitude of scores.

Projective techniques Projective techniques are one method of assessing personality. The test taker gives free response to a series of stimuli, such as inkblots, pictures, or incomplete sentences. It is assumed that individuals will project their own perceptions, feelings, and attitudes in their answers.

Psychomotor test A psychomotor test measures fine and gross motor skills. The psychomotor domain—unlike the cognitive and affective domains—organizes and classifies psychomotor behaviors in terms of the amount of concentration required.

Public Law 94-142 Public Law 94-142, entitled the Education of All Handicapped Children Act, was passed in 1975 and established the requirements for free and appropriate education for all handicapped children. It also restricts the use of tests and assessment procedures with handicapped individuals.

Questionnaire   A questionnaire is similar to a structured interview; it contains a list of questions on a topic or issue. A questionnaire is usually administered to a group of individuals to find out about their attitudes, beliefs, behaviors, and so on.

Range   Range is a statistic used to measure the variable or spread of the scores. It is the difference between the highest and lowest score in a distribution.

Rapport   Rapport is a warm and friendly relationship or interpersonal environment. An examiner wants to ensure valid results by establishing this type of positive environment and thereby encouraging the proper motivation and cooperation of the test taker.

Rating scale   A rating scale is a measure that requires the rater to estimate the value of a person or thing or assess the presence of some trait or characteristic. Sometimes the scale calls for self-ratings; at other times ratings are given by peers, teachers, parents, and so on.

Ratio scale   The ratio scale has equal units of measurement and has a true zero point. Time, height, and weight are examples of measurements that utilize the ratio scale. Most educational and psychological variables cannot be measured on the ratio scale.

Raw score   Raw score is the unadjusted number of correct answers.

Readiness test   A readiness test measures the extent to which the test taker has acquired the skills and knowledge necessary to learn a more complex skill.

Regression   Regression is a statistical technique used to help individuals predict x when they know y and the relationship between x and y. A linear equation can be compared to predict criterion scores with one or more predictor variables.

Reliability   Reliability refers to the degree to which test scores are consistent, dependable, or repeatable. Reliability is a function of the degree to which test scores are free from errors of measurement.

Response set   Response set refers to the tendency of a test taker to respond to test items in a stereotyped or fixed way. The test taker may consciously or unconsciously choose the most socially desirable answers or perhaps true rather than false options.

Scatter plot   A scatter plot is a bivariate graph that shows the paired values of two variables being correlated.

Scholastic aptitude test   A scholastic aptitude test measures the cognitive skills necessary for success in school. It is used to predict how well individuals will do in educational contexts.

Screening test   A screening test makes broad categorizations as a first step in a selection or diagnostic process in school or industry.

Situational test   A situational test is a performance test in which an individual is placed in a realistic but contrived situation and then is rated on her role competence and problem-solving abilities.

Skewness   Skewness is the degree of asymmetry in a frequency distribution. In positively skewed distributions the scores are piled up at the lower end of the distribution, to the left of the mode. In a negatively skewed distribution the scores are piled up at the high end of the distribution, to the right of the mode.

Social desirability response set   The social desirability response set is active when an individual tries to portray himself in a socially desirable light. The individual fakes "good" instead of putting down what is truly descriptive of his behavior.

Spearman-Brown prophecy formula   The Spearman-Brown formula is used to estimate the reliability of a test if the test length is increased. Theoretically, a longer test samples more behavior and covers more items from the measured domain, thereby increasing the reliability of the test.

Speeded test   A speeded test measures performance by the number of tasks performed in a given time period. Clerical speed and accuracy, typing, and coding tests are examples of this type of test.

Split-half reliability Split-half reliability is a method of computing the reliability of a test from one administration of the test. An internal analysis coefficient is obtained by using one-half of the items on the test for one score, and the other half for the second score. These scores are then correlated and corrected for a full-length test, using the Spearman-Brown Formula. The method provides an estimate of the alternate form reliability.

Standard deviation The standard deviation is the square root of the variance; it is a statistic that describes the spread or dispersion of scores. Standard deviation is used with a derived scores as an index of how far above or below the mean the score falls.

Standard error of measurement The standard error of measurement is the standard deviation of the errors of measurement associated with the test scores for a specific group of test takers.

Standard score A standard score describes the location of an individual's score within a set of scores. Its distance from the mean is expressed in terms of standard deviation units. Such a score is used in norm-referenced measurement contexts.

Standardized test A standardized test is administered under standard directions and conditions.

Stanines Stanines are a 9-point scale having a mean of 5 and a standard deviation of 2. All but stanines 1 and 9 are one-half standard deviation in width. They are used to describe an individual's position relative to the norming group.

Statistics Statistics are an area of mathematics focusing on the collection, organization, and interpretation of numerical data. A statistic is a number used to describe some characteristic, such as the central tendency or variability of a set of scores.

Subtest A subtest is a grouping of items measuring the same function.

T-score A *T* score is a derived score on a scale usually having a mean score of 50 and a standard deviation of 10.

Test anxiety Test anxiety is a psychological state of stress and fear caused by testing situations. Although some anxiety may be beneficial, extreme test anxiety can disrupt performance.

Test-retest reliability Test-retest methods require giving the same test to the same group of examinees on two different occasions and correlating the two sets of scores. The resulting coefficient gives an indication of the stability of the results.

True score The true score in classical test theory is the average of the scores earned by an individual on an unlimited number of perfectly parallel forms of the same test.

Usability Usability refers to the practical factors that must be considered in selecting a test—for example, cost, time, ease of administration, and ease of scoring.

User's guide The user's guide contains a statement of the purpose of the test, its content, and appropriate uses. The guide often contains information on how to administer, score, and interpret the test.

Validity Validity is the degree to which a certain inference from a test is appropriate or meaningful.

Variance Variance is the average squared deviation from the mean or the standard deviation squared. The statistic is a measure of variability or dispersion of the scores.

Verbal test A verbal test is a test requiring oral or written responses to test items.

z score A *z* score is a type of standard score in which the mean is zero and the standard deviation is 1. A *z* score represents the raw score in standard deviation units.

References

Aiken, L. R. (1985). *Psychological testing and assessment* (3rd ed.). Boston: Allyn & Bacon.

Alderman, D. L., & Powers, D. E. (1980). The effects of special preparation on SAT-Verbal scores. *American Educational Research Journal, 17,* 239–253.

Allred, L. J., & Harris, W. G. (1984). Personal communication cited in B. F. Green (1984), *Computer-based ability testing.* Washington, DC: American Psychological Association, Scientific Affairs Office.

Aman, M. G., Hammer, D., & Rojahn, J. (1993). Mental retardation. In T. H. Ollendick & M. Hersen (Eds.), *Handbook of child and adolescent assessment.* Boston: Allyn and Bacon.

American Association for Counseling and Development (AACD). (1980). *Responsibilities of users of standardized tests* [APGA Policy Statement]. Falls Church, VA: Author.

American Association for Counseling and Development & Association for Measurement and Evaluation in Counseling and Development. (1989, May). The responsibilities of test users. *AACD Guideposts,* 12–28.

American Association of Mental Retardation. (1993). *Manual on terminology and classification in mental retardation.* Washington, DC: Author.

American Association of School Administrators, National Association of Elementary Principals, National Association of Secondary School Principals, & National Council on Measurement in Education. (1994). Competency standards in student assessment for educational administrators. Educational Measurement: Issues and Practices, *13*(1), 44–47.

American Counseling Association. (1993). *Code of ethics.* Alexandria, VA: Author.

American Educational Research Association, American Psychological Association, & National Council on Measurement in Education. (1985). *Standards for educational and psychological testing.* Washington, DC: American Psychological Association.

American Psychiatric Association. (1980). *Diagnostic and statistical manual of mental disorders* (3rd ed.). Washington, DC: Author.

American Psychological Association. (1988). *Code of fair testing practices.* Washington, DC: Joint Committee on Testing Practices, American Psychological Association.

American Psychological Association. (1990). Ethical principles of psychologists. *American Psychologist, 45*, 390–395.

American Psychological Association. (1992). *Ethical principles of psychologists* (Rev. ed.). Washington, DC: Author.

American Psychological Association. (1994). *Publication manual of the American Psychologi-cal Association* (4th ed.). Washington, DC: Author.

Anastasi, A. (1982). *Psychological testing* (5th ed.). New York: Macmillan.

Arnold, M. B. (1962). *Story sequence analysis: A method of measuring and predicting achievement*. New York: Columbia University Press.

Assessing assessments: Testing issues were hot on Capitol Hill in '90. (1991, January, February). *APA Science Agenda, 4*(1), 6–8.

Bailey, D., & Wolery, M. (1989). *Assessing infants and preschoolers with handicaps*. Columbus, OH: Merrill.

Bailey, R. C., and Siudzinski, R. M. (1986). *The FAST Profile Instruction and Reference Manual: The Florida Analysis of Semantic Traits Profile*. Dallas: BALI Screening Co.

Baker, F. B. (1989). Computer technology in test construction and processing. In R. L. Linn, *Educational measurement* (3rd ed.). New York: Macmillan.

Baldwin, J. A., & Bell, Y. R. (1985). The African Self-Consciousness Scales: An Africentric Personality Questionnaire. *Western Journal of Black Studies, 9*(2), 65–68.

Bandura, A. (1986). *Social foundations of thought and action: A social cognitive theory*. Englewood Cliffs, NJ: Prentice-Hall.

Bannatyne, A. (1971). *Language, reading, and learning disabilities*. Springfield, IL: Charles C. Thomas.

Bannatyne, A. (1974). Diagnosis: A note on the recategorization of the WISC scaled score. *Journal of Learning Disabilities, 7*, 272–273.

Barbe, W. B., & Swassing, R. H. (1979). *Teaching through modality strengths: Concepts and practices*. Columbus, OH: Zaner-Bloser.

Barclay, J. R. (1983). *Barclay Classroom Assessment System manual*. Los Angeles: Western Psychological Services.

Barnett, D., & Zucker, K. R. (1990). *The personal and social assessment of children*. Boston: Allyn & Bacon.

Barrious, B. A. (1993). Direct observation. In T. H. Ollendick & M. Hersen (Eds.), *Handbook of child and adolescent assessment*. Boston: Allyn & Bacon.

Baruth, L. G., & Manning, M. L. (1991). *Multicultural counseling and psychotherapy. A life-span perspective*. New York: Merrill/Macmillan.

Bellak, L. (1975). *The TAT, CAT, and SAT in clinical use* (3rd ed.). New York: Grune & Stratton.

Bender, L. (1938). A visual motor Gestalt test and its clinical uses. *Research Monographs of the American Orthopsychiatric Association*, No. 3.

Bennett, G. K., Seashore, H. G., & Wesman, A. O. (1977). *Counseling from profiles: A casebook for the DAT* (2nd ed.). New York: Psychological Corporation.

Bergan, J. R. (1977). *Behavioral consultation*. Columbus, OH: Merrill.

Berk, R. A. (1986). Minimum competency testing: Status and potential. In B. S. Plake & J. C. Witt, *The future of testing*. Hillsdale, NJ: Erlbaum.

Bersoff, D. N., & Hofer, P. J. (1991). Legal issues in computerized testing. In T. B. Gutkin & S. L. Wise (Eds.), *The computer and the decision-making process*. Hillsdale, NJ: Erlbaum.

Beutler, L. E., & Berren, M. R. (Eds.). (1995). *Integrative assessment of adult personality*. New York: Guilford.

Binet, A., & Simon, T. (1916). *The development of intelligence in children*. (E. S. Kite, Trans.). Baltimore: Williams & Wilkins.

Bishop, J. H. (1988). Employment testing and incentives to learn. *Journal of Vocational Behavior, 33*(3), 404–423.

Boehm, A. E., & White, M. A. (1982). *The parents' handbook on school testing*. New York: Teachers College Press.

Bradley-Johnson, S., & Evans, C. D. (1991). *Psychoeducational assessment of hearing-impaired students: Infancy through adulthood.* Austin, TX: Pro-Ed.

Bromly, D. B. (1986). *The case-study method in psychology and related disciplines.* New York: John Wiley & Sons.

Brown, D., Pryzwansky, W. B., & Schulte, A. C. (1995). *Psychological consultation: Introduction to theory and practice* (3rd ed.). Boston: Allyn & Bacon.

Brown, D., Wyne, M. D., Blackburn, J. E., & Powell, W. C. (1979). *Consultation: Strategy for improving education.* Boston: Allyn & Bacon.

Brown, F. G. (1983). *Principles of educational and psychological testing* (3rd ed.). New York: Holt, Rinehart & Winston.

Buck, J. N. (1970). *The House-Tree-Person technique: Revised manual.* Los Angeles: Western Psychological Services.

Bunderson, C. V., Inouye, D. K., & Olsen, J. B. (1989). The four generations of computerized educational measurement. In R. L. Linn (Ed.), *Educational measurement* (3rd ed.). New York: Macmillan.

Burger, S. E., & Burger, P. L. (1994). Determining the validity of performance based assessments. *Educational Measurement: Issues and Practices, 13*(4), 9–15.

Burns, R. C., & Kaufman, S. H. (1972). *Action, styles, and symbols in Kinetic Family Drawings (K-F-D).* New York: Brunner/Mazel.

Buros Institute of Mental Measurements. (1994). *Psychological assessment in schools.* Lincoln, NB: Author.

Byham, W. C., & Thornton, G. C., III. (1986). Assessment centers. In R. A. Burke (Ed.), *Performance assessment.* Baltimore: Johns Hopkins University Press.

Campbell, D. T., & Fiske, D. W. (1959). Convergent and discriminant validation by the multitrait and multimethod matrix. *Psychological Bulletin, 56,* 81–105.

Canino, I. A., & Spurlock, J. (1994). *Culturally diverse children and adolescents. Assessment, diagnosis, and treatment.* New York: Guilford.

Caplan, G. (1963). Types of mental health consultation. *American Journal of Orthopsychiatry, 33,* 470–481.

Caplan, G. (1964). *Principles of preventive psychology.* New York: Basic Books.

Caplan, G. (1970). *The theory and practice of mental health consultation.* New York: Basic Books.

Caplan, G., & Caplan, R. B. (1993). *Mental health consultation and collaboration.* San Francisco: Jossey-Bass.

Casenada, A., McCandless, B. R., & Palermo, D. S. (1956). The children's form of the Manifest Anxiety Scale (CMAS). *Child Development, 27,* 317–326.

Cattell, R. B. (1963). Theory of fluid and crystallized intelligence: A critical experiment. *Journal of Educational Psychology, 54,* 1–22.

Chase, J. B. (1986). Psychoeducational assessment of visually impaired learners. In P. J. Lazarus (Ed.), *Psychoeducational evaluation of children and adolescents.* New York: Grune & Stratton.

Chiodo, J. J. (1986). The effects of exam anxiety on grandma's health. *Chronicle of Higher Education, 32*(23), 68.

Chun, K. T., Cobb, C. S., & French, J. R., Jr. (1975). *Measures of psychological assessment: A guide to 3000 original sources and their application.* Ann Arbor, MI: Institute for Social Research.

Conoley, J. C., & Kramer, J. J. (Eds.). (1994). *Supplement to the eleventh mental measurements yearbook.* Lincoln, NB: Buros Institute.

Cook, M., & Cook, M. (1988). *Personnel selection and productivity.* Chicago: Dryden.

Cooper, J. M. (1984). Observation skills. In J. M. Cooper (Ed.), *Developing skills for instructional supervision.* New York: Longman.

Cooper, J. O. (1981). *Measuring behavior* (2nd ed.). Columbus, OH: Merrill.

CRESST. (1992, Spring). *Principles of learner centered assessment*. Los Angeles: Author.

CRESST. (1994, February). *Portfolio assessment*. Los Angeles: Author.

Cronbach, L. J. (1951). Coefficient alpha and the internal structure of tests. *Psychometrika, 16,* 297–334.

Cronbach, L. J. (1984). *Essentials of psychological testing* (4th ed.). New York: Harper & Row.

Dana, R. H. (1985). Thematic Apperception Test (TAT). In C. S. Newmark (Ed.), *Major psychological assessment instruments*. Boston: Allyn & Bacon.

Dana, R. H. (1993). *Multicultural assessment perspectives for professional psychology*. Boston: Allyn & Bacon.

Davidson, M. L. (1992). Test scores and statistics. In M. Zeidner & R. Most (Eds.), *Psychological testing: An inside view*. Palo Alto, CA: Consulting Psychologists Press.

Deffenbacher, J. L. (1978). Worry, emotionality, and task-generated interference in test anxiety: An empirical test of attentional theory. *Journal of Educational Psychology, 70,* 248–254.

Dragus, J. G. (1989). Dilemmas and choices in crosscultural counseling. The universal versus the culturally distinctive. In P. B. Pedersen, J. G. Draguns, J. Lonner, & J. E. Trimble (Eds.), *Counseling across cultures* (3rd ed.). Honolulu: University of Hawaii Press.

DuBose, R. F. (1982). Assessment of severely impaired young children: Problems and recommendations. In J. T. Neisworth (Ed.), *Assessment in special education*. Rockville, MD: Aspen Systems.

Dunn, R. (1983). Learning style and its relation to exceptionality at both ends of the spectrum. *Exceptional Children, 40,* 496–506.

Dunn, R., Dunn, K., & Price, G. E. (1983). *Learning style inventory*. Lawrence, KS: Price Systems.

Dustin, D., & Ehly, S. (1984). Skills for effective consultation. *The School Counselor, 31,* 23–29.

Educational Testing Service. (1988). *Test-taking tip sheet. General*. Princeton, NJ: Author.

Educational Testing Service. (1993). *Testing in America's schools*. Princeton, NJ: Author.

Educational Testing Service. (1994). *Computer based testing: From multiple choice to multiple choices*. Princeton, NJ: Author.

Eisen, J. (1984). Researchers examine learning styles. *APA Monitor, 15*(5), 34.

Elam, S. M. (1990). The 22nd annual Gallup Poll of the public's attitudes toward the public schools. *Phi Delta Kappan, 72,* 41–55.

English, H. B., & English, A. C. (1958). *A comprehensive dictionary of psychological and psychoanalytical terms*. New York: Longman.

Erdberg, P. (1985). The Rorschach. In C. S. Newmark (Ed.), *Major psychological assessment instruments*. Boston: Allyn & Bacon.

Exner, J. (1974). *The Rorschach: A comprehensive system*. New York: John Wiley & Sons.

Exner, J. (1978). *The Rorschach: A comprehensive system: Vol. 2. Current research and advanced interpretations*. New York: John Wiley & Sons.

Exner, J., & Weiner, I. B. (1982). *The Rorschach: A comprehensive system: Vol. 3. Assessment of children and adolescents*. New York: John Wiley & Sons.

Eyde, L. D., Moreland, K. L., & Robertson, G. J. (1988). *Test user qualifications: A data-based approach to promoting good test use*. Washington, DC: American Psychological Association.

Farr, R. (1994). *Portfolio and performance assessment*. San Antonio: Psychological Corporation.

Feld, S. C., & Lewis, J. (1969). The assessment of achievement anxieties in children. In C. P. Smith (Ed.), *Achievement-related motives in children*. New York: Russell Sage Foundation.

Feldt, L. S., & Brennan, R. L. (1989). Reliability. In R. L. Linn (Ed.), *Educational measurement* (3rd ed.). New York: Collier Macmillan.

First, P. F., & Curcio, J. L. (1993). Implementing the Disabilities Act: Implications for educators. *Fast Back #360*. Bloomington, IN: Phi Delta Kappa.

Fisher, C. T. (1985). *Individualized psychological assessment*. Monterey, CA: Brooks/Cole.

Fisher, J., & Corcoran, K. (Eds.) (1994). *Measures for clinical practice. Vol. 1: Couples and families* (2nd ed.). New York: Macmillan.

Fisher, T. H. (1993). Perspectives on alternate assessment: What's happening nationally. *Research Bulletin—Florida Educational Research Council, 25*(1), 11–16.

Flanagan, J. C. (1954). The critical incidents technique. *Psychological Bulletin, 51,* 327–358.

Florez, J. (1991, January, February). Quoted in Assessing instruments. *Science Agenda, 4,* 6–7.

Ford, V. (1973). *Everything you wanted to know about test-wiseness*. Princeton, NJ: Educational Testing Service.

Frederiksen, N., Saunders, D. R., & Wand, B. (1957). The in-basket test. *Psychological Monograph, 71*(9).

Friedman, T., & Williams, E. B. (1982). Current uses of tests for employment. In A. K. Wigdon & W. R. Garner (Eds.), *Ability testing: Uses, consequences, and controversies (Part 2)*. Washington, DC: National Academy Press.

Fuchs, D., & Fuchs, L. S. (1986). Test procedure bias: A meta-analysis of examiner familiar effects. *Review of Educational Research, 56*(2), 243–262.

Gabel, S., Oster, G. D., & Botnik, S. M. (1986). *Understanding psychological testing in children*. New York: Plenum.

Gallup, A. M. (1986). The 18th Annual Gallup Poll on the Public's Attitude Toward the Public School. *Phi Delta Kappan, 68*(1), 43–59.

Gardner, H. (1983). *Frames of mind: The theory of multiple intelligence*. Cambridge: Cambridge University Press.

Gardner, H. (1993). *Multiple intelligences: The theory in practice*. New York: Basic Books.

Gardner, P. M., & Parker, P. (1993). Eating disorders. In T. H. Ollendick & M. Hersen (Eds.), *Handbook of child and adolescent assessment*. Boston: Allyn & Bacon.

Garfield, N. J., & Prediger, D. J. (1982). Testing competencies and responsibilities: A checklist for counselors. In J. T. Kapes & M. M. Mastie (Eds.), *A counselor's guide to vocational guidance instruments*. Falls Church, VA: National Vocational Guidance Association, American Personnel and Guidance Association.

Gatewood, R., & Perloff, R. (1990). Testing and industrial application. In G. Goldsten & M. Hersen (Eds.), *Handbook of psychological assessment*. New York: Pergamon.

Gatewood, R. D., & Feild, H. S. (1990). *Human resource selection*. Chicago: Dryden.

Gazzaniga, M. S. (1985). *Social brain: Discovering the networks of the mind*. New York: Basic Books.

Glaser, R. (1994). Criterion referenced tests: Part II. Unfinished business. *Educational Measurement: Issues and Practices, 13*(4), 27–30.

Glaser, R., & Bond, L. (1981). Testing: Concepts, policy, practice, and research. *American Psychologist, 36*(10), 997–1000.

Golden, C. J. (1990). *Clinical interpretation of objective psychological tests* (2nd ed.). Boston: Allyn & Bacon.

Goldman, B. A., & Mitchell, D. F. (1990). *Directory of unpublished experimental mental measures*. Dubuque, IA: William C. Grown.

Goldman, L. (1971). *Using tests in counseling* (2nd ed.). Pacific Palisades, CA: Goodyear.

Goldstein, G. (1984). Comprehensive neuropsychological assessment batteries. In G. Goldstein & M. Hersen, *Handbook of psychological assessment*. New York: Pergamon.

Goldstein, K. M., & Blackman, S. (1978). *Cognitive styles: Five approaches to theory and research*. New York: John Wiley & Sons.

Grady, M. P. (1984). *Teaching and brain research*. New York: Longman.

Grayson, H. H., & Tolamn, R. S. (1950). A semantic study of concepts in clinical psychologists and psychiatrists. *Journal of Abnormal and Social Psychology, 45,* 216–231.

Graziano, W. G., Varca, P. E., & Levy, J. C. (1982). Race of examiner effects and the validity of intelligence tests. *Review of Educational Research, 52*(4), 469–497.

Greaud, V. A., & Green, B. F. (1986). Equivalence of conventional and computer presentation of speeded tests. *Applied Psychological Measurement, 10*, 23–34.

Green, B. F. (1984). *Computer-based ability testing.* Washington, DC: Scientific Affairs Office, American Psychological Association.

Green, B. F. (1991). Guidelines for computer testing. In T. B. Gutkin & S. L. Wise (Eds.), *The computer and the decision-making process.* Hillsdale, NJ: Erlbaum.

Gregorc, A. F. (1982). *Gregorc Style Delineator: Developmental, technical, and administrative manual.* Maynard, MA: Gabriel Systems.

Griggs, S. A. (1991). *Learning styles counseling.* Ann Arbor, MI: ERIC Counseling and Personnel Services Clearinghouse.

Griggs v. Duke Power Co., 401 U. S. 424 (1971). 3EPD P8137, 3FEP175.

Grossman, H. J. (Ed.). (1977). *Manual on the terminology and classification in mental retardation.* Washington, DC: American Association on Mental Deficiency.

Groth-Marnat, G. (1984). *Handbook of psychological assessment.* New York: Van Nostrand Reinhold.

Groth-Marnat, G. (1990). *Handbook of psychological assessment* (2nd ed.). New York: John Wiley & Sons.

Guilford, J. P. (1967). *The nature of human intelligence.* New York: McGraw-Hill.

Gutkin, T. B., & Curtis, M. J. (1982). School-based consultation: Theory and techniques. In C. R. Reynolds and T. B. Gutkin (Eds.), *Handbook of school psychology.* New York: John Wiley & Sons.

Hambleton, R. K., & Eignor, D. R. (1980). Competency test development, validation, and standard setting. In R. M. Jaeger & C. K. Tittle (Eds.), *Minimum competency testing: Motives,*

models, measures, and consequences. Berkeley, CA: McCutchan.

Hammer, A. L. (1992). Test evaluation and quality. In M. Zeidner & R. Most (Eds.), *Psychological testing: An inside view.* Palo Alto, CA: Consulting Psychologists Press.

Hammer, E. F. (1985). The House-Tree-Person Test. In C. S. Newmark (Ed.), *Major psychological instruments.* Boston: Allyn & Bacon.

Hansen, J. C. (1990). Interest inventories. In G. Goldstein and M. Hersen (Eds.), *Handbook of psychological assessment* (2nd ed.). New York: Pergamon.

Hanson, J. C. (1986). Computers and beyond in the career decision-making process. *Measurement and Evaluation in Counseling and Development, 19*(1), 48–52.

Hargrove, L. J., & Poteet, J. A. (1984). *Assessment in special education: The educational evaluation.* Englewood Cliffs, NJ: Prentice-Hall.

Haring, N. G. (Ed.). (1982). *Exceptional children and youth* (3rd ed.). Columbus, OH: Merrill.

Hartshorne, H., & May, M. A. (1928). *Studies in deceit* (Vol. 2). New York: Macmillan.

Hathaway, S. R., & McKinley, J. C. (1943). *Manual: The Minnesota Multiphasic Personality Inventory.* New York: The Psychological Corporation.

Hawley, G. A. (1988). *Professional manual for measures of psychosocial development.* Odessa, FL: Psychological Assessment Resources.

Hembree, R. (1988). Correlates, causes, effects and treatment of test anxiety. *Review of Educational Research, 58*(1), 47–77.

Herr, E. L., & Cramer, S. H. (1984). *Career counseling through the life span* (2nd ed.). Boston: Little, Brown & Co.

Herrnstein, R. J. (1971, September). IQ. *Atlantic Monthly*, pp. 43–64.

Herrnstein, R. J., & Murray, C. (1994). *The bell curve.* New York: Free Press.

Hirsh, S., & Kummerow, J. (1990). *Introduction to type in organizations* (2nd ed.). Palo Alto, CA: Consulting Psychologists Press.

Hodges, K., Kline, J., Stern, L., Cytryn, L., & McKnew, D. (1982). The development of a child assessment interview for research and clinical use. *Journal of Abnormal Child Psychology, 10,* 173–189.

Hodges, K., & Zeeman, J. (1993). Interviewing. In T. H. Ollendick & M. Hersen (Eds.), *Handbook of child and adolescent assessment.* Boston: Allyn & Bacon.

Holland, J. L. (1979). *Professional manual for the self-directed search.* Palo Alto, CA: Consulting Psychologists Press.

Holland, J. L. (1985). *Making vocational choices* (2nd ed.). Englewood Cliffs, NJ: Prentice-Hall.

Holland, J. L. (1985). *Occupational finder.* Odessa, FL: Psychological Assessment Resources.

Holland, J. L. (1985). *Self-directed search.* Odessa, FL: Psychological Assessment Resources.

Holland, J. L. (1986). New directions for interest testing. In B. S. Plake & J. C. Witt (Eds.), *The future of testing.* Hillsdale, NJ: Erlbaum.

Holt, R. R. (Ed.). (1968). *Diagnostic psychological testing* (rev. ed.). New York: International Universities Press.

Horn, J. L. (1989). Cognitive diversity. A framework for learning. In P. L. Ackerman, R. J. Sternberg, & R. Glaser (Eds.), *Learning and individual differences: Advances in theory and research.* New York: W. H. Freeman.

Howard, E. R., & Keefe, J. W. (1991). *The Case-IMS School Improvement Process.* Reston, VA: NASSP.

Hoyt, C. J. (1941). Test reliability estimated by analysis of variance. *Psychometrika, 6,* 153–160.

Hurt, S. W., Reznikoff, M., & Clarkin, J. F. (1995). The Rorschach. In L. E. Beutler & M. R. Berren (Eds.), *Integrative assessment of adult personality.* New York: Guilford.

Inghram, C. F. (1980). *Fundamentals of educational assessment.* New York: D. Van Nostrand.

Jackson, D. N. (1985). *Computer-based personality testing.* Washington, DC: Scientific Affairs Office, American Psychological Association.

Jackson, D. N. (1991). Computer-assisted personality test interpretation: The dawn of discovery. In T. B. Gutkin & S. L. Wise (Eds.), *The computer and the decision-making process.* Hillsdale, NJ: Erlbaum.

Jaeger, R. M. (1994). What parents want to know about schools: A report on school report cards. *Evaluation Perspectives, 4*(2), 2–3.

Jensen, A. R. (1969). How much can we boost IQ and scholastic achievement? *Harvard Educational Review, 39,* 1–123.

Jensen, A. R. (1980). *Bias in mental testing.* New York: Free Press.

Jensen, A. R. (1988). Armed Services Vocational Aptitude Battery. In J. T. Kapes & M. M. Mastie (Eds.), *A counselor's guide to career assessment instruments.* Alexandria, VA: National Career Development Association.

Johnson, M. E., & Holland, A. L. (1986). Measuring clients' expectations: The 15 Personal Problem Inventory. *Measurement and Evaluation in Counseling and Development, 19*(3), 151–156.

Joint Committee on Testing Practices. (1988). *Code of fair testing practices.* Washington, DC: American Psychological Association.

Jung, C. G. (1910). The association method. *American Journal of Psychology, 21,* 219–269.

Jung, C. G. (1918). *Studies in word association.* London: Heinemann.

Kachigan, S. K. (1986). *Statistical analysis: An interdisciplinary introduction to univariate and multivariate methods.* New York: Radius.

Kachigan, S. K. (1991). *Multivariate statistical analysis: A conceptual introduction* (2nd ed.). New York: Radius.

Kagan, J. (1966). Reflection-impulsivity: The generality and dynamics of conceptual tempo. *Journal of Abnormal Psychology, 71,* 17–24.

Kagan, J., Rosman, B. L., Day, D., Albert, J., & Phillips, W. (1964). Information processing in the child: Significance of analytic and reflective attitudes. *Psychological Monograph, 78*(578).

Kamphaus, R. W. (1993). *Clinical assessment of children's intelligence: A handbook for professional practice*. Boston: Allyn & Bacon.

Kane, M. T. (1986). The future of testing for licensure and certification examinations. In B. S. Plake & J. C. Witt (Eds.), *The future of testing*. Hillsdale, NJ: Erlbaum.

Kapes, J. T., & Masstie, M. M. (1994). *A counselor's guide to career assessment instruments* (3rd ed.). Alexandria, VA: ACA.

Katz, L. (1991). *A practical guide to psychodiagnostic testing* (2nd ed.). Springfield, IL: Charles C. Thomas.

Kaufman, A. S. (1976). Verbal-performance IQ discrepancies on the WISC-R. *Journal of Consulting and Clinical Psychology, 44*, 739–744.

Kaufman, A. S. (1979). *Intelligence testing with the WISC-R*. New York: John Wiley & Sons.

Kaufman, A. S., Kamphaus, R. W., & Kaufman, N. L. (1985). The Kaufman Assessment Battery for Children (K-ABC). In C. S. Newmark (Ed.), *Major psychological assessment instruments*. Boston: Allyn & Bacon.

Kaufman, A. S., & Kaufman, N. L. (1983). *Kaufman Assessment Battery for Children*. Circle Pines, MN: American Guidance Service.

Kazdin, A. E. (1993). Conduct disorders. In T. H. Ollendick & M. Hersen (Eds.), *Handbook of child and adolescent assessment*. Boston: Allyn & Bacon.

Keefe, J. W. (1979). Learning style: An overview. In *Student learning styles*. Reston, VA: National Association of Secondary School Principals.

Keefe, J. W., & Languis, M. L. (1983, August). *Operational definitions*. Paper presented to NASSP Learning Styles Task Force, Reston, VA.

Keefe, J. W., & Monk, J. S. (1988). *Manual to Learning Style Profile*. Reston, VA: National Association of Secondary School Principals.

Keesling, J. W., & Healy, C. C. (1988). USES General Aptitude Battery. In J. T. Kapes & M. M. Mastie (Eds.), *A counselor's guide to career instruments* (2nd ed.). Alexandria, VA: National Career Development Association.

Kelly, E. L., & Fiske, D. W. (1951). *The prediction of performance in clinical psychology*. Ann Arbor: University of Michigan Press.

Kline, P. (1993). *Handbook of psychological testing*. New York: Routledge.

Klopfer, B., & Davidson, H. H. (1962). *The Rorschach technique: An introductory manual*. New York: Harcourt, Brace, & World.

Klopfer, W. G. (1960). *The psychological report: Use and communication of psychological findings*. New York: Grune & Stratton.

Kolb, D. A. (1976). *Learning Style Inventory*. Boston: McBer.

Koppitz, E. M. (1968). *Psychological evaluation of children's human figure drawings*. New York: Grune & Stratton.

Koppitz, E. M. (1975). *The Bender Gestalt Test for Young Children: Vol. 2. Research and applications 1963–1973*. New York: Grune & Stratton.

Koppitz, E. M. (1982). Personality assessment in the schools. In C. R. Reynolds & T. B. Gutkin (Eds.), *Handbook of school psychology* (pp. 273–295). New York: John Wiley & Sons.

Korchin, S. J., & Schuldberg, D. (1981). The future of clinical assessment. *American Psychologist, 36*(10), 1147–1158.

Kovacs, M. (1982). *The longitudinal study of child and adolescent psychopathology: I. The semistructured psychiatric interview schedule for children*. Unpublished manuscript.

Kubiszyn, T., & Borich, G. (1987). *Educational testing and measurement* (2nd ed.). Glenview, IL: Scott, Foresman.

Kuder, G. F., & Richardson, M. (1937). The theory of the estimation test reliability. *Psychometrika, 2*, 151–160.

La Greca, A. M., & Stringer, S. A. (1985). The Wechsler Intelligence Scale for Children–Revised. In C. S. Newmark (Ed.), *Major psychological assessment instruments*. Boston: Allyn & Bacon.

Lanyon, R. I., & Goodstein, L. D. (1982). *Personality assessment* (2nd ed.). New York: John Wiley & Sons.

Lawrence, G. (1982). *People types and tiger stripes* (2nd ed.). Palo Alto, CA: Consulting Psychologists Press.

Lee, J. A., Moreno, K. E., & Sympson, J. B. (1984, April). *The effects of mode of test administration on test performance.* Paper presented at the annual meeting of the Eastern Psychological Association, Baltimore.

Lerner, B. (1981). The minimum competence testing movement: Social, scientific, and legal implications. *American Psychologist, 36*(10), 1057–1066.

Lien, A. J. (1971). *Measurement and evaluation of learning* (2nd ed.). Dubuque, IA: William C. Brown.

Linn, R. (1982). Ability testing: Individual differences, prediction and differential prediction. In A. K. Wigdor & W. R. Gainer (Eds.), *Ability testing: Uses, consequences, and controversies* (Part 2). Washington, DC: National Academy Press.

Loehlin, J. C., Lindzey, G., & Spohler, J. N. (1975). *Race differences in intelligence.* San Francisco: Freeman.

Machover, K. (1949). *Personality projection in the drawing of the human figure.* Springfield, IL: Charles C. Thomas.

Madsen, D. H. (1986). Computer applications for test administration and scoring. *Measurement and Evaluation in Counseling and Development, 19*(1), 6–14.

Mann, L., & Sabatino, D. A. (1985). *Foundations of cognitive process in remedial and special education.* Rockville, MD: Aspen Systems Corporation.

Marcus, L. M., & Schopler, E. (1993). Pervasive developmental disorders. In T. H. Ollendick & M. Hersen (Eds.), *Handbook of child and adolescent assessment.* Boston: Allyn & Bacon.

Martin, W. T. (1982). *Self-Perception Inventory.* Creve Coeur, MO: Psychologists & Educators.

Matarazzo, J. D. (1983). Computerized psychological testing [Editorial Comment]. *Science, 221*(4608).

Matey, C. (1984). Leiter International Performance Scale. In D. J. Keyser & R. C. Sweetland (Eds.), *Test critiques: Vol. 1.* (pp. 411–420). Kansas City: Test Corporation of America.

McBride, J. R., & Martin, J. T. (1983). Reliability and validity of adaptive ability tests in a military setting. In D. J. Weiss (Ed.), *New horizons in testing.* New York: Academic Press.

McDaniel, C., & Gysbers, N. C. (1992). *Counseling for career development: Theories, resources, and practices.* San Francisco: Jossey-Bass.

McDermott, P. A. (1980). A systems-actuarial method for differential diagnosis of handicapped children. *Journal of Special Education, 50,* 223–228.

McGrew, K. S. (1994). *Clinical interpretation of the Woodcock-Johnson Tests of Cognitive Abilities-Revised.* Boston: Allyn & Bacon.

McKee, P., & Wilt, R. (1990). Effective teaching: A review of instructional and environmental variables. In T. B. Gutkin & C. R. Reynolds (Eds.), *Handbook of school psychology* (2nd ed.). New York: John Wiley & Sons.

Meehl, P. E. (1954). *Clinical versus statistical prediction.* Minneapolis: University of Minnesota Press.

Mehrens, W. A., & Lehman, I. J. (1986). *Using standardized tests in education* (4th ed.). New York: Longman.

Meier, S. T., & Geiger, S. M. (1986). Implications of computer-assisted testing and assessment for professional practice and training. *Measurement and Evaluation in Counseling & Development, 19*(1), 29–34.

Merz, W. R., Sr. (1984). Kaufman Assessment Battery for Children. In D. J. Keyser & R. C. Sweetland (Eds.), *Test critiques: Vol. 1.* (pp. 393–405). Kansas City: Test Corporation of America.

Messick, S. (1980). *The effectiveness of coaching for the SAT: Review and reanalysis of research from the fifties to the FTC.* Princeton, NJ: Educational Testing Service.

Messick, S. (1989). Validity. In R. L. Linn (Ed.), *Educational measurement* (3rd ed.). New York: Collier Macmillan.

Messick, S., & Yungeblut, A. (1981). Time and methods in coaching for the SAT. *Psychological Bulletin, 89,* 191–216.

Miller, M. D., & Seraphine, A. E. (1993). Can test scores remain authentic when teaching to the test? *Research Bulletin—Florida Educational Research Council, 25*(1), 21–29.

Millman, J., Bishop, C. H., & Ebel, R. L. (1965). An analysis of test-wiseness. *Educational and Psychological Measurement, 25,* 707–726.

Miner, M. G. (1976). *Selection procedures and personnel records.* (Personnel Policies Forum Survey No. 112). Washington, DC: Bureau of National Affairs.

Mitchell, J. V., Jr. (Ed.). (1985). *Ninth mental measurements yearbook.* Lincoln, NB: Buros Institute of Mental Measurements, University of Nebraska Press.

Moos, R. H. (1973). Conceptualizing human environments. *American Psychologist, 28,* 652–665.

Moos, R. H. (1974). *The Social Climate Scales: An overview.* Palo Alto, CA: Consulting Psychologists Press.

Moos, R. H. (1976). *The human context.* New York: John Wiley & Sons.

Moreland, K. L. (1992). Computer assisted psychological assessment. In M. Zeidner & R. Most (Eds.), *Psychological testing: An inside view.* Palo Alto, CA: Consulting Psychologists Press.

Moreno, K. E., Wetzel, C. D., McBride, J. R., & Weiss, D. J. (1984). Relationship between corresponding Armed Services Vocational Aptitude Battery (ASVAB) and computerized adaptive testing (CAT) subtests. *Applied Psychological Measurement, 8*(2), 155–163.

Moses, J. (1990, August). Report of the National Commission of Testing and Public Policy. *APA Monitor, 21*(8), 8.

Munsterberge, F. (1955). *Relationships between some background factors and children's interpersonal behavior.* Unpublished doctoral dissertation, The Ohio State University, Columbus, Ohio.

Murphy, L. L., Conoley, J., & Impara, J. C. (1994). *Tests in print IV.* Lincoln, NB: Buros Institute.

Murray, H. A. (1938). *Explorations in personality.* New York: Oxford University Press.

Nairn, A., and Associates. (1980). *The reign of ETS: The corporation that makes up minds.* Washington, DC: Author.

National Association of College Admissions Counselors. (1991). Statement on counselor competencies. Alexandria, VA: Author.

National Association of School Psychologists. (1978). *Standards for the provision of school psychological services.* Washington, DC: Author.

National Board for Certified Counselors (1989). *Code of ethics.* Alexandria, Va: Author.

National Commission on Excellence in Education. (1983, April). *A nation at risk: The imperative for educational reform.* Washington, DC: U.S. Government Printing Office.

National Commission on Testing and Public Policy. (1990). *From gatekeeper to gateway: Transforming testing in America.* Washington, DC: Author.

National Council of Measurement in Education. (1994, February). *Alternate assessment standards.* Washington, DC: Author.

National Council of Teachers of Mathematics. (1993). *Assessment standards for school mathematics.* Reston, VA: Author.

Nazzaro, J. (1979). Assessment of minority students [Fact Sheet]. Reston, VA: ERIC Clearinghouse on Handicapped and Gifted Children.

Nevo, B., & Jaeger, R. S. (1993). *Educational and psychological testing: The test taker's outlook.* Toronto: Hogrefe and Huber.

Newmark, C. S. (1985). The MMPI. In C. S. Newmark (Ed.), *Major psychological assessment instruments.* Boston: Allyn & Bacon.

Nowicki, S., & Strickland, B. (1973). Nowicki-Strickland Locus of Control. *Journal of Consulting and Clinical Psychology, 40,* 148–154.

Nutall, E. V., Romero, J., & Kalesnik, J. (1992). *Assessing and screening preschoolers: Psychological and educational dimensions.* Boston: Allyn & Bacon.

Oakland, T. (1982). Nonbiased assessment of minority group children. In J. T. Neisworth (Ed.), *Assessment in special education.* Rockville, MD: Aspen Systems.

Oakland, T. D., & Parmelee, R. (1985). Mental measurement of minority group children. In B. B. Wolman (Ed.), *Handbook of intelligence: Theories, measurements, and applications.* New York: John Wiley & Sons.

OSS Assessment Staff. (1948). *Assessment of men.* New York: Holt, Rinehart, & Winston.

Ownby, R. L. (1990). *Psychological reports: A guide to report writing in professional psychology* (2nd ed.). Brandon, VT: CPPC.

Pennock-Roman, M. (1988). Differential Aptitude Test. In J. T. Kapes & M. M. Mastie (Eds.), *A counselor's guide to career assessment instruments* (2nd ed.). Alexandria, VA: National Career Development Association.

Perkins, M. R. (1982). Minimum competency testing: What? why? why not? *Educational Measurement: Issues and Practices, 1*(4), 5–9, 26.

Perloff, R., Craft, J. A., & Perloff, E. (1984). Testing and industrial application. In G. Goldstein & M. Hersen (Eds.), *Handbook of psychological assessment.* New York: Pergamon.

Piacentini, J. (1993). Checklists and rating scales. In T. H. Ollendick & M. Hersen (Eds.), *Handbook of child and adolescent assessment.* Boston: Allyn & Bacon.

Piaget, J. (1970). *The science of education and the psychology of the child.* New York: Orion Press.

Pipho, C. (1978). Minimum competency testing in 1978: A look at standards. *Phi Delta Kappan, 59,* 585–588.

Plake, B. S., & Witt, J. C. (Eds.). (1986). *Buros-Nebraska Symposium on Measurement and Testing: Vol. 2. The future of testing.* Hillsdale, NJ: Lawrence Erlbaum.

Popham, W. J. (1981). *Modern educational measurement.* Englewood Cliffs, NJ: Prentice-Hall.

Prediger, D. J. (Ed.). (1993). *Multicultural assessment standards: A compilation for counselors.* Alexandria, VA: Association for Assessment in Counseling.

Prell, J. M., & Prell, P. A. (1986, November). Improving test scores—teaching test-wiseness: A review of the literature. *Research Bulletin of the Center on Evaluation, Development, and Research.* Bloomington, IL: Phi Delta Kappa.

Prentice Hall/American Society for Personnel Administration. (1975). *Prentice-Hall Survey: Employee testing and selection procedures—Where are they headed?* Englewood Cliffs, NJ: Author.

Public Law 94–142, Education for All Handicapped Children Act of 1975, Nov. 29, 1979.

Rapport, M. D. (1993). Attention deficit hyperactivity disorders. In T. H. Ollendick & M. Hersen (Eds.), *Handbook of child and adolescent assessment.* Boston: Allyn & Bacon.

Reiff, J. C. (1992). *Learning styles.* Washington, DC: NEA.

Reiling, E., & Taylor, R. (1972). A new approach to the problem of changing initial responses to multiple choice questions. *Journal of Educational Measurement, 8,* 177–181.

Reitz, R. (Ed.). (1989). *Test anxiety.* Bloomington, IN: Phi Delta Kappa.

Reynolds, C. R., & Brown, R. T. (1984). Bias in mental testing. In C. R. Reynolds & R. T. Brown (Eds.), *Perspectives on bias in mental testing.* New York: Plenum Press.

Richardson, M. W., & Kuder, G. F. (1939). The calculation of test reliability coefficients based on the method of rational equivalence. *Journal of Educational Psychology, 30,* 681–687.

Rogers, C. R. (1942). *Counseling and psychotherapy.* Boston: Houghton-Mifflin.

Roid, G. H. (1986). Computer technology in testing. In B. S. Plake & J. C. Witt (Eds.), *The future of testing.* Hillsdale, NJ: Erlbaum.

Roid, G. H., & Gorsuch, R. L. (1983). Development and use of test interpretive programs on microcomputers. In M. Schwartz (Ed.), *Guide to the clinical use of computers*. New York: Haworth.

Rorschach, H. (1942). *Psychodiagnostics: Methodik and ergebnisse eines warhenhumungs diagnostischen experiments. [Psychodiagnostics: A diagnostics test based upon perception]*. Bern, Switzerland: Hans Huber.

Ross, M., Brackett, D., & Maxim, A. B. (1991). *Assessment and management of mainstreamed hearing impaired children*. Austin, TX: Proed.

Rossetti, L. M. (1990). *Infant-toddler assessment*. Austin, TX: Pro-Ed.

Rotherman, M. J., & Phinney, J. S. (Eds.). (1986). *Children's ethnic socialization: Pluralism and development*. Newbury Park, CA: Sage.

Rothman, R. (1990). Ford study urges new test system to "open the gates of opportunity." *Education Week, 9*(36), 1, 12.

Rothman, R. (1990). News on tests. *Education Week, 9*(36), 1.

Rotter, J. B. (1966). Generalized expectancies for internal versus external control of reinforcement. *Psychological Monographs, 80*.

Rotter, J. B., & Rafferty, J. E. (1950). *Manual: The Rotter Incomplete Sentence Blank*. New York: The Psychological Corporation.

Rubin, R. B., Palgreen, P., & Sypher, H. E. (Eds.). (1994). *Communication research measures. A source book*. New York: Guilford.

Russell Sage Foundation. (1970). *Guidelines for the collection, maintenance and dissemination of pupil records*. New York: Author.

Saklofske, D. H., & Kowalchuk, V. L. (1992). Influences on testing and test results. In M. Zeidner & R. Most (Eds.), *Psychological testing: An inside view*. Palo Alto, CA: Consulting Psychologists Press.

Sampson, J. P., Jr., & Pyle, K. R. (1983). Ethical issues involved with the use of computer assisted counseling, testing, and guidance systems. *Personnel and Guidance Journal, 61*, 283–287.

Sarason, I. G. (Ed.). (1980). *Test anxiety: Theory, research, and application*. Hillsdale, NJ: Erlbaum.

Sarason, S. B., Davidson, K. S., Lighthall, F. F., Waite, R. R., & Ruebush, B. K. (1960). *Anxiety in elementary school children*. New York: John Wiley & Sons.

Sattler, J. M. (1992). *Assessment of children's intelligence and special abilities* (3rd ed.). Boston: Allyn & Bacon.

Scherer, M. (1985). How many ways is a child intelligent? *Instructor, 94*, 32–35.

Schmidt, F. L., & Hunter, J. E. (1981). Employment testing: Old theories and new research findings. *American Psychologist, 36*(10), 1128–1137.

Schuler, H., Farr, J. L., & Smith, M. (Eds.). (1993). *Personnel selection and assessment*. Hillsdale, NJ: Lawrence Erlbaum.

Science Directorate of the American Psychological Association. (1993). *Finding information about psychological tests: A guide for locating and using both published and unpublished tests*. Washington, DC: Author.

Shapiro, E. S., & Cole, C. L. (1993). Self-monitoring. In T. H. Ollendick & M. Hersen (Eds.), *Handbook of child and adolescent assessment*. Boston: Allyn & Bacon.

Shavelson, R. J., Hubner, J. J., & Stanton, G. C. (1976). Self-concept: Validation of construct interpretations. *Review of Educational Research, 46*, 407–442.

Sherrod, B. (1985, November). Jobs for left brainers; Jobs for right brainers. *Career World*, 19–21.

Shertzer, B. (1986). Integrating computer-assisted testing and assessment in the counseling process: A reaction. *Measurement and Evaluation in Counseling and Development, 19*(1), 27–28.

Shertzer, B., & Linden, J. D. (1979). *Fundamentals of individual appraisal: Assessment tech-*

niques for counselors. Boston: Houghton-Mifflin.

Shimberg, B. (1981). Testing for licensure and certification. *American Psychologist*, *36*(10), 1138–1146.

Shore, M. F., Brice, P. J., & Love, B. G. (1992). *When your child needs testing: What parents, teachers, and other helpers need to know about psychological testing*. New York: Crossroad.

Simeonsson, R. J. (1986). *Psychological and developmental assessment of special children*. Boston: Allyn & Bacon.

Slosson, S. W., & Callisto, T. A. (1984). *Observational analysis*. East Aurora, NY: Slosson.

Spearman, C. (1927). *The abilities of man*. London: Macmillan.

Spielberger, C. D., Gorsuch, R. L., & Lushene, R. E. (1970). *Manual for the State-Trait Anxiety Inventory*. Palo Alto, CA: Consulting Psychologist Press.

Standards for educational and psychological testing. See American Educational Research Association (1985).

Sternberg, R. J. (1980). Factor theories of intelligence are all right almost. *Educational Researcher*, *9*, 6–13.

Sternberg, R. J. (1985). *Beyond IQ: A triarchic theory of human intelligence*. Cambridge: Cambridge University Press.

Sternberg, R. J. (1990). T & T is an explosive combination: Technology and testing. *Educational Psychologist*, *25*(3 & 4), 201–222.

Stiggins, R. (1987). Design and development of performance assessments. *Educational Measurement: Issues and Practices*, *6*(3), 33–42.

Stockwell, S., Schaeffer, B., & Lowenstein, J. (1991). *SAT coaching coverup: How coaching courses can raise scores by 100 points or more and why ETS denies the evidence*. Cambridge, MA: Fair Test.

Stoddard, G. D. (1943). *The meaning of intelligence*. New York: Macmillan.

Strauss, C. C. (1993). Anxiety disorders. In T. H. Ollendick and M. Hersen (Eds.), *Handbook of child and adolescent assessment*. Boston: Allyn & Bacon.

Strong, E. R. (1927). Vocational interest test. *Educational Record*, *8*, 107–121.

Sue, D. W., Arrendondo, P., & McDavis, R. J.(1992). Multicultural counseling competencies and standards: A call to the profession. *Journal of Counseling and Development*, *70*.

Super, D. E., & Crites, J. O. (1962). *Appraising vocational fitness by means of psychological tests* (rev. ed.). New York: Harper & Row.

Super, D. E., Thompson, A. S., & Lindeman, R. H. (1988). *Manual to Adult Career Concerns Inventory*. Palo Alto, CA: Consulting Psychologists Press.

Tallent, N. (1958). On individualizing the psychologist's clinical evaluation. *Journal of Clinical Psychology*, *14*, 243–244.

Tallent, N. (1994). *Psychological report writing* (4th ed.). Englewood Cliffs, NJ: Prentice-Hall.

Taylor, J. A. (1953). A personality scale of manifest anxiety. *Journal of Abnormal and Social Psychology*, *45*, 285–290.

Ten Brink, T. D. (1974). *Evaluation: A practical guide for teachers*. New York: McGraw-Hill.

Tenopyr, M. L. (1981). The realities of employment testing. *American Psychologist*, *36*(10), 1120–1127.

Tenopyr, M. L. (1986). Needed directions for measurements in work settings. In B. S. Plake & J. C. Witt (Eds.), *The future of testing*. Hillsdale, NJ: Erlbaum.

Terman, L. M. (1954). The discovery and encouragement of exceptional talent. *American Psychologist*, *9*, 221–230.

Test Alert. (1990). Chicago: Riverside.

Thorndike, E. L. (1927). *The measurement of intelligence*. New York: Teachers College Press.

Thorndike, R. L., & Hagen, E. P. (1959). *Ten thousand careers*. New York: John Wiley & Sons.

Thorndike, R. L., Hagen, E. P., & Sattler, J. M. (1985). *Examiner's manual for the Stanford Binet Intelligence Scale: Fourth Edition*. Chicago: Riverside.

Thurstone, L. L. (1938). *Primary mental abilities* (Psychometric Monograph No. 1). Chicago: University of Chicago Press.

Tobias, S. (1979). Anxiety research in educational psychology. *Journal of Educational Psychology, 71*, 573–582.

Touliatos, J., Permutter, B. F., & Straus, M. (Eds.). (1990). *Handbook of family measurement techniques*. Newbury Park, CA: Sage.

Tucker, B. P., & Goldstein, B. A. (1991). *The educational rights of children with disabilities: A guide to federal law*. Horsham, PA: LRP Publications.

Tyron, G. S. (1980). The measurement and treatment of test anxiety. *Review of Educational Research, 50*, 343–372.

Urman, H. (1983). *The effect of test-wiseness training on the achievement of third or fifth grade students*. Paper presented at the annual meeting of the National Council on Measurement in Education, Montreal, Quebec.

Vale, C. D. (1990). The Minnesota Clerical Assessment Battery: An application of computerized testing to business. *Measurement and Evaluation in Counseling and Development, 23*, 11–19.

Valencia, R. R., & Aburto, S. (1991). The uses and abuses of educational testing: Chicanos as a case in point. In R. R. Valencia (Ed.), *Chicano school failure and success: Research and policy agendas for the 1990s*. Basingstoke, England: Falmer Press.

Vernon, A. (1993). *Developmental assessment and intervention with children and adolescents*. Alexandria, VA: American Counseling Association.

Vernon, P. E. (1960). *The structure of human abilities* (rev. ed.). London: Methuen.

Viadero, D. (1990, June 20). Georgia ends performance-based tests for teachers. *Education Week*, 18.

Wagner, E. E. (1983). *The Hand Test* (rev. ed.). Los Angeles: Western Psychological Services.

Wakelee-Lynch, J. (1990, December). Testing in the workplace. *APA Guideposts, 33*(9), 1, 6.

Wallace, G., & McLoughlin, J. A. (1979). *Learning disabilities: Concepts and characteristics*. Columbus, OH: Merrill.

Watkins, M. W., & McDermott, P. A. (1991). Psychodiagnostic computing: From interpretive programs to expert systems. In T. B. Gutkin & S. L. Wise. (Eds.), *The computer and the decision-making process*. Hillsdale, NJ: Erlbaum.

Wechsler, D. (1958). *The measurement of adult intelligence*. Baltimore: Williams & Wilkins.

Weiner, E. A. & Stewart, B. J. (1984). *Assessing individuals: Psychological and educational tests and measurements*. Boston: Little, Brown.

Whitman, N. A., Spendlove, D. C., & Clark, C. H. (1986). *Increasing students' learning: A faculty guide to reducing stress among students*. ASHE-ERIC Executive Higher Education. Report 4.

Wigdor, A. K., & Garner, W. R. (Eds.). (1982). *Ability testing: Uses, consequences, and controversies* (2 vols.). Washington, DC: National Academy Press.

Wiggins, G. P. (1989). A true test: Toward more authentic and equitable assessment. *Phi Delta Kappan, 70*(9), 703–713.

Wiggins, G. P. (1993). *Assessing student performance: Exploring the purposes and limits of testing*. San Francisco: Jossey-Bass.

Wiig, E. H. (1982). Communication disorder. In N. G. Haring (Ed.), *Exceptional children and youth* (3rd ed.). Columbus, OH: Merrill.

Wine, J. D. (1980). Cognitive-attentional theory of test anxiety. In I. G. Sarason (Ed.), *Test anxiety: Theory, research and application*. Hillsdale, NJ: Erlbaum.

Wise, S. L., & Plake, B. S. (1990). Computer-based testing in higher education. *Measurement and Evaluation in Counseling and Development, 23*, 3–10.

Witkin, H. A. (1949). Perception of body position and of the position of the visual field. *Psychological Monographs, 63*(1, No. 302).

Witkin, H. A., Moore, C. A., Goodenough, D. R., & Cox, P. W. (1977). Field-dependent and field-independent cognitive styles and their educational implications. *Review of Educational Research, 47*, 1–64.

Wolman, B. B. (Ed.). (1985). *Handbook of intelligence.* New York: John Wiley & Sons.

Wonder, J., & Donovan, P. (1984). *Whole brain thinking: Working from both sides of the brain to achieve peak job performance.* New York: William Morrow.

Wylie, R. C. (1979). *The self-concept: Theory and research on selected topics.* Lincoln: University of Nebraska Press.

Wylie, R. C. (1990). *Self-concept instruments.* Lincoln, NB: University of Nebraska Press.

Ysseldyke, J. E., & Christenson, S. L. (1987). *Instructional environment scale.* Austin, TX: Pro-Ed.

Zachary, R. A., & Pope, K. S. (1983). Legal and ethical issues in the clinical use of computerized testing. In M. D. Schwartz (Ed.), *Using computers in clinical practice.* New York: Haworth.

Zeidner, M., & Most, R. (1992). *Psychological testing: An inside view.* Palo Alto, CA: Consulting Psychologists Press.

Zuckerman, E. L. (1991). *The clinician's thesaurus: A guidebook for writing psychological reports and their evaluation* (2nd ed.). Brandon, VT: CPPC.

Zytowski, D. G., & Warman, R. E. (1981). The changing use of tests in counseling. *Measurement and Evaluation in Guidance, 15*(2), 147–152.

Name Index

Subject Index

Test Index